Index to English

Index to English both supplements and augments *Writer's Guide*. It includes articles on grammar, parts of speech, sentence structure, diction, punctuation, mechanics, logic, rhetoric, and style, as well as entries on individual words and phrases and special kinds of writing—all arranged alphabetically for easy reference. The Correction Chart inside the back cover lists articles that are especially useful in revising papers.

Writer's Guide and Index to English

Sixth Edition

Writer's Guide and Index to English

Sixth Edition

Wilma R. Ebbitt
The Pennsylvania State University

David R. Ebbitt

Scott, Foresman and Company
Glenview, Ill.
Dallas, Tex.
Oakland, N.J.
Palo Alto, Cal.
Tucker, Ga.
London

Library of Congress Cataloging in Publication Data

Ebbitt, Wilma R
    Writer's guide and index to English.

    Fifth ed. by P. G. Perrin.
    1.   English language—Rhetoric.   I.   Ebbitt,
David R., joint author.   II.   Perrin, Porter Gale,
1896–1962. Writer's guide and index to English.
III.   Title.
PE1411.E22   1978   808'.042   77–21370
ISBN 0–673–15109–3

Acknowledgments of sources granting permission to reprint
copyrighted material appear on pp. 689 ff.

3 4 5 6 7 8-RRC-86 85 84 83 82 81 80 79

Preface

Writer's Guide and Index to English combines a rhetoric, *Writer's Guide,* with a comprehensive handbook, *Index to English.* In this sixth edition we have made a special effort to render both parts accessible to a broader range of students. Recognizing the rhetorical situation (as we urge students to do in all their papers) has meant, not omitting and oversimplifying, but writing in a style freshmen will find readable and using illustrative material they will be interested in. Sources of such material are by no means limited to popular journalism. *Sports Illustrated* and *Newsweek* are represented here, but so are *The New York Review of Books* and *The American Scholar.*

In both parts of the book, we have offered practical instruction and realistic advice. We have told students the truth—that writing well requires concentrated effort—but we have also reminded them now and again that it needn't be a grim ordeal, that college papers can give pleasure to the writer as well as to the reader.

We encourage students to take responsibility for their own progress in writing. From the first pages of the *Guide,* we insist that at the heart of the composing process must lie a sense of personal commitment, personal engagement, personal responsibility. At the same time, we give most attention to practical problems of execution—problems that recur in drafting and redrafting papers, in revising and rewriting. Like the earlier editions, the sixth proceeds on the assumption that writing can be most satisfactorily discussed and practiced in the context of a range of choices—rhetorical, syntactic, and lexical.

Both *Guide* and *Index* have been largely rewritten. The *Guide* has also been reorganized. Chapter One, "Getting

Started," introduces the student to the concept of the rhetorical situation: the combination of writer, subject, purpose, and audience that determines what methods and what style will be most appropriate in a particular paper. As long-time users of *Writer's Guide and Index to English* are aware, appropriateness is the key principle that Porter G. Perrin recommended in the early editions of this textbook.

Chapter One deals with prewriting and writing and re-writing. It gets the student started by offering an overview of the whole process of writing papers in college – deciding on a manageable topic, arriving at a statement of pur-pose, gathering material, choosing methods of developing ideas (and in the process generating content), writing drafts, revising, and editing. All through the text the need for rewriting and revising is repeatedly emphasized. Chapter One suggests steps and procedures, but it does not present *a* procedure, *a* formula for writing. Instead, it urges students to experiment, to find out what works for *them*.

In both *Guide* and *Index* the labels "general," "formal," and "informal" are applied not only to words and phrases but to punctuation, to sentence patterns, to transitions, and to the styles that are the end result of the countless choices every writer makes, deliberately or intuitively. For writing – certainly good writing – is all of a piece, and even worse than the categorical separation of words into "right" words and "wrong" is the separation of usage from style and of style from rhetoric. Thus while the varieties of usage are treated in detail in Chapter Nine, "Choosing Words," the broad differences among general, informal, and formal styles are introduced in Chapter One in con-nection with the rhetorical situation and are appealed to throughout the text as a basic element in rhetorical choice.

Chapter Two consolidates into one long chapter what was spread over three chapters and part of a fourth in the last edition. Description and narration are presented not as separate modes of discourse but as methods of developing expository and argumentative papers, along with division, comparison and contrast, classification, cause and effect, and definition.

Chapter Three takes up the organizing of papers, and Chapter Four the building of paragraphs – not only single paragraphs but paragraph sequences. Chapter Five deals with persuasive writing – with argument, with general fallacies, and with refutation. In the earlier chapters ex-planatory and persuasive writing are treated together;

here the special rhetorical techniques and the ethical dimension of persuasion are examined.

Chapter Six, "Testing Logical Relationships," is restricted to formal logic. Those instructors who approved the coverage of induction and syllogistic reasoning in the fifth edition will find it much the same in this one. Those who lack the time or don't feel the need to take up formal logic will be able to introduce their students to the general fallacies and to refutation in Chapter Five.

Chapter Seven, on sentences, takes the place of two chapters in the fifth edition. The reduction in space has been achieved largely by omitting any comprehensive treatment of grammar. Students who need to review particular grammatical problems are led by a self-test to the item-by-item coverage in the *Index*. The material in "Shaping Sentences" has been reordered so that revising for clarity is separate from and precedes revising for style. Chapter Eight, a brief review of punctuation, is keyed to correction articles in the *Index*.

Chapter Nine deals with words, their use and their misuse. Again, the material moves from the elementary to the more sophisticated, from finding out what a word means to using words with precision or with originality and flair.

Chapter Ten, "Doing a Close Reading," describes, with an example, a single, specific approach to an extremely broad subject—writing about literature. Chapter Eleven, "Writing the Research Paper," has been carried over from the fifth edition but expanded, revised, and reorganized.

In every chapter of *Writer's Guide* students are offered frequent opportunities to test their mastery of the principles of invention, structure, development, and style that are discussed in the text. Sometimes writing tasks are sharply focused; sometimes students are invited to discover and shape their own topics, establish their own rhetorical situations. In addition, they are regularly asked to analyze and sometimes to revise the writing of others, both amateurs and professionals, so that they can develop criteria for judging their own work as they expand their rhetorical horizons. Revising the work of others is the quickest way for students to acquire the objectivity they must have in order to revise their own work intelligently. And, as instructors and students alike must recognize, revising is an indispensable part of the process of writing. While spontaneity has its virtues, for the most part writing that meets college standards is rewritten writing.

Supplementary material for class assignments, as well as suggestions for using the *Guide,* will be found in

A Teacher's Guide to the Writer's Guide, available from the publishers.

In the *Index to English* we have retained the alphabetical arrangement of articles and the extensive system of cross references that permit users of this handbook to find what they want quickly and easily. The introduction, addressed to the student, describes the book and tells how it can be used – for course work, for individual reference, for browsing.

To help students write so that what they have to say will be understood, respected, even enjoyed by readers, we provide them with some rules, remind them of certain conventions, and suggest some of the uses that can be made of both highly formal and decidedly informal English. Recognizing, however, that the practical functions of formal and informal are sharply limited for undergraduates, we recommend that they set out to master general American English, the variety of English that all educated Americans read and that all need to be able to write. The great majority of the illustrative passages in the *Index* – whether taken from books, learned journals, popular magazines, and newspapers or adapted from the writing of students – represent this most useful and versatile variety.

On the issue of standards, we endorse neither anarchy nor absolutism. We don't believe that college students, or college graduates, should be encouraged to think that just any rush of words on paper necessarily has value. Nor do we believe that students should be misled into thinking that there is only one Good English – least of all the Good English that demands observance of rules embalmed in prescriptive handbooks and guides to linguistic etiquette.

On certain matters, students need, and will find, unequivocal advice. In the articles keyed to the correction chart we have made the *Index* as prescriptive as honesty and realism permit. The correction articles answer directly and explicitly such questions as "What mark of punctuation do I need here?" "Should this verb be singular or plural?" "What can I do to improve the continuity of this paragraph?" But they also take into account appropriateness to the writer's subject and purpose and audience and to the writer's self. And in most of the articles relating to usage, style, and rhetorical strategies, appropriateness is the primary criterion students are urged to apply.

In usage articles, after identifying the current status of a locution – standard or nonstandard; if standard, formal, informal, or general—we often include the alternatives: the "*pretty* good time" of informal and the "*fairly* good time" of general; the formal *arising* and the general *getting up*. The student who has read the *Guide* knows that the varieties overlap and that on occasion good writers deliberately shift from one variety to another. In a paper that is predominantly in general English, then, the informal *about* may be used instead of *almost* ("I was about done") as a means of moving a bit closer to the reader. Here and elsewhere we neither deny students a choice nor simply list alternatives and invite them to take their pick. What we try to do is guide them toward making intelligent choices that reflect their awareness of the rhetorical context in which they are writing.

Discussion in *Index to English* is not limited to small writing problems that can be safely detached from the context in which they occur. Many of the articles bear on the composing of whole essays—on prewriting and getting started, on the choice of details, on the means of achieving logical sequence, on the organization and development of special kinds of papers, on how to stop. And many articles, like those on grammar, linguistics, usage, the English language, and the origin of words, introduce readers to broad areas of scholarship. From these as well as from many of the shorter articles, references open the door to further study.

Here, then, is a rhetoric that guides the student, by a choice of routes, through the process of writing papers for college courses. And here is a handbook he can turn to, as he writes and revises and as he goes over papers that have been corrected and returned, to find solutions to particular problems and answers to specific questions. A general index coordinates the two. The sixth edition of *Writer's Guide and Index to English* is, we hope, a book worth keeping, a resource for writers not just for the duration of a composition course but through college and after. In looking for new ways to help today's college students of writing develop confidence and gain competence, we were guided by the principles of Porter G. Perrin, who made *Writer's Guide and Index to English* a resource for generations of teachers as well as students.

Before work was begun on this sixth edition, an undertaking initiated by Richard Welna of Scott, Foresman and Company, the *Guide* chapters of the fifth edition were reviewed by Mark Ashin of the University of Chicago,

Douglas B. Park of The Pennsylvania State University, William D. Payne of the University of Illinois, Mina P. Shaughnessy of the City University of New York, William B. Stone of the University of Illinois at Chicago Circle, and Gary Tate of Texas Christian University. We thank all of them for their criticisms and advice. We are particularly grateful to Professors Payne and Tate, who read the copy for the new edition as well and made many helpful suggestions.

Among the teachers whose comments influenced the revision of the *Index* were Julia A. Alexander of the Colorado School of Mines, Ronald E. Buckalew and Martha Kolln of The Pennsylvania State University, Don Norton of Brigham Young University, and William H. Pixton of Troy State University. Again, as in the fifth edition, we warmly acknowledge the contributions to the *Index* of James Fitzpatrick of Masonite Corporation, Jay Robinson of the University of Michigan, James Sledd of the University of Texas, and Joseph M. Williams of the University of Chicago.

Our thanks to Margaret A. Martin and Robert C. Gruen for their care and patience in seeing the manuscripts of the *Guide* and the *Index* through the press.

Wilma R. Ebbitt
David R. Ebbitt

Contents
Writer's Guide

Contents
Index to English

The Index, pp. 381–685, contains articles in alphabetical arrangement that fall roughly into six categories:

Articles on particular words and constructions, like *among, between; definitely; like, as; not about to; who, whom.*

Articles to be used in correcting and revising papers, indicated by longhand abbreviations.

Articles on composition, such as Prewriting, Thesis statement, Transition; rhetoric, such as Argument, Cause and effect, Comparison and contrast; and style, such as Diction, Figurative language, Periodic sentence.

Articles offering information and advice on a range of topics that are useful in special writing situations, such as Research papers (and the related articles Bibliographical form and Footnote form), Business letters, and Technical writing.

Articles on grammar, offering definitions and discussions of standard grammatical terms and concepts, such as Collective nouns, Parts of speech, Relative clauses, Subjunctive mood.

Articles about language and language study, such as British English, English language, Linguistics, Sexist language, and Usage.

Writer's Guide

Chapter One
Getting Started

What's my subject? What do I want to say about it? Do I have enough information, or do I need to look for more? Can I depend on what's in my head — my mind, my memory — or should I turn to outside sources?

Who will my readers be? What kind of people are they? What are their tastes, values, prejudices? What common ground is there between us? What assumptions do we share?

How much do my readers know about my subject? How do they feel about it? Can I expect them to be interested in what I have to say? What will they be willing to take for granted, and what will I have to prove?

How can I make them see what I want them to see, think the way I want them to think, do what I want them to do?

Do I need to make my style more personal, more relaxed, or does my relationship with my readers call for a more formal style, one that keeps more distance between us?

Is this the fact to be emphasized, or is that the one? Where should I place it to give it the most emphasis?

How can I make this sentence say exactly what I mean? How can I phrase this idea to make it both clear and persuasive?

Will *this* phrase, *this* word, *this* punctuation mark work with *this* audience?

Questions like these, which range from large matters to small, need to be faced up to whenever you set about writing a paper. Essentially, they're questions of rhetoric — how to gather, organize, and present your facts, ideas, feelings, and impressions so as to achieve a specific purpose as you address a specific audience on a specific topic. Good writing doesn't just happen. It comes about because a person who is interested in a subject wants to communicate something about it. Before you begin to write, you should have clearly in mind the particular circumstances in which you're writing — the rhetorical situation.

The Rhetorical Situation

The rhetorical situation is made up of writer, subject, purpose, and audience, each interacting with the others.

Let's start with *audience*. In conversation you adjust to the group you're in. Among automobile enthusiasts you talk about makes and models, mileages and speeds. Among nature lovers you compare notes on hikes and trails, wildlife and ecology. And just as you choose appropriate subjects, so you adjust your speaking style to the company you're in. Though you may make precisely the same judgment about a college course when talking to a dean, to your parents, and to your roommate, you will certainly express that judgment in different ways. You'll adjust your language to your audience.

When you write, you need to make comparable adjustments. If this is sometimes hard to do, it's mainly because your sense of the rhetorical situation is seldom as keen when you're writing as when you're talking. In a composition course you may be bothered by the artificiality of a situation in which you're called on to write papers that will all be read by the same audience, your instructor. But your instructor will probably set up hypothetical audiences for you to address or urge you to specify the readers you have in mind. To ward off the feeling that you're writing in a vacuum, get in the habit of visualizing a specific audience for each of your papers—the head of your dorm for a protest about noise in the halls, readers of the campus newspaper for a letter about the problems of bike riders, prospective guitar buyers for an appraisal of the different makes. For other topics, other audiences will seem plausible—the brightest person in your class, say, or a childhood friend, or a group of sixth-graders, or the members of a campus organization, or the readers of *Newsweek* or *Rolling Stone* or *Harper's*. This last kind of audience is a broad one, made up of thousands of nameless, faceless individuals; but it's the kind you may be addressing someday in a sales letter or an annual report or some other sort of business writing. Only when you have an audience, real or assumed, are you operating in a rhetorical situation, and only then can you judge realistically how to say what you want to say.

There's much more to the rhetorical situation than your conception of your readers—their tastes, their interests, their views on the subject you're discussing. There's the *subject* itself—your response to an incident or situation or problem or idea. There's your *purpose* in discussing the subject—to inform, to persuade, to amuse, or whatever. Together they determine the kind of writing you're setting out to produce—a term paper in sociology, a movie review for the campus newspaper, an account of freshman registration for the college literary magazine. This element in the rhetorical situation—the occasion—is closely related to the audience but at times specifies the writing job more narrowly. Though many of the same people read the literary magazine and the campus newspaper, they bring to their reading quite different expectations. They know that the articles in the magazine are likely to be more ambitious, more carefully written and revised, more personal than the newspaper stories.

The final element in the rhetorical situation is *you*, the writer. The way you see yourself and the way you want your audience to see you will determine many of the choices you make as you write.

Whenever you begin a paper, you should ask yourself who is writing. Naturally, the writer is you; but which you is writing this particular paper? The you who argues about course requirements is not the same you who reminisces about a grandfather in southside Chicago or in small-town Nebraska. The you who tells how to tune up a motorcycle is different from the you who criticizes a television program. And in addition to these real selves, there are imagined ones: the strategist advising a basketball coach, the reformer pointing out ways to improve living conditions in the neighborhood, the laid-off worker telling of the psychological effects of being unemployed. As a writer you speak in different voices and play different roles.

You also assume different relationships with different audiences. You may be an expert addressing experts, an expert addressing amateurs, an amateur addressing experts, or an amateur addressing amateurs. And your relationship with an audience may be characterized by almost any degree of formality or familiarity, of hostility or affection. Each different relationship calls for adjustments not only in what you say but in how you say it.

The audience-writer relationship determines a great deal about your approach to writing a particular paper. It gives a rough indication of where your writing should fall in the range from very informal to highly formal, where it should fall in the range from simple to complex. And it suggests the degree of intimacy you should assume or seek to establish. The language, you'll find, offers choices for registering closeness, remoteness, and every degree of distance in between.

■ *For Writing*

Write a three-minute talk in which you introduce yourself to your classmates. You can't possibly tell everything about yourself in that length of time, and a recitation of facts — date and place of birth, schools attended, and so on — won't make very interesting listening when you read the paper aloud. So focus on something in your background that will give your listeners an idea of the kind of person you are.

Now write a letter of the same length in response to a "Help Wanted" ad for a part-time job you'd very much like to have. Tell your prospective employer (someone you've never met) just what your qualifications are.

Look closely at the two papers. Explain how the different rhetorical situations have made them differ.

Prewriting

"Writing a column is easy," Red Smith has said. "I just sit down at the typewriter, open a vein, and bleed it out, drop by drop."

The work habits of writers vary. Some can't write at all until they know just what they want to say. Others have to write in order to find an idea. Some make elaborate plans before they begin to write. Others work out the structure as they go along. Some write a first draft at top speed, without paying any special attention to sentence structure, word choice, or punctuation. Others proceed slowly and carefully, trying to perfect each sentence before going on to the next.

There is no one way to write. What works for one writer doesn't necessarily work for another. So if one route turns out to be a dead end for you, there are others to travel, and at least one of them will take you where you want to go. Try out different approaches, and settle on the methods of composing that seem to work best for you most of the time. All the evidence suggests that finding your own way to handle writing projects will increase both your confidence and your competence. And you'll still have plenty of opportunity for improvising, because no two writing projects are exactly alike.

Looked at from the outside, writing is the act of joining words into sentences on paper. To anyone who's ever tried to write, that's a misleading definition. Certainly a large part of composing takes place in the mind. But if writing isn't just exercising the fingers, neither is it necessarily the act of finding words to express definite, fully formed ideas. For some writers, it is – they "think the whole thing out" before they put words on paper. For others, the physical act of writing stimulates their thinking and gives them ideas. Like E. M. Forster, they ask, "How can I know what I think until I see what I say?" (Another writer, Joan Didion, has said, "I write entirely to find out what I'm thinking, what I'm looking at, what I see and what it means.") Whatever the action, whether external or internal or both, this initial stage of composing may be called *prewriting*. Without sustained and inventive prewriting, a good paper can only be a lucky accident.

Prewriting is discovering what you think and feel about your subject; it's finding the perspective from which you'll write about it. It includes whatever goes on before you make a purposeful effort to produce a first draft. Depending on your subject and your habits of work, prewriting may be a period of thinking that ranges from idle musing to hard concentration. Or it may include talking, reading, taking notes, making more or less systematic outlines. Or it may mean scribbling away in an attempt to get at a hazy notion that could turn out to be the core of what you write. Some of us think on paper.

Whether your hands are busy or still, prewriting is the process of discovering your ideas – how you view your subject, what meaning it has for you, what you want to say about it. From this it follows that a central requirement of prewriting is, in the words of Gordon Rohman and Albert Wlecke, an "absolute willingness to think one's own thoughts, feel one's own feelings." Only by becoming involved with the subject will you make it your own.

Making the subject your own doesn't mean that all your writing will be personal. It means that all your writing will be motivated by a kind of personal concern that we'll call the writer's commitment. It's a commitment – intellectual or emotional or both – that's developed during the prewriting stage, an awareness of how you as an individual relate both to your subject and to your prospective readers. Writing that lacks such commitment is very likely to be dull stuff, expressing nothing but trite ideas and conventional attitudes. At times, both in college and later on, you'll have to do kinds of writing that make personal commitment difficult. But with enough effort in the prewriting stage, you can almost always find your way into the subject you're to write about. And the more you get into any subject, the more likely you are to get caught up in it. At the very least, you can always be personally concerned with the quality of what you produce, making sure that it represents your best effort.

Writing that grows out of personal concern sounds as though the writer believes what he says. Whether the style is rough or smooth, what comes through is the voice of a living human being. Certainly personal concern need not and should not express itself in ego trips — turning an account of a local housing problem, say, into a display of your own sympathy and sensitivity. In a research paper personal concern may require nothing more — *but nothing less* — than your determination to give a faithful and coherent account of facts scholars have discovered about your subject. In this sense, you can be just as committed to writing a solid, well-documented research paper as to expressing yourself in an uninhibited autobiography.

Your Resources

In your prewriting you have a unique resource to draw on — your memory. If it's less efficient than an electronic memory bank, it has the advantage of being yours alone. No one else can program it; no one else can tap it. Besides providing the substance of autobiographical papers, your personal experiences can provide the basis for an opinion, give authority to an explanation, add conviction to an argument. While memory won't provide a printout at the push of a button, it can be coaxed. When it offers only blurred impressions, keep working on it. Hunt up snapshots, souvenirs, news items. Get in touch with relatives or old friends who can help. The fog may clear. Often you'll find your memory coming through under pressure.

You can teach yourself to be a better observer, too. For the most part, we see only what we want to see and what we've been brought up to see; but with conscious effort all of us can expand the circle of our awareness. By observing with an open mind as well as open eyes, we can literally see more. Train yourself to see beyond the surface of things. Instead of settling for a general impression, look for parts and the ways they fit together. Single out the specifics that will make your writing concrete and individual. Close, deliberate observation turns up good material.

Ideas for papers come from listening, reading, and studying — from what you hear in conversations with your friends; from what you read in newspapers, magazines, and books, listen to on the radio, and watch on television; from what you hear in lectures and class discussions and from what you study in course assignments. Ideas also come from talking and writing—from what you say yourself and what you put down on paper. And ideas spark ideas. In the course of converting a vague notion into words, you may find the words themselves sparking a train of thought that leads to a conclusion you'd never considered.

Reading lots of good prose can do more for your writing than provide content. It won't guarantee that you'll become an expert writer any more than regularly visiting art exhibits will make you an expert painter. But wide reading will probably do more than anything else to help you improve your own use of language. No matter how heavy the reading assignments for your courses, try to read a variety of current magazines and books, both fiction and nonfiction. Paying attention to the ways professional writers organize and express their ideas can help you considerably in presenting your own. But most of all read for enjoyment, not just for the good it may do you. While you're enjoying yourself, you'll be absorbing the rhythms of the written language.

Material for short papers will come chiefly from your experiences, past and current, and from your thinking about topics that are making news. Longer, more comprehensive papers will call for the kind of specialized, factual information your courses and the library can supply. Sometimes information from a course can be combined with personal experience: perhaps you can illustrate (or challenge) a sociological theory about city or suburban or rural life from your personal knowledge. In other cases, what you've learned in a course equips you to deal with topics outside your experience: a physics course may help you make sense of a proposal for further space exploration; a course in economics may help you understand the monetary policy of the Federal Reserve Board.

Lack of expert knowledge of a subject shouldn't make you shun it. Though you've never designed a spacecraft or controlled the money supply, you can have strong convictions about the relative importance of the investigation of distant planets and the development of new energy sources on earth, and you can be personally concerned about an increase in tuition. As long as you know enough about a subject to be able to support your opinions with facts, you're qualified to write about it.

Your basic qualifications for writing on a wide range of topics are, first, your ability to collect data—facts—and, second, your ability to think about this information. Of all your resources, the most important is your power to reason and reflect. Use your papers as testing grounds for the ideas you're incubating, ideas you've formed in response to what you've read and heard. Your mind, which sets you apart from everyone else, gives your writing its individuality. Until it begins to work on material, the data remain data and nothing more. Whether you're drawing on personal experience, observation, discussion, or reading, you need to keep thinking. Think *through* your material, sifting it, sorting it, evaluating it. When you're recalling personal experience, you're the only one who can separate what really happened from what you wish had happened. When you're dealing with what you've read or what you've been told, it's up to you to decide what information is most reliable and which sources are most trustworthy. In the end, you must decide what you believe, and why. Writing the truth as you know it or as you see it (without ever forgetting that you may be wrong) is not only the right thing to do in the moral sense; it's also likely to produce the direct, forceful style that reflects conviction.

■ *For Writing*

1. *Take any activity that interests you—singing, surfing, cooking, camping, walking, whatever—and keep turning the subject over in your mind until you know how you feel about it and what you want to say about it. There's no best way to do this, but you might try the method of comparison. See how many resemblances, even accidental and partial ones, occur to you when you think of the activity in terms of another that seems somehow like it. What new perspectives do you gain if you think of surfing as flying, of cooking as composing poems, of walking as attending a religious service? Such thinking may give you a controlling idea ("A good singing group is like a top basketball team") that will help you say what you feel about your subject.*

Or try treating the activity as unique. Ask yourself what qualities it has that make it—at least for you—different from everything else. You may find this approach just as effective in opening up the subject. ("Bike riding doesn't just get you there; it lets you get yourself there, and have a great time doing it.")

Now write a paper saying in one or two pages what the activity you've chosen means to you. For your own information, keep a record of how you went about thinking through the material and writing the paper.

2. *For several days in a row, spend fifteen or twenty minutes looking at and writing about the same thing—a building, a*

tree, a cat. Observe it and write about it at different times of day. Each time you look at it try to see it afresh, and each time you write about it try to record a sharp image of what you see at that time. After a week or so review the five or six passages you've written. If they all sound much the same, you weren't looking hard enough, or you didn't work hard enough to find the words that would convey exactly what you saw.

Settling on a Topic

Assigned topics that don't awaken any immediate interest call for special effort in the prewriting stage. Special effort of a different kind is called for by an assignment that's wide open—a "free choice"—or by one that invites you to stake out a topic for yourself from a very broad area like sports or politics. For a free choice, don't spend too much time deciding what to write about. You may have to mull over several possibilities, but don't prolong the process until indecision becomes paralysis. You can keep it from reaching that stage if you recognize the simple truth that you're a person of many experiences, interests, and talents and that there are probably a dozen topics you can write on with as much authority as anyone else in the classroom, including the instructor. Without wasting time waiting for the ideal topic to suggest itself, you should be able to find a subject that's not only a good one for a paper but the right one for you.

The subject you settle on should be close enough to your own experience for you to feel comfortable with it. Or it should be something you've read about and thought about enough so that you can write about it with some confidence. You're apt to flounder if you launch into something like "The Outlook for the Year 2000." But though your subject should be one you're capable of handling, it shouldn't be one you know is trivial. The more it stirs your imagination and stretches your mind, the more likely it will be to interest your audience.

Often you'll arrive at a good topic by building up and out from a particular incident—something that's amused or stirred you, given you pleasure or caused you pain. If you keep a journal, you'll find that entries in it can be excellent starters for topics, reminding you not just of things you've done and seen but of the impression they made on you and the way you felt about them. When you're faced with a broad, general subject like education, you have to find ways of making it manageable. Perhaps the best way is to cut in on the subject where you have some personal experience with it. Last summer you tutored some teen-agers? Then don't write about education, or high-school education, or the problem of dropouts, or teaching dis-advantaged children. Write about tutoring your tenth-graders. If you want to generalize about reaching unmoti-vated tenth-graders, let the generalizations develop out of your summer work.

Defining Your Purpose

Once you've moved in on your topic and become fully en-gaged with it, you'll find it helpful to frame a tentative statement of your purpose—what you want to explain or explore or demonstrate or describe. True, your purpose may change as you gather more material or even when you're well along in your first draft. But to give your think-ing some direction, to have some criterion to help you sort out the relevant from the irrelevant and spot the leads worth following up, you need to have some notion of what you're setting out to do.

Though a few of the papers you write may be wholly autobiographical, in most of what you write in college you'll be asked to clarify, interpret, explore, support, or challenge. That is, most of the papers will be explanations or arguments. Many of them will be based on course read-ings, but for some you'll be able to draw on your own ex-perience. And whenever you can, you should. What you write is likely to be more alive and more convincing if it includes references to what you know firsthand.

Sometimes the same experience will provide material for different kinds of essays. Your part in a show put on by the senior class in your high school could be written up as a straight autobiographical narrative. Handled differ-ently, the experience could be used as an explanation of the process of presenting an original musical. And you could draw on the same experience for evidence if you wanted to argue that school administrators should leave the activities of student organizations in the hands of the members.

Exposition and Persuasion. Traditionally, a distinction has been made between explanatory (or expository) writ-ing and argumentative (or persuasive) writing. How do they differ? Clearly not in the source of the material. Either exposition or argument can draw on a personal experience; either can be based on reading and research.

And they don't differ in subject. Hundreds of explanatory articles have been written about wildlife conservation, and so have hundreds of persuasive articles. The only sound basis for differentiating between the two kinds of papers is the use to which the material is put. And use is determined by purpose. In an explanatory paper your purpose is to *inform* your readers, to clarify the subject for them. In a persuasive paper your purpose is to *influence* your readers to think or act in a certain way. Having one of these purposes doesn't mean you can't also have the other. Informing may be the first step toward influencing. But in a good paper one purpose is usually the more important, and that's the purpose you should spell out for yourself.

Statement of Purpose and Thesis Statement.   Spell it out either in a *statement of purpose* or in a *thesis statement*. Both indicate what you intend to accomplish. Both help keep you on target. If your purpose is to record, describe, or explain (an expository paper), you'll find the statement of purpose more useful:

This paper will give an account of the expenses an entering student has to face during the first two weeks of the term.

Here is a description of the way a typical issue of the *Daily Collegian* is put together.

I want to explain how I developed my ideas about women's rights.

My intention in this paper is to present both the advantages and the disadvantages of having the local economy dominated by a single corporation; I will use Westend and the Giant Electric Corporation as my example.

Statements of purpose like these are for your own use, not for inclusion in the papers you write. One paper based on the first statement of purpose in the preceding list began this way: "During the first two weeks of the semester I was shedding money the way a tree sheds leaves in November."

If your purpose is to support an idea or advance a proposition (an argumentative paper), you can use the same form: "My purpose in this paper is to show that entering students are being overcharged by practically every institution in University City, on campus and off." Or you can use the more direct thesis statement, or thesis, worded as it might appear in the final paper:

Entering students are being overcharged by practically every institution in University City, on campus and off.

Our newspaper should concentrate on this college and keep out of politics.

The feminist movement on campus needs new leadership.

Westend, where I come from, is a much more pleasant place to live than University City.

Once you've phrased your statement, you're ready to set about discovering specific things to say. Depending on what you're writing about, this may or may not involve reading and research to collect facts and assemble evidence. It should mean settling on ways of carrying out your intention. It will certainly mean digging into your own experience for relevant details and images, ideas and opinions.

All the while your mind has to be active. It has to make something of the material you're assembling, something that's the product of your thinking and bears the mark of your individuality. When you're reading and taking notes, keep asking yourself what functions the notes can serve. When you're figuring out how to present and develop material, ask yourself what your readers will need in the way of illustration and definition. Don't just think *about* your topic. Think *through* it; make it yours.

A Reminder. What we're outlining here is a straightforward progression from planning to performing. But not everyone writes that way, or writes well that way. You may be one of those people who discover their purpose or their thesis only after they've begun to write. You may not find out whether you have a thesis until then. If that's the case, don't worry about it. Keep writing until you know where you're going, until you find out what your paper's going to be. Then compose your statement, or pick it out of the sentences you've already set down.

If you've written a statement of purpose or a thesis statement in advance, don't be afraid to change it or even abandon it. Thinking through the topic may lead you to change your mind about just what you want to accomplish. Writing the first draft may make you question your thesis. In either case, don't hesitate to back up and take a new route. The essential thing is to believe in what you end up writing. You can't expect your readers to accept what you have to say if you're not fully convinced by it yourself.

■ *For Writing*

1. Choose three of the general subjects listed below. After turning them over in your mind, narrow each subject to two topics, one for a paper of 400 to 700 words, one for a paper of 800 to 1200 words. Consult with your instructor, and write on the one that you both agree is best for you. Either before, during, or after you've written your paper (depending on your habits of composition), phrase a statement of purpose or a thesis statement that makes clear your intention. Specify the audience you're addressing.

admission to college	rock	family life
television	junk food	coed housing
equality of the sexes	fashion	race relations
meditation	finding a job	movies
comic strips	sports fans	sci-fi
prestige symbols	religious training	citizen's band radio

2. Professional writers often begin with nothing in mind but a phrase, an image, just the hint of an idea. See if you can develop a paper from such a small beginning. Start with a word, a line from a song, a feeling, the memory of a place or an incident, and expand it into a subject for a paper of 300 to 500 words. You'll want to work from your own experience, not anyone else's; but here are starting points that two students used:

The memory of a visit to the refrigeration room of a wholesale-retail meat market was developed into an argument for vegetarianism.

The phrase "April green" triggered a paper on the colors of the months in a Midwestern state.

Building Content

Even after you know pretty clearly what you want to do in your paper, you may find yourself complaining that you're short of ideas ("I've got nothing to write about") or that you can't express what you mean ("I know what I want to say, but I don't know how to say it"). In fact, you're never totally bankrupt of material. No matter what the subject, you can always come up with a few ideas about it. But sometimes you may have trouble settling on an approach to the subject, relating your ideas to each other so that your paper makes good sense, fleshing out the topic so that readers get something worth reading and worth thinking about. ("Fleshing out" doesn't mean padding. It means putting meat on the bones – developing ideas, not just adding words.) This section will make some suggestions about how you can generate content as you think and write your way through a topic.

Suppose you've been given the broad assignment of writing about the place you come from – the city or city neighborhood, the suburb, the small town, the farm or ranch. After turning the subject over for a while, you decide that all you can say about Westend, your city, is that it's a pleasant place (or that it's peaceful, quiet, dull; or noisy, exciting, terrifying; or ugly or beautiful or ordinary). That gives you a general idea of what point you want to make – not a very precise one but something to work with. What you need to do next is find out what you have to say on the subject.

How do you go about that?

If we omit all the sudden twists and turns of thought, the false starts and dead ends that characterize the prewriting stage, the main thread of your thinking – in your mind or on paper – might go like this: "I like Westend. It was a good place to grow up in. It's pleasant. Why? Well, it's a pretty place – lots of trees, some good parks and playgrounds. Except when the shifts change at Giant Electric, there's not much heavy traffic since the bypass was built. People get along well together. Certainly the kids do. There's work for just about everybody. Nobody goes hungry. . . ." You're collecting particulars that support your thesis. You're also developing content.

Or perhaps your musing reminds you of some incidents that show how pleasant life in Westend can be – stories to tell by way of illustration. Or you think of the activities that make up the daily round of your friends and neighbors – a typical workday, a typical weekend. Again, you're generating substance.

Another possibility: "Let's see. How can I make my point? Compare Westend with the *un*pleasant places you read about in the papers? Compare it with *this* place. Peace and quiet there, noise and hassle here. Tick off the differences, one after another." Or maybe, to make clear that Westend isn't one of those all-of-a-kind places, you could classify the residents by ethnic background, income, education, and so on. Or by discussing the positive things Westend has to offer in the way of job opportunities, education, recreation, and entertainment, you could convince a reader that it's an attractive city.

At this head-scratching or scribbling stage, you may find that while you're generating some content, it isn't going to stretch very far. So you plug away: "All right, I can nail down the fact that Westend is a nice place to live, but then what? How about explaining *why* it's the kind of place it is? Is it because of the location? Because of all the different kinds of jobs at Giant Electric? The kinds of people those jobs attract?" Perhaps thinking about why Westend is pleasant will lead you to come up with a new thesis: "Although the job opportunities at Giant Electric make Westend fairly prosperous, the city might be better off if it didn't depend so much on one employer." Could you make a good case for that statement?

What you know about Westend might serve as a springboard for a paper defining a one-industry city. The aim of the definition could be simple explanation, with Westend serving as a typical example of a city dominated by a single industry. Or the aim could be to persuade the reader that life in a small industrial city is better (or worse) than life in a big city or a suburb or a small town.

By the time you've thought through your subject—and, in the process, built content for your paper—you will probably have refined, modified, narrowed, or expanded your original generalization ("Westend is a pleasant place") into a proposition that indicates with some precision what your paper will do. Mulling over approaches in the prewriting stage will have pointed you in the direction of a specific, manageable central idea. And it may have led you to change your original thesis. Instead of setting out to convince your audience that Westend is a pleasant city, you may decide to settle on a thesis like "Growing up in the security of Westend is poor preparation for getting along in University City, with its tensions, pressures, and competitiveness." Serious prewriting effort may have led you to the discovery that your initial generalization doesn't stand up, that when you examine it closely, Westend isn't such a pleasant place after all.

Prewriting may have that effect because it involves being honest with yourself, deciding what you really believe about your subject. It also involves selecting the most promising approaches to your subject—comparing, classifying, dividing, and so on. And it does more than lay the groundwork for a successful paper. In considering how you'll approach your subject, you don't think of comparing in the abstract; you think of comparing Westend with University City. Thus prewriting generates content; it makes you aware of the specific things you want to say.

■ For Writing

Write three beginnings for a paper on the community where you grew up. Each beginning should be at least 150 words, and each should point to a different method of developing your main generalization about the community. Then, in a paper of about 1000 words, complete the beginning that interests you most. Address your paper to a college friend you'd like to take along on your next trip home.

Writing

Prewriting and writing overlap. Preparing a paper isn't a mechanical, linear process in which each operation is wrapped up before the next one is begun. Instead, all the vital activities continue as the project moves from one stage to another. Some authors prewrite well into the stage of putting sentences on paper.

Even so, writing proper brings in a whole new dimension of creative activity. You have to juggle and weigh varying (and sometimes conflicting) demands. You must do justice to your material and at the same time reach your audience, not just say what you mean but say it so that it will interest, inform, and influence others.

Writing and Rewriting

Find the way into your paper that suits you best. Will you begin by making a detailed plan for your paper, or will you let the plan develop as you write? Some professionals like to build the organizational framework before they have much to put into it. They start with a few phrases or sentences, push them into the pattern of an outline, and keep working until they have a series of statements representing the main points they want to make in the order they want to make them. Only then do they start writing consecutive sentences. Others like to coax the structure out of the material. Whatever procedure you follow, leave your mind open to the new possibilities for developing ideas and the new ways of arranging them that the actual process of composing may suggest.

Use an outline or not, as you see fit, but above all get started. Students aren't the only ones to inflict the self-punishment of putting off the job. Commenting on the habits of professionals, Malcolm Cowley has said, "Apparently the hardest problem for almost any writer, whatever his medium, is getting to work in the morning (or in the afternoon, if he is a late riser . . . or even at night)." Instead of thinking up reasons and excuses for not getting on with the job, plunge in, and keep going. Don't waste time trying to dream up the perfect opening. Chances are that when you've finished the paper, you'll have a much better notion of what will make a good first paragraph.

Once you're started, stick with it long enough to write several pages—if possible, a complete draft. Writing done in one sitting is likely to have better continuity, more consistency, more life than writing that's done in bits and pieces. Though some professional writers like a bare-bones first draft, most find it a good practice to make their first draft a full one. If you're in doubt about some of your material, include it. When you've finished, you'll be in a better position to decide whether or not a particular passage is relevant. Make your paragraphs full-bodied, too, with plenty of details. In revising, it's easier to reduce an outsize paragraph than to fatten up an undernourished one.

Unless you're the most careful and deliberate kind of writer, your first draft will be rough and uneven. Some sentences will be rambling, clumsy, perhaps unintelligible. Even if the paragraphs are more or less related to your purpose, they may show little relation to each other. But writing the first draft should have clarified your thinking, given you some notion of the shape the paper ought to take, and shown you what needs to be done to produce a strong, unified essay. Possibly you need hard evidence to support your generalizations. Possibly you should build what's now a minor point into a major one. Certainly you should give attention to linking paragraphs to show the connection of ideas, revising sentences to make the thought come clear, finding words and images that will sharpen and freshen your meaning. One of the main objectives of this text is to help you rework early drafts.

As you revise and rewrite, keep your mind open to new ideas. If the process of setting down your thoughts has made you realize that some of them contradict others or that some of them are plain foolish, it should also have generated sounder, more consistent ones. And keep your mind open to new ways of expressing your ideas. The biggest obstacle to improvement in writing is the notion that once a sentence is written, it's finished, fixed, frozen. Don't guard your first phrasing of an idea as if it's sacred. Take the attitude that anything you write can be improved—or thrown away.

A Word About Style

When we write a first draft, most of us are so intent on getting our meaning straight that we pay little attention to matters of style. In revising, we have to work over our sentences carefully to make them say what we want them to say *in the way we want to say it*. So a good part of the process of writing consists of revising not for meaning and not for correctness but for style.

The basic rule for finding the right style is simple to state: Your style should be appropriate to the rhetorical situation. The informality appropriate in a newsy letter to a younger brother or sister is inappropriate in a letter applying for a scholarship grant. A term paper on the origins of mercantilism should be more formal than a review of a rock concert for the campus newspaper. But most college work neither permits total relaxation nor requires rigid formality. Stylistically, it belongs to that broad middle area represented by what we see regularly in current books and magazines.

The interaction of writer, subject, purpose, and audience should influence both choice of words and syntax—the way words, phrases, and clauses are shaped into sentences. Later chapters will deal in some detail with these matters of style, as well as with paragraphs and paragraph sequences. Here we'll merely sketch styles that can be called informal, formal, and general and examine some of their more obvious traits.

I. Informal
Once you're off the campus this place is no big deal. Pretty horrible, actually. I guess you could say that the U is honcho here like Giant Electric is there, but the difference is that here the kids are just passing through and paying their dues. So nobody really gives much of a damn about University City except to get out of it. And that's the way it looks.

II. Formal
Westend, a city of medium size in the northeastern corner of the state, differs from University City in a number of significant respects. Although each city is dominated by a single institution—the one industrial, the other educational—the two societies are quite unlike. The great majority of the residents of Westend are permanent: they hold steady jobs at Giant Electric Corporation; they own their own homes; and they look forward to eventual retirement in Westend or its environs. By contrast, the great majority of the residents of University City are temporary: they hold part-time jobs, if any; they rent their living quarters, whether dormitory rooms, apartments, or houses; and they depart as soon as they have received their degrees. These marked differences in the life-styles and attitudes of the populations are reflected in both the physical environment and the ambience of each city.

III. General
Westend, the city I grew up in, is a stable sort of a place compared to University City. Most of the people work in the Giant

Electric plant. They start young, and they stick with it till they qualify for their pensions. Unlike University students, who keep their suitcases under their beds, Westenders put down roots. Residential neighborhoods in Westend give an impression of neatness and self-respect, while here off-campus housing is likely to be rundown and dirty.

The first passage might appear in a letter from a student to a hometown friend. Because both know Westend well, the writer can tell the reader a lot about University City by simply suggesting the comparison; there's no need to say what Westenders do instead of "pass through." The style is casual, with some of the flavor of easy talk. The word choice and phrasing — "actually," "really," "honcho," "no big deal," "pretty horrible," "paying their dues," "like Giant Electric is," "giving much of a damn" — contribute to a dominant impression of informality. So does the syntax, particularly the fragmentary second sentence and the loose-jointed second last sentence, which won't stand up to logical analysis. The writer hasn't gone to any special effort. The reader will catch the writer's tone of voice and get the drift of what's said, and that's enough.

In contrast, the second passage gives the impression that the writer has done a good deal of preliminary planning and then worked over the sentences carefully. The style is about as formal as undergraduate writing ever should be — suitable, perhaps, for a term paper in one of the social sciences. Word choice and phrasing — "eventual," "environs," "depart," "ambience," "a number of significant respects," "dominated by a single institution," "the one industrial, the other educational" — are characteristic of written rather than spoken English. The arrangement of words in the sentence — especially the placing of modifiers and the use of parallel structures — and even the punctuation marks all help point up logical relationships. The distance between writer and reader is much greater than in the informal passage. Although the audience of the second would probably know as much about University City as the audience of the first would know about Westend, the writer of the formal passage has taken no shortcuts. The contrast is balanced throughout.

In the third passage neither word choice nor phrasing nor sentence structure calls attention to itself. If we examine the vocabulary, we find it more precise than in the first passage ("stable," "residential neighborhoods," "neatness and self-respect"), less bookish than in the second ("sort of a place," "there's," "stick with it"). Similarly, the sentences are more carefully constructed than in the letter home, less obviously arranged than in the term paper. (As a metaphor for transience, keeping the suitcase under the bed might be said to counterbalance the well-worn putting down roots for permanence, but the reader gets no impression that the pairing was planned.) It's a kind of straightforward, readable style that we call general, a kind you'll find most useful in the writing you do both in and out of college.

In identifying styles as informal, formal, or general, we go by dominant impressions. In fact, general styles aren't sharply separate from the other two types. When writing in a general style, you can borrow the contractions of informal—*you'll, she's, can't,* and so on—and when you need them, you can take words from the scholarly vocabulary of formal. Thus a style can lean to either formal or informal while remaining predominantly general. As a college student you'll have few occasions to write in an informal style, except in your diary or journal and in your personal correspondence. In term papers, research reports, and critical essays, you'll probably be expected to write toward the formal end of your range. In most of your writing a general style will be appropriate.

In choosing a style for college work, students are most likely to err in the direction of formality and produce a stilted, stuffy prose that has no particular relationship to subject or audience or writer. But a general style can be poorly handled, too. The many options it offers are of no advantage if you don't know what they are or how to choose among them. Guiding you toward making the right choices is one major purpose of this book. The most important thing to keep in mind is that the stylistic choices you make should be appropriate to the rhetorical situation, which is created by the interaction of your purpose in writing, your subject, your audience, and yourself.

For further discussion of informal, formal, and general English, see Chapter Nine.

■ *For Writing*

In a letter to a close friend who doesn't attend your college, describe a current campus fad. Then write an account of the same fad for a national magazine whose readers are mainly college graduates in their thirties, forties, and fifties. For each paper, consider what role you want to play. Are you writing as a participant in the fad or as an observer of it? Are you defending it, attacking it, or simply reporting it? The two papers should probably differ somewhat in content and should certainly differ in style.

Revising and Editing

Even with the most thorough prewriting, a paper should go through several drafts. Good writing is rewritten writing. Rework your papers—and the emphasis is on *work*—until you're satisfied that the content, organization, and style represent the best you can do with the topic in the time you have and until you've said what you want to say to your audience in the way you want to say it.

In the final stage of composition, get outside your paper. Look at it from the perspective of a critical reader. Try to be objective about your work. That usually calls for letting a day or two pass before writing the last draft and doing the final revision.

Taking a fresh look at what you've written may persuade you to make substantial changes in content. A new idea may hit you. For the first time you may see that dropping paragraph 5 and merging paragraphs 4 and 6 will make the organization tighter and more economical. But if you've given enough thought to composing and if you've gone through enough drafts to produce a version that satisfies you, most of the job of revising will consist of reworking sentences. Slash unnecessary phrases, the ones you wrote just to get your thinking started or just to fill up space. Pare and prune. Try to pack more meaning into fewer words.

As you give your paper this last revision, read it aloud once or twice. Your ear will catch some weaknesses that your eye has missed. A shapeless sentence will betray itself by making you stumble over it. You'll hear clichés and flabby phrases that will make you wince. Even errors in spelling and punctuation sometimes call attention to themselves if you're listening hard. Keep your dictionary open. Check anything that raises doubt in your mind.

Finally, type a clean draft, following the manuscript form your instructor prescribes. Before submitting the paper, give it a careful proofreading to get rid of typing errors.

A Checklist

Before you've established your own habits of composing and developed skill in sizing up the requirements of an assignment, you may find it helpful to have a list of steps to follow in producing a paper. Any division of the writing process into steps is bound to be somewhat artificial and arbitrary, but for most college writing you're likely to go through the stages summarized here. Depending on the method of composing that turns out to be best for you, prewriting may merge into writing as early as the first step or as late as the fifth.

1. Focusing on a subject, locating a topic in the subject, and phrasing a tentative statement of purpose or a thesis statement.

2. Gathering material—from memory or reflection, or from reading or study—sifting it, and evaluating it.

3. Choosing ways of developing the material (and in the process generating material).

4. Organizing the material, using an outline or some other method to map out the structure of the paper.

5. Writing drafts of the paper, rewriting until the thought comes clear within a sound structure, in a style that fits the rhetorical situation. (During this stage be prepared to reconsider all the decisions you've made up to this point.)

6. Revising and editing the paper—deleting, adding, rewording to make the meaning clearer and the style smoother, correcting errors in spelling, grammar, and punctuation.

7. Preparing and proofreading the manuscript—following prescribed form and correcting all copying errors.

Self-Analysis and Evaluation

Our main concern in this chapter has been to make clear that good writing springs initially not from formulas but from creative activity, from the desire and need to express particular information, thoughts, and feelings to a specific audience. Even when it's not at all personal in the sense of being about you, your writing always deserves a personal commitment, not only to the subject but to the actual job of composing. If you're to take full responsibility for what you write, you need to develop habits that work for you (though not necessarily for anyone else), and you need to learn to appraise the strengths and weaknesses of what you write. Commitment to writing calls for both genuine involvement and candid self-criticism.

As a means of self-appraisal, you should find it helpful

now and then to keep a running account of how you go about preparing an essay. Try to adopt a double vision: watch yourself as you work, and jot down notes on how you go about the job. Identify the trouble spots at every stage from prewriting to final revision. Note how you try to solve (or sidestep) each problem. When you've finished the paper, write an account of what you did, and make an honest attempt to evaluate the paper you produced.

■ For Analysis and Writing

1. Take stock of your strengths and weaknesses as a writer. In a short paper addressed to your instructor, tell about your experiences in writing. How much and what kinds have you done? What's frustrated you? What's given you pleasure? What kind of writing do you think you do best? What, in your judgment, do you need to do to improve your writing?

Here are three responses to this assignment:

a. In general, I don't particularly enjoy writing. I don't dislike writing, but I would rather be working with numbers than with letters.

I do not consider myself a particularly good writer because I feel it takes me too many words to get my point across. I've always received good grades on papers mainly because they contained some good ideas, not because they were well expressed.

If I follow through with my major (accounting) I don't think I'll be doing much writing (other than numbers), but I would like to learn to write better, mainly because I don't think I could do a very good job on some of the things necessary in college, such as term papers, resumés, etc.

I think that my main problem in writing is due to a fairly limited vocabulary.

As for what kind of writing I like best, I really don't have any preferences.

I haven't done too much voluntary writing of any kind.

b. I have a great deal of trouble expressing myself in any form of writing, forced or not forced. Due to this problem I seldom write about anything, unless I am forced to. In high school I did have some training in writing different types of papers such as expository and critical. It might have helped a little except for the fact that I don't like to write and therefore didn't practice very much. I also had training in writing the research paper.

The only type of writing which I really don't mind is writing a letter. I only write letters when I have something to say. I also don't mind writing research papers that much. This is because I am not forced to think of any original ideas, but I am taking the ideas of other people and putting them together. The times I have trouble come when I have to write original poetry or something like that. I guess my imagination isn't big enough. I just seem to have trouble coming up with the right words in the right spots.

c. Until the last half of my senior year in high school I didn't do much writing except what I had to for course work. Once in a while when I was twelve or thirteen I would write a poem and I had a spell of science fiction writing one summer. But mainly I just wrote for courses – biology and history and of course English where I remember writing book reports and some critical essays. I have always preferred reading to writing. I suppose it was because I got interested in some modern writers last year and because I had a teacher who encouraged me to try different kinds of writing that I began to take pleasure in expressing my ideas and feelings in different styles. Anyway, last spring writing became important to me for the first time in all the years I've been in school.

Our teacher encouraged us to write in a journal every day. We didn't have to do it, but when I got in the habit I found I enjoyed it. Our teacher told us to single out just one thing that had happened, one mood, or one idea we'd had and write about that. So the journal wasn't as much a diary as a record of moments that had made an impression on us.

Another thing I learned last year was to write for different kinds of people. Unlike other courses, where we had to please only the teacher, we were expected to write our papers for senators or movie stars or news commentators or parents or whoever we wanted to express an opinion to. But we *had* to have something to say. Our teacher always knew when we were faking it. As a result I had to get rid of empty, flowery phrases that just use up space. I've found that my best papers were those which came from my heart. If I have a strong opinion about a subject the words seem to flow naturally. By looking at my writing as a learning situation or chance to express an idea, instead of an assignment which needs completing, I've learned to enjoy writing a lot more.

I still have a lot to learn about how to put on paper the ideas in my head. Usually I leave too much for the reader to figure out. I have to say what I mean more fully, in more detail, and more expressively so that the reader will read what I write with some pleasure as well as understanding. Hopefully I will learn to do this in college.

2. *Write a paragraph of advice to the author of 1a, b, or c.*

3. *Choose a subject that you're interested in and that you feel competent to write about. Take any approach to it that you wish, specify an audience, and write a paper of about 750 words. While prewriting and writing the paper, make notes on how you go about it. Be as accurate as you can in reporting the procedures you follow in generating content for the paper and in presenting the content for the audience you've chosen. Turn in your notes with your paper.*

4. *The following paper and the accompanying analysis were produced at the end of the second week of an advanced composition course in response to the preceding assignment. As you read the paper and the analysis, ask yourself these questions:*

Did the writer choose a good subject?

Has the writer found a satisfactory way of approaching the subject? Can you visualize the scene? Does the writing re-create the experience clearly and vividly enough for you to share the author's feelings?

Has the writer made a sound evaluation of the paper? Do you think it went through enough drafts? What are its strengths? Its weaknesses?

Write a letter to the author of "An Island Perspective," proposing solutions to the problems she recognizes and suggesting specific ways her paper could be improved.

An Island Perspective

I suppose everyone on the island had a favorite spot. Mine was a little cove about a quarter of the way around the coast from the hotel. If none of the guests were around — we had to preserve a conservative image for them — I would take off my shift and, in my swim suit, test the freedom of my limbs against the stability of the rocks, running and leaping from one to another. It was simple happiness then, but here at college I wonder that it didn't approach the ecstasy I know I would feel now if somehow I could be back at Star Island.

I would arrive at the cove breathless, quickly dive in, and then in one continuous movement slide from the water to a prone position on the rocks. For the first few moments I could do nothing more than lie there, still breathing hard, and feel the rays from the omnipresent sun weave their way through the cool ocean breeze. The regularity of the waves as they broke against the rocks was nothing short of a lullaby for me after the frantic business of serving breakfast to two hundred guests. I would let the sound gradually replace the echo of banging dishes, chattering girls, and shouted orders, until my mind was blank except for the rhythmical song of the sea.

It must have been an ambitious nature that made me plan reading and letter writing each time I went to the cove. Whatever it was, it fought a losing battle all summer, never giving up the hope that maybe *today* would be the day I would finally accomplish something "productive." But I was in the sea world, and the most productive thing I could do was to become a part of that world. That meant, at first, letting the sounds of gulls and waves override my mind's activities, and allowing the sun, air, and spray to relax my tense body. It meant giving in to the hypnotic power of the sea.

Later, though, after I'd become like a mussel on the rocks — part of the rocks, yet not a rock — my mind would begin to respond to the sea. Thoughts flowed in and out, short, almost wordless impressions as quickly gone as they had come. Gently they came, yet more and more pervasively, like the rising tide, and I'd begin to play with them, holding them a little longer, asking a little more of them. Thoughts that had been troublesome and seemed complex drifted to their natural place and, feeling at home there, could relax and stop demanding attention by pretending they were more important than they were.

I don't know if I was experiencing Contemplation, Meditation, or just Peaceful Solitude as I lay there on the rocks in the cove. Now that I'm back on the mainland, it seems impossible to find time to be alone, to empty myself as I did by the sea, and then to explore my thoughts with such curious, sometimes amusing, sometimes startling objectivity. If I miss the sea, it's because it expected nothing of me, yet gave me its perspective on my often confused thinking, a perspective of simplicity and naturalness.

Self-Analysis

At first mention of writing about a personal experience, I thought of Star Island, one of my most recent and more unusual experiences. But I hesitated a few days, considering topics not quite so immediate that I could perhaps handle more objectively. There was also the fear that anything I wrote about Star would lose something in the telling and fail to communicate to the reader the experience that had meant so much to me. I finally decided that the topic must be Star, because I rejected all other ideas as less interesting. Besides, it was a good justification for thinking about Star as much as I wanted to without feeling that I was shirking school responsibilities.

I started several times, the first a light description of some of the more amusing aspects of living on an island for ten weeks. Now I think perhaps I should have continued with that idea, rather than switching to a more serious topic. It's easier to convey the humor in incidents than it is to convey feelings. I began the submitted essay on Monday. I wrote two paragraphs after reliving the experience I wanted to re-create several times earlier that day. I rejected a first paragraph about how I got the job as irrelevant and made the second paragraph the opening one. At the point where I mention feeling like a mussel on a rock, I was stuck for a transition to describe the gradually increasing activity of my mind. I was also bothered that my feelings sounded too "romantic" and unreal. My problem—that of describing a situation that at the time wasn't analyzed or "metaphorized" (I can't think of any other word for it), yet now, in retrospect, doing both. I did not solve that problem, so I am not accurately describing to the reader my feelings of the moment, but rather the significance they have taken in my memory—my feelings *now*, at college, about *then*, at Star.

My ideas grew more complex, thus harder to express, and further away from the simplicity I wanted to convey. Tuesday I did quite a bit of piecemeal composition. I went to bed Tuesday night wanting to change topics but forced by the schedule to stay with the one I had chosen. Wednesday morning I reread what I had written, crossed out one whole paragraph, and gave up on a transition I had been trying to make from the experience on Star to the problem of re-creating the situation here. Wednesday afternoon I rearranged a few sentences, reworded several phrases, and bought paper for the final typescript. I have to admit that the essay falls short of my expectations by a more than usual distance. However, I am satisfied with several of the sentences and out of necessity must for the present consider the essay finished.

Chapter Two
Developing Papers

In Chapter One we looked at some ways of generating content in prewriting. Here we'll examine those methods and techniques more carefully, paying special attention to how they can be used in developing and organizing different kinds of papers.

We'll begin by discussing generalizations and particulars, the building blocks of all writing, and then move on to the chief methods of developing papers—description, narration, division, comparison, classification, analysis of causes, definition. Traditionally, description and narration have been classified with exposition and argument as major types of prose discourse. Here we'll treat them mainly as means of supporting exposition and argument, the kinds of writing you'll do most often in college.

Keep in mind as you study each section that a method of development rarely occurs alone in a paper. Normally the methods are used in combination, to support one another, to share in carrying out the writer's purpose. An explanation of why something happened (why a candidate won, why a team lost) may be presented within a narrative account of what took place (the political campaign and the election, the events leading up to the game and the game itself). Comparing is one way of defining ("Aikido, *like judo,* is one of the martial arts, but . . ."). And so on. But taking up the methods one by one makes it easier to single out their special uses and the problems in planning and writing they sometimes raise. What's said about each method applies whether the method is used in developing part of a paragraph, a whole paragraph, a sequence of paragraphs, or (more rarely) a whole paper.

Generalizations and Particulars

One way to look at a piece of writing is to see it as made up of generalizations and particulars. Particulars often take the form of examples or details.

Some statements can immediately be identified as generalizations ("Italians love music") and some as particulars ("The black-eyed peas were served with bits of bacon"). But the terms *generalization* and *particular* are relative; often we can tell which a statement is only in context. "The Olympic Games are held every four years" would probably be a generalization in a paper that looked back on the last Olympic Games. It might be a particular in a paper that dealt with the history of amateur and professional sports.

Though generalizations may dominate in some kinds of writing and particulars in others, usually there's a regular interplay, with the particulars giving support to the generalizations and the generalizations giving point to the particulars. The following passage shows a typical interweaving. Of the generalizations, the broadest occurs in the first sentence. Note the successive narrowing from "real life" to "your life" to "my mother's house." The glitter in the mother's house is particularized by clusters of details about furnishings and clothes, details that justify the writer's making two further generalizations—"size, quantity, and glitter always count" and "it all seems somehow gayer that way."

The drabness of real life seems to affect taste. If your life is exciting you are likely to decorate in stark Danish and wear simple unadorned black classics. But in my mother's house there is glitter —a dazzling wall clock that bongs every half-hour, an oversized, wood-inlaid painting of Chinese dancers (à la Coney Island), painted figurines of bongo players, and a giant Buddha perched atop the TV. In her clothes my mother prefers bright reds to black. She will choose the flashy fakes over subdued pearls, big beads over smaller ones, and three strands over one. Size, quantity, and glitter always count. Her car is an orange and white Mercury (now in its declining years), and her hair is of rather similar hues—it all seems somehow gayer that way.—Patricia Cayo Sexton, *Harper's*

Generalizations

Generalizations perform many different functions. They may sum up a number of experiences: "Growing up black means growing up angry." They may bring out the meaning of a single experience: "Those first few days in the hospital taught me that there's a time when just surviving is enough." They may express an opinion or a judgment: "The drabness of real life seems to affect taste"; "All in all, our team would have been better off if it had stayed in the locker room"; "That is certainly the best of Altman's movies."

Because generalizations show relationships, bring out meanings, and draw conclusions, you'll find them indispensable in any papers that criticize or evaluate. At times you may find an entire essay spinning from or building toward the single generalization that is your thesis.

A bold, dramatic generalization can pull a reader into a piece of writing as nothing else can. When Irving Howe writes, "The day *Native Son* appeared, American culture was changed forever," he captures the attention not only of those already convinced of the significance of Richard Wright's novel but of those who are either unfamiliar with it or unimpressed by it and ready to challenge what Howe has to say. Don't, however, let the urge for dramatic effect tempt you into producing a journalistic opener like "Americans love violence" or "Our school totters on the brink of disaster" or "Marriage is obsolete" unless you can support your headline with convincing particulars. Unsupported generalizations are a major cause of weakness in any writing.

Examples

Citing a member of a group or class — using the Labrador retriever as a member of the class *retrievers,* or beets and carrots as members of the class *hardy vegetables*, or "Marriage is obsolete" as a member of the class *generalizations* — is the most common way of bringing in examples. But it's not the only way. Anecdotes, or small-scale narratives, can serve as examples: an account of an experience you had when you were five might illustrate, or lead to a generalization about, how impressionable children are. Comparisons can serve as examples: a comparison of social dancing in the 1940s and social dancing in the 1970s could support some generalizations about young people in those two periods.

What turns an anecdote or a comparison into an example is its connection with a general statement. The connection may be explicit, as in the second sentence and the last phrase of this passage:

Among the fans of astrology everyone has his or her favorite item of proof. John Dryden's melancholy reading of his newborn son's horoscope is a fair example. He predicted disasters at the ages of eight, twenty-three, and thirty-three. At eight the child was involved in an accident with a stag. At twenty-three he fell from a tower. He drowned at thirty-three.

The amazing batting average of Nostradamus, who appears to have foretold the Great Fire of London, the French Revolution, and the rise of Russian power after World War II, is everywhere cited as evidence of the astrological imperative. — Linda Lewis, *Atlantic*

For example and *for instance* are the familiar introductory tags, but often no such signals are necessary:

Many slang words pass into standard use and once they do, of course, they don't sound slangy at all. Among such now-sturdy-respectables are *club* (social), *dwindle, flout, foppish, freshman, fretful, glib, hubbub, nice, ribaldry, scoundrel, simper, swagger, tidy, tantrums, tarpaulin*, and *trip* (journey). — Bergen Evans, *New York Times Magazine*

How many examples you need in a piece of writing depends on the rhetorical situation, especially on how familiar your audience is with your subject and how much authority you speak with. Provide too few examples and uninformed readers will be confused or unconvinced. Provide too many and informed readers will be bored. (Because it's addressed to an audience with widely varied backgrounds and interests, this book cites many more examples than it would if it were addressed to a homogeneous group.) The number needed depends also on the nature of the subject and the kind of examples it calls for. In the passage by Lewis, two striking examples are enough to support the opening generalization. In the excerpt from Evans, seventeen examples aren't excessive in supporting the generalization about "many slang words." The subject is specialized, and the fact that all the words in the list were once considered slang is likely to interest and inform readers as well as convince them that the statement is true.

Examples that will be immediately familiar to your audience need only be mentioned: "Freestanding sculpture may be small enough to hold in one's hand or huge, *like the Statue of Liberty*." If your examples are unfamiliar or if you're using them to prove as well as to clarify, you'll want to develop them, explain them, support them with details. That would be the case if you based a thesis about high-school education on your own experiences and the experiences of students you've talked with since coming to college.

In revising your papers, examine your generalizations to see if they need to be supported or clarified by examples. If they do, ask yourself whether it would be better to mention half a dozen instances or to develop one or two in some detail. Decide whether, in the particular rhetorical situation, the examples should lead up to the generalization or follow it. And make sure that the relevance of the examples to the generalization is immediately apparent.

Details

If it's true, as we said in Chapter One, that in order to write well you must become involved with your subject, it's equally true that your audience must become involved with it. The readers' involvement will come about if you make it possible for them to visualize what you write about and to experience the sounds, smells, sensations, and emotions you've experienced. This you can do through your use of sensory details: the *flashing blue lights* of the police cars, the *saw-toothed blade* of a knife, the *webbed toes* of the Labrador retriever; amplified enough *to make your nose bleed;* walking *arm-in-arm.*

Like examples, details can make your generalizations clear and convincing. And they can do more than anything else to give your writing individuality, immediacy, concreteness. During an actual experience – say a trip to the dentist – sense impressions predominate. In telling about the experience, you should try to convey those impressions, not just the generalizations that come to mind later. Don't talk about having felt pain; make the pain real. Abstractly, pain is "a distressing sensation of a part of the body." Concretely, it's the constant throbbing of an abscessed molar or the shocking twinge of a pinched nerve.

Details are essential if your readers are to share your experiences and your feelings about those experiences. They're equally necessary when you're dealing with literary works and with abstract ideas. A review of a novel calls for details of plot, character, style. A discussion of the abstraction *virtue* might use as details the individual virtues honesty, kindness, generosity, and so on. Every subject has its details. Much of the art of writing consists in choosing the right details and making them do what you want them to do. These are matters we'll consider more fully in the next two sections.

■ *For Analysis and Writing*

1. Recall an experience you've had, and in two or three substantial paragraphs present it so that the reader will be able to relive it with you. Your purpose is not to tell a story with a beginning, middle, and end but to use sensory details to re-create a scene or recapture the feel of an experience.

Here's a procedure you might follow in preparing the paper. First, choose a scene or an incident from your experiences that, for one reason or another, appealed to your senses. It doesn't have to be dramatic; a particular meal or bus ride or day in the sun may be memorable. Second, decide how you feel about the experience. Third, relive it in your mind, listing as you do as many details as you can. Try to draw on every one of your five senses. Fourth, select from your list the details that best re-create the feel of the experience, and arrange them so that they work together to give a unified impression. As you write, keep in mind that your aim is to share *the experience, not just talk about it. Don't tell your readers how you felt; let your sensory details do that.*

When you submit your paper, turn in your complete list of details with it.

2. For each of the following passages, identify the main generalizations and explain why you think the writer's use of detail is or is not satisfactory. Has he used enough details to support the generalizations? Are they the right details? In your answers, take into account the rhetorical situation. You can make a pretty good guess about the audiences by noting the publications in which the selections appeared. If you aren't familiar with them, look for copies in the library.

a. My gym suits fit me only in sports shop dressing rooms. By the time I got them to school they'd be several sizes too small. I don't think I ever passed a happy hour in a gym suit, and at no time was I unhappier than during the week we had coed gymnastics. All the equipment was set up in the girls' gym, and I guess the Phys. Ed. department figured it would be logistically too difficult to have the boys and girls trade gyms for a couple of weeks.

Nowhere was I flatter of foot, spindlier and paler of leg, more equivocal of shoulder, and heavier of acned brow than in the girls' gymnasium. We would have to line up boy-girl-boy-girl in front of the parallel bars, and it was no picnic when my turn came. I could never straighten my arms on the parallel bars, and spent a lot of time swinging from my armpits and making exertive noises.

We had to jump over horses in gymnastics class. We were supposed to run up to the things, grab them by their handles, and swing our legs over them. This seemed to me to be an unreasonable expectation, and I always balked on my approach. "You're always balking on your approach," the woman gym teacher would shout at me. "Don't balk on your approach." Thus lacking momentum, I would manage to grab the bars and kind of climb over the things with my knees. My only comfort was in watching Richard Walters try to clear the horse, which he never did, even by climbing.

The balance beam was probably the least threatening piece of equipment as far as I was concerned. I had a fair sense of balance and enormous, clutching feet, and I could make it across all right. But when the exercise called for straddling, and my flaring shorts endangered coed decorum, I would pretend to slip from the balance beam and then hurry to the next piece of equipment.

Coed gymnastics was in some ways a mixed bag, for while there was always the agony of failing miserably and almost nakedly before the fair sex (as it was known at the time), we were afforded chances to observe the girls exercising in their turbulent Danskins. I hope I'll never forget how Janet Gibbs moved along the balance beam, how Denise Dyktor bounced upon the trampoline, how Carol Dower arched and somersaulted across the tumbling mats. Perhaps one of the true high points of my adolescence was spotting for Suzie Hawley, who had the most beautiful, academically disruptive calves in Greenwich High School, and who happened once to slip from the high bar into my startled and grateful clutches.

But that was a fleeting delight in a context of misery. Mostly I remember just standing around, or ducking from the end of one line to the end of another, evading the apparatus and mortification of coed gymnastics as best I could.—Andrew Ward, *Atlantic*

b. I've always had a special liking for old men. Once when as a boy I saw some friends catch a fish and clean it without first killing it, I found myself thinking that an old man wouldn't do such a thing. I listened to the stories strangers told—old people who sat next to me on a bus—and recognized that their pride in what they said was not random boasting, that a man's life story summarizes plainly enough the stamina, concentration and energy he has had over the years, as well as his luck; loyalty, friendship, sanity, imagination—those old words too. Old men are usually joyful men at heart. Ulcers and hypertension have winnowed away the more fretful fellows to the peace of the grave. Old men are those who have bobbed to the surface in time of flood, who have smiled to themselves and let their hurts heal.—Edward Hoagland, *Walking the Dead Diamond River* (appeared originally in *Village Voice*)

c. Even in the wilds of Texas, where ranchers still nail dead coyotes and chicken hawks to their fence posts as a taunt to wild predators in general, times seem to have changed. The two small Texas towns of Noack and Lometa held their rattlesnake round-ups this spring, as they have done every spring for years. Thousands of the creatures were captured, exhibited, beheaded, and fried. But this year, in addition to the participants, there was also a group of dissenters who made the indisputable point that the hunt was hard on the snakes. "There are a growing number of people," one member of this group wrote in the Austin *American-Statesman*, "who recognize specieism as the bigotry that it is. Mistreatment of any animal, human or nonhuman, is wrong." A few weeks later, Austin's Armadillo World Headquarters, the country-music palace that had been second only to the Astrodome as an outlet for Lone Star Beer, cut off its Lone Star contract because the company persisted in sponsoring live armadillo races. "The only way to protect an armadillo," said

Eddie Wilson, the Armadillo's manager, "is to leave it alone, rather than rounding them up and capturing them." – James Fallows, *Atlantic*

Describing: Showing How It Looks

A small, puckish-looking man with round, heavy-lidded eyes, always with dark circles under them, and with fingers and teeth stained a deep yellow by nicotine, he had an engaging yuk-yuk of a laugh, and as he told stories he would swing back and forth in his swivel chair, rather like a child riding a hobby-horse. – Brendan Gill, *Here at the New Yorker*

The height of the grass at Wimbledon is three-sixteenths of an inch. The mower that keeps it at that level is a sixteen-inch Ransome Certes, which has a high-speed, precision-ground, ten-knife cylinder, makes a hundred cuts every thirty-six inches, costs forty-one pounds twelve and six, and hums with the high sound of a vacuum cleaner while it moves. – John McPhee, *A Roomful of Hovings and Other Profiles*

The first of the two passages above pictures a man as a friend remembers him. The second describes a mower used on the grass tennis courts at Wimbledon as it might be seen and heard by any careful observer. The purposes of the two writers are quite different. Gill wants to produce a sketch in which his feeling for his subject comes through. McPhee wants to impress upon the reader the precision and professionalism with which the grounds-keeper at Wimbledon approaches the task of maintaining the courts for championship tennis. To achieve their different ends, they use the same means – concrete details and comparisons.

Gill's details give us the whole man ("small, puckish-looking"), the dominant feature of his face ("round, heavy-lidded eyes . . . with dark circles under them"), his yellowed teeth and fingers, the sound of his laughter ("engaging yuk-yuk"), a characteristic movement (swinging "back and forth in his swivel chair"). McPhee's details give us the exact height at which the grass is kept ("three-sixteenths of an inch"), the size and make of the mower, the kind of cylinder it has ("high-speed, precision-ground, ten-knife"), the number of cuts it makes per yard, its cost, and its sound. Each writer also uses a comparison: Gill's friend swings in his chair "rather like a child riding a hobby-horse"; McPhee's mower hums "with the high sound of a vacuum cleaner."

Selecting Details

Perhaps the most common weakness in descriptive writing is to rely on generalizations to do the work that should be done by details—to say no more, for instance, than "The park is not old, but it is going slightly to seed." When the same generalization is supported by the details that made it true for the writer, it becomes true for the reader too:

The park is not old, but it is going slightly to seed. Grass pushes through the concrete in some places, there's graffiti on the handball courts and benches have boards missing. By the basketball court, some of the slats are broken on the bleachers, and the bolts of one of the baskets have been yanked loose, probably by a future pro practicing his sky-hook slam-dunk.—Al Harvin, *New York Times*

The basis of all good description is close observation. To start with, you need a store of particulars to draw on. From these you select the ones that suit your purpose. Details that fit one aim may not fit another. Read the description of an escaped criminal on a "Wanted" bulletin put out by the police, and imagine how the same fugitive might be described by a loving parent and by a frightened or embittered victim of his crime.

If your purpose is to picture an object or a person or a place as any careful observer would see it, the details you choose will supply specific information about size, shape, weight, color, and so on. If your purpose is to have your audience experience the subject as you've experienced it— take *your* view of it—you might select different details, or you might use the same details but treat them differently, emphasizing some, subordinating others, and choosing modifying words and phrases that convey your mood or attitude or judgment. The objective "navy blue" of literal description could become a "drab" or a "depressing" or a "sturdy" or a "comforting" blue, depending on the way you saw it.

If you want your reader to share your impression of your brother, try to capture the features that are unique to *him*, not those that apply equally well to most of his friends. If you want to catch the special flavor of an experience, don't bother with the details that apply to whole classes of people or places—the shrill voices of small children, the bustle of shopping centers—but concentrate on what makes the particular person or place distinctive. On the other hand, for the kind of description that contributes to definition—what a human being is, what a Sioux encampment was—present details that characterize all human beings, all Sioux encampments.

In choosing details, pay close attention to the rhetorical situation and be guided by your readers' probable knowledge of your subject. If you're describing your basset hound for an audience that doesn't know a basset from a beagle, concentrate on details that apply to all bassets. If your audience already knows what bassets look like and how they act, concentrate on the characteristics that make your dog an individual among bassets.

Arranging Details

Once you've chosen your details, your next job is to arrange them so that readers will be able to see what you want them to see. In the description on p. 35 of the park that's going to seed, the writer first calls attention to the cracked concrete, the graffiti on the walls of the handball courts, and the broken benches—things a casual visitor would notice in just glancing around. Then he focuses on the basketball court, its bleachers and one of its baskets, because his subject is the decline of one of the great launching pads for professional basketball stars.

In this description there's no need for the writer to establish a specific viewing point. But sometimes deciding where you are in relation to what you're describing will help you settle on a logical progression of details and keep the scale of the description right—the relation of large elements to small, of more important to less important. In describing the block you live on, you might imagine yourself standing across the street from your home and begin your description with the building on the corner to your left. In describing the statehouse, you could spot yourself at the foot of the steps leading to the front doors and arrange your details in vertical order, from the steps upward or from the dome of the building downward.

The more complicated your physical point of view, the more necessary it is to make sure you're not losing or confusing your readers. But indicate changes in position as unobtrusively as possible. No reader likes to be elbowed into place. In presenting the sights and sounds you experienced on a Sunday stroll in the park, you might keep a narrative thread running through your description:

Coming out of my apartment building, I turned left and crossed the bridge into our city's largest park. . . . Enjoying the sunshine, I walked about a mile west through crowds of picnickers to the hill in the center of the park, always the scene of the liveliest action. . . . After an hour or so I moved to a bench near the bandshell at the foot of the hill and waited for the open-air concert to start. . . .

In describing a large city or a stretch of country, you might decide to present it as seen from an automobile or a plane. Here the writer has hit upon a highly imaginative device — the flight of a seagull — to help him give a picture of a vast area, the Pacific Northwest:

A seagull's view of this region would start in the north, in the Strait of Georgia, which separates Canada's Vancouver Island from the forested mainland. Flying south, with sedate Victoria at the tip of Vancouver Island in view from one side, and metropolitan Vancouver, B.C., on the other, the gull will wing down broad Puget Sound, where dotted islands, timbered to the shorelines, are connected by state-owned ferryboats ceaselessly crisscrossing the Sound as if it were a street. The Sound is protected water, unlike the stormy ocean coast to the west. Beginning at Everett, the gull will be flying over a metropolitan complex that includes Seattle at its center, extends past Tacoma, and thins out at Olympia, whose gray capitol dome looms over the tideflats at the foot of Puget Sound. At this point the seagull had better don shoes, to travel down the farmlands and scrub timber of the Cowlitz Valley and arrive at the Columbia. Just beyond lies Portland, sitting busily astride a tributary of the Columbia, the Willamette.

The Willamette Valley is where the American settlement of the Pacific Northwest began. — Thomas Griffith, *Atlantic*

Dominant Impression

Sometimes the purpose of your description will be to present not a photograph of whatever you're describing but a sketch that captures the features you want to emphasize and that creates a dominant impression. The writer of the paragraph about the rundown park made no attempt to cover the park in detail or to map out the relation of its parts. Instead, he chose details that stressed its seediness and arranged them so that they focused the reader's attention on the neglected basketball court. As the following description shows, precise details about size, color, diet, and so forth can be coordinated with a writer's personal reactions ("immense," "grotesque and revolting," "alarming") to support the dominant impression conveyed in the "fabulous and ridiculous" of the first sentence. (Rhetorical situation: the book, well illustrated with photographs, is written by an expert naturalist for an audience of general readers.) From the section on sea elephants:

Even a photograph cannot give a true picture of these fabulous and ridiculous creatures. Not only are they immense, males growing to eighteen feet in length and as much as fifteen feet in girth, but this sex is adorned with an eighteen-inch trunk that normally flops down over the mouth but which is also connected with the nasal passages and can be inflated and raised almost straight up. Worse still, these animals are clothed in very short sparse greyish brown hair, which they moult once a year and in doing so not only lose their fur but also their whole outer skin; they are then bright pink and present the most grotesque and revolting appearance, especially when they lounge around on shore in great misshapen, heaving masses under a hot sun, moaning, groaning, gurgling and roaring. They live on cuttlefish, seaweed, and shellfish and are fairly agile in the water but spend a lot of time on land. The great bulls heave their immense bulk up gently sloping beaches and into the tussocky tall grass of the islands they most prefer and then go to sleep. Nothing is quite so alarming as to stumble up against one of these animals at such a time since they come "unstuck" with a veritable explosion and rise to full height, blowing and snorting. — Ivan T. Sanderson, *Living Mammals of the World*

■ *For Analysis and Writing*

1. For your instructor, re-create in a paragraph of 150–200 words a recent encounter you had with yourself in the bathroom mirror. Before you begin to write, choose a specific circumstance. Was it just before an early class, after a very late party, before an exam, before a vacation break, after a good night's sleep, in the midst of an attack of flu? Don't include this background in your paper. Your purpose is to make your reader understand what you saw and how you felt, not why you looked and felt as you did.

Here's one student's response to the assignment:

Bleak Beginning

At 7:05 the echo of the alarm still throbs dully in my ears. I grasp the cold, white porcelain of the sink and stare at the face in the mirror, which stares blankly back, mealy-white and blurred, vacant green wall behind. Straggly, broth-colored hair hangs down around the face in wisps and tangles. The eyes are puffed and half-closed, blinking, trying to focus. *Warm bed. Crawl back in, just for a minute.* The face stares indecisively. The distant thunder of trucks echoes, magnified, throbbing in my head, fading into the undercurrent of traffic. My tongue moves leaden in my stale, dry mouth; air whistles faintly through my clogged nose. *There's time. Go back just for a minute.* My whole body feels heavy, as if liquid cement had hardened in my veins overnight. *Too late to go back.* My hand gropes for the cold-water faucet.

2. Describe a place that has some special significance for you — the room you had when you were a child, the park you played in, the candy store you patronized, the church you attended, or the beach or pool you went to in the summer. Select and arrange the details so that the reader will see the place clearly and also understand why you feel about it as you do. So far as possible, make the details do the job of telling the reader how you feel. (To make sure you haven't relied too heavily on generalizations, read your first draft through, skipping all the general statements. If the details don't make you feel you're there—in the place you're describing—you need to replace some of your generalizations with particulars.)

In a note at the beginning of the paper, identify the reader you have in mind and briefly define your relationship. It should be someone you want to share your feeling about the place, someone you can count on being a sympathetic audience.

3. *Review Sanderson's description of sea elephants. Write a description of a person or an animal in which precise physical details are coordinated with a personal reaction to produce a dominant impression.*

4. *Describe someone you know well, using only details of physical appearance and mannerisms and examples of typical behavior to convey personality and character. Don't generalize at all.*

5. *Describe two houses or apartments you know well—your family's home and the home of another, very different family. Select details that reflect the occupants' personalities, habits, tastes, interests, values. Address your descriptions to an audience that doesn't know either family. Don't tell what the occupants are like. If you've chosen the right details, readers will get a clear picture of them.*

6. *Write two descriptions of the same thing, each for a different purpose. Example: Describe your desk or your bike. Make one account a "For Sale" paragraph to be posted on a bulletin board. Give particulars that will identify your desk or bike and tell a prospective buyer what he needs to know. Write the other account for a good friend. Describe the desk or bike in such a way that the friend will know how you feel about it and about the activity (intellectual/physical) that it represents to you. In the first passage your desk or bike is an object. In the second, make it a symbol—beat-up old friend, thing of beauty, comfort or curse, whatever.*

7. *You're the editor of a school newspaper. The paragraph below has been submitted for publication. You like it, but you're not satisfied with the way the writer has expressed himself. So you rewrite the paragraph, keeping the central idea and feeling but improving the expression so that the thought and emotion will come through more clearly.*

Keep in mind that a good rewrite is one that the author will recognize as an improvement. It will also, of course, meet the standards of edited written English.

[No title. Supply one.]

I had been here since September and not realized, or observed, or knew where I was. One overcast, snowy afternoon I saw for the first time the environment I was in. At first I detected how large the university really was. The high-rise dorms stood naked against the sky. The brick and glass structures were noticeably out of place. Then I realized there were no dogs, children, or old people. The thought of being in an environment where there was no birth or death hit me. I remembered growing up in the city where the children and dogs ran wild, the noise of cars, buses, and ambulances constantly clouded the air; and the old people were always visible. The university was full of people, young people, my age. On this afternoon I saw their faces. I detected a loneness, yet a happiness and on some a blankness. The awareness that I was away from home was projected on my face for the first time. I had been like a brick and glass structure lost in some remote area surrounded by enormous white covered mountains. I was conscious of a nakedness, a feeling I had not known before. The sensation of cold and the snowflakes manifested itself in and on my body. I experienced the pressure of the sky on the earth and I was caught in the middle, out of place with the real world.

8. Study the use of details in each of the following passages. Is the writer's purpose to show you what he saw or to show you what any careful observer would see? In answering the question, define as precisely as you can what the writer is describing and the point of view from which he's describing it. Then go on to analyze the kind of detail he uses to accomplish his purpose.

a. Tuttle's San Francisco studio (he has branches in Los Angeles and Fresno) is situated next to the Greyhound bus station in a district of cheap hotels and racetrack touts. The visitor climbs a long flight of stairs to a brightly lit lobby, the walls of which are covered with numbered examples of Tuttle's tattoo designs, his "flash." Just off the lobby, behind a railing, is an area that has somewhat the feeling of a barber shop, with chairs, mirrors, a sterilizer for tattoo needles, and containers for black, red, green, yellow, and blue India ink. Most of the tattooing is done there, but two private rooms with padded benches are available for working on the less public parts of the body, and for extensive jobs which might take up to five hours at a crack. Pervading the entire studio is the sharp, aseptic smell of surgical soap. — George Leonard, *Atlantic*

b. Just then, I see a tall, powerfully built, khaki-colored young man in skintight shorts and nothing else, a leather belt wrapped around his waist like a bracelet, five or six necklaces around his neck, who has climbed a tree just behind the musicians. Holding one foot in the fork, he slowly stretches his other leg along the branch as he reaches up to the next branch and extends his arms along it until his entire body is stretched taut. Then he begins to flex and writhe to the beat, now and then extending one hand and moving it back and forth, like an exotic benediction. His eyes are as inward as the drummers'. His "dancing" is as dark and potent and on the edge. There is a hint of the jungle here as well as of the San Juan honky-tonks, a mixture of the primitive and the urban, of lust and fear. . . . — Theodore Solotaroff, *New York Times Magazine*

c. For centuries Englishmen and others in temperate climates of Western Europe had been building their wooden houses (or houses with wooden frames) in a certain traditional manner. To insure strength and durability, the house was built on a sturdy frame of heavy timbers about a foot thick. These were held together by cutting down the end of one beam into a tongue ("tenon"), which was then fitted into a hole ("mortise") in the adjoining beam. When there was a pull on the joint, the pieces were held by a wooden peg fitted into an auger hole through the joined timbers. This kind of construction was generally supposed to be the only proper way to build a house. It also required a great deal of skill: shaping tongues and grooves, boring auger holes, making wooden pegs, and finally fitting all these neatly together required the tools and training of a carpenter. — Daniel J. Boorstin, *The Americans: The National Experience*

d. As he waded out, his big right arm swung back and forth. Each circle of his arm inflated his chest. Each circle was faster and higher and longer until his arm became defiant and his chest breasted the sky. On shore we were sure, although we could see no line, that the air above him was singing with loops of line that never touched the water but got bigger and bigger each time they passed and sang. And we knew what was in his mind from the lengthening defiance of his arm. He was not going to let his fly touch any water close to shore where the small and middle-sized fish were. We knew from his arm and chest that all parts of him were saying, "No small one for the last one." Everything was going into one big cast for one last big fish. — Norman Maclean, *A River Runs Through It*

Narrating: Telling What Happened

Narration and description occur together more often than not. As we said in the last section, you'll sometimes want to keep a narrative thread running through a description. And it's hard to find a narrative that doesn't include some descriptive detail. Both narration and description appear in many papers that explain or analyze, and brief passages of both are common in persuasive and critical essays. An argument for slum clearance may open with a description of life in a decaying neighborhood. A movie review usually includes a narrative summary of the plot.

You'll adopt the chronological arrangement typical of narrative when you present the development of an idea, a fashion or a fad, a theory in science, a movement in art or literature or politics, a strategy or technique in sports, a trend in television. You'll also adopt it in explanations of how things work and how things grow and in "how-to-do-its" (how to play tennis, how to cook spaghetti, how to set up a particular experiment), where directions are typically combined with descriptions of equipment.

Purpose is central to the kind of narrative you write. If you want to re-create an event in which you took part—a dance marathon, for example—you'll tell what you did and what you saw. You'll concentrate on actions and sensations. If you want to report the event so that readers will understand what happened and why and what came of it, you'll give reasons (to raise money for scholarships) and point out significance (college students, as represented by the organizers and participants, are willing to give generously of their time and energy to help others). If you want to explain how to organize and conduct a dance marathon for a good cause, you'll outline a procedure, telling not what happened at a particular contest but what should always happen to make such a contest a success.

The first account, which tells what happened, is a personal narrative. The second, which explains what happened, is expository narrative. The third, a special variety of expository narrative that tells how it was done, is called a process paper. Though all three may be rooted in the same personal experience, their purposes and possibly their readers differ, and so will the approaches used in the accounts and the material they contain.

Point of View

In narrating as in describing, you may want to make clear where you are in relation to the action. In a personal narrative, you're likely to adopt a restricted point of view, reporting only what you could see and hear, and what you could hear about, while the event was taking place. As a reporter giving a comprehensive account of the same event, you might want to use an unrestricted point of view, so that you can jump from one incident to another ("Meanwhile, outside the building . . ."). You're then free to be wherever you want to be, both in space and in time ("Two days earlier . . ."). In a process paper the unrestricted point of view permits you to coordinate stages of the process that take place simultaneously: "During this time other members of the committee have been looking for sponsors among the local merchants"). For some processes you may adopt a restricted point of view, identifying yourself with the reader and going through, or watching, the process with him step by step. In explaining a specific undertaking—making an omelette, changing a tire, setting up lab equipment—your paper may be clearer and more interesting if you take up the steps in proper sequence, limiting each one to what a performer of the action could do at any one time.

The advantage of the restricted point of view is its realism: you are there, and the reader is there with you. Even as an observer rather than a participant, you may choose to swap the freedom of the unrestricted point of view for the realism of the restricted. Once you've adopted it, though, you should stick to it. You shouldn't suddenly announce that at the very moment you were dozing on your partner's shoulder, or standing on the sidelines taking notes, a restaurant manager was deciding to send over a van-load of pizzas. The pizzas can enter the narrative only when you first saw or smelled them or when someone told you they were on the way.

In the passage that follows, the narrator tells in chronological sequence what he heard and saw on a moonless night in the desert as he sat by a campfire. First, two yellow lights appeared miles away on the horizon. Soon they illuminated "a swirling, humming cloud of dust." Then:

> The hum became a buzz, a grumble, then a roar; each light split, and now four lights crashed through the dust to reveal an off-white Chevy Blazer. Just when it seemed as if the Blazer was going to stampede through the campsite, the lights bent away and the truck slid to a stop, driver's door next to the fire. The lights flicked black; the hot engine creaked quiet; dust drifted down in the silence and settled over the campsite, on the men. A match was struck inside the Blazer to light a cigarette, and newborn shadows slipped around a felt cowboy hat. The face and body under the hat climbed out of the Blazer and stretched. Pearl shirt snaps glowed like polished mescal buttons, and a sterling silver belt buckle reflected so sharply it seemed to be a tiny window into the man's belly, where a campfire was burning. His filigreed blue cowboy boots had no cow dung on their pointy toes.
>
> The man took a sullen drag on his cigarette, tilted the gray Stetson off his forehead with the side of an index finger and said with a sudden grin, "Damn, I need a tequila."—Sam Moses, *Sports Illustrated*

Physical point of view indicates your location in space and time. Psychological point of view indicates your attitude toward your subject, the role you've assumed. As a participant, you may be so intensely involved that you almost pull the reader into the action with you. As a reporter who's trying hard to be objective, you may be quite unemotional. But a reporter can also be amused, or bored, or admiring, or disgusted. This applies whether you're reporting something you witnessed or something that took place in Nazi Germany or the Dakota Territory or czarist Russia or imperial Rome. If you react strongly to the event you're telling about, it may suit your purpose to share that response with your audience. Traditionally, process papers stress exactness of observation and clarity of presentation, but given the right rhetorical situation, you may choose to communicate your own curiosity about the subject or your enthusiasm or distaste for it.

As with physical point of view, a psychological point of view, once established, should be maintained. Don't make fun of a dance marathon for two thirds of your paper and then expect your readers to believe you when you express great admiration for the organizers and participants in the final paragraphs. Don't switch back and forth between the invisible, all-knowing reporter of a happening and the "I" who takes part in it. In a process paper you may choose to keep the reader at arm's length with the formal, impersonal "one" ("At this stage one should be careful not to . . .") *or* reduce the distance with the less formal "you" ("You would be wise at this point to . . .") *or* go arm-in-arm with "we" ("Now let's see if we can run through those steps again"), depending on the rhetorical situation. Once you've settled on the appropriate relationship, stay with it.

Personal Narrative

The following two passages from papers by students show how feeling or attitude can be communicated through narrative. In the first the writer describes his emotions as the incidents occur:

The bus was coming to a stop. I pushed my way into the crowd to get on before some of the others. The doors opened. I felt pushing people behind me and resistance from those in front. Suddenly, I sensed something was wrong, or maybe I heard something. I glanced over my shoulder. I saw an old man (perhaps sixty) with an expression of horror on his face. I was shocked and looked more closely. Behind him was poised a tall, nondescript man. His hands were under the old man's long coat. His right had found the old man's right hip pocket; his left hand, the left pocket. As if lightning had hit me, I froze. My heart beat furiously. After a moment, I realized what the situation was. Suddenly, I felt superhuman. I felt as though I could have run a mile in three minutes; I felt as though I could have defended myself against anyone. I realized the old man was only five feet from me. If some man would help me. . . . But then I was nauseated as I saw the old man struggling futilely. He reached behind him to grasp the robber's hand. He wheezed. His tortured, plump face was deathly pale. His cap fell off, his white hair was mussed. The robber still did not have the wallet. They struggled. I heard the bus driver shout, "Somebody help. . . . That man is being robbed!" Several women said, "Why doesn't somebody do something?" Still they struggled.

The last person got on the bus, and the driver closed the doors. I watched from the window. Still they struggled. The robber spun around, throwing the old man down. He hit him hard, I do not know where but I think near the head. The old man gave up the struggle. The robber turned the old man over, reached into his pocket, and pulled out the wallet. As the bus pulled away, I saw the robber running north, up Wentworth. I also saw the old man, lying face down in the gutter, in the spit, and dirt, and rain water, and cold darkness, alone.

In the second the writer simply presents details, withholding comment until the final sentence:

The camp counselors would occasionally take us to a riding stable, where the horses would try to rub us off against fence posts, or to a monster swimming pool, where the sun never shone and the wind always blew. One day I remember as a series of particularly grotesque experiences. It was very hot and we started a forced march down an interminable road, ankle deep in dust. Eventually we arrived at a large deserted quarry, where the rock had been extensively exposed but not deeply excavated. I wandered off from the group and found myself confronted by two dogs that had apparently died at each other's throats. Their seams had burst and I suppose they would have looked horrible to some, but to me they somehow looked natural in that jumbled rock setting. When I returned to the group I said nothing. Everybody was gathered around a green pond, and a boy named Charlie had just hit a small fish with a large rock. "What a shot!" The fish fluttered down into the reeds, smoking dark brown.

The road back to the shelter was all uphill. Looking back on the day, I see it as a basic lesson in surrealism.

A personal narrative should have some central meaning. It should make a point. Building that point into your statement of purpose—the general indication of what you're trying to do—will help give direction to your planning and writing. Since your point of view and your descriptive details will affect your readers' understanding of the significance of the event you write about, choose them so that they help make that significance emerge. You can, of course, spell out the meaning the experience had for you, but if you do, be careful not to inflate modest personal significance into cosmic importance. While "My First Date" should have enough point to be worth writing, no reader will expect it to arrive at a profound truth. And few readers will put up with the moralizing tone that sometimes creeps into retrospective comment ("That experience taught me a lesson I've never forgotten: Hard work is the straightest road to self-respect").

To avoid crossing the line that separates interpreting from moralizing, you can work at selecting details that will lead readers to make the comment for you. In writing about accidentally killing a songbird, a student chose to avoid making any explicit statement about his emotional reaction. Instead he made his point through a series of contrasts. Before the incident, everywhere he looked he saw beauty; after it, everywhere he looked he saw ugliness. Not that he used the abstract nouns *beauty* and *ugliness*. He relied on contrasting images – the colors of falling leaves, the taste of an apple, the glance of a girl; later, rubbish in the gutter, dirty words scrawled on a bus, a drunk lurching by.

One way or another, directly or indirectly, any narrative should carry its own meaning. Whether that meaning is clear to you in the prewriting stage or becomes clear to you only as you write the paper, you should have it firmly in mind as you revise. Weed out incidents and details that blur the impression you want to get across. Keep only those that sharpen the impression. On paper as well as off, the bad storyteller is always bogging down in details that are unnecessary and irrelevant. By so doing, he regularly leaves his audience wondering what the point of his story was. The more superfluous, distracting details you can get rid of, the greater the impact of your narrative will be.

Be honest, though. If the meaning you want to get across requires omitting facts that are essential to a truthful account, then you're writing fiction, and you should label it as such.

This passage is an account of an incident that the author didn't experience himself but that he presents partly as it may have been experienced:

On the third lap of the Italian Grand Prix at Monza last week, just as the cars were approaching the wrenching curve known as *La Parabolica*, a rabbit darted out of the infield grass and ended its life under the wheels of Jackie Stewart's Matra. Sixty-five laps later, with the rabbit little more than a blur of fur on the line through that treacherous corner, Stewart swept under the flag to win both Monza and the world driving championship. The only casualty of the day, if you discount a few thousand pinched bottoms in victory lane, was the unfortunate rabbit. Nobody mourned him, but let's try to imagine his last impressions: the sudden approach of the pack — 15 cars flat-out, black dots emerging from the Ascari curve and magnifying almost instantly into giant torpedoes of blue and red and marigold orange. The noise ripping upward from a moan through a snarl to a steady explosion. The drivers barely visible within their bonedomes. Stewart's close-set, sensitive, mud-colored eyes, with one drooping lid masked behind the smoky visor of his helmet, the eyes of a hunter flicking down and seeing the rabbit sprint and freeze on the track, widening, holding firm on the line ahead. The broad reach of the Dunlop tire blurring into treadlessness, rising above the doomed animal. Thump.

Arrivederci, rabbit. — Robert F. Jones, *Sports Illustrated*

With "let's try to imagine his last impressions," Jones signals a shift from straight narrative to dramatic reenactment — from the rabbit's point of view. Through the rabbit's eyes and ears the reader experiences the head-on approach of fifteen Grand Prix racing cars traveling at top speed. In the sentences about the drivers generally and Stewart in particular, the angle of vision would require a very tall rabbit, but the final blur of the Dunlop tires restores a believable perspective.

Pace

In most of the narratives you write, you'll want to compress — that is, to summarize — some parts of your account, while treating the significant episodes or stages in appropriate detail. By so doing, you inform readers of what is important from your point of view and what isn't; you keep the story moving instead of letting it stall; and you perk up your readers' interest with the changes in pace.

If you're a good oral storyteller, you already have the knack of compressing here and stretching out there for dramatic purposes. If you're not a natural storyteller, you still can work on the proportions of your narrative in the revision stage. Look carefully at any narrative that proceeds at an even pace from beginning to end. If it's an account of a process or the record of an experiment, such balanced, comprehensive coverage may be exactly what you intend. Otherwise, you'll want to slow down actual time in some parts and speed it up in others.

■ *For Writing*

1. In 500–700 words, write about a personal experience that has in some way been significant for you. Your reader is someone you can count on to be interested in you and your experiences. Tell about a violent incident that you were involved in or that you witnessed. Or report an episode in which you had a sharp disagreement with a close friend, a parent, or someone in a position of authority. Or write a chapter of your autobiography, telling about a stage — unpleasant or delightful, disillusioning or inspiring — in your growing up.

Here is one student's response to the assignment:

Winning — The Only Thing?

It was a very hot, summer day. My family and I were sitting in the stadium at the local high school. The Annual Track and Field Day always drew a large crowd; it was one of the biggest events of the year in our area. I remember how close together everybody was sitting and how noisy the people were. Because I was little I had to sit in my father's lap, pressed against his sweaty, tee-shirted chest. At the close of the day's activities there was an announcement of an unplanned, special event — a race for all four-year-old girls in the stands. Everyone in my family looked at me. I was four years old and a girl and therefore eligible to run in the race. My brothers and sisters encouraged me, saying, "Come on, Missy, if you win we can all hang up our ribbons in the family room. Why don't ya? All of *us* did." Although I was frightened by the large crowd, I decided to run in the race so that I could be just like my older brothers and sisters, who had each won a ribbon that day.

As I stood at the starting line the butterflies in my stomach went wild and I thought that I was going to get sick. Dust kept flying in my face, clogging my throat and stinging my eyes, making them water. There was only one other girl in the race. She looked very delicate and lady-like in her short dress and white patent leather shoes, which were starting to turn brown from the dirt track. When the gun went off, I ran.

The crowd was cheering and screaming their support and the dirt and gravel flew beneath my feet, biting my ankles. When I was half-way up the track I looked to my side and realized that my competitor was not nearby. I stopped and turned around and saw that she was still standing at the starting line. Her clothes were filthy from the dust and she was sobbing. I ran all the way back, grabbed her hand, and started to pull her along behind me. As we ran together I was laughing and the girl turned to me and smiled.

When we reached the midpoint the girl's mother, who was standing at the finish line, started calling to her daughter. "C'mon baby, you can do it," she yelled in a harsh voice. "Pour it on, now's your chance!" Suddenly, heeding her mother's advice, the girl threw down my arm and took off. The crowd laughed uproariously as I stood in mute, shocked surprise. The little girl crossed the finish line before me and ran straight into the arms of her gloating mother. I was even more hurt when, after I finally crossed the finish line, the girl's mother leaned down and growled, "My daughter could beat you any day of the week!"

The girl won a blue ribbon for first place; I won a red one for coming in "second." During the announcement of the other girl's first-place award the crowd remained quiet, but when my second-place ribbon was presented the yelling, cheering, and whistling began again. I was confused and embarrassed and scared because I couldn't find my family. It was then that the winner turned to me, laughed, and repeated childhood's ancient taunt, "Hah-hah, you can't beat me."

I began to cry.

2. *What are the major differences between "Winning—The Only Thing?" and "How I Got There," reprinted below? In responding to the question, consider such matters as quantity and kind of detail, point of view, pace, and means of conveying significance. When you've listed the major differences, try to account for them in terms of the writers, their subjects, and what you assume to be their purposes and their audiences.*

How I Got There

In 1962, I, a black woman, ran for election to the Texas House of Representatives. I live in populous Harris County, which includes Houston. The county was not divided into districts. *Baker v. Carr*—one man, one vote—had not yet arrived in Texas. It was necessary for me to run countywide. All eligible voters in the million-plus county voted for each representative. The political experts gave me no chance of winning, but in my political naïveté I believed that I was more articulate than my opponent, and sensitive to people's needs and aspirations. These qualities, I felt, would help me overcome the odds against my election to the Texas House.

I rarely saw my opponent in person, but was confronted by his face on many billboards and on the television screen. He was obviously well financed. I had borrowed my filing fee of $500. I felt that if politicians were believable, and pressed the flesh to the maximum extent possible, the people would overlook race, sex, and poverty—and elect me. They did not. In that race, I received 46,000 votes; my opponent more than 65,000. I tried to rationalize the outcome by saying that I had a victory of sorts, but that of course wasn't really true. To win a seat in the Texas House of Representatives, it was necessary to be backed by money, power, and influence. The candidate's qualifications seemed to matter very little. My name on the ballot brought out a heavy black vote in 1962; every other "liberal" candidate running for the House won. The black vote helped them win, but it didn't help me. It was clear then that if I was to win the right to represent some of the people of Texas, I had to persuade the moneyed and politically influential interests either to support me or to remain neutral.

In 1964, I tried again for the same position in the Texas House. I went to the newspaper publishers and acknowledged their probable difficulty in supporting me editorially, but urged them not to support my opponent—just to take a chance on the people making the best choice. One of the major papers in Houston made no endorsement; the other endorsed my opponent. A half-victory of sorts. But I lost the election. I received 66,000 votes; my opponent received in excess of 66,000. I made some inroads into my opponent's stronghold. This time there was identifiable support in traditionally white, conservative precincts. I was "on the move," according to my supporters, but I was dispirited.

I considered abandoning the dream of a political career in Texas and moving to some section of the country where a black woman candidate was less likely to be considered a novelty. I didn't *want* to do this. I am a Texan; my roots are in Texas. To leave would be a cop-out. So I stayed, and 1966 arrived. *Baker v. Carr,* and reapportionment had inched its way across the Texas political borders. *People* were to be represented, not vast acreage. The Texas Senate was reapportioned. I lived in a newly created Texas senatorial district which contained more than 70 percent of the precincts which I had carried in my two previous unsuccessful races. I would run for the Senate. It was a different kind of race from the one I had run before, because my opponent was a liberal who had served in the Texas House for several terms. He called me before the filing deadline and asked if I was planning to run for the Senate. I said I was. He said he was going to run no matter what I did. It was a friendly and candid conversation.

The new district was 38 percent black; the balance was comprised of Chicanos and whites. Many laborers affiliated with the AFL-CIO lived in the district. My opponent asked, "Can a white man win?" My supporters were angered by the seeming intrusion of racism, and answered the question with: "No, not this time." I was elected to the Texas Senate by a margin of two to one.

On the day I was sworn in to the Senate, the gallery was filled with proud supporters. Although demonstrations are not permitted, my supporters cheered when I walked onto the floor. They didn't know about the rules. I looked up at them and covered my lips with my index finger. They became quiet instantly, but continued to communicate their support by simply smiling. Finally I had won the right to represent a portion of the people of Texas. What next?

The leadership of the Senate was white, conservative, and male. Indeed, of the thirty-one members, thirty were white and male, and twenty-four were "conservative." The black who preceded me served in 1883. (There had been eighty-three anemic years!) The Texas Senate was touted as the state's most exclusive club. To be effective I had to get inside the club, not just inside the chamber. I singled out the most influential and powerful members and was determined to gain their respect. "Texan" frequently evokes images of conservatism, oil, gas, racism, callousness. In my judgment, the myths should be debunked, or at the least, should include the prevalent strain of reasonableness, compassion, and decency. Willie Morris, in *North Toward Home,* wrote accurately of a pervasive Texas characteristic: "There was a kind of liberality of spirit there, an *expansiveness* which, as I was one day to learn, is one of the most distinctive qualities of Texans, even though it can be directed toward things that do not deserve being expansive about." Individuality and populism are constant components of the stuff of a Texan. We have a sense of humor and do not take ourselves *too* seriously. These admitted generalizations apply equally equally to politicians. Lyndon Johnson was the prototype of the Texas politician; tough, expansive, and pragmatic. Yet he was largely responsible for unprecedented civil rights legislation which brought our country closer to the constitutional ideal of equity.

Dorsey Hardeman of San Angelo, then chairman of the Senate State Affairs Committee, and Tom Creighton of Mineral Wells, then chairman of the Privileges and Elections Committee, exemplified what I have tried to describe as the typical Texan—and Texas politician. Senator Hardeman knew the rules of the Senate better than any other member. In order to gain his respect, I, too, had to know the rules. I learned the rules. One day I sought to pass a pollution control bill by obfuscating some parliamentary fine points—a tactic for which Hardeman was noted and which he practiced masterfully. I almost succeeded until Senator Hardeman started to listen to what I was saying. He raised questions. He asked, "What are you trying to do?" I said, "It's simple, I'm using the tricker's tricks." Hardeman could not contain his appreciation for what I was doing, nor his mirth. His respect for me was affirmed at that time, and our friendship continues.

Senator Creighton sponsored a bill, the effect of which would be to restrict the Texas electorate severely and compound the difficulties of voter registration. He needed twenty-one votes to gain consideration of the bill. I opposed it, and needed ten other senators to join me. I made a list of ten senators who were in my political debt. I went to each one and said I was calling in my chit. I needed their votes in order to keep the Creighton proposal from Senate deliberation. Armed with ten commitments, I went to Senator Creighton and asked when he planned to bring the bill to the floor of the Senate. He smiled, but with resignation, and said, "I, too, can count; the bill is dead, Barbara." These men, and others, were conservative, decent, and practical. I respect them.

At the conclusion of my first term, the Senate unanimously passed a resolution citing me as the outstanding freshman member. In spite of the unanimous voice vote adopting the resolution, Senator Hardeman asked that the names of all senators and the lieutenant governor be added for unquestioned unanimity.

In 1968, I ran for re-election to the Texas Senate. I was unopposed. My next political race was in 1972, when I won 81 percent of the vote and was elected to the United States House of Representatives.

I'm glad I stayed in Texas. —Barbara Jordan, *Atlantic*

The Process Paper

The basic structure of any narrative is the sequence of actions in time, and the simplest pattern is straight chronology, with one action following another as it did in the actual event. (The student paper on pp. 48–49 is an example.) As in all the other kinds of writing you do, your first responsibility in narration is to make your material understandable to your audience. That means linking the successive actions with words and phrases (*then, later, next, after that, meanwhile,* and so on) that make the temporal relationships clear to readers. In expository narrative and process papers, where you're not only telling what happens next but explaining why, there's the further need to provide such indicators of cause and effect as *because, thus, therefore,* and *as a result,* to make these more complex relationships equally clear.

As we said earlier, process papers are one kind of expository narrative — the kind that explains how to do something or how something is done. In a process paper you tell your readers how to bake bread or make a hook shot or chair a meeting, or you tell them how a combination lock or an antibiotic or a state legislature works. Everyone knows how to do something or how something is done.

In how-to papers your job is to present the process so clearly and completely that your readers will be able to perform it. Such clarity and completeness call for a chronological ordering of *all* the steps in the process, sometimes with warnings against *mis*steps. Being clear also means adjusting vocabulary and coverage to the audience. For a reader who doesn't know what a jack or a lug wrench is, you'll have to define more terms and explain steps in much greater detail than for a reader who knows what's in the trunk of his car. Providing a complete account means leaving out nothing that's essential to performance of the operation. Don't choose as subject a process so complicated that you can't cover it adequately in the space allotted — or one so simple that you'll have to pad the paper.

If how-to instructions are to be included in a driver's manual or a cookbook or some similar publication, reader interest is no problem. Only people who want to be instructed will seek them out. But with some how-to material and in much other informational writing, the interest of the audience has to be aroused and sustained. Clarity will continue to be the primary goal: make sure you neither baffle readers by using undefined technical terms nor confuse them by failing to explain how Step 3 leads to Step 4. But you'll also need to persuade readers that your subject is worth reading about. Certainly the best way to do this is to choose a topic that interests you and to have a reason for writing about it.

This opening of an article on the mechanization of post offices tells what the job of operating a Ziptronic Mail Translator machine entails:

You are seated in front of a green plastic keyboard. Sixty times a minute, a rotating metal arm reaches into a tray of letters and deposits one onto the chain conveyor 16 inches in front of your eyes. You have six-tenths of a second to read the zip code on the letter before you hear the click. Then, within the next four-tenths of a second, you must press the right three keys, like staccato notes on a piano. When a full second is over, a rubber finger snaps the letter out of your line of vision and onward toward its intended destination. Simultaneously, the metal arm deposits another letter 16 inches in front of your eyes, and you have six-tenths of a second before you hear another click. . . .

Your job as operator of a Ziptronic Mail Translator machine goes on like that, 45 minutes out of every hour, eight hours a day, all year long. – Joseph Albright, *New York Times Magazine*

Note the use of the present tense. Unlike pure narrative, which tells what *did* happen ("Once upon a time"), the process paper tells what always happens and always will happen under a given set of circumstances ("Whenever the temperature drops below freezing"). It's natural, then, to adopt the present tense in writing about a process.

Besides telling what goes on in a process, you will usually want to tell why. You may need to point out the significance of each stage and the procedure by which one stage merges into the next. Or you may decide to begin by giving an overview of the process, emphasizing its function or usefulness and so directing the reader's attention to the whole scheme before dealing with its separate stages.

Below are two how-to papers written by students. One is serious, the other lighthearted. The first gives a good deal of space to describing the situation in which the technique is used and to explaining what its principle is and why it works. The how-to section is a single paragraph. The second paper consists largely of instructions, including plenty of warning about the risks of not following them.

The Heimlich Maneuver

Imagine that you're eating in a restaurant and suddenly hear someone at a nearby table gasping loud and hard. He is conscious but cannot speak. His friends are slapping him on the back, but the man continues to gasp. You realize that he is choking on something he was eating. Unless the obstacle is removed, he will die within minutes from lack of oxygen. What can you do?

The answer is to use the Heimlich Maneuver, a technique devised by Dr. Henry J. Heimlich, director of surgery at Jewish Hospital, Cincinnati, Ohio. This technique has proven most effective in forcing large bites of food from the windpipe.

Choking occurs when food is sucked into the windpipe instead of being swallowed. Usually the gag reflex makes a person cough out the food before it becomes lodged, but sometimes – particularly when alcohol has dulled the gag reflex — the big bite of meat or other food "sticks in the throat." Because this can occur only during inhalation, there is normally a small amount of air in the victim's lungs. The principle of the Heimlich Maneuver is that of a piston action — to compress the air out of the lungs with a force that will also propel the food up and out of the mouth.

Stand behind the victim, and instruct him to lean forward, bending at the waist and letting his upper body, arms, and head hang down. Then wrap your arms around him just below his rib cage. (If the arms are wrapped around the rib cage, broken ribs may result.) Make a fist with one hand and grasp it with your other hand. Then exert a sudden, strong, upward pressure, repeating it if necessary. This pressure on the victim's abdomen should force the diaphragm upward, compress the lungs, and cause the air expelled from the lungs to dislodge the chunk of food stuck in the windpipe.

CAUTION: T-bars May Be Hazardous to Your Health

One of the trickiest techniques for a beginning skier to learn is how to use the T-bar, a type of ski tow still found in many areas. Once you have learned the knack, the T-bar will take you from a loading station at the bottom of a slope to an unloading station at the top. A cable runs from the bottom station to the top one, then around a pulley and back down again. The T-bars, which are hooked onto the cable at set intervals, are upside-down T's of metal, equipped with a spring to prevent them from jerking at take-off. Two people use each T-bar. One stands on either side of the vertical main bar, holding onto it with one hand while leaning his rear end against his half of the horizontal cross bar.

I would like to suggest that before you attempt to tackle the first problem, which is the loading procedure, you stand back and observe a few other skiers to pick up some pointers. The effortless manner in which experienced skiers glide into place and get whisked away will also give you confidence. Of course, if the other skiers happen to be novices like you, you may see them falling every which way all over the slope, and that won't do a thing to build up your courage. But concentrate on the experts.

Once you decide that you are ready to give it a try, take your place in line with your partner and wait your turn. Well before that time arrives, the two of you should decide which person will be on which side of the T-bar. It is best for the more experienced skier to take the far side, so that he can guide his partner into place. As a safety precaution, be sure to take the straps of your ski poles off your wrists and hold both poles in the hand that will be on the outside when you are on the T-bar. If you fall and try to throw the poles away while they are still hooked to your wrists, they will probably come right back and conk you — or your poor, defenseless partner.

As soon as the couple in front of you takes off, whichever one of you agreed to be on the far side should move into position. Then the other gets into the snow tracks beside him. If you are on the near side and don't wait until your partner is in place, chances are that you will run over your friend's skis, causing both of you to land in a heap at the feet of the lift attendant.

Once you're in place, *don't* relax! Look back so as to be prepared to grab the vertical shaft of the approaching T-bar with your free hand when the lift attendant places it between you and your partner. Make sure the T-bar is correctly positioned. If it hits you behind the knees, you can go over backwards and be dragged up the hill feet first.

You *must* bend your knees. Bent knees act as shock absorbers, lessening the initial jolt when the T-bar grabs you from behind. If you insist on standing stiff-legged, you will most likely end up with your nose in the snow while your T-bar sails on, laughing silently at its latest victim.

Another common mistake is to sit on the T-bar. This is an error you must avoid at all costs! The T-bar was not made to be sat on. It's supposed to pull you and push you, not carry you up the hill. If you sit on it, it will not support you. Instead, its spring will stretch until you and your partner find yourselves sitting on the cold, hard snow feeling very foolish.

But let's imagine that you have avoided all these pitfalls. You are on your way up the slope. What fouls up many beginners at this point is the snow tracks. You must concentrate on keeping your skis in these deep ruts, for if one of them strays, you're in trouble. Once a ski is out of the track, it will behave as if it has a mind of its own. The harder you try to get it back where it belongs, the farther out it will move. Eventually you may find yourself doing a full straddle split in the middle of the slope. Once again, the T-bar will not stop and wait for you. Leave it, and you're stranded.

If you do get separated from your T-bar, remember to get out of the path of oncoming skiers as quickly as you can. Many a painful pile-up has been caused by the stunned novice sitting open-mouthed in the middle of the tracks.

The last hurdle is the unloading procedure. While some beginners have at least as much trouble getting off as they do getting on, leaving the T-bar is really quite simple. All you need to do is twist the main bar. This will cause the cross bar to become vertical so that it can slip between you and your partner and the whole contraption can continue on its way. Just be sure not to twist before you reach the flat ground at the top of the slope, or you may find yourself speeding downhill backwards.

After successfully parting company with the T-bar, step carefully from the tracks, and you are ready to start down the slope. Although worn and tired from your nerve-wracking encounter with the mechanical monster, you will be fully restored by an exhilarating descent. Then all you have to do is to face once again that murderous modern convenience, the T-bar.

■ *For Writing*

In 500 words write an account of a process. It can be in the form of instructions (how to play stickball, how to weave a rug or upholster a chair, how to prepare for moving from one house or apartment to another or from home to dormitory) or a description of an operation (how a sewing machine works, how a building is demolished, how an auction is conducted) or step-by-step advice about how to organize and carry out a fund-raising project like a car wash, a bake sale, or a raffle.

Dividing: Finding the Parts

When your purpose is to explain or explore a subject, consider the method called division, or analysis. By dividing — by sorting out the parts — you can gain control of your subject. By analyzing the subject, you can generate ideas to build on later, and you can find a way of presenting what you have to say. Often you'll discover that dividing is as useful a method for developing your paper as it is for thinking about your subject in the prewriting stage. An initial sorting of ideas will help you understand the internal structure of your subject — whether it's the many committees and subcommittees of student government or the parts of a protozoan. The same procedure, refined by what you've learned during prewriting, can make a complex subject clear to your readers as well.

If you wrote the process paper proposed as an exercise in the last section, you've already had some practice in dividing. You almost certainly presented the skill or operation or activity in stages. But while strict process relies heavily on chronological development, many divisions do not. You can divide an object (an automobile, a shark) or an institution (a social club, a corporation) in order to distinguish its parts and show how they fit together and function together. You can even divide an abstraction, like courage or capitalism, which doesn't have parts in any physical sense. In such cases, the "dividing" you do consists in recognizing elements that can most usefully be singled out for discussion.

Purpose in Dividing

The same thing can be divided in a variety of ways, according to different principles of division. For the user of a textbook, who is primarily interested in what the book contains and how to find it, the table of contents may represent the most important method of division. For the editor who worked out the allotment of pages while the book was being produced, the significant division may have been front matter, text, and end matter, perhaps with subdivisions of each of these. And for the person who had to estimate the manufacturing costs of the same book at the planning stage, a simple breakdown into paper, printing, and binding may have been adequate.

The kind of division you make depends on the principle you apply, and that principle depends on your purpose. For some purposes, dividing an automobile into chassis, engine and driving parts, and body would be enough. Simple as it is, it's consistent (only one principle of division is applied) and it's complete (it takes in the whole car). By contrast, a division into chassis, engine and driving parts, and fenders wouldn't satisfy any principle because it omits so much—all the body parts except the fenders. And a division into chassis, body, and dependable transportation doesn't work because it's both incomplete and inconsistent. The third "part"—dependability—introduces a new principle of division—performance.

Making a complete and consistent division is easiest when the subject is a physical object like a car. It becomes more difficult when the subject is an institution, like a university, and much more difficult when the subject is an abstraction, like patriotism or communism or love. Discussing the right to commit suicide, one student wrote, "The question involves morals, values, and perhaps selfishness." Since values and morals overlap and selfishness may be considered a kind of value, no single principle of division can be identified.

Whenever you can, find a principle of division that reflects your own interest, your way of looking at your subject, your purpose in exploring it. In the following passage the author makes a division of the highly complex activity of listening to music, admits that the division is somewhat arbitrary, and then points out its usefulness for his purpose:

> We all listen to music according to our separate capacities. But, for the sake of analysis, the whole listening process may become clearer if we break it up into its component parts, so to speak. In a certain sense we all listen to music on three separate planes. For lack of a better terminology, one might name these: (1) the sensuous plane, (2) the expressive plane, (3) the sheerly musical plane. The only advantage to be gained from mechanically splitting up the listening process into these hypothetical planes is the clearer view to be had of the way in which we listen.—Aaron Copland, *What to Listen for in Music*

Dividing to Organize

The Copland passage illustrates a point we made earlier: division is an aid to organizing. You make use of it every time you outline one of your own papers or a chapter in a textbook. First you divide the material into main topics; then you divide each of these into subtopics; and so on. Just as the outline helps you test the structure of your own paper or grasp the structure of a textbook chapter, so making a division of your subject at the beginning of your paper will forecast for your readers the topics you're going to discuss and the order you're going to discuss them in. Especially when your subject is a complex one, this technique will help you as well as your readers. By setting up the organizational scheme for them, you'll plant it firmly in your own mind; and you can then go on to develop each part of the division with appropriate details.

Here's the opening paragraph of a student's term paper on the traits used in selecting beef cattle:

The goal of commercial beef production is to market animals that return a maximum profit. Just as animals differ in their genetic makeup, they differ in the quality of their meat. Therefore the quality of beef can be improved through selective breeding. Only those traits that increase the rate and efficiency of production as well as the quality of the meat are economically important to the beef cattle industry. These traits, frequently referred to as performance traits, are (1) reproductive performance, (2) longevity, (3) mothering or nursing ability, (4) growth rate, (5) efficiency of gain, (6) conformation, and (7) carcass merit.

There followed a section for each of the numbered traits and a concluding summary:

It is through these seven major traits that beef production is improved. Change through selection is slow but tends to be permanent. These permanent traits increase the quality of beef, meeting consumers' demands, and decrease the production costs, making them economically feasible for breeders.

An undergraduate who described himself as "a knowledgeable science student" first divided a nuclear reactor into three parts: "the reactor core and its component parts, the power plant, and the safety devices." In his second paragraph he analyzed the nuclear core, discussing the radioactive fuel, the fuel rods, and the control rods and showing how the heat that's produced turns water into steam, which operates the power plant. In his third paragraph he subdivided the power plant into turbine, generator, and condenser, describing each one and explaining its function. In his fourth, he discussed the numerous safety devices that are built into the reactor. In a brief concluding paragraph he summed up: a nuclear reactor operates on a very simple principle; it has very few major parts; these parts work together "to produce what our society needs so much of—electricity."

Thus, through dividing and subdividing, this writer accomplished his purpose—explaining how a nuclear reactor produces electricity. It's unlikely that any approach other than division would have produced such a clear and economical explanation.

Normally in expository and argumentative prose, you'll use division as a means to the end you're aiming for. You'll analyze a poem not just to analyze it but to explore its strengths and weaknesses. You'll set up alternative courses of action not just to set up alternatives but to argue that one is superior to the others. Unless you're using division as a means to generate content, then, you should have the purpose of your paper clearly in mind as you divide. If you disliked a movie because you thought its plot was stupid, there's no reason to launch your review by proposing a division into characters, direction, plot, and photography. Make such a division only when your judgment of the film takes all these elements into account.

A great many things—automobiles, anatomies, governments, nations, plays, leagues, and so on—have ready-made divisions: mechanical, physical, political, what-have-you. Even so, a writer may find it possible, and enjoyable, to suggest a new twist, as in the following:

It's time to start over.
Oh, I don't mean to raze the entire country and plunge it into the sea—there are still too many nice things about this land, bless its heart. No, it's simply that it has now become too elephantine, too lumbering, too ponderous to work efficiently in the modern world. It can't control the oil nations, it can't get anyone to respect the dollar, it can't even destroy a place like Vietnam, and there's a whole host of problems at home, from crime to inflation to game shows, that it can't begin to wrestle with. It's just too big.
We sometimes forget that we started this nation with only 4 million people. But now here we are with 215 million, heading to 230 million by 1980, and we've become bloated and turgid, like some gluttonous dinosaur—and with as much chance of survival. And inevitably, because of our size we've become disputatious and contradictory as well, too large to have common assumptions and mutual sympathies any longer, too vast to hold the same values, share the same life-styles. Hence black against white, young against old, left against right, hip against square, straight against gay . . .
The solution, it seems obvious, is not to *destroy* the country we have spent the last 200 years in creating, but simply to *divide it up*, to make smaller, sleeker, more efficient nations out of the cumbersome one we have now—and then to give like-minded people their own separate areas to move to. Like the ancient Greeks with their city-states, the Swiss with their cantons, the modern Europeans with their hodgepodge of nations, we should decide that that which governs least—geographically, at any rate—governs best.
In countries, as in art, less is more.
As a small step in this direction, may I suggest the following

model of a future America? Let's say, just for starters, that we divide the country up into five new nations, each with 40 million people or so—that was a good number for Frenchmen, you may remember, and it's large enough to get things done, small enough not to cause too much trouble. And, following the birds-of-a-feather principle, we might arrange them thus:

The Northeast.   This would be made up of the dozen states from Maine to Ohio, the homeland of the Yankees, and would be set aside for intellectuals, scholars, students, academics, poets, romantics, people of that sort, the kind that seem to be so numerous in that region already. For its flag—of course each newly created nation needs a flag—this land might choose some version of the Union Jack, since most of them will probably be Anglophiles anyway, and for an anthem, let's say "Yankee Doodle."

The Southeast.   Not much juggling needed here: this would contain all the states of the old Confederacy except Texas, and would naturally be the homeland of all the superpatriots, right-wingers, fundamentalists, racists, antifeminists and would-be Southern belles. Its flag, needless to say, would be the Confederate banner, its national anthem "Dixie," and for currency it could use old Confederate dollars brought out of the attics.

The Southwest.   Here, in the vast region from Texas to southern California, would be a natural site for all the scientists and engineers, aerospace and computer types, military and defense contractors, most people with crewcuts and most retired folks over 65. This country would probably pick the Lone Star flag of Texas as its standard, since most of the area is settled by Texans, and, given a free vote, would most likely end up with "Rhinestone Cowboy" as its national anthem.

The Northwest.   This nation, from San Francisco to Seattle, from the Pacific through the Rockies, would undoubtedly be the most beautiful and hence naturally the home for nature lovers, ecology folks, beach and ski bums, young people in general, hippies and, just to make sure they stay in one place, all radical types of whatever party or age. As a flag, the old Yippie banner with the huge marijuana leaf would seem to suggest itself, and for an anthem perhaps they might select "Rocky Mountain High" or, for the more traditional, "Roll On, Columbia."

The Midwest.   Finally, for everyone else left over, every place else left over: the heartland from the Dakotas to Indiana. Anyone who doesn't fit into any of the other areas would be free to move here, but if the division elsewhere was done right they'd mostly be quiet, staid, simple, farm-loving folks anyway, rather like the ones who live there now. It figures to be such a quiet place that they'd probably not even need an anthem, but they'd undoubtedly want a flag—and since the traditional Stars and Stripes seems to be left over, we might work it out so that they could adopt that.

There, see how simple it all is?

Now, we haven't quite solved all the problems. There's Alaska and Hawaii left over—but maybe the former could be a congenial home for American Indians who didn't want to live elsewhere, and the latter similarly for the black population that wanted space of its own. And there's the problem of Washington, D.C. —maybe that could be closed off as a museum, and all those Federal types who cling to their bureaucratic lives could stay there as the caretakers.

Yes, true enough, there are a few wrinkles that may need working on. But the underlying principle of the *de*-unification of the United States seems to make preponderantly good sense: not only do you get smaller and more workable governments, but you get more homogeneous and harmonious societies as well. And as long as there was free choice, as long as the borders stayed open and people could take up citizenship in whichever state they found the most congenial, that arrangement could last for a long, long time to come. — Kirkpatrick Sale, *Newsweek*

■ *For Writing*

1. *Identify the parts of a mechanism — a can opener, a pencil sharpener, a lawn mower, an automobile engine — that are related to the function or use of the mechanism. In an essay intended for junior-high-school students, describe each part and explain how it functions in the working of the mechanism.*

2. *For a campus magazine, analyze the humor in a comic strip, a television comedy series, a movie, or any recent happening. You may want to explain why you think people laugh at the things they laugh at.*

3. *Describe the structure of a college organization or the activities of a club, showing how the structure or the activities relate to the purpose. Your audience is a friend you want to have join the organization or club.*

4. *Propose four different ways of analyzing your neighborhood. Write a paper developing the one that would be most useful to someone who is organizing a political campaign in the area.*

5. *Argue for assigning the baseball teams in the major leagues to different cities or for dividing the teams or talent of major leagues in any professional sport in some new way.*

6. *Describe the composition — the structure — of a painting or photograph. In the course of your analysis, make clear what central idea or feeling the work conveys and explain what each part contributes to the effect of the whole. Submit with your paper a reproduction or copy of the painting or photograph.*

Comparing and Contrasting: Finding Likenesses and Differences

Often you can generate ideas for your papers by asking how your subject is like or unlike another subject. In conversation we constantly make comparisons—of movies, teams, books, clothes, and so on. In writing we go through the same procedures more thoroughly and systematically in order to clarify our meaning or make an idea more persuasive. (Strictly, *comparison* implies likeness and *contrast* implies difference, but ordinarily *comparison* is applied to discovering and presenting either similarities or differences.)

Whenever your main intention in a paper is to bring out similarities and differences, comparison is naturally central. But it may also be essential in papers with other aims. A good way of explaining how a new mechanism works is to compare it with a familiar one, using a known to shed light on an unknown. To establish a generalization about television audiences, you might compare shows that enjoy high ratings with shows the public rejected. The technique of comparing is also useful in argument—inevitable, in fact, in controversies about which action should be taken, which policy adopted, which candidate elected.

Points of Comparison

A point of comparison is a significant question you can ask about each of your subjects. (What is significant will be determined by your purpose in comparing them.) About two presidential candidates you might ask, "What do they plan to do about the three issues that are bothering most Americans—unemployment, inflation, and defense?" These three issues would then be points of comparison, topics you would discuss in connection with your subjects.

Notice that you arrive at your points of comparison by dividing each of your subjects. What you're looking for, however, is not *all* the parts, as in a division, but a manageable number that will yield significant likenesses and differences when applied to your subjects.

You're most likely to discover relevant points of comparison if you begin by investigating your subjects as fully as possible. Study each one, jotting down all the details and aspects of it that occur to you. Keep turning it over in your mind; keep asking questions of it. Once you have two full lists (if you're comparing two subjects), review them, looking for points of contact that suggest relationships worth exploring. As you examine these relationships more closely, you'll begin to make finer distinctions, asking yourself whether the likenesses you're uncovering are fundamental or superficial and whether the differences are differences in degree or differences in kind.

A difference in degree is expressed in terms of more or less, or better or worse, or stronger or weaker: "Both *A* and *B* are enjoyable, but *A* gives more lasting pleasure than *B*." Uncovering differences in kind is often the most satisfactory way of accounting for the existence of differences where one would expect to find similarities. In this excerpt a scientist explores reasons for the differences between his own conclusions and those of a colleague:

As each of us draws opposite conclusions about the significance of the Mariner data regarding life on Mars, it is difficult to escape the impression that we are both interpreting it in the context of differing *a priori* views of the planet.

Since Sagan and I respect each other greatly as scientists and find much stimulation in each other's thoughts, why should we find it so difficult to read the record similarly? One can look first to our scientific backgrounds. He aimed at the planets and research from his undergraduate days. My first love was—and is— the Earth, and my initial postgraduate activities were of an applied nature. I didn't return to a university for a research career until I was twenty-nine years old. Carl has emphasized synthesis and conjecture about how things are, might be, or could be beyond the Earth. If he is lucky, his great passion, the search for extraterrestrial life, especially intelligent life, will blossom during his lifetime. I, on the other hand, have been mainly concerned about distinguishing fact from fiction in a subject moldy with misconceptions and inherited prejudices. My passion is to understand how things *really* are on Earth as well as in space.— Bruce Murray in *Mars and the Mind of Man* by Ray Bradbury et al.

Once you've discovered the points of comparison that have a bearing on your purpose, you have the criteria you need to select from your lists just those characteristics and qualities and details of your subjects that have a bearing on what you want to demonstrate or prove. Then you're ready to consider how you can best organize your comparison.

■ *For Analysis*

Initial cost, operating cost, and repair record are points of comparison that might be used to evaluate two or more makes of car. What points of comparison would you use to bring out significant similarities and differences between two musicians or groups of musicians (you name them), two courses that you're now taking (you select them), two methods of learning a skill (a skill you're qualified to teach)? In each case, state what interest you have in making the comparison—what you're trying to demonstrate or prove—and what audience you're addressing. (In making a comparison of cars for an audience of wealthy readers, you might ignore matters of cost entirely.)

Structuring a Comparison

Essentially, a passage of comparison consists of several points of comparison filled out with details, examples, facts. How you arrange the points and the supporting information will usually depend on the material itself, on your audience's familiarity with it, and on your purpose. Here are three patterns frequently used in balanced comparisons—comparisons in which roughly the same attention is given to each of the subjects being compared:

I. Whole-to-Whole

Thomas Jefferson grew up among the landed gentry of Virginia, and he remained a confirmed Virginian throughout his life. He was a thoughtful man, a scholar and a philosopher, always eager to add to his knowledge of the arts and sciences and to explore the mysteries of the universe and of the human spirit. Though reluctant to take part in the clamor and conflict of politics, he became a powerful political leader, working for the welfare of his nation. A patriot and statesman, he devoted his life to the development of the Republic he had helped to create. His writings reflect a hopeful view of human nature, a belief that under the right conditions men will improve. That faith is implicit in the great Declaration of Independence, of which he was the author. It is the basis of his dream of a happy land of free men, living together in natural harmony. And that faith is, of course, the root of his objection to any kind of government that would stifle individual liberty and hamper individual growth. Both his faith and his dream became permanent parts of American democracy.

Alexander Hamilton came from a background very unlike Jefferson's. He was born into a poor family on an island in the Lesser Antilles. He became a New Yorker, joining a society of men as competitive and aggressive as himself. A gifted organizer and administrator, he used his brilliant mind as a weapon with which to fight not only for personal success but also for the practical policies he supported. His patriotism was as great as Jefferson's, but his view of the future of the nation was dictated by a very different reading of human nature. He believed that men will act upon the same selfish motives whatever the form of government and that therefore a government with sufficient authority to impose order and stability is always essential. Only through a strong central government, he thought, could America achieve peace, progress, and prosperity. This idea, powerfully expressed in his *Federalist* papers, had great influence upon the organization of the new republic and upon its subsequent history.

II. Part-to-Part

Thomas Jefferson and Alexander Hamilton were two of America's most influential statesmen in the early period of the Republic. Jefferson grew up among the landed gentry of Virginia; Hamilton was born into a poor family on an island in the Lesser Antilles. Only with great reluctance did Jefferson accept a political career, with its accompanying clamor and conflict. A thoughtful man, he would have preferred to spend his life in his native state, free to add to his scholarly knowledge of the arts and sciences and to explore the mysteries of the universe and of the human spirit. Hamilton, on the other hand, found his natural milieu in New York City, in a society of men who shared his competitive, aggressive spirit, and he entered politics with the enthusiasm and efficiency of the born organizer and administrator. His brilliant mind served him admirably in his fight for personal success and for the political policies he supported. His *Federalist* papers are among the greatest documents of the period, ranking in historical importance with Jefferson's Declaration of Independence. Both are the works of great patriots.

Jefferson's political philosophy was optimistic; he believed that, given the right conditions, men would improve. By contrast, Hamilton was convinced that, regardless of environment, human nature does not change. Accordingly, while Jefferson dreamed of a happy land of free men, living together in natural harmony, Hamilton worked for order and stability, for system and organization. The Virginian feared that the machinery of a strong central government would stifle individual liberty and hamper individual growth; the New Yorker believed that government must have authority in order to ensure peace, progress, and prosperity. Regardless of the differences in their views, both men devoted their lives to the welfare of the new nation, which both had helped to create and which both helped to survive. And their different views had permanent influence upon the history of America.

III. Likeness-Difference

Thomas Jefferson and Alexander Hamilton were fellow patriots and fellow statesmen. Men of true brilliance, the powerful influence that they exerted upon the Republic at the beginning of its history had an effect that has persisted to the present day. To them we owe some of our greatest historical documents—to Jefferson the Declaration of Independence and to Hamilton a number of the famous *Federalist* papers. Both were powerful political leaders, working for the welfare of the new nation which they had helped to create and which they helped to survive.

At the same time, their differences were numerous and profound. They were unlike in background, in temperament, in habit of mind, and in political philosophy. Jefferson grew up among the landed gentry of old Virginia; Hamilton was born into a poor family on an island in the Lesser Antilles. Throughout his life, Jefferson remained a confirmed Virginian, but Hamilton became a New Yorker, flourishing in a society of men as competitive and aggressive as himself. Jefferson shrank from the clamor and conflict of politics; Hamilton had the zeal of a born organizer and administrator. Jefferson was a thoughtful man, a scholar and a philosopher, always eager to add to his knowledge of the arts and sciences and to explore the mysteries of the universe and of the human spirit. Hamilton used his mind as a keen weapon with which he fought not only for personal success but also for the practical policies he supported.

They differed markedly in their views of human nature. An optimist, Jefferson believed that, under the right conditions, men would improve; Hamilton was convinced that, regardless of environment, human nature would never change. Because of their different readings of human nature, they had different views about the role of government. Since he could not believe that a new type of government would result in a new type of citizenry, Hamilton worked for the old objectives—order and stability, system and organization; he sought to build a government with traditional authority, which he considered essential to peace, progress, and prosperity. Just as naturally, considering his philosophy, Jefferson fought against a strong central government, fearing that it would stifle individual liberty and hamper individual growth, seeing it as a threat to his dream of a happy land of free men, living together in natural harmony.

These examples show that the same material can be organized in three ways, each giving the reader a slightly different view. The first, in which the writer has his say about one of the subjects before turning to the other, presents each subject as a whole rather than focusing on precise similarities or differences. The part-to-part scheme, with its perfect symmetry, highlights specific points of comparison, leaving the reader with a sharp impression of how the subjects relate to each other on each point. (Notice how the symmetry extends even to the individual sentences. Many of them are balanced, the two halves built just alike.) The third pattern begins with similarities but emphasizes differences; what is given most space and placed last is usually remembered longest.

Comparisons don't often fall into patterns as neatly balanced as these. If you were comparing the British and American political systems in order to explain the British system to American readers, you'd naturally give the American "whole" briefer coverage. A few generalizations would be enough to remind your readers of what they already knew and to open the way for the contrast. The same unequal coverage would make sense if you used the part-to-part structure: whenever you introduced a point of comparison, you'd touch on its application to the American political system only briefly, giving much more space to the corresponding details of the British system.

If you were using comparison to establish the superiority of public schools over private schools, you'd naturally give most attention to the strong points of public schools

—and to the weak points of private schools — since these would be what had convinced you of the superiority of public schooling in the first place. If you intended to bring out hidden likenesses between two things normally thought of as strikingly different — tap dancing and ballet, perhaps — there wouldn't be any point in reviewing the differences. You'd acknowledge them very briefly and move on to what you were really interested in — the similarities.

There are valid reasons, then, for giving more attention to one of your subjects or for otherwise modifying the basic patterns of organization. But if you commit yourself to making a full, balanced comparison, you must work at doing just that. And in making a comparison you'll find that each of the patterns poses some problems. In the whole-to-whole the two halves of your paper will drift apart if, in dealing with the second whole, you lose sight of the points you made about the first. Part-to-part has the advantage of keeping the topics in view, but unless they're smoothly related, the paper will seem choppy and disjointed. And if the third pattern is less common than the other two, it's probably because many subjects yield such a random collection of either likenesses or differences that half the comparison turns out to be weak and uninteresting.

In choosing among the patterns, try to decide which best suits your material, your purpose, and the needs of your audience. Suppose you were writing an article for a popular magazine about the pollution of waterways and you used as evidence a comparison of the Concord and Merrimack rivers as they are today with the rivers as Henry David Thoreau knew them in 1839. Doing a part-to-part comparison probably wouldn't suit your purpose. You'd be more likely to offer a brief sketch of the rivers as Thoreau wrote about them and then move on to a detailed account of their present deplorable state. Your overriding pattern would be *un*balanced whole-to-whole.

When you write an extended, analytical comparison for an audience that knows a good deal about your subjects, you'll probably use the part-to-part pattern. Close analysis of separate points can be sustained longer in that scheme than in the whole-to-whole. A detailed comparison of the techniques and accomplishments of two film directors, supported by examples of their work, would be easier to follow in the part-to-part scheme than in whole-to-whole, and relationships could be stated with greater precision than in the likeness-difference pattern.

Likeness-difference is a good choice when your readers not only know a lot about your subjects but have a strong opinion about them that you want to change. If your purpose is to persuade them that subjects generally regarded as similar are actually unlike, begin with the likenesses and go on to the differences, perhaps showing that the likenesses are more apparent than real. If you want to persuade them that subjects generally regarded as different are actually much alike, acknowledge the differences first and then go on to reveal likenesses that are more significant.

In making a choice of methods, ask yourself questions like these: Will my purpose be best served (and my readers best informed) if I present a general view of each whole? Or should I set certain aspects of each side by side to sharpen the contrast? Or will it be more effective to talk entirely in terms of *like* and *unlike*? Do *like* and *unlike* need equal attention, or should I pass over the likenesses quickly and get on to what really counts – the differences?

Of course, the assumption behind all these questions is that you already have a definite thesis in mind, that you intend more than a mere list of particulars, that you have selected every point of comparison for a specific reason. Don't focus so closely on the procedures of comparing that you forget the purpose you want the comparison to serve. And remember that though the structure of a comparison must be clear, symmetry doesn't guarantee a good paper. Organization is only a means of calling attention to the similarities and differences. To convince the reader that they are real ones, you must present the details, the examples, the facts that make your subjects alike or different in respects you consider important and interesting.

In the following newspaper article comparison is used to support a thesis. The structure is clear-cut, and the proportions are balanced, but these virtues are functional. The writer is comparing two sports not simply to compare them but to make a point about their sociological significance.

Baseball and football nicely reflect, sociologically, their respective eras of inception, development and maturation. They reflect, rather directly, the evolution, or demise, of the American dream. It is no accident that in terms of media popularity, football, a game clearly defined by time and space, is the No. 1 sport in America today. Football in many ways mirrors contemporary America; baseball preserves an image of the America we have lost.

For baseball is a game in which the passage of time is incidental; the season turns, but no clocks run out in baseball games. Baseball is the summer game, reflecting a society still rural and thus fitting perfectly into the languid season between sowing and reaping. Deeds matter in baseball: hits, runs, errors and outs rather than mere time make the inning.

Nor has space, time's twin, much to do with baseball. There were no fences early in the game and even today they are seen as rather arbitrary.

There are home fields but no enemy territory to penetrate, no home territory to defend. The entire field is open to both teams equally. This befits a society in which land is abundant. Baseball is the Homestead Act with bases.

Although there are teams in baseball, there is little teamwork. The essence of the game is the individual with or against the ball: pitcher controlling, batter hitting, fielder handling, runner racing the ball. All players are on their own, struggling (like the farmer) to overcome not another human being but nature (the ball).

This individualism is demonstrated when the shortstop, cleanly fielding the ball, receives credit for a "chance" even if the first baseman drops the thrown ball. It is demonstrated when a last-place team includes a Cy Young Award-winning pitcher or a league-leading hitter. It is perhaps most clearly manifest in the pitcher-batter duel, the heart of the game, when two men face each other.

Baseball is each man doing the best he can for himself and against nature within a loose confederation of fellow individualists he may or may not admire and respect. This reflects a society in which individual effort, drive and success are esteemed and in which, conversely, failure is deemed the individual's responsibility.

Like life itself, baseball is full of surprising twists and turns and there can be no game plans. The season contains all the stuff of the old American dream. Disappointments are softened by the realization that one game, one defeat or even a series of defeats does not spell failure. Such a situation weakens any tendency toward winning at all costs and by any means.

In football, losing is worse than death because after losing there is nothing. In baseball, there is always tomorrow or at least next year. The baseball season ends with harvest time; the football season ends with the plunge into deepest winter.

Baseball is everyman's game; that is, it is not a big man's game: Phil Rizzuto, Bobby Shantz, Pee Wee Reese and Joe Morgan are among the greatest players and not big. Henry Aaron is barely above average in size.

Nor is baseball a specialist's game. Except for pitchers and catchers, many players can readily shift positions, but who ever heard of a utility linebacker?

In baseball we see perpetuated one of the guiding myths of America — egalitarianism, equal opportunity, every man potentially a champion. Neither smallness of stature nor a computer analysis precludes everyman's attempt to make the team and to attain glory. Baseball is perhaps the only team sport in which a good small team can beat a good big team — provided the small team has a superior pitcher.

These factors account in large part for the almost total absence of physical contact, to say nothing of physical violence, in baseball. This rarity of physical violence reflects a time when America itself, as a nation among nations, was incapable of great violence, having neither contiguous enemy or potential enemy states nor a significant standing army.

But America has changed. After World War II, in a clear break with our history, America became a military power of the first order and in the last 25 years we have used that power often: Massive violence, or the threat of it, has been our lot for a generation.

In such a context, football has matured. In football, violence is an essential characteristic; it is a team sport played by specialists who must submerge their personalities for the sake of the corporation; it is a game of big men whom lesser mortals may passively watch but not emulate; it is a game severely circumscribed by time and space factors; it is a game (unlike baseball, of "democratic" origins) that originated among college elites and was purveyed to the masses as a commodity.

Baseball appears as a relic from a simpler, richer, more leisurely past. Its enduring popularity attests to the strength of the myth it re-enacts, of individuals in their lonely struggle against nature. Football is a manifestation of that stage in the evolution of America when highly specialized organization men, inured to violence, confronted a world increasingly limited in economic time, space and resources. Now that "limits to growth" have been perceived, perhaps the situation is ripe for a new American pastime, in which space, time and organization factors are predominant but in which there is room for individualism as well.

Soccer, anyone? – Gerald J. Cavanaugh, *New York Times*

■ *For Analysis and Writing*

1. Review the three methods of structuring a comparison, and then write a paper of about 1000 words on one of the following topics.

a. For a sympathetic audience, such as an old friend or a school counselor, compare and contrast your views and attitudes with those of your parents on matters that are especially important to you. (Suggestions: religious or moral views; social activities; dress; education; money.)

b. For the sports section in a newspaper or magazine, compare and contrast two games or sports, like table tennis and paddleball, handball and jai alai, basketball and hockey, baseball and stoopball, golf and tennis.

c. For a TV magazine, write a comparison of the styles of two comedians or two serious actors with a view to demonstrating that one is more talented or more entertaining than the other. Audience: TV fans.

2. Write a comparison of your own family and another, very different family that you know well. In making the comparison, rely chiefly on details about their homes—furniture, drapes, color schemes, pictures on the walls, knickknacks,

*and so on — that seem to you to reflect the occupants' personali-
ties, tastes, interests, and values. (The details you chose for
assignment 5 on p. 39 could be used for this comparison.)
Your audience is acquainted with both families but hasn't
visited their homes.*

3. *Examine the following paper. What purpose does the comparison serve? Is it intended simply to show likenesses and
differences, or is it used to support a thesis? What method of
comparison has the writer used? Is it a good one for the purpose, or would another have been better? Are the details well
chosen? Do they make the generalization believable? Are the
tone and style appropriate to the audience proposed in 1a?
Why or why not?*

Old Is Right?

Many members of the older generation are under the impression that their values and ways of life are the only right ones.
They think that their children must inherit these qualities or
they, the parents, have failed. They refuse to acknowledge that
teenagers might have some legitimate ideas of their own. I am
tired of having my opinions put down by my parents simply
because of my youth and relative lack of experience.

Family ties are extremely important to my father and mother.
They feel that their children should prefer to do things with the
family rather than on their own. Unfortunately, their attitudes
make me unwilling to spend time with them.

"Conservative" is a good word to use to describe my parents.
They find it hard to accept any sort of change. When I was growing up, all the girls were wearing pants to school, but I wasn't
allowed to until the seventh grade, and even then I was restricted
to dress pants. It was my senior year in high school before I was
permitted to wear jeans — once a week. I consider myself a liberal
to a certain extent. At least I see nothing wrong in dressing in a
casual, comfortable way.

My father and mother are very straitlaced Protestants who
firmly believe that going to church every Sunday is an integral
part of religion. I see religion as a more personal thing. I feel that
I can be just as close to God, if not closer, through my own
private, nightly prayers. Although I believe strongly in the love
of God, I am not interested in organized religion. Rather than
accepting and respecting my views, my parents are constantly
trying to convert me to their way of thought.

Politics is another sore point. My parents are devoted Republi-
cans and always vote for the party's candidate because they are
sure he must stand for Republican principles and ideals. I chose
to register as an Independent, believing that I should vote for
the candidate whose personal qualities I most admire, regardless
of his party label. My parents disapprove.

My father and mother are convinced that one of the most important things in life is working to earn money for later years.
For them, work has nothing to do with enjoyment or even interest. It is a duty you must perform for yourself and your family.
I feel that work is part of life but that life is something to be
relished. So I would rather work for low pay in a job I like than

be stuck in a high-paying dull job. My parents can't understand this. One of the worst shocks of their lives was when my sister dropped out of college, leaving behind a relatively secure career in fashion merchandising, to become an apprentice sailor on a square-rigged ship.

I don't mean to sound like my parents are inhuman. My mother and father have always been more than generous, giving me everything I ever needed. I love them both dearly and don't mean for it to appear otherwise. They have taught me many valuable lessons. But though I appreciate their efforts to give me the best upbringing possible, according to their standards, I think we would get along much better if they would only try to understand my feelings and remember that I am an independent adult with ideas of my own, however different they may be from theirs.

Classifying: Making Groups

Classifying is a method of developing and organizing papers that is closely related to dividing and also requires skill in comparing. In dividing you separate something into parts to see what it's made up of. In classifying you sort a collection of individual things—cars, people, sports, foods, books, wars—into groups or classes on the basis of likenesses, so that they'll be easier to understand and easier to think and talk about. Much of human knowledge is organized by classification, in the humanities as well as in the physical sciences and the social sciences (note this classification). So is much human prejudice, as in racial, ethnic, regional, social, and sexual stereotypes (note this classification). What we're primarily concerned with here are the criteria you should keep in mind as you make new groupings in the course of expressing your ideas about your subject.

Consistency

Like division, classification should be consistent—that is, only one principle of classification should be applied at a time. You can classify cars by make or by size or by price, people by age or by weight or by nationality, and so on. Once you've classified your subject according to one principle, you can classify it by another; but don't shift principles in mid-classification.

For your grouping to be reasonably sound, the classes must be reasonably separate and distinct. In a paper describing the football fans at his college, a student set up four groups: alumni, students, serious fans, and "the ones that party." As a classification this is a mishmash. Both alumni and students may attend tailgate parties, and whether they do or not, they may be serious fans. Beginning with a single principle of classification—main purpose in attending—would have permitted a division into those who come primarily for love of the game, those who come primarily for love of the school, and those who come primarily for social reasons. Then these groups could have been subdivided. For example, those who come primarily for love of the game would probably include students, alumni, and fans who have no connection with the college.

In some situations logical consistency is neither possible nor necessary. In the passage below, a classification of the "new" students of the 1970s produces four groups that are "distinctive but overlapping." Some of the members of the third group, for instance, also fit into the fourth group. For anyone interested in higher education in the 1970s this overlapping wouldn't be troublesome. What's important is that ethnic minorities, whether the members are men or women, make up one significant group of "new" students. Another significant group is made up of women who are gaining admission through "public conscience and Affirmative Action."

> The new clientele for higher education in the 1970s consists of everyone who wasn't there in the 1940s, 1950s and 1960s. There are four distinctive but overlapping groups: (1) low academic achievers who are gaining entrance through open admissions; (2) adults and part-time learners who are gaining access through nontraditional alternatives; (3) ethnic minorities; and (4) women who are gaining admission through public conscience and Affirmative Action.—Patricia Cross, *Change*

In classifying a subject with which you're personally associated—say sorority or fraternity members—you may make the mistake of using individuals you know as the basis for establishing groups. If you do, your classification is likely to emerge as a series of character sketches. A classifier must concentrate on the type, not the individual. The main concern is not the idiosyncrasies that make two people different but the characteristics that they share when they're looked at from a particular perspective—as students, perhaps, or as voters or as consumers of junk food. What the classifier says, in effect, is that *for the purpose he has in mind,* some people can be grouped with some other people. Despite their many differences in respects unrelated to the point he's making, they are alike in terms of the principle of classification he's applying.

Completeness

The classifier's interest in the type rather than the individual often makes necessary some relaxation of the rule that a classification must be complete—that is, that it must assign a place to every item in the collection of items being classified. Formal classifications, like those used in the sciences, seek to organize all the available data according to objective criteria. But making your classification all-inclusive when its aims are modest and its criteria personal may be unwise as well as unnecessary. For most purposes the rule can be modified to something like this: A classification should be as complete as your knowledge of the subject permits and as your purpose requires.

In classifying a large group of people, there's no necessity for pigeonholing every last individual. A too-conscientious effort to do so may result in the major groupings getting lost among minor divisions and catchalls with labels like "borderline" and "miscellaneous" and "other." The writer who says that there are four types of students or five types of statesmen or three types of singers is not saying that *every* student or statesman or singer fits comfortably into one of these groups. What he is saying is that four (or five or three) classes can be differentiated in ways that are significant for the purpose he has in mind. If the classification is relatively inclusive, if each class is substantiated by enough details to make it a real one, and if the classes are adequately differentiated from one another, the reader will be satisfied.

Many informal classifications have a highly personal flavor. In her book *The OK Boss,* for example, Muriel James classifies types of bosses as the critic, the coach, the shadow, the analyst, the pacifier, the fighter, and the inventor. Another classifier of bosses might come up with a completely different set of labels. In discovering and offering a new way of looking at a subject, you may learn and reveal something about yourself as well.

■ *For Analysis*

Examine the following groupings. Explain why you think each grouping is or is not logically sound (or as sound as the subject permits). If you find a grouping satisfactory, tell what kind of paper it might be appropriately used in. If you think a grouping is unsatisfactory, propose a better one.

a. College students: those who want an education, those who want a job, those who want a diploma

b. Crime-and-detection TV programs: criminal-centered, police-centered, private-detective-centered

c. Cars: those that look good and those that give good service

d. Churchgoers: the devout, the insecure, the socialites

e. Political extremists: the ultraconservatives, the ultraliberals, the know-nothings

f. Approaches to social problems: know-nothing, know-it-all

Sometimes you'll be interested not in setting up a classification of your own but in fitting your subject into an existing classification. When you want to make a judgment about a movie, you often start by placing it in a class—comedy, satire, melodrama, musical, or whatever. Then you can go on to make further distinctions by comparing it with other members of that same class. Sometimes you can draw interesting conclusions about your subject by showing that it doesn't fit into existing categories. A fondness for branding mavericks can lead to competing labels: the music of Willie Nelson has been classified as, among other things, progressive country and redneck rock.

Observers with an eye for new trends and new variations on old themes are constantly creating classifications or making fresh applications of existing ones. In the prewriting stage, when you're mulling over possible approaches to a subject, you can often generate good ideas by putting your subject into as many different classes as you can think of. So long as things are in the process of changing—and they always will be—there are endless opportunities for giving a fresh reading of experience and inventing new classifications.

Writing a passage or a whole paper that classifies calls on many of the skills you use in comparing. Similarities cause you to put a number of objects in a single class; differences cause you to create separate classes. So as you classify, keep your emphasis on those similarities and differences. And make them convincing through the use of descriptive details.

■ *For Analysis and Writing*

1. Propose five different principles or bases for classifying each of the following subjects: clothes, vegetables, liberation movements, songs, humorists, notions of physical beauty. (Example: Students might be classified on the bases of their reasons for being in college, their study habits, their recreational choices, their places of origin, and their manner of dress — not necessarily in that order.) Not every principle need be serious. Use your imagination. Once you have your five principles, set up the classes that each principle yields. Then choose one of the classifications and write a paper that makes use of it.

2. A stereotype is a classification that's applied unthinkingly and without regard for individual differences. It may reflect the user's bias and may be in part responsible for that bias. With a few descriptive labels — "weak," "strong"; "honest," "dishonest"; "hard-working," "lazy"; and so on — sketch a popular stereotype of each of the following: college students, politicians, mothers, males. Write a short paper about a college student, a politician, a mother, or a male who doesn't fit the stereotype. Then sketch a new class — not a stereotype — that accounts for that person.

3. Analyze the people you went to high school with according to some principle of classification that interests you. Write for a specific audience — your high-school counselor, a student who attended a different high school, a student who will be attending your high school next year, your parents. Make your classification support a generalization — some point or some conviction you want to express about your high-school classmates.

Analyzing Causes and Effects: Finding Out Why and What Then

I'm disorganized because my mother's always been super-organized.

We wouldn't have lost if he hadn't fouled out.

If they win the election, taxes will go up.

All of us are constantly crediting or blaming *A* for causing *B* or predicting that *C* will result in *D*, and in ordinary conversation this free-swinging approach usually goes unchallenged. When you write, though, your readers have time to examine and think about what you have to say. If the causal (*not* casual) connection you assert doesn't make sense, they'll reject it. If it's sensible enough but you provide no evidence to back it up, they'll treat it as no more than a possibility.

Causal connections help give coherence to material that's organized chronologically—sets of instructions and descriptions of processes as well as narratives told for their own sake. In a paper on a natural process like soil drifting, you generate content by asking yourself why the drifting takes place. By explaining why—by providing the causal statement—you help your reader understand the whole process.

In other papers cause-effect analysis is the chief method of development. The writer searches out the causes of (or reasons for) an event or situation or policy or belief. He traces the effects (or results or influences) it has had or will have. Or he conducts both inquiries in the same paper, first setting forth the events that led to a certain state of affairs, then revealing what developments have ensued or predicting what developments will ensue. In an essay on the *causes* of student apathy toward politics or the psychological *effects* of abortion, the writer's interest is centered not so much on the situation itself as on what led to it or on what it led to or will lead to. His main concern is to present, and perhaps argue for, the relationships and connections he's arrived at by reasoning about origins and results.

Like any other kind of reasoning, reasoning in terms of cause and effect can be done well or badly. If you approach a cause-effect analysis too blithely, you're likely to oversimplify: bureaucracy is to blame for high taxes; slavery caused the Civil War; the poor representation of women in top executive positions is the result of male chauvinism; progressive legislation will put an end to all sexual discrimination. You'll match one cause to one effect, often without providing any evidence that your one cause is, in fact, a cause at all, and in that way turn what should be a reasoned discussion into a dogmatic statement of opinion.

Or, convinced that only an omniscient being can assign causes or attribute results, you may refuse to commit yourself. You load your discussion with cautious qualifications, present an endless list of "possible" causes, or trace the "possible" immediate causes back to such remote and virtually meaningless causes as "civilization," "chance," or "human nature"—thus World War II (or

World War I or the Trojan War or the Vietnam War) was caused by human nature. Whether your tendency is to oversimplify or to overqualify, you need to develop a realistic notion of how to go about answering *why* questions.

Discovering Causes

The procedure in answering *why* questions always involves two steps—investigating the facts and reasoning from the facts to a causal explanation. Anyone accustomed to thinking of cause-effect relations in the context of scientific experiments knows that two phenomena are causally related only if the existence of one *requires* the existence of the other. A causal relation between A and B can be established with certainty only if it can be demonstrated that whenever B occurs, A is present; that B never occurs when A is absent; and that the presence of A is always accompanied by the occurrence of B. A laboratory worker tries to isolate all variables and then puts strict controls on one variable after another until eventually he determines what condition or set of conditions operates as a cause. He runs experiments again and again until he either verifies or disproves his hypothesis—his hunch or guess that A is the cause of B.

In attempting to answer many of the *why* questions that matter most to us, we can't set up controlled laboratory experiments. We can't call into existence the actual circumstances in which a fatal accident took place or a game was lost or a war was won. And even if we could rerun such happenings, we would rarely be able to isolate a single cause that inevitably led to the given effect. "In the world of reality," a logician observes, "there is no such thing as *the* cause of anything. There are many causes, or necessary antecedents, for everything that happens." An investigation into the collision of two cars may have to take into account such *necessary* antecedents as weather, traffic, and road conditions, the mechanical condition of the cars, and the competence of the drivers. The investigator may be able to demonstrate that one of many *contributory* causes had a more immediate connection with the accident than the others and was in itself *sufficient* to have caused the accident. But he may have to be satisfied with listing three or four contributory causes, none of which can be said to have been decisive.

When you're writing about social and moral problems like alcoholism, drug addiction, the divorce rate, the failures of our educational system or the system we use for dealing with crime, and the hardships faced by many of our old people, you'll probably want to list several causes, not just one, and distinguish immediate causes from remote ones. In a thoroughgoing causal analysis you may need to examine the evidence for conflicting explanations, show that a commonly accepted cause can't be held solely responsible, distinguish between conditions that made an event likely to occur and conditions that triggered the event, perhaps rank contributory causes in order of importance—any or all of these.

In any case, your reader will be interested not just in the list of causes you offer but in your demonstration that there's a probable relationship between each cause you cite and the effect. Merely asserting causal connections isn't enough: you must supply enough details to join "cause" to "effect." Causal analysis usually has an argumentative edge. There's no point in writing about cause-effect relations that are obvious to everyone (touching a hot stove causes pain). There *is* some point in exploring relationships which can, when shown to be probable, increase a reader's understanding of the subject and suggest solutions as well. (Why do so many students have difficulty with math? Why has the Midwest lost industries to the "sun states"? Why have there been a number of car-truck collisions on Amato Road within a period of weeks?) And it is demonstration, not mere assertion, that establishes probability—demonstration in the form of concrete, relevant details and facts that knit cause to effect.

Attributing Effects

You'll want to concern yourself primarily with effects in two different writing situations. In one you work from a current state of affairs or a current policy to its effects (the effects of coed housing, for example), with a view to arguing that since the effects have been desirable, the state of affairs or the policy should be continued, or that since the effects have been undesirable, the state of affairs or the policy should be changed. Here, the procedure is much like the one you'd use in discovering causes and in persuading readers that your analysis was plausible. As in identifying causes, you must take care not to attribute to one cause a condition that might just as logically be the effect of another cause. Good relations in a housing unit may be less the result of social arrangements than of pleasant surroundings and a fair distribution of responsibilities.

In the second writing situation you *predict* effects as part of your argument for accepting or rejecting a proposed policy. The element of prediction imposes on the responsible writer the need to bring in all the evidence he can to show that the results he projects are likely to occur. We're all familiar with predictions about the bad consequences that will flow from courses of action or habits that the speakers or writers don't approve of—continued attempts to integrate schools will destroy the American educational system; rock concerts will deafen a generation; anti-pollution legislation will wreck the economy; television will wipe out literacy; and so on. The political candidate's routine prediction of horrendous consequences if his opponent should be elected is not taken seriously by many intelligent voters. To make sure *your* analysis of effects is taken seriously, make every effort to proportion effects to causes (field mice don't cause landslides) and to establish through detailed evidence reasonable links between the policy or event or situation and the results you say it will bring about.

Tracing a sequence of probable effects, linking one effect to another, is a natural way of making predictions. Although the following passage isn't a full discussion of the complex subject, it gives a good idea, in summary fashion, of how a scientist interprets a phenomenon, reasoning from a limited effect to a much more sweeping one.

Throughout the eons, habitats have undergone frequent change, and Lepidoptera, like other life forms, have become extinct through the processes of evolution. According to the new preservationist society which has adopted its name, however, Xerces blue is "the first butterfly to become extinct in North America due to human impact."

Modern man's impact on butterflies, as well as other harmless insects, is of deep concern to many scientists today. Their reasoning goes something like this: About the only way man can totally eliminate a butterfly or moth species from the earth— intentionally or accidentally—is by destroying its habitat (which contains its food plant), leaving no possibility for regeneration in the foreseeable future, as when a meadow is paved for a shopping mall, a woodland cleared for a subdivision or a marsh drained for an industrial site. This habitat, however, is not the butterfly's alone. It is something the butterfly has shared with other living creatures, including man. And when man thus molds a habitat to his exclusive use, asserting his claims there over those of all the other life forms in it, he is destroying *his* natural environment as well as theirs.

So it isn't just a question of the butterfly's world going down the drain; the world in which man in his present form has been able to flourish so successfully for half a million years or so is going down the drain, too, leaving in its place a very dubious synthetic substitute. It is with such a set of interlocking relationships in mind that Robert M. Pyle, the Xerces Society's executive director, has called butterflies "excellent monitors of environmental change and of rises in pollution levels." From this viewpoint, moths and butterflies are the barometers of our industrial civilization; their elimination from our human habitat is a danger signal we must heed. – Paul Showers, *New York Times Magazine*

■ *For Analysis and Writing*

1. *"At night the noise in the dorm makes sleeping, as well as studying, almost impossible." Take this statement or a similar one based on your own experience and develop a paper in which you first investigate the causes of the situation and then discuss its effects. You might go on to propose a remedy. Your audience is the director of housing on campus.*

2. *To support his contention that the side effects of technical innovation may be more influential than the direct effects in transforming the behavior, outlook, and moral ethic of a civilization, Jacob Bronowski in 1969 used this illustration:*

Who would have thought that the unfortunate character who invented photographic film would have been responsible for the California film industry? And thus, indirectly, for contracts that would prevent film stars from having affairs that might give rise to gossip and scandal? That consequently stars would lead their love life in public, by repeated divorce and marriage? That therefore the beautiful pin-ups of film would, in time, become the models of the divorce business? And the climax, that one-third of all marriages contracted this year in California are going to end in divorce – all because somebody invented the process of printing pictures on a celluloid strip? – Jacob Bronowski, *Saturday Review*

First comment on the Bronowski paragraph as causal analysis, and then try your hand at the same sort of thing. Write a paper – serious or humorous – showing the unanticipated side effects of a recent discovery or policy.

Defining: Telling What It Is

Whatever your subject, definitions may be used not only to explain unfamiliar terms but to give new meanings to familiar terms or to indicate the exact sense in which a word is to be understood. And besides these uses, which, though often vital, occupy very little space in a paper, definition can serve as the chief means of explaining a subject or persuading an audience to respond to it in a particular way.

Technical terms and the special vocabulary of a subject can be serious obstacles to communication between writer and reader, and even everyday words can cause misunderstanding. Some words—*rhetoric, liberal, realistic*—are used in so many different ways that it's often wise to specify the meaning you intend. On some occasions you may need to distinguish between the popular and the scholarly senses of a term.

At the beginning of *The American Myth of Success,* Richard Weiss writes:

I do not use the word "myth" to imply something entirely false. Rather, I mean it to connote a complex of profoundly held attitudes and values which condition the way men view the world and understand their experience.

A *stipulative* definition like this one establishes common ground for the discussion and so makes communication easier. Communication won't be made easier if you stipulate a meaning never before given the word. Nobody will pay much attention to a writer who in a serious discussion decides, like Humpty Dumpty in *Alice in Wonderland,* that *glory* is to mean "a nice, knock-down argument."

A good grasp of the rhetorical situation will help you decide when to define and when not to. If you neglect to supply a definition your readers need, you'll lose touch with them. If you persist in providing definitions they don't need, you may lose them altogether. How you phrase a clarifying definition also depends on your awareness of your audience, its needs and its capabilities. Don't confuse a general audience by defining a technical term in terms that are entirely technical. Don't insult an intelligent audience by simplifying so much that your definition lacks precision. So far as you can, harmonize the definition with its immediate context. Using zoological terminology to define *bush baby* is appropriate in a course paper for Zoology 101 but out of place in a paper describing the attractions of the local zoo.

Though you may occasionally want to call special attention to a key term you're defining, you can usually slip the explanation in casually and unobtrusively, without delaying the forward movement of the discussion. There are many ways of working a brief definition into a sentence:

So far, 24 bodies have been placed in "cryonic suspension," a process that involves replacing the blood with an antifreeze solution and placing the corpse in a thermos-shaped capsule cooled with a frequently replenished supply of liquid nitrogen. — *Newsweek*

If our universities were interested in education, which is to say in helping the young grow in self-awareness, it would follow that they would be deeply interested in teaching. — Martin Duberman, *New Republic*

From the start, book publishing has been a prime instance of what Max Weber called the Protestant ethic: to serve God by making money. — Stanley Kauffmann, *New Republic*

Dr. King was a radical in the truest sense: he insisted at the same time upon the terrible reality of our problems and upon their solubility, and he rejected everything that was irrelevant to their solution. — *New Yorker*

Extended Definitions

Defining as a method of developing a subject goes beyond the defining that functions solely as an aid to clarity. In some papers you may find that the question you're raising about your subject can best be answered by explaining what a term means or by asserting what it ought to mean. Is the world at peace when there is violent conflict in a number of small — that is, economically, politically, and militarily weak — countries? That depends on what you mean by "the world" and by "peace." Is violence a legitimate form of protest? That depends on your conception of both violence and protest. Should universities adjust their course offerings to the job market? The question can hardly be answered without defining the proper function of a university.

To answer questions like these, you can't simply report on how the term is used — though you may need to do that, too. You have to examine carefully the *class* of events or objects designated by the term — the world, peace, violence, protest, universities — seeking out distinctive characteristics, properties, qualities, or functions. Once you've isolated these, you'll have a sound basis for answering the question you've posed.

The aim of extended definition is not to say simply what a word means or how it's used (a *lexical* definition) but to say what the thing or concept is that the word stands for. The difference between these two kinds of definition is plainly stated in this passage:

Let us start by agreeing on one small but plaguey matter: we are interested in learning more about a certain concept. This is the concept evoked for critics by the word *literature* — but evoked also by such other terms as *poetry, great books, the classics, serious writing, verbal art.* We are *not* interested in the word *literature* itself. Questions about the deployment of the word *literature* by the critics, and by others, are questions lexicographers will try to answer. We already know that the word *literature* is used in a variety of different — even inconsistent — ways. We want to know about that "thing" that literary critics are talking about, the thing they refer to with, among others, the word *literature.* The question I am here phrasing, "What is literature to literary critics?" might be phrased by someone else as, "What is *poetry* [or *good books*, or *serious writing*, or *verbal art*, etc.] to literary critics?" Literary critics feel that, whether profoundly or superficially, accurately or inaccurately, they are all talking about the same thing, and it is this thing we want to learn more about. — Thomas J. Roberts, *College English*

There are many ways of defining. When you write an extended definition, you usually want to make several different approaches to your subject. Each can give you a grip on your subject, some a more secure grip than others.

Etymologies, the histories of words, are of very uneven value in developing extended definitions. To point out that the word *car* goes back to the Latin *carrus*, a word of Celtic origin that meant a four-wheeled wagon, doesn't offer a very promising start for a definition of the class of objects we call cars. But etymologies do have force in some rhetorical situations. For example, reminding readers that the word *radical* comes from the Latin *radix*, meaning "root," may be a successful way of opening up a discussion of a political issue. Many readers are attracted by the notion of getting to the root of a problem.

Synonyms are more generally useful as a means of defining. Though no two words mean exactly the same thing, several words may mean roughly the same thing; and synonyms can indicate the general area of meaning. If you want to tell what a dilemma is, you may find it useful to begin with "something-likes" — *predicament, quandary, plight, jam*, and so on.

Examples help make distinctions between synonyms (*tempt* versus *lure*). They can also introduce the reader to the general area of meaning, as when having breakfast in bed on a Sunday morning is used to illustrate *contentment*. While such use of example doesn't constitute a full definition, it does stimulate the imagination and often works well in relaxed rhetorical situations. Specific examples can be extremely helpful in defining groups and classes: a detailed examination of one member of a school of poetry (Wordsworth) can contribute a good deal to a definition of the school (Romanticism).

An example helps define in an informal context, as in this case, where it gives point to an extremely broad definition:

My definition of music is anything that sounds good to the ear. If a peanut rolling across the floor sounds good, that's music. — Willie Nelson, quoted in Douglas Martin, *Wall Street Journal*

Connotations — the associations a word has — may be spelled out in a definition to make sure that readers will be aware of the writer's emotional response to the subject ("To me, *winter* means physical discomfort and mental depression").

Formal definitions, as they are sometimes called, offer a traditional way of establishing denotative meaning — that is, of pointing to the objects or events named by a term. You're probably familiar with this method of defining from textbook definitions, and you may have used it yourself in answering examination questions and in writing course papers. First you specify the genus or set to which the class designated by the term belongs ("A ballad is a song"), and then you differentiate it from other classes in the set ("that tells a story"). "A ballad is a song that tells a story" puts the class *ballad* into the larger class or set *song* and then selects the quality — storytelling — that differentiates it from other kinds of songs. For some terms one differentiating characteristic is enough. For others, several may be required to isolate the precise combination of qualities that characterize the class.

Framing definitions on this pattern gives excellent training in precise, literal statement. Before you begin, consider carefully which of several possible genuses you might use in defining your term. Should you, for *ballad,* choose *rhyming narrative, popular song,* or simply *song*? Should you, for *rabbit,* choose *mammal,* the Latin label for its biological genus, or simply *member of the hare family*? Your purpose and the rhetorical situation will affect your choice.

Choosing the right characteristics to set the genus apart is also of vital importance. In telling a story a ballad may praise a heroic deed or mourn a lost love or whatever, but these characteristics are shared by other kinds of songs and therefore would not be sufficiently limiting. Finally, the differentiating characteristics must really mark the class and not just individual members of it. "A ballad is a song that tells a story drawn from folklore" introduces a characteristic shared by a good many individual ballads but not by ballads as a class. It would be too limiting for an accurate definition.

A genus-plus-differentiae definition is often at the heart of an extended definition, with the genus and each of the differentiae receiving detailed discussion. But for many purposes the pattern seems too confining or smacks too much of textbook-encyclopedia style. Not all definitions call for such rigor.

Negation has its uses in definition. Telling what the class you're establishing is *not* may lead effectively to an explanation of what it *is*. You may also use negation or contrast to correct current misconceptions, rejecting fuzzy or wrong notions of the meaning of a term before offering more accurate explanations. Or you may begin with a single explicit negative like "A composition text is not a book of etiquette" or "Loyalty is not conformity." Defining by negation can be a risky technique—you can become so wound up in telling what the subject isn't that you never get around to telling what it is—but it's necessary when you have to dislodge connotations that you know your audience clings to. In addressing readers to whom *youth* equals *irresponsibility,* no one committed to the thesis that most young people are at least as responsible as their elders can afford to sidestep either the job of attacking the entrenched definition or the obligation to create a more accurate one.

In the following passage, negation is one of several means the writer chooses to define the concept of protest:

How does protest differ from revolution? The word "revolution" is often used for any radical change in an aspect of government or society, but in its strict and more correct historical usage revolution is the great exception, whereas protest is the norm. Protest is an attack on the prevailing system in an intellectual or organized way. Revolution is a sickness in society, a breakdown of the social order, the kind of general demoralization and civil war that the ancient Greek philosophers called *stasis*. Protest uses violence, but it is strictly controlled and specific in its purposes—the seizure of a building, a riot, a political assassination—designed to shock and bewilder the elite and to advertise a grievance. Revolution is unchecked violence in which social groups war against one another for dominance, although violence usually becomes an end in itself and the groups often lose sight of their original purposes.

Revolution occurs only when an old regime defends itself against protest by becoming more reactionary and oppressive but, once having radicalized the middle class and stirred the workers and the poor to involvement, is too inefficient or guilt-ridden to carry out the necessary slaughter and imprisonment of protesters. The political and legal system then splinters, and uncontrolled violence takes over. Finally, some army or police leader takes advantage of middle-class fear of extermination and working-class hunger and establishes a new tyranny. Protest in the twentieth century has led to social change and, more often than not, to social melioration; revolution has been the road to chaos, civil war, and new tyranny. – Norman F. Cantor, *The Age of Protest*

In reading the preceding paragraph you will have recognized not only some specific ways of defining – stipulative definition (the strict historical use of the term *revolution*) and formal definition (in the third and fourth sentences) – but several of the other techniques we've discussed in this chapter. The writer has used comparison and contrast, analysis of causes (government responses that lead to revolution), process (the stages in the fall of a regime), and attribution of effects (the contrasting results of protest and revolution). What this demonstrates is that there are many ways of building an extended definition.

The Center of the Definition

To define is to limit and to exclude – to narrow down to the characteristics or properties that set the class off from other classes. This is the process that brings you to the real center of your definition. One helpful means of finding that center has already been suggested and illustrated in the discussion of the formal genus-plus-differentiae definition. Weaknesses in definition papers often stem from the writer's failure to give serious thought to the class the thing belongs to and to the characteristics that make it different from other members of that class. "A scholar is a student who wears thick glasses, avoids fresh air, and never has a good time" is a trivial definition because it doesn't establish a significant class.

The elements that are central to any particular definition naturally depend on what's being defined. They may relate to the origin of the subject or its history or what it's made of or what it looks like or what it's used for or what effects it produces. A physical object like a lathe will be defined in different ways from a concept like responsibility, and a concept will be defined in different ways from a school of economic thought.

What the central elements in your definition are will also depend on where your interest in your subject lies. "Man is a talking animal" is a good definition for some purposes. "Man is a laughing animal" is a good one for others.

Once you've decided on the center of your definition, you'll find yourself drawing on other methods of development. These summaries of what some students have done in writing definition papers suggest a range of possibilities:

The center of a paper defining a stapler was a statement of its use. From there the student went on to tell what a stapler looks like, what its parts are, what materials it is made of, and how it operates. The paper was developed mainly by division and objective description.

A definition of Cubism first placed the movement in time, giving a narrative account of how and why it arose, explaining the theory on which it was based, and showing how it differed from other contemporary philosophies of art. By using examples of major Cubist artists and describing some of their chief works, the student arrived at the characteristics of form, color, and handling of subject that make a painting representative of Cubism.

A definition of brainwashing centered on the purpose, contrasted the methods and effects of brainwashing with those used in psychiatric treatment, and drew examples and details from a factual study of American captives in the Korean War and the novels *1984* and *The Manchurian Candidate.*

An essay on electronic music compared it with traditional music in terms of method of production, role of composer, range of sounds used, and kind of appeal. It reviewed various definitions of music in order to see whether they would admit electronically produced sounds as a legitimate class. Finally, it proposed a definition of music broad enough to include electronic music.

These summaries are not intended to represent the only ways of developing definitions or the best ways; in each case you should be able to think of other good approaches. They simply suggest the great variety of resources at hand when you set about the task of defining — not only etymologies, synonyms, examples, and connotative and denotative meanings but also description, narration, comparison and contrast, classification, division, analysis of causes and effects. Choosing wisely among these techniques of defining will help you make clear the properties or characteristics of your subject — those distinctive features that set it off from everything else. And this is why we use definition.

■ *For Analysis and Writing*

1. Choose a slang term that you enjoy using, explain its meaning, illustrate its use, and offer some reasons for its popularity. Your audience is your grandparents.

2. *Explain what you mean when you speak of sin (or pain or tolerance or courage or prejudice or any other concept that can mean different things to different people). Your audience is someone you want to help understand you better.*

3. *Define a political ism you favor (conservatism, liberalism, radicalism, or any other) for readers who are hostile toward it.*

4. *Through examples and personal anecdotes, show how love or fear or hate or happiness has come to have a new meaning for you.*

5. *Write a paper on some group you're familiar with, one that can be identified or defined by its habitual activities; its moral or social standards; its dress, language, or ceremonies. Make clear through concrete details the distinguishing characteristics of the group, its typical behavior, and the shared attitudes that give it unity and explain its actions. Your audience is a class in sociology.*

6. *Compare the meanings given* rhetoric *(and* rhetorical) *in the passages below. Which uses are favorable? Which neutral? Which unfavorable?*

a. There are extremes of exaggeration here that I must suppose to be rhetorical if I am to avoid attributing an implausible degree of ignorance to those of my interlocutors who indulge in them. — Louis J. Halle, *New Republic*

b. When the action is hot, keep the rhetoric cool. — President Richard M. Nixon in a television address, May 1970

c. But to those devoted to other concepts of science, Erikson often seems inexact, elusive, rhetorical, and even mystical. — Kenneth Keniston, *Science*

d. Rhetoric, therefore, is the method, the strategy, the organon of the principles for deciding best the undecidable questions, for arriving at solutions of the unsolvable problems, for instituting method in those vital phases of human activity where no method is inherent in the total subject-matter of decision. — Donald C. Bryant, *Quarterly Journal of Speech*

e. ". . . do you think back on the fight?"
"Not as much as I thought I would," Ali answered. "Fighting is more of a business now than the glory of who won. After all, when all the praise is over," and he shifted into the low singsong voice that he uses for rhetoric and poetry, "when all the fanfare is done, all that counts is what you have to show for. All the bleeding; the world still turns." — George Plimpton, *Sports Illustrated*

f. Rhetoric, we argued, is concerned primarily with a creative process that includes all the choices a writer makes from his earliest tentative explorations of a problem in what has been called the "prewriting" stage of the writing process, through choices in arrangement and strategy for a particular audience, to the final editing of the final draft. — Richard E. Young, Alton L. Becker, and Kenneth Pike, *Rhetoric: Discovery and Change*

Chapter Three
Organizing Papers

In discussing methods of developing content, we said some things about arranging it as well. In this chapter we'll focus directly on arranging material — on organizing complete papers.

Looked at from the outside, the structure of a successful piece of writing seems inevitable: This is the way it should be; this is the way it had to be. We speak of the organization of a good article or essay as if what appears on the page represents the only possible arrangement of the content. When you're writing, however, and particularly when you're prewriting, the process of organizing is scarcely more than an attempt to piece together a collection of facts and a jumble of ideas. Even in your early drafts you may still be searching for order, trying to make out patterns in your material and working to bring the particulars of your subject into line with what is still only a half-formed notion of purpose.

In your search for order you should be guided primarily by two considerations — what you've thought out, and found out, about your subject and what you want to say about your subject to the particular audience you're addressing. The structure you settle on is likely to be the result of reconciling the demands of your material, your purpose in writing about it, and the needs and interests of your readers. As you write and rewrite, you'll compress here and expand there, possibly changing the order of major blocks of material. Such shifts are a natural part of the writing process because for the writer, unlike the reader, no structure is inevitable. What the writer wants to do is settle on a structure that will strike the reader as the right one.

Types of Order

There are two basic types of order for material: *chronological* or *spatial* order, which to some degree reflects or adapts an order in time or space that the writer perceives in the material; and *logical* order, which represents a pattern that the writer invents and imposes on the material. Even chronological or spatial order is imposed, of course, in the sense that the writer must first recognize the existence of that order and then represent it. In the process of representing it, he almost always modifies it in some way.

A third type of order, *associational,* is highly personal. The subject, or some phase of it, reminds the writer of something, which he associates with something else, and so on.

Chronological or Spatial Order

Whenever you give a physical description of your subject or treat it in a chronological framework, the structure of your paper is rooted in the space order or time order of the material. For some purposes, you'll reproduce that arrangement as accurately as you can. For others, you'll alter it. Even when your prime obligation is to make an accurate report, you have some options. You can choose a space order and then proceed systematically from left to right, top to bottom, inside to outside, suburbs to city center, and so on. Or you may decide that you can give a clearer, more unified account by using a time order based on the sequence of your own observation—first, perhaps, the major features, visible from a distance, then successively smaller details as you (and your readers) come closer to the subject. In yet another adaptation of spatial order, you might first single out the most striking feature (not necessarily the largest) and from there move backward or forward, up or down, right or left.

Whenever you use description to support a thesis, the order you give your visual impressions will be strongly influenced by what that thesis is. Think of the different ways you might describe registration day, depending on whether the impression you want to get across is purposeful activity or aimless confusion. In either case, if your intention is to produce a factual account, the spatial arrangements you indicate in your paper should be recognizable to anyone who looks at the same scene. He should be able to see what you saw, even though he might interpret it in a different way. The college registrar may see the long lines on registration day as gratifying design. Your impression may be quite different.

For any material presented in a time sequence—an account of a process, a summary of a plot, a personal narrative—the typical movement is chronological (raw material to product, opening to closing, 1970 to 1977). But again you can modify the actual sequence in various ways. You can describe the finished product before giving the instructions for making it. You can begin with the climax of a plot and then work backward and forward from it. You can start with the concluding episode of a personal narrative and use flashbacks to fill in the action. Whatever the modifications, the order should make sense, and the reader should be able to reconstruct the actual order of events.

And whether or not you spell out your point of view, it should be consistent. Organizational weaknesses in descriptive and narrative papers can often be traced to a physical point of view that falters or shifts unaccountably or to a psychological point of view that's confused or unclear. If, in describing the scene on registration day, for example, you abruptly changed your physical point of view from that of an observer on the sidelines to that of a student enduring the long delays—or if you changed your psychological point of view from that of objective reporter to that of disgusted critic—the organization of your paper would be weakened. When such shifts occur, the reader simply can't tell where you stand, literally or figuratively, in respect to the subject.

Logical Order

Except when it clearly lends itself to space order (as in physical description) or to time order (as in narration), a subject seldom suggests and scarcely ever requires a definite order of discussion. There's no necessary order, for instance, in a criticism of a movie or an argument about sexist language or an analysis of the problem of adjusting to college life. The structure of any paper that explains an idea or presents an argument is an outgrowth of the writer's purpose and his estimate of the rhetorical situation—what aspects of the subject to discuss, in what order, and with what emphasis. The structure is good if it makes the writer's ideas and convictions about the subject clear and sensible to his audience.

Any order other than time order, space order, and associational order (p. 100) may be called *logical*. Logical order covers a great variety of organizational patterns. You may set your readers straight on some matter by showing how wrongheaded other ideas about the subject are.

You may examine the many particulars of a subject in order to arrive at a generalization about it. You may list and support six reasons for holding a conviction, ordering them from weak to strong or from strong to weak or from middling strong to strongest. You may explore three proposed courses of action, demonstrating that one isn't feasible, that another is feasible but not desirable, and that the third is both feasible and desirable. You may make a systematic investigation into what the subject is like and unlike, what caused it, what effects it has, and perhaps what good it is.

There are other possibilities, more than can be listed here. Whatever the structure, the good paper has direction and destination. The thought moves. It gets somewhere. Sound logical order reveals the relation among clusters of details or between ideas and carries a reader smoothly from one stage of the discussion to another. Faulty order makes a reader puzzle over the relation of, say, the sixth paragraph to the fifth and makes him wonder why a topic is treated *here,* not *there* – or why it's treated at all.

Though many variations occur, the skeleton organization of an expository paper is likely to follow one of three basic schemes. In the *support* structure the paper develops *from* the central idea – an assertion, a generalization, a thesis. In the *discovery* structure the paper develops *toward* a generalization, a thesis, a solution. In a *pro-and-con,* or *exploratory,* structure the writer investigates the subject by weighing its strengths and weaknesses or by looking at it from different points of view; the conclusion he arrives at often represents the correction, qualification, or refinement of the generalization or hypothesis with which he began.

Support Structure.   Early in a paper that follows the support plan, the writer advances the idea or cluster of ideas that he intends to analyze or defend or attack. This paragraph from a textbook forecasts the topics that will receive detailed discussion in the succeeding pages, discussion that will substantiate the generalizations that open and close the paragraph:

Americans in the years following the Civil War – a time which has become known as the Gilded Age – lived in a nation quite different from that of their fathers. It had become a nation where traditional ideas of democracy were modified by the values of a new industrial and urban society. The most important single change was the rise of industrial capitalism and the burgeoning of corporations that controlled nationwide industries. But American life was altered by other far-reaching developments: settlement of the last American West, construction of the transcontinental railroads, revolutionary change in agriculture, urban growth with all its attendant problems, the rise of the labor movement, a huge influx of immigrants, and the emergence of the United States as a world power. These developments gave the period its dramatic character and its importance in our history. They also established the foundations of modern America. – Vincent P. De Santis in Carl N. Degler et al., *The Democratic Experience*

The opening paragraph reprinted below is equally informative. A commonly accepted generalization has been tested, and the investigation has shown that the generalization is true for one group but not for another.

One would suppose, in view of all the household appliances that have been introduced over the past 50 years, that American women must spend considerably less time in housework now than their mothers and grandmothers did in the 1920's. I have investigated the matter and found that the generalization is not altogether true. Nonemployed women, meaning women who are not in the labor force, in fact devote as much time to housework as their forebears did. The expectation of spending less time in housework applies only to employed women. – Joann Vanek, *Scientific American*

In writing a paper on the support pattern, you can follow your initial statement with roughly equal blocks of material (single paragraphs or paragraph sequences), each developing an aspect of your lead-off idea. Or you can narrow your opening assertion to a particular application (a general opinion about school busing followed by an account of your own experiences when you were being bused to school) and then conclude with a recommendation for action in a current case. Or you may state your opinion, drop immediately to the most specific aspect of the subject, and then build back to your generalization, now giving it more decisive statement.

Discovery Structure. The typical procedure for a paper on the support pattern is *analytic:* the writer slices or divides his opening block of material. In the discovery pattern the procedure is *synthetic:* the writer pulls together, gathers up, as he builds toward his thesis. Again, there are many variations. You can begin with a particular aspect of the subject, move to a related aspect, then to another and yet another, unfolding your ideas step by step. You can start your paper small and end broad, in inverted pyramid fashion. (You might open a discussion of a campuswide or statewide or nationwide issue with an account of a single incident that you saw or took part in.) Or you can start small, move to a generalization, and go on to a new particular that can be inferred from it. (You might begin with one aspect of your elementary-school education, move to a generalization about elementary-school teaching, and then relate that generalization to some habits and attitudes of yours that persist now that you're in college.)

One common application of the discovery pattern is the *problem-solution* (or *question-answer*) structure. The occasion for the paper lies in a problem that needs solving, an issue that needs settling, a happening or situation that needs explaining. The paper comes to a close when the solution has been offered, the course of action shown to be wise or unwise, the happening or situation explained. In such a paper you may move directly from your analysis of the problem to your solution, or you may explore alternative proposals, showing them to be inadequate and all the while piling up evidence for the solution you're going to propose. Though the content of papers that follow this pattern may be complex, the bare structure can often be reduced to some such simple formula as

To solve *X*, we need to take steps *A*, *B*, and *C*.
or
What caused *X*? Not *A*. Not *B*. Not *C*. But *D*.
or
What is the right course of action? Not *A*. Not *B*. Not *C*. But *D*.

Because the sense of investigation is strong in the problem-solution structure, you'll find the approach particularly useful for persuasive papers. It's also suitable for expository papers in which you present various other explanations before offering your own.

Pro-and-Con, or Exploratory, Structure. You set out to write an evaluation—of a movie, a book; a musical group, a team; an actor, a singer, an athlete, a poet, a political candidate; a policy, a theory, a technique. You're familiar with your subject, but you quickly become aware that you've never reached any firm conclusion about it. Just how good or bad is the work, how competent or incompetent the performer, how wise or unwise the idea? In the prewriting stage you find your opinions zigzagging, with a "yes, but" or an "and yet" following immediately after each point for or against: "She did an excellent job in Movie *A* . . . but in *B* she overacted. Maybe comedy just isn't her thing . . . though two years ago she almost won an Oscar for her performance in that very funny picture called *C*." So it goes, as you explore the subject and finally reach a judgment, with strengths balanced against weaknesses and your own system of values determining the decision, or perhaps end up still undecided but with a much clearer understanding of the reasons for your indecision.

When you write a paper based on such internal conflict, or ambivalence, reproducing the zigzag movement of your thoughts may create a good pattern of organization. And you can use the same pattern when the conflict is external — when you begin with the opinions of two critics, one strongly pro and the other con, or the differing interpretations of two historians, or the projections of two economists, or the theories of football coaches or astronomers or psychologists. In all these cases you first undertake to present the opposing points of view and then give your support to one of the positions, explaining why you find it superior, or identify the common ground that makes it possible to reconcile them, or admit to an inability to choose between them.

Though the pro-and-con, or exploratory, structure resembles an organizational pattern used in comparisons, the purpose of these papers is not simply to compare but to arrive at a decision or a conclusion: Good or bad? Strong or weak? Right or wrong? The question can be phrased as a generalization to be examined and tested: Team *X* is the best in the league; Writer *Y* is a mediocre poet; Admissions policy *Z* is turning this college into a joke. But even when two opposing generalizations are involved, a question is still implicit: Sociologist *A* says that young people today are more religious than their parents; Sociologist *B* says that, for college students, religion is largely a fad; who's right? Whether it begins with a question, a generalization, or two generalizations, the exploration should lead to a judgment, an answer. Or the conclusion — the discovery — may be that the question can't be answered, that the problem can't be solved, or that the truth isn't found in either point of view.

The opening of a discussion of British colonialism in India shows the use of the pro-and-con pattern to probe competing generalizations. The first paragraph states the opposing points of view:

The British Raj: imperialist aggressors, exploiters of the Indian subcontinent, repressive tyrants betraying the principles of their own civilization. Or the British Raj: benevolent despots, peacemakers in India, enlightened rulers bringing order and efficiency where chaos had reigned and training in the most precious element of the Western tradition, democracy. Two views: one couched in the rhetoric of Indian nationalism, the other in that of the British administrators of India.

In the four paragraphs that follow, the author turns to the Indian charge of economic oppression and finds it essentially unproved. He does not, however, dismiss the charge out of hand; his method is to moderate and refine the initial generalization rather than to reject it. Notice the repeated use of *but* in the paragraphs analyzing the nationalists' claim. The pro-and-con movement is well suited to the practice of making distinctions that qualify an initial generalization.

The theme of economic distress and oppression was a fundamental part of the rhetoric of Indian nationalism. Nationalists pointed to India's poverty and charged – but did not prove – that this poverty was the fault of the British Empire. The authors of this charge were themselves generally middle-class Indians enjoying at least fair economic security. Their argument was simple: India was poor; it was ruled by Britain; British interests took goods and money out of India to Britain; therefore India's poverty was caused by British rule.

To describe the source of the charge is not to prove it false, but the failings of British economic policy in India show evidence of negative rather than of positive harm. Nineteenth-century Indians spoke often of the "drain" on India caused by the British by which they meant that there was a steady flow of gold and goods out of the country which was not balanced by an equal influx of goods of any kind. This drain, they claimed, impoverished India and caused the rural poverty and periodic famines that plagued the country.

There had been an actual drain of goods from India during the latter part of the eighteenth century and probably extending into the nineteenth, but it resulted less from British actions than from failures to act. Tariffs are a good example. British economic policy, the famous laissez-faire, prevented the creation of protective tariffs on goods coming into India; emergent Indian industries were thus left to the mercies of general competition. Only once did the British government take positive action directly against Indian interests – and that was to establish a tariff on Indian cotton in order to protect the Lancashire wool industry. But this move was the exception. British economic failure in India was generally the result of the absence of any action at all.

Not that the British Empire in India did not operate in the long run against the interests of Indians. The destruction of village industries through European competition and the failure to establish modern industries are probable evidence of the destructive effects of British rule. It has been argued that the passion of the British governors for caution and economy kept them from undertaking programs that would have been beneficial to the

country and policies that might have led to the eventual indus-
trialization of India. But if India failed to progress, it seems fair
to say that it was less because of the conscious policy of its rulers
than because of the combination of current economic fashion
and the unconscious, though consistent, British pursuit of imperial interests. British policy *may* have damaged the Indian
economy, and India's poverty *may* have been a function of
British rule. But twenty years after independence and partition,
it is more difficult and less convincing to charge British imperialism alone with the responsibility. — Norman F. Cantor, *The Age
of Protest*

In the remainder of the passage, the author examines
the British claim that imperialism brought enlightenment
to India and gave training in democracy. Again he makes
distinctions, demonstrating that while *political* oppression was sporadic, psychological oppression was chronic
and its effects widespread. Again the pro-and-con structure affords the means of testing and refining the initial
generalization. The upshot of the discussion is a new view
of "the British Raj" — one different from either of those
presented at the start.

Choosing a Structure. The actual organization of most
long papers is more complex than the patterns we've outlined so far. Often a paper includes several generalizations
of roughly equal importance, and instead of being lumped
at either beginning or end, they're distributed so that each
is the core of one section of the paper. Even so, the progression within each section is likely to approximate one of the
patterns:

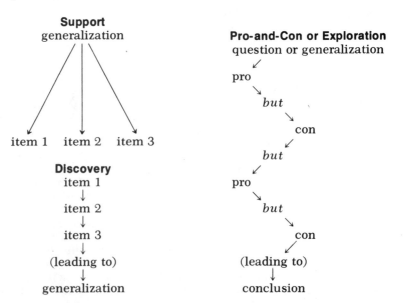

Support
generalization

item 1   item 2   item 3

Discovery
item 1
↓
item 2
↓
item 3
↓
(leading to)
↓
generalization

Pro-and-Con or Exploration
question or generalization

pro

but

con

but

pro

but

con

(leading to)
↓
conclusion

These are the basic movements. Of course, you'll need to arrange your examples (or details or pieces of evidence) in a sequence that makes sense — chronological, simple-to-complex, increasing importance, or whatever suits your purpose.

As we saw in Chapter Two, division is treated in a support structure, with the various parts or stages set forth at the outset and then taken up in turn. In a classification, use either support or discovery. If you're classifying television commercials, you might say at the start that you've turned up four main kinds of appeal, identify each in a sentence or two, and then discuss them in turn, moving from the least common to the most common or according to some other principle. Or you might begin with a description of one commercial as representative of its class, move to a striking example of a second class, and so on. The first option emphasizes the class; the second highlights individual examples.

When you organize a passage of causal analysis, you can first list the causes (or effects) and then take them up one by one, or you can introduce them one after the other until your analysis is complete. If your aim is to weigh and judge several possible causes, you may use the pro-and-con movement ("Some evidence points to this cause, but . . ."; "However, this doesn't seem likely because . . ."; and so on). You have comparable options when you define.

We've already examined three common organizational patterns for comparisons (pp. 64–70). Which you choose will depend on how complex your material is and what your purpose is. If you decide to summarize the upshot of the comparison before going into it in detail ("The United States as we know it represents the philosophy of Alexander Hamilton far more than it does the philosophy of Thomas Jefferson"), you'll be using the support structure. For some papers you may find that shaping your comparison into either the discovery or the pro-and-con pattern will suit your purpose better.

A paper needn't follow only one pattern from start to finish. Indeed, a long paper is unlikely to. It may be made up of a half-dozen sections or paragraph sequences, each with a recognizable movement of its own — particular-to-general, general-to-particular, pro-and-con. The key to firm structure is being sure that though each section has its own identity and makes its own contribution to the writer's purpose, it's also a functioning part of the design of the whole.

■ *For Analysis and Writing*

From a book of readings or a current magazine, choose an explanatory or a persuasive essay or article. Describe its large-scale organization, and consider alternative ways the material might have been presented. Taking into account the author's purpose and the probable audience, explain why you think he did or didn't find a good way of structuring his discussion. (Turn in the book, the magazine, or a photocopy of the selection with your analysis.)

For this exercise, read the selection several times to get firm control of the content, and then prepare any kind of summary that will help you indicate the large-scale features of the organization.

Associational Order

Instead of basing your paper on a perceived order in time or space or on an order that another writer could invent and impose on the same material, you may follow a pattern suggested by the associations the subject sets off in your mind. Though not often suitable for college papers, associational order can work well when a distinctly personal flavor is appropriate. Instead of giving a chronological account of the building of a house or using a space order in describing its interior, you might open your paper with a description of the house as it appeared to you when your family first moved into it, perhaps, and then drift from one memory to another as you recall the years you lived there. Such a paper would probably end up telling more about you and what your memory clings to than about the house and what it looked like, but if done well it could have charm, drama, humor, tragedy. Unless it's handled skillfully, however, associational order may be confusing, and the paper as a whole may seem rambling and pointless.

■ *For Analysis and Writing*

1. Examine this complete paper, paying special attention to its organization.

So Much Going On

¶1 Because his air bubble nest wasn't ready, he attacked her savagely, his jaws clamping down on her tail fin. She wriggled free and like a gray bullet streaked to the other side of the aquarium, where she took refuge in a web of twisted underwater plants. Having defended his home, the male Siamese Fighting Fish returned to his secluded corner and continued to blow bubbles of air coated with saliva. Each pearl of air rose dizzily to the surface of the water, bobbed momentarily, and then adhered to the other bubbles. Within a week there were hundreds of these jewels of air floating in a mass. The nest was near completion. As each new bubble rose, the female, swollen with eggs, became more desperate. Finally she left her grove of protective vines and once again approached her future mate. This time his nest was ready and he could devote himself to the beautiful creature before him. In anticipation of a mating, her sides were no longer a dusty gray but boldly streaked with glistening blue.

¶2 The male put on his show. He fanned out his plumes of dark violet streaked with a lighter shade. He shook his body, and the sailing fins waved furiously. Gracefully he dropped to the rocks below, the female following his every move. Suddenly from below her abdomen, the eggs spewed. The male quickly passed over them several times, depositing a cloud of sperm. Now the female was hungrily eyeing her fertilized eggs. Her mate opened his mouth in a wide "O" and darted toward her. She had felt his wrath before, however, and was gone before he reached her wake. Because of her voracious appetite for her own young, the male would never again let her come near them. Scooping a cluster of fertilized eggs into his mouth, the male Fighting Fish transported them up to the floating air bubbles. Due to the care of their father, the new-born young would be assured of plenty of oxygen when they hatched.

¶3 Peering into the microscope, looking at the drop of pond water sandwiched between the slide and the lens, one feels that he's stealing his way into a fantastic subworld of nimble beasts a hundred times smaller than a speck of sand. They dart three-quarters across the field of vision, stop, then whirl about and cavort away. Here comes another tumbling about. One can only stare in awe at his enormous littleness. The seemingly playful antics often disguise their true nature. Give them half a chance and they will attack tissue and tear it to pieces like crazed, silent assassins.

¶4 But this new, mysterious world under the microscope can be inhabited by other things besides strange animals and plants. Under the glass a few slivers of hair are transformed into great rough logs. One steps back, awed at the outlandish perfection of the sting of a worker bee or the barbed leg of a mosquito or the thousand light receptors on the "eye" of a fly. What a thrill to see the orange, sun-shaped egg of a sea urchin bombarded by thousands of tiny, comet-like sperm. When one finally crashes through the membrane, a new organism is born under your eyes. With the right simple mixture under the lens, one can see a co-acervate, the pre-cellular form that gave rise to life—and you don't have to go back millions of years to see it.

¶5 The other chicks have pecked their way out of their wonder-fully protected shells. But one little fellow hasn't the strength to peck out more than a small window. The air circulates in, hardening the blood and membranes. The protective shell has been transformed into a suffocating, binding prison. Soon he will die unless you free him. Bit by bit you peel off the shell flakes. He peeps in pain when the dried membrane is stripped from his delicate feathers. Soon the exhausted chick lies prostrate on the paper. Propped up by your hand, he toddles on wobbly legs that quickly collapse. He lies flat, his legs bent crazily sideways. They punch outwards with astonishing vigor, but they never get under him. He gropes and fumbles, raising false hopes. But it is to no avail. He is a splay chicken. The tendons in his legs never took hold, and he will never walk. Humans like this are put in wheelchairs and fed. Not chickens. It's a sad paradox that you have to take this chick whose life you've saved and plunge him head first into a beaker of water. His mouth closes and opens frantically, gasping for air. But all that enters is heavy, suffocating water. Soon his lungs are filled, and he stops struggling. Your own face feels uncomfortably hot and your shirt is all sweaty.

¶6 Dissecting a shark's head, one is appalled by the vast subway system of olfactory organs that lies beneath the tough leather hide. The horseshoe-shaped canal, with turnstile plates that first sense the moving chemicals in the water, is fascinatingly intricate. As commuters on subway trains are moved from place to place, so the chemical sensations are transmitted from organ to organ until they reach the brain. A big-thumbed male frog jumps on a female frog ripe with eggs. He holds her in his powerful grip and punches her sides until the eggs come flowing out. At the same time his sperm mixes with the eggs. Why do the frogs fertilize externally rather than internally? In an hour the fertilized eggs divide once, then twice. Soon a cluster forms, then a hollow ball. Then a turning-in occurs, a neural plate arises from the buckling outer layer, an elongation slowly takes place, and soon a tadpole is swimming about. The pleasant, powerful aroma of the sea that still clings to seaweed is overwhelming. A paramecium bumbles upon a salty concentration of water and begins to shrink. Why? And to take it a step further, what can it tell a nurse who must prepare an intravenous feeding mixture? A decapitated frog still shows a scratch reflex—how come? A pregnant mouse toddles with the weight of twelve youngsters in her. Placing her little paws around her head, she bears the pain of dropping them out one by one. One tiny pink tyke strays away from the nest. It's easy to pick him up by the tail and return him to his mother. And all the friendly, sour, grateful, crabby, shy, carefree, happy, apprehensive, funny, and serious classmates that come are just as fascinating as the marvellous things already there.

¶7 To think that some students say it's all in the book so there's no sense wasting one's time in the Biology lab!

a. *Describe the organization of "So Much Going On." To begin with, what are its main parts or divisions? What's the writer's purpose? Is that purpose stated explicitly? If so, where? Do all the parts of the paper contribute to the chief point the writer is trying to make?*

b. *Has the writer made clear his psychological point of view, his attitude toward his material? Has he established a physical point of view (a viewing point) and maintained it consistently? Study his use of personal pronouns to see how he locates himself in relation to his material.*

c. *Now that you've described the organization, evaluate it. Is the material developed according to any plan you can recognize? Is there a spatial movement that permits you to visual-*

*ize the laboratory? Is there a chronological movement — events
arranged in a time sequence or according to the order in which
objects or activities are observed? Is there a progression that
makes sense in terms of bringing out the significance of
what's being observed? If not, should there be? Or is this kind
of material suitable for an essay that is ordered largely on the
basis of the writer's associations? If so, what are the associations that apparently govern the order of details?*

*d. If you think the organization is weak, try to identify the
main source of the weakness. Is it the writer's uncertainty in
handling point of view? Is it his uncertainty about what impression he wants to leave with the reader? Or what?*

*e. Sketch three plans for organizing the material in this
paper, one relying mainly on spatial relations, one on temporal relations, and one on association. Specify an audience
and a purpose for each. Which of these plans do you think
would make the best paper in the rhetorical situation? Are any
or all of your plans better than the one you assume the writer
followed? If so, in what respects?*

*f. Try rewriting the paper, using the bulk of the material
but rearranging it as you think best. Pay special attention to
the beginnings and endings of your paragraphs.*

*g. Reread the paper, taking into account the content and
style as well as the organization. What are the strengths?
What are the weaknesses?*

*2. Describe the organization of the article reprinted below.
State the writer's purpose, and show how the organization of
the material helps him accomplish it.*

Apple & Beech, Birch & Oak

¶1 Woodcutting is full of sensuous and kinesthetic rewards.
There is the rhythmic *thock* of the ax, with every second stroke
freeing flat-spinning chips of yellowish wood. The special alertness of felling builds up during preliminary notching cuts and
rises to a breathless moment when the treetop loses the symmetry of its sway, hovers against the sky for a moment, and then
sweeps over with fierce cracking as the trunk thunders to the
ground with branches thrashing. When limbs are cut free with
diagonal-slicing ax strokes, the ellipses of fresh-cut wood gleam
against the bark in the soft forest light. As wood is bucked into
portable lengths, measured multiples of what your fireplace
accepts, the saw generates little conical hills of cuttings; coarser
than carpentry sawdust, these tiny cubes of pale damp wood
creep into boot tops and pockets. When wood is split in the yard
by the woodshed there comes a time when a husky billet of hardwood, almost too big and cross-grained to be ax-splittable, nevertheless responds to a precise blow by dropping apart in two even
pieces, their inner faces moist and fragrant at this first exposure
to light and air. Toward dusk there is an enjoyably tired feeling
as the day's yield is stacked for seasoning, the wedge-sectioned

pieces fitted evenly, like a carefully built stone wall. Only stove-wood is allowed to remain in a tumbled heap.

¶2 Getting in your own firewood has much to recommend it, if not done of necessity. Felling, limbing, bucking, and splitting are the four basic steps in the process, none difficult to bring off passably, and yet none so simple that your technique cannot be bettered. Prodigious exertions are not called for, although it is somewhat more strenuous than golf or other conventional absorbents of leisure. It is work that is likely to blister the hands or crick the back unless undertaken along a gentle slope of habituation.

¶3 You can do a considerable amount of creative resting in the woods, seated on a log, absently rubbing tired muscles, studying the intricate topography of bark, reading the now-ended calendar of tree rings, smelling the fresh woody fragrances, watching the chipmunk or bluejay come closer to scout the meaning of your silence. Almost alone among outdoor pursuits, woodcutting is unaffected by weather, and can be engaged in at all times except drenching cold rain or driving sleet (it is quite magical during a snowstorm). You automatically work at a tempo attuned to the temperature, easily enough to keep from steaming on a golden day in Indian summer, briskly enough to keep comfortable when north winds icily rake the woods.

¶4 Unlike many leisure activities, woodcutting delivers a product in return for time and effort, a pile of beautiful, well-split hardwood, abounding in promise of bright fires radiating their magic on winter nights. The degree of satisfaction is curiously high. It is not altogether clear why a filled woodshed should be so reassuring, more so than shelves of cans and jars in the cupboard, or a freezer chest chock full of frosted parcels. Some shadowy motivation is buried here, something to do with the peripheral rewards of possessions, and with a need for making experience tangible and visible to others.

¶5 Perhaps a clue can be sensed by considering people whose leisure activities do *not* afford a product. If you observe the cameras carried in such profusion by returning travelers as they flow through customs weirs, it is possible to conclude that the profoundest need filled by vacation photography is documentation. Pictures, studied and shown about, function as a kind of certification of experience, and generally they don't bleach as fast as memory. Returning travelers carry, in addition to luggage and cameras, an extraordinary volume of gifts and bric-a-brac. From the balcony above the arrival pens at an international airport, a jetload of tourists tends to look as if most of them were victims of besetting generosity or compulsive connoisseurship. The scene suggests that possessions bought abroad and carried home have high value as confirmation of time well spent, proof less evanescent than airline tags left dangling and customs symbols chalked on luggage.

¶6 People appear to buy knickknacks for the oddest of motives, not the least of which is the conversation that can be casually constructed about them later. Evidently recollection is for many persons simply not sufficient, and a physical thing or image supplies welcome additional testimony.

¶7 As for the filled woodshed, it is true that few countrymen whip out a camera to document the achievement of several cords

of beech, but it *is* noticeable that conspicuous supplies of firewood are frequently stacked in an open shed in no way concealed
from those driving past. Firewood is after all not as inherently
invisible as those parcels in the freezer, and a possession that is
invisible is somehow slightly diminished.

¶8 Getting in firewood is a many-faceted activity, and not the
least of its benefits is a sense of calm. You may stride off to the
woods bearing, along with ax and saw, a well-nourished grievance; you are almost certain to return with, if you think of it at
all, detached surprise that the matter could have been so troublesome. Woodcutting is a sovereign remedy for a churny mind, a
specific for festering concern. It works its spell not so much by
substitution (which is what skiing does, it being difficult to
cherish a grievance while hurtling downhill in continuous alarm
over narrowly averted catastrophe) as by the more subtle method
of transference. Using an ax or splitting sledge is of course a
form of sanctioned violence, and it takes only a half-hour's tussle
with some mulish hickory to mop up any likely supply of hostility. This is nothing so simple as venting one's spleen on poor,
harmless trees: it is instead a kind of cancellation, perhaps a
physiologic process related to the sensations of using the large
muscles.

¶9 Woodcutting also provides a second form of psychotherapy
by presenting a series of small, engrossing, and delightfully
soluble problems. A tree is felled exactly where it is supposed to
fall, despite a slight lean in another direction; threatened pinching of the saw kerf is avoided by reordering the natural sequence
of bucking cuts; an unsplittably gnarled crotch is finessed by
relocation of fireplace lengths. It is not necessary to pretend that
these are substantial achievements, nor anything more than
routine to a woodsman; it is just that the successful solution of
random problems, however small, is tonic to the spirits. Certainly
it could not have been by chance that Wilhelm II, the last of the
German emperors, his restlessly proud and never very stable
mind corroded by an awareness of a world war disastrously lost,
spent time each exiled day in woodcutting. But it is not necessary
to have the Marne, and Verdun, and the utter ruin of an empire
on your mind to find reliable serenity in the woodlot.

¶10 Of course it doesn't always go well. Sometimes a tree
chosen for cutting because it looks peckish, no longer a sturdy
member of its company, falls with a distinctively hollow thump
and shatters, revealing a punky interior so far gone in corruption
as to be worth no more work. (A fireplace fire is contemptuous
of punky wood, burning it sullenly, as a reluctant duty.) Occasionally the felling goes awry, from miscalculation of lean or
veering of the wind during the wavery moment when a tree has
concluded to fall but has not yet fixed on direction. It may ma-
liciously slant off course and lodge, half fallen, propped by the
upper branches of a neighboring tree. This is a woodcutter's
embarrassment, impossible to explain to anyone who happens
by as something intended, and impossible to abandon, being a
deadfall peril. If it cannot be jounced free, the choice is either to
fell the second tree too, or to dislodge the hang-up by rolling it or
by using a log chain to drag the butt out until the top breaks free.
The work is arduous, a little dangerous, and thoroughly frus-
trating.

¶11 On those infrequent days when malign spirits flit through the woods to perch on branches nearby, all woodcutting can grow cranky. With each bucking cut the trunk rolls to new positions of inconvenience, and the saw binds inexplicably, and the ax glances wickedly, and the footing is precarious while you are trudging with a heavy four-length log on your shoulder. It is prudent to gather up your tools and depart on such a day. Don't even stop to split what's been cut: the first piece will simply swallow three wedges, and smile. — Frank Rowsome, Jr., *Atlantic*

3. *Paying special attention to selecting and maintaining your point of view, write an account of a high-school graduation, a memorial service, or some other ceremonial occasion. Your reader is a member of your family who was not present. Your purpose is to make this reader see the occasion as you saw it and react to it as you did.*

Strategies of Ordering

The structure of a paper is always strongly influenced by the nature of the material and the writer's purpose. In most writing the third major influence should be the audience. With the audience in mind you decide whether to organize your material according to the rhetorical strategy of *announcing* or the rhetorical strategy of *disclosing*.

Announcing and Disclosing

In announcing, you make the structure of your paper explicit, either in a fairly elaborate program paragraph early in the paper or in guidepost statements at key points throughout (or, sometimes, in both). A *program paragraph* previews the organization by indicating the divisions of the subject or by listing the topics to be treated; it may or may not include a thesis statement or a direct statement of purpose of the "This-essay-will-attempt-to-show" type. In any case, one way or another you tell the reader what you're going to do before you do it. When the announcing is done by sentences interspersed through the paper, they often summarize as well as forecast, reminding the reader of what ground has already been covered besides giving clues to what lies ahead.

You use the strategy of announcing when you begin a paper by saying that the decline in the President's popularity has been caused by a series of administrative decisions or that you propose to record the sequence of events that has led to the decline in the President's popularity or that news analysts are offering five reasons for the decline in the President's popularity. When you announce, you keep few organizational secrets from the reader. The structure of your paper is exposed or at least lies close to the surface.

In the strategy of disclosing, your structure lies deeper. Your beginning doesn't forecast your ending, and you proceed from stage to stage without revealing to the reader just how each is related to the point you'll eventually make. When you use the strategy successfully, the subject seems to unfold according to its own inner pressure, and the climax sometimes brings an element of surprise. (In the good paper the surprise is immediately followed by a "Why, of course!")

Although announcing may seem to be the likelier strategy for a paper that moves *from* a generalization and disclosing for a paper that moves *toward* a generalization, this isn't always the case. A problem-solution paper may begin with an announcement of what procedures are being followed, what alternatives excluded, and so on. Or it may be handled in such a way that the reader is gradually brought to realize that a problem exists and then given a sense of sharing in a joint inquiry that leads to a solution.

Choosing a Strategy

For some of your papers it will seem natural to adopt one strategy rather than the other. But often you can use either. In making your choice you should be guided by your estimate of the needs, interests, and predispositions of your audience. If the material is difficult or the organization necessarily complicated, you may decide that readers will find the paper hard going unless you announce at some length, offering a blueprint to show how each topic or section fits into your whole scheme. Or you may decide that instead you should begin with material your readers are familiar with and gradually work up to the more complex aspects of the subject, disclosing your full scheme only toward the end of the paper. (You can find both approaches in the textbooks on your desk.)

If you can count on your readers having a strong interest in the subject, you may decide to plunge in without offering any guidance to the structure. Or you may conclude that sketching the course of your discussion in a program paragraph will make it easier for readers to concentrate on the content as they move confidently through the paper. If you suspect that their interest is so slight that they'll go woolgathering while you're expounding, you have a harder decision to make. Can you announce in such a way that your promise of interesting things to come will counteract their indifference? Or does the strategy of disclosing seem more likely to capture their attention? If you're writing an argument, size up the probable attitude of your audience. Is it largely hostile to your position, or sympathetic to it, or indifferent? Will announcing increase the hostility or diminish it?

Answers to questions like these depend on the individual writing situation. Few rhetorical problems are solved by formulas. Handled well, either strategy can result in strong, satisfying organization. But each has its drawbacks. Though announcing ensures that readers know where they're going, it may make the structure seem too mechanical. The strategy of disclosing escapes this danger; but unless the parts of the paper have a tight, organic connection, making the logic of a shift from one part to another immediately clear, readers may not see what direction the paper is taking. And if they have difficulty detecting the general drift, they'll probably miss the significance of many of the details. A good writer always provides clues to structure, even if he plants them deep.

One strategy doesn't necessarily rule out the other. In long papers you often have occasion to use both. In the first half you lay out your subject, perhaps by giving a chronological sketch of the origins of a problem, analyzing its current dimensions, and offering a method for solving it — all this in a structure strong in announcing. In the second half you shift the technique, now organizing the discussion as an exploration in which you and the reader are carried forward by the logic of the inquiry.

Whether you choose to announce or to disclose (or to announce and disclose by turn), your motive should be to involve your readers in your discussion as deeply as you're involved in it. You want them to understand what you have to say, to take an intelligent interest in it, and finally to accept it.

Parts and Paragraph Sequences

As we've already suggested, in all but the shortest and simplest papers the discussion moves through stages. In most writing you can better control the organization if you think of the paper as consisting of a few parts, each performing one significant role in relation to your purpose, rather than as consisting of three or four times that many separate paragraphs. The beginning is a part, whether it's a single sentence, several sentences, a paragraph, or three or four paragraphs in sequence. The ending of a paper is a part, no matter how long or short it is. Each bridge between one stage of the discussion and the next is a part. And each paragraph or sequence of paragraphs that forms one of those stages is a part.

In revising a paper, you can work more efficiently once you've identified the paragraphs that belong together, those so related that an attentive reader will recognize that they perform one main function in the total scheme. You can make sure that such paragraphs are grouped in a sensible order, and you can shift or drop any paragraph that appears in a sequence where it doesn't belong. Revising one sequence, or block, of paragraphs before turning to the next is more likely to produce a paper that has direction and point than simply revising paragraph by paragraph without paying attention to these groupings.

Once you have the parts of your paper mapped out, you should be able to answer such basic questions about its structure as these:

Are the parts in an order that makes the best sense in terms of my purpose?

Will the connections between the parts be clear to my readers?

Are the beginning and ending suitable in this rhetorical situation?

Are the proportions satisfactory? Have I given most space and emphasis to what's most important?

These matters we'll consider in the remainder of this chapter.

■ *For Analysis*

Turn back to the article on woodcutting by Rowsome, pp. 103–06. Mark off the main parts, and explain how each part is related to the writer's purpose.

Signals of Transition

Strong organization demands that the parts of a paper be in the right order, an order that permits you to say what you want to say to your particular audience. It also requires that the order be apparent to the audience and that it seem at least reasonable, at best inevitable. Though what you write may meet the first requirement, it will fall short of the second if you don't provide connecting links. Remind yourself regularly that while you know how the parts fit together, your readers don't have your inside information.

Sometimes the connections are in the material, and the movement from one part to another seems entirely natural and necessary. More often they're in your insight into the subject, your approach to it, your analysis of it. You *make* the connections, and in composing your paper you must be sure they come clear to your readers. At the structural breaks where one stage of a discussion ends and another begins, you should consider using explicit transitions, bridges that will carry your reader from one topic to the next.

Explicit Signals

In themselves, explicit transitions seldom advance a discussion. They signal relationships, establish connections. Often they comment directly on the structure of the essay, as in this passage, where the first paragraph looks back and the second ahead:

> Such are the four basic processes by which air carries its moisture aloft. They can work alone or together to produce an infinite variety of cloud forms and combinations.
>
> Now suppose we spend two or three days observing the sky during the approach and passage of a typical warm front. This means we start with a cold air mass around us. The air behind the front is comparatively warm. What kinds of clouds do we see as the boundary between cold and warm air approaches? – Richard M. Romin, *Natural History*

The machinery of transition is also visible in the following key paragraph, which comes exactly in the middle of the article. The first sentence summarizes the discussion to this point; the last forecasts what's to come:

> These, then, are the negative effects of the scientific literature I have observed in the course of teaching scientific writing. I am glad to say that there are also definite positive findings. The most striking observation is that by teaching writing you can actually strengthen students' ability not only to write but also to read more attentively and to think more logically and rigorously. – F. Peter Woodford, *Science*

Paragraphs like these announce their function directly. Other transitional paragraphs are less obvious; only in context can they be seen to be gathering up and pushing on.

Because transitional paragraphs have some of the imperative force of a police officer directing traffic, they should be used only to mark major turns in a discussion. In short papers their function can be performed by single sentences, which gather up less material and usually provide gentler guidance. The transitional sentence normally comes either at the beginning or at the end of a paragraph. It signals a shift from one idea to another, indicates that the discussion is to take a new turn, or marks a digression from the main thread:

A word, finally, about the isolation of our colleges, particularly those not attached to great universities. – Henry Steele Commager, *Saturday Review*

But this is only part of the truth. – Charles A. Siepman, *New York Times Magazine*

Before I try to look into the future, I would like to present a debit and credit sheet on mankind. – C. L. Stebbins, *Saturday Review*

While in no way central to his development as an artist, Tennessee Williams' career as a shoe salesman is worth recalling at this point.

Transition can be provided by a question:

In contrast, what are our hopes for the United States? – Alvin C. Eurich, *Reforming American Education*

A question like this one structures the discussion very clearly. Although it doesn't disclose precisely what the writer's position on the new topic is, it does promise an answer. Used sparingly, the question is a good transitional device. Overused, it quickly becomes tiresome (as does any other transitional device). Misused – as when the question doesn't rise naturally out of the discussion – it's clumsy and distracting.

Most transitional paragraphs and some transitional sentences are like road signs: they tell readers where they're going and perhaps where they've been. Other transitions indicate connections readers must make and relationships they must perceive if they're to follow the discussion. A good many words and phrases perform this function, among them *however, moreover, therefore, on the contrary, on the other hand, likewise, consequently, incidentally, as a result, nevertheless, in the first place, in short*. The function of such transitional words and phrases in achieving coherence will be discussed in some detail in the next chapter.

Explicit transitions serve you well when they point out connections that your readers wouldn't otherwise per-

ceive. If you use too few, your writing will seem disconnected, and readers may fail to see relationships you count
on their recognizing. But if you use too many, you'll weigh
your writing down, slow its movement, and make the
machinery of expression seem to take precedence over
what's being expressed. When the direction of your paper
is clear and the order of its parts readily apparent, announcing in the form of the authoritarian "First it is
important to consider . . ." or the chatty "Now let's examine . . ." is wasteful and sometimes annoying; and too
many *howevers* and *therefores* create a lumbering effect.

Implicit Signals

A skillful writer uses explicit transitions where he needs
them – especially to mark a sharp turn in the discussion
and to relate paragraphs in which the ideas aren't obviously consecutive. The skillful writer also knows the value
of less obvious means of establishing continuity. Instead
of standing outside his material and pointing readers in
the right direction, he makes the language of the discussion do the work. These lexical means include repeating
or echoing key words and phrases. A phrase at the beginning of a paragraph ("The notion that busing could be a
'remedy' for official school segregation was encouraged
by . . .") may allude to a use of *remedy* three paragraphs
earlier. Or, in moving from one paragraph to another, the
writer may carry over a key word or synonym that echoes
the idea. Here a slight variation ("undignified" – "lack of
dignity") accomplishes the transition:

> . . . And the statement becomes undignified – if not, indeed,
> slanderous.
>   The lack of dignity in such statements is not in the words, nor
> in the dictionaries that list them, but in the hostility that de-
> liberately seeks this tone of expression. – Bergen Evans, *Atlantic*

Organic transitions – those that depend on meaning –
bind a discussion together without stopping its flow. These
lexical means of establishing continuity, as well as such
grammatical means as the use of pronouns and parallel
constructions, will be discussed in the next chapter.

■ *For Analysis and Writing*

*1. Identify the major transitional devices (phrases, sentences,
paragraphs) in the article by Rowsome on pp. 103–06.*

2. *Identify the transitional paragraphs and sentences in three articles of 2000 words or more in current magazines. (Turn in either the magazines or photocopies of the articles.) If one article has a much higher proportion of these overt signals than the other two, what accounts for the difference — the subject matter? the writer's purpose? the audience? Do you find any relation between the use of transitional devices and the general strategy (announcing or disclosing)?*

In one of the articles identify the words and phrases that serve as explicit transitions from paragraph to paragraph. What devices other than explicit transitions are used at the beginnings and ends of paragraphs to establish continuity?

3. *Review "So Much Going On" (pp. 100–02). Identify the transitional sentences and paragraphs. Suggest sentences and paragraphs that would provide more explicit transitions.*

Beginnings and Endings

The beginning of a paper may be a paragraph, less than a paragraph, or — if the paper is a long one — several paragraphs. The same is true of endings. Although some good papers don't have identifiable sections that can be labeled "beginning" or "ending," how your paper opens and how it closes have a decided bearing on the reader's interest in and acceptance of what you have to say.

Beginnings

For most readers, interest and understanding are closely related. If they don't understand what a writer is up to, they won't be much interested in what he has to say. If an opening captures their interest, they'll work harder to understand what follows. If it doesn't interest them, all the clarity in the world won't help much. Your beginnings should be clear, then, for understanding, and they should catch the attention of your readers, for interest.

You might think that the sure way of achieving clarity would be to use the strategy of announcing. But a labored statement of purpose can kill off a reader's interest: "This paper is going to discuss. . . . The four chief topics to be treated are. . . . First in importance is. . . ." This sort of blueprinting works in some stereotyped situations, as in technical reports, where the only considerations are accuracy and system; and in special circumstances it can be dramatic, as when a trial lawyer begins, "I am going to prove to you that. . . . First, I will describe. . . . Second, I will trace.... Third, I will expose.... And finally I will demonstrate...." But for most purposes the announcing should be done more subtly.

And it need not be done in the first sentences of a paper. The program paragraph—the announcing paragraph—is not necessarily the leadoff one. In a long paper it's often the last in the sequence of paragraphs that makes up the opening section, sometimes the first paragraph of the second section. In such cases it's preceded by a stretch of material that contrives to bring the reader into the paper less formally and less abruptly—a short anecdote, a passage of descriptive details (giving, say, the look of clouds in a summer sky as a way in to a precise account of what causes cloud formations and how clouds are classified), the larger context that points up the significance of the issue being debated, and so on.

Worse than a dull opening is an opening that tries to manipulate readers or that misleads them. When attempts to whip up interest can be recognized as no more than that, they do more harm than good. Sensational details, forced enthusiasm, and chitchat actually draw attention away from the subject, not toward it. One trouble with a wildly provocative opening is that it robs you of the opportunity to build to a climax; the paper can only run downhill. And concentrating on grabbing the reader's attention often produces an opening that has little connection with the real subject of the paper and therefore misleads the reader. The short, dramatized narrative used as a standard opening in popular magazines is sometimes relevant to what follows, often no more than a gimmick. Remember: A good beginning arouses expectations that the body of the paper satisfies.

In general, a beginning should point not only to the real subject of the paper but to the way the discussion will be handled; the opening sentences should set the tone. Compare these two beginnings, each of which is entirely in keeping with what follows:

I have at least one qualification for writing about the generation gap. I have lived with two, if not three, of them during my lifetime. To be sure, practice does not make perfect. But it does teach one to realize an important human truth. The movement of events is almost always a great deal faster than the movement of our own minds.

In my youth, for example.... —Walter Lippmann, *Harper's*

I've grown damned sick and tired of having the youth culture, whatever that is, rammed down my throat by members of my own generation. I am all, as I said here last month, for the self-determination of the old, or getting on for old, and I do not think that a mindless and guilt-ridden capitulation to the questionable values of the young will set my people free. Those of us who were born before, say, 1935, have some values and some virtues of our own, and I think it's high time one of us spoke up for them.

In the teeth of a perfect gale of mass-media propaganda to the contrary, I'd like to suggest that the middle generation possesses a greater share of skill, subtlety, discipline, and judgment than its juniors. . . . – L. E. Sissman, *Atlantic*

Common types of openings include the anecdote, often in the dramatized form already mentioned; the generalization followed by a quick narrowing down to the specific subject; the quotation; the citation of statistics; and the rhetorical question. Here are some examples:

Anecdote
The strapping rodeo bull rider grabbed Jerry Jeff Walker's arm in a vicelike grip and stared angrily at the singer, who bore a beatific, faraway expression on his face. "Didn't you hear me, boy?" he growled. "I told you to play that song about red-necks. Now play it. Fast."

Stoned and drunk and uncertain if he was in a honky-tonk in Austin or in Oklahoma City, Walker struggled to concentrate on his dilemma. If he played the song, which he knew the cowboy hated, he would probably be beaten up. If he refused the request, he would also be beaten up. Finally, he began to play. The cowboy hit him three times, smashed his guitar and left him bloody. "Situations like that," Jerry Jeff explains cheerfully, "are what being an outlaw is all about."

The outlaws of country music need all their dark memories these days; tales of brawls, drug busts and rejection slips seem to be their best means of coping with the fact that they are suddenly rich and fashionable. – Pete Axthelm, *Newsweek*

Generalization
More and more people are seeking out islands, I read in the newspaper recently, in the hope of finding freedom from neighborhood blight, crime, atmospheric pollution, noise, and the general fears and insecurity of a troubled world. The law of supply and demand having asserted itself, the article continued, habitable islands are becoming almost impossible to acquire.

I live during the more moderate months of the year on a small island close to the coast of Maine, and perhaps I can furnish a footnote on the prizes – and shortcomings – of island life. – Caskie Stinnett, *Atlantic*

Quotation
"There are no such things as incurables," said Bernard Baruch. "There are only things for which man has not found a cure." A lifetime in medical practice, education and research has convinced me, too, that we need not accept disease as an inescapable human destiny, despite our lack of information about many forms of human illness. – Michael E. DeBakey, M.D., *Saturday Review/World*

Statistics

Ben-Hur, as everyone knows, cost $15,000,000 to make, runs for almost four hours, has a cast variously estimated at 50,000 (by Metro-Goldwyn-Mayer) and at 10,400 (by *Time*), was directed by William Wyler, and has had the biggest advance sale ($500,000) in film history. But what no one knows who hasn't seen it is that it is lousy. – Dwight Macdonald, *Esquire*

Rhetorical Question

How much bureaucratic stupidity do we have to put up with? – University newspaper

English teachers and editors who have been swamped with openings that are phony or plodding or pointless sometimes advise throwing away all first paragraphs and letting second paragraphs stand as openings. It's true that a short paper scarcely needs a paragraph that can be identified as a separate, distinct "beginning." But both writer and reader must have a sense that the starting point is a logical or natural one, and throwing out the first paragraph doesn't guarantee that the next one will make a strong start. The best course is to cut in on your material at a point that has caught your own interest and *get started.* It's much better to build up some momentum than to sit around trying to compose the perfect opening. If you can't find a way in, try writing your introduction last. Then you can gear it to the rest of the paper.

Endings

Short papers seldom need formal conclusions. When the process has been described, the narrative completed, the problem solved, nothing more need be said – or nothing but a brisk comment or two, perhaps an allusion to something at the start to round out the paper.

But discussions that move through several stages need recognizable endings if they're not to give the impression that they've been cut off or that they've simply run down. You can turn this necessity to your own advantage. The ending is your last chance to win acceptance for your ideas – to establish your generalization, to drive home your thesis, to clinch your argument. A good conclusion brings out the significance of all you've written. A mechanical summary on the order of "In this paper I have shown that . . ." is lifeless, but some sort of restatement of the course of your discussion is appropriate in papers four or five pages long and may be necessary even in short papers when the material is difficult.

When you've built up evidence throughout a paper, you can end by stating authoritatively what you presented at the start as no more than a possibility. Or you may finish up by recapitulating only the strongest of the points you've made. Even when it's little more than a summary, your ending can take on freshness from a slight change in style —a sharpening of the tone or a relaxation of tension or a touch of humor.

Your ending should make clear that the paper has arrived at its destination. It should strike a note of finality and completeness. Don't use it for apologies, for after-thoughts, for bringing in ideas that should have been treated in the body of the paper, or for introducing a brand-new issue. Make it as affirmative and positive as your discussion justifies. Point to broader implications, indicate the significance of your findings, make predictions or recommendations, or throw out a challenge to your readers. An ending that brings a paper to a totally satisfying conclusion may at the same time generate a follow-up paper.

One good way to test the effectiveness of an ending you've written is to see how well it fits the beginning of the paper. In the following paired passages, the expectations set up in the second half of the opening paragraph are fulfilled by the summary of the "serious weaknesses" of American football—weaknesses which have been discussed in detail in the body of the article:

Like many American institutions, the game of football was acquired from England. Rugby football, as it is played throughout the British Commonwealth, Ireland, and France, contains most of the ingredients out of which the American game has been developed—such as running with the ball, passing, kicking, and tackling—but in the American game these ingredients have been complicated, padded, and shot through with specialized operations. The result has been that the more salutary technique and the better spirit of Rugby football have been lost.

. . . .

The general mood which most distinguishes the Rugby scene from American football is that of temperance; and this temperate mood is made possible to a considerable extent by the simplicity of the game. The intemperance which is associated with American football may have a number of causes, but frustration is a prominent one. The American game will not allow many able-bodied and interested people even to join a team; it will not allow many of the members of a team to play a full game; and of those actually playing, only a few can engage in the full range of activity. These are serious weaknesses in the American game, and anyone interested in getting rid of them ought to observe how Rugby football is played in England.— Allen Jackson, *Atlantic*

In the next pair the opening narrative raises the question of why the "deadly device" had been planted. The last one-sentence paragraph is a reminder, in a play on words, of the opening. The substantive conclusion, which makes up the second last paragraph, is characteristic of inquiries of this kind. It both indicates the limits of our present knowledge and points the way to investigations that urgently need to be made.

It was just after dawn on a chilly November morning, and the three surveyors were scratching about the barren earth southwest of Fort Stockton, Texas, looking for the old cedar stakes that would give them their bearings. The men were members of a seismic team, jolting and bullying the earth out of its geologic secrets on behalf of a major petroleum company. One of them, 49-year-old Raymond Medford, reached down to tug at a gray pipe protruding from the chalky soil; as he did, there was a sharp report and something tore upward into the fleshy part of his hand. "What happened?" one of the other men shouted. Medford, confused and shocked, was running in circles. Then he calmed and said, "That thing went off! It had an explosion, whatever it was." A doctor in Fort Stockton looked at the bloody hand, administered first aid and sent the surveyor off to bed. An hour later Medford was dead.

Investigation showed that the pipe in the earth was a so-called "coyote-getter," a deadly device loaded and cocked and set to shoot a cyanide charge into the mouth of any animal that pulled at its aromatic wick.

•   •   •   •   •   •   •   •

One comes away from a discussion with this plain-spoken biochemist — and other experts in the field — with the uneasy feeling that there are serious gaps in the toxicological profile of sodium fluoroacetate. Whole tables and booklets have been prepared on such practical matters as the exact amount of 1080 required to kill kangaroo rats, ferruginous rough-legged hawks, Rhode Island red hens and Columbian ground squirrels, but no one seems to have done much research into an equally practical matter: What is the total amount of 1080 and other poisons that the sodden soils and polluted waterways of the West can absorb without becoming lethal agents themselves? One asks, and one is told: "Nobody knows."

Someday we may be dying to find out. — Jack Olsen, *Sports Illustrated*

In the following pair the ending, with its guarantee that "you will become stronger" as a result of practicing jujitsu and other martial arts, reminds the reader of the weak, helpless victim the writer presented herself as at the start of the article.

My involvement with the martial arts began the day I spread my arms out from my sides (unconsciously asking, I suppose, to be crucified) to stop a thief from leaving my office. Grabbing my left wrist, he flipped me as easily as he would a pancake. Later, grimly contemplating the black and blue marks which ran across the right side of my body, I was forced to realize not only how vulnerable I was but how naive as well.

Like most women, I had little knowledge of how to defend myself. . . .

•   •   •   •   •   •   •   •

Of course, the martial arts are not a panacea. Learning any martial art is a painstaking process, which is why you must have a competent instructor who will let you go at your own pace. One woman in my first jujitsu class broke her collarbone because she tried a forward roll she did not feel ready for, but had been urged to do by her instructor. That was a painful, bitter lesson: learn to trust your own instincts. A good instructor will teach you to tap or slap your thigh, your partner, or the mat, as a signal to your partner that she or he is hurting you.

While a broken collarbone is the exception rather than the rule, you *can* expect to be occasionally black and blue, to suffer minor sprains, pulled muscles. And, as with any new subject, you may at first feel apprehensive and awkward. However, as you acquire competence, you will probably feel exhilaration at overcoming your fears of pain and violence. You will begin to become aware of the potential power of your body. Yes, you will become stronger. — Victoria Pellegrino, *Ms.*

Here a brief, generalized anecdote opens a discussion and evaluation of eyewitness testimony. The paragraph that concludes the article indicates that the "impressive testimony" in the opening should not impress jurors as much as it does.

The woman in the witness box stares at the defendant, points an accusing finger and says, loudly and firmly, "That's the man! That's him! I could never forget his face!" It is impressive testimony. The only eyewitness to a murder has identified the murderer. Or has she?

Perhaps she has, but she may be wrong. . . .

•   •   •   •   •   •   •

It is discouraging to note that the essential findings on the unreliability of eyewitness testimony were made by Hugo Münsterberg nearly 80 years ago, and yet the practice of basing a case on eyewitness testimony and trying to persuade a jury that such testimony is superior to circumstantial evidence continues to this day. The fact is that both types of evidence involve areas of doubt. Circumstantial evidence is tied together with a theory, which is subject to questioning. Eyewitness testimony is also based on a theory, constructed by a human being (often with help from others), about what reality was like in the past; since that theory can be adjusted or changed in accordance with personality, with the situation or with social pressure, it is unwise to accept such testimony without question. It is up to a jury to determine if the doubts about an eyewitness's testimony are reasonable enough for the testimony to be rejected as untrue. Jurors should be reminded that there can be doubt about eyewitness testimony, just as there is about any other kind of evidence. — Robert Buckhout, *Scientific American*

In this last pair a serious proposal is introduced by bold appeal to a precedent that the writer knows his readers will find distasteful. The last paragraph is intended to clinch the argument that has been made in the body of the article. The wry humor of the last line echoes that of the proposal, with its "lock, stock, and burglar's kit."

Stalin did establish one useful precedent. He made it a practice to bump off whoever served as head of his secret police. He never let anybody stay in the job too long. As a successful dictator, Stalin seems to have felt that anybody who had collected so many secrets would be a No. 1 menace to security if he ever went sour. Stalin thought it safer not to wait.

I think we ought to take Stalin's example one step further. I think we ought to get rid of the CIA altogether, lock, stock, and burglar's kit.

•   •   •   •   •   •   •   •

A government, like an individual, hates to hear what it doesn't want to believe. This is why no intelligence agency in any society ever really understands — or can afford to let itself understand — what is going on. The bigger the intelligence agency the more powerfully its sheer inertial weight reinforces the misconceptions of the ruling class it serves. Hence the paradox: the more "intelligence" a government buys the less intelligently it operates. The CIA will go down in the books as a vain attempt to change history by institutionalizing assassination. It deserves a dose of its own favorite medicine. — I. F. Stone, *New York Review of Books*

■ *For Analysis and Writing*

1. Here are the openings of two papers on the fluorescent lamp, the first prepared for beginning high-school students, the second for college students with some knowledge of physics. State in detail the differences between them and discuss their appropriateness to their intended audiences.

a. You turn the switch. For an instant, nothing happens. Then light flickers along the tube. And finally there is full, steady illumination. As contrasted with the ordinary bulb, which lights up as soon as its switch is turned, the fluorescent tube always provides a moment of dramatic uncertainty. Why the hesitation?

b. The fluorescent lamp is a device which utilizes a relatively low voltage electric current to provide artificial illumination. Unlike an incandescent light, it employs an electrical discharge through tenuous mercury vapor to convert electrical energy into light energy. The discharge produces invisible ultraviolet light. The long glass tube through which the discharge passes is coated on the inside with a substance that transforms the ultraviolet light into visible radiation. That the visible light comes from

this coating rather than directly from the discharge differentiates the fluorescent lamp from other types of discharge lamps.

2. *Describe and evaluate the beginning and ending in each
set quoted below. What expectations does the beginning
arouse? How do you know that the ending is an ending? In
making your evaluation you may find it useful to take into
account the publication in which the essay appears.*

a. People like getting something for their money, even when
the money is going to a good cause. That's why fund-raising
events often are more successful than outright solicitations for
contributions.
All kinds of groups—service clubs, school and church organizations, charities, civic associations, community agencies, political organizations—are putting on fund-raising events these
days. For some, an annual fund-raiser is the only method used to
get financial support.
Don't get the idea that staging a successful fund-raiser is a
cinch. It's not. To succeed, the event must be well planned. All
sorts of details have to be carefully worked out for even a fairly
small-scale project. And there are some pitfalls that must be
skirted. . . .

•   •   •   •   •   •   •   •

When the curtain has fallen on your event, the receipts tallied
and the bills paid, follow up by sending thank-you notes to every
person and firm that contributed in any way to its success. Even
the most altruistic volunteer workers and helpful business firms
like to be recognized for their contributions.—*Changing Times*

b. They still tell in our family how the 14-year-old, my father,
came off the boat with a rope around his waist to hold up his
pants. When he bent to kiss the ground, the rope loosened and
his pants fell down. "America!" he cried.

•   •   •   •   •   •   •   •

The cataclysmic assaults upon faith and myth, innocence,
invincibility all came after my father's death. I cannot imagine
what he would think today, but I suspect that he would still hear
America singing. It was a sound so sweet that he could never
have borne to relinquish it.—Martha Weinman Lear, *New York
Times Magazine*

c. Many members of the older generation are under the impression that their values and ways of life are the only right ones.
They think that their children must inherit these qualities or
they, the parents, have failed. They refuse to acknowledge that
teenagers might have some legitimate ideas of their own. I am
tired of having my opinions put down by my parents simply
because of my youth and relative lack of experience.
Family ties are extremely important to my father and mother.
They feel that their children should prefer to do things with the
family rather than on their own. Unfortunately, their attitudes
make me unwilling to spend time with them.

•   •   •   •   •   •   •   •

I don't mean to sound like my parents are inhuman. My mother and father have always been more than generous, giving me everything I ever needed. I love them both dearly and don't mean for it to appear otherwise. They have taught me many valuable lessons. But though I appreciate their efforts to give me the best upbringing possible, according to their standards, I think we would get along much better if they would only try to understand my feelings and remember that I am an independent adult with ideas of my own, however different they may be from theirs.

d. Karen Tucker is a 35-year-old reservations clerk with Ozark Airlines. "Just a clerk," she says. "You know, like 'just a housewife.' I sit all day with earphones that are too heavy—all the girls get ear infections from them. But 'just housewives' have rights. Clerks have rights, too. In small-town U.S.A., just like everywhere else."

Mrs. Tucker is an outspoken feminist and a union organizer in a town so renowned for its conservatism that the very word *Peoria* has become a mass-media synonym for Middle America. She is one of the many energetic examples of the influence exerted by the women's-liberation movement in an area of the country where people do not take quickly to new fashions or new social trends.

•   •   •   •   •   •   •   •

The concrete advances represented by women found on the assembly line are accompanied by subtle psychological changes, which are difficult to measure.

Last year a writer for the local newspaper, the *Journal-Star,* was asked to prepare a list of Peoria citizens who would appear on the "David Frost Show." He made notes about each potential participant for Frost's staff. A lawyer's wife—an old friend of the writer—asked one of Frost's assistants why she and her husband had been asked to appear on the show. He looked at the writer's notation and told the woman, "Well, the slip says that your husband is a brilliant attorney and you're very beautiful."

Sitting in his office, the writer recalled how his woman friend came to him in tears. "She said to me, 'You've known me all these years, and all you can say about me is I'm beautiful.' I was stunned. Of course, this woman is a lot more than beautiful. But there it was—what I had written down was that her husband was brilliant and she was beautiful. Like everyone else, I have a lot of thinking to do."—Susan Jacoby, *Saturday Review*

e. An acquaintance of mine from Alabama served in Poland for seven years with the U.S. State Department. His children, now 10 and 12, went to Polish schools, having learned the language with the ease of the very young. Now back in Virginia, the two children, despite their pure Anglo-Saxon Baptist features, are the constant object of playground abuse. Children shout "goulash!" at them. They are called "Hunky." They are the constant butt of "dumb Polack" jokes. On one occasion when the older lad could bear the humiliation no longer, he had an inspiration. He turned on those who were taunting him with a challenge: "Can you speak Polish?" The others fell silent and then he hit them: "How does it feel to be dumber than a Polack?"

Too many Americans make a joke out of Polish jokes. They expect people of Slavic descent (all of whom suffer under these jokes; no one can tell us apart) to take these jokes as funny, to show our own sense of humor, gracefully to laugh at ourselves. If mere graciousness were at stake, we could easily oblige.

The intent of Polish jokes, however, is not humor alone. . . .

• • • • • • • •

Cannot some major center of learning conduct a study of how much damage is done to the psyches of people constantly stereo-typed in public? Can't the American Civil Liberties Union and a wide range of anti-defamation societies join in protests to the magazines, television channels and gatherings of (otherwise) sophisticated people who tell ethnic jokes of the inherently demeaning kind? We don't need Supreme Court decisions, per-haps, but we do need a basic sense of public fairness. Eastern Europeans cannot halt Polish jokes alone. The help of all is required.

This is supposed to be a nation of civility toward all, bigotry toward none. It is not. But when the laughter rings, it rings for thee. – Michael Novak, *Newsweek*

Proportion and Emphasis

A paper needs to have shape as well as direction. A bulge will develop if you let a minor point get out of control and take up more space than it deserves. Good proportions depend on your own sense of the relative significance of your separate ideas about your subject, modified by your sense of the needs of your audience. If your readers are unfamiliar with the subject, spend time breaking ground. If they're likely to reject one of your ideas, pile up evidence at that point. If your discussion has been complicated, be especially careful to pull things together at the end.

Proportion is related to emphasis. What deserves most emphasis usually gets most space. Position can provide emphasis, too: beginnings and endings offer major op-portunities. Beginnings can arouse curiosity and over-come resistance, and endings – of sentences and para-graphs as well as of whole papers – can serve as clinchers. If you use a comparison to prove that one product is su-perior to another, put its strongest claim either at the beginning or at the end – the beginning if you sense initial resistance, otherwise the end for climax.

Failures in proportion and loss of emphasis often result from writing by association and from excessive qualifying. Associational thinking may be a great help in prewriting (writer in search of a topic) and in early drafts. One idea, or image, or word can remind you of another. At this early stage you aren't selective. You pursue your subject through related pictures in your mind or through the connotations of the words you're setting down – even through puns and other kinds of word play. You're hospitable to all ideas. Approaching a subject this way helps get you into a first draft. But a paper isn't a duffel bag. You can't stuff everything into it. At some point you've got to select and shape. Otherwise you'll never focus on a single theme. As your real topic comes clear, you've got to throw out the extraneous material that associational thinking produced and distribute the relevant material with attention to proportion and emphasis.

Most of us don't do enough qualifying when we write. We generalize about "people," "men," "women," "students," and so on, without a "some" or a "many" or a "most" to indicate that our statements aren't all-inclusive. As you strive for accuracy and truth in what you write, you'll need to qualify some of your generalizations, take note of exceptions, ward off unwarranted inferences. Simply adding "based on my own experience" or words to that effect will often make acceptable a statement that readers might otherwise reject: "On the basis of my own experience, I'd say that women bosses are harder on women employees than men bosses are." In some rhetorical situations you'll want to establish yourself as a person of moderation, not given to extremes either in the ideas you advance or in the tone of your discourse; and so you'll qualify and temper your remarks. All this is reasonable, often admirable. But don't carry it so far that you weaken your organization and deaden your style. There are always exceptions if you hunt for them hard enough (just about every statement on writing in this book could be qualified); but introducing them when they have little point or significance can damage your paper in a half-dozen different ways.

Aids to Organizing: Outlines

Opinions differ sharply on the value of outlining in the prewriting stage. Some professional writers never make outlines of any kind. Others can't write without an outline. Of those who use outlines, some work from sketchy notes, others draw up extremely detailed plans, and still others *think* the whole thing through, so that they have a complete structure in mind before they write a word.

What sort of writer are you? If your papers read as if you're mechanically ticking off points one, two, three, then perhaps you're being cramped by your outlines and should use them more flexibly. If your papers — particularly the longer ones — are criticized for being disorganized, you probably need to try outlining, in your head or on paper, before you write. But never let an outline freeze a paper. As you write, always be prepared to move away from your plan. The act of writing down one recollection may spark another that throws a different light on the event; a new example may point toward a conclusion quite unlike the one that originally seemed logical. Whenever you have to choose between following your outline and following your ideas, go with your ideas. Change your outline. Keep your mind open and active.

Types of Outlines

The working outline (or scratch outline or informal outline) is a private affair — fluid, subject to constant revision, made without attention to form, and destined for the wastebasket. But enough working outlines have been retrieved from wastebaskets that something can be said about them.

A working outline usually begins with a few phrases and some descriptive details or examples. From them grow fragmentary statements, tentative generalizations, hypotheses. One or two of these take on prominence, shaping into the main ideas that seem worth developing. New examples bring to mind new ideas, and these find a place in the list of phrases, canceling out some of the original ones. The writer keeps adding and subtracting, juggling and shifting, until he has his key points in an order that makes sense to him. He scribbles a sentence, works in a transition, adds examples.

Depending on his habits, he may discard his working outline as soon as it has served the purpose of getting the direction and shape of his essay clear to him. Or he may keep it beside him as he writes, checking off points as he covers them, rejecting those that prove unsatisfactory, taking out time to rethink and reorder before finishing the first draft. By then, if he has kept expanding and correcting it, his outline comes close to being a rough summary of the essay itself.

Here, minus crossings-out, arrows, and general untidiness, is a working outline for a paper about the impact of Alex Haley's bestselling book *Roots* and the very popular television production that was based on it.

How explain the enormous appeal of *Roots*? Awakened longing for sense of heritage.

Haley's story, beginning with amazing search, captured imagination of millions.

A few clues led to uncovering of long-buried facts that the author made into a gripping story.

Really three stories in *Roots* – Kunta Kinte and succeeding generations, the black experience in America generally, and Haley's search.

Publishers and TV producers were sure they had a hit on their hands.

First printing of 200,000 copies.

TV production cost $6 million for 8-episode series shown on consecutive nights.

Results outdid expectations. A million copies of book in print five months after publication. TV series drew 130,000,000 viewers.

Good effect on U.S. race relations. New sense of identity, pride for blacks. For whites, new understanding of blacks, new appreciation of their history.

Upsurge of interest in genealogy. Blacks *and* whites hungry for knowledge of own roots.

Where the working outline is ragged, the formal outline is tidily schematic. Though not necessarily a public affair, it may be; and when it's intended for eyes other than the writer's, it should observe certain conventions. Some of these conventions make the formal outline more remote from the actual paper than the working outline is. Following the title, for example, stands a thesis statement, which may or may not appear in the paper and, if it does, may or may not occur at the beginning. The outline itself passes over introductory and transitional material as well as most illustrations and restatements. In its final version it reflects a process of logical division. The statement of the thesis is broken down into its parts, each represented in the outline by a main heading. These main heads are in turn analyzed into their parts, with subdivisions indented to show relationships of coordination and subordination. Theoretically, the subdividing can go on indefinitely; practically, it's rarely carried beyond the third level. On the logical principle that division always produces at least two units, no single subdivision (a *1* without a *2* or an *a* without a *b*) is permitted in the formal outline.

Following are two versions of the formal outline—the topic outline and the sentence outline—both based on parts of the paper we saw taking shape in the working outline above. The versions overlap: the topic outline covers the first three of the four sections of the paper; the sentence outline covers the last two. Note that the topic outline uses phrases or words for heads; the sentence outline uses complete sentences. In both, logically parallel ideas are presented in matching grammatical structures. First, the topic outline:

Roots: Not One Man's Story

The dramatic account of one man's successful search for his roots fascinated millions and inspired thousands to begin investigating their own.

I. The search: a story in itself
  A. Few clues
    1. Grandmother's stories
    2. Names from the past
  B. Sources
    1. Scholars, museums, ships' manifests, libraries
    2. African tribesmen and *griots*
    3. One memorable voyage

II. The book
  A. A mixture of fact and fiction
    1. 2500 items of information
    2. Factual errors
    3. Psychological re-creation
  B. A spellbinder
    1. Chronicle of Kunta Kinte and his descendants
    2. Panorama of black life in America
    3. Saga of Haley's search

III. The TV series
  A. Elements of success
    1. Good story
    2. Lots of publicity
    3. Big production budget
    4. Decision to show episodes on consecutive nights
  B. Phenomenal response
    1. 130 million viewers
    2. Zooming book sales
    3. Fame for author

The sentence outline:

III. The TV dramatization brought the story into millions of homes.
  A. It was almost assured of success.
    1. It had a story that offered excitement, sentiment, romance, melodrama.

2. It was given extensive promotional tie-in with the book.
3. It was allotted a production budget of $6 million.
4. It was presented on consecutive nights to hold viewer interest.
  B. The success it achieved was beyond expectation.
    1. It attracted 130 million viewers.
    2. It spurred tremendous demand for the book.
    3. It made Haley a celebrity.
IV. *Roots'* phenomenal impact was both personal and social.
  A. Response to the TV version was biracial.
    1. Both blacks and whites said that *Roots* on TV made them see the reality of the black experience.
      a. It gave both a greater appreciation of black history.
      b. Among blacks, it spurred a sense of pride and identity.
      c. It made many whites more sensitive to the black situation.
    2. It led to new discussions of racial questions.
      a. Its success caused newspapers and magazines to reexamine the state of race relations in America.
      b. As a national event, it became a natural topic for discussion whenever people came together.
  B. The fascination of *Roots'* theme is universal.
    1. The average American longs for a sense of heritage.
      a. All of us—regardless of race—want to know who we are and where we came from.
      b. We want to trace our roots—not to uncover distinguished forebears but to learn about the ordinary people most of us are descended from.
    2. *Roots* sparked an upsurge of interest in genealogy.
      a. Inquiries for information to libraries and the National Archives doubled or tripled.
      b. Schools had students search out their family trees as course projects.
      c. Tourist offices geared up to help travelers search out family connections while abroad.
    3. The appeal of *Roots* was linked to the growing interest in social history.
      a. Historians were placing new emphasis on reconstructing the behavior, culture, and quality of life of ordinary persons.
      b. At least 250 college courses immediately adopted *Roots* as a textbook.

■ For Writing

Complete the topic outline by converting into topics the heads in section IV of the sentence outline.

The topic outline is the usual choice if you're preparing an outline to accompany a short or medium-long paper. A sentence outline is always the best choice for long papers, especially reference papers, when you plan to ask your instructor for advice and criticism before proceeding with the project. Because the ideas are expressed in complete sentences, inconsistencies and lapses in logical progression are more obvious in the sentence outline than in the topic outline or the working outline. And the need to write complete sentences forces you to examine the *purpose* of each paragraph or other subdivision of your paper. Though a sentence outline takes time to prepare, it remains the most informative of all outlines for the writer as well as for the reader.

Testing Organization

Whether or not they find it helpful to prepare an outline in the prewriting stage, most writers would probably agree that reducing a completed essay or article to an outline is an excellent way to expose its structure and test the progression of ideas. Making a detailed outline on the model of the sentence outline is the surest means of gaining control of any difficult reading you're assigned. And making an outline, however rough, of your own papers is one of the best ways to determine whether they have genuine unity and continuity. For this purpose, begin by making a paragraph-by-paragraph summary (a sentence for each paragraph is enough).

Unless your paper is very short, this first step will make clear that not all your paragraphs are of equal importance. It will also show you that many of your paragraphs fall into groups, each of which performs one main function in the total scheme. Bracket the sentences representing such paragraph sequences, to show that the block as a whole is one of the parts into which your paper is divided, and compose a sentence that states the point of each of these stages in the discussion. Indent the sentences that state secondary points.

A paper twelve to fifteen paragraphs long may fall into three or four sequences of closely related paragraphs, connected either by transitional paragraphs or by transitional sentences that stand at the end of one sequence or the beginning of the next. Ending with almost as many parts—that is, major headings—as you have paragraphs suggests that you should consider reducing the number of points you're making, concentrating on the most significant and developing them in paragraph sequences.

Once you've made this rough approximation of a sentence outline, including the formal statement of a thesis, you can move quickly to close gaps, improve sequences, and in general give your rewrite a stronger, firmer organization. Unquestionably, bad papers are sometimes written from splendid outlines; but accurate outlining does expose structural weaknesses, and exposure clears the way for intelligent revision.

■ *For Writing*

Write a paper on how, at this stage in the course, you go about writing a paper. Before you begin the final draft, test the organization of what you've written by outlining it, using the sentence outline on pp. 127–28 as a model for the format. Now write your final draft, taking into account what your outline has told you about the unity and progression of your paper. Turn in both versions of the paper as well as the sentence outline.

Chapter Four
Building Paragraphs

Content paragraphs—paragraphs that do the work of conveying ideas rather than fulfilling special functions of transition, restatement, and emphasis—are groups of related statements that a writer presents as units in developing a subject. They strike the eye as units because they're set off physically from what precedes and what follows, either by indention or by spacing above and below. They strike the mind as units because the sentences that make them up are logically connected. Each of these clusters of related statements forms a stage in the flow of the writer's thought (as this paragraph defines the subject and the next one expands on the function of paragraphing).

Experience leads readers to expect that each new paragraph will take a somewhat different tack. They read indention as a signal that a shift in thought or tone is going to take place, and they adjust their attention accordingly. If you do your job well, your paragraphing will help make the movement of your ideas clear. If you do it carelessly, your readers will have difficulty following your line of thought.

If you've been given practice in writing single paragraphs, you may have come to think of them as "compositions in miniature." Whatever validity this notion may have for some individual paragraphs, it doesn't hold when applied to paragraphs in context. Some paragraphs do have a self-contained wholeness, but in tightly organized papers most do not. Detached from context, they're obviously incomplete. And even when a paragraph makes perfectly good sense standing alone, it usually doesn't say precisely what it says when it speaks in company with its neighbors.

Function and Length

You can make paragraphs work for you in a variety of ways. You can use one to lay the groundwork for a discussion that you'll carry on through the next five or six paragraphs. Then you can move to a new topic by way of a transitional paragraph—one that serves as a structural guide rather than a conveyor of ideas. Or, before you move ahead, you can help your reader by restating in a short paragraph a complicated part of your discussion.

You can write a sequence of three linked paragraphs, using the first to make a major point and the next two to amplify, illustrate, and support it. You can write another three that stand in a first-second-third relationship, all of roughly the same importance. You can write pairs of paragraphs that complement each other—one cause and the other effect, one positive and the other negative, one listing advantages and the other disadvantages.

How long should your paragraphs be? That depends on two things: function and convention. Though a transitional paragraph is typically very short, paragraphs that serve other functions are not likely to be. A good content paragraph should present a succession of logically related sentences that add up to something. While there are exceptions, the typical content paragraph focuses on a single subject or part of a subject; it gives a reader the sense that it's a logical unit. Does that mean three sentences or thirty? It's impossible to answer the question in the abstract. A three-sentence paragraph *could* be all right. But in most college writing, a three-sentence paragraph would be skimpy. The three sentences could be in logical order, and they could make a single, sensible point; but the result wouldn't be satisfying. The point wouldn't be sufficiently developed, or the problem wouldn't be explored in sufficient detail. Adequate length is related to adequate thought.

A thirty-sentence paragraph could be all right, too. Certainly in a long paper—say a twenty-page term paper based on research—thirty logically ordered sentences could form one unified phase of the subject. But whether the thirty sentences *should* be presented as a single unit would depend not only on the continuity and cohesiveness of the stretch of thirty sentences but also on the audience. Long paragraphs demand sustained concentration. While a succession of very short paragraphs gives a choppy, jerky effect, a short paragraph is easier to read than a long one. And very long paragraphs look forbidding. Convention calls for breaking them up to provide some visual relief and to slice the text into manageable bites.

If a first draft of yours includes a thirty-sentence paragraph, examine it carefully. Does it hold together? Does it proceed logically? Does it convey the message you intend, with the emphasis you want? If so, good. But you should also ask yourself whether your readers will be able and willing to make their way through it without getting lost or bored. If you're doubtful, look for a satisfactory dividing point. Two paragraphs that your audience can read comfortably are better than one paragraph that intimidates or overwhelms. (The two paragraphs that precede this one could be joined. They're separated for easier reading, a brisker tone, and brisker movement.)

■ *For Analysis*

1. *Count the words in each of three complete paragraphs (other than opening and closing paragraphs) and calculate the average number of words per paragraph*

   a. in this chapter

   b. in two essays in a scholarly journal such as *PMLA, The American Historical Review, American Psychologist, Science*

   c. in two nonfiction articles, without dialog, in one or more of the following: *The Atlantic, Harper's, Saturday Review, The New York Review of Books, The New Yorker, Esquire, Scientific American*

   d. in *Newsweek, Time, National Review,* or *The New Republic*

   e. on the front page, the editorial page, and the sports pages of a newspaper.

2. *What tentative generalizations can you make about the relation between paragraph length on the one hand and, on the other, what is being written about and who the audience is, as indicated by the nature of the publication? Do your findings in b and c suggest that writers for the same publication use paragraphs of roughly the same length or of very different lengths? Through further sampling try to estimate the relative importance of content, expected audience, and a writer's individual style and taste in determining paragraph length.*

3. *Make a word count for paragraphs 2, 3, and 4 in a recent paper of yours. Can you justify the average length as appropriate to the rhetorical situation?*

Unity and Development

As you write, it's helpful to visualize each paragraph—at least each content paragraph in an expository paper—as an organic unit built around a nucleus, linked to what precedes and what follows but with its own center, a core of meaning that justifies including the paragraph in your paper. Every paragraph must *do* something for the sequence of paragraphs it belongs to or for the paper as a whole or for both – make a point, convey an idea, create an impression. It *will* do something only if all the sentences that make it up contribute to its core of meaning and if that meaning is an integral part of the stream of ideas that runs through the essay.

Cores of meaning are what you look for whenever you outline or summarize something you've read. How do you get the key statements that go into your outline? Some you can copy straight from the text. Others you produce by combining and condensing several of the author's sentences. Still others you compose, setting down the gist of a paragraph; it's all there, but you have to pull it together.

In writing paragraphs it's well to remind yourself of your experience in reading paragraphs. They make their points in different ways. The core of meaning may be explicitly stated in a single sentence (called the *topic sentence*), or it may be scattered through several sentences, or it may be the unstated idea underlying all the particulars of the paragraph – sometimes of the entire block of paragraphs to which the paragraph belongs. And if it is to have an impact and not just make an assertion, this core of meaning must be developed.

Topic Sentences and Pointers

Every content paragraph you write should have a topic *idea*. Whether or not it has a topic sentence is secondary; normally the question won't enter your mind. When you're intent on formulating and expressing ideas, you don't think in terms of topic-sentence-and-support-for-it any more than you consciously decide that the paragraph is to develop by definition or by causal analysis or whatever. You follow the flow of your ideas. But when the flow is down to a trickle, you'll probably start trying to figure out what general point you want to make next. Hitting on a core idea gives you the sense of direction you need, and framing a sentence that expresses the idea gives you something to work toward or away from. Once you have a topic sentence – either in mind or on paper – you'll find it easier to write a paragraph that's a meaningful unit, not just a collection of statements.

Whether in your final draft you give the paragraph a topic sentence or allow the central idea to emerge without one depends on the rhetorical situation – your subject and what you want to do with it, your relation to your readers, and so on. Certainly your readers will be no more concerned with singling out topic sentences than you are with writing them, but if the material is difficult or if the subject calls for interpretation and judgment, they probably will be looking for guidance. Usually you'll find it most convenient to provide guidance through the companion devices of topic sentences and pointer statements.

A *topic sentence* gives the gist of the discussion or states the central proposition to be explained or defended: "The drabness of real life seems to affect taste" (Sexton, p. 28). Though it seldom represents the central idea in every detail or with every qualification the writer intends, the topic sentence is the most explicit statement he can make, or cares to make, of the meaning he wants the paragraph as a whole to convey. In rhetorical situations where clarity is of first importance, a topic sentence may be restated – sometimes with greater precision or greater fullness – either immediately or after an intervening passage has offered illustration or proof.

Instead of telling the reader the central idea – what the paragraph says – a *pointer statement* tells him what the paragraph is going to do. Pointers are part of the strategy of announcing, as in this paragraph opener: "Here is what happens when you heave to" (William F. Buckley, Jr., *New Yorker*). They include some questions ("What of the future?") and many transitional sentences ("Before deciding whether it's a good idea, let's look at the alternatives"). In any case, they indicate the scope of the discussion. "Basically there are four types of college students" signals precisely what's to come. "*Equality* means different things to different women" tells the reader to expect an account of various interpretations of the term. "There are problems about thinking of the purpose of a college education in either of these ways" forecasts the next stage of the discussion.

Their function as guideposts makes pointers extremely useful in organizing a paper. But, as always, keep the rhetorical situation in mind. Guidance where no guidance is needed will irritate readers, and too many guideposts can make them feel they're being herded. On the other hand, when the material you're dealing with is complex and you know your readers will welcome all the help they can get, you may want to use both topic sentences and pointer statements to characterize and control the content of a paragraph or of a sequence of paragraphs. Notice how these two pointer statements, which stand at the beginning of a paragraph, together give readers a good deal of guidance to what follows:

> A word is needed at this point to explain in fuller detail what is meant by the *structure* of a subject, for we shall have occasion to return to this idea often in later pages. Three simple examples – from biology, from mathematics, and from the learning of language – help to make the idea clearer. – Jerome S. Bruner, *The Process of Education*

Though at this point the reader doesn't know the outcome of the discussion – what *structure* means – he does know, as he reads on, what purpose the example from biology is intended to serve. And at the close of the paragraph he finds the promised definition, expressed in a topic sentence and then, for clarity and emphasis, restated:

> Grasping the structure of a subject is understanding it in a way that permits many other things to be related to it meaningfully. To learn structure, in short, is to learn how things are related.

These twin topic sentences sum up the content of the paragraph just as the opening pointers predict it.

Expanding the Core

Whether or not you express the central idea of a paragraph in a topic sentence, the real work of explaining or persuading remains to be done. A topic sentence may be the most inclusive sentence in a paragraph but also the least interesting. What convinces readers is not so much the idea a topic sentence expresses as the clarification and enrichment offered by the other sentences in the paragraph – sentences that restate, refine, and qualify the central idea, sentences that illuminate and support it with anecdotes, descriptive details, and examples.

If you fail to recognize the need to expand and clarify and support your key generalizations, you may end up with undeveloped paragraphs and unconvincing papers. Such failure is natural enough, for in framing a general statement, you assimilate, and so in a sense discard, the particulars that led you to it. But bare assertions and propositions can't convey anything like the fullness and complexity of thought processes. If readers are to share in your thinking and find their way to the same conclusion, they must be led over some of the same ground.

Recall the differences between an article or a chapter you've read and the outline you've made of it. Reviewing the outline several times while the complete reading is fresh in your mind is an excellent way to get control of the material. But if you go back to the outline a few weeks later – or if you look over notes you took in a lecture course some weeks or months ago – you're likely to get very little help. In the interval you'll have forgotten all the particulars – the details, the examples, the evidence – that originally supported and clarified the key statements you assembled.

This paragraph is both abstract and undernourished:

Americans have more difficulty verbalizing their political ideology than many Europeans do. Historical reasons are mainly responsible for their comparative inarticulateness on both domestic and foreign policy.

Fleshed out as it was originally written, it's a good deal more interesting and more convincing:

An educated Russian can give a coherent statement of his beliefs and can argue ideology effectively with persons from other nations; so can an educated Englishman. Even many who have not had university training can do quite well. But most Americans have difficulty explaining to foreigners what their fellow citizens believe in. This is one of the paradoxes that, as Kluckhohn has stated, characterizes the American culture. We talk much of "the American way of life," but we are almost incapable of telling others about it. Much of the political ideology we do have stems from an intellectual movement of the late eighteenth century, a development discussed in later chapters. It was beautifully expressed by the most "egghead" of American Presidents, Thomas Jefferson, but since his time we have had difficulty in organizing our changing thoughts about beliefs. The Jacksonian movement of a generation later, for example, never had a philosopher who could systematically state its beliefs. The credo of the American businessman, dating from the post-Civil War days, is also a haphazard set of ideas. Furthermore, America had little in the way of a systematic foreign policy until the time of World War II, and hence until recently we learned a political rhetoric that concentrated on domestic issues rather than on foreign policy. In contrast, the Englishman's basic ideology concerning relationships with other nations has been relatively clear and has not changed fundamentally in 400 years. For that reason alone, he is far more likely to be able to state his nation's position in international affairs. – Charles R. Adrian and Charles Press, *The American Political Process*

In expanding the core of a paragraph, you have two obligations. One is to keep the paragraph unified. Stuffing a paragraph with ideas that head off in different directions weakens the force of the central idea; if the paragraph is to have an impact, all the statements in it must have a bearing on its core of meaning. The second obligation is to expand the core adequately. A broad assertion may be a good starting point for a paragraph, but if left to stand alone, it's likely to be unsatisfactory. To improve the paragraph, ask yourself why you made the assertion in the first place. Once you're clear on that, try to figure out what kind of support the assertion needs to make it convincing or memorable—specific details, examples, definitions, comparisons, and so on. Some of the dozens of ways of substantiating a generalization were touched on in Chapter One (pp. 13–15) and discussed in Chapter Two.

■ *For Analysis and Writing*

1. For each of the four paragraphs in this passage, pick out the topic sentence or pointer, or, if the paragraph has neither, compose a sentence that expresses the topic idea. Then state the chief method or methods used in developing the paragraph.

Whatever is different about the scientist must begin with the particular kind of intelligence such a man possesses. It is said that the scientist must have an inquiring mind—which is true; and that he must also be one of those people who take deep pleasure in learning—which is also true, and also superficial; because both these qualities are demanded also by any number of other disciplines. The particular kind of sensibilities required by a scientist are more complicated.

Begin with his intense awareness of words and their meanings. While the poet's affinity for words makes him sensitive to their sound, emotion, and rhythm, the scientist uses them as instruments of precision. He must be capable of inventing new words to express new physical concepts. He must be able to reason verbally by analogy—to explain "how this thing is like that thing," and to be able to fit the many resemblances into one single generalization that covers them all.

The scientist must also think graphically, in terms of dynamical models, three-dimensional arrangements in space. The dynamical model of a bacterial cell, for example, is a hollow rigid capsule that may be either spherical or tubular, containing an otherwise shapeless living cell enclosed within a soft sac, the plasma membrane. Niels Bohr's dynamical model of an atom is a miniature solar system with relatively enormous electrons orbiting about an almost inconceivably small sun—the atomic nucleus—a tremendous distance away. Scientists keep these three-dimensional pictures in mind as vividly as if they were actually seeing them. Formulas and equations printed on a two-dimensional page have three-dimensional meanings, and the scientist must be able to read in three dimensions to "see the picture" at once. There is nothing "abstract" about a scientist's thinking.

This visualization is so vivid that a scientist examining a theoretical problem is really like a jeweler peering through his loupe at a gem which he holds close to his eye, turning it over and over in his fingers. To Einstein, there was nothing abstract about his theory of relativity. Even the slightest apparent deviation from the hard world of physical reality made him intellectually uncomfortable. For more than a decade, meeting at international science conferences, he and Bohr, by then both in middle age, had monumental arguments over the meaning of the uncertainty principle, with Einstein the one who stuck stolidly to the basic mechanistic principle of cause and effect. "I cannot believe that God throws dice," he said. — Mitchell Wilson, *Atlantic*

2. *Compose a generalization about yourself, about college life, about some issue that interests you — or, if you prefer, choose one from the list below. Treat it as the topic idea that you develop in a sequence of two or three or four paragraphs. After you've written the sequence, examine the paragraphs. Explain why each does or does not contain a topic sentence or pointer.*

   a. The child of divorced parents has no real sense of security.

   b. To sell their products, advertisers make appeals that have nothing to do with the quality of the products themselves.

   c. My family has some unusual traditions.

   d. Though sometimes laughed at, such terms as *blitzing, red-dogging, stunting,* and *shooting the gap* have precise meanings for knowledgeable football fans.

   e. Popular songs fall into several groups.

3. *Here's a student's explanation of why he values his stereo. Is it a satisfactory response? Why or why not?*

   I think the type of music a person listens to says a lot about that person. It is not the stereo that really means that much to me, but the quality of the music that comes out of it. Without it all there is to listen to is quiet, or the noise in the hallway.
   I listen to my stereo when I'm in a good mood, I listen to it when I'm in a really bad mood, and I also listen to it when I'm feeling pretty mediocre. It has a real advantage since it has a turntable. This way I can control what comes out of the speakers. I can put on whatever I'm in the mood for. Since this is the only stereo I've ever owned, it is the only one I've ever been able to do all these things with. That is why it means so much to me.

   4. *Write two paragraphs telling why you value a possession of yours as you do. Develop each point you make, and in revising your paper, make sure you've related one point to another in a sensible way. Most important, make sure your reader ends up knowing why you feel as you do.*

Paragraph Structure

To worry about the structure of your paragraphs while you're writing a first draft is more inhibiting than helpful.

It's when you turn to revising and rewriting that you should ask whether each paragraph has a satisfactory internal structure and whether the sentences in it track one another logically and smoothly.

Ask yourself, too, whether each paragraph satisfies whatever expectations it arouses. Have you committed yourself to giving examples, to justifying a position, to attacking or modifying a generalization? Does the opening of the paragraph forecast an account of an episode? Once you're aware of what obligation you've assumed, you can visualize the underlying structure or "plot" the paragraph should have. Like a whole paper, a paragraph may use chronological or spatial order, logical order (support, discovery, pro-and-con), or associational order. Recognizing that you've committed yourself to a certain order in the opening sentence or two is the first step toward repairing a broken-backed paragraph – one that heads one way at the start, and midway through veers off in another direction.

■ *For Analysis and Writing*

The two paragraphs below begin a paper. How do they fail to satisfy the reader's expectations? What suggestions can you make for improving them? Should the order of the sentences be changed? Should some of the sentences be dropped? New ones added? Try rewriting the passage to strengthen its organization and to make each paragraph better unified.

Last June I went to England for a summer of archaeology and travel. I was to work for three weeks at the site of Fishbourne, near the city of Chichester. I was to be a "voluntary labourer" in the trenches and to otherwise help in every possible way. I had gotten interested in archaeology in the eighth grade during an ancient history course and since then had continually read journals about Roman excavations, called "digs." From these magazines, I learned the language and something about the technology of the archaeologist. One very widely used method of dating material is the Carbon-14 test, in which the amount of carbon in some artifact is measured. Its date of manufacture can then be estimated within about fifty years. Another method of dating sites, or levels of sites, is by identifying particular styles and types of earthenware. Often it is possible to even tell the place of origin of pottery by marks on the bases of the pieces, or by the way the pottery has been made.

The Romans were very helpful to archaeologists because usually when they tore something down they left the foundation and would rebuild over it. The actual process of archaeology consists of digging rectangular trenches vertically downward at strict right angles (for dating and photographic purposes) with the soil taken off in layers so as to keep the trench and all the uncovered artifacts within the same period. Trench digging is sometimes done to sample an area and see if there is anything worth uncovering with an excavation. I got involved with the English dig through a teacher at my high school who went to England each year to work at different sites. Last year he invited me and some other classmates to accompany him to the Fishbourne excavation.

Functional Units

To test the structure of a paragraph, you'll naturally look closely at individual sentences, asking whether and in what way each one furthers the topic idea. Does each one particularize it, illustrating it or comparing it or supporting it in some other useful way? If the function of a sentence isn't clear to you, ask yourself whether you should omit the sentence or move it to another position in the paragraph or revise it to link it more closely with its neighbors. But as you work to strengthen the continuity of the paragraph, you'll find it useful not just to look *at* sentences but to look *for* functional units. Perhaps you'll see your paragraph as a two-part structure that can be described as cause+effect or problem+solution or positive+negative or topic+illustration. Or you may see it as consisting of three parts, or four, or more, each relating in some significant way to the others and to the whole paper. Whatever general plan your paragraph follows, identifying the functional units in it will help you see its structure more clearly and decide whether it has a consistent logical movement.

The paragraph below is made up of just two functional units—a generalization that's a topic sentence (the first) and particulars that illustrate it (the other seven):

[1] Frequently the colonists made an old word serve with slightly different meaning. [2] The American red-breasted thrush, for example, was called a *robin;* the European bird which they had called a *robin* in Old England is somewhat smaller and has a yellowish-red breast. [3] *Blackbird,* which in Europe denotes a wild bird allied to the thrushes, was applied in America to any of various birds having black plumage. [4] A number of different brightly colored birds not closely related to the orioles of Europe were nevertheless given that name in this country, for example, the *Baltimore oriole.* [5] Similarly, the European partridge is not the same as its American namesake, or rather namesakes, for in New England *partridge* designates the ruffed grouse and in Virginia the bobwhite quail. [6] *Corn* was applied here to an altogether different cereal and lost its older general meaning "grain." [7] *Huckleberry* is a variant of *hurtleberry,* which is in turn an older form of *whortleberry* "bilberry"; but the American huckleberry is quite a different fruit. [8] *Beech, hemlock, walnut,* and *laurel* also acquired new meanings in the colonies.—Thomas Pyles, *Words and Ways of American English*

The format is open-ended, in the sense that illustrations could be put in or pulled out and the paragraph shortened or lengthened without changing the basic structure. Though the examples that validate the opening statement don't come at random—we would be disturbed if, say, the last sentence broke into the cluster of examples in sentences 2–5—the four categories of examples could be shifted around, and other categories could be added.

When you write such a paragraph, ask yourself questions like these: Do the examples really bear on the opening statement? Is each one interesting in its own right? Are they of roughly the same significance, so that the order doesn't matter much, or are some more important than others? Should I leave the paragraph open-ended, or should I close it out with an example that's clearly climactic?

In the paragraph that follows, the abstract pattern—the underlying "plot"—also has a two-part structure. The "roles" of the first sentence are elaborated on in the next three. But because the sentences lengthen and the details become increasingly specific, this paragraph has a climactic effect:

> [1] In the media, women appear primarily in supportive roles as housewives, secretaries and girl friends. [2] They usually are incapable of initiating actions of their own; they get into difficulties from which they must be extricated by their men. [3] When not treated as weak and scatter-brained, women are likely to be portrayed as devious, dehumanized sex objects, the ornaments of male egoism. [4] In media advertisements women seem exclusively concerned with getting a fluffy glow shampooed into their hair, waxing "their" floors, making yummy coffee for hubby, getting Johnny's clothes snowy white, and in other ways serving as mindless, cheery household drones.—Michael Parenti, *Democracy for the Few*

The simple two-part structure of topic+illustration or topic+development can be extended by adding functional units. Thus you can write a paragraph of three units—topic+restriction(or development)+illustration. The middle stage, which may consist of several sentences, modifies or restricts the topic idea, narrows and limits it, defines it, or extends it. The following paragraph has three related units—topic (sentence 1), specification or development (sentences 2 and 3), illustration (sentences 4–6):

> [1] Once in a great while, a man all of a sudden finds himself completely happy and content. [2] His stomach feels good; he's breathing fine and easy; there's nothing whatever bothering him in his mind; the sun is shining, perhaps, but it doesn't have

to be; a breeze is blowing gently, perhaps, but it doesn't need to be; and nearby there is something or somebody he has a deep fondness for. [3] What he's fond of can be a boat, or a woman, or a horse – anything at all. [4] About eleven o'clock in the morning on Tuesday, April 14th, I was silently grateful to find myself in that pleasant fix. [5] At that hour, I was sitting alone in a warm and comfortable room no more than thirty yards away from the stall in which stood the race horse Native Dancer. [6] I have a deep fondness for Native Dancer. – John McNulty, *New Yorker*

As the preceding paragraph indicates, combinations of functional units are used not only in scholarly formal prose but in personal writing that's relaxed in tone. Still, a long, closely reasoned paragraph is likely to have the greater number of functional units; and before submitting a paper that has special importance for you, you may want to keep on subdividing units and seeing how they relate to each other until you can account for parts of sentences as well as for whole sentences and groups of sentences.

The General Plan

The three paragraphs quoted in the preceding section (from Pyles, Parenti, and McNulty) are all built on the support plan. This is the favorite plan in exposition and argument because it offers the easiest way of keeping the reader informed about what's coming next. Probably most of the expository paragraphs you write will follow this order. The opening sentence (or the one following any transitional material) more or less establishes the dimensions of the discussion by telling either what the subject is (topic sentence) or what procedure will be followed (pointer). After this initial statement come other statements that illustrate, interpret, extend, explain, qualify, or refute. (Sentences that "support" an opening generalization don't necessarily back it up or prove it. They may even contradict it. The point is that in one way or another they're all related to it.) The supporting statements may be roughly equivalent to each other, as in Pyles, or they may be built one upon another to reflect a train of reasoning or to move to a particular situation, as in McNulty.

In writing a paragraph on the support plan, you can make it move clearly toward a conclusion – a *therefore* – or establish its scope with a pointer opening like "Three qualities make her recordings consistently successful." You can leave it open-ended: "She has several qualities that contribute to the success of her records. She is. . . . She is. . . ." And so on. You can round it out with a climactic particular or signal the ending with a close like "These are the qualities the public applauds when it buys her records." Restatement of the initial generalization – perhaps with more emphasis, perhaps with qualifications – is common when the material is complicated or the paragraph long. Even a fairly short paragraph will be improved by a restatement that doesn't just repeat but gives fresh expression to the leading idea – perhaps, as in this example, through the use of a telling quotation:

> Neighborhoods – Boston is a city of neighborhoods. That, aggravated by racism, is the crux of its busing problem. To outsiders, the violence has been shocking, for Boston was long considered a mellow citadel of high culture, liberalism, old money and young students – the Athens of America. But the reality is far different: This is largely a working-class city, shaped by a unique history. The wealth and the liberals are in the suburbs now. Beyond the cosmopolitan center of town lie distinct, easily defined neighborhoods bracketed by ethnic origin and economic status. The neighborhood boundaries are reflected in postal zones, political wards, police districts and the jurisdictions of the lower courts. City Councilor "Dapper" O'Neil, a roseate-faced pol of the old school who can fly into a paroxysm of wrath at the drop of a judicial gavel, winds up his orations with a ringing defense of "our neighborhood churches, our neighborhood schools, our neighborhood shopping centers."
> – John Kifner, *New York Times Magazine*

Whether or not the end of a support paragraph should be signaled by restatement or some other device can usually be decided only in context. At the end of a sequence of paragraphs you'll naturally want a firmer conclusion than for a paragraph within a sequence.

Though less common than the support structure, the discovery structure – the paragraph that leads the reader through a series of particulars to an inference or a generalization – has distinct advantages in some rhetorical situations. You may have any one of several motives for withholding the topic idea until the end of the paragraph: to make readers feel they're sharing in the process of discovery; to give them easier access, through specific details, to a complicated or difficult generalization; to counteract initial hostility; to achieve dramatic impact. In any case, when the movement is *toward* a generalization, it's especially important that the particulars feed logically into one another and so into the generalization. The readers won't know just what the discussion is leading to, but they should have a sense that every detail is making its contribution.

Many paragraphs that aren't clear-cut discovery in format gain their persuasiveness through an accumulation of evidence that gives the impression of discovery. In the following passage each paragraph has the kind of movement we call discovery, the second to a greater degree than the first. That the two paragraphs form a block is indicated by the connection between sentences 3–4 of the first paragraph – "Firewood, in essence, is mysterious. For example, when it is kindled and burned it almost completely disappears" – and the last sentence of the second – "Logs burning in a fireplace are making and burning gasoline." The first paragraph introduces a mystery. By the end of the second, the mystery has been solved.

There was a time when New England farmers preferred to cut firewood under the influence of a waning moon. Something to do with the tides. Firewood, in essence, is mysterious. For example, when it is kindled and burned it almost completely disappears. The nature of firewood seems to be in the mind of the believer. Some people believe that black cherry, burning, sends out clouds of befouling soot. It no doubt does, in their houses. Others smell cherries when black cherry burns, smell apples in smouldering apple. Some people say that wood splits more easily when it is freshly cut; others say to wait until it has seasoned and checked. Still others say that it depends on the wood: you can't split fresh apple with a pile driver, but at the tap of an axe fresh oak will fall apart into boards. Most people have thought that green wood is wood that has been recently cut from a living tree, no matter at what time of year, and that seasoned wood is wood that has been drying for at least six months. This has been the impression of silviculturists, dendrologists, and foresters, for example, who go to universities and are taught that trees are full of water in the winter as in summer.

Science was once certain that firewood was full of something called phlogiston, a mysterious inhabitant that emerged after kindling and danced around in the form of light and heat and crackling sound – phlogiston, the substance of fire. Science, toward the end of the eighteenth century, erased that beautiful theory, replacing it with certain still current beliefs, which are related to the evident fact that green wood is half water. Seasoning, it dries down until, typically, the water content is twenty per cent. Most hardwoods – oak, maple, cherry, hickory – will season in six months. Ash, the firewood of kings, will season in half the time. When firewood burns, it makes vapor of the water. The rest of the log is (almost wholly) carbon, hydrogen, and oxygen – the three components of cellulose, also of starch and sugar. When a log is thrown on the fire, the molecules on the surface become agitated and begin to move vigorously. Some vibrate. Some rotate. Some travel swiftly from one place to another. The cellulose molecule is long, complicated, convoluted – thousands of atoms like many balls on a few long strings. The strings have a breaking point. The molecule, tumbling, whipping, vibrating, breaks apart. Hydrogen atoms, stripping away, snap into oxygen atoms that are passing by in the uprushing stream of air, forming even more water, which goes up the chimney as vapor. Incandescent carbon particles, by the tens of millions, leap free of the log and wave like banners, as flame. Several hundred significantly different chemical reactions are now going on. For example, a carbon atom and four hydrogen atoms, coming out of the breaking cellulose, may lock together and form methane, natural gas. The methane, burning (combining with oxygen), turns into carbon dioxide and water, which also go up the flue. If two carbon atoms happen to come out of the wood with six hydrogen atoms, they are, agglomerately, ethane, which burns to become, also, carbon dioxide and water. Three carbons and eight hydrogens form propane, and propane is there, too, in the fire. Four carbons and ten hydrogens—butane. Five carbons . . . pentane. Six . . . hexane. Seven . . . heptane. Eight carbons and eighteen hydrogens—octane. All these compounds come away in the breaking of the cellulose molecule, and burn, and go up the chimney as carbon dioxide and water. Pentane, hexane, heptane, and octane have a collective name. Logs burning in the fireplace are making and burning gasoline.—John McPhee, *Pieces of the Frame* (appeared originally in *The New Yorker*)

The pro-and-con movement has a more complex structure than those illustrated so far. After opening with a generalization, which is given support, the paragraph takes a turn in another (but related) direction, signaled by *but, still, however,* or some similar contrast. This two-stage movement is well suited to balancing a positive against a negative—advantages against disadvantages, say—and it's a natural choice for a paragraph in which you set out to qualify or refute a widespread notion:

It's an unattractive human truth, but every now and then someone should put it on record: most people—Christians used to acknowledge this fact without embarrassment—most people are not particularly talented or beautiful or charismatic. Set free to discover "the true self," very often they find nothing there at all. Men and women who determine "to do their own thing" commonly learn that they have little of note to do. Yet these people are harassed, shamed by the Zeitgeist and its glib armies into disparaging their conventional roles. The bubble-gum tune goes like this: American civilization, through some spiteful, stupid conspiracy, means to thwart self-expression. We are all frustrated painters, explorers, starlets, senators. But there are times when it's more healthful to be frustrated than to have one's mediocrity confirmed in the light of common day.—D. Keith Mano, *Newsweek*

The pro-and-con movement is also useful for refining and qualifying your own generalizations. In the paragraph that follows, the pro-and-con movement is repeated several times, and the regular alternation of negative and positive statements about the average man of Lincoln's generation permits the writer to move judiciously to a final generalization that's considerably stronger than the initial one:

The average Western American of Lincoln's generation was fundamentally a man who subordinated his intelligence to certain dominant practical interests and purposes. He was far from being a stupid or slow-witted man. On the contrary, his wits had been sharpened by the traffic of American politics and business, and his mind was shrewd, flexible, and alert. But he was wholly incapable either of disinterested or of concentrated intellectual exertion. His energies were bent in the conquest of certain stubborn external forces, and he used his intelligence almost exclusively to this end. The struggles, the hardships, and the necessary self-denial of pioneer life constituted an admirable training of the will. It developed a body of men with great resolution of purpose and with great ingenuity and fertility in adapting their insufficient means to the realization of their important business affairs. But their almost exclusive preoccupation with practical tasks and their failure to grant their intelligence any room for independent exercise bent them into exceedingly warped and one-sided human beings. — Herbert Croly, *The Promise of American Life*

Organizing a paragraph on the pro-and-con pattern will make it possible for you to indicate your awareness of conflicting opinions and of the need to modify and qualify your own generalizations. Handled well, it suggests that you've explored the subject thoroughly. Handled badly, it can give the impression that you're sitting on the fence, evading the responsibility of making clear what your own ideas on the subject are. Usually a pro-and-con paragraph needs to end with a forceful, positive statement that leaves the reader in no doubt as to the writer's final judgment.

Not every content paragraph you write will conform to one of the patterns illustrated here, but every paragraph you write should have some discernible pattern. Each should be built in such a way that your readers will sense the direction in which your thought is moving, be able to follow it through the functional units you incorporate, and end up with a feeling of comprehension and satisfaction. In all but the shortest papers you'll naturally vary the structure of your paragraphs to accommodate your material.

■ *For Analysis and Writing*

1. Describe and evaluate the structure of each of the paragraphs below. Consider these questions: What are the main functional units in the paragraph? Is the paragraph tightly unified, in the sense that all the sentences in it bear directly on the core of meaning? Or do some of the sentences relate to the core only loosely? Is the paragraph tightly structured, in the sense that the order of the sentences couldn't be altered without damaging the unity of the paragraph, or could some of the sentences be interchanged? If you find that one paragraph is less unified than the others or looser in structure, can you justify the difference in terms of the subject and general style?

a. In American cities the size of Kansas City, a careful traveling man has to observe the rule that any restaurant the executive secretary of the chamber of commerce is particularly proud of is almost certainly not worth eating in. Its name will be something like La Maison de la Casa House, Continental cuisine; its food will sound European but taste as if the continent they had in mind was Australia. Lately, a loyal chamber man in practically any city is likely to recommend one of those restaurants that have sprouted in the last several years on the tops of bank buildings, all of them encased in glass and some of them revolving — offering the diner not only Continental cuisine and a twenty-thousand-word menu but a spectacular view of other restaurants spinning around on the top of other bank buildings. "No, thank you," I finally said to the twelfth gracious host who invited me to one of those. "I never eat in a restaurant that's over a hundred feet off the ground and won't stand still." — Calvin Trillin, *American Fried*

b. Right from the beginning I understood that flirting had its own rules and its own chivalry. I knew I should not flirt a serious favor out of someone; a small favor was OK. I knew that I must not as a woman abuse my privilege to flirt, that I should not flirt to inflame the jealousy of a present love or to tease the passion of a prospective one. Then flirting became a weapon and to my mind just wasn't flirting any more. To me flirting was the delicate eye-play, talk-play, touchless touching by which I could show affection or approval for someone else, tell him he was pleasing to me, without promising anything or hurting anyone. — Anne Taylor Fleming, *Newsweek*

c. Fort Hood. Fort Bragg. Fort Leavenworth. Fort Benning. Fort Lewis. The big army bases in the United States are tight societies, forts in more ways than one. A man and his family need never leave the post, not for birth, marriage, or death, not for shelter, food, fuel, or clothing, not for golf, drinks, dinner, dancing, or movies. A man is encouraged to spend his money on the base — as who would not, considering the bargains? One hundred and fifty dollars for an AKAI tape recorder worth two hundred, fifty cents for a V.O. and soda at the NCO club. A man can worship a nondenominational God ("army God," a senior soldier described Him) and putt on an army green and have a tooth pulled by an army dentist, and all the time call it home. There is only one thing that the Army doesn't have. It doesn't have schools for the children, at least at the bases in the United States it doesn't. — Ward Just, *Atlantic*

d. The informer—the Judas figure—has been an odious creature in the popular mind throughout history. Even so, governments have always used his services, and one measure of freedom in any society is the extent to which the informer flourishes.
In a tyranny, the informer contributes a basic necessity to the
tyrant's survival—the people's fear of him—by demonstrating
that any deviant political expression or behavior may be reported
to the state, and then punished. In a democracy, on the other
hand, the sovereignty of the people is supposed to encourage
diversity of thought and allow open dissent and outright opposition to the public policies of those who are elected to run things
temporarily. But even the most democratically conceived government comes to behave as if its own survival, rather than the
people's welfare, is the paramount good. This happens not because democracy inevitably degenerates into tyranny through repressive leadership at the top but because the government's
ordinary day-to-day operations depend on entrenched "public
servants"—the bureaucracy—who are always most concerned
about protecting and expanding their own power. In time, bureaucrats transform government into a kind of private institution
that exists for their sake, and this makes them deeply committed
to preserving the system—*their* system—as it is. The deeper
their commitment, the more alarmed they are likely to be by anything that seems to threaten the system; and the more alarmed
they become, the more likely they are to resort to extreme measures to meet the threat. One extreme measure that is being increasingly resorted to by government in the United States today
is the official use of informers from the bottom to the top of our
society.—Richard Harris, *New Yorker*

2. *Drawing on subjects of your own choosing, write a paragraph that follows closely the* structure *of one of the paragraphs you've analyzed in 1 above. You might, for instance,
write a paragraph on motels that imitates the structure of
Trillin's paragraph on restaurants, or a paragraph on gossiping that imitates the structure of Fleming's on flirting.*

3. *Compose a paragraph that sets forth both the advantages
and the disadvantages of a proposed course of action. Make
sure that by the end of the paragraph the reader will know
whether you do or do not support the proposal.*

Paragraph Coherence

A paragraph is coherent if it hangs together as a whole (if
it has unity) and if the thought flows smoothly and consecutively from sentence to sentence (if it has continuity).
Initially, coherence is an intellectual matter. It has its
origin in a writer's sure grasp of what he wants to say. To
convey to your readers the relationships you perceive
among your ideas, you can use a variety of techniques—
repeating, partially repeating, or echoing key words and

ideas; repeating grammatical patterns; introducing overt transitions like *but* and *therefore;* and, on occasion, telling readers explicitly what the preceding paragraph (or sequence of paragraphs) has done and what the next one will do. But if you're to use these various ways of linking sentences and paragraphs successfully, you must first know what it is you want to say.

If you don't think through what you want to say, you're likely to produce paragraphs like this one:

> Many good citizens find it hard to convince themselves that their vote will make any difference. Men of good will have been voting for generations with little effect. The same hacks and manipulators seem to get into office every time, and the same corrupt Establishment runs the show. When a young person becomes eligible to vote in a national election, he should either acquaint himself with the issues and the policies of the candidates or use the day to catch up on lost sleep. Voting Republican or Democratic because that's how your parents vote is irresponsible if not stupid. A thoughtless vote can cancel an intelligent one, and this country has no intelligent votes to spare.

Three sentences on one topic, three on another—the structural gap suggests that the writer made two different stabs at his subject. That might have turned out all right if he had thrown one away, settled down to work on the other, and developed it adequately, but instead he simply jammed the two together. The result: an incoherent paragraph. And tinkering with it won't help. Merely inserting transitional words, for instance, would be useless. Before he can revise it sensibly, the writer must decide what he wants to talk about and what he wants to say. Coherent writing requires coherent thinking.

Though unified content and orderly movement are necessary for coherence, they're not enough to guarantee it. Even if every sentence in a paragraph has a bearing on the central point, and even if the order of the sentences is sensible, the paragraph may fail to give readers a sense of wholeness and an understanding of how one thought relates to another. The grammatical aspect of coherence has to do with the writer's skill in making clear to his audience the connections he himself perceives in his material. The following paragraph is hard to read because the sentences seem to be sealed off from one another; the reader gets no help at all in trying to move from one statement to the next.

> When Richard Nixon was elected President, bringing the American people together was supposedly one of his primary

goals. It can be argued that President Nixon made no attempt to unify America. There were no discernible gains in national unity during the Nixon administration; in fact, disunity increased. The trouble with a slogan like "Bring us together" was that it had no specific meaning. With a population as large as ours, it was ridiculous to expect everyone to agree on such issues as the war in Vietnam, race relations, national and personal goals, and life-styles. The American people have seldom been unified for long, and their unity has always been limited. World War II was supported by a large majority of Americans. Some of our parents and grandparents hated Hitler; some feared Japan; some wanted to save Western civilization from barbarism; some got rich on defense contracts and black marketeering. After the collapse of the Axis and the death of Franklin Roosevelt, the public demanded the immediate disbanding of our military forces and the abandonment of wartime controls.

Probably the habit of thinking in single sentences is at least partially responsible for the lack of cohesiveness in this paragraph. Or you might produce something like it in a first draft if you simply copied down the notes you'd made in the prewriting stage. In either case, the sentence-at-a-time procedure results in a series of independent units rather than the sequence of *related* statements that coherence requires. In the revision below, the sentences reflect a logical train of thought. Words and phrases have been added to bring out the connections in the material and so guide the reader. Each sentence looks back to the one before it, and this interdependence of the sentences makes the whole paragraph cohere. Now it strikes the mind as a unit, not simply as a collection of sentences.

When Nixon was elected President, bringing the American people together was supposedly one of his primary goals. Whether he made any attempt to achieve that goal is debatable; that he failed to do so is not. But could anyone have succeeded? Presumably success in bringing us together would have meant securing general agreement on issues and problems like the Vietnam War and race relations, on national goals, perhaps even on personal goals and life-styles. But the fact is that the American people have never been "together" except on limited issues for limited periods of time. Even during World War II, a period frequently pointed to as one of maximum national unity, those who supported the war (and a sizable minority did not) supported it for divergent reasons – from the most noble and idealistic to the most crass and self-serving. The war – and Franklin Roosevelt – brought Americans together, but with the end of the war and Roosevelt's death, the temporary and superficial nature of that unity was quickly revealed.

You can use both lexical and grammatical means to make your paragraphs coherent. *Lexical means* include repeating key words and introducing transitional words and phrases to connect sentences. *Grammatical means* include continuing the same grammatical subject or its equivalent (a pronoun, for example) through successive sentences and repeating grammatical patterns — that is, giving sentences and parts of sentences the same grammatical form. All these devices will contribute to the sentence-by-sentence consecutiveness of your paragraphs.

Repetition and Parallelism

The repetition of key words and grammatical patterns is illustrated in the passage by McPhee that appears earlier in this chapter. Note, for example, how the author gives focus to his paragraphs by repeating "firewood," "wood," and the related pronoun "it":

> There was a time when New England farmers preferred to cut *firewood* under the influence of a waning moon. Something to do with the tides. *Firewood*, in essence, is mysterious. For example, when *it* is kindled and burned *it* almost completely disappears. The nature of *firewood* seems to be in the mind of the believer. . . . Some people say that *wood* splits more easily when *it* is freshly cut; others say to wait until *it* has seasoned and checked. Still others say that it depends on the *wood*. . . .

In the last two sentences quoted, McPhee uses consistent grammatical patterns. Though "wood" continues to echo through the passage, the emphasis shifts to the beliefs people have about it: "Some people say . . . ; others say. . . . Still others say. . . ."

Repeating key words and their synonyms and putting into similar grammatical structures (phrases, clauses, sentences) ideas or details that are logically coordinate are devices for achieving coherence that you probably use without thinking about it. If you're having difficulty with coherence, though, you'll want to make use of them consciously and deliberately. Just be careful that you don't give them such prominence that your writing seems labored and artificial. Notice the casual remark that McPhee drops in as his second sentence in the passage just quoted. And note that he keeps his parallel structures flexible, varying their length and avoiding complete parallelism at times ("Some people say that wood splits . . . ; others say to wait until it has seasoned . . .").

In revising your first drafts, then, check each paragraph for coherence and, where necessary, introduce whatever grammatical and lexical repetitions are needed to make clear the focus you intend and to guide readers through the sequence of ideas you're presenting. Meanwhile, look out for—and get rid of—unintentional repetitions that either make your prose boring to read or suggest connections in meaning where none exist.

The combination of a key word and its related pronouns and synonyms—all the words and phrases that in the context have roughly the same meaning or that refer to the same thing—creates an *equivalence chain*. The simplest chain is a pronoun and its antecedent ("it," "wood") or a pair of words or phrases that are synonymous ("wood," "log"; "flue," "chimney"); sometimes a chain consists of a dozen variations on the central meaning of the key term. In this example the words in italics show how a dominant equivalence chain can link all the sentences of a paragraph:

No other living *writer* has yielded himself so completely and recklessly as has *Isaac Bashevis Singer* to the claims of the human imagination. *Singer* writes in Yiddish, a language that no amount of energy and affection seems likely to save from extinction. *He* writes about a world that is gone, destroyed with a brutality beyond historical comparison. *He* writes within a culture, the remnant of Yiddish in the Western world, that is more than a little dubious about *his* purpose and stress. *He* seems to take entirely for granted *his role* as a traditional *storyteller* speaking to an audience attuned to *his* every hint and nuance, an audience that values *storytelling* both in *its* own right and as a binding communal action—but also, as it happens, an audience that keeps fading week by week, shrinking day by day. And *he* does *all this* without a sigh or an apology, without so much as a Jewish groan. It strikes one as a kind of inspired madness: here is a *man* living in New York City, a sophisticated and clever *writer,* who *composes stories* about Frampol, Bilgoray, Kreshev AS IF THEY WERE STILL THERE. *His work* is shot through with the bravado of a *performer* who enjoys making *his* listeners gasp, weep, laugh, and yearn for more. Above and beyond everything else *he* is a great *performer,* in ways that remind one of Twain, Dickens, Sholom Aleichem.—Irving Howe, Introduction to *Selected Short Stories of Isaac Bashevis Singer*

In the fifth sentence, "his role," one item in the dominant chain, initiates the sequence "storyteller," "his," "storytelling," "its," "all this," "composes stories." In the same way, "his work" introduces "performer." These words and phrases, all stemming from the key word "Singer," make a network of relationships linking the ideas. The paragraph contains other equivalence chains, among them "audience," "listeners." Parallelism of verbs strengthens continuity not only by the repetition of "writes" in three successive sentences but also by the consistent use of the present tense: "seems," "does," and so on. And parallelism of other words and phrases plays a role in keeping the stress where the author wants it. But by far the strongest cohesive force in the paragraph is the recurrence of the same grammatical subject, or its equivalent, from sentence to sentence. A new subject is introduced only when it's needed to mark a shift in the point of view ("It strikes one" in the third-to-last sentence).

What you should work to avoid in your own writing is not *every* shift in point of view but only shifts that are erratic, unmotivated, illogical – the changes in person, voice, tense, and structural pattern classed as shifted constructions. Consistency in these matters contributes to the grammatical cohesion of a paragraph; lack of consistency detracts from it and gives even a well-unified paragraph a general air of incoherence.

Though using similar grammatical subjects is a dependable means of maintaining continuity, it's not always feasible. The process of reasoning from premises to conclusion or of relating causes to effects calls for a different procedure. Instead of invariably returning to the one subject (or a related subject), a writer may knit his sentences together by having the subject of a sentence grow out of the predicate of the preceding sentence. Even in informal writing, the strongest links may occur not between grammatical subject and grammatical subject but between the end of one sentence and the beginning of the next, as in the paragraph by Harris on p. 149 and the paragraph beginning "When Nixon" on p. 151.

■ *For Analysis and Writing*

Rewrite the following paragraphs to make them more coherent. Pay special attention to getting rid of unnecessary shifts in grammatical subject and in point of view.

a. Counselors often rely very heavily on test scores for an insight into a student's mental ability and interests. Children are subjected to I.Q. tests all through elementary school. The most important of these tests is taken in the eighth grade. Advisors use these results to determine what kind of program a student is capable of following. It may seem very reasonable, but test scores are not always an accurate measure of a person's mental ability. Another kind of test that is popular is the interest test. I remember taking one of these tests and scoring high in business. Business has always seemed loathsome to me. But when asked questions like, "What would you rather be, a garage mechanic, a termite exterminator, or a secretary?" I quickly answered, "A secretary." Such tests are clearly not only worthless as guides to ability but are also an absolute waste of time.

b. At the opening whistle the two sides burst into action. They had been preparing themselves for this for weeks. Many long hours of tiring practice were behind us, and now was the time to prove just how much endurance we had built up. Sweat began flowing in streams and breath came in gasps. The first time the ball sailed through the air, the clean swish of the net was met with deafening applause. Every bounce, twist, and turn of the orange sphere was alertly followed by all eyes. The players felt the pressure more and more as the game progressed and the figures on the scoreboard remained ever so close. "Push yourself harder, harder!" I kept repeating to myself as my limbs began to ache with tiredness.

Transitions

The most overt signals of movement in paragraphs—as between them—are connecting words, phrases, and clauses that spell out the relations between ideas and, in so doing, help make the paragraphs coherent. Most common of these signals are the coordinating conjunctions (*and, but, or, nor, for, so, yet*), the conjunctive adverbs (*however, indeed, moreover,* and so on), and phrases like *of course, for example, in the first place.* In some of their uses, subordinating conjunctions (*because, since*) and simple adverbs (*then, here*) also mark transitions.

What the scores of transitional words, phrases, and clauses all have in common is the function of calling the reader's attention to the role played by a statement or by a paragraph. As such, they make for cohesiveness, binding ideas together and bringing out connections in the material. They can also be misused: an *and* may disguise a break in logical continuity; a *therefore* may suggest that an argument has been clinched when in fact nothing relevant has been proved.

Transitional words and phrases are italicized in the paragraph below. Note that the favorite position for transitional markers is at or near the beginnings of sentences. A connector placed early in a sentence will usually do its job most efficiently.

What unites the horror movie and the science fiction film is their concern with the phenomenon of fear. *To be sure,* there are many differences between their approaches. The horror film, *for instance,* ordinarily locates its dangers in the realm of the supernatural or in the murky twistings and turnings of abnormal psychology, while the science fiction movie most often finds the frightful in a futuristic and misguided technology. *And* where the menace in the horror movie usually attacks an individual or at most a small group, the nemesis in the science fiction film tends to be a potential threat to society as a whole. *But* whether it's mankind or the individual who is the potential victim, science or magic or man himself who acts out the part of villain, the terror these films present us with must, to be genuinely terrifying, address some universal concern. — Joy Gould Boyum, *Wall Street Journal*

While transitional markers seem to be the simplest of devices for achieving coherence, using them well calls for care and discrimination. If you use too few, your sentences may strike a reader as unrelated to one another, as in the example on pp. 150–51, and the train of thought will be hard to follow. If you use too many, your style will be heavy-handed. *For example* is the typical marker to indicate that what follows illustrates what has come before or particularizes it in some way; but if you use *for example* to signal every such instance, readers will feel you're lecturing them.

The need for explicit signals of transition depends partly on your subject and your purpose. When the thought drives straight ahead, they're unnecessary. When the thought is complex, it's your responsibility to mark its path. You'll also use more explicit transitions when your purpose is to inform or instruct than when your aim is simply to suggest a possibility or propose an interpretation.

The need for overt signals of transition should also be judged in relation to other means of achieving coherence. In a paragraph that already has consistent focus and well-made equivalence chains, logical relationships may not have to be indicated by connectors. You don't need to tell your readers twice how one statement relates to another. When they get their clues from the language of the discussion itself, they'll prefer not to be elbowed from one sentence into another by a *therefore* or an *as a result*. And some clues are wordless: as in this sentence, a colon can do the work of *for example*. Indeed, just placing one sentence immediately after another can signal a relation of addition or, in other contexts, of contrast or causality. Transitions can be implied as well as expressed.

The following paragraph, which begins a long paper, uses no explicit signals of transition, yet the thought develops clearly and smoothly from the first sentence to the last:

Even a casual reader of Ernest Hemingway's stories about Nick Adams will leave that collection with at least a vague sense of continuity, emotional if not chronological. The characteristic emotion is an almost overwhelming anxiety, which is simply intensified by arranging the stories chronologically. One leaves these stories, almost all of them, with a sense of dread: an unrelieved tension pervades and projects from them. Writing on a different topic entirely, T. S. Eliot described very well the narrative method used by Hemingway in the stories about Nick Adams. Eliot speaks of "a set of objects, a situation, a chain of events which shall be the formula of that *particular* emotion; such that when the facts, which must terminate in sensory experience, are given, the emotion is immediately evoked." The impact of the stories is remarkably consistent because Hemingway repeatedly uses a set of objects (a long, yellow house or a swelling river), a situation (characterized by traumatic violence), or a chain of events (culminating in a wound) to evoke a particular emotion – anxiety.

In selecting a transitional marker, then, be sure first of all that you need one. If you're convinced you do, be sure the one you choose expresses the logical relationship you intend. And when you have a choice of markers to signal the relationship, pick the one that best suits your style and that provides the emphasis you want.

■ *For Analysis*

Identify and explain the function of the transitional words and phrases in the paragraph by Adrian and Press on p. 137. Explain why these transitional markers are or are not necessary to the reader's comprehension of the ideas.

Development and Coherence in Paragraph Sequences

Plainly there are many techniques for developing paragraphs and for binding ideas together, in paragraphs, in paragraph sequences, in whole papers. Which ones you should choose will depend on the nature and complexity of your subject and on your purpose in dealing with it. On occasion, particularly in examinations, you'll find that restrictions of time or space or both make it necessary for you to discuss a broad subject briefly. But even then, though you're forced to deal in large generalizations, you'll find that the means of relating ideas and achieving coherence are much the same as when you're treating subjects of smaller scope in greater detail.

The complete article reprinted below is a good example of how a professional writer handles a very large subject for a general audience of readers who are interested in keeping up with what's going on and who are therefore presumably familiar with the major events of the recent past. (Allusions to "Potomac fever" and the Gulag Archipelago are probably safe. Reference to Kossuth is more of a gamble.) Though the article is short, it has a distinct movement. The author's ideas progress through stages — represented by parts, or paragraph sequences — and the means of achieving coherence are nicely adjusted to the methods used to develop and organize the discussion. In the commentary, S stands for "sentence," Ss for "sentences."

¶s 1–2 form the first part, or paragraph sequence. ¶1 defines the United States as an idea. The definition is built by contrast (Ss 1, 3, 4) and, more important, by division. The "idea" is partitioned into its elements, and beginning with S2, coherence is achieved through the use of "it" as subject of every sentence. Ss 2, 3, 5, and 6 are all on the same level of generalization. S4 particularizes S3. Parallelism, used throughout the article, is especially noticeable in the three clauses that end ¶1.

¶2 uses the same devices as ¶1: "it," the subject of S2, makes "idea," the subject of S1, the center of the paragraph. The simple series of nouns in S1 and the more elaborate parallelism of S2 provide the writer with very economical ways of qualifying and particularizing in S2 the assertion that "the idea" remained dominant for "the first 100 years."

¶s 3–4 form a second paragraph sequence. ¶3 opens with a transitional sentence, with "idea" pointing back to ¶s 1–2 and the second clause ("it was never . . .") introducing the notion of opposing forces. These are dealt with throughout ¶3. S2 and S3 are closely linked, S3 particularizing S2 and establishing a

¶1 [1] The United States is a nation consciously conceived, not one that evolved slowly out of an ancient past. [2] It was a planned idea of democracy, of liberty of conscience and pursuit of happiness. [3] It was the promise of equality of opportunity and individual freedom within a just social order, as opposed to the restrictions and repressions of the Old World. [4] In contrast to the militarism of Europe, it would renounce standing armies and "sheathe the desolating sword of war." [5] It was an experiment in Utopia to test the thesis that given freedom, independence and local self-government, people, in Kossuth's words, "will in due time ripen into all the excellence and all the dignity of humanity." [6] It was a new life for the oppressed, it was enlightenment, it was optimism.

¶2 [1] Regardless of hypocrisy and corruption, of greed, chicanery, brutality and all the other bad habits man carries with him whether in the New World or Old, the founding idea of the United States remained, on the whole, dominant through the first 100 years. [2] With reservations, it was believed in by Americans, by visitors who came to aid our Revolution or later to observe our progress, by immigrants who came by the hundreds of thousands to escape an intolerable situation in their native lands.

¶3 [1] The idea shaped our politics, our institutions and to some extent our national character, but it was never the only influence at work. [2] Material circumstances exerted an opposing force. [3] The open frontier, the hardships of homesteading from scratch, the wealth of natural resources, the whole vast challenge of a continent waiting to be exploited, combined to produce a prevailing materialism and an American drive bent as much, if not more, on money, property, and power than was true of the Old World from which we had fled. ⁴ The human resources we drew upon were significant: every wave of immigration brought here those people who had the extra energy, gumption or restlessness to uproot themselves and cross an unknown ocean to seek a better life. ⁵ Two other factors entered the shaping process – the shadow of slavery and the destruction of the native Indian.

¶4 ¹ At its Centennial, the United States was a material success. ² Through its second century, the idea and the success have struggled in continuing conflict. ³ The Statue of Liberty, erected in 1886, still symbolized the promise to those "yearning to breathe free." ⁴ Hope, to them, as seen by a foreign visitor, was "domiciled in America as the Pope is in Rome." ⁵ But slowly in the struggle the idea lost ground, and at a turning point around 1900, with American acceptance of a rather half-hearted imperialism, it lost dominance. ⁶ Increasingly invaded since then by self-doubt and disillusion, it survives in the disenchantment of today, battered and crippled but not vanquished.

¶5 ¹ What has happened to the United States in the twentieth century is not a peculiarly American phenomenon but a part of the experience of the West. ² In the Middle Ages, plague, wars and social violence were seen as God's punishment upon man for his sins. ³ If the concept of God can be taken as man's conscience, the same explanation may be applicable today. ⁴ Our sins in the twentieth century – greed, violence, inhumanity – have been profound, with the result that the pride and self-confidence of the nineteenth century have turned to dismay and self-disgust.

¶6 ¹ In the United States we have a society pervaded from top to bottom by contempt for the law. ² Government – including the agencies of law enforcement – business, labor, students, the military, the poor no less than the rich, outdo each other in breaking the rules and violating the ethics that society has established for its protection. ³ The average citizen, trying to hold a footing in standards of morality and conduct he once believed in, is daily knocked over by incoming waves of venality, vulgarity, irresponsibility, ignorance, ugliness, and trash in all senses of the

causal relation. S4 and S5 are on the same level of generalization as S2. Mainly because S1 promises an enumeration, sentence-to-sentence connectives are unnecessary in this paragraph. S5, however, does have two devices for maintaining coherence: "other" (in "other factors") and "the shaping process," which repeats in another way the verb "shaped" in S1.

¶4 takes up the "opposing force" introduced in ¶3. S2 sets up the conflict between the "idea" and "material success." A chronological thread makes time indicators of first importance: "through its second century," "in 1886," and so on. In S5 "but" provides transition to the decline of the "idea." Second in importance in maintaining coherence is an equivalence chain ("idea," Ss 4–5; "it," Ss 5–6), like the one in ¶s 1–2.

¶s 5–6 form a third paragraph sequence. ¶5 consists of an explanation or causal analysis of the onset of "self-doubt and disillusion" (¶4, S6). Related terms, "dismay and self-disgust," occur in the last sentence of ¶5.

¶6 extends and particularizes the sins of greed, violence, inhumanity (¶5, S1). S2 particularizes S1. (The "average citizen" of S3 prepares us for ¶7 by indicating that while lawlessness pervades our society, most of us struggle against the breakdown in ethical behavior.) Ss 4–6 make an attack on the government, with "government" and "it" creating a minor equivalence chain.

¶7, the last part of this four-part article, opens with the conjunction "yet," marking a contrast with what precedes. S1 takes us back to the end of ¶4, where "the idea" was last mentioned. Ss 2–4 support S1 with increasing specificity ("Americans" in S2, "we" in S2, "some group" in S3). S5 repeats in a new way the case against America that has been made in ¶6. Again, the assertion is followed by a transitional conjunction marking a contrast ("nevertheless") and introducing a comparative statement. S7 makes a generalization. S8 restates the point made in S5 and ends appropriately with the word "here" – taking us back to the opening words of the article and the references to the United States in ¶s 2, 4, 5, 6, 7. This last paragraph has a pro-and-con structure that achieves coherence chiefly through the use of conjunctions that contrast or qualify.

word. [4] Our government collaborates abroad with the worst enemies of humanity and liberty. [5] It wastes our substance on useless proliferation of military hardware that can never buy security no matter how high the pile. [6] It learns no lessons, employs no wisdom and corrupts all who succumb to Potomac fever.

¶7 [1] Yet the idea does not die. [2] Americans are not passive under their faults. [3] We expose them and combat them. [4] Somewhere every day some group is fighting a public abuse – openly and, on the whole, notwithstanding the FBI, with confidence in the First Amendment. [5] The U.S. has slid a long way from the original idea. [6] Nevertheless, somewhere between Gulag Archipelago and the featherbed of cradle-to-the-grave welfare, it still offers a greater opportunity for social happiness, that is to say, for well-being combined with individual freedom and initiative, than is likely elsewhere. [7] The ideal society for which mankind had been striving through the ages will remain forever beyond our grasp. [8] But if the great question, whether it is still possible to reconcile democracy with social order and individual liberty, is to find a positive answer, it will be here. – Barbara Tuchman, *Newsweek*

■ *For Analysis and Writing*

1. *When a paragraph is unsatisfactory, the trouble may be caused by (1) lack of development – not enough details; (2) lack of unity – no controlling idea; (3) lack of continuity – insufficient indication of the relationship between statements; (4) lack of consistency in point of view or tone or style. Using this checklist as a guide, identify the weaknesses in each of the following, and rewrite to improve the paragraphs.*

a. It is imperative for a show horse to look perfect when walking into the ring. That includes a brushing program and a bath every so often. My hardships began before the show. I gave Chappy a bath and scrubbed until the white coat glistened. I put her in the stall with the amount of straw rationed to all the horses. I packed all my tack for Saturday, turned out the lights and left. I strolled over to the barn in high spirits for the show. When I entered the barn I was appalled at what I saw. The straw was gone and huge stains covered her right side. I hurriedly washed her again. This was the beginning of a ritual I had to perform every week for the show season.

b. The first step in rebuilding a motorcycle is to dismantle the cycle and clean all the parts. All metal parts that aren't chromed should be cleaned with an oil solvent, making sure all build-up of dirt and foreign particles is removed. The parts are then soaked in gasoline, then wiped, dipped in an alcohol solution, then again wiped clean. Chromed parts are cleaned with a light oil solution, rubbed clean, then alcohol-dipped and dried. You should clean the painted parts with plain soap and water. When they are dry, they should be covered with a paint remover. After fifteen minutes, the paint is scraped and sandpapered off until only the bare metal is showing. The metal is then polished with 00 sandpaper until smooth. The only non-metal parts are the battery, lights, tires, and seat, all of which should probably be replaced. When I rebuilt my motorcycle I had a new seat made to my specifications.

c. In *Our Blind Children,* Berthold Lowenfeld discusses four criteria for deciding whether to send a blind child to public or residential school: the personality of the child; his home environment; the geographic relationship between the home and the public school where the special program is available; and the quality of the school. In regard to the first factor, Lowenfeld suggests that consideration be given to how well the blind child has interacted with sighted peers in nursery school experiences. His intelligence is also very important, as Eric T. Boulter points out, for the slow-learning blind child should definitely be placed in a school for the blind. Blind students need from 40% to 60% more time than sighted students to complete assignments. It is obvious, therefore, that blind students having a below-average I.Q. should be placed where the subject matter can be presented more slowly. A blind child's talents and abilities should also be considered. One of the students I interviewed for this project had belonged to her school orchestra. Most blind students could not join an orchestra, for they would have to memorize all their music before they could play. This girl had perfect pitch and could learn the music after hearing it only once or twice. This is more important than it may seem, for there are not many opportunities for a blind student to integrate with sighted students outside of classes. Another blind student, who seemed very timid, told me that she had never joined any organizations in school. The residential school would be a better placement for such students, unless their parents would encourage them to join clubs. In a school for the blind, I am certain this girl would have participated in many activities.

d. I personally prefer prose over poetry, for reasons I'll explain later. I enjoy fiction and non-fiction very much. I do like non-fiction better, though. Nothing can beat a well-written biography, or autobiography. The details and explanations in someone's life are fascinating, and elucidate the human spirit in the individual, and in all of us. *The Diary of Anne Frank* is a good example of this. Her problems with adolescence, combined with her Jewish identity in Nazi Germany, while living in hiding, are written with sensitivity and insight, making her diary a famous autobiography, and wonderful reading material. At the same time, however, I derive great enjoyment out of novels and short

stories. I have been concentrating on novels for the past few
months, and am now realizing the beauty of the novel. I have
said that I prefer non-fiction: I like to read about reality. However, I now recognize the power fiction has in expressing truth
and reality. The more abstract forms of human emotions, such
as freedom and guilt, are beautifully portrayed in such novels
as *1984* and *The Scarlet Letter*, two books that held me spell-
bound this summer. One book I read, *The Fox in the Attic*, was
a combination biography/novel based on the facts of pre-WW II
Europe, but developing fictitious characters. It was a tremendous
book, and showed to me the overlapping of fiction and non-
fiction can be successfully done.

2. *Below is part of a paper analyzing a neighborhood for someone who is trying to decide whether to retire there. The writer
analyzed the subject into three parts: "socializing, property
responsibility, and recreation." This paragraph is the complete part on "socializing."*

*Examine the paragraph to see how it could be improved. Are
all the details necessary and useful? If not, cut the ones that
aren't. Should details be added? If so, make up some and add
them. Is the movement of thought from sentence to sentence
clear and smooth, or should you introduce transitions? Revise
or rewrite to produce a better paragraph.*

Socializing with neighbors will only be accomplished if you
make the first move toward friendship. Many people will not
bring themselves to you, but once you show that you want to
know them, then their hearts are warmed. We have had neighbors move in before who have alienated themselves completely
by never showing or trying a friendship with the family next
door. Our neighborhood will keep to themselves unless you make
the initial move. You will find them quite friendly. Since you are
a senior citizen, you will find that my neighborhood is mostly
adult-oriented. I'm sure you wouldn't prefer a teenage hangout
outside your driveway every night. This is not the case. Only
three teenagers live in the development, and that is with their
parents. However, your tolerance for kids may be tested at times.
You might love kids and no problem will exist. I'm stating this
because I learned you were never married. Some of the older
couples are quite rich and show it off. But most others are middle
income families. We have no poverty problems and like to keep
it that way.

3. *In a paper of 500–750 words, either contrast the version of
love and marriage presented by popular TV programs with the
version presented in recent movies you've seen; or explain
how your own view of love and marriage conforms to or conflicts with another current view of them—that of your parents
or of your friends or of your church, TV, Hollywood, or any
other individual, group, or institution.*

Chapter Five
Persuading Readers

When we think of attempts to persuade, the first examples that come to mind are likely to be television commercials or, if it's around election time, campaign speeches — all-out efforts to sell products or candidates. What we're concerned with in this chapter is persuasion of a more reasoned and reasonable sort. The persuasive papers you write may, like commercials and campaign speeches, urge your audience to *do* something — go out and buy, get out and vote — or they may simply try to win a hearing for a point of view you support. The purpose of this chapter is to suggest methods of persuasion that will help make your arguments work while keeping them fair and honest.

Whether your style is clumsy or slick, the papers you write should grow out of ideas you believe in, principles you hold to be true. And in trying to persuade your readers, you should make every effort to show them that you have good reasons — the best reasons — for holding the beliefs and supporting the positions you do. Don't try to win arguments by slanting the evidence, by blustering and brawling, or by ignoring reason. That persuasion can be dishonest, we all know. It can also be fallacious — that is, based on faulty or illogical reasoning. What you should aim to do is to write *honest* arguments that are *logically sound* and, at the same time, as persuasive as you can make them.

The Ends and the Means of Persuasion

A persuasive paper isn't just an exploration of a topic. It affirms something about the topic. It sets forth and supports a proposition. An expository paper about a college club may explain how the club's activities are related to its purpose. A persuasive paper about the club may shape the same material to support the proposition that, because the club performs valuable functions, it should be subsidized by the college administration; or that, because of certain activities, it should be censured; or that, because the membership rules are discriminatory, it should be disbanded.

Issue, Thesis, Proof

In choosing a topic for a persuasive paper, you must first of all see an *issue* in it. An issue exists when there is disagreement, and the best kind of issue for you is one about which you have convictions you want to express and about which you have, or think you can acquire, adequate information to support those convictions.

Given a live issue, the two essential elements in a persuasive paper are the *thesis* and the *proof*. The thesis, or central proposition, is the conviction—emotional or intellectual or both—or the recommendation for action that represents your stand on the issue. The proof is the evidence you offer to support it. Thesis and proof make up the *what* and the *why* of argument.

Proof in persuasive papers is not the same as scientific demonstration. If we could settle a dispute by demonstrating conclusively that one side was right and the other wrong, presumably there would be no further debate. But the things we argue about from week to week and even from generation to generation (questions of morals and ethics, of crime and punishment, of priorities, of policies, of taste) are precisely those things that are not subject to indisputable demonstration. When sensible people of good will honestly disagree about whether a particular course of action is just or wise—or whether this person is better than that one at a certain skill or job or profession, or whether a movie or play or poem or painting is good—it's because the evidence in issues like these very often can't be conclusive.

From the point of view of the writer, proving means giving reasons why a belief should be held or an action taken—reasons strong enough to lead readers to share the belief or agree that the action is wise. Not all such reasons are *logical* proofs, addressed to the intellect. Some are *emotional* appeals. Appeals to the emotions are not by their nature inferior to appeals to the intellect. They are *alogical*, not illogical but simply outside the province of logic. (The term *illogical* refers primarily to mistakes in reasoning.) In most great arguments—speeches or essays that argue with compelling power for a course of action or a principle or a belief or a judgment – logical and emotional, or alogical, appeals work together, reinforcing each other. The crucial distinction is not between the kinds of appeal but between the ways either kind is used. Unethical or immoral arguments as well as ethical and moral ones can be logically sound. Good arguments as well as bad ones may make deliberate appeals to the emotions.

Working Within the Rhetorical Situation

How should you go about persuading others to accept your views, to share your beliefs, to act in ways you think right? To begin with, size up the rhetorical situation, and then work in that context. Aim for a paper that will exhibit adaptation *by* a writer *to* an audience *of* an argument *on* a specific subject. The whole art of persuading consists of maintaining the right balance among these elements.

The "I" of Argument.   "Who am I," you need to ask yourself, "in this particular rhetorical situation? How do I want to appear to my audience?" You're always yourself, of course; but a self is the sum of many selves, and in any particular writing situation one of them dominates. That's natural. The way you think about, talk about, and argue about love is different from the way you think about, talk about, and argue about movies or sports or politics. And (leaving aside love) you shape your argument on an issue one way when you're talking to a neutral but receptive listener, another when you're having a dispute with someone who's sold on the opposing point of view. To be persuasive in both situations requires a good deal of flexibility.

Flexibility doesn't mean fakery. If you try to assume a pose that's totally alien to you – the cool, disinterested observer, for example, when you're naturally a feisty partisan – the strain will probably make itself felt. A professional writer can sometimes successfully wear the mask of bland, humble inquiry when he's actually in a rage ("So I decided to try to learn something about how justice is dispensed in our traffic courts"). Worn by someone less experienced, the mask usually slips, and the deception is exposed. Nothing so quickly destroys a sympathetic relation with the reader as evidence of insincerity.

Then why not sidestep this problem of the "I"? Wouldn't it be smart to conceal yourself altogether, to cancel yourself out of the writer-reader-subject equation? No. For in situations that require judgment, the qualities and qualifications of the person who is judging constitute the most powerful of the alogical (*not* illogical) arguments in favor of that judgment. Logically, the worth of an idea has nothing to do with the character of the person advancing it; but in areas where differences of opinion exist among people of good will, it *is* a matter of importance for the audience to have confidence in the writer. Indeed, it has such weight that some students of rhetoric, following Aristotle, give a separate label to this dimension of the rhetorical situation: they use the term *ethical proof* for all those appeals that relate directly to the character and authority of the person who's attempting to persuade.

In the persuasive papers you write, in and out of college, you should have no problem making clear the ways in which you're qualified to argue for a particular thesis. As for character, you should present yourself in your writing as you present yourself in person to someone whose respect and attention you value. By creating a favorable impression, you make your readers want to identify with you, and identification opens the way to assent. In general, what wins confidence is a discussion conducted with intellectual vigor by a person who knows the subject, has a good grasp of the issue being debated, is fair in examining alternatives, but at the same time shows a strong commitment to the solution he's convinced is right.

Beyond that, different circumstances call for different strategies. In one situation, crisp, incisive, confident argument is appropriate; in another, a tentative searching out of the truth works better. Some situations require zealous advocacy of a cause; in others, the audience may be more responsive to cool, detached counsel. (But remember the limits to role-playing: no faking.) On the face of it, adapting an argument to readers might seem to mean that you start by telling them what they want to hear. At times it does. At other times it means telling them at the outset what they *don't* want to hear. Tough talk sometimes succeeds where sweet talk does not. Readers may be moved to grudging admiration for the writer who's not afraid to stand up for an unpopular idea. Grudging admiration may make them receptive to arguments on the issue itself. But if you do come out swinging, in the course of the argument you must find ways to bring yourself and your readers around to the same side. The prickly individualist may command respect, but he's unlikely to make many converts. Remember that your goal is not to win an argument but to win minds — to persuade your readers that the position you support is the position that deserves their support as well. At the least you want to persuade them to open their minds to your ideas.

You should be able to make your presence felt in your papers without either insulting your audience or harping on your own tastes, feelings, and attitudes and relating all your arguments to your own ego. Don't simply announce that you know what you're talking about ("As an expert on stereo components . . ."); earn the respect and trust of your audience. The "I" dimension of persuading is one more of the rhetorical matters that call for the right balance between too much and too little.

The "You" of Argument. The more sharply you can characterize your readers, the more likely you are to speak directly to them. (In seeking to address all Americans, Presidents sometimes fail to give the impression that they're speaking directly to anyone.) In accommodating your argument, take into account the general state of their knowledge as well as their grasp of the particular issue. Are they, on the whole, naive or sophisticated? Are they, compared with you, novices or experts? What basic attitudes, values, and prejudices can you expect them to have? What is their probable initial response to your thesis—hostile, critical, skeptical, open-minded, tolerant, sympathetic? Is there apathy to be overcome, tension to be relieved, fear to be allayed?

If you can accurately assess your readers' acquaintance with the issue, you'll know how much background information you should provide, how much specialized or technical data you should include, and, perhaps, how you can relate the issue to other issues in which your readers have a stake. If you know what their values and prejudices are, you'll be less likely to insult them without meaning to. Though some writers specialize in insolence (witty insolence, that is), in general it's prudent to show respect for entrenched positions and basic prejudices even as you urge the need for change and for an *un*prejudiced stand on the particular issue. There are times when a direct appeal to self-interest is necessary (as in persuading purchasers to pay an extra 30 percent for optional safety equipment on a new car); there are other times when an audience must be urged to rise above self-interest (as in persuading the elderly and childless to vote for higher taxes to improve schools). In such cases you need to know what your readers construe to be to their own advantage.

Direct appeals to the audience usually entail alogical proofs ("Open your hearts; give generously; don't let a single child go hungry"). These should support the rational appeals, not take their place. Don't substitute emotion for reason when the proposition requires logical proof. On the other hand, when circumstances call for action as well as for intellectual conviction, don't hesitate to supplement logical proof with honest appeals to your readers' hopes and fears, their sense of what's right and just, their sentiments of love and pity. Emotional responses are bad if they block out rational ones, but rational responses alone, and rational commitment alone, may stop short of any action. In some situations – particularly when self-sacrifice is involved – moral exhortation has its place. Readers may need to be told not only that they *can* take a certain action but that they *should* take it.

Your sense of your audience's mood and convictions will help you decide how much space you should give to refutation – to attacking opposing views. Others have lined up in support of the counter proposition, or there wouldn't be any need for you to press your argument. If they've made a strong case for it, you'll need to give that case your serious attention. Whether you need to make refutation a major part of your paper or an incidental one depends in part on how much your audience has been swayed by the opposition. Anticipating and dealing with objections your readers are likely to raise is an excellent rhetorical technique. (Refutation is discussed on pp. 195–98.)

Taking into account the special characteristics of your audience will help you hone the edge of your positive argument. Every appeal for funds to support the university library gives primary attention to the library's need; but an appeal to one alumnus may emphasize school pride, and an appeal to another may stress the financial advantages of a tax write-off. Both appeals are legitimate attempts to accommodate an argument to a particular audience. (Such genteel blackmail as proposing to publish the names of those who fail to contribute might work with some lukewarm alumni, but as accommodation it could hardly be regarded as ethical.)

The broader the audience you address, the less specific knowledge of it you'll have. Someday you may be called on to write an appeal for contributions that will be mailed out to all the members of your graduating class. Or you may feel so strongly about an issue that you'll write a letter to a major metropolitan newspaper, trying to win its readers over to your views. In such cases, since your purpose will be to persuade as many as possible, you'll aim your argument at the kind of reader you think would be representative of the majority. You can imagine a reader of each sex, give them homes, jobs, interests, problems, even names if that will make them more real for you. Just be sure that the circumstances and characteristics you assign to them aren't so special that your Mary and John stop being typical of the audience you want to reach.

The Limits of Accommodation.   You don't accommodate an argument to an audience by just adding a few personal remarks or some emotional appeals to an argument you've already worked out in detail. Accommodation involves the method and manner of developing the entire argument — what evidence you use and how you use it, what appeals you make and how you make them. Accommodation affects the order in which you set forth the separate arguments and the weight and emphasis you give to each of them. It determines many features of style.

If accommodation isn't just adornment, neither is it the con man's bag of tricks. It's a necessary dimension of argument. The need for it begins as soon as you undertake to argue at all. "What's the distance," you ask yourself, "between the view my readers hold and the view I want them to hold? If it's great, how do I go about reducing it so that I'll get a fair hearing?" Finding common ground, however limited, is a necessary first step in persuading.

Finding common ground doesn't mean that you should start by buttering up your readers — flattering them, implying a closeness that doesn't exist, or telling jokes just to get them in a good mood. A joke may be the way in, particularly when there's something special in the relationship between you and your readers, but the technique of the after-dinner speaker rarely succeeds in print. Nor does accommodation mean putting your virtues on display in an effort to persuade your audience to accept your position just because you're you. Everyone is familiar with such attempts to subordinate issues to personality, to win friends *to* influence people. The devices are used, and sometimes they work. But they don't represent accommodation within the bounds of honest, ethical behavior.

Accommodation in this sense means finding ways to bring your readers to feel the force of the reasons that have led you to believe in your thesis. In persuading, you're not selling a piece of merchandise that can be returned tomorrow through the complaints department. You're contributing to the responsible discussion of ideas. Probably the best protection against the shoddier devices of accommodation is to remind yourself that whether you "win" the argument or not, you're trying to lead your audience to see the truth as you see it. The right procedure is to find good reasons for supporting the position you've taken and then to use all the resources of *responsible* communication to persuade your readers to assent to it.

The criterion of responsible communication puts limits both on what you say and how you say it. In accommodating your argument to your audience, don't compromise either your best self or your best arguments. We give our serious attention to the writer who, as we say, knows his subject (meaning that he knows more about it than we do) and who gives solid reasons why we should accept the position he's taken. The position may be a minority one; his views may be unpopular. But we read what he has to say if we have the impression that he is testifying to the truth as he sees it. In honest persuasion the writer adjusts neither his thesis nor his evidence to his notion of what his audience wants to read. Though he adapts his arguments to a particular audience, he doesn't alter his basic beliefs. He doesn't write in support of a point of view for an audience favorably disposed toward it and then write against that point of view when he's addressing an audience he knows is strongly critical of it. Accommodate your argument to your readers, yes. But don't accommodate it out of existence.

■ *For Analysis and Writing*

1. Select a campus issue that interests you and use it as the basis for two papers, about 750 words each, in which you try to persuade two distinctly different audiences to share your judgment or support your recommendation. (An illustration — but only an illustration: Write to the curriculum committee asking that specific changes be made in a course you've taken. Write to a friend urging him not to sign up for the course until these changes have been made.)

Though your two papers will present the same general views about the issue, they should differ in the space you give to each reason, the order in which you present your reasons, the way you open and close, and the general style and tone. Your task is to adapt the same argument to two very different audiences and to lead them both to the same conclusion.

2. What is the thesis of the passage below? What arguments are used in support of the thesis? Do you regard these appeals as logical or alogical? Why? What can you infer about the writer's conception of his audience? (The figures are out of

date because the article was written in 1969. Do you think the
sentiments are out of date, too?)

I hope that the cynicism that pervades so much of modern life
has not yet grown to exclude the demands of common morality.
The black man was brought to these shores in chains, enslaved
for 250 years, kept in peonage for most of the past hundred years,
and now suffers disproportionately in all areas of life. Common
decency demands that this situation be changed. The growing
anger of the black masses, especially among the younger people
who see through the hypocrisy of this society, will not lessen
unless such a national commitment is swiftly implemented.
Countering such protest with increased repression can only fan
the flames of anger and eventually lead to the kind of police-state
that will enslave all Americans.

Those in this morally underdeveloped nation who do not
readily respond to the demands of conscience may be more responsive to self-interest. The black minority, disproportionately
disadvantaged as it is, constitutes a huge market that cannot be
ignored. Negroes earn about $30-billion, form up to 50 per cent
of the total consumer market for certain goods, and will be in the
majority in about a dozen major cities well before 1980. Economic equality would mean enlarging this market by about $25-
billion, and it would also mean the creation of a stable urban
middle class.

Our economy can ignore this huge market and the implications
of equality only at its peril. The question really becomes: Does a
society dominated by white-run institutions have any kind of
future in a world that is three-fourths non-white? And can a
business-oriented society survive when its major centers of
power and commerce are populated by poverty-stricken, angry
black majorities? – Whitney M. Young, Jr., *Saturday Review*

Discovering Proof

To win readers over to your point of view, you have to
give them compelling reasons to believe that it's the right
one. Discovering good reasons is a strenuous activity. You
don't stumble on arguments ready-made. You need to
hunt for them, both in the subject itself – the internal
sources of argument – and in external sources, those that
lie outside the subject.

Internal Sources of Argument

A real issue will yield any number of lively arguments.
You can generate some of them by studying the nature of
what you're arguing about, by investigating its causes and
effects, and by finding out what it's like and unlike. To see
how, we'll refer again to some of the methods of develop-

ing ideas discussed in Chapter Two. Definition, example, classification, division, causal analysis, and comparison can all be given an argumentative thrust that shapes them into support for a belief or a proposal.

Argument from the Nature of the Thing. If you take the position that college students should have certain privileges and if you offer as a reason the assertions that college students are mature and that mature people deserve these privileges, you're drawing your argument from the nature of the thing—the subject—here, the nature of college students. A vital part of the argument is the case you make for putting students into the class of mature people: you need to give evidence about their habits, attitudes, and so on. (For the moment we're not concerned with the details of the proof but only with the general lines of the argument.)

Making a similar approach to a different issue, you might argue that a high-school diploma should guarantee competence in the basic skills—reading, writing, arithmetic —on the ground that the public schools are responsible for developing such skills. Or you might argue that tuition fees should be abolished in all schools supported by public funds, on the ground that, according to our democratic principles, every citizen has the right to be educated to the limit of his intellectual ability. In each case you're saying that something—the something your thesis is about —is a member of a class: college students are mature people; teaching competence in fundamentals is the responsibility of the public school system; free tuition is a right of citizens in our society. It follows that any assertion you can make about the class as a whole, you can make with equal confidence about your subject—so long as you've persuaded your audience that your subject is indeed a member of the class.

In arguing from the nature of the thing—the subject— your essential task is to fit your subject into a class that your audience will accept and respond to. *Maturity* (in connection with privileges), *responsibility* (in connection with the public schools), *rights* (in connection with American citizenship)—relating your particular subject to classes like these assures you at least of a hearing, if not of agreement with your thesis.

In building your argument, work hardest at supporting the proposition that your readers are least likely to find acceptable. In most rhetorical situations, arguing that college students are mature would be more to the point than arguing that mature people deserve specific privileges. It would usually be more telling to argue that a high-school diploma should guarantee competence in fundamentals than to argue that the public schools are responsible for teaching fundamentals. But sometimes the proposition on which you base your thesis may need defending. If you did some investigating before writing a paper on the right of every citizen to be educated to the limit of his intellectual ability – that is, before arguing that no one who is qualified intellectually should be denied an education for economic or other reasons – you might find that some of your prospective readers believed only that all young people should have the *opportunity* to be educated to the limit of their ability – that is, that schools should be open to all who can meet their intellectual requirements *and* pay their fees. Those who viewed as a right not education but the opportunity to be educated would be trying to dislodge your subject from the class you put it in. So if you were committed to arguing the issue on the ground of citizens' rights, you would in this case first need to persuade your audience that those rights do indeed include free tuition.

Though arguments from the nature of things can often be stated concisely, the beliefs they reflect are so much a part of your thinking that you may scarcely be aware of them. These beliefs – about human nature, ethics, government, education, and so on – shape your convictions on issues and stand as unstated *assumptions* behind every serious argument you take part in. (Anyone who argued that the availability of pocket calculators made the teaching of mathematics unnecessary would be revealing questionable assumptions about the nature of calculators, the nature of mathematics, and the nature of education.) As a writer, take pains to recognize what your assumptions are. In some rhetorical situations you'll want to state them openly. Readers who begin by opposing your position on an issue but share your basic assumptions can be led to see that your position follows logically from those assumptions. Such an audience can sometimes be won over. And even when you know that your readers don't share your assumptions, stating them may clarify your stand.

The bare statement of a shared assumption can have great rhetorical force. Consider this assertion by John T. Rule: "To punish all to prevent the transgressions of the few is, on the face of it, unjust." In the context, "on the face of it" clearly indicates that the writer believes no proof is needed. Any reasonable person, he says in effect, will accept as an axiom, or at least as an assumption he can go along with, that it's unjust to punish everyone in order to prevent a few from breaking the law. Another unstated assumption stands behind this one: A policy that's unjust shouldn't be pursued. Again the writer takes it for granted that any reasonable person would accept that assumption.

To the degree that evidence is offered in support of them, assumptions take on the character of definitions or statements about membership in a class. Typically, in an argument based on classification, you refer the specific issue to a larger context. You discuss a question about university policy in the context of what a university should be. You refer a question about the quality of a particular dictionary to the question of the nature and function of dictionaries. Once you've dealt with the larger question, you can turn to the particular instance with confidence that your argument is solidly grounded.

Working in terms of definitions and classes is not the only way of conducting an argument based on the nature of the subject. Examples (see pp. 29–31) are powerful persuaders when they can be shown to be representative of the whole. And division (see pp. 56–61) opens the door to two common, if sometimes risky, ways of arguing. One is to make inferences about part-whole relationships – to argue that what is true of a part is true of the whole ("The recall of thousands of cars with defective door latches indicates that this is a poorly designed model, carelessly constructed of shoddy materials") or that what is true of the whole is true of a part ("In a university with a fine reputation, you can be confident that the faculty is first-rate"). The other is to examine each part in turn and come to some judgment. The parts may be constituent elements, as plot, character, and theme are constituent elements of a novel; or they may be alternative courses of action, in which case the typical procedure is to show that since one course is impracticable or unwise or impossible, the other should be adopted.

When arguments go wrong, it's because of false premises (starting points that we accept as true or believe we have proved to be true) or faulty reasoning or both. Fallacies related to the nature of the subject can be traced to a misconception of what the nature of the subject is (as in the case of pocket calculators and the teaching of math), to the use of examples that are inadequate or unrepresentative, or to an analysis that's incomplete or illogical. Some of the potential trouble spots were identified in Chapter

Two, and more will be taken up later in this chapter. To summarize and anticipate: Arguments based on the nature of the subject, like all arguments, are susceptible to faulty generalizations (as in the condemnation of the automobile model because some of the cars had a defective door latch) and such fallacies as question-begging (assuming the truth of a conclusion that needs to be proved) and clouding the issue with irrelevant emotional appeals. Arguments based on the nature of the subject are especially susceptible to the use of stereotypes ("She has the hot temper typical of redheads") and of classes that can be counted on to stir deep but irrational feelings — either unexamined "God-terms" (*democracy, free enterprise, law and order*) or unexamined "devil-terms" (*communism, revolution, filth*). A responsible argument deals not with words but with what words stand for. The groundwork for sound argument is fair and accurate analysis of the subject. Later we'll see that faulty analysis leads to fallacious *either-or* arguments — arguments that ignore the existence of more than two alternatives — and that faulty inferences about part-whole relationships can lead to the fallacy of equivocation, in which the meaning of a key term is changed in the course of an argument.

■ *For Analysis and Writing*

1. The three passages that follow all date from the period of student rebellion in the late 1960s. Read each one carefully, and then answer the questions that follow it.

A

¶1 All of us have heard of the so-called "student revolt." Some who have taken part claim they learned more from their participation than from all their classes. If this was so, their time in college was ill spent, and both they and the university they revolted against would have been better off if they had never enrolled.

¶2 If your years as students are not to be a period of intense living, if you are going to sit in your classes like inert bodies, if what you study and what it does to you are not going to change your whole life — in short, if you close yourself to intellectual discoveries — even the best instructors will bore you. But then you should not have come. There is no greater abdication of self than when a student says he did not learn about life from the intellectual venture that a university *is*. If he did not learn about life from his studies, why did he study — to evade the draft, to find a marriage partner, to enjoy a paid vacation without working for it?

¶3 This is not to say that one cannot learn about life through political activities, or that you should not participate in them. Of course you should. But the university is not the ground on which to carry on politics, nor does the learning that can be gained from political action belong in a university. Certainly *something* can be learned about life through taking part in a revolt. That's the wonderful thing about life – there is practically no human situation from which we cannot learn a great deal about ourselves and our world. But this happens only if the setting is germane to the type of learning we are after.

¶4 There is only one purpose for which a university exists: to enable you to live the sometimes disappointing, often strenuous, but always exciting life of the intellect. The only true gains to be won on a campus are the intellectual virtues. The purpose of a university is to *study* political revolt, not to engage in it; to *examine* how peace might be won and maintained, not to crusade against war; to *investigate* and *plan* for social reforms in the university and outside it, not to carry them out. Thus, the sole objective of a university is to study every possible question, but to fight for only one cause: *freedom of inquiry and thought.*

¶5 For example, if one wishes to demonstrate for or against the draft or the war in Viet Nam, there are appropriate places to do so – but they are not the university. Here one should study objectively whether there should be a draft and what alternatives exist. Demonstrations interfere with such unbiased, in-depth investigation, which requires research, quiet concentration, and a careful weighing of all arguments.

¶6 All of us are familiar with Camus and his conviction that one ought to live an engaged and committed life. I could not agree more. But what, exactly, the engagement should consist of depends on what, at the moment, forms the center of our lives. If it is politics, then *that* should engage us. But the life of action is not that of carefully examining all sides of an issue; revolt is the opposite of contemplation. If you opt for a life of violent action, you may find in it self-realization. But the university is the least suitable place for this way of finding yourself. Indeed, if at this moment, strife *is* your way of finding yourself, you have no business being here because it is a way that only destroys what a university is for *without* adding to the general weal. – Bruno Bettelheim, *Rochester Review*

What clues in ¶4 indicate that Bettelheim is basing his argument on the nature of the thing – the purpose of a university? Is his view of the purpose of a university consistent with his statement in ¶2 that a student's years in college should be "a period of intense living"? Why or why not? Now explain why Bettelheim condemns so severely the life of action represented in "the student revolt." What evidence does the excerpt offer that he's aware that others hold different views of the purpose of a university?

The argument was originally presented in an address to students. Look closely at the language, especially in the last sentences of ¶s 1, 2, and 6. What tone of voice comes through? How does Bettelheim characterize himself through the language he uses and through his method of arguing? In what ways does he accommodate himself and his argument to his audience? What function is served by the reference to Camus in ¶6?

Explain how you, as a student, respond to Bettelheim's argument and why you respond as you do. If you disagree with his thesis, is it because you don't accept his argument of what a university is for, or is it because of the way he advances his ideas, or is it for some other reason? If you agree with him, draw evidence from your own experience as a student to support his position.

B

¶1 Turning back to the fifties, I will assert that we were right on one absolutely vital point: we knew what the university was for: learning. The university is for learning – not for politics, not for growing up, not for virtue, except as these things cut in and out of learning, and except also as they are necessary elements of all good human activity. The university is for learning as an airplane is for flying. This is its elemental and defining purpose. There is both affirmative and negative reason for this purpose: no other institution has this mission, and no other mission justifies the university.

¶2 One word is not a philosophy of academic life, but to begin with the right word is crucial. I choose "learning" rather than "scholarship" or "education" because "scholarship" puts too much emphasis on faculty alone, and "education" too much on students. Moreover, "scholarship" suggests what the scholar does to knowledge, and "education" suggests what someone does to a student. "Learning" suggests what professors and students do with knowledge, with thought, and with one another. Whitehead had it right and I repeat him: "uniting the young and the old in the imaginative consideration of learning." What helps with that is good for the university. What hinders it, hurts. For the academy this is the first and great commandment. – McGeorge Bundy, *Daedalus*

Explain why Bundy in ¶1 tells what a university is not *for. Would he do this if he were simply writing an explanatory statement about the nature and purpose of a university? Do you find the negative statements useful in sharpening your sense of what Bundy understands a university to be? When he says, "The university is for learning as an airplane is for flying," what new element enters into the definition of the purpose of a university?*

Show how the technique of arguing in ¶2 is similar to the technique used in ¶1. What does this tell you about how to conduct an argument based on definition?

Compare ¶2 of this passage with ¶4 of the passage that precedes it. Do Bundy and Bettelheim agree on the purpose of a university? If not, what differences do you find?

Compare the two passages in terms of accommodation to the audience. Do you recognize any significant differences in tone? Explain why you do or do not have as much sense of a specific audience in Bundy as you do in Bettelheim.

C

¶1 The educational premise behind demands for student power reflects the notion that people learn through living, through the process of integrating their thoughts with their actions, through testing their values against those of a community, through a capacity to act. Education which tells students that they must prepare to live tells infants that they learn to walk by crawling. College presidents who invoke legal authority to prove educational theory—"if you don't like it, leave. It's our decision to make"—assume that growth is the ability to accept what the past has created. Student power is a medium through which people integrate their own experience with a slice of the past which seems appropriate, with their efforts to intensify the relationships between the community within the university.

¶2 Let this principle apply—he who must obey the rule should make it.

¶3 Students should make the rules governing dormitory hours, boy-girl visitation, student unions, student fees, clubs, newspapers, and the like. Faculty and administrators should advise—attempt to persuade, even. Yet the student should bear the burden of choice. They should demand the burden.

¶4 Students and faculty should co-decide curricular policy.

¶5 Students and faculty and administration should co-decide admissions policy (they did it at Swarthmore), overall college policy affecting the community, even areas like university investments.

¶6 Student power brings those changes, and in the latter cases, it means that the student view will be taken seriously—that it will be treated as a view, subject to rational criticism or acceptance, not simply as "the student opinion which must be considered as the student opinion—*i.e.*, the opinion of those lesser beings in the university."

¶7 Student power brings change in the relationships between groups within the university, as well as change in attitudes between the groups of a university. It renders irrelevant the power of factions outside a university who impose external standards on an internal community—Trustees, alumni.

¶8 Student power should not be argued on legal grounds. It is not a legal principle. It is an educational principle.—Edward Schwartz, quoted in Immanuel Wallerstein and Paul Starr, eds., *The University Crisis Reader,* I.

Schwartz also argues from definition, but his interest is in a definition of the learning process. What is it, according to him? Show how this view of the learning process determines the position he takes on the issues in ¶s 3–5.

How does Schwartz support his assertion that student power is "an educational principle"? Would Bettelheim agree? Would Bundy? Schwartz doesn't argue directly on the topic that's central to Bettelheim and Bundy—the purpose of a university. What do you infer he would say on the subject? Would he or wouldn't he agree with Bettelheim? With Bundy? What do you infer that Bettelheim and Bundy would say about the issues Schwartz discusses in ¶s 3–7?

Do you find significant differences between the tone in the passage by Schwartz and the tone in the passages by Bettelheim and Bundy? If so, how do you account for those differences?

2. *What is the purpose of a college or university? Is it to help students learn, to give them a taste of political activity, to provide them with time to grow up, to help them develop moral standards, or something else? Write a persuasive paper in which you make the best case you can for your view of the purpose of an institution of higher learning. Adapt your argument to a particular audience and state what that audience is.*

3. *Using comparison and contrast, write a convincing explanation of why your view of the nature of a college or university differs from the view of the student radicals of the late 1960s — or why it does not. Address the explanation to someone you know who was in college in that period.*

Argument from Causal Relations.   Often a productive line of argument will open up if you inquire into the causes or the effects of a situation or a policy or an action. Here the main emphasis is not on the nature of the thing but on its origins or its consequences — how it came about or what it will lead to and sometimes, though not always, what should be done about it. In some situations, what you want to do is simply replace a mistaken analysis of causes with a more accurate one. In the following passage the author rejects one explanation for the decline in movie attendance after World War II and argues for an explanation he considers more valid:

When the artist, in whatever medium, provides *all* the stimuli necessary to keep his audience awake and fully informed, the audience, having nothing to do, goes limp. This is not to say that audiences at today's sound films, which blaze with color and screech with car-skids, are limp. But there was a time when they were. In the late 1940's and early 1950's, audience attention at films dropped so spectacularly that thousands of film houses closed and the studio system itself was destroyed. The decline is normally attributed to television. But in certain Rocky Mountain states where television was not yet available, the falloff was exactly as precipitous. Filmmakers had put their audiences to sleep. They had done it by taking care of everything — smoothing the way with slow dissolves that made transitions plain, firmly ending sequences with fade-outs followed by a few seconds of blankness to indicate the passage of time, beginning new sequences with fade-ins that made adjustment easy, *always* indicating shifts of time and place with calendar leaves slipping from the wall, candles burning down, railroad wheels racing. Movement within a scene, no matter how many shifts of position the camera might record, was complete: long establishing shot in which we could identify the room and see a character entering it, pickup shot from the doorway as the character moved deeper into the room, reaction shot from another character watching him come closer—the whole clock accounted for moment by moment. Of course there were graceful elisions, interesting camera-made metaphors, as there always had been. But if film had nearly, and too literally, ground to a halt, it was partly because it had learned to be too helpful.—Walter Kerr, *The Silent Clowns*

An argument from causal relations (or argument from consequences, as it's also called) is the natural approach whenever you're urging that a new policy be adopted or an old one changed.

Many social issues are debated largely in medical terms of diagnosis and prognosis or of diagnosis, prognosis, and prescription, terms that imply analysis of causes and prediction of effects. Typically the argument moves through four stages: an analysis of conditions ("Among teenagers in our central city, unemployment has reached 60 percent . . ."); an investigation of causes ("With no incentive to stay in school, these young people enter the job market lacking any real qualifications . . ."); a proposal designed to correct, control, or improve conditions ("What we need are tax adjustments that will enable companies to provide job training . . ."); and a call for action to put the proposal into effect ("So write your representative in the legislature, urging support for immediate revision of the tax structure so that . . .").

An argument based on cause-effect relations may lead you in any of several directions. If you can pinpoint the probable cause of a bad situation, your way is clear to argue that the situation will be improved if the cause is eradicated. But as our earlier discussion indicated (pp. 76–79), there may be no single cause but a whole network of causes. And even if a single cause can be isolated, removing it may be difficult or dangerous, if not impossible. In these circumstances you may find yourself arguing that the only feasible course of action is to treat the symptoms —that is, to alleviate the effects. Or you may take instead the radical position that anything short of uprooting the fundamental causes is futile. Often the crux of the argument is not what the causes of the situation are but what should be done to correct it.

In the following passage the argument against wage and price controls is made in terms of the bad effects such controls have:

When excess demand is pulling prices up, wage and price controls work against the basic forces. If firms and unions in some sector of industry are induced or compelled to hold prices or wages down, that is like pinching one corner of a large balloon. The lucky buyers of the goods pay less and have more left to spend elsewhere – driving other prices up still higher and not reducing over-all inflation at all. Jobs in the industry become unattractive, so it will be short of labor. The amount produced will be less than the amount demanded, so buyers will have to be rationed somehow. Distortion of output, black markets, government controls, inefficiency – these are the clearly predictable results. Repressed inflation rolls merrily on, doing far more harm than open inflation. – Milton Friedman, *Newsweek*

One form of argument from causal relations – the argument from circumstances – neglects causes completely and denies the existence of any real choice among cures. In this kind of argument the writer devotes his energy to establishing that a current situation dictates a particular course of action. He hammers away at the point that the circumstances are overpowering – that pollutants from the internal-combustion engine are killing us *now*, that the strike has brought the corporation to the very brink of bankruptcy, that the costs of higher education are intolerable. Essentially he tells his audience, "Given this situation, there is only one thing we can do" – not because it's a good or wise or appealing action but because the only alternative is death or ruin or an end to higher education or some other unacceptable choice.

Arguments based on causal relations are vulnerable to a number of fallacies, known collectively as *false causes*. They include failing to recognize that a number of causes are responsible for a situation, identifying as a cause something that's merely an accompanying circumstance, and establishing a cause-effect relationship between two events when there is only a chronological one (*post hoc* fallacy, pp. 192–93). Arguments from circumstances include the special kind of *either-or* argument known as the *dilemma,* in which both of two alternatives are unpleasant. Such argument is also susceptible to the *prodigious* fallacy – gross exaggeration or hysterical overstatement.

■ *For Analysis*

The following excerpt shows a typical use of the argument from circumstances – first the situation, then the solution, then the call for action. Look for weaknesses in the argument. If you find any, explain why you regard them as fallacies.

Ten percent of the human beings ever born are now alive and breeding like bacteria under optimum conditions. As a result, millions live at famine level. Yet even with the fullest exploitation of the planet's arable land — and a fair system of distribution — it will not be possible to feed the descendants of those now alive. Meanwhile, man-made waste is poisoning rivers and lakes, air and soil; the megalopolis continues to engulf the earth, as unplanned as a melanoma and ultimately as fatal to the host organism. Overcrowding in the cities is producing a collective madness in which irrational violence flourishes because man needs more space in which to *be* than the modern city allows. . . .

To preserve the human race, it is now necessary to reorganize society. To this end, an Authority must be created with the power to control human population, to redistribute food, to purify air, water, soil, to repattern the cities. . . .

These, then, are the things which must now be done if the race is to continue. Needless to say, every political and economic interest will oppose the setting up of such an Authority. Worse, those elements which delight in destroying human institutions will be morbidly drawn to a movement as radical as this one. But it cannot be helped. The alternative to a planned society is no society. If we do not act now, we shall perish through sheer numbers, like laboratory rats confined to too small a cage. — Gore Vidal, *Esquire*

Argument from Likenesses and Differences.   Ideas about what a thing is like and what it's unlike can provide a lead-in to productive argument. The main function of difference arguments is to make distinctions among things normally thought to be the same. And the main function of likeness arguments is to persuade the reader that things not normally thought of as alike are, in fact, alike in important respects that bear directly on the point at issue. Likeness and difference relations enter into a great many arguments where the aim is not to establish good or bad or right or wrong or to propose solutions but to make a comparative judgment: to prove that one book is better than another, to show that the choice is between a stronger candidate and a weaker one, and so on.

A typical use of likeness arguments is to urge that a program or policy be adopted — or rejected — because the same program or policy, or a similar one, has — or has not — been successful in a comparable situation. One argument for some universal form of health insurance in the United States is that socialized medicine functions well in Great Britain. (And one argument against universal health insurance in the United States is that the British medical system does *not* function well.) For those who attribute criminal behavior to a disorder of the individual personality, it's reasonable to argue that it be treated medically, as other physical and psychological ailments are.

In this passage the writer clarifies and reinforces the point he makes in his first two sentences with the likeness argument in sentence 4 and the difference argument in sentence 5:

[1] The responsible man is not capricious or anarchic, for he does acknowledge himself bound by moral constraints. [2] But he insists that he alone is the judge of those constraints. [3] He may listen to the advice of others, but he makes it his own by determining for himself whether it is good advice. [4] He may learn from others about his moral obligations, but only in the sense that a mathematician learns from other mathematicians — namely by hearing from them arguments whose validity he recognizes even though he did not think of them himself. [5] He does not learn in the sense that one learns from an explorer, by accepting as true his accounts of things one cannot see for oneself. — Robert P. Wolff, *In Defense of Anarchism*

The last two sentences of the passage just quoted bring us to the variety of likeness-difference argument called analogy. We argue from analogy when we say that because the period we're living in is strikingly similar to some period in the past, we should adopt a policy now that proved successful then. We argue from analogy when we say that the methods used to solve an economic or social problem in an industrial city in Italy can be successfully applied in Seattle, or that blacks can work their way out of the slums as white ethnic minorities have done. Some years ago, members of the women's liberation movement who saw the position of women as analogous to (comparable to) that of an exploited racial or ethnic group called for a program of action like the one then being pursued by black militants. These are all literal analogies, in which things of the same class are compared — historical periods, industrial problems, people. When you use a literal analogy, your argument will be persuasive if the similarities between the two cases have a direct bearing on the point at issue.

In a figurative analogy, the writer sees a relationship that involves members of different classes — governments and housewives, for example; he may argue that just as a housewife can spend no more on her family than she has in her pocketbook, so a government should spend no more than it takes in, keeping its budget in balance. You can use figurative analogies to throw new light on a subject, to open up an avenue of speculation, to give colorful support to an argument. The author of the following passage has suggested that clothing is a language with its own vocabulary and grammar:

Moreover a costume, like a sentence, does not appear in a vacuum, but in association with a specific person in specific circumstances, any change in which will alter its meaning. Like the remark "Let's get on with this damn business," the three-piece tan business suit and boldly striped shirt and tie which signify casual conformity at an office meeting will have quite another resonance at a funeral or picnic. And the meaning of this costume will alter according to whether it is worn by a fifty-year-old man, a thirty-year-old woman, or a ten-year-old child.—Alison Lurie, *New York Review of Books*

Seeing similarities between things is essential to thinking, and seeing similarities that others have overlooked can open the door to a fresh, inventive approach. But the use of analogy in argument does involve risks. No matter how many similarities have been uncovered, no two situations are identical, and therefore a solution that works in one may be worthless in another. And many analogies break down at a point that's crucial to the argument. (A lot of housewives have charge plates in their pocketbooks and depend heavily on credit.) Even so, analogies have great persuasive force and can be extremely useful so long as they're not expected to carry the entire burden of proof. (Could Friedman, in the quotation on p. 181, have extended his pinched-balloon analogy successfully?)

In offering an analogy a writer doesn't claim that two things are alike in all respects or even in most respects. He says only that they're alike in some respect that's relevant to the point at issue. And he may, quite fairly, make an inference based on that one resemblance. An analogy isn't fallacious because it ignores differences; it's fallacious when the differences it ignores are highly significant. An analogy between a bird and a plane wouldn't serve much purpose in an argument about the consumption of petroleum products. Most faulty analogies result from using similarities that aren't relevant, from pressing the analogy too far, from treating a figurative analogy as a literal one, and from reasoning from partial resemblance to complete correspondence.

■ *For Analysis and Writing*

1. Discover an analogy that expresses your attitude toward five of the following:

April	the FBI	hitchhiking
traffic	racial conflict	marriage
guilt	loneliness	hair

Now write a brief argument in which you make a point about one of these subjects. Make your argument grow largely, if not entirely, out of your analogy.

2. *Examine the following argument, written just before the Bicentennial. What is the issue, as Schlesinger sees it? What evidence does he offer that the issue is worth considering? What position does he take? What arguments does he offer in support of his position? To what extent does he argue from the nature of the subject? From cause-effect relations? From likenesses and differences? Do you find his argument convincing? Why or why not?*

¶1 At last the great day is almost upon us, and a great day it will be. There is something extraordinarily exhilarating in a contemplation of the changes two centuries have wrought on the North American continent. Still the parades and the fireworks and the men and women in colonial costumes reenacting the glorious past confront us, I think, with an anomaly. Despite our ostentatious ransacking of history for the Bicentennial rites, we have become, it would seem, a people to whom history in fact seems to mean singularly little — much less certainly than it meant to the Founding Fathers.

¶2 History, for example, is a declining subject in our secondary schools. In many communities it has steadily lost ground to an amorphous hybrid known as "social science" or "social studies" and characterized by emphasis on current events and on "problem-solving." Some states — among them New York, Indiana, Iowa, Oklahoma and Oregon — require practically no prior training in history for high school history teachers.

¶3 The situation is different but hardly better in our universities. The number of college students concentrating in history or even taking history courses has been shrinking remarkably in the last few years. The bottom has fallen out of the academic job market for historians. The oversupply of history Ph.D.s has led some of our best graduate schools to cut back on their post-graduate admissions in history. The projections for the future have cast a pall over the profession. The Organization of American Historians produced last year a cogent and pessimistic report "The State of History in the Schools," from which many of the facts I cite have been taken. This year Professor Frank Freidel of Harvard devoted a somber OAH presidential address to the proposition, "The historical profession is in a state of crisis."

¶4 This spring *The New York Times* administered a test of American historical knowledge and attitudes to nearly 2,000 freshmen at nearly 200 colleges. It was unfortunately one of those infernal multiple-choice examinations, which so often penalize students bright enough to perceive the ambiguities in the answers. Still it had four eminent historians as consultants, and it can be taken as a rough measure of the quality of historical information students pick up in high school. "The main conclusion one must draw," said Professor William

Leuchtenburg of Columbia, one of the consultants, "is . . . that this group of students knows remarkably little American history. Their knowledge of the colonial period is primitive. Two-thirds do not have the foggiest notion of Jacksonian democracy. Less than half even know that Woodrow Wilson was President during World War I."

¶5 Why should the young know so little about the history of their own land when, as Professor Freidel has said, "Never has American history been more in the public eye than in this Bicentennial year"? Yet history as decor is one thing, history as consciousness is another. One doubts whether the parents of the 2,000 college freshmen would have done much better on the *Times* test. (In fact, they didn't when the *Times* administered a similar test 33 years ago.) How is one to account for the decline of historical consciousness among the American people?

¶6 It was not always so. The Founding Fathers had a vigorous sense of history. They were steeped in the classics of Greece and Rome as well as in the English historians. They read Plutarch, Polybius, Livy, Sallust, Tacitus. Madison, before going to the Constitutional Convention, composed an historical essay called "Of Ancient and Modern Confederacies." After giving three long Federalist papers over to a review of the history of confederations, Madison and Hamilton wrote that they made "no apology for having dwelt so long on the contemplation of these federal precedents. Experience is the oracle of truth; and where its responses are unequivocal, they ought to be conclusive and sacred."

¶7 The intense historical-mindedness of the Founding Fathers did not last very long. Something happened to attenuate the national sense of America as part of the web of history. Perhaps it was because so many Americans were themselves fleeing from, or brutally torn from, their own histories. For all the show-business clatter of the Bicentennial, we seem to have become in these two centuries an essentially historyless nation. Our intellectuals reject history in their infatuation with the ahistorical behavioural science. Our businessmen — and our youth — observe, in the style of the elder Henry Ford, that history is bunk, or at least a bore and an irrelevance. Even our political leaders, who need most to know history and who used to know more of it than the generality of their fellow-countrymen, have fallen by the wayside.

¶8 Theodore Roosevelt and Wilson were, among other things, professional historians. Franklin Roosevelt and Truman had a vast amount of historical lore at their fingertips. Kennedy was our last historically literate President. George McGovern was a history Ph.D. — and look what happened to him. Reading Jimmy Carter's appealing autobiography, one is struck by the meagerness of the historical reference — all the more odd because the South until recently prided itself on its historical consciousness. The historical reference in Ronald Reagan's autobiography, it need hardly be said, is even more meager.

¶9 I do not suggest that simple lessons can be simply drawn from history. Historical analogy has been very often the bane of statesmanship. Still a sense of the great and intricate stream of historical experience is exceedingly helpful in making intelligent judgments about current policy. It is particularly helpful

in distinguishing between real and phoney crises. If Nixon had
not been an historical illiterate, he might not have responded in
so hysterical a fashion to the supposed threats to national security mounted by the Weathermen, the Black Panthers and the
dissident young in 1970. Even worse, as America's historical
consciousness has thinned out, a messianic sense of unique and
sacred national destiny has flowed into the vacuum.

¶10 Is there a remedy? Can historical consciousness be re-
vived and restored? It will not be easy. For one thing, the historical profession itself is in a condition of intellectual as well as
economic disarray. The old idea of history as one of the humanities is under assault from historians who think the computer can
transform it into a science. The old idea of history as a means of
providing a common core of necessary knowledge is under assault from historians who see that common core, traditionally
construed, as a means of reinforcing insidious bias – the superiority of the West over the East or of whites over non-whites,
or of men over women. The old idea of narrative history is under
assault from historians who feel that narrative glides over the
basic questions as formulated by sociology and anthropology.

¶11 Some historians try to rescue the discipline by accommodating themselves to new tastes and fashions. There has been
much emphasis on innovation in teaching methods – "concepts"
rather than facts, film strips, do-it-yourself historical projects,
role playing and the like. Much of this is worth trying; some of it,
however, simply abandons any distinctive contribution history
can be thought to make to a civilized society. Advocates of history outside the profession sometimes think the solution lies in
making American history a compulsory subject. Too often this
results in the misguided notion of "positive history" – the notion,
that is, that history courses ought to teach students how perfect
the United States is, how blameless our national motives are,
how harmonious our national development, how marvelous our
system of free enterprise. History that omits conflict, frustration,
folly and failure is worse than useless.

¶12 There is no easy remedy because the causes of the decay
of historical consciousness are so deeply rooted in the national
culture – a culture dominated by technology, by incessant and
accelerating change, by forebodings about the future. My own
old-fashioned belief is that, if anything is likely to restore our
historical consciousness, it is narrative history, which after all
did so much to create it. Written history tends to tidy up the past,
to smooth it out, to make everything seem mechanical and inevitable. But very little seems inevitable as it happens. Narrative
history at its best can remind us that the past, like the present,
was filled with surprise and unpredictability, with hard-pressed
men making difficult choices on the basis of inadequate information, with struggle, dream and tragedy.

¶13 As we celebrate our heritage on July 4, perhaps we should
not conclude that watching the holiday fireworks discharges our
obligation to the American past. It might be useful to begin the
third century by serious reflection on the meaning of our national
experience – that long quest, still unfinished, forever problem-
atic, to fulfill for *all* our citizens their unalienable rights to life,
liberty and the pursuit of happiness. – Arthur Schlesinger, Jr.,
Wall Street Journal

External Sources of Argument

Internal arguments grow out of the issue itself or, rather, out of the writer's development of his views on the issue. The case is decided on its merits: a product should be used because it's well made and serviceable; a policy should be adopted because it's wise and humane. External arguments don't relate directly to the issue or the writer's analysis of it but to evidence brought to bear on it from the outside—the testimony provided by documents or by statistics or, most commonly, by other people: a certain type of tennis racket should be used because the Wimbledon champion uses it; a foreign-aid bill should be enacted because the Secretary of State has spoken in its favor.

Argument from Authority. In structure, the argument from authority could hardly be simpler: it asks for the reader's assent or belief on the basis of the recommendation of somebody (or a number of somebodies) presumed to be better informed or wiser than either the writer or his audience. To use this kind of argument responsibly, you must first of all be sure that your authority *is* an expert. If you ask your readers to take his word on a factual matter, they have the right to assume that he has access to the relevant information and that his integrity guarantees honest reporting. If you ask them to accept his opinion, they should be able to count on his ability to form sound judgments. Thus the ethical dimension of argument bears as strongly on the external sources you use as it does on the internal ones. You must choose authorities whose integrity and competence on the particular issue are generally recognized.

When equally respected authorities offer testimony supporting different sides of the same issue, you have to go beyond the simple use of authority. You need to make clear to your readers why you find this expert's view more convincing than the opposing view, why you've chosen this expert rather than that one.

Argument from authority is so frequently abused that it must be handled with special care. It's misused, logically and ethically, when it's substituted for reasoned discussion: "Dr. Rogers says so, and that settles the matter." Authority and issue must be precisely matched: not only can a television star's opinion of toothpaste or an evangelist's opinion of fiscal policy be inexpert and irrelevant, but a psychologist may lack authority in psychiatry, and a historian who specializes in medieval France may have no expert knowledge of Victorian England. And the right authority must not be used in the wrong way. Don't misrepresent the views of an authority by selective quotation or other distortion in order to strengthen your argument.

One of the common abuses of argument from authority is to cite not any identifiable individual but a vague, general class: "Scholars tell us . . . ," "Scientists say . . . ," even "Everybody knows. . . ." The next step is the fallacy known as *hypostatization* or *reification*—appeal to an abstraction: "Science tells us . . . ," "History says . . . ," "Democracy teaches. . . ."

Sometimes you may want to present testimony from a respected or revered document like the Bible or the Constitution. The effectiveness of such testimony will depend on the attitude of your audience toward the document you quote, but it's well to remind yourself that the Constitution is open to conflicting interpretations on many points, and that "the devil can cite Scripture for his purpose." Which brings up the use of quotations, maxims, proverbs, platitudes—miniature testimonials that are supposed to distill the wisdom of the ages but that actually carry no weight in serious discussion. As grounds for arguments, they're unreliable. An alert reader can usually find another bit of wisdom that directly contradicts the one he's been asked to accept: "Look before you leap," but remember that "He who hesitates is lost."

Use of Statistics.   The testimony of statistics is used so widely that it deserves special consideration. The basis for its persuasive appeal is the maxim that figures don't lie. But of course they do lie—when opinion polls are not representative, when rating systems have biases built into them, when the figures are irrelevant, or when they are used dishonestly. Like the human authorities you appeal to, your statistical authorities must be carefully examined and responsibly presented. Announcing that 274 students signed a petition may help your argument, but if you hide the fact that 742 refused to sign it, you're grossly distorting the situation.

Even when accurate statistics are honestly presented, an argument based on them is not necessarily sound. Establishing the fact that a sizable majority agrees with you proves only that a sizable majority agrees with you—not that your audience should therefore agree. Use of the *bandwagon* fallacy — vote for the candidate who's going to win, buy the product that "everyone" buys, read the best seller, join the crowd — is an appeal not to authority but to the herd instinct.

So far as everyday matters go, it's advisable to use authority and testimony only as *supporting* evidence. As such, it can strengthen a paper whose main substance has been drawn from internal sources of argument. In research projects, where the use of authority and testimony is essential, wise and scrupulous use is of first importance not only in doing justice to the subject but in convincing the reader of your own fairness and accuracy.

Some acquaintance with the sources of argument, both internal and external, will help you size up realistically what you have to do to prove your thesis. In its skeleton form, proof consists of a chain of related propositions, one anchored to another and all giving support, direct or indirect, to the thesis. Once you've visualized your argument as a series of key assertions moving from *here* (the problem) to *there* (the solution), you can turn to the question of proof in the particular context, asking which of the assertions can stand unsupported and which, without support, are likely to strike your readers as arbitrary or shaky or unreliable. Making wise decisions at this point is the essential rhetorical task. If you belabor the obvious, you'll bore your readers. If you assert as truths what they regard as debatable issues, you'll outrage them.

For each of your key assertions, then, ask yourself these questions:

Is this a basic assumption I can count on my audience sharing, or does it need support?

If it needs support, what route will I take in developing the particular point?

What possibilities open up when I try to support the assertion by analyzing the nature of the thing? By investigating causal relations? By making comparisons?

What concrete evidence will convince my readers that the definition is reasonable? The causal analysis sound? The comparison legitimate?

For what instances, what particulars, can I draw on my own knowledge and experience? What kind of support can I find in the writings of others? If authorities disagree, how shall I choose among them?

Good answers to these questions will generate the substance of your paper.

■ *For Analysis and Writing*

1. *From each of two newspapers or magazines that are known to have basically different political viewpoints* (National Review *and* The New Republic, *for instance, or the* Chicago Tribune *and* The New York Times), *make a copy of an editorial or column dealing with a topic of social or political importance. (If possible, choose articles on the* same *topic.) Or check through back issues of weekly magazines* (Newsweek, Time, The New Yorker) *until you find two sharply conflicting reviews of the same movie. Submit them with a paper in which you compare and contrast the two articles. Give the best explanation you can for the similarities and differences in the opinions you find stated in the articles, in the assumptions underlying these opinions, in the kinds of arguments used, and in the style and tone. Be objective; don't express your own opinion on the issue.*

2. *From the subjects below, choose one that interests you. Specify an issue related to it, and when you've committed yourself to a thesis, write a persuasive essay for an audience of your choice. For some of the subjects you may want to support your thesis by offering the testimony of experts. If you do, give some attention to establishing their credentials.*

meditation	psychiatry
drinking	sex discrimination
a college education	work and the workweek

Keep asking questions about your subject until you can see a problem in it. For example, about work and the workweek: What are the psychological effects of working? Of not working? If you found you could meet expenses by working only ten hours a week, would you choose to work only ten hours? Would a three-day workweek be desirable? What should a person do whose job brings him a good paycheck (which he wants and needs) but no satisfaction? What should a person do whose job brings him great satisfaction but not enough money to live on?

3. *From the areas of education, politics, social reform, art, and popular culture, draw up a list of assertions or propositions that you're prepared to support—for example, that students should have a voice in promoting and firing faculty members, that voting rights in the United States should be restricted to property owners, that adults should be made legally responsible for the welfare of their aged parents, that transistor radios should be banned from public transportation, parks, and beaches. (The propositions can be more specific—that the management of the cafeteria or the bookstore should be replaced, that Instructor X was treated unjustly because of sex discrimination.) Settle on a proposition that your instructor approves. Write two short papers (about 400 words each) on*

the same topic, one addressed to a neutral audience, one to an audience that's at least mildly opposed to the action you propose or the judgment you make.

4. Review the passage by Schwartz on p. 178. Write a persuasive paper expressing your views about student power in one of the areas he refers to—fees, admissions policy, and so on. Your audience is the faculty.

General Fallacies

Below is a listing of the more common fallacies, arranged in groups. Some have been mentioned earlier in the chapter, in connection with particular kinds of argument. The categories frequently overlap; and it's well to remember that recognizing an argument as fallacious is much more important than labeling the fallacy precisely. Even so, the names can help remind you of what to check as you revise your own arguments and what to look for as you read the arguments of those you disagree with. Fallacies in syllogistic reasoning are taken up in Chapter Six.

1. *Hasty generalizations* are based on inadequate, scanty evidence. *Faulty generalizations* are based on weak, unrepresentative, or irrelevant evidence, or on emotion rather than evidence. Deliberately slanting or suppressing or disguising contradictory evidence is a variety of faulty generalizing known as *card-stacking, special pleading,* or *dealing in half-truths.* Generalizations that don't stand up under careful examination represent one of the most common of all fallacies in argument.

Stereotyping is the practice of applying group labels to persons or things without regard for individual differences and sometimes without regard for the significant characteristics of the group. There are popular stereotypes for hundreds of groups—scientists, schoolteachers, Swedes, redheads, athletes, Baptists, bird watchers, Rotarians, Texans, New Yorkers, "the enemy," and so on—including college students and young people generally. Stereotypes in your thinking, or non-thinking, may reflect unexamined assumptions that weaken your entire argument. You can guard against stereotyping by citing numerous examples and by recognizing contradictory evidence.

2. *False cause* embraces all the fallacies relating to causal reasoning—*post hoc,* mistaking an accompanying circumstance for a cause, failing to recognize multiple causes. Logicians give the label *post hoc, ergo propter hoc* ("after this, therefore because of this") to the fallacy of assuming that what comes after an event is necessarily a result of it. The mere fact that one event follows or precedes another in time doesn't necessarily indicate any causal relationship. *Post hoc* is the most common fallacy of causal relations.

3. *Faulty analogy* results from making comparisons that aren't relevant to the issue, from pressing an analogy beyond legitimate similarities, from treating a figurative analogy as a literal one, or from insisting that analogical resemblances constitute adequate proof. The fallacy of the *perfect analogy* occurs when you reason from a partial resemblance to an entire and exact correspondence.

4. *Begging the question* means assuming the truth of a proposition that you actually need to prove. "This unfair method of voting" assumes that the method *is* unfair. ("Unfair" is a question-begging epithet.) Though the writer who uses that phrase hopes to take advantage of a general predisposition in favor of virtue over vice, in begging the question he is himself engaging in an unethical tactic. One common form of begging the question is *arguing in a circle*. At its simplest, the circular argument asserts that X is true because X is true: "In our society it is necessary to keep up with the latest styles because it is essential to be fashionably dressed." This evasion is often hard to recognize when it's buried in a long chain of argument; but in developing an argument, you should be sufficiently aware of the steps you take to avoid tripping over your own heels.

Another version of begging the question is the *false* or *complex question*. "When is the Administration going to stop bankrupting the country with its illegal expenditures?" begs at least two questions—whether the Administration is bankrupting the country and whether its expenditures are illegal.

5. *Ignoring the question* is a broad label for various kinds of irrelevant argument. It consists in shifting the grounds of the argument from the real issue to one that's not under consideration. In one characteristic form, *argumentum ad hominem*, the attack is not on the issue itself but on those who support the view that's being opposed: "It should be mentioned that this noble champion of academic freedom recently had his license suspended for driving while intoxicated." The trial lawyer's tactic of seeking to discredit hostile witnesses usually depends on *ad homi-nem* argument. Related to it is the tactic of *damning the source*—dismissing the opposing view because of its origin ("After all, that was Hitler's line"), sometimes called *poisoning the well* (or *spring*).

To set up a *straw man* is another form of ignoring the question. The strategy is to argue not against the opposing point of view but against a caricature of it which supports propositions it does not support and may even expressly condemn—that is, to attack an opposition that doesn't exist. To use a *red herring*—still another form—is to introduce an issue that diverts the discussion from its proper course: "Before we permit this rock festival to be held in our town, let us remember that not many years ago hundreds of long-haired young radicals went to Communist Cuba to help harvest the sugar cane."

Two more forms of ignoring the question are the *argumentum ad populum* and *name-calling*. The *argumentum ad populum* (which usually incorporates a variety of other fallacies) speaks to the jealousies, hatreds, fears, resentments, prejudices, and passions of audiences: "Are you going to continue to allow your hard-earned tax dollars to be handed over to a bunch of immoral bums who are too lazy to work?" Name-calling includes not only insulting racial epithets and crude slurs like *commie, fascist, bum,* and *pig* but labels chosen for their connotations for particular audiences: *liberal, controversial, Eastern, Southern, conservative, intellectual, foreign.* Irrelevant emotional appeals can take many forms and can be subtle or blatant. Epithets may be slanted to arouse admiration, sympathy, anger, disgust. Propaganda regularly substitutes diabolical abstractions for human beings. Vocabulary may be deliberately used to impress: sometimes a parade of technical terms will hoodwink an audience into accepting claptrap.

6. In the fallacy known as *shifting the burden*, the writer asserts his case and dares the audience to prove him wrong. All manner of beliefs and superstitions fall into this category, from the Great Conspiracy theory of national and international affairs to the conviction that toads cause warts.

In testing your arguments, be sure to examine all the appeals you've used to support your thesis—the alogical ones as well as the logical ones. Appeals to emotions and ideals—to pride, to justice, to morality—can be extremely persuasive. They are properly used when they're brought to bear on the real issue. To use them to cloud or misrepresent or smother the issue is to argue unfairly and dishonestly.

■ *For Analysis*

Which of the following do you find convincing and which unconvincing? In each case explain why.

a. The Democrats are warmongers. Every time this country gets involved in a war, it's when they're in power.

b. And the reason for all the trouble with our young people can be identified in two words: permissive parents.

c. Peckham was a New Englander through and through — cold, narrow, tight-fisted, self-righteous, and smug as a Persian cat.

d. Like a skyrocket, he has made a colorful ascent in our political skies; but no skyrocket can climb forever. In the end it must return to earth — with a resounding thud. We can safely predict the same fate for Candidate Kent.

e. The reason students today are more willing to accept authority than were students of the 1960s is that today's students are obsessed with grades and the high-paying jobs that they think high grades will guarantee.

f. Franklin D. Roosevelt's Communist connections are a matter of record: he allied himself with Joseph Stalin, supplied the Soviet Union with weapons of every variety, and traveled halfway round the world to confer with Communist leaders.

g. Training and practice? Forget it. A musician like that is born, not made.

h. Returning from his three-day inspection trip, Congressman Flood reported that both civilian and military morale was high, that the rebels' strength had been shattered, and that victory was being rapidly achieved by government forces.

i. Parents have no right to criticize the public schools. After all, they don't tell their surgeons how to operate.

j. America today has adopted the repressive tactics of Nazi Germany; and just as Nazi Germany went up in flames, so will America.

k. I oppose the registration of firearms. History shows that registration leads to confiscation.

Refuting Arguments

In the background of every piece of persuasion lurks the opposing thesis. And very often it looms in the foreground.

In fact, the procedures you follow in revising your persuasive papers – testing the logical relationships in your argument and checking for fallacies – are the same procedures you'll follow when you set out to correct a misinterpretation or to refute an opinion, though then you'll be probing logical relationships and searching for fallacies in the writings (or speeches) of others.

In preparing any argument, find out what's been said on the other side or figure out what might be said. Even if you give no explicit recognition to the opposing view in your paper, knowing what arguments its proponents present will help you decide what kind and quantity of evidence you need, what reasons give strongest support to your thesis, and how they can best be ordered. In some of your papers you may limit yourself to constructive argument – affirmative support of your thesis – but in others you'll probably want to meet objections, demolish misconceptions, and in general strengthen your own thesis by showing the weaknesses in the counter-thesis.

Especially when you have reason to believe that your readers lean to the opposing view, you may find it useful to open your paper by analyzing it and exposing its weaknesses. Launching a brief and temperate offensive at the start can clear away obstacles to a sympathetic hearing for your own view. On the other hand, it's ordinarily a bad tactic to recognize and deal with the opposition at the very end of the paper, no matter how briefly. The conclusion should strongly reaffirm your own thesis.

Refutation is an attack on the evidence and the reasoning that make up the proof for the other side. In most cases attack isn't enough; you must bolster it by building an affirmative argument for your own thesis. But the term *refutation* properly applies only to proving the opponent wrong. Full-scale refutation goes to the roots of the opposing argument. If it's to be convincing, it must attack the fundamental assertions or premises of the argument, not merely its conclusions. If it's to win respect, it must scrupulously avoid those tactics that it criticizes the opponent for using.

In a ten-paragraph article on school busing, Irving Kristol begins with a list of the premises originally used in the arguments for busing:

What were the premises on the basis of which school busing was originally urged? There were three:
1) Legal segregation of the races, as embodied in the "Jim Crow" legislation of the South, was in violation of both the spirit and the letter of the Constitution. Also in violation of the Con-

stitution were those cases of *de facto* segregation which were the result of deliberate official policy (e.g., school districting along racial lines).

2) The close and daily association of white and black school-children would in and of itself engender greater interracial understanding and harmony.

3) Black students, once brought into closer contact with more highly-motivated and better-prepared white students, would themselves become better students.

He goes on to assess each premise. The first he finds "incontestable," but he sees no reason why busing had to be used to combat segregation. The second and third he attacks as false assumptions, based on theories that have been disproven. After completing his refutation, Kristol shifts the discussion to what he presents as the real issue:

The truly interesting questions are: What are the sources of this ideological fanaticism? How is it that people, who are perfectly sensible in other respects, succumb to it? We really don't need any more research on busing – we know that, though a truly integrated society is certainly our ideal, there is no point marching up that hill. We could indeed use new research on *alternatives* to busing – on more effective ways of achieving amicable race relations and better black education. But we need even more urgently new research on the peculiar social psychology of the busing crusade – this could give us some valuable insights into our contemporary distemper. – Irving Kristol, *Wall Street Journal*

There are other ways of refuting an argument besides attacking its premises. Refuting by analogy often involves *reductio ad absurdum* – pushing the thesis or the proposed course of action to an illogical extreme. The main argument for the control of handguns is that handguns are used to kill people. Opponents of gun control have argued that if the use of guns is to be regulated because they are sometimes used to kill people, then the use of knives, hammers, cars, and hands should also be regulated. The counter-argument (really counter-counter-argument) typically rejects the analogies by pointing out that whereas knives, hammers, cars, and hands have various legitimate uses, the only function of a gun is to destroy. Or it may point out a difference in degree, relying on statistics to show that most murders are committed with guns. Or it may itself advance a *reductio ad absurdum* by inquiring whether the sale of atomic bombs should be unrestricted.

Drawing out the implications of a proposal is an effective technique in refutation and, if it's done fairly, a reputable one. If used unscrupulously, it will distort and misrepresent the original argument, creating a straw man.

Making a lucid, accurate statement of the view that you're refuting is the best protection against misrepresenting it in the course of your paper. Caricaturing comes easy in refutation because normally anyone who undertakes a rebuttal has been stirred—emotionally as well as intellectually—to disagree. But setting up a straw man or distorting the position that's being opposed means there will be no real debate. Ask yourself: Have I represented my opponent's case in such a way that he would find it an acceptable statement of his position?

It's also easy, when feelings are strong, to berate and scold and ridicule. But no one who is seriously interested in dealing with the issue, as contrasted with cowing the opposition, uses language as a club. A temperate tone in refutation is not incompatible with strong, incisive assertion of a different point of view. Most important for responsible refutation, perhaps, is to have respect for your opponent. Unless you *know* him to be otherwise, assume that he's the kind of person you'd like to think you are— open, intelligent, reasonable. And as you proceed with your refutation, remember that the purpose of argument is to get closer to the truth. Much sound refutation is devoted not to rejecting the opposing position outright but to refining and modifying it.

■ *For Analysis and Writing*

1. Make a copy of a newspaper editorial or column or a magazine article that expresses an opinion or makes a recommendation you strongly disagree with. Make a careful analysis of the selection, singling out the premises on which the argument hinges and examining the evidence offered in support of it. Then write a "Letter to the Editor" in which you make clear exactly why you disagree with the position advanced in the editorial, column, or article. Depending on what the issue is, you may or may not decide to go on to make a constructive argument for the position you favor.

Submit the selection you're refuting along with your own paper.

2. Here's a section of an article on an issue of current interest. After you've analyzed the argument, prepare answers to the questions at the end.

¶1 One argument used against national health insurance is cost. In fiscal year 1975, American expenditures for health care reached $118.5 billion, a figure that is 8.3 per cent of the gross national product. Remember, this astronomical sum is what we pay now, *without* national health insurance. Opponents of the plan say that national health insurance inevitably will mean higher health-care costs for the individual citizen. But why should that be? Dollars paid in premiums to a national-health-insurance program will cancel out the dollars we now pay in medical bills and in private and semiprivate health-insurance premiums. And for our money, we should have better distributed and more inclusive health-care services. For all of us.

¶2 Wait, opponents argue. What about the scandals and rip-offs in medicare and Medicaid? It's true, there are dishonest doctors, dishonest hospitals and nursing homes and dishonest patients. But their crimes are small potatoes compared with the enormous good these programs have done for millions of Americans. Furthermore, for me, the claim that there have been abuses in the past is a poor argument against something new we need; it is an excellent argument for running the new plan effectively. We don't close down the Defense Department because defense contractors have overrun costs or offered bribes. We need to be defended and President Ford's "realistic" budget asks for an additional $10 billion for the department this year. We also need to be healthy. Therefore, let's create a national-health-insurance plan that is well administered and that has heavy penalties for anyone who abuses it.

¶3 Finally, the oldest argument against national health insurance is that it will bring us "socialized medicine" and get us into the mess in which Britain now finds itself. First, we should understand that despite the current troubles of Britain's National Health Service, the system has been of incalculable value to the British people for 30 years. No government, Labor or Conservative, would dream of trying to take it away. Second, no one is proposing for America a system like England's in which the doctors *do* work for the government. Instead, what is asked for here is simply a government insurance system. Under such a plan, doctors would work for themselves, we would choose the one we like, pay his bill and then submit a reimbursement claim, just as millions of us now do with our private and semiprivate insurance plans.

¶4 The difference would be that everybody would be covered. In America today, private insurance companies pick and choose among various risks, trying to avoid the bad ones. Group major-medical plans have maximum coverage ceilings that may be too low to cover the expenses of catastrophic illness. Sometimes, insurance companies put pressure on employers not to hire people who are handicapped or chronically ill. Self-employed people have to struggle to get good medical insurance. Indeed, more than 50 million Americans, one-quarter of the population, now have no health insurance at all, not even basic hospital insurance. What happens to them when they become seriously ill?

¶5 The problem, basically, is to get a substantially better distribution of the miracles of modern medicine and to ensure that people get the care they need, not the care they can afford. The solution is strictly political. We have only to inform 536 people in Washington that national health insurance is very important to us and that this time we're not kidding. — Robert K. Massie, *Newsweek*

What is Massie arguing for? *How much space does he give to positive or constructive argument? How does he organize his attack on the views of those who oppose him?*

How does Massie refute the argument he takes up in ¶1? What method does he use in ¶2?

In ¶3 he advances two reasons for rejecting "the oldest argument." What are they? How do they differ? Are both necessary? Why or why not?

What's the function of ¶4?

Evaluate the effectiveness of the final paragraph. What does Massie imply when he says that the solution "is strictly political"? Is the solution he offers a practical one? Explain why you are or are not persuaded by his argument.

3. *Analyze the arguments in the two articles that follow. Show how each writer interweaves positive argument with refutation. What arguments does van den Haag advance in favor of the death penalty? What arguments does Shapiro advance against it? Does van den Haag meet all of Shapiro's arguments? Does Shapiro meet all of van den Haag's? Do they agree or disagree in interpreting Ehrlich's statistical studies? To what extent does each writer rely on arguments from definition, from consequences, from likeness, from testimony and authority? Finally, explain why you do or do not think that one of these writers could persuade the other to change his mind.*

A. Pro Argument

¶1 Is the death penalty a greater deterrent than equally irreversible but revokable penalties such as imprisonment? Evidence collected mainly in the last 10 years indicates that the threat of probable and severe punishment does deter most people. Still, it's possible that the death penalty adds little or nothing to what long imprisonment could accomplish. Indeed statistics in the past did not show that lower rates of capital crimes occurred with the death penalty.

¶2 However, recent more sophisticated statistical studies, relying on actual execution rates rather than on laws alone, show, in the words of Isaac Ehrlich of the University of Chicago, that over the period 1933–1969 "an additional execution per year . . . may have resulted on the average in seven or eight fewer murders."

¶3 Professor Ehrlich, who is opposed to the death penalty on moral grounds, reached his results by feeding the data into simultaneous equations far too complex to recount here. He carefully neutralized factors which influence capital crime, such as age, income or employment.

¶4 Much more research is needed, but Mr. Ehrlich's methods and tentative conclusions have withstood many attacks so far. We must assume that for each non-execution of a convicted murderer we do in fact run the risk of between seven and eight murders by other murderers who could have been deterred by the execution. Surely, the loss of a convicted murderer's life weighs less heavily in the balance than the risk of losing seven or eight additional victims.

¶5 Since most murderers are irrational, it is sometimes argued that they are unlikely to be deterred by the threat of death. This is an argument *for* the death penalty, suggesting that the threat of death has deterred all but the irrational (whose "crimes of passion" are usually not punished by death). The absence of the death penalty, finally, confers an undesirable immunity on "lifers" who murder fellow prisoners or guards, and on anyone who, already threatened with life imprisonment for his crime, murders the arresting officer or the kidnapped victim. The credible threat of execution here too may deter and save victims from being murdered.

¶6 Those who, frivolously rejecting all calculations, pride themselves on objecting to the death penalty on purely moral grounds, usually insist that the sacredness of human life is violated by executions. Actually, the inviolability of human life is proclaimed and protected best by the credible threat of death against anyone who violates what should be inviolable—as enjoined in the Bible and by all major religions. (It is hard to understand what is meant by "the sanctity of human life" outside a religious context.)

¶7 Sometimes it is argued that the death penalty barbarizes society, yet there is as much evidence that the absence of capital punishment does. Or, oxymoronically, that capital punishment amounts to "legalized murder." Yet the difference between a crime and a non-crime is not physical, but legal. Murder is an unlawful killing, just as stealing is an unlawful taking. Lawful execution is not murder any more than lawful confiscation is stealing. And we often do to the criminal as he did to his victim, e.g., we lawfully imprison those who unlawfully imprisoned others.

¶8 Discrimination against the poor and the black in the distribution of the death penalty has often been alleged. (Recent statistical investigations throw some doubt on this allegation, particularly outside the South.) Penalties can be applied unjustly. Discrimination, however, is an argument not against penalties but against their improper application. Discrimination by courts is corrected not by changing penalties, but by rectifying discrimination by the courts.

¶9 It is for the voters to decide whether they wish some crimes to be punished by death as authorized by the Constitution. The Fifth Amendment says: "No person shall be held to answer for a capital . . . crime . . . nor be deprived of life, liberty or property without due process of law." In other words, it recognizes *capital* crimes and a "due process" to deprive a person "of *life*, liberty or property."

¶10 The Eighth Amendment, prohibiting "cruel and unusual punishment," hardly was meant to contradict the Fifth adopted at the same time. How can the death penalty have become unconstitutionally cruel (irrational?) or unusual (capricious?) since? Polls show that most people favor capital punishment. Should the moral sentiments of judges have more weight than those of the people? Should the people be denied the right to legislate to protect their lives in accordance with the Fifth Amendment?

¶11 In passing, it should be noted that while most convicts prefer life imprisonment to death, some, such as Gary Gilmore, prefer death. Decency requires that his preference and his courage be respected. Any competent person sentenced to death is surely entitled to execution. To deny a man's responsibility for his conduct and his life is ultimately to deny his dignity and liberty. How can it be a "civil liberty" to be denied one's final choice? — Ernest van den Haag, *Wall Street Journal*

B. Con Argument

¶1 Down through the ages the only proposition the death penalty has ever proved is that the state itself can kill as mercilessly and as premeditatedly as the most cold-blooded killer. Of course this killing is always done in the name of decency, integrity and reinforcing the moral fiber of society.

¶2 With few exceptions, such as Prof. Ernest van den Haag's book, "Punishing Criminals," most of the arguments in favor of capital punishment have been primarily based on appeals to raw emotion and grounded in a lynch-mob psychology.

¶3 The principal argument is usually the unproven notion that the death penalty deters. There is absolutely no proof that the taking of a human life by the state has ever been, or will ever be, a deterrent to prevent others from murdering or performing other heinous crimes. Indeed, all our experience in comparing statistics of states which have capital punishment with those which do not has shown that there has been no discernible difference in the murder rate between these states. Many times these states were almost of identical composition and indeed bordered on each other.

¶4 Recently, capital punishment adherents have been widely quoting Isaac Ehrlich's study, which finally lends some support to their contention that the death penalty has deterrent value. Prof. Ehrlich argues, contrary to all other serious studies previously done in this field, that there is a correlation between the murder rate and the actual use of the death penalty. This is an interesting variation to previous studies.

¶5 Yet even Prof. Ehrlich concluded his study by stating that, "These observations do not imply that the empirical investigation has proved the existence of the deterrent or preventive effect of capital punishment." He further concludes that ". . . these results do not imply that capital punishment is necessarily a desirable form of punishment."

¶6 Thorsten Sellin, who analyzed a large mass of this homicide data, concluded in "The Death Penalty," published by The American Law Institute, that "Anyone who carefully examines the . . . data is bound to arrive at the conclusion that the death penalty, as we use it, exercises no influence on the extent of fluctuating rates of capital crimes. It has failed as a deterrent."

¶7 If the existence of capital punishment served as a deterrent to crime, then 18th Century England would have been one of the most crime-free havens in the world since children were hanged for stealing a loaf of bread. But, as Dr. Samuel Johnson observed during that same period many centuries ago, the surest place to find most of the pickpockets in London at one time plying their trade was in a crowd assembled to witness one of their own being hanged.

¶8 Although there is no real proof that killing by the state acts as a deterrent to murder or other serious crime, there is excellent proof that those who are the victims of legalized killing by the state are usually the poor, the blacks, and the pleaders for unpopular causes. To quote Justice Douglas' concurring opinion in Furman v. Georgia, where he cites with approval the definitive study of The President's Commission on Law Enforcement and the Administration of Justice, "Finally there is evidence that the imposition of the death sentence and the exercise of dispensing power by the courts and the Executive follow discriminatory patterns. The death sentence is disproportionately imposed and carried out on the poor, the Negro, and the members of unpopular groups."

¶9 Nor has there ever been any evidence that the moral fiber of society has been substantially improved and uplifted by a good hanging, either privately or publicly. Indeed, the very converse is true. It is ironic to note, according to Prof. van den Haag, that Prof. Ehrlich is himself against capital punishment for moral reasons; he feels it destroys the very moral fiber of society to have the state engage in killing. For the state to engage in the death business morally debases us all.

¶10 The one undeniable conclusion about the death penalty upon which we can all agree is its finality. Far too often in the past, an innocent person has been executed and years later the guilty party was either discovered or confessed. But death cannot be undone.

¶11 The absolute faith adherents of capital punishment have in the infallibility of our justice system is a constant source of amazement to me. Our justice system itself does not claim infallibility in any other area of human concern. The answer, to those who claim that without the death penalty crimes of violence will flourish and increase, is that there has been no validation for that claim either by experience or by morality. — E. Donald Shapiro, *Wall Street Journal*

4. *Write a paper in which you argue for or against the death penalty. In the course of your argument, take into account the opposing views. If you like, address your argument to either van den Haag or Shapiro.*

Chapter Six
Testing Logical Relationships

Chapter Five sketched some ways to build content in any persuasive paper. Now we turn to the logical underpinnings of particular arguments. To win your audience over to your side, you must make a good case for it. In writing your paper—and especially in revising it—you need to anticipate the questions a skeptical reader will raise: Is this assertion accurate? Is this generalization convincing? Does this statement follow from that one? In answering these questions, you can rely to a considerable extent on your own good sense, but you'll also find some helpful clues in the procedures of formal logic. These procedures can be applied both in developing persuasive papers and in testing them—your own and others'.

Traditionally, the terms *induction* and *deduction* identify two ways of reaching conclusions. In argumentative writing, inductive reasoning and deductive inference mix freely; but because different methods are used to test the conclusions they lead to, we'll discuss them separately.

Testing Induction

An inductive inquiry is grounded in particulars. It moves from the observation and analysis of facts, characteristics, attitudes, or circumstances to an inclusive statement or generalization. It has its origin in a puzzle or a question. (Why was Cortez with a few hundred men able to conquer the Aztec nation?) Essentially it's a search for a pattern or an explanation. The inquiry is set in motion by a hunch or guess—a hypothesis (something had weakened the Aztecs) —that is then tested by further investigation (the Aztec capital was being ravaged by smallpox, to which the Spaniards were immune).

The generalization that's the outcome of an inductive

inquiry may describe and classify, or express a causal relation, or make a comparison. Induction is the procedure
you're most likely to use when you approach your subject
from the various perspectives we discussed as the internal
sources of argument (pp. 171–84); it's the pulling together
of evidence that will make your particular assertions convincing. When you base your argument on external
sources, you're asking your readers to accept the results of
the inductive investigations that were carried out by others
—the authorities you cite (pp. 188–90).

Establishing Inductive Generalizations

What makes a sound induction? That depends, first of all,
on what's being asserted. Criteria for reliability are easy to
state, and reliability is easy to assess, when the hypothesis
takes the form of a generalization that can be either verified or shown to be false. If the assertion "All our entering
students graduated from high school with averages of B
or better" is based on an examination of the grade records
of all the freshmen, and if the calculations are accurate,
the statement is true. (This is actually nose-counting rather
than rhetorical induction.) But significant arguments seldom rest exclusively on factual statements that can be
definitely confirmed or contradicted. The evidence is less
certain, less "hard," and altogether more difficult to weigh
when you're generalizing, say, about campus attitudes
toward politics or about the merit of a musical group or
about the extent of regional bias in the United States. Even
when you can examine all the data (listen to all the recordings of the musical group, for example), inspection alone
won't produce a sound generalization. You need to interpret and judge.

For the vast majority of the generalizations that figure
in persuasive writing, you can't examine all the data. At
some point in your thinking about the subject, you make
the *inductive leap*—a shift from a descriptive or statistical
observation about this item, that item, and the next one to
an assertion about the whole class of items, including
those members of the class not available for inspection.
Whenever unexamined data are included in a generalization—and no one has ever examined all men or all women
or all robins or all Datsuns—the logician insists that the
inference (in contrast to a nose count) is not certain, however high its degree of probability. Even death and taxes,
according to this principle, may not be inevitable. For you
as a writer, such skepticism is a useful reminder that in-

ductive generalizations need the best support you can give them. Each one stands or falls on the amount and kind of evidence that backs it up.

Take a relatively simple generalization: "Students on this campus have practically no interest in national politics." Unsupported, it doesn't convince. Backed up by well-chosen examples, it may be highly persuasive. But how many examples, and what kind? Probably no reader would be persuaded by a single instance—"My roommate pays no attention to the political news on TV" or "The Young Democrats had to disband this year for lack of members" or "Only a handful turned out to hear Senator Patch." Nor will a reader be impressed by a quantity of evidence if he has reason to believe that the instances you cite are unrepresentative. To decide that students are politically apathetic on the basis of the indifference shown by your roommate would be premature: the sample is too small and the generalization hasty. To base the judgment on the indifference shown by all students majoring in music or in forestry would be unwise: because the sample is unrepresentative, the generalization is faulty.

Naturally, when you're gathering evidence for your persuasive papers, you haven't time to conduct comprehensive polls, nor do you have at your command the complicated statistical systems that make some polls reliable. But with care and thought you can strengthen the key generalizations your argument depends on.

In arriving at a generalization, don't brush aside contradictory evidence. Suppose you want to follow up a hunch that your roommate's apathy toward politics is an attitude shared by a great many other students. On the basis of that hunch, or hypothesis, you start to investigate —carefully reading the campus newspaper, including letters to the editor, and talking to as wide a range of students as you can, particularly to those who've made attempts to stir up interest in political organizations or in talks by visiting politicians. The hypothesis is necessary; without it you could hardly launch an inquiry. But if your investigation doesn't turn up support for your hypothesis, abandon it, no matter how much you wish it were true. Sticking to it in the face of evidence that contradicts it would be foolish. Suppressing or disguising the evidence would be dishonest.

This doesn't mean that all the evidence you turn up must support your hypothesis. Inductive generalizations offer only probability, not certainty. So if you come upon some negative evidence, acknowledge it in your paper. Admitting that exceptions exist can damage a persuasive paper less than ignoring them. And if you can offer plausible reasons for the exceptions, your generalizations will be all the sturdier.

Establishing Causes

So far we've been concerned with the making of an inductive generalization that describes or classifies, that makes an assertion about the nature of the thing. (If you have enough evidence and the right kind of evidence, you assert that students on your campus are in the class of people who are uninterested in national politics.) Inductive inquiries that set out to establish causal relations need to be handled with special care, particularly when they're presented as guides to future action. Some causal relations are indisputable: no one who puts a plastic dishpan on a very hot burner will consciously do it a second time. But in other situations causal connections are much harder to establish.

Suppose you hear that not one of the last ten students to come to your college from the high school you attended managed to graduate. Upset by the information, you decide that you haven't a chance of ever earning a diploma. You've formed a causal connection between coming-from-Monitor-High and failing-in-college.

Are you right? Probably everyone would agree that the causal connection is less sure than the one established between the hot burner and the ruined dishpan. The capacity to withstand heat isn't likely to vary much from one plastic dishpan to another. But you can't count on such uniformity when you're dealing with the quality of instruction in a high school from year to year or with the capacity of individual students to succeed in spite of poor instruction.

Did the ten students who preceded you fail *because* they came from Monitor High? The evidence might be enough to suggest this as a hypothesis, but it can do no more than that. You need to go on to make inquiries about the students who failed, about Monitor High, and so on. Such inquiries might make it possible for you to confirm the hypothesis about the ten students, or they might force you to alter it or reject it altogether. Determining cause is the most rigorous stage of any inductive inquiry, for only a good deal of analytical skill can distinguish coincidental circumstances from genuine causes. (See pp. 76–79, and remember the *post hoc* fallacy referred to on pp. 192–93.)

Even if you found strong support for a causal relation

between attendance at Monitor High and failure in college for the other ten students, you'd have difficulty convincing others that *you* were therefore doomed to failure. A prediction of future effects is much more difficult to support with evidence than an assertion of past causes.

Most of the issues you'll debate in college papers are too complex to be argued on the basis of a single cause. You can acknowledge the complexity by ranking causes in terms of probability, by classifying different kinds of causes, and by proposing solutions that take into account a variety of causes.

Analogies

The logical form of analogy (pp. 183–84) is a partial induction: two things alike in certain respects are presumed to be alike in another respect. As we've already pointed out, analogies generate material by suggesting arguments, provide support for argumentative positions, and frequently have great persuasive force. But they do not have strict logical validity. Though they may persuade an audience to give your thesis serious consideration, in themselves they don't prove it. A frank admission of precisely where your analogy breaks down—where the similarities run out—is rhetorically much more effective than pressing it to the point where it becomes ridiculous.

In sum, the two chief features of the inductive procedure are the framing of the hypothesis and the inductive leap. The three chief fallacies, or sources of error, are (1) hasty generalization, (2) mistaken identification of cause, and (3) faulty comparison or analogy. Knowing the possible sources of error can guide you in testing the reliability of the generalizations you use in your persuasive papers.

■ *For Analysis and Writing*

1. *Make copies of eight or ten typical advertisements in current magazines, and submit them with an essay in which you first generalize about the techniques used in the ads and then, on the basis of your inductive investigation, make an inference about the nature of the audiences aimed at—age, sex, economic bracket, and so forth. (For the second part of the paper you'll be relying on many inductions you've performed and many assumptions you've formed in the past.)*

2. *How would you go about testing the hypothesis that all graduates of a particular high school would succeed in col-*

lege? How much evidence and what kind of evidence would convince you that the hypothesis could be accepted as a sound generalization? How much evidence and what kind of evidence would persuade you to abandon the hypothesis? Give your answers in a unified 500-word paper.

3. You have a friend (or relative or pen pal) in another country who has asked you to explain the nostalgia craze in the United States. Write a letter saying why you think Americans— particularly young Americans—have been attracted by the songs and movies, fashions and styles of the 1950s or the 40s or 30s or 20s. Does it reflect discontent with the present? Were those happier times? How do you feel about the current fascination with one or another past decade?

4. In the following excerpts identify the generalizations, both explicit and implicit, that seem to have been arrived at by induction or by partial induction (analogy), and explain why you do or do not find them reliable. In your own words, reproduce the train of reasoning in each excerpt and explain why you do or do not find it convincing. Then try composing a different argument to prove the point each excerpt makes.

a. When mosquitoes are a problem, it is standard practice to get rid of stagnant water and to cover windows with screens. Nobody calls that coddling mosquitoes. But when somebody proposes spending money to clean up slums, and to screen society from crime by building humane jails and by hiring many more honest, well-trained cops, the outcry against coddling criminals always kills the budget.—Robert Sherrill, *Life*

b. Every winter those of us who attend plays at the Auditorium come away with only a faint notion of what the actors were saying. This is because of the endless hacking and coughing that makes hearing the actors' lines almost impossible. During last night's performance, however, there was a sudden silence that lasted for minutes. It occurred during the nude scene. Here, then, is the solution to our problem. From now on, let's have all plays presented in the nude. While eye strain may increase, ear strain and throat irritation will be wiped out. And everyone will be happy.—From a letter to a campus newspaper

c. Everyone would agree that poetry needs rhythm, but some people still cling to the notion that a poem is not a poem unless it has rhyme as well. In connection with this, one is reminded of a woman wearing an extraordinary diamond necklace. The necklace enhances her costume, but whether or not she *needs* it is questionable. The jewelry may be so distracting that perhaps we will not notice the fact that she is not attractive. If she is really beautiful, the necklace will serve only as a charming incidental. Similarly with poetry. If the work is a piece of great writing, rhyme acts only as an incidental. If, however, the work is poor, the rhyme may serve to distract us from that fact.

d. We find it easy to imagine superhuman robots, but now science is showing us that our own abilities are even more remarkable. For example, recent experiments by Dr. Barbara

Sakitt, a physicist-psychologist now at Stanford University, have shown that the unaided human eye can detect a *single quantum* of light—that is, the smallest amount of energy possible in our known universe. The quantum is a unit of energy so small that the energy a piece of chalk releases falling one-thousandth of an inch would be 1 trillion quanta. Then, too, we find it easy to be dumbfounded by the amount of information that can be stored in an advanced computer, until we begin to consider that a single ordinary-sized gene can be arranged in some 10^{600} different ways. (To get an idea of the magnitude of this number, you might bear in mind that the entire universe contains only an estimated 10^{80} atoms.) A gene is made of DNA, the basic blueprint for all life as we know it. A virus, the simplest form of life, consists of a gene or genes with a protein cover. Thus, it may be said that the world of viruses, submicroscopic entities so small that they will pass through most filters, has informational possibilities that would stagger the largest computer.

But let us expand our imagination from viruses to a single human being with 100,000 or more genes and with trillions of individual cells arranged in any number of complex patterns. And let us focus for a moment on that particular concentration of information-carrying cells or neurons called the brain, and on all the multifarious interactions of those neurons—the complex pathways of synapses, the domains of cooperating neurons, the pulse of the information-carrying waves, the constant, flickering electrochemical changes within neurons and between neurons, the information-multiplying capacities between brain and "mind," the constant interplay between areas of the brain and every muscle, organ, nerve, and sensory receptor in the body. And the interplay between all of this and what is outside the skin, with nature and culture, and perhaps with zones of information we have not yet identified. Indeed, the number of possible interactions within the brain alone is beyond the current skill of our best mathematicians to compute in a meaningful manner. The best way of expressing the total creative capacity of the human central nervous system in layman's language is that for all practical purposes it is infinite.—George Leonard, *Saturday Review*

Testing Deduction

In reasoning inductively we pull particulars into an inclusive generalization that describes or explains them. In reasoning deductively we draw a conclusion from propositions that we accept as true or that we have already proved to be true, or probable, by inductive procedures. We reason deductively when we say, "If this is true, that *must* be true." If Jack is a National Merit finalist, he must be smart. Why *must*? Because we take it for granted, or are convinced on the basis of our own inductive inquiries, that all National Merit finalists are smart. The essence of the deductive process is the *must*—drawing an inevitable conclusion from propositions known or assumed to be true.

Some assertions can be proved both deductively and inductively. A cluster of examples, each giving evidence of Jack's braininess, would lead inductively to the same conclusion as the deductive inference. For sound induction you would have to know a lot about Jack. For sound deduction you would need to know only the one fact about him, so long as you could get agreement on your general principle about *all* National Merit finalists.

To test conclusions arrived at deductively, you ask two questions: Are the premises true? Is the reasoning valid — that is, does the conclusion follow logically from the premises? Only if you can answer *both* questions affirmatively is your argument sound.

Though logic offers some rules of thumb for testing the reliability of inductive generalizations, it doesn't tell whether a specific generalization is true or untrue, probable or improbable. This you can determine only by examining the material — the facts or instances that have gone into the making of the induction. Similarly, logic can't tell you whether the premises you're working from in a deduction — many of them inductive generalizations — are true or false. (Are all National Merit finalists smart? Is the generalization true beyond a doubt, or is it only highly probable? The question is a complex one, involving among other things the meaning of *smart*.) What logic can do is provide rules for testing the validity of the conclusions you draw from your premises.

As an intelligent, responsible person, you should never be careless about the logic of your arguments. But it's undeniable that some writing situations — particularly some combinations of topic and audience — call for more thorough testing of deduction than others do. When these occasions arise, some knowledge of formal logic and the formal fallacies can be a real advantage to you as you revise your papers.

To begin with, you want to uncover the chain of reasoning — reduce complex propositions to simple ones, sort out premises from conclusions, and bring into view whatever generalizations are not stated but simply implied in the argument (in the example above, "All National Merit finalists are smart"). In this preliminary analysis your aim is to reduce your reasoning to a pattern that will conform to the three-part structure of assertions known as the *syllogism*. Once your reasoning is laid out in syllogistic form, you can begin testing your premises for reliability and your conclusion for validity.

The three parts of the syllogism are the *major premise*,

the *minor premise,* and the *conclusion.* The phrasing of the major premise allows us to distinguish three common patterns: the hypothetical syllogism (If P, then Q), the *either-or* syllogism (Either P or Q), and the categorical syllogism (All P is Q). You can often reduce an argument to more than one of these patterns, but ordinarily one will seem more natural and easier to deal with than the others.

Hypothetical Syllogisms

The pattern of the hypothetical syllogism is familiar from mathematics:

Major premise	If P, then Q		If P, then Q
Minor premise	P	*or*	Not Q
Conclusion	Therefore Q		Therefore not P

The major premise asserts that if the antecedent P is true, the consequent Q is true. The minor premise asserts that P is true, and the conclusion drawn is that Q must be true. Or the minor premise denies that Q is true, leading to the conclusion that P is not true. These are the two valid forms of inference in a hypothetical syllogism.

Suppose you've written a paper on why you're in college and you've begun by saying, "I'm going to college because I want to be financially secure." Your reasoning would seem to run like this:

If a person goes to college, he'll achieve financial security in later life (If P, then Q).

I'm going to college (P).

Therefore I'll achieve financial security in later life (Therefore Q).

The inference is valid. The major premise ("If a person . . .") asserts a causal relation based on induction. If the causal relation is sound, the conclusion is true as well as valid.

Certainly you know that future financial security is by no means inevitable for everyone who goes to college. What you probably mean is that graduating from college makes future financial security more likely than dropping out, flunking out, or never going would. But let's assume that your major premise is sound and see what inferences can, and can't, be drawn from it.

Using that premise, you could infer from a person's financial failure that he had *not* gone to college. The syllogism would look like this:

If a person goes to college, he'll achieve financial security in later life (If P, then Q).

Bob Burns is not financially secure (Not Q).

Therefore Bob Burns didn't go to college (Therefore not P).

The minor premise has denied the consequent Q. From this it follows that the antecedent P can be denied.

But look at these two inferences from the same major premise:

Steve Johnson didn't go to college, so he'll never be financially secure.

Jane Smith is the richest person in town; she must be a college graduate.

Both inferences are incorrect. The *if . . . then* relationship isn't reversible. The major premise asserts that P implies Q, but it doesn't rule out the possibility of other antecedents for Q—other sources of financial security than P. Nor does it assert that Q implies P—that every case of financial security can be attributed to going to college.

To summarize, the two patterns of valid inference are these: affirming the antecedent (P) entails affirming the consequent (therefore Q), and denying the consequent (not Q) entails denying the antecedent (therefore not P). It's fallacious to move from denying the antecedent (not P) to denying the consequent (therefore not Q) or to move from affirming the consequent (Q) to affirming the antecedent (therefore P). The argument will also be unsound, of course, if the implication stated in the major premise is untrue.

Look again at the conclusions that we've labeled invalid: "Steve Johnson will never be financially secure" and "Jane Smith must be a college graduate." It may turn out that Steve never does become financially secure and that Jane did graduate from college—that is, we may discover that both conclusions are true. They're true, however, for reasons *other than* those given in the premises we were working with. In other words, invalid inference may yield a conclusion that happens to be true, just as valid inference may yield a conclusion that happens to be false. To repeat: For a *sound* argument, you need valid inference from true premises.

Note that in each of the examples in the preceding paragraphs—about "I," about Bob Burns, about Steve Johnson, about Jane Smith—the major premise has been unstated; we've had to supply it in constructing a syllogism. In some other examples we'll use, the minor premise will be omitted. These combinations of a single premise and a conclusion are called *enthymemes*. We use them constantly in speech and writing – far more often than we use full syllogisms. And, as with the first causal statement we proposed – "I'm going to college because I want to be financially secure" – they frequently represent probability rather than certainty. Finding out through the testing procedure that an enthymeme you've written falls into this category does *not* mean that you should abandon it. It does mean that you should try to assess the degree of probability and adjust the rest of your paper to it. Don't claim to be establishing truth when you're presenting only what is likely to be true. But don't, on the other hand, reject everything that's less than absolutely certain. If you do, you'll find yourself with very little to say.

Although the *if . . . then* pattern is particularly appropriate for expressing causal relations, it's not limited to them. The reasoning of the senator who says, "I oppose this bill because it's unconstitutional" could be put into the *if . . . then* framework:

If this bill is unconstitutional, then I oppose it.

This bill is unconstitutional.

Therefore I oppose it.

But the senator gives little attention to establishing the necessary relation between the unconstitutionality of a bill and his opposition to it. For him, that's a *given,* an assumption. His real job is to prove the minor premise, and this requires making a careful analysis of the bill to show that it is unconstitutional. Definition and classification, not causal relations, lie at the heart of this syllogism.

If . . . then is central to many problem-solution arguments. The final section of an article on "the new tyranny of sexual liberation" opens with an *if* (actually several *if*s) summarizing the problem and a *then* that points the way to the solution:

If we are to be truly liberated, if we are to understand and explore the contribution sexual arousal can make to relationships, if we are to make it possible once again for this activity to kindle the imagination and intellect, and if we are to do justice to the fact that man has a single nervous system whose functions are integrated and interdependent, then we must evolve a way of thinking about sex which sees it as embedded in a personal context.
– Derek Wright, *Life*

The author counts on his audience to agree with him that the *if*s are desirable and that the consequent can therefore be affirmed. In the rest of his essay he develops the consequent, outlining the steps that must be taken to achieve the new way of thinking about sex. (Once again, note that if the argument is to be sound as well as valid, the major premise must be true—the consequent must *necessarily* follow from the antecedent. Does it? Or can you offer another *then* clause that is equally convincing?)

Reasoning in *if . . . then* terms can sharpen an issue, making an audience face up to the implications of a widely held but perhaps unexamined view. The following assertion brings out the logical consequence of the notion that the price consumers are willing to pay provides an adequate and accurate index to the value of goods and services:

> If price were the only criterion of value, we should really have to accept the phrase *de gustibus non disputandum* [there's no disputing about taste], and concede that the desire for heroin was to be regarded by society as equal in every regard to the desire for education.—Eugene V. Rostow, *California Management Review*

Rejecting the consequent (which, it can be assumed, any reasonable person would do) involves rejecting the antecedent, and this in turn paves the way for reconsidering what criteria should be used in determining the value of goods and services.

■ *For Analysis and Writing*

1. Keeping Rostow's antecedent in the passage quoted above, substitute a number of other consequents; for example, "If price were the only criterion of value, everyone would agree that owning a huge diamond is preferable to having adequate housing." Then, keeping Rostow's consequent, substitute a number of other antecedents; for example, "If heroin addicts have made valuable contributions to society, the desire for heroin should be regarded by society as equal in every regard to the desire for education." Use your list of assertions to demonstrate why it's possible to move from affirming the antecedent to affirming the consequent but not the reverse, and from denying the consequent to denying the antecedent but not the reverse.

2. Note the form of this statement:

> If capital punishment is ever necessary for the preservation of public welfare, and it is at times necessary for that end, then according to reason capital punishment is lawful.—John J. Ford, *Catholic Mind*

Using the statement as a model, build several sentences that move through the three stages "If ..., and ..., then ...." *Then choose one of your sentences, and write a paragraph that supports the minor premise—the one phrased in the* and *stage.*

Either-Or Syllogisms

In arguments that weigh possibilities—courses of action, judgments, points of view—you'll find yourself using the *either-or* pattern. For testing such arguments, you have two forms of *either-or* syllogisms to work with:

	Disjunctive	*Alternative*
Major premise	Either A or B but not both	Either A or B
Minor premise	A	Not A
Conclusion	Therefore not B	Therefore B

The major premise in the disjunctive syllogism is exclusive—one or the other *but not both.* The major premise in the alternative syllogism is not exclusive: either *or* both can be true. The minor premise of the disjunctive affirms; it offers one of the possibilities. But the minor premise of the alternative syllogism denies; it excludes one of the possibilities.

An alternative syllogism with a positive minor premise can have no valid conclusion. If we write, "The senator could either run for reelection this year or try for the presidency two years from now, and he's decided to run for reelection," our readers can't assume that the senator is no longer a possible candidate in the next presidential election. He could return to the Senate and then make a bid for the presidency.

In fact, disjunctive syllogisms usually appear as simple *either-or* arguments, with "but not both" implied but unstated: "The senator must either win reelection this year or return to his law practice." Then the assertion that the senator has campaigned successfully means that he's not returning to his practice, and the assertion that he's returning to his practice means that he has lost his bid for reelection.

The most common *either-or* fallacy is an error in content, not in inference: it results from a major premise that poses incorrect alternatives (*false dichotomy*) or that fails to offer all the alternatives (*incomplete enumeration*). The untrue claim or implication that there are two and only two alternatives is extremely common. The militant says, "You're either with me or against me," canceling out neutrality. Traditionally, our society has told women they could have motherhood or a career but not both. In increasing numbers, women have proven society wrong. In the late 1960s the American people were told that they had to choose between inflation and recession. They got both.

A choice between inflation and recession is a mild example of the *dilemma,* the form of *either-or* argument in which both alternatives are unpleasant. The fight against pollution frequently creates true dilemmas — for example, either permit a lake to continue being polluted by industrial wastes or close down the industrial plant and so create unemployment.

Either-or arguments are inviting because they're simple, dramatic, direct. But the real world is complex, not simple like the world of *either-or.* Often there's another alternative, and there may be a dozen more. Whenever you find yourself writing, "We must make this change or accept defeat," or "We must choose either law or justice," or posing alternatives like "He's on our side, or he's an enemy," stop and ask yourself, "Really?" Perhaps if no change is made, the situation will remain about the same. Law with justice is a possibility. He may be neither ally nor enemy. Between black and white there are many shades of gray.

The fundamental test of an *either-or* argument is less often a matter of logic than of truth — the truth of the major premise. That premise always reflects a classification or division of the material under consideration; it will be true only if it proceeds from rigorous and accurate analysis. (See pp. 56–61.) If other alternatives can be shown to be feasible, the argument is unsound. A systematic consideration of genuine alternatives offers an excellent way of structuring and developing a persuasive paper. But shrill insistence on an *either-or* premise that stems from a faulty analysis of the material can be damaging to the very case you're trying to make.

■ *For Analysis and Writing*

In the following paragraph, the author says, "I don't see why it's an either/or situation." Just what is the "either/or situation"? Explain why you do or do not think that the argument should be framed as either-or alternatives.

Professional historians' groups concede that the news is better from some school districts than from others, but on the whole they are gloomy. That is because courses in ancient and modern history have been giving way at a rapid rate to such substitutes as ecology and consumer education, which are thought to be—in the words of one report—more "practical" and "related more significantly to problems faced by the society at the present time." I don't see why it's an either/or situation. But if it is, I would, on *practical* grounds, go with Charlemagne every time. For I think a knowledge of history is, to use the dread term, "relevant" above all other things to our immediate concerns, both as a society experiencing great internal strains and as a country whose interventions abroad have enormous consequences.—Meg Greenfield, *Newsweek*

In a column written two weeks later, the same writer says of abortion that it is "an issue that is exceptionally resistant to the classic middle-ground, I-am-a-moderate formulations." She goes on to ask

A moderate what? A moderate proponent of murder? A moderate proponent of denying women the right to decide whether they will bear a child?

After discussing the issue, the writer sets forth her own position and once again insists that abortion is an issue that has to be treated as either-or:

I think abortion is a choice that must be made by the woman involved and that her rights take precedence over the rights of an unborn and unformed human being and that abortion is not murder in any sense that should be covered by our criminal laws.

Having reached that conclusion by way of much anguish myself and not regarding it as the sort of thought that can be handily reduced to bumper-sticker size, I can appreciate the politicians' terror and turmoil—especially as they are trying to get elected to office and I am not. But this time and on this one I think they have no choice. They have to do the one thing that displeases them most. They have to say yes or no.—Meg Greenfield, *Newsweek*

Do you or don't you agree that the issue of history in the schools and the issue of abortion are different kinds of questions, that one is appropriately argued in terms of either-or *alternatives and the other isn't? Give reasons for your answer in a paper of 500 words.*

Categorical Syllogisms

A categorical syllogism asserts a series of class relationships. "All actors are egotists, and Van is an actor; so Van is an egotist." The major premise makes an assertion about all members of a class (actors), the minor premise relates the subject of discussion (Van) to that class, and the conclusion states what necessarily follows.

Each of the three assertions in the categorical syllogism contains two terms. The major term (P) is the predicate of the conclusion, the minor term (S) is the subject of the conclusion, and the middle term (M) appears in both the premises but – naturally – not in the conclusion. Diagrams show the relationships among the terms: the class M falls within the larger class P, and so on.

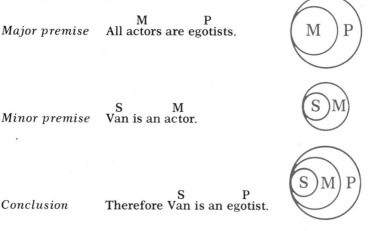

Major premise	M P All actors are egotists.
Minor premise	S M Van is an actor.
Conclusion	S P Therefore Van is an egotist.

In ordinary prose the categorical syllogism is sometimes hard to recognize, for the assertions may occur in any order and one of them may be omitted altogether:

Van is an actor [Minor premise], so he must be an egotist [Conclusion].

Van must be an egotist [Conclusion]: he's an actor [Minor premise].

All actors are egotists [Major premise]; so naturally Van's an egotist [Conclusion].

Van is an actor [Minor premise], and actors are egotists [Major premise].

All but the last of these examples are enthymemes. In the first and second the premise that all actors are egotists is omitted. The third implies that Van is an actor but doesn't say so.

Here are some other examples of enthymemes with the full syllogisms they're based on:

1. We should give this plan serious consideration because it offers a possible solution to the deadlock.

All plans that offer possible solutions to the deadlock are plans that should be given serious consideration (All M is P).

This plan is a plan that offers a possible solution to the deadlock (S is M).

This plan is a plan that should be given serious consideration (S is P).

2. I know some of my friends are real fans; they wouldn't have bought season tickets if they weren't.

All who buy season tickets are real fans (All M is P).

Some of my friends bought season tickets (Some S is M).

Some of my friends are real fans (Some S is P).

3. It's unreasonable to suppose that Laux, a staunch Republican, voted for a Democratic governor.

No staunch Republican is a person who votes for a Democratic governor (No M is P).

Laux is a staunch Republican (S is M).

Laux is not a person who votes for a Democratic governor (S is not P).

The tests for the categorical syllogism are precisely the same as for the other types of syllogisms. To be sound, the conclusion must make a valid inference from true premises. And once again, truth and validity must be examined separately. But the first step is to reconstruct the syllogism so that you can see exactly what's being asserted as true and what inference is being made. In everyday argument it's often the suppressed premise that contains an error. In "All fish have gills, so whales must," the concealed minor premise, "Whales are fish," is false, and so the conclusion is unsound. In "Jack must be a Democrat; he's in favor of socialized medicine," the concealed major premise, "Anybody who favors socialized medicine is a Democrat," is false, and so it's unsound to conclude that Jack is a Democrat. In both instances, as we shall see, the inferences are valid. But validity does not imply truth.

To test the validity of an inference, you often need to rephrase an assertion as well as to expand an elliptical statement into a full syllogism. The terms in the premises of a formal categorical syllogism are qualified in only three ways: *all, no, some. Few* and *most* are always translated into *some, every* and *any* into *all.* The trickiest qualifiers are *the only* and *only.* "The only people in favor of socialized medicine are Democrats" is clearly the equivalent of "All the people in favor of socialized medicine are Democrats." But "Only Democrats are in favor of socialized medicine," when rephrased as an *all* assertion, must have the term following *only* transferred to the predicate: "All who are in favor of socialized medicine are Democrats."

Diagramming offers a visual test for the validity of deductive inference. An inference will be valid only if the premises yield enough information to locate each circle (representing a class) in relation to the other two. "Jack must be a Democrat; he's in favor of socialized medicine" is valid because the premises tell us where M (supporters of socialized medicine) is in relation to P (Democrats) and where S (Jack) is in relation to M. But "Jack's a Democrat so he must favor socialized medicine" is invalid. "All who favor socialized medicine are Democrats" does not say that all Democrats favor socialized medicine. So Jack's being a Democrat doesn't prove he favors it. In our diagram we can't tell whether the S circle falls inside M or in the part of P that lies outside M. For valid inference we must know whether a circle lies inside another, lies outside it, or intersects it. A circle with no fixed location indicates that the inference is invalid.

Diagramming will tell you that an inference is valid or invalid, but to know exactly why it's invalid you need to apply the rules for inference. Two of the rules rely on the concept of *distribution*. A term is said to be distributed when the proposition in which it appears affirms or denies something about the entire class for which the term stands.

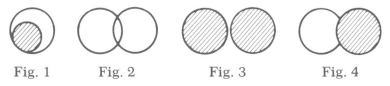

Fig. 1   Fig. 2   Fig. 3   Fig. 4

The shaded circles represent the distributed terms.

In "All men are mortal" (Fig. 1), the subject term *men* is distributed; mortality is said to be an attribute of the whole of the class. The predicate term *mortal* is undistributed, for no assertion is made about the whole of the class. In "Some men are liars" (Fig. 2), both terms are undistributed: some men (not all) are in the class of liars, a class whose limits are not specified. In "No men are four-legged" (Fig. 3), both terms are distributed: the class of men is excluded from the entire class of four-legged things. In "Some men are not liars" (Fig. 4), the subject term is undistributed; an assertion is made about some members of the class but not about all of them. The predicate term is distributed, however, for something *is* asserted about the entire class of liars — that some men are not in the class.

Knowing how the terms are distributed provides one quick test for validity. Here are the rules for valid inference in the categorical syllogism.

1. The syllogism contains three terms, and the meaning of these terms is the same every time they appear.

The *fallacy of four terms* is illustrated in this sequence of statements: All intellectuals are aesthetes, and Pete is an incessant reader; so Pete is an aesthete. If you try to diagram the sequence, you'll find there's no way to relate Pete to aesthetes.

The most common variant of the fallacy of four terms is *equivocation*, which results from a shift in the meaning of one of the three terms in the syllogism:

All other democratic republics are acceptable as allies of the United States.

East Germany is the German Democratic Republic.

Therefore East Germany is acceptable as an ally of the United States.

A sly or inadvertent shift in the meaning of a term (as in "democratic republic" above) results in invalid inference. A related error occurs in inferences whenever it's incorrectly assumed that what holds for a class collectively holds for every member of the class. Though Americans *as a whole* may have the highest standard of living in the world, it does not follow that every American lives well. Nor does the truth of the part guarantee the truth of the whole: the fact that migrant workers in the United States often suffer from malnutrition and have wretched housing does not mean that the American people are ill-fed and ill-housed.

2. The middle term must be distributed at least once in the premises — that is, an assertion must be made about *all* or *none* of the class.

The *fallacy of the undistributed middle* is the most common of the formal fallacies. It is illustrated in this pattern:

American flags are red, white, and blue.

This flag is red, white, and blue.

Therefore this flag is an American flag.

No inference about "this flag" can be drawn because neither premise has supplied any information about the whole class of red, white, and blue flags. In a diagram, "this flag" would fall somewhere within the circle of red, white, and blue flags, but there would be no way of knowing whether it would fall inside or outside the smaller circle of American flags.

3. No term can be distributed in the conclusion unless it was distributed in at least one of the premises.

Illicit process results from distributing in the conclusion a term that was not distributed either in the major premise (the *fallacy of the illicit major*) or in the minor premise (the *fallacy of the illicit minor*).

All good citizens are nature lovers.

No thief is a good citizen.

Therefore no thief is a nature lover.

In this syllogism "nature lover," distributed in the conclusion, is undistributed in the major premise. The inference is invalid because even though thieves are excluded from the smaller circle of good citizens, they may still fall within the larger circle of nature lovers. Do they? We can't tell.

Four other rules will help you spot invalid inference without going through the analysis of terms and their distribution:

4. From two particular premises (assertions about some — not all — members of a class), no conclusion can be drawn. (From "Some men are honest" and "Most thieves are men" we can infer nothing about the honesty of thieves.)

5. From two negative premises, no conclusion can be drawn. (From "No thieves are honest" and "Some men are not thieves" we can't infer that some men are honest.)

6. If one premise is negative, the conclusion must be negative.

7. If one premise is particular, the conclusion must be particular.

Non sequitur (does not follow) is a comprehensive category covering all those errors of reasoning in which the stated conclusion does not follow from the premises that have been supplied — the fallacies of undistributed middle terms, denial of the antecedent, and so on. But often what looks like a *non sequitur* to the reader is simply a lapse in continuity, a failure to make the relationship clear. It can occur whenever you skip a step in the argument and so leave the reader confused about how one assertion connects with another. Take the statement, "If you really love Lake Baikal, boycott Gogol's products." The reader who knows that the Gogol Company has been responsible for polluting Lake Baikal will grasp the relationship between antecedent and consequent. The reader who doesn't know will be puzzled. In this case, the impression of a *non sequitur* can be avoided by supplying the missing link in the reasoning. In other cases, where the error lies in the reasoning itself and not in the phrasing of it, the relation of the premises must be reexamined and strictly logical tests applied.

The criteria for valid inference in the categorical syllogism apply, with appropriate modification, to other types of deductive reasoning that are variations on the basic three-statement pattern. In a chain argument the inferential process is extended through four or more premises, with any two successive ones sharing a common term: "India was poor; it was ruled by Britain; British interests took goods and money out of India to Britain; therefore India's poverty was caused by British rule." Still other trains of deductive reasoning have their basis not in the kinds of relationships that can be represented by circles but in relationships that involve comparisons—one thing is better than another, or stronger than another, or older than another: "If their new release is better than 'Shriek,' it must be better than 'Groan,' because 'Shriek' was the best thing they'd done."

Logical inference offers general guidance but no sure criteria for the arguments we use most commonly in persuasion. By following the rules for valid inference, we could achieve certainty (not just probability) if we knew we were arguing from statements that were unquestionably true. But for the most part our reasoning is not grounded in universals (*all* or *none*) and does not yield— or claim to yield—certainty. More often we argue and act on the basis of probability in enthymemes like this one: "The Corner Bookstore carries a good stock of new novels, so I'll probably find Rogers' latest there." To say that you'll certainly find the novel you want is to commit the fallacy of the undistributed middle; to say that you'll probably find it is a reasonable inference. Weighing the probabilities is the crucial test for a good many of the deductive inferences we make and for our inductive generalizations as well.

■ *For Analysis and Writing*

1. Examine these brief bits of deductive reasoning. Sort out premises from conclusions; where necessary, uncover and examine concealed premises; and decide whether or not the conclusions are sound. If a conclusion is unsound, identify the fallacy.

a. If the Constitution was wisely conceived, the United States was destined to become a great and powerful country. The United States has become a great and powerful country. Therefore, the Constitution was wisely conceived.

b. Why study logic? It certainly has no bearing on the things that matter most to us — love, faith, and so on.

c. He must be either very foolish or very stupid; he's left all his money to charity.

d. He's a drunk, all right. Birds of a feather flock together.

e. More students go to college every year. Unfortunately, our mental institutions are getting more crowded all the time. There's obviously something wrong with the education our colleges are giving.

f. Studying logic improves reasoning power. Literature is not logic, so studying literature does not improve reasoning power.

g. Style is choice. Choice reflects personality. Writers differ in their personalities. Therefore writers differ in their styles.

h. No wonder the book is a best-seller. Look at the sex in it.

i. He doesn't really believe that human life is sacred. He drives his car every day.

j. He's a distinguished atomic scientist, so the President should seek his advice on this international problem.

k. No sentimentalists are tough-minded; some businessmen are tough-minded; therefore some businessmen are not sentimentalists.

l. All underdeveloped countries are countries where the standard of living is low. All countries where the standard of living is low are countries susceptible to Communist influence. So all countries susceptible to Communist influence are underdeveloped countries.

m. The notion that college students are unconcerned about the hereafter is absurd. Millions of them go to church every Sunday.

n. I can't understand why he spends so much time in Canada. He must be un-American.

o. You believe in free enterprise in business, so why won't you support competition in the postal service?

2. Analyze the following passage. First, decide whether the reasoning is or is not valid. Then write a brief paper in which you argue, on the basis of your own experience and investigation, that the conclusion is or is not true.

Teachers of writing courses in which a good deal of time is spent analyzing readings assume that there's a significant connection between the ability to read and the ability to write. There is. But it's important to get straight the logic of that relation. If a student can't read well, he can't write well. But it does not follow that if he can read well, he can write well.

3. Analyze the train of reasoning in each of the following excerpts and explain why you find it sound or unsound. If it's unsound, identify the fallacy.

a. I see no reason in morality (or in aesthetic theory) why literature should not have as one of its intentions the arousing of thoughts of lust. It is one of the effects, perhaps one of the functions, of literature to arouse desire, and I can discover no ground for saying that sexual pleasure should not be among the objects of desire which literature presents to us, along with heroism, virtue, peace, death, food, wisdom, God, etc. — Lionel Trilling, quoted in Kenneth Tynan, *Esquire*

b. The remaking of American education will not be possible without a new kind of synergistic relationship between the colleges and universities and the public schools. The schools cannot be transformed unless the colleges and universities turn out a new breed of teachers educated to think about purpose, teachers who are themselves, in Dewey's phrase, students of teaching. But the colleges and universities will be unable to train the kinds of teachers we need unless they, working with the schools, create classrooms that afford their students models of what teaching can and should be like. — Charles Silberman, *Atlantic*

c. All life and property are now in jeopardy because the foreign policies of the national sovereignties produce total anarchy. It is necessary, therefore, for people to stretch their minds, their concepts and their demands in order to bring about a government over governments. Anything else is irrelevant to their safety and indeed to their destiny. — N[orman] C[ousins], *Saturday Review*

d. The newspaper should stop reporting local incidents of rape and assault. Such reports arouse fear in our citizens and do harm to the image of our town as a safe, pleasant place to live. The ill effects of such news items certainly outweigh any benefits. — Letter to the Editor

e. Every discovery of a true correspondence is an act of reason and an instruction to the mind. For intelligence does not consist of masses of factual detail. It consists of seeing essential likenesses and differences and of relating them, allowing for differences with the likenesses and for likenesses with the differences. Mentality is born of analogy. — John Ciardi, *Saturday Evening Post*

f. The college administration has gradually recognized that dorms are private residences of students who may see whom they wish, when they wish, in their homes. Administrators have ceded their right to restrict our personal actions in dorms except in the most destructive or violent cases. Drinking is neither.

Granted underage drinking is illegal in this state, and the college is bound to obey state law. But a second Prohibition will be no more successful than the first. Most of us demand liquor. If we're denied it, the dorm supervisors will all have writer's cramp from filing disciplinary charges, the bureaucratic gears will grind to a halt when faced with their processing, the administration will have its back to the wall, and the students will still be merrily boozing it up.

All students, whether "wet" or "dry," should oppose any attempt to force us back into a childhood we have outgrown. — Adapted from a college newspaper editorial

g. The way I understand the law and any other subject is to understand it in its context, in its relations to all other subjects that bear upon it. In the case of the law, philosophy, history, psychology, and all the social sciences bear upon it, and it bears on all of them, and I venture to suggest that it is this, this centrality, this intellectual centrality, this bearing that the law has on all intellectual subjects and the bearing that they have on it, it is this that makes the law a university subject. If the law is not taught this way, then there is no reason why it should not be relegated to trade schools—and I mean trade schools that are admittedly trade schools, in name as well as in fact.

Any section of the university that cannot have an intellectual connection with the rest of the university has no place in the university and should be abolished. Since all other disciplines in the university today are in the same shape that the law is in, and since a university does not exist in my opinion unless it is an intellectual community, it follows that almost no universities exist in the United States, for almost none of them is or can be an intellectual community. — Robert M. Hutchins, *Change*

4. From the seven excerpts in 3 (above), select any assertion that interests you and write an argument supporting or attacking it.

Chapter Seven
Shaping Sentences

Whether the sentences you compose turn out to be clear or fuzzy, limp or emphatic, rhythmical or stumbling depends on how skillful you are in putting them together and particularly in revising and rewriting them for your final draft. This chapter will focus on individual sentences; but keep in mind all we said in Chapter Four about the need for relating sentences to one another and grouping them in paragraphs. It's always better to think in—and to write—blocks of sentences rather than single sentences. No matter how well made a sentence is, unless it works well with its neighbors, it doesn't do what it should for your paper.

As you shape a particular sentence, then, you also have to take into account the sentences that precede it and the sentences that will follow it. Should its structure contrast with the structure of the sentence before it, or should it repeat that structure? Should the emphasis fall at the beginning or at the end, close to the next sentence? Whether a sentence is long or short, straightforward or involved, it should do what you want it to do in its context.

When we compare two versions of a sentence in this chapter and indicate that one is better than the other, we're saying that *in most contexts* it would be better. The important thing is for you to be in control of a variety of ways of expressing your ideas, so that you can meet the rhetorical demands of the immediate context. Satisfying these demands is part of the job you face when you sit down to prepare a final draft.

When you're revising, don't just look at individual sentences and decide to subtract words from one or add them to another. Concentrate on separating, combining, and regrouping *ideas*. More often than not, your purpose in breaking up one sentence or combining two will be to iron out an inconsistency, to introduce a needed qualification, to give a statement the right emphasis—most of all, to bring out logical relationships.

Combining Sentences

In revising, you may find that you've used too many sentences in your first draft, perhaps giving a full sentence to an insignificant detail, perhaps saying the same thing twice, perhaps separating ideas that belong together. If your sentences are consistently short—say under seventeen words—you're probably fragmenting your ideas.

To make sure we have a vocabulary for discussing syntax, the order and relation of sentence elements, we'll briefly review the traditional system of classifying sentences:

Sentences are called simple, compound, complex, and compound-complex according to the number and kind of clauses (subject-predicate combinations) they have.

Clauses may be independent or dependent. Grammatically, an independent clause can stand alone as a complete sentence. A dependent (or subordinate) clause can't. Dependent clauses are introduced by subordinating conjunctions like *if, when, although* or by relative pronouns like *that, who, which,* though these relative pronouns may sometimes be omitted from the clauses they introduce ("I knew [that] you would come").

A *simple* sentence, like this one, consists of one independent clause. It's often short but needn't be. Like the other three sentence types, a simple sentence can contain compound subjects, compound verbs, compound objects, and compound modifiers; prepositional phrases; verbals and verbal phrases; adjectives, adjectives in series, and adjective phrases; and nouns and noun phrases used as appositives. The long sentence you've just read is grammatically a simple sentence.

A *compound* sentence consists of two or more independent clauses. The clauses are usually joined by coordinating conjunctions like *and, but, or,* but sometimes two clauses are joined by a pair of correlative conjunctions like *either . . . or* or *not only . . . but also.* (The preceding sentence is a compound sentence.) They may also be linked by a semicolon; in such cases the second clause often begins with a conjunctive adverb like *however, nevertheless, hence.* (The preceding sentence, too, is compound.)

A *complex* sentence consists of one independent clause and one or more dependent clauses. When you write a complex sentence, you can often place the dependent clause either before or after or within the independent clause, as you choose. (The preceding sentence is a complex sentence.)

A *compound-complex* sentence consists of two or more independent clauses and one or more dependent clauses. A compound-complex sentence can be very long, or it can be as short as "If he did it, find him guilty; if not, set him free."

Coordinating and Subordinating

As the preceding definitions suggest, two ways to combine sentences are by coordinating and subordinating. The simplest way is to join them with a coordinating conjunction:

The United States is a conservative country. Its working class is one of the anchors of its conservatism.

The United States is a conservative country, and its working class is one of the anchors of its conservatism. — Richard Hofstadter, *Harper's*

Often, though, simply tying two sentences together won't work. Take these two sentences:

The principal urban characters in the comic strips — Maggie and Jiggs, Moon Mullins, Dick Tracy — were Irish. These were early comic strips.

Turning them into a compound sentence — "The principal urban characters . . . were Irish, and these were early comic strips" — wouldn't make sense in most imaginable contexts. Instead, the second sentence could be converted into a dependent clause:

When the comic strips began, the principal urban characters — Maggie and Jiggs, Moon Mullins, Dick Tracy — were Irish. — Nathan Glazer and Daniel Patrick Moynihan, *Beyond the Melting Pot*

Sensible subordination of separate sentences puts information together that belongs together, gives writing a brisker pace, and makes it sound more adult, less like the prose in grade-school readers. The two sentences

She left without Jack. He was the man she had come with.

can be rewritten as a single sentence in various ways:

She left without Jack, the man she had come with.

She left without Jack, though she had come with him.

Though she had come with Jack, she left without him.

Making Choices. When you combine sentences, what you want to say will ordinarily determine whether you use coordination or subordination. But often you can say what you mean in either a compound sentence or a complex sentence, and then you choose one rather than the other in order to make a smoother transition, to break up a succession of sentences with the same structure, or for some similar reason. Though there may be slight differences in emphasis and degree of explicitness, in some contexts either of these paired sentences could be used:

He shouted, *but* the crowd paid no attention.
Although he shouted, the crowd paid no attention.

You must enroll for the course, *or* you will not receive credit.
Unless you enroll for the course, you will not receive credit.

He appealed the decision, *for* everyone advised him to.
He appealed the decision *because* everyone advised him to.

Both coordinating and subordinating offer further choices. Take these two statements:

He kept making eloquent speeches against corruption.

The Council remained indifferent.

If you want to point up the contrast, you can coordinate them in any of these ways:

He kept making eloquent speeches against corruption; the Council remained indifferent.

He kept making eloquent speeches against corruption, but the Council remained indifferent.

He kept making eloquent speeches against corruption; however, the Council remained indifferent.

He kept making eloquent speeches against corruption; the Council, however, remained indifferent. Or: . . . remained indifferent, however.

Or you might have reason to reverse the order of the clauses:

The Council remained indifferent, but he kept making eloquent speeches against corruption.

And so on. Instead of *but* or *however*, you might use any one of a number of other connectives that indicate contrast: *yet, still, nevertheless, in spite of that* are examples.

If you want to point up the contrast by subordinating, you have to decide which clause should be the independent clause — where the emphasis in the sentence should fall—and also whether it should follow or precede the dependent clause. If you settle on *though* as the subordinating conjunction, you have these possibilities to choose from:

Though he kept making eloquent speeches against corruption, the Council remained indifferent.

He kept making eloquent speeches against corruption, though the Council remained indifferent.

Though the Council remained indifferent, he kept making eloquent speeches against corruption.

The Council remained indifferent though he kept making eloquent speeches against corruption.

The Council, though he kept making eloquent speeches against corruption, remained indifferent.

He kept making, though the Council remained indifferent, eloquent speeches against corruption.

Stylistic considerations alone would rule out the last, with its awkward interruption of verb and complement, and probably the second last as well. Choices among the others should be made largely on the basis of context— what the neighboring sentences call for, what emphasis is needed. Compare:

Though he kept making eloquent speeches against corruption, the Council remained indifferent. So he gave up. Indifference was the one response he could not tolerate.

Nobody else in town showed his persistence. Though the Council remained indifferent, he kept making eloquent speeches against corruption.

The first passage begins by emphasizing the indifference of the Council and thus points the way to the third sentence, which has *indifference* as its subject. The second passage begins with a generalization about his persistence and supports the generalization with a sentence so arranged that his persistence is emphasized.

Placing Clauses. In subordinating, it's good stylistic practice to experiment with the position of the dependent clause. You'll find that some kinds of clauses are more mobile than others and that some shifts in the position of clauses will clarify your meaning while others will obscure it. At times the position of an adverbial clause (introduced by words like *when, if, although, because*) makes no difference in the meaning:

When he spoke in support of the bill, he was in Washington.

He was in Washington when he spoke in support of the bill.

He was, when he spoke in support of the bill, in Washington.

In other sentences the placing of the adverbial clause makes a decided difference in meaning:

While he was in Washington, he argued that the bill should be passed.

He argued that the bill should be passed while he was in Washington.

Note, too, that the second of these sentences can be interpreted in at least three different ways: Was he arguing that the passage of the bill should be accomplished during the time that he was in Washington, not after he had left? Was he two-faced—arguing for the bill in Washington but against it elsewhere? Or does the sentence mean that though he argued for the bill while he was in Washington, he soon had to leave the capital? Although context could probably be counted on to resolve the ambiguity, the adverbial clause should be placed so that the meaning is unmistakable. If that's impossible, the sentence should be rewritten.

Clauses used either as nouns or as adjectives (usually introduced by *who, which, that,* though the introductory word is sometimes omitted) are less mobile than adverbial clauses. When a clause used as an adjective is placed near a word it can't logically modify, there's not so much a change in meaning as a loss of sense:

No one was interested in meeting Oscar or his new bride, who had come to the reunion to show her off. [The *who* clause doesn't modify "bride."]

We drove over an old bridge into the village, which grumbled under the weight of our camper. [The *which* clause doesn't modify "village."]

In cases like these, simply shifting the clause either creates confusion:

No one was interested in meeting Oscar, who had come to the reunion to show her off, or his new bride.

Or it causes an awkward interruption:

We drove over an old bridge, which grumbled under the weight of our camper, into the village.

In both cases, the best solution is to rearrange the sentence so that the word being modified and the clause that modifies it come together at the end:

No one was interested in meeting Oscar's new bride or in meeting Oscar, who had come to the reunion to show her off.

We drove into the village over an old bridge, which grumbled under the weight of our camper.

In other cases, shifting the clause to a different position in the sentence will make the intended meaning clear:

The stanza in the poem that I prefer is only two lines long.

The stanza [that] I prefer [in the poem] is only two lines long.

The bracketed words might be omitted.

When a dependent clause can come before, after, or in the middle of the independent clause without altering the meaning, weigh the advantages of one position against another as you revise your draft. Putting the clause first usually produces a neater sentence:

When we finally got to her house, she was packed and ready to leave.

Putting it last produces a looser, more casual style:

She was packed and ready to leave when we finally got to her house.

When it's placed first, readers have the circumstance or qualification or concession in mind while they're reading the main assertion; and this is often an advantage. But you may decide to put the dependent clause last or in the middle so that you can make a smoother transition into or out of the sentence. What's important is to recognize the difference between a situation in which you have a choice and one in which you don't and, when you have a choice, to select the alternative that helps you say best what you want to say.

In either subordinating or coordinating, the choice of conjunction is often automatic, but in revising your early drafts you should keep reminding yourself of the context. Out of context, *and* clearly adds and *but* contrasts. Just as clearly, the *and* of the first passage below conveys a different meaning from the *and* of the second:

Yesterday I had news of the two Smith boys for the first time since they left home. John is a bank manager in New Orleans, and James is a forest ranger in Idaho.

Although he modeled himself on his brother for years, James Smith finally showed some independence. Now John is a bank manager in New Orleans, and James is a forest ranger in Idaho.

In conversation, the clause introduced by the second *and* would have something of a "what-do-you-know" effect, with the *and* close to the usual meaning conveyed by *but.*

Context, then, can give an overlay of meaning — even a new meaning — to the commonest of conjunctions. What causes trouble is the use of *and* in contexts that call for decidedly different conjunctions:

He went to church every Sunday, and he never put a cent in the collection plate.

The sentence seems to cry out for *but* instead of *and.* If the first clause was subordinated, *although* would be the natural choice of conjunction, expressing the same contrast that *but* does.

Here the contrast expressed by *however* is decidedly illogical:

Admittedly the high cost of automobile liability insurance is a real burden to some drivers. However, the protection it affords is so limited that the insured may still be stuck with tremendous bills.

Furthermore or *besides* would be a logical choice.

Even when a conjunction isn't misleading, it may be less precise than it should be. In this pair of sentences, *because* makes explicit what *and* can only imply:

The film upsets traditional notions about morality, and conservatives are agitating to have its audience restricted.

Because the film upsets traditional notions about morality, conservatives are agitating to have its audience restricted.

While cause shouldn't be assigned casually, use *because* whenever you have good reason to do so. Explicit conjunctions give combined sentences a strength and vigor seldom found in their separate parts.

Embedding Words and Phrases

Combining sentences needn't involve either coordinating or subordinating. Sometimes in revising you'll reduce one sentence to a few words and add them to, or embed them in, another sentence:

Parts of the world are becoming overrun by tourists. They are the most beautiful parts.

The most beautiful parts of the world are becoming overrun by tourists.

You can also make subjects, verbs, and modifying words compound. In the following example the single sentence that expresses the content of the separate sentences has a compound subject ("Both radio and TV") and compound adjectives ("short, unrelated") as well as the compound adverbs ("between and within") that appear in the first version:

Radio offers short programs, interrupted between and within by commercials. They are often unrelated. TV does this too.

Both radio and TV offer short, unrelated programs, interrupted between and within by commercials. — Edmund Carpenter, *Explorations in Communication*

Verbs and objects may also be made compound when words from one sentence are embedded in another in this way.

Often, in combining sentences, you'll find that you have to change the form of a word you're transferring. Frequently you'll change verbs to verbals — gerunds, participles, and infinitives — and embed them either singly or in phrases, as in these examples:

I *read* the book. It was a shock, a thrill, a wild adventure.

Reading the book was a shock, a thrill, a wild adventure.

This flood of rhetoric had an effect. It *befuddled* the outside world with the view that China was indeed being aggressive, as the West already assumed.

The effect of this flood of rhetoric was *to befuddle* the outside world with the view that China was indeed being aggressive, as the West already assumed. — John K. Fairbank, *New York Review of Books.*

And you will shift some adjectives from predicate position and turn them into modifiers of the subject:

The citizens of Winesburg are *frustrated* and *distorted.* They are *violent* or *passive.* They are also *aggressive* or *self-destructive.* They are the living dead. They are victims of truths which are limited and which deny life, and they are guilty for having chosen them.

Frustrated, distorted, violent or *passive, aggressive* or *self-destructive,* the citizens of Winesburg are the living dead, victims of limited, life-denying truths and guilty for having chosen them. — Brom Webster, *Sherwood Anderson*

When you combine sentences, you can also use nouns — singly or in series or in phrases — as appositives, naming or further identifying or describing the other nouns they follow. In this example a series of nouns in apposition specifies who is hunted:

And none of those he hunts — thieves, drug pushers, Murphy men, assault and robbery men, killers — wants to confront him on anything resembling even terms. — James Mills, *Life*

Separation into two sentences would produce something flatter like

He hunts thieves, drug pushers, Murphy men, assault and robbery men, and killers. None of them wants to confront him on anything resembling even terms.

■ *For Analysis and Writing*

Revise the items below according to the instructions.

a. The parasite is a tiny worm. The parasite can penetrate the skin of a human. The parasite can enter the bloodstream of a human. The parasite lays eggs in the bloodstream. (Make one sentence.)

b. At first I found her attractive. She wore a bit too much makeup. Underneath, her facial bone structure was strong and pleasing. (Rewrite as one or two sentences, using conjunctions to bring out a sensible relationship among the observations.)

c. The main reason I began college in the summer term is that it will take me several years to complete my formal education. The sooner I start, the sooner I will be through. (Join the two sentences so that the causal relation is clear and logical.)

d. Scientists face many conflicts between their work and moral standards that seem insoluble. (Revise to make clear what "that" modifies.)

e. Teachers who are interested in their subjects do the best work. The same is true of students. (Make one sentence, first by joining these two and then by reducing one of them to a phrase and embedding it in the other.)

f. There are also study lounges on every other floor of the dorm if you don't want to leave the building where you can study. (Shift the position of the *if* clause for clarity and smoothness.)

g. Many nations that have built up a military caste have lived to regret giving power to those with the skill and inclination to use it. A good many people feared the prospect of a professional army in this country. (Make one of the independent clauses dependent.)

h. With a bedroom, a kitchen, a living room, and a bathroom up the hall that rented for $125 a month, the apartment was a great bargain. (Make clear what rented for $125 a month.)

i. Because the mainland was convulsed in civil war, news of the massacre received little world attention. The news was reported by a few foreign journalists on the spot. (Make one sentence by reducing one of these sentences to a dependent clause or a phrase.)

j. Laguna Diablo is about 175 miles down the Baja California peninsula. It is surrounded by mountains of brown rock. It is dry. It is desolate. It is miles from the nearest plumbing, the nearest freeway. — Sam Moses, *Sports Illustrated.* (Combine into one simple sentence.)

k. They made their first homes in dugouts or sod cabins. These dugouts or cabins were dark. They were badly ventilated. The windows were covered with blankets or hides. So were the doors. (Combine into one sentence.)

Breaking Up Sentences

In revising your first drafts you may come upon sentences that need breaking up. And in going over revisions in which you've combined sentences, you may find that at times you've stuffed in more than you should have. The sentences that most urgently need breaking up are those that join unrelated ideas and so lack unity. The two assertions in the following sentence belong in separate — and separated — sentences:

The desert country of New Mexico presents a striking contrast to the mountain beauty of Colorado, where the citizens are strongly opposed to any increase in the state income tax.

It would be hard to imagine any possible connection between the attitude of Colorado's citizens toward a state income tax and the geological contrast between Colorado and New Mexico. So simply turning the subordinate clause ("where the citizens . . .") into a separate sentence ("The citizens of Colorado are . . .") wouldn't improve things. The new sentence probably belongs in a different paragraph.

Less obviously illogical but still troublesome is the sentence that brings together ideas that have some relationship but not a close enough one to justify joining them. The lead sentence of a book review or news story is sometimes too loaded for clarity:

The Merry Month of May, a title used ironically, is a novel of dissolution, the dissolution of a family of American expatriates at the time, and partly because, of the student riots in Paris in the spring of 1968, which when the unions and the apache

joined in brought all France to a standstill. — Edward Weeks,
Atlantic

Mr. Nader's criticism of pollution caused by Union Carbide's
Ferro Alloy Division here, which results in a 24-hour pall of
black, yellow and orange smoke and soot that nearly blots out
the sun and has forced the Roman Catholic Church to enclose
an outdoor statue of St. Anthony in a transparent plastic case,
was contained in a letter to . . . the Carbide board chairman in
New York. — *New York Times*

In the second example the details about pollution compete so strongly for attention that the reader is distracted
from the main point. Separating out some of the details
about the pollution would improve sentence unity. But
the main point is hard to grasp for still another reason:
the grammatical subject ("criticism") is separated from
its verb ("was contained") by a long string of phrases and
dependent clauses. Reordering the main elements and
replacing abstract "criticism" with an active verb ("criticized") would make the sentence clearer and more direct:
"In a letter to the Carbide board chairman . . . Mr. Nader
criticized the pollution caused by. . . ."

Degrees of interruption are illustrated in this sentence:

But one cannot keep, in looking at documents which might
establish a context for a last inference about the Nixon Administration, finding signs, in government in recent years, of something, in economic terms at least, radically amiss. . . . — Renata
Adler, *Atlantic*

The delays caused by separating "help" from "finding"
and "something" from "radically amiss" are troublesome. While the separation of "signs" from "of something" may be less noticeable, three delays in one sentence are likely to bother most readers.

Long modifiers that break up the basic structure of a
clause can so interfere with the forward movement of a
sentence that the reader loses track of the really important assertion. And when repeated embedding places two
verb phrases side by side, the reader has to go back over
the sentence to match the right verb with the right subject:

All these forces, added to the other deterrents which combinations of Powers, great and small, ready to stand firm upon the
front of law and for the ordered remedy of grievances, would
have formed, might well have been effective. — Winston S.
Churchill, "The Munich Agreement"

Even short interrupters can spoil a sentence if they're
allowed to create an erratic, jerky movement:

American drama, it is generally agreed, continues, as it has over a long period, to be in a seriously bad way. —Nathan A. Scott, Jr., *Broken Center*

If you find yourself writing sentences that contain several paired commas or dashes or parentheses, examine the elements they enclose to see, first, whether you're making necessary, useful qualifications. Repeated interruption to qualify unnecessarily can make you sound indecisive or evasive or prissy. And if the enclosed elements are no more than asides or extraneous details (often in the form of prepositional phrases), they overload your sentences and slow them down.

Be sure you haven't produced a sentence so long or so complicated that the reader gets lost in it. For a house-that-Jack-built sentence that stitches several dependent clauses together, separation is often the best remedy. This one, with its ten dependent clauses—most of them built one upon the other—needs to be separated into at least two sentences and, in the process, reduced to its essential meaning:

He admitted that the course of study which he was taking was the wrong one for him because it could never lead to a job that would give him the kinds of satisfaction that he would expect if he agreed to put up with the restrictions on his time that would certainly be the result of taking a position in the field for which he was currently preparing himself.

He admitted that the course of study he was taking was the wrong one for him. It could only lead to a job that would restrict his freedom and deny him the satisfactions he sought.

And so sentences string together one independent clause after another, flattening out logical relationships so that everything seems to have equal importance. Unless there's a rhetorical justification for this effect— unless, that is, you have a reason for wanting to give just that impression—restructure any *and so* sentence you find in your writing. Ordinarily a stringy sentence like the following will strike the reader as unemphatic, imprecise, and tiresome:

I found my eyes blurring, and so I took my usual headache pills, and after a couple of hours my head didn't hurt so much and my vision cleared, and so I went back to work.

In revising, look for natural breaking points (here, after "and so I took my headache pills"), and then consider whether using subordination to bring out chronological and causal relations would improve the sentence. In revising the preceding example, you might end up with something like

When I found my eyes blurring, I took my usual headache pills. After a couple of hours my head didn't hurt so much, and since my vision had cleared, I was able to go back to work.

■ For Writing

Break up each of these long sentences into shorter sentences. Don't try to see how many sentences you can produce. Instead, reshape the material into enough sentences to make it easier for you to read and understand.

  a. Swimming slowly, the four of them swam out in the green water, their bodies making shadows over the clear white sand, bodies forging along, shadows projected on the sand by the slight angle of the sun, the brown arms lifting and pushing forward, the hands slicing in, taking hold of the water and pulling it back, legs beating along steadily, heads turning for air, breathing easily and smoothly. – Ernest Hemingway, *Esquire*

  b. Claudia McNeil, the star of *Tiger*, an enormous woman, very dark, glared silently each day at Logan, measuring him, seeming to possess in her attitude the secret of his weakness and the power to destroy him; and Joshua Logan, at fifty-four, white-haired, white-mustached, big and broadshouldered but somehow soft and very pale, stood in front of the Negro cast of this play about a mother who dominates her children in a dream world she has created in Louisiana – a play that gradually, as rehearsals progressed, churned up more and more memories for Logan, haunting memories of his days in Mansfield, Louisiana, on his grandfather's cotton plantation, where, in his boyhood dreams, he often saw himself as a strong man riding through the streets of Mansfield standing on a horse, arms folded across his chest. – Gay Talese, *The Overreachers*

Emphasis, Directness, Economy

As you revise and rewrite, keep trying to make your sentences say what you want them to say with the emphasis you intend. For the most part, this means expressing yourself directly and economically.

Achieving Emphasis

In reviewing your early drafts, examine your sentences to see that you've placed emphasis where it belongs. Decisions about such matters as whether to combine or separate sentences and where to place elements within sentences determine what's emphasized and what isn't.

Separating for Emphasis. In speaking, a pause allows what's just been said to sink in or throws emphasis on what follows. In writing, something of the same effect can be gained by separating. Consider this sentence:

The trouble with modern English spelling is that it does not spell or even approximately spell modern English but instead spells the English of the Late Middle English period around 1470 A.D.

Here is the much more emphatic form in which it originally appeared, as three separate sentences:

The trouble with modern English spelling is that it does not spell modern English. It does not even approximately spell modern English. What it does spell is the English of the Late Middle English period around 1470 A.D.—Harold Whitehall, *Structural Essentials of English*

Now contrast this pair of sentences:

It promises and delivers a civilized, casual, and colorful account of a phenomenon unfamiliar to many of us but important to our times.

It promises a civilized, casual, and colorful account of a phenomenon unfamiliar to us but important to our times; and it delivers.—Dan Wakefield, *Atlantic*

In the second version Wakefield's use of two clauses instead of one and his choice of a semicolon (instead of a comma) between them give "delivers" an emphasis that's completely lacking in the first.

In smaller units, repeating the conjunction or preposition in a series of parallel items isolates and emphasizes each item. Here, in an article on the position of women in America, the repetition of *her* underlines the division of the sexes:

It is not exactly a posture in which she has much of a chance to enjoy her life, her liberty, or the pursuit of her happiness. —Clare Boothe Luce, *Saturday Review/World*

Ordering for Emphasis. The natural points of emphasis in a sentence are the beginning and the end. You'll waste them if you launch your sentences with empty introductions or let them run down into trivial detail. In revising sentences (or paragraphs) for emphasis, look for ways to build to some sort of climax. It may be simply a matter of making your point at the end, or of making the last word a word that has impact (*victory, disaster, ridiculous, magnificent—if* the context justifies such words), or of using a short, punchy sentence to bring a paragraph to a close. When you list items, see if you can't order them in some logical way — either the order of climax, with the biggest, oldest, richest, or most something in the list coming last, or possibly in order of diminishing importance, moving down the scale.

Often, of course, no rise or fall is inherent in the content: a list of a city's manufactures or a state's farm produce may offer no rationale for ordering the items. But when there is an opportunity to give direction to a list, failing to do so may result in a flabby, boneless sentence or sometimes in silly anticlimax:

The driver of the other car was in much worse shape, with a sprained ankle, a crushed pelvis, a severe concussion, and a bruised elbow.

In this case, as in many others, the items should be pruned as well as reordered. Here, the bruised elbow should probably be eliminated as a trivial detail.

The introductions *It is, It was, There is, There were* are properly criticized as sentence openers when they substitute unnecessary filler for a strong subject-verb combination:

[There are] some people [who] read history to increase their own self-esteem. [It is a fact that] the past offers such an array of villains that almost anyone reading about them can feel some moral superiority.

The words in brackets could be omitted — and should be, unless the context provides some excuse for the longer version. In revising your papers, check every sentence that you've begun with *It is* or *There is*, and unless the opener is serving some real function, drop it. Breaking the habit of beginning sentences with these words is one of the quickest and easiest ways to improve a writing style.

This doesn't mean you'll never open a sentence with *It is, It was, There is,* or *There were,* but when you do, it will be with a purpose. These openers can perform useful — even necessary — functions. They may assert the existence of what follows: "There are six major martial arts." They may provide special emphasis: "Quarreling about words is silly" emphasizes *silly;* "It's silly to quarrel about words" emphasizes *words.* And using the expletive *It is* to begin one sentence often opens the way for a smooth transition into the next one:

It is important to the purposes of history to remember that the twenty blacks who arrived in Jamestown in 1615 were not, strictly speaking, slaves. They were permitted to become "indentured servants."—Larry L. King, *Confessions of a White Racist*

An alternate version of the first sentence—"Remembering that the twenty blacks . . . is important to the purposes of history"—would shift the emphasis to "the purposes of history" and blur the transition to the following "They."

Mechanical Devices and Word Choice. You can indicate emphasis by underlining, by capitalizing, and by using exclamation marks, but depending on these methods is primitive practice—like shouting to gain attention. If your content is strong and you're expressing yourself well, the mechanical devices aren't necessary. If your content and style are weak, the devices won't help.

Slightly less obvious are the adverbs commonly tacked onto adjectives (*very* beautiful, *extremely* successful, *terrifically* loud); the adjectives that once carried real force but now, through overuse in conversation, do little more than express approval or disapproval (a *wonderful* time, a *terrible* exam, a *horrible* day); and the superlatives most of us overuse in speech (the *greatest* game, the *wildest* time, the *craziest* driver). In serious writing, reliance on any of these weakens rather than strengthens what's said. Nouns that are themselves emphatic in meaning—the *victory* and *disaster* we cited earlier, *triumph*, *genius*, *tragedy*, *sensation*—have their legitimate uses, but when applied indiscriminately ("The new sweater was a sensation"), they make a writer sound like a fraud or a fool.

You're not likely to achieve successful emphasis—that is, emphasis that convinces the reader—by using mechanical devices and exaggerated word choice. Instead, choose words that are appropriate to the context and the rhetorical situation and place them where you want the emphasis to fall.

Repetition. Thoughtless, accidental, or lazy repetition always weakens style, but consciously repeating words and phrases that are genuinely significant emphasizes ideas. (The function of repetition in binding sentences together and making paragraphs cohere has been discussed on pp. 152–54.) Controlled repetition of the key terms in a paper keeps the reader's attention focused and makes for clearer, more honest writing than shifting from synonym to synonym ("the Supreme Court . . . the high court . . . the highest tribunal").

In the first sentence of the passage that follows, James Baldwin makes careful discriminations in word choice ("chilling," "cruel," "bitter"); in the second he uses repetition deliberately and purposefully:

> He could be chilling in the pulpit and indescribably cruel in his personal life and he was certainly the most bitter man I have ever met; yet it must be said that there was something else in him, buried in him, which lent him his tremendous power and, even, a rather crushing charm. It had something to do with his blackness, I think—he was very black—with his blackness and his beauty, and with the fact that he knew that he was black but did not know that he was beautiful.—James Baldwin, *Notes of a Native Son*

Notice that both nouns ("blackness," "beauty") and adjectives ("black," "beautiful") are involved in the repetition.

Often, as here, the effect of verbal repetition is enhanced by the repetition of sounds. Together the two sentences offer many examples of alliteration—in addition to the insistent *b*'s, the patterns of sound in "indes*cr*ibably *cr*uel," "*cr*ushing charm," and so on. But like aimless repetition of the same word, aimless repetition of the same sound can become obtrusive and distracting, as in the hiss and clatter of "excessively successful executives." So can unintentional rhymes and off-rhymes, as in "I treated the wound, but the *pain* re*main*ed the *same*." Generally, in prose, words that rhyme shouldn't be allowed to come close enough together to create accidental comic effects (or bad verse). To find out how your own writing sounds, read your papers aloud or—better—have someone read them to you.

Repetition must be controlled. Like repeated drum beats or high notes or dramatic gestures, emphases that come in bunches soon cease to impress. Indeed, they soon cease to be emphatic. To make your writing genuinely emphatic, use emphasis sparingly.

Long and Short Sentences. Besides combining some first-draft sentences and splitting others to make them clearer, you may want to reshape sentences to improve them stylistically. At their best, short sentences have a simplicity and directness that makes them easy to understand and a briskness and drive that carries the reader along. But they can become choppy and jerky, breaking ideas into units too small to be followed easily; and several in succession can result in monotony and a loss of emphasis. Long sentences, on the other hand, can be so complicated or so rambling that the reader (if not the writer) loses track of the main idea. But handled well, a long sentence—even a very long one—can gather up and convey the full meaning of a complex thought, with all its distinctions and qualifications.

If there's no special virtue in either long sentences or short ones, there *is* a virtue in making the length of your sentences appropriate to what you're saying. Short sentences can separate details, keeping them apart so that each one gains significance:

> City church bells aimlessly ringing announced the temblor. Waves formed on the ponds in John McLaren Park. In a block of Victorian houses on Union Street, the chimneys snapped off at the roof-line. Approaches to the Bay Bridge and the Golden Gate collapsed. Concrete slabs of freeway spun through the air like Frisbees. Overpasses to highways 101 and 280 crumbled. The Candlestick causeway was under six feet of water. San Francisco was closed off.—Ted Morgan, *New York Times Magazine*

A long sentence coming after a series of relatively short ones can pull particulars together into an inclusive statement that summarizes or interprets or evaluates, rounding off a paragraph or a stage in the discussion or the discussion itself. Or it can open a discussion, as in this first paragraph of a movie review:

> "Marathon Man" starts with the amplified sound of breathing. What is it? Some rough, snuffling beast? With embarrassment, one recognizes the nasal-clogged exertions of Dustin Hoffman running around the Central Park reservoir. Has a parodist taken over the sound controls? No, it's just that "Marathon Man," a project that seemed a lead-pipe cinch to be the kind of visceral thriller that makes audiences almost sick with excitement, has fouled up right from the word go, and nothing in it works quite the way it was meant to.—Pauline Kael, *New Yorker*

And a short sentence following one or more long ones can often bring a paper to a dramatic close. The variation in sentence length creates tension in this paragraph:

> I would expect an instant rebuttal by the anthros. They will say that my sentiments do not represent the views of all Indians —and they are right, they have brainwashed many of my brothers. But a new day is coming. Until then, it would be wise for anthropologists to climb down from their thrones of authority and pure research and begin helping Indian tribes instead of preying on

them. For the wheel of karma grinds slowly, but it does grind fine. And it makes a complete circle. — Vine Deloria, Jr., *Custer Died for Your Sins*

Achieving Directness

Most good expository writing is direct and economical. It says what it has to say without being stuffy or round-about or long-winded. This doesn't mean that using the fewest and simplest words is always best. It may result in oversimplifying your ideas. A style can become too economical — too packed — to be read with ease or pleasure. In some circumstances you can increase the clarity and impact of a main idea by repeating it in more concrete terms. But saying the same thing twice in slightly different words usually means you're just spinning your wheels. *Unnecessary* words and *pointless* repetition work against clarity and directness and create a style that bores and frustrates readers.

In most good writing, sentences are built on concrete subjects and active verbs. While nominalization — changing a whole clause to a noun or a noun phrase — is a great help in combining sentences, it can ruin a prose style. If you let nominalization become a habit, you'll find yourself writing the kind of prose that comes out of committees:

There was an affirmative decision in regard to the implementation of a policy concerning a reduction in employment levels on the part of management.

Either of these short sentences captures the gist of that long-winded pronouncement:

The Board of Directors has decided to employ fewer workers.

The Company is going to fire some of you.

It could be argued that the writer of the first version, with its nominalization and its string of prepositional phrases ("in regard to . . . of . . . in . . . on the part of . . ."), accomplished his rhetorical purpose — to muffle the unpleasant truth in a cloud of abstraction. But much writing of this kind results not from conscious choice but from a failure to assign action to the active — that is, a failure to make *people* the doers, the subjects of your verbs:

A state of fury existed among the ticket-holders after their learning of the failure of the rock stars to appear.

Simply by asking yourself "Who did what?" you come around to this rewrite:

The ticket-holders became furious after they learned that the rock stars hadn't shown up.

If you find yourself using abstract nouns, especially nouns ending in *-ence, -ity, -ment, -tion,* every six or seven words, make a habit of asking yourself "Who did what?"

Asking yourself that question will also help you avoid overuse of passive verbs. Passives can't be, and shouldn't be, avoided entirely. In describing an industrial process or recording a laboratory experiment, there may be good reason to keep the focus solely on what takes place, ignoring the operators or researchers or other human agents involved. There are times when the doer of the action isn't important or can't be identified: "The oil is loaded aboard tankers in the Gulf of Aden"; "For a week no garbage was collected." And there are times when being acted upon is what you're writing about: "I was laughed at by every kid on the block." But despite these exceptions, the general rule holds: Use active verbs to make your writing direct and vigorous—and honest. Active verbs are more likely to assign responsibility; instead of reporting that tuition was increased, they state that someone raised tuition. Hiding behind passives is a rhetorical strategy of dishonest bureaucrats.

Usually directness and economy go together, but that's not always the case. Here, abstraction is shorter:

What we say is true depends more on what we believe is true than on what is really true.

Truth depends more on belief than on reality.

In some rhetorical situations the more specific statement would be well worth the extra words.

When you're revising your papers, four steps will make your sentences more economical.

1. Reduce subject-verb combinations by combining and embedding.

The leaves covered the ground. *They looked* like a carpet.

The leaves, which looked like a carpet, *covered* the ground.

The leaves covered the ground like a carpet.

The leaves carpeted the ground.

Each of the first two versions contains two subject-verb combinations; each of the last two contains one. Which is the most appropriate sentence would have to be decided in context. From the point of view of economy, the last two versions are better.

2. When you have a choice between long and short constructions, use the shorter form.

The man [whom] I spoke to is my counselor.

He knew [that] the cause was lost.

Political success was limited to those [who were] skilled in public debate.

In formal styles the constructions are often filled out. In general styles the short forms are preferred.

You can often make deletions in a series of parallel structures:

A light rain was called a bird sweat, a sprinkle was a shirttail shower, a heavy rain a frog-strangler.—Helen Bevington, *The House Was Quiet and the World Was Calm*

"Was called" in the first clause is reduced to "was" in the second and omitted altogether in the third without loss of clarity.

3. Choose direct phrasing instead of circumlocution. "Have the idea that" instead of "believe," "in rather short supply" instead of "scarce," "destroyed by fire" instead of "burned"—these are typical circumlocutions. (The example of committee prose on p. 247 is full of them.) In context there may be a sound reason for using several words where fewer would be more direct and just as clear, but as a characteristic of style, circumlocutions create pomposity or flabbiness or both. And they may hide, or at least blur, the central subject-predicate idea. In each of the following pairs, the action statement comes through less clearly in the first version, with its circumlocution, than in the second:

The way psychologists measure ability is by the use of tests.

Psychologists use tests to measure ability.

As far as the mission is concerned, there is no question that it was a success.

The mission succeeded.

My answer is in the affirmative.

Yes.

Like nominalization and overuse of prepositional phrases and passive verbs, circumlocution is a characteristic of institutional prose – the kind of writing churned out by government agencies, corporations, and administrative offices, sometimes to inform, sometimes to mislead.

4. Prune the deadwood. Deadwood is words and phrases that add nothing to the meaning. The bracketed words in the following sentences can be omitted with no loss at all and, of course, with a gain in economy:

All thinking persons [these days would] probably agree [with the conception] that the world has gone mad.

Anyone familiar with violin-making knows that the better the wood is seasoned, the better [the result will be as far as] the tone [of the instrument is concerned].

In [the course of] an hour we reached [the spot where] the red flag [was situated].

Deadwood is particularly annoying when it repeats what's already said, as when *size* is added to a word that can only mean size – large *in size* – or when an unnecessary adverb doubles the meaning of a verb: continue *on*, repeat *again*, return *back*. And it's especially wasteful when it takes the emphasis from more important words. Giving a sentence an empty introduction ("What I would like to say is that . . .") means losing the chance to make a firm assertion.

Pruning the deadwood from your prose is part of the job of revising. Occasionally, for rhythm or change of pace or emphasis, you may want to keep a locution that's more wordy than need be or that's not essential to your meaning, but as a rule you'll find that getting rid of it results in stronger as well as leaner prose.

Though writing can be so compressed that it's hard to follow, more writers need to work for economical expression than for expansion. Length in a paper should come from working out ideas, not from piling up words. The right kind of economy means using no more words than you need to say what you want to say in the way you want to say it.

■ *For Writing*

Rewrite each of these passages according to the instructions.

a. The first thing to do is choose the right pack for your size and weight. Do not buy a pack that is bigger than you are, because you will have an extremely hard time carrying it. The best idea is to get a pack with a frame. The frame will spread the weight of the pack across your body better than a pack without a frame, making your load much easier to carry. (Make the passage more economical and direct, the connections between the statements clearer.)

b. When you start living in a fraternity, you have to pay house fees and social dues. The cost usually amounts to about the same amount you would have been charged for living in a dorm. (Rewrite as one compact sentence, getting rid of unnecessary words and careless repetition.)

c. In college an exposure to many views of government, morality, and society is beneficial not only because weaknesses can be detected but also because strong points might also be discovered that can be borrowed and incorporated into the American way of life. (Begin the sentence with "College students" and turn passive verbs into active ones.)

d. A good indication that the human animal is still a brute at heart is to be found in the fact that there is an endless stream of books and articles on manners and etiquette, in all of which the purpose is to urge on us the desirability of introducing into our lives some of the amenities of gracious living. (Condense and make the phrasing more direct. Start by finding out what the real subject of the sentence is.)

e. The central character is admirable; she is conscientious, she is marvelously sensitive and humane, and she is considerate of her associates. (Make the sentence more emphatic.)

f. When someone suggested in late afternoon to the several hundred students who waited almost five hours in intermittent sleet and snow to receive the A&E Committee's response to their demands for a budget review that the group sing, "We Shall Overcome," the new activists made an embarrassing discovery: hardly anyone knew the lyrics.—*Brown Alumni Monthly.* (The dependent clause is too long, with far too many prepositional phrases. Rewrite, correcting these flaws. Making two sentences might be the best solution.)

g. In our discussion we will be enabled by a typical quotation from each of the authors to increase our understanding of an actual LSD experience. (Turn passive verbs into active ones.)

h. As this record was slipped across this reviewer's desk, the initial response was: ". . . You're kidding! . . ."
But, knowing an assignment is an assignment and seeing that the "Alma Mater" was the first selection, solace was taken in the prospect of becoming one of the apparent few who actually know the "G-- ---- words" to that hallowed dirge. . . .
As the record spun through the last "dear old State, dear old State," first impressions seemed to be confirmed. . . .
However, the sardonic smile began to fade after awhile as the mellow timbre of blended male voices caressed one of the more delicate selections on the album. An appreciation grew for the extra touches and a seductive urge to harmonize began to well in the throat.—Charles C. Dubois, *The Centre Daily Times.* (Rewrite in the first person, using active verbs.)

i. My parents and I have different opinions on the importance of money. My parents were raised in a society where money was scarce and people placed a high value on it. As a result of this, my parents place a high value on money, and it is a very important aspect of their lives. They tend to be money-hungry and strive to be well-off. I, on the other hand, place less importance on money and try not to let money run my life. I have seen too many people who have let money run their lives. These are the people who end up unhappy. I am more interested in enjoying life than getting rich. (Rewrite, combining some of the sentences and getting rid of the repetition.)

Parallelism and Order

From the discussion of types of sentences, you know that the compound sentence joins an independent clause to an independent clause. You also know that in the complex sentence the order of elements may be dependent-independent or independent-dependent. Here we'll have more to say about balance and order, and we'll talk some more about the relation between how you shape your sentences and what you want your sentences to say.

Using Parallelism

Early in this chapter we combined two simple sentences to make a single compound sentence:

The United States is a conservative country,

and

its working class is one of the anchors of its conservatism.

The coordinating conjunction *and* joins two independent clauses. When clause is matched to clause in this way — or phrase to phrase, noun to noun, verb to verb, and so on — they are said to be parallel. As you work to untangle a confusing first-draft sentence or to smooth a ragged sentence in a second draft, you'll often find that parallelism, by providing grammatical similarity, offers the best way to bring related details and ideas together.

Grammatical Uses. Our speech and our writing are full of parallel structures:

young and *old*	*laughing* and *crying*
red, white, and *blue*	*for richer,* for *poorer*
men, women, and *children*	*come rain* or *come shine*

All of us use parallelism all the time without even think-ing about it. Because we're so accustomed to it, its absence where we expect it can bother us. Try reading this sen-tence:

One group favors gradual desegregation, another demanding immediate integration, and from the third, total opposition to integration.

With some effort we can figure out what the writer means; but the way he's expressed it strikes us as garbled, and it's certainly no pleasure to read.

The first thing to do to improve the sentence is to recog-nize what we've got there. The sentence is contrasting three attitudes toward the same thing. Suppose, then, that we treat the three attitudes in a series. Group 1 *favors*. What does Group 2 do? *Demanding?* No, to parallel *favors*, we want *demands*.

One group favors gradual desegregation.

Another demands immediate integration.

What about Group 3? To be in step with the first two groups, it must *do* something, not have something—"op-position"—coming *from* it. Let's turn this noun back into the verb it came from:

The third group opposes integration altogether. ("Totally op-poses integration" would be all right, too.)

One more thing: we've got two *integration*s, one *de-segregation*. Sticking with the same key term throughout would increase clarity, and since gradual desegregation would result in gradual integration, we can substitute *integration* in the first sentence:

One group favors gradual integration.

Now we combine the three sentences, retaining the parallel forms:

One group favors gradual integration,
another demands immediate integration,
and
a third opposes integration altogether.

Repetition and parallelism work together to produce a smooth, clear, unified sentence. Roughly the same effect would be achieved if a *but* was introduced to emphasize contrast:

One group favors gradual integration,
but
another demands immediate integration,
and
a third opposes integration altogether.

Since parallelism is a form of coordination, failures in parallelism may occur in pairs of any kind or in series of three or more items. Faulty parallelism is a variety of shifted construction: you use the wrong form to fill a specific position in a sentence that seems to call for matching structures. What goes with what is the key question. Here are a few examples:

Parallel: *Swimming* and *playing the piano* were her hobbies.
Parallel: *To swim* and *to play the piano* were her hobbies.
Not parallel: *Swimming* and *to play the piano* were her hobbies.

Parallel: I've heard about her *swimming* every day and *playing the piano* every evening.
Not parallel: I've heard about her *swimming* every day and *that she plays the piano* every evening.

Parallel: She *swam* in the mornings and *spent* her evenings playing the piano.
Not parallel: *She swam* in the mornings, and *her evenings were spent playing* the piano.

The last sentence isn't "wrong," but you shouldn't shift subjects and go from an active to a passive verb in a compound sentence without good reason.

So far we've examined sentences that would be clearer and stronger if parts of them were made parallel. But the parts made parallel must be logically related. You'll seriously mislead your readers if you put into parallel structures details or ideas that can't sensibly be paired. What do you make of this sentence?

The artist's method of composition gives the painting a harmonious arrangement, a kind of stability, a confidence that after looking at every detail our eye will find its way back to the center.

Of the three elements in the series, only the first two— "a harmonious arrangement" and "a kind of stability"— belong together. With the third ("a confidence") the reader is puzzled: Can a painting have confidence? If he has the patience to reread, he'll realize that the writer has shifted in mid-series from a description of what the artist's method gives the painting to a description of the impression the painting makes on its viewer. The parallelism is illogical; it can't be justified.

Besides keeping order in a sentence, parallelism — rightly used — can contribute to economy in writing. It offers a way to combine sentences and to embed the gist of several sentences in one:

On Monday we went to a movie. The next day there was nothing to do but hang around the house. Then we spent a day in the park. Finally we went back to school out of simple boredom.

We *went* to a movie on Monday, *hung* around the house on Tuesday, *spent* Wednesday in the park, and finally *got* so bored that we *went* back to school.

The first version is superior in conveying the sense of time passing, but in a context where the passing of time has no significance, the brisker one-sentence version might well be preferable.

Whether used to point to similar ideas, to distinguish closely related ideas, to set off opposing ideas, or to combine ideas, parallelism can work so unobtrusively that the reader is barely aware of the structural repetition; or it can work so insistently that the reader can't ignore the symmetrical design. Here we move into the rhetorical effects of parallelism. If you don't use parallelism for such effects, you're not making an error in grammar or mechanics, but you are wasting a valuable resource.

Rhetorical Uses. The careful patterning in the following sentences comes clear when the parallel structures are italicized and made graphically parallel:

Many of the young people of the past decade and today are considered
    to have a profound sense of moral awareness,
    to be a truly moral generation.
Outraged at
    the injustices,
    the hypocrisy,
    the baseness
        they have observed in the adult world,
they have expressed their moral concern
    by rejecting the materialistic values
                and
                conventions
                    of older generations
       and
  by seeking personal redemption
        in
      protest movements,
      new life styles,
      and
      service to the community.
      —Alan Pifer, *The Chronicle of Higher Education*

Though you may not often have occasion to build so much parallelism into a two-sentence passage of your own, you can, by a moderate use of parallelism, pack more meaning into your sentences and at the same time make your writing more forceful and rhythmical, as in this passage by a student:

My parents complain that I am *arrogant, thoughtless,* and *rebellious.* I tell them they misunderstand me. *What they see as arrogance* is my attempt to be a person in my own right. *What they see as thoughtlessness* is usually just forgetfulness. *What they see as rebelliousness* is a drive to be independent.

The student concludes the passage with parallel sentences. In each, she defends herself against what she considers her parents' misinterpretations of her conduct. The same opening for three sentences in a row is justified because each has the same rhetorical purpose.

When the parts of a sentence are matched to a noticeable extent in grammatical form and even in vocabulary, the sentence is said to be balanced:

> The world will little note nor long remember what we say here but
>
>   it   can never forget   what they did here.

Grammatically, the balanced sentence is made up of parallel structures. Rhetorically, the parallelism points up the similarity or the opposition of ideas. Balance can match a positive statement with a negative one, an abstract statement with a concrete expression of the same idea. You can use it, as it's used here, to give an assertion a forthright, authoritative tone:

They have been educated to achieve success; few of them have been educated to exercise power. — Walter Lippmann, *A Preface to Morals*

In formal contexts, parallelism may be sustained and deliberate. (Balanced sentences are a hallmark of formal prose and particularly of oratory.) In informal contexts, where the series is just as common as in formal contexts — though the structures are usually not so elaborate — you're likely to give a sentence a twist that signals to the reader that you're *not* working at matching word with word or phrase with phrase. Here, for example, the writer achieves economy and rhythm with a fast-moving series but rejects a dramatic stance with the closing, informal "whatever":

He carried his faith into the country like baggage and hung onto it, with that fierce urgent immigrant's grip, through the sweatshops, through the Crash, through the wars, the political scandals, the Coughlins, the Ku Klux Klanners, the lynchings, whatever. — Martha Weinman Lear, *New York Times Magazine*

As usual, then, context counts. Though sustained parallelism within and between sentences is appropriate in writing situations that call for gravity, for judiciousness, for carefully thought-out pronouncements, and for stirring emotional pleas, in more relaxed situations parallelism should be treated more casually:

What made the house a home was the runaround porch, a screen that stuck or slammed, a wire basket of dead ferns, a swing that scuffed the paint off the clapboards, a rail to lean on when you threw up, a stoop to sit on when you watered the grass. — Wright Morris, *God's Country and My People*

There's enough parallelism here to hold the sentence together and give it an easy, casual rhythm but not so much that it becomes monotonous or seems contrived. (If you try attaching a *that* clause to each of the nouns after *was* — "porch," "screen," "basket," "swing," "rail," "stoop" — you'll see how stiff and affected parallelism can make everyday material sound.) The modern writer often feels no need to press parallelism to the point of exact symmetry:

Warsaw to many who arrive from Paris is drab and joyless; to those who arrive from Moscow it is colorful, joyous, swinging. — David Halberstam, *Harper's*

Would the sentence be any better if "drab and joyless" had been matched with "colorful and joyous"?

Making a fetish of parallelism will hurt any style. Regardless of context, the parallelism in the following passage falls flat:

Although some were shouting, like the men and women on the pier, although some were hysterical, like the men and women crowding around the plank, although some were dazed, there was a difference between them and the people who awaited them. — Leane Zugsmith, *Home Is Where You Hang Your Childhood*

The repetition of "although some" at the beginning of three clauses builds up the reader's expectations. The writer fails to deliver. After all the careful structuring of the dependent clauses, the independent clause is a dud.

Get in the habit of using parallelism for clarity. Use it for rhetorical effect when the ideas you're expressing justify the emphasis parallelism gives. But don't strive for a series of three parallel clauses when all you have to say can be put in one clause or two. If you do, the elaborate structure will only emphasize the emptiness.

■ *For Writing*

Rewrite the following items to improve parallelism.

a. You need to know when to begin the job and knowing what to do in which order.

b. In the dorms there is usually too much noise, and too many people are continually walking up and down the corridors and in and out of rooms.

c. The resort was quiet. There was not much to do besides taking walks or the local movie house.

d. The law serves a double purpose; first, it protects the people, and second, the capture of criminals.

e. The university has grown so rapidly that it is short of facilities, instructors, and is faced with a discipline problem.

f. Besides basketball, field hockey, and tennis, she keeps in shape by running up three flights of stairs instead of using the elevator.

g. He said that we should either live according to our beliefs or that we were hypocrites and ought to face the fact.

h. Because he had failed the course and having no chance of graduating, he packed up and left.

i. Considering the low rent, the house is a bargain even though the roof leaks, some window panes are missing, and it is not what you would call modern plumbing.

j. Malamud creates characters that are real yet eccentric, and his recurring themes of suffering and poverty are presented with a twist of absurdity that tickles and also horrifies.

Composing Cumulative Sentences

The fully balanced sentence represents sentence form at its most symmetrical. Two other patterns you may find useful contrast sharply both with the balanced sentence and with each other. In one, you make your main assertion at, or near, the beginning and then add details or reasons or qualifications. In the other, you don't complete your sentence grammatically or disclose your meaning fully until the last few words. Especially in long sentences, the rhetorical effects of these two patterns are distinctly different.

The first pattern is called the *loose,* or *cumulative,* sentence. It occurs most distinctively in narrative and descriptive writing, as in this passage from a novel:

> . . . we walked up the beach. We kept on walking until we left the public part behind and started passing the houses of the rich people, houses so rich and elegant that they didn't have to look it but sat back almost inconspicuously there among the palms and sea grape, each with its own little flight of steps leading up from the sand to the green lawn, each with its low cement groin projecting out into the sea to keep the beach from washing away.
> — Frederick Buechner, *Lion Country*

The cumulative sentence opens with a base structure, usually a short independent clause. Added to it are modifiers built on what precedes ("each with its own little flight of steps") or parallel to what precedes it ("each with its low cement groin"). The cumulative sentence of description and narration is often open-ended, giving the impression that more phrases could be added. (See, for example, the Hemingway sentence on p. 241.)

The modifiers in descriptive-narrative sentences typically add details. In expository sentences they typically interpret, extend, explain, justify, or exemplify the main assertion. Here is a cumulative sentence from the Inaugural Address of President John F. Kennedy:

> Let the word go forth from this time and place, to friend and foe alike, that the torch has been passed to a new generation of Americans, born in this century, tempered by war, disciplined in a hard and bitter peace, proud of our ancient heritage, and unwilling to witness or permit the slow undoing of those human rights to which this nation has always been committed, and to which we are committed today at home and around the world.

On the whole, the cumulative sentences of exposition and argument are less open-ended than the cumulative sentences of description and narration. The "and to which" at the end of the sentence just quoted gives a distinct sense of closure. It's hard to imagine anything following the last clause.

Because it follows the normal order of speech — main statement first, then qualifications and particulars — the cumulative sentence can give the impression of naturalness and spontaneity, of following the workings of the writer's mind. As modifier is added to modifier, the thought can grow, sharpen, change. But writing a good cumulative sentence calls for control over both content and structure.

If your modifiers don't strengthen your original assertion, if they wander away from it, if they get into a tangle, you've written a bad sentence. See how this one drifts, as detail is added to detail:

It was a new experience for us, waking before sunrise, the wind quiet then, the countryside still except for the first bird calls, the blackbirds whistling in the bushes, the pale light streaking the windows on the east side of the cabin, facing the barn, empty now, unused for years, its doors nailed shut to keep out tramps, waiting for the day to begin.

When modifiers are stacked like this, their grammatical relations must be clear. The sentence above drifts grammatically with its final verbal phrase, "waiting for the day to begin," which belongs just after "waking before sunrise." In any position after that, the phrase dangles.

In brief, then, you can achieve an impression of ease and flexibility with the cumulative sentence *if* you're careful to see that the order of its elements makes your meaning immediately clear.

Shaping Periodic Sentences

Because its base structure stands first, the cumulative sentence can be cut off after the initial assertion (and often at several points beyond that) and still be intelligible. Because its base structure stands last, the *periodic* sentence will be intelligible only if it's complete, or very nearly so. When you write a periodic sentence, remember that the reader has to hold the elements of the sentence in mind as he goes along, instead of getting the central message and then adding to it, detail by detail, as he does with the typical cumulative sentence.

In a simple example, this is no great burden:

Tired, cold, and hungry, and discouraged by my failure to find a job, I crawled into bed.

In a longer sentence, introduced by more elaborate structures, the elements must be related to each other so that the reader can easily keep them in mind as he moves toward the main assertion:

Not so long before he died, still receiving carloads of honors as he always had, and still receiving, as also he always had, from Right or Left in turn, fanatic attacks on his social views, Mann remarked that he was a "great, unloved name." — John Thompson, *Harper's*

Nervous, strewn with knotty or flashy phrases, impatient with transitions and other concessions to dullness, willfully calling attention to itself as a form or at least an outcry, fond of rapid twists, taking pleasure in dispute, dialectic, dazzle—such, at its best or most noticeable, was the essay cultivated by the New York writers.—Irving Howe, *Decline of the New*

As a musical composition remains in suspension until the final chords provide resolution and release, a periodic sentence achieves its effect by withholding its full meaning until its last words. Building a lengthy periodic sentence, then, can be a tour de force, with the reader kept in suspense as to how both structure and meaning are going to come out. But unless there's a rhetorical reason for withholding the full meaning, a long, complicated periodic sentence may seem decidedly artificial. And unless parallelism provides order among the elements piled up before the final clause, both sense and grammar may become tangled.

Cumulative and periodic sentences sometimes offer alternative ways of expressing the same idea. As you revise a paper, you may decide to make a loose sentence periodic for reasons of emphasis or to make a periodic sentence cumulative so that your writing will have a less formal, more open style. Ordinarily it's the long cumulative sentence or the long periodic sentence that calls attention to itself; and when any sentence calls attention to itself, it should do so for the right reason—because its form not only fits but strengthens the idea it expresses.

The study of good cumulative sentences and good periodic sentences suggests one simple, practical rule: Keep your main assertion short and direct. Whether you place your modifiers early or late or spread them through the sentence, your writing will be clearer if your main assertions—your action statements—are short clauses rather than long ones.

Self-Test

This self-test is a review of trouble spots in grammar and sentence structure. Some of the items are satisfactory. Some contain grammatical errors: a plural subject may have a singular verb; the reference of a pronoun may be unclear; a modifier may be placed so that it doesn't seem to be related to the word it's meant to modify or may be punctuated so that the intended meaning doesn't come through; and so on. Some are grammatically correct but should be more direct and economical. Revise the unsatisfactory items to make them acceptable in college writing. Then see the comments on pp. 264–65 and, when necessary, read the articles in Index to English *that are referred to there.*

1. Why don't people give their pets warm food before they leave for work these cold mornings?

2. Reaching sixteen, my parents agreed to let me drive.

3. The major fault of the black powder were the dense clouds of smoke it generated.

4. In strict Puritan households, dancing, music, and the theater — indeed, all manner of entertainment — was condemned.

5. Coming into the open, he could see the tracks plainly.

6. Since sponges are capable of consuming food, making cells, and reproducing its own kind, they are living organisms.

7. The club is sponsoring a dance, and it plans to give the proceeds to charity.

8. Women won the right to vote, which happened in 1920.

9. Many people take pills without a doctor's prescription. This is unwise. They begin by taking habit-forming sedatives only when they cannot sleep or when they are tense. But it is not long before they can't do without them, and they increase the dose until all it does is make them worse.

10. The only correct standard of English is that which is appropriate to the occasion and accepted by the people with whom you are.

11. He asked me who I thought would win the election.

12. From the attic window of our home, one can command a view of our entire neighborhood. Situated in the northeast corner of this quiet suburb, it is a perfect spot from which to observe the community.

13. Settled at last in Greensboro, it is my understanding that he was loved or admired by everybody in the place. . . . – John Crowe Ransom, *Southern Review*

14. Our entire air-frame and aircraft engine industry — immense contributors to employment and vital in the free world's defense – are as fundamentally sick. – Henry J. Taylor, syndicated columnist

15. Those people with whom you went to high school but who didn't go on to college now have very different interests than yours.

16. Hotels are booked solidly for the convention.

17. The Democratic organization, as many other organizations, are concerned about young people's disenchantment with politics.

18. Residents object to the cutting down of trees which the officials say is necessary.

19. Having written Quentin Reynolds' Class Day address for him, West's own graduation in 1924 was the climax to a history of what appears to have been lighthearted chicanery. – Mark Shorer, *Atlantic*

20. I spent the next two months in a house the roof of which leaked.

21. They invited my roommate and I for the next weekend, but we decided it would be safer to refuse.

22. Everyone should write their papers two days before they hand them in.

23. If the mixture tastes bitterly, dump it down the sink. You made a mistake in your measurements.

24. Even though she drunk more than I did, she was full of pep the next morning.

25. When he left the building he was so tired that he was thankful he brought his bike to ride home on.

26. It has always been felt by me and by my friends that to study the subject of physics is to waste a lot of time on material which will soon be outdated.

27. These two stories deal with Americans in Europe who suffer conflicts of love and questioning of the standards of European society.

Comments on Self-Test

1. Change "before they leave" to "before leaving" to avoid any suggestion that the pets are employed. See Reference of pronouns 1a.

2. Change "Reaching" to "When I reached." See Dangling modifiers.

3. Change "were" to "was." See Agreement 1a.

4. Change "was" to "were." See Agreement 1a.

5. OK.

6. Change "its" to "their." See Agreement 2.

7. OK, though "is sponsoring a dance and plans to give" would make the sentence tighter. More formal style might reduce the second clause to an absolute phrase: ". . . dance, the proceeds to go to charity." See Absolute phrases 3. More informal style would switch to the plural in the second clause: ". . . dance, and they plan to give the proceeds to charity." See Collective nouns.

8. The simplest revision deletes the comma and "which happened." Rearrangement – "It was in 1920 that women won the right to vote" – gives a different emphasis. See Reference of pronouns 2.

9. A clutter of pronouns. "This" in the second sentence isn't ambiguous, but for economy that sentence might well be embedded in the first one: "Many people unwisely. . . ." Similarly, though the reader can sort out the *them*s, the chore should be made less difficult. The shift from "cannot" to "can't" is a needless inconsistency. "All it does" in the last sentence brings the vagueness and fuzziness to a climax. A general rewrite is needed. See Reference of pronouns 1d, 2, 4.

10. Ending with a preposition ("the people you are with") would make the sentence less awkward. Changing "The only correct standard of English" to "Good English" would reduce the wordiness. See Prepositions and style 4; Wordiness.

11. OK. If you changed it, better see *who, whom.*

12. Loose. "It" refers to "attic window," but it's the house that's situated; and so forth. One revision would reverse the sentence order: "Situated in the northeast corner of this quiet suburb, our house is a perfect spot. . . . From the attic window I [*or* you] can. . . ." Or: "Our house is situated. . . . The attic window gives a view. . . ." See Reference of pronouns 3; Point of view 1; *one.*

13. Though there's no real problem here, the conservative reader would be troubled by "it is my understanding that" coming between "Settled at last in Greensboro" and "he." Such a reader might prefer "I understand that, after he had finally settled in Greensboro, he was loved or admired by everyone in the place." See Dangling modifiers.

14. "Industry" calls for "is," not "are." "Contributors" in the cumbersome interrupting phrase misled the writer. See Agreement 1a.

15. "With whom" doesn't mix well with "didn't" and "than yours," and "from" as a preposition is preferable to "than": "Those people who went to high school with you but didn't go on to college now have interests very different from yours." See *different;* Shifted constructions.

16. Change "solidly" to "solid." See Adverbs and style 1b.

17. Change "as" to "like" and "are" to "is." See *like, as;* Agreement 1a.

18. Change to: ". . . trees, but the officials say it is necessary." At the very least, put a comma between "trees" and "which." See Reference of pronouns 2; Restrictive and nonrestrictive 2.

19. This type of dangling modifier, in which the word the writer means to modify is in the genitive, or possessive, now appears fairly often in print. But conservative stylists would insist on making the participle modify "West," not "West's graduation," and that would call for rewriting. See Dangling modifiers.

20. Change "the roof of which" to "whose roof." See *which* 2.

21. Change "I" to "me." See Case 2a; Hypercorrectness.

22. OK, but see Agreement 2.

23. Change "bitterly" to "bitter." See Predicate adjectives.

24. Change "drunk" to "drank." See list in Principal parts of verbs.

25. Change "brought" to "had brought." See Tense 2.

26. Get rid of the weak opener and the unnecessary words: "My friends and I have always felt that to study physics. . . ." See Passive voice 1; Wordiness 1.

27. Make the coordinate elements grammatically similar: " . . . who suffer conflicts of love and who question the standards of European society." See Shifted constructions.

Chapter Eight
Punctuating Sentences

Punctuation marks separate sentences and indicate the relationships of words and word groups within sentences, joining them, separating them, or setting them off. Properly used, punctuation controls and emphasizes meaning. Misused, it distorts meaning and confuses the reader. Though accurate punctuation can't redeem a mixed-up sentence—one that requires rewriting—it may save a weak sentence from ambiguity, and it can make the meaning of a complicated sentence precise and clear.

Convention and Choice

Some punctuation marks are substitutes for, or reminders of, elements in speech for which we have no written equivalents—a pause, for example, or a raising or lowering of the voice's pitch. But though we should listen to what we're writing and punctuating, the correspondence between punctuation and features of speech is by no means complete. We can't always hear the difference between a pair of commas and a pair of dashes, nor can we hear the apostrophe in an apostrophe-*s* like "Bill's." Some uses of punctuation marks must be learned as arbitrary conventions—rules for writing that have become established through practice.

The conventions governing the apostrophe and such matters of mechanics as capital letters are so well established that every careful writer observes them. But you still have a considerable range of choice. In deciding whether to use a particular mark of punctuation, you may be guided by the emphasis, tone, and movement in a sentence or perhaps by the intention of a whole paragraph. Some uses of punctuation marks are almost entirely stylistic. For example, when either a comma or a semicolon can be used before the coordinating conjunction in a compound sentence, the semicolon is the more formal choice:

He deplores the Easter Rising as willful and unnecessary; [a comma would be equally correct] but in deploring it he sounds as if he thought that an Irishman in, say, 1914 should have been content to find himself represented by the squires of the Irish National Party. – Denis Donoghue, *New York Review of Books*

Besides making specific choices in specific contexts, you can choose between two styles of punctuation – open and close. Close punctuation puts a comma before the conjunction in every compound sentence and a comma after an introductory clause or phrase. Open punctuation does not, except to prevent misreading. Close punctuation typically encloses interrupters like *however, of course, too*. Open punctuation seldom sets off *too*, often leaves *of course* unpunctuated, and may omit commas around other interrupters.

Although punctuation in general is more open than it was a generation ago, good writers adjust their punctuation to their subject matter and to their audience. The difficult concept probably won't be expressed in such elaborate, heavily punctuated sentences as it would have been in 1900, but it still may call for complicated sentence patterns with supporting punctuation. Casual general-to-informal writing can usually get by with a minimum of punctuation, but the writer needs to keep his audience in mind. A sophisticated reader skims such writing rapidly, and if a lack of punctuation invites even momentary confusion, he may quit rapidly, too. An unsophisticated reader needs the help that conventional punctuation can provide.

In punctuating as in writing generally, the claims of your readers should come first. Use punctuation marks to help readers understand what you have to say. Beyond that, a good rule of thumb is to use no more punctuation than *current* convention calls for. Punctuation marks that are too numerous or too heavy – as colons and semicolons may be in a relaxed style – call attention to themselves just as words that are too heavy or too pretentious do. But limiting yourself to a subsistence budget of commas and periods is no more essential to good writing than sticking to one- and two-syllable words.

A Review of Punctuation

The chart on page 268 and the sections that follow are intended to refresh your memory of punctuation rules you were told about in grade school and high school and to suggest some of the ways you can adjust your use of punc-

The Principal Marks and Their Main Functions

Period •   to end statements

Comma ,   to separate words and word groups within sentences

Paired commas , ··· ,   to set off words and word groups that are not part of the main structure of the sentence

Semicolon ;   to link clauses that would otherwise be separated by a period

Colon :   to link words and word groups to the sentence element that introduces them

Other Punctuation Marks

Question mark ?   to mark a direct or a quoted question

Exclamation mark !   to mark an exclamation—a word or a word group or a sentence that is vigorously stressed

Dash —   to link to a word group an example or an unexpected addition

Paired dashes —···—   to set off words and word groups that are less closely related to the main structure than they would be if set off by commas

Parentheses ( )   to set off words and word groups that are less closely related to the main structure than they would be if set off by dashes

Quotation marks " "   to identify what is directly quoted

Brackets [ ]   to enclose insertions in quotations

Ellipses • • •   to indicate omissions in quotations

Apostrophe '   to indicate the genitive, or possessive, case and omitted letters in contractions

Hyphen -   to link words and to link syllables

The uses of all the marks of punctuation are explained in separate articles in the *Index to English*.

tuation marks to the rhetorical situation. For fuller explanation of particular problems, follow up the references to articles in the *Index to English*.

At Ends of Sentences

Most sentences are statements and should end with a period. Use a question mark after a clear-cut question: "When does the balloon go up?" Don't use one after an in-

direct question: "We asked when the balloon would go up."
When you phrase a request as a question, you can end it
with a period: "Will you please give this matter your immediate attention."

Reserve the exclamation mark to express strong emotion
—outrage, incredulity, determination—or, in dialog, high
volume. The single-word exclamations range from powerful ones like *Ouch,* which almost always call for an exclamation mark, to mild ones like *Oh,* which may deserve
only a comma. Outside of dialog, use exclamation marks
only when special emphasis is fully justified. And don't
use multiple exclamation marks. Dialog that's punctuated
as though it consists of an exchange of shouts should be
restricted to comic strips.

When you punctuate a dependent clause or a phrase or
some other part of a sentence as if it were a separate
sentence (a *fragment*), you may need to remind yourself
of what a sentence is. Usually you can eliminate such
flaws from your work by reading it carefully as you revise.

■ *For Punctuating*

*The following items include fragments as well as sentences
that are complete and correctly punctuated. If you think that
some of the fragments should be acceptable in college writing,
mark them "OK" and be prepared to defend your judgment.
If you think a fragment is unacceptable, rewrite to make the
item satisfactory.*

a. When I go to the movies, I go for a good time. Not to be
depressed.

b. Magnificent, but is it art? Certainly not. Art follows rules
based on our tiny comprehension.—Jacques Barzun, *God's
Country and Mine*

c. Under the American system, the civilians have to control
the military because there is no mechanism for the military to
control itself.

d. One solution is to remove portions of the bottom of the bay
for purposes of navigation, land fill, and mining. If the water is
deepened only in selected areas, the bay bottom becomes irregular, and circulation of water through the deeper portions
decreases. Thus cutting down the amount of available oxygen in
the water and increasing anaerobic activity of harmful, pol-
lution-causing bacteria.

e. In the final minutes of the trial, he clenched his fist and
shouted. Actions that showed how passionately concerned he
was for the welfare of the children.

f. The book treats the Revolution under three topics. First, the
causes of the war; second, the events; third, the effects.

g. On the other hand, if the ratings turn out to be as striking as NBC expects, even in the face of Sunday prime-time competition on the other networks, all future World Series Games are likely to be nocturnal. So much for tradition. — *Sports Illustrated*

h. Many young people of college age automatically make two assumptions. One that all men are individuals. The other that in America every individual has a right to a good deal of freedom. They themselves have been brought up in a permissive atmosphere and have rarely been disciplined. Which means they have little fear of authority and even less respect for the traditions of the past.

If you have trouble with these items, see the Index to English *article "Fragment."*

Between Main Elements

As a mark of separation, a single comma doesn't belong between the main elements of a clause — between subject and verb or between verb and object or complement. When you separate a subject from its verb with a comma, it's often because the noun phrase you've used as the subject is a long one:

Students who spend their summers having an exciting time in some colorful location[,] don't return to campus with much enthusiasm.

Try reducing the noun phrase:

Students who have exciting summers don't return to campus with much enthusiasm.

You won't feel the need for a comma, and you'll probably end up with a better sentence.

When you separate a verb from its object or complement, the reason may be that you've used an interrupting phrase:

So I telephoned *without much hope*[,] the cab stand at the corner of Lake and Park.

Sunday is *in other words*[,] the day I look forward to all week.

In the first example, the best revision would probably be to shift the phrase so that it stands just before the subject: "So *without much hope* I telephoned. . . ." In the second, the phrase could be left where it is, but another comma is needed to set it off from the main structure: "Sunday is, *in other words*, the day. . . ." (Commas might also be used around "without much hope" in the preceding example.)

Paired commas like these set off the interrupting element rather than separate main elements. Commas in series may also come between main elements:

The group with *flute, drums, mandolin, and zither* won the most applause.

Although punctuation rules usually forbid the use of a comma to separate the verbs in a compound predicate, many accomplished writers of general-to-formal prose occasionally use such punctuation – to point up a contrast, to prevent misreading, or simply to mark a pause in a long, involved sentence. But in most general styles separating predicates with a comma creates an unnecessary interruption:

He listened patiently to our questions[,] and answered them as if they deserved serious discussion.

Between Coordinate Clauses

Formal writing ordinarily has a comma between the clauses of a compound sentence connected by *and, nor, or, yet.* General writing may omit the comma if the clauses are short or have the same subject. In both styles commas are usual when the clauses are connected by *but* or *for* or *so.* Always use a comma between coordinate clauses if leaving it out would encourage misreading, as in this sentence:

The dog ate the cold eggs[   ] and the burned toast was thrown out for the birds.

Even though a reader would quickly discover that the dog hadn't eaten the toast, a comma after "eggs" would prevent even momentary confusion.

A semicolon – *not* a comma – should ordinarily be used to link independent clauses when there's no connecting word. (When one independent clause runs into another with no punctuation in between, the result is called a *fused* sentence.) A semicolon should also be used when the connecting word is a conjunctive adverb (*however, therefore, nevertheless* . . .). While a conjunctive adverb may be set off by commas within a clause ("She is, however, an excellent administrator"), it should be preceded by a semicolon – *not* a comma – when it connects clauses:

Her performance in the classroom has been uneven; however, she is an excellent administrator.

A colon—or, in less formal writing, a dash—is used between coordinate clauses when the first clause introduces or points to the second:

Some of the supporting performances are rather odd: Dorothy Tutin is wooden and rather withdrawn as Charles's Catholic queen.—David Denby, *Atlantic*

■ *For Punctuating*

In most of the following items, commas are used to separate independent clauses not joined by a conjunction. Correct all those that you judge to be comma faults, *either by substituting a semicolon, by making separate sentences, or by some other means. If you think some of them should be acceptable in college writing, mark them "OK." Be ready to defend your judgment. Correct any fused sentences you find.*

a. In conclusion, artists use specific colors for special reasons, whether for organization or for communication is for the artist to decide.

b. No cars crossed the bridge, no policemen came to ask what we were doing.

c. A big effort is put forth to meet people most of the students in the dorm are ready to be friends.

d. White, yellow, and gray are the colors most anglers prefer, however, the color of the lure is actually of little importance.

e. Black audiences and white audiences feel distinguishably different. Black audiences feel warmer, there is almost a musical rhythm, for me, even in their silent responses.—*The Autobiography of Malcolm X*

f. Not only could she write well, she had something to say.

g. When I was a child, the city meant excitement and the country meant boredom, now the reverse is true.

h. When we got there the door was locked there was nobody home.

i. Mississippi is different now, it is going through its own amazing revolution, but then it had a special darkness; for a variety of reasons it lacked freedom of speech.—David Halberstam, *Harper's*

j. It is the writer's job to persuade his readers that he knows what he is talking about, nearly all good writing rests on the solid ground of experience and knowledge.

k. Now my own involvement with Zen is slight, but as I understand it in Salinger, the deeper we go into this world, the further we can get away from it.—Philip Roth, *Commentary*

l. The course isn't teaching me anything I will ever need to know, therefore, I think I should be allowed to drop it.

If you have trouble with these items, read the Index to English *articles "Comma fault" and "Fused sentence."*

After and Before Subordinate Elements

In formal styles a comma is ordinarily used to separate a dependent clause from the main clause it precedes:

Whenever he was too exhausted to face the crowded subway, he took a taxi.

In general styles the comma is often omitted if the dependent clause is short and closely related to what follows, especially if the two clauses have the same subject as in the example above. For consistency, some writers use a comma after all introductory clauses and after any introductory phrase that contains a verbal ("Having passed mathematics, . . ."; "To get an early start, . . ."). But most writers now punctuate short introductory phrases ("In the morning . . ."; "Behind the building . . .") only when the comma is needed to prevent misreading or to provide special emphasis.

But and other coordinating conjunctions are a part of the clauses in which they appear and should not be followed by a comma either when they join coordinating clauses or when they begin a sentence:

We won the game in overtime, but[,] that was our last victory.

And[,] I hope that if he calls again, someone else answers the phone.

Placing a comma after initial *And* or *But* probably results from punctuating for the ear: the writer wants a pause after the conjunction.

Whether you use a comma before words, phrases, and clauses that follow the main clause depends on how close they are to the core of the sentence. The question can be treated in terms of restrictive and nonrestrictive modifiers. A modifier that limits the meaning of the word it modifies in the main clause is not separated from the main clause. The principal modifier of this type is the restrictive relative (or adjective) clause:

Latecomers repeatedly disturbed the people *who had aisle seats.*

Similarly, an adverbial clause that follows the main clause and restricts its meaning shouldn't be separated from it:

He left *because he could stand no more of it.*

A modifier that comes after the main clause and is not a part of the central structure of the sentence is separated from the main clause by a comma. One such modifier is the nonrestrictive relative clause, which doesn't alter the meaning of the word it modifies. (In the preceding sentence the clause "which doesn't alter the meaning of the word it modifies" is an example of a nonrestrictive clause. In the sentence you've just read, the same clause is restrictive.)

In many cases only you, the writer, can decide whether a modifier is a part of the main structure. Omitting a comma indicates that it is. Using a comma indicates that it isn't. Compare:

Newspaper stories which imply value judgments by the very way they order their facts can be powerful political weapons.

Newspaper stories, which imply value judgments by the very way they order their facts, can be powerful political weapons.

The punctuation in both sentences *may* be correct, depending on the writer's meaning. The omission of commas in the first sentence makes the modifying clause part of the main structure; the writer is singling out stories that go beyond presenting the facts. The use of commas in the second sentence separates the modifying clause from the main structure; the writer is talking about newspaper stories in general (which, he believes, imply value judgments).

Around Interrupting Elements

Traditionally, a word, phrase, or clause that is introduced within the main structure of a sentence but is not a part of that main structure is set off by commas or, in some cases, by dashes or parentheses. As we've noted, however, usage is divided over enclosing single words like *incidentally* and short phrases like *of course*. Some writers consistently set them off; some do so only to prevent misreading; and some use or omit them depending on the emphasis and tempo they're aiming for. But if you shift aimlessly from one practice to the other, it's likely to distract your readers. Here as elsewhere in writing, consistency is a good habit to develop.

If you feel that an interrupting word or word group is more separate from the core of the sentence than commas would indicate, you can enclose it in dashes. And if you feel that the separation needs to be made still more definite, you can put parentheses around it. *Feel* is the right word here, for the choice is often a subjective one that can't be reduced to a "rule."

If you doubt this, try substituting a lesser sin — say gossiping — for adultery in this passage. . . . — Wayne C. Booth, *English Journal*

And from the same article:

It is exactly the same claim that we teachers want to make about a book like *Catcher in the Rye* (though few of us would go as far as one theologian who has called it a piece of "modern Scripture").

Dashes may be said to make a word group more separate but also more emphatic than commas. Parentheses make it more separate still but less emphatic.

In Series

Commas separate the items in a series of words or word groups. (If the word groups contain commas, semicolons may provide the separation.) Practice is divided over using a comma after the item in the series that precedes the conjunction: "literature, painting, sculpture, music[,] and drama." The close style of punctuation uses this comma consistently; the open style omits it unless leaving it out could cause misreading. If you switch styles in the course of a paper, you're likely to puzzle your readers.

Commas are used to separate a series of adjectives before a single noun:

When the long, cold, lonesome evenings came, we would gather around the old wood stove.

In this sentence there are commas between "long — cold — lonesome" because each stands in the same relation to the noun "evenings." But there's no comma between "old" and "wood" because "old" modifies "wood stove" rather than just "stove." Stylistic considerations may also affect the punctuation of a series. Note the difference in emphasis in these two versions of a line in Robert Frost's poem, "Stopping by Woods on a Snowy Evening":

The woods are lovely, dark, and deep

The woods are lovely, dark and deep

The first version is purely descriptive. The second — Frost's version — suggests a definition of "lovely" that affects the interpretation of the poem.

For Clarity

Using enough punctuation to make your meaning clear does *not* mean inserting marks at every possible opportunity. Overpunctuating creates an obstacle course that encourages readers to drop out. But often a comma that's not essential can help a reader understand a sentence without having to go back over it. A comma between clauses connected by *but* or *for,* for example, signals the reader that the word is being used as a conjunction and not as a preposition. Have a friend read your paper aloud and listen for stumbles and stalls. Then check the places where they occurred to see if the trouble calls for rewriting or if punctuation will solve the problem.

With Quotation Marks

The chief use of quotation marks is to enclose the spoken or written words of others, quoted directly. A comma ordinarily separates the quotation from the words that introduce it:

He said, ". . . ."
As Dickens wrote, ". . . ."

unless the quoted words are built into the structure of the sentence:

He said "So long" and headed for the door.

When the quoted word or words are followed by a comma or a period, the punctuation comes inside the closing quotation marks. A question mark or exclamation mark is placed inside if it is part of the quotation, outside if it belongs only to the enclosing sentence:

Collins looked around and said, "Have they gone?"
I insist that you say "I'm sorry"!

When the quotation is followed by a colon, semicolon, or dash, the punctuation comes outside the closing quotation marks:

They waited in line until the agent said, "That's it for today"; then the door closed and they were left standing in the cold.

■ *For Punctuating*

1. Copy the items below, supplying appropriate punctuation. If a mark of punctuation is optional, bracket it.

a. Here is a letter that gives a clue to his mysterious behavior and perhaps explains his Mona Lisa smile

b. Isnt this the letter the clue to the mystery

c. When the war ended the trials of the traitors began

d. When the war ended the tourist business he reenlisted

e. The Constitution guarantees us our civil rights but does not set up the machinery to investigate violations of these rights

f. The Constitution guarantees us our civil rights unfortunately it does not set up machinery to investigate violations of them

g. We walked in the park at night as though we were in our own garden

h. He told us we could feel perfectly safe walking in the park at night as though we needed reassurance

i. We walked in the park at night as though we were in our own garden because the grounds were always well patrolled

j. The election of Jackson brought one era of our history to a close it represented the triumph of the masses over the classes

k. An era ended with Jacksons election the masses had triumphed over the classes

l. Adamss administration ended one era Jacksons election began another

m. It is the student who works diligently and steadfastly who succeeds

n. The women in the office who do the same work as the men should get the same pay

o. Its the worlds oldest profession he says

p. These were Lincolns words Four score and seven years ago in 1776 our fathers brought forth on this continent a new nation

q. Hers is a happy life she trusts her parents she likes her work she has many friends and a grey cat

r. All of us have some beliefs we cannot prove by induction or deduction basic assumptions standards of value articles of faith

s. Not all superstitious people are ignorant however superstition usually stems from ignorance its not only ignorant people though who are superstitious

t. The difference between man and mans is a matter of case

u. The difference between man and boy is hard to state

v. As we drove along we found that Chile was just like the travel posters towering mountains winding roads wayside chapels and glimpses of the blue blue Pacific *w.* The storm was violent but freakish straws were driven into concrete posts feathers were blown off chickens trees were stripped of branches yet frail flowers remained undamaged

x. Packed in his suitcase were a few clothes including a turtle neck sweater two pairs of socks and a handkerchief the Bible a hymnal and a pocket dictionary and a loaded revolver

y. At Laredo Tex the flooding Rio Grande forced 2500 persons from their homes and about the same number fled from homes on the Mexico side of the river in the worst inundation in ten years maybe even in twenty

z. The psychologist Henry G Wegrocki explains abnormal delusion in these words the patients delusion is an internal resolution of a problem it is his way of meeting the intolerable situation

2. Supply appropriate punctuation marks for the following paragraph, from which all marks have been removed. First, read the passage to get a general grasp of the content. Then copy it, inserting punctuation. Bracket punctuation that you consider to be optional.

Words are not obscene naming things is a legitimate verbal act And frank does not mean vulgar any more than improper means dirty What vulgar does mean is common what improper means is unsuitable Under the right circumstances any word is proper But when any sort of word especially a word hitherto taboo and therefore noticeable is scattered across a page like chocolate chips through a tollhouse cookie a real impropriety occurs The sin is not the use of an obscene word it is the use of a loaded word in the wrong place or in the wrong quantity It is the sin of false emphasis which is not a moral but a literary lapse related to sentimentality It is the sin of advertisers who so plaster a highway with neon signs that you cant find the bar or liquor store youre looking for Like any excess it quickly becomes comic — Wallace Stegner, *Atlantic*

Chapter Nine
Choosing Words

Much of the craft of writing comes in choosing words that *in context* will mean to your reader exactly what you intend them to mean. The groundwork for our treatment of words in context was laid in Chapter One, where we discussed the need for fitting language to the rhetorical situation. Now we turn to the question of how to find words and how to choose among them. Though at times we may seem to treat words in isolation, keep in mind that the most important qualities and powers of a word come alive only in context—the immediate context of the sentence, the larger context of the paper, and the still larger context of the rhetorical situation.

We begin with the assumption that you want to express your ideas as clearly and directly as you can. As a general rule, clarity should be your prime objective. And achieving that objective—choosing words that express your meaning precisely rather than skew it or blur it—isn't always easy.

Some of your problems in choosing words stem from the difference between your recognition vocabulary, the words you understand when you read them or hear them, and your active vocabulary, the words you speak and write with confidence and assurance. When a word is in your recognition vocabulary but not in your active vocabulary, it may come out sounding not quite right—"the dominating cause," for instance, instead of "the dominant cause." Or it may come out sounding quite wrong—"dominant parents" instead of "domineering parents," or "the element of mysticism" when you intend "the element of mystery," or (as in a campus newspaper story) "the utmost in human suffrage" instead of "the utmost in human suffering." To increase your control of these borderline words—to keep words moving from your recognition vocabulary into your active vocabulary—listen, read (and read and read), and get into the habit of using dictionaries. Own a good dictionary, and open it often.

Using Dictionaries

There's no such thing as *the* dictionary, one that can be quoted to settle every question about words. But there's a real difference between a dictionary that's newly compiled or that's kept up to date by experts constantly recording current usage and a dictionary that's patched together from older dictionaries. The following dictionaries, appropriate for the personal libraries of college students, are listed alphabetically: *American Heritage Dictionary of the English Language* (Houghton), *Funk & Wagnalls Standard College Dictionary* (Funk), *Random House College Dictionary* (Random), *Webster's New Collegiate Dictionary* (Merriam), *Webster's New World Dictionary* (Collins and World). When you buy a dictionary, get the newest edition. And don't ever choose a dictionary simply because it has "Webster's" in its title. While the two in the preceding list will serve your needs, some others won't. "College" and "text" editions are designed especially for the student market.

Entries

To make good use of your dictionary, first read the introductory material. Lexicographers—dictionary makers— have to resort to space-saving devices wherever possible. The shortcuts they have used, as well as their general policies and purposes, will be explained in the front matter. Here, too, you'll probably find instructions for using the dictionary.

After you've read the introductory sections and acquainted yourself with the arrangement of material, read a page or two of consecutive entries. Then look up a few words that you know and a few that you've heard or seen but aren't certain about. Try pronouncing some words, familiar and unfamiliar, to see how the pronunciation key works. Examine some entries in detail to see what information they give. Typically, the following are included:

Spelling and Division of Words.   A word is entered in a dictionary under its most common spelling. When more than one spelling is given, both are in good use: *esthetic, aesthetic; judgment, judgement;* but often the first is preferred or more current. The entry shows where a word should be hyphenated at the end of a line, as in *mor ti fi ca tion, dis par ag ing ly.* It also shows whether, in their search, the editors have found a compound word most often as two words, as one word, or with a hyphen:

> **baby-sit** (bā′bē·sit′)   *v.i.* **-sat, -sit·ting**   *U.S.* To act as a baby sitter.
> **baby sitter** *U.S.* A person employed to take care of young children while the parents are absent: also called *sitter*.

From FUNK & WAGNALLS STANDARD COLLEGE DICTIONARY. Copyright 1974. Reprinted by permission of Funk & Wagnalls Publishing Company, Inc.

Pronunciation.   Dictionaries respell words in specially marked letters to show their pronunciation. The key to the sounds represented by the symbols is usually printed at the bottom of the page and further explained in a discussion of pronunciation in the front matter. If more than one pronunciation is given without qualification, as in the following example, each is acceptable:

> **bo·vine** (bō′vīn, -vin, -vēn), *adj.* **1.** of the ox family, *Bovidae.* **2.** oxlike; cowlike. **3.** stolid; dull. —*n.* **4.** a bovine animal. [< LL *bovīn(us)* of, pertaining to oxen or cows = L *bov-* (s. of *bōs* ox) + *-īnus* -INE¹] —**bo′vine·ly,** *adv.* —**bo·vin·i·ty** (bō vin′i tē), *n.*

From the RANDOM HOUSE COLLEGE DICTIONARY, Revised Edition. Copyright© 1975 by Random House, Inc. Reprinted by permission.

Linguistic Information.   A dictionary entry indicates the part or parts of speech, the transitive or intransitive use of a verb, the principal parts of irregular verbs, plurals of irregular nouns, and any other distinctive form a word may assume. An entry may also give the history of the word — its etymology. Sometimes this is merely a statement of the language from which the word came into English; sometimes, using such abbreviations as *L* for Latin and *OE* for Old English, it traces a chain of sources and changes in form, as here:

> **sil·ly** \′sil-ē\ *adj* **sil·li·er; -est** [ME *sely, silly* happy, innocent, pitiable, feeble, fr. (assumed) OE *sǣlig,* fr. OE *sǣl* happiness; akin to OHG *sālig* happy, L *solari* to console, Gk *hilaros* cheerful] **1** *archaic* : HELPLESS, WEAK **2 a** : RUSTIC, PLAIN **b** *obs* : lowly in station : HUMBLE **3 a** : weak in intellect : FOOLISH **b** : exhibiting or indicative of a lack of common sense or sound judgment <a very ~ mistake> **c** : TRIFLING, FRIVOLOUS **4** : being stunned or dazed <scared ~> <knocked me ~> *syn* see SIMPLE — **sil·li·ly** \′sil-ə-lē\ *adv* — **sil·li·ness** \′sil-ē-nəs\ *n* — **silly** *n or adv*

From WEBSTER'S NEW COLLEGIATE DICTIONARY. © 1977 by G. & C. Merriam Co., Publishers of the Merriam-Webster Dictionaries. Reprinted by permission.

Definitions.   The definitions of words take up most of the space in a dictionary. When you check an entry to find out what a word means or to sharpen your understanding of a word that's only in your recognition vocabulary, keep three points in mind. First, a dictionary doesn't authorize or forbid a particular sense of a word but records the various senses in which people use the word. It reports facts about words, including perhaps the fact that a word is acquiring a new sense or that its customary sense is being altered. Second, the purpose of the definition, together with any examples or illustrations, is to help you understand what, in the world of objects and ideas, the word refers to—its denotation. Third, as we shall see later, a dictionary definition can scarcely hint at the associations or overtones a word has—its connotations. Since these overtones are what can make a word strikingly appropriate in one context but thoroughly inappropriate in another, it's unwise to use a word solely on the basis of what you learn about it from a dictionary. Before using it, you should hear it or read it in various contexts and so know it in part through experience.

The order in which most dictionaries offer definitions of a word is either oldest meaning first or oldest last. In a third form of entry, a "psychologically meaningful" order is followed:

> **style** (stīl) *n.* **1.** The way in which something is said or done, as distinguished from its substance. **2.** The combination of distinctive features of literary or artistic expression, execution, or performance characterizing a particular person, people, school, or era. **3.** Sort; kind; type: *a style of furniture.* **4.** A quality of imagination and individuality expressed in one's actions and tastes. **5. a.** A comfortable and elegant mode of existence: *living in style.* **b.** A particular mode of living: *the style of a gentleman.* **6. a.** The fashion of the moment, especially of dress; vogue: *out of* (or *in*) *style.* **b.** A particular fashion. **7.** A customary manner of presenting printed material, including usage, punctuation, spelling, typography, and arrangement. **8.** *Rare.* A name, title, or descriptive term. **9.** A slender, pointed writing instrument used by the ancients on wax tablets. **10.** An implement used for etching or engraving. **11.** The needle of a phonograph. **12.** The gnomon of a sundial. **13.** *Botany.* The usually slender part of a pistil, rising from the ovary and tipped by the stigma. **14.** *Zoology.* Any slender, tubular, or bristlelike process. **15.** *Obsolete.* A pen. **16.** A surgical probing instrument; stylet. —See Synonyms at **fashion.** —*tr.v.* **styled, styling, styles. 1.** To call or name; designate: *"whatever is mine, you may style, and think, yours"* (Sterne). **2.** To make consistent with rules of style. **3.** To design; give style to: *style hair.* [Middle English, from Old French, from Latin *stilus†,* writing instrument, style.] —**styl′er** *n.*

The front matter of your dictionary will tell you which order is followed in the entries.

Labels. Words that are unlabeled in a dictionary are assumed to belong to the general vocabulary; other words, or senses of words, may be labeled *dialectal, obsolete, archaic, foreign, informal, colloquial, slang, British,* or *United States* or may be referred to some field of activity—*medicine, aeronautics, law, astronomy, base-*

ball, printing, electronics, philosophy. (Labels may be abbreviated—*dial., colloq., U.S., aeron.,* etc.) Subject labels indicate that a word is restricted to one field or has a special meaning in that field.

> **push·er** (-ər) **n.** **1.** a person or thing that pushes **2.** an airplane with its propeller or propellers mounted behind the engine: also **pusher airplane** ☆**3.** [Slang] a person who sells drugs, esp. narcotics, illegally

With permission. From WEBSTER'S NEW WORLD DICTIONARY, Second College Edition. Copyright© 1976 by William Collins + World Publishing Company, Inc.

Because labels can be only rough guides to usage, you need to supplement the advice they offer with your own judgment of the appropriateness of a word in a particular rhetorical situation. While the labels *nonstandard, substandard, illiterate,* and *vulgar* can be taken as fair warning that the words or word forms would not normally be appropriate in college writing, you'll sometimes find that the dictionary editors' point of view is out-of-date. Some words marked *dial.* or *colloq.* or *slang* may fit perfectly well not only in informal writing but also in general styles. On the other hand, many words that carry no label are rarely used (*pursy, lucubration*) and would be out of place in most writing.

The labels themselves are descriptive. *Colloq.,* for example, simply means that the word is characteristic of ordinary conversation and of general rather than formal writing, though some readers persist in interpreting it as condemning the words or word forms it's attached to. Because dictionaries vary in the labels they use and in the amount of labeling they do, you'll often want to consult several when you're trying to determine the status of a word.

Synonyms. Most dictionaries gather words of similar senses into a group and show in what ways the words are alike and in what ways different, as in the following:

> **ex·clude** (iks klo͞od′) *vt.* -clud′ed, -clud′ing [ME. *excluden* < L. *excludere* < *ex-*, out + *claudere*, CLOSE²] **1.** to refuse to admit, consider, include, etc.; shut out; keep from entering, happening, or being; reject; bar **2.** to put out; force out; expel —**ex·clud′a·ble** *adj.* —**ex·clud′er** *n.*
> *SYN.*—**exclude** implies a keeping out or prohibiting of that which is not yet in [to *exclude* someone from membership]; **debar** connotes the existence of some barrier, as legal authority or force, which excludes someone from a privilege, right, etc. [to *debar* certain groups from voting]; **disbar** refers only to the expulsion of a lawyer from the group of those who are permitted to practice law; **eliminate** implies the removal of that which is already in, usually connoting its undesirability or irrelevancy [to *eliminate* waste products]; **suspend** refers to the removal, usually temporary, of someone from some organization, institution, etc., as for the infraction of some rule [to *suspend* a student from school] —*ANT.* admit, include

From WEBSTER'S NEW WORLD DICTIONARY, Second College Edition. Copyright© 1976 by William Collins + World Publishing Company, Inc. Reprinted by permission.

Unabridged and Specialized Dictionaries

For reading and writing in special fields, you'll need to supplement your desk dictionary.

Unabridged Dictionaries.   The most complete dictionaries of present-day English are called unabridged, meaning that they are not selections from larger works as, in effect, many desk dictionaries are. The three most widely used American unabridged dictionaries are the *Funk & Wagnalls New Standard Dictionary of the English Language* (Funk), the unabridged edition of the *Random House Dictionary of the English Language,* and *Webster's Third New International Dictionary of the English Language* (Merriam).

Historical Dictionaries.   The *Oxford English Dictionary,* twelve volumes and a supplement, is the great storehouse of information about English words. It traces the various forms of each word and its various senses, with dates of their first recorded appearances and quotations from writers to illustrate each sense. The *Supplement* gives material on new words and evidence on earlier words not found in the original work. The complete work is also available in the two-volume *Compact Edition.*

   The Dictionary of American English, four volumes on the same plan as the *OED,* is especially useful in reading American literature, for it gives the histories of words as they have been used in the United States. An entry begins with the first use of the word by an American writer and continues, with quotations, to 1900. The more recent *Dictionary of Americanisms* presents only those words and word meanings that have entered the language in this country.

Dialect Dictionaries.   Two standard dialect dictionaries are Joseph Wright's *English Dialect Dictionary,* which gives words in the various dialects of England, and Harold Wentworth's *American Dialect Dictionary.* Wentworth and Stuart Flexner compiled the *Dictionary of American Slang.* Eric Partridge's *Dictionary of Slang and Unconventional English* is a historical dictionary of English slang.

Dictionaries in Special Subjects.   For the vocabularies of special fields, you can find dictionaries in education, law, business, medicine, philosophy, psychology, sociology, economics, mathematics, and so on.

■ *For Analysis and Writing*

1. Examine your dictionary and write out answers to these questions: What is the title, the date of original copyright (on the back of the title page), the date of the latest copyright? Who is the publisher? Do the editors say what they believe the function of a dictionary is? What sections precede and follow the main body of your dictionary? Approximately how many entries does it have? Is there a supplement of new words? Where are biographical and geographical names listed? Where is the key that explains the symbols used in giving pronounciations? When several definitions of a word are given, in what order do they appear—in historical order, in order of frequency, or in some other order? What.labels does your dictionary use, and what does each label mean? Is profanity labeled?

2. Look up the following words to see what usage labels, if any, your dictionary applies. Then examine other desk dictionaries to see what labels they apply. How do you account for differences?

bobby	deadhead	hush puppy	pester	T formation
boss	dead pan	joint	snide	turn on
clepe	fain	nobby	snoot	uptight
clime	honky-tonk	old-timer	strung out	whiz

3. Does your dictionary include synonyms and antonyms? If so, where in the entry are they placed? Does your dictionary discriminate among synonyms, explaining the differences between words that have similar meanings? Does it help you distinguish between argue, dispute, *and* contend? *Does it help you decide in what situations you would use* done in, tired, *and* fatigued?

4. Would your dictionary help a writer who was trying to make a choice between each pair of words in parentheses?

He had the (temerity, timidity) to suggest that he alone could solve the (issue, problem). As it turned out, his solution was (ingenious, ingenuous) but showed no (perceptive, perceptible) difference from one that had (failed, faltered) last year. What he was counting on was the (affect, effect) of the special appeal he directed to the (new, novice) voters—those who had just turned eighteen.

Are the choices offered by these seven pairs all of the same kind? If not, how do they differ?

5. Write at least six sentences in which the word dog *has different meanings. Write six using* bug, run, horse, *or* cast.

6. *Although* lucid *means "clear" in such contexts as "lucid instructions" and "a lucid speaker," we don't talk about "a lucid liquid" or "a lucid day." We say "humid day" but not "humid towel." Explain why a person who didn't grow up speaking English could, or couldn't, avoid lapses like "lucid day" and "humid towel" by consulting a dictionary.*

7. *Choose the word in parentheses that's most closely synonymous with the italicized word. Then test your answer by checking with your dictionary. Does it permit you to say with assurance that you've selected the right word?*

   a. The speaker's remark was entirely *apposite* (foolish, fitting, irrelevant, unintelligible, to the point).

   b. The date of the ceremony was left *tentative* (indefinite, undecided, provisional, uncertain, contingent).

   c. The well-dressed guest seemed strangely *diffident* (indifferent, shy, fearful, evasive, embarrassed).

   d. Many causes have been suggested to explain the *deterioration* of moral standards in Roman society (degeneration, decadence, lowering, decline, decay).

   e. The essay was badly written, but it was *sincere* (candid, simple, honest, guileless, frank, plain).

   f. The affairs of the nation have now reached a *crucial* stage (dangerous, decisive, critical, ticklish, difficult, delicate).

Connotation

Your dictionary can keep you from using a "wrong" word—a word that doesn't convey your meaning. It can help you distinguish between look-alikes (*insidious, invidious; incredible, incredulous*) and sound-alikes (*write, right; born, borne; bridle, bridal*). It can give you some help in finding synonyms, words with such a large overlap of meaning that in at least one of their senses they are interchangeable in some contexts. But it can't tell you all you need to know to make the best choice between words that are very similar in meaning.

Scarcely any words in the language duplicate each other to the extent of being interchangeable in all contexts. *Shiver* and *quiver* are very close and can often be substituted for each other, but the overlap isn't complete. Though we say "She quivered with rage," we don't ordinarily say "She shivered with rage." *Pail* and *bucket* are used in different parts of the country to refer to the same thing, but people who normally use *pail* find *bucket* old-fashioned. The difference between the words in each of these pairs lies not in their denotations – they refer to the same action or thing – but in their connotations, in the associations they have for speakers and hearers, for writers and readers.

English is rich in words that carry different shades of meaning:

joke/jest average/mediocre childish/childlike flashy/striking
cheap/inexpensive intelligent/smart

obedient/dutiful/amenable/docile/yielding/compliant

old-fashioned/antiquated/passé/dated/out-of-date/old hat

What sometimes makes it difficult to discriminate among synonyms is that though the related words have a common core of meaning, they carry different connotations that make it inappropriate to substitute one for another freely in all contexts. Though a dictionary may define *mediocre* as "average," normally the connotations of *mediocre* are derogatory, while *average* is sometimes derogatory, sometimes favorable, often neutral, depending on the context. You say, "He's an average student" with no derogatory intention; but "As a driver, he's no better than mediocre" means you have little respect for his skill behind the wheel. Making the right choice between words you're not entirely familiar with requires care and thought and information. A thesaurus – a book of words and their synonyms – may offer a dozen words with the same general denotation, but to make a wise choice among them you need to know what their connotations are.

The context in which a word has been regularly used, the variety of usage to which it belongs (standard or non-standard; formal, informal, or general), and the prevailing social attitude toward what it refers to and toward the people who generally use it (politicians, prizefighters, secretaries, writers of television commercials, college students, teachers, children, seamen) – all these things contribute to a word's connotations. And connotations change with changing attitudes. The associations of much slang and profanity have altered in recent years with their widening use by adults of high social and economic status and by respected publications. Historically, connotations change as the people, things, or actions the words refer to move up or down in social esteem: *Methodist* and *Quaker* originally had derogatory connotations but are now either simply denotative or approving. For the general public, *drugs* has acquired wholly new connotations in the last generation, though these connotations differ from group to group.

Words that are heavily connotative are sometimes referred to as emotive, evaluative, intentional, loaded, or slanted. As these labels suggest, such words are often regarded with suspicion; and it's true that slanting—in headlines, in advertisements, in political speeches, in discussions of social problems—can range from inconsequential to deliberately malicious and deceptive. But connotation is rightly an element in our use of language, and it's a resource that can greatly enrich our writing. We use words not only to give information about things but to express our attitudes toward them and our feelings about them and to influence the attitudes and feelings of others. It's natural for us to apply words that have favorable connotations to actions we honestly admire (*courageous*) and to apply words with unfavorable connotations to actions we deplore (*foolhardy*). Doing so is irresponsible only if we assume that by giving a name to the action, we've proved that it is indeed courageous or foolhardy or whatever. (Remember the "God-terms" and "devil-terms" of persuasion, p. 175.)

If we're to be persuasive, we need to make good use of connotation, not to evade it by trying to find words that are as purely denotative as possible. To describe a family in desperate need, *penniless,* with its emotional connotations, may be a more responsible choice than the flatly factual *without funds.*

Words pick up associations not only from the way we regard what they refer to but from the contexts in which they're commonly used. Connotation provides much of the basis for classifying words as standard and nonstandard and for dividing standard English into formal, general, and informal. The words *stasis* and *eschew* are so unfamiliar to most of us that we probably have only a faint emotional response to them, but we do have a definite sense that they're formal—which is in itself a kind of emotional response for most people—and so we would find them out of place in casual contexts. Whenever you ignore the social side of connotation by using a formal word where the rhetorical situation calls for a casual one, or the reverse, you distract your readers from what you're trying to say—amusing them, perhaps, or annoying them, but in any case creating a barrier to communication. Like style in the broad sense, diction should call attention to itself only if, by so doing, it strengthens what's being said.

■ *For Analysis and Writing*

1. *Explain what these words have in common and how they differ*: svelte/slender/slim/thin/lean/skinny/scrawny. *Compose sentences to show which you would use and how you would use them if you wanted to be complimentary, neutral, insulting.*

2. *Explain, with sample sentences, why the words in each of the following pairs are not interchangeable in all contexts*: fair/objective; polite/courteous; clamor/uproar; stubborn/obdurate.

3. *What connotations or associations does each of these words have for you*: soul, booze, politics, hunter, business woman, science? *Which of the connotations do you believe to be generally shared (at least by your contemporaries)? Which are private associations of your own?*

4. *In a newspaper or magazine, find a discussion of a current issue in which words are, in your opinion, used irresponsibly, in a slanted fashion. Rewrite the article, removing the slant. (Be careful that your own feelings about the issue don't lead you, instead, to reslant in another direction.) Turn in both the original and your rewrite.*

5. *Write three one-paragraph descriptions of the same building (your home, your dormitory, your church, a skyscraper, a city hall, a shack)—one as objective as you can make it, one affectionate or admiring, one hostile or contemptuous.*

The Varieties of English

Even if you keep a stack of good dictionaries on your desk, the right answer to the question "What word should I use?" is usually "It depends." *Request* and *ask* are both correct; which one is preferable depends on the style of your paper, and that in turn depends on your purpose and your audience. Both *can't* and *cannot* appear regularly in print; in a specific context, one would be better – more appropriate – than the other. (In a paper in which *can't* is stylistically appropriate, *cannot* might be introduced to provide special emphasis.)

Questions about usage arise because there are different varieties of English and because these varieties don't fit equally well into every social and rhetorical situation. What's appropriate in casual talk isn't always appropriate on paper. What sounds natural to an audience of teen-agers may baffle an audience of old people. What amuses readers in one context antagonizes them in another. Knowing what kinds of English there are and recognizing how and why the alternatives differ puts you in a position to suit your style to your subject and to your audience and to the occasion. When you write English that's appropriate to the rhetorical situation, you're making the right use of language. Good English isn't just arbitrarily "good." It's good because it's right for the job. (In these last few sentences, *right* is used in a functional, not a moral, sense. If your purpose in writing is dishonest, then your use of language – whatever it may be – is morally wrong.)

There are many ways of classifying the Englishes we use, both the spoken and the written. This book is concerned primarily with written varieties of the language in their edited form – that is, with writing that's been gone over with some care. Its purpose is to help you increase your skill and confidence in writing standard English.

Standard and Nonstandard English

Standard English is the dialect used, and therefore approved, by the middle class, the dominant class in American society. The other cultural variety of English is nonstandard English, which includes usages from numerous regional and social dialects. In speech the distinction between standard and nonstandard hinges on a fairly small number of pronunciations, words, word forms, and grammatical constructions habitually used by people whose educational backgrounds and social standings are noticeably different from those of members of the middle class. In writing, the distinction is chiefly based on a carry-over of those speech habits, with spellings taking the place of pronunciations:

He et a apple.

Youse ain't wrote in months.

She seen them kittens get drownded.

Nonstandard English, which appears in published writing chiefly in dialog and in other prose that attempts to reproduce nonstandard speech patterns, is inappropriate in the writing that you'll normally be expected to do in college.

We introduced the idea of informal, general, and formal styles of writing in Chapter One. These styles are based on the informal, general, and formal varieties of standard English – categories of usage that correspond broadly to the social and rhetorical situations in which the stylistic varieties commonly occur. Since they shade into each other, with large areas of overlap, the categories shouldn't be rigidly interpreted nor the labels rigidly applied. While some words are clearly more formal than others — *disputatious*, for example — and some more informal — like *hassle* — many can be labeled only in context. A word that stands out as inappropriately formal in one paper might, in a different paper, pass as general. To say that a passage is formal, then, doesn't mean that the vocabulary and sentence structure are exclusively formal. It means that there are enough traits usually associated with that variety of the written language to give the passage a formal feel or tone, even though much of it — perhaps most of it — may be general in style.

The boundaries between the varieties continue to shift, as they have been doing for hundreds of years. Today's good formal English is close to what would have been considered general English in the essays of a half century ago, while what might be called the High Formal of the 1800s has almost disappeared. General English, meanwhile, has become increasingly relaxed, taking in more and more words, phrases, and constructions from informal. Even short periods of time bring changes in the status of individual usages. A word or phrase that's looked on as informal one year may appear often enough in well-edited publications to be considered general a year later, as the verb *bug* (to plant a secret listening device) did in the early 1970s. A word from the formal vocabulary may catch on in general English (as *charisma* and *détente* did), enjoy a vogue, and then either return to its original, restricted use or become a permanent part of the general vocabulary. Given such short-term change, the best way to keep in touch with what's going on in the language is not by relying on dictionaries and guides to usage, which are inevitably out of date, but by reading current books and newspapers and magazines and by listening to all the voices that reach your ear, directly and by way of radio and television. As you do, you'll become increasingly aware that the language is a living, changing thing; you'll expand your range of choices; and if you read and listen intelligently and critically, you'll also increase your ability to choose well.

Formal English

Old-fashioned formal English — what we've referred to as High Formal — survives today chiefly in oratory: in some political speeches, some sermons, some eulogies and other ceremonial addresses, as at graduation time. At its best, old-fashioned formal demonstrates that the English language can not only disseminate information with clarity and precision but also spark the imagination, stir the emotions, lift up the heart. At its worst, it's empty verbal posturing, a pompous parade of "big" words and stilted phrases.

Formal written English is found today in some text-books—particularly those for advanced courses—and in some learned journals. Outside academic circles it appears in books and articles addressed to well-educated audiences willing to make a greater intellectual effort than is called for by a newspaper or a popular magazine. Formal is appropriate (though not obligatory) for writing on philosophy, religion, aesthetics, literature, theoretical science, and so forth. Though its subject matter is likely to be intellectual, its tone need not be solemn. Wit and formal English are often happily allied.

The vocabulary of formal English smacks of the literary, the scholarly, the philosophical. It includes words seldom used in ordinary conversation (*desultory, ubiquitous, importunate*) and a high proportion of nouns like *hiatus, resurgence, retaliation,* which generalize about experience rather than present it directly. For those familiar with them, the words are often rich in suggestion (*omen, luminous, transcend*) or have some special appeal of sound or rhythm (*immemorial, quintessence*), while the abstract nouns and technical terms permit the exact and concise statement of ideas.

Though formal English uses short, compact sentences for emphasis, its typical sentence is fairly long, and the elements in it are carefully ordered. Here's an example of current formal English:

The children, we hear, are badly taught and cannot read, spell, or write; employers despair of finding literate clerks and typists; the professions deplore the thickening of jargon which darkens counsel and impedes action; scientists cry out in their journals that their colleagues cannot report their facts intelligibly; and businessmen declare many bright people unemployable for lack of the ability to say what they mean in any medium. — Wilson Follett, *Modern American Usage*

Such deliberate, studied arrangement of elements in a series ("employers despair . . . ; the professions deplore . . . ; scientists cry out . . ."), as well as careful, often self-conscious word choice ("the thickening of jargon which darkens counsel and impedes action"), characterizes formal writing, making its impact quite different from that of most general and all informal English.

When you set out to write a paper in formal English, you run some risks. The bad imitations of formal called officialese are prize exhibits of unreadable prose, while literary efforts are plagued by words selected more to impress than to inform and by styles so self-conscious that they divert attention from the content. And there is the problem of sustaining a formal style – not writing just one or two neatly balanced sentences but continuing to show control of phrases and clauses, mastery of the rules of close punctuation, informed conservative taste in usage, and a vocabulary adequate to the demands of the subject and the style. In short, writing a successful essay in formal English is a challenging undertaking. Meeting the challenge when the occasion arises is one measure of your sophistication as a writer.

Informal English

Informal written English is the variety of standard English that most of us use naturally in letters to members of our families and to close friends, in diaries and journals, and in other kinds of personal, intimate expression. It's also used – sometimes appropriately, sometimes not – when writers who share no intimacy with the readers they're addressing try to reduce the distance between themselves and their audiences.

Although it actually differs a good deal from the English we use in casual, spontaneous conversation, informal written English suggests speech in several of its characteristics. It swings over a wide range, sometimes mixing vocabulary from formal English with verb forms from nonstandard. It makes free use of slang and draws on the shoptalk that develops in every occupation and the in-group vocabulary that attaches to every sport. The writer takes many syntactic shortcuts, sometimes omitting subjects, usually skipping optional relative pronouns ("I hear he's in town" instead of "I hear that he is in town"), regularly using contractions. Some of the sentences of informal are short and elliptical ("Bet I won more than you" instead of "I'll bet that I won more than you did"); others are unusually long, with asides and afterthoughts keeping the structure loose and rambling. The following passage, from a book that was first talked into a tape recorder and then transcribed and carefully edited, manages to keep the feel of informal while ending up in the general-to-informal range.

> The football season is almost upon us, so I got to thinking about some basic differences in the two games for the players. Baseball players play so many games it's impossible to get emotionally high for any one of them. Football players get all gung-ho in the locker room. They chant and shout and jump up and down and take pills and hit each other on the helmet and shoulderpads and spit and kick and swear and they're ready to go out and bust some heads. If a baseball player got that emotional, he'd go out swinging hard — and miss. I think baseball is more of a skill sport than any other. Hitting is the single most difficult feat in sports. Second most difficult is preventing hitting. — Jim Bouton, *Ball Four*

The one thoroughly informal sentence in the whole paragraph is the fourth.

In published nonfiction the extended use of informal English is limited to some periodicals addressed to special audiences (rock fans, surfers, motorcyclists), to the columns of determinedly personal columnists in more general publications, and to letters from readers. Often, published informal represents the hyped-up "Hey, there, you guys and gals" school of artificial intimacy, but it may also echo the flatness of much ordinary speech, as in these excerpts from campus newspapers:

> I can't see why girls should be given a free ride. They're just being used as the window dressing and guys are being played for suckers.

> Joanne Woodward gets to use a southern accent and drink a lot for her role. She is quite good but it is not much of a part.

In small doses, however, informal English appears in a great variety of newspapers, magazines, and books, where writers of general English use informal words and phrases to move closer to their readers. The following sentences, from a range of sources, share the feel of informal and the personal note that's one of its chief characteristics:

> You can bet your sweet patootie they haven't. — Richard Dougherty, *Newsweek*

> Both parties have been stuck with old geezers in their sixties ever since. — James Reston, *New York Times*

> Around 3:30 in the afternoon, he'd been fooling with his hair, spraying, setting, combing, until it was perfect. — Lawrence Gonzales, *Playboy*

> When I was 10, gangs of hoods would stone us Jewish kids. — Audrey Gellis, *Ms.*

A single outing with one dame when he was 60 later cost him a couple hundred grand in paternity suit fees. — Tony Hiss, *New York Times Book Review*

And, of course, there is his behind. He has a fabulous behind. — Sally Quinn, *Washington Post*

If you have a chance to write a paper in informal English, don't make the mistake of assuming that it won't be any more of a problem than writing to your kid sister or your best friend. Your readers probably won't include your sister or your friend, but they will include your instructor and your classmates. And while no one should be applying the standards of formal written English or even the more relaxed ones of general English, all of them have a right to insist on being able to understand what you say. In a letter to family or hometown friends, you can take a lot for granted: they know the local places and people and happenings you refer to without needing to have everything spelled out in detail; they know the special connotations of some of the words you use; they know your regional and social dialects. But it's certain that not everyone in your class knows these things, nor will everyone be as willing as family and friends to puzzle over what you're getting at.

So your job will be to put informal English to work for you — to preserve its easy, casual tone while ridding it of its sloppiness and vagueness. That takes some doing.

General English

Occupying the broad middle ground between formal and informal is general written English. It's the variety of standard English that educated people most often read and that they themselves most often write. The words in its vocabulary include *spacious* as well as *roomy, precipitation* as well as *rainfall, nutty* as well as *eccentric, rip off* as well as *steal;* but unless there's a special reason for using the formal or informal words, *roomy, rainfall, eccentric,* and *steal* will be its choices. Writers of general English are likely to use words that are concrete, close to experience, referring to things, people, actions, and events more than to abstractions. The turns of phrase reflect those of speech (*look into, give up, take over*); coordinating conjunctions like *and* and *so* are much more common than conjunctive adverbs like *furthermore* and *consequently.* Typical sentences are moderate in length, with few interrupting phrases or elaborate constructions.

General written English is much less conservative than formal, more controlled than informal. Though it's more likely than informal to follow strict conventions of subject-verb agreement, it doesn't do so as consistently as formal does. It often ignores formal distinctions, as between *can* and *may, raise* and *rear*. Yet it's slower than informal to accept slang. And while the writer of general English is less conservative than the writer of formal English, he may be quite as careful. Indeed, because his style is not so restricted by conventions, he has more choices to make than the formal writer does.

General English is the most versatile and the most serviceable of the three varieties of standard written English this book deals with. It's the variety this book uses, because general English can reach more people than formal or informal can. For the same reason, it's the variety you'll use in most of your writing while you're in college and after you've graduated. But keep alert to the opportunities informal and formal English offer you. Mixing the varieties of English is common practice in current writing. In many magazine articles, you'll find an informal phrase dropped into a passage whose predominant tone is general or formal – possibly for shock effect, possibly because the writer wants to show a new side of himself, possibly because he wants to mock his own seriousness or an attitude held by his audience. Or an essay that's been light and casual may move to a thoughtful, measured, formal conclusion.

Sudden shifts in style that have no discernible motive distract the reader and suggest that the writer has lost control. Sometimes he has. But a good writer knows what he's doing: by calling attention to *what* he's saying by the *way* he says it, he makes shifts in style perform double duty. Even though most of your writing may be general, then, the more you acquaint yourself with the alternatives that formal and informal English offer, the better you'll be able to use them for rhetorical effects that rely on contrasts in style.

Barriers to Communication

No word, no type of word, is in itself good or bad, right or wrong. All kinds of words can be put to good use. You'll have reason to use abstract words like *rage, honor, symmetry, evil* as well as concrete words like *show, onion, motorcycle, flower*. You'll need to decide whether, in a

particular context, you want to use the broad term *headache* or the more specific *migraine,* the broad term *typewriter* or the specific *my Olympia portable.* You'll have to
decide whether a highly connotative word would be better
or worse than a relatively neutral one. You'll have to decide whether to choose from the formal or the general
or the informal vocabulary. Whether a word is actually
put to good use can be judged only in context, for good
diction is diction appropriate to the rhetorical situation.
But something can be said about ways of using words
that are likely to weaken writing and handicap you in your
attempts to communicate.

Pretentiousness

You throw up a barrier to communication when you try
too hard—when you set out to impress readers rather than
to inform them. Perhaps this means using five words
where one would do ("prior to the time that" instead of
"before"); perhaps it means choosing a formal word where
a general one is more suitable ("ameliorate" instead of
"improve"); perhaps it means adopting the special vocabulary of a subject—the jargon of literary critics or
sociologists or psychologists or economists, for example—
when doing so is unnecessary or inappropriate.

Many of the words selected more to impress an audience
than to express meaning are what are sometimes called
"big" words—*emulate* for *imitate, inculcate* for *teach,
valiant* or *intrepid* for *brave.* Though "big" words are
often long, length alone doesn't make them objectionable.
Long words are the only words for some things: *poly-
unsaturated* and *sphygmomanometer* have their place.
Short or long, "big" words are words that are too heavy
for the subject, too pretentious for what the writer is
saying. In the proper rhetorical situation, they may be
exactly the right words. Where they don't fit, they're "big"
words.

Triteness

You throw up a barrier to communication by not trying
hard enough—not working to find the words that express
your ideas and feelings. It's easy to slide into the ready-
made expression, the phrase that's on everyone's lips
("Winning is the name of the game"). It takes less effort
to use a trite phrase, a cliché, than to find your own words
to express your meaning.

A word or a combination of words isn't trite simply because it's familiar. Phrases like "in the first place" and "on the other hand" can be used again and again without attracting attention to themselves (though *not* in the same paper), and the names of things and acts and qualities don't wear out from repetition. But unlike transitional devices and nouns and verbs that perform essential functions, formulas like "a sunny smile," "a necessary evil," "a tower of strength," "the acid test," "the crack of dawn," "a whole new ball game," and scores of similar expressions have become almost meaningless. A phrase doesn't have to be ancient and corny to be trite. Thanks to the saturation made possible by the mass media, last year's vogue expressions can be as thoroughly drained of substance as frayed quotations (and misquotations) from Shakespeare and the Bible. *Massive* was so widely applied in the late 1960s that it lost all its former impact. Often there's an inverse relation between how widely a word or phrase is used and its rhetorical strength.

If you turn in a final draft that's littered with clichés, your readers are going to sense that you didn't bother hunting for words that would accurately express what *you* thought. And if you write in all seriousness that "there are two sides to every question" or that "life is what you make it," your readers will have reason to suspect that you didn't bother to think. Triteness is a matter not only of using worn-out words but of using worn-out ideas. When the word comes before the idea, the trite expression can lead to the trite thought. If you write in clichés, you'll think in clichés. And vice versa. Here's an example of trite ideas, tritely expressed:

The world of fashion shows free enterprise in action—the good old American way. Spending six months as a salesgirl in a dress shop made me realize that most women are slaves to fashion, that few know the value of a dollar, and that there's lots of truth in the old saying "It takes all kinds." Some of the customers made my life miserable. On more than one occasion I had to bite my lip to keep from giving them a piece of my mind, and sometimes it was difficult to keep from crying. But there was laughter as well as tears, and I learned many valuable lessons in interpersonal relations. After all, getting along with others—even featherheaded spendthrifts—is a must if we want to make this old world a better place to live in. And if our economy is to stay healthy, we'll have to put up with women (and men too) breaking down the doors to grab up bargains that aren't bargains and making fools of themselves as they adjust to the winds of fashion, season after season.

One reason the paragraph lacks focus is that the writer follows the lead of clichés instead of expressing her own perceptions and substantiating them from her own experience. Even when she's talking from her experience, the phrases she uses – "bite my lip," "a piece of my mind," "laughter as well as tears" – have been repeated so often that they carry no personal flavor. When she deals in generalizations, she's so locked into clichés – "world of fashion," "free enterprise in action," "good old American way," "interpersonal relations," "healthy" economy, "winds of fashion" – that whatever ideas she may have had are lost in the blizzard of trite words and phrases.

If triteness is a problem in your writing, the cause isn't necessarily laziness. Perhaps you're simply unaware that the phrases you use are worn out. Possibly you haven't read enough or listened carefully enough to know that your figures of speech are stale. The first step in replacing stock phrases and senile images is to recognize them for what they are. Compare these three descriptions:

I.

A grey mist overhung Nature like a pall. The somber shroud wrapped in oblivion lifeless forms which had been so beautiful in their summer splendor. The branches of the trees, shorn of their green raiment, appeared like spectral fingers reaching up to the somber, low-hanging clouds. Stunted shrubs, less bold, groveled to the ground. Closer still to the earth huddled withered blades of grass, corpses of the gallant, green-clad knights of early May. The staunch little soldiers of spring and summer were no more; they had succumbed in the battle with wind and storm. Faded autumn leaves stirred restlessly with every puff of wind, but seemed unwilling to leave the protection of Mother Earth's embrace.

II.

A tall lonely tree in the distance remained silent in the calm night breeze. The tree stood like a proud mother with her branches reaching out welcoming arms into the darkness. She had a straight stately trunk which was surrounded by her children. The small pines, dressed in white, stood close together under her outstretched arms to be protected by her. Their branches touched each other, holding hands for comfort in the darkness. The mother and her children stood against the horizon, and above them the stars shone brightly in the clear sky. The hilltop, which was their home, smelled crisp and clean.

III.

The oak trees on our street were honest and forthright. The bark was not just a grey skin but a solid dark coat. In the winter they stood heavy and black against the sky, while other trees threw up mere bundles of twigs. In the spring, they did not creep out in pale green mistiness, like the other trees; they waited until they were sure, and then they put out their leaves in great confident clots. When summer winds blew, the oaks never trembled. They surged mightily, sighing fiercely. And in the fall, their leaves felt like stiff wrapping paper, and their seeds, which were not of membrane and cotton but of wood, bounced smartly when they fell on the sidewalks, and popped loudly in the fires.

In the first passage the clichés—including much old-fashioned personification—make the description both flat and pretentious. The student who wrote it had done some reading and had been much influenced by it. And that's the trouble: The description is derived not from life but from literature. If the student kept on reading, he'd find that generations of writers have used the same similes and metaphors. But even without doing any further reading, he could expose the artificiality of his description simply by being honest with himself. Has he ever seen a pall? A shroud? Knights, "green-clad" or otherwise? Does he wear "raiment"? Does he really picture plants as "staunch little soldiers"? Does he spontaneously think of "Mother Earth" embracing anything? The whole paragraph smells of the library, not of nature with or without a capital N.

The writer of the second passage began with a single cliché—the personified tree—and then got all tangled up in triteness and sentimentality. The "lonely," "silent" tree turns into a "proud" mother with "welcoming" arms. Next the loneliness is forgotten: a whole family of "children" is disclosed, holding hands. The mother's welcoming arms become protective. The stars are bright; the sky is clear; the hilltop smells crisp and clean. The inspiration in this case seems to be, not literature and certainly not nature, but a combination of Walt Disney, greeting cards, and television commercials. There's no sign of a controlling idea, no coherent attitude, no consistent emotion.

In the third passage personification persists; but here it's fresher because the student has looked squarely at what he's writing about and presented it as *he* sees it, in forceful prose.

The ways to avoid triteness, then, are first of all to do your own thinking and your own seeing and then to say what *you* think and to record what *you* see. A good deal can be accomplished by simply rejecting combinations that come to mind automatically: "godless communism," "capitalist imperialism," "male chauvinism," "the weaker sex," "crooked politicians," and so on. Often the phrase that comes to mind without active thought performs no function in the context. The "godlessness" of communism may have no relevance to the thought in the passage you're writing. And even if you want to express the idea a stock phrase stands for, you'll do better to express it in a different way so that, in fresher form, it can make some impression on your readers.

Jargon

You throw up a barrier to communication when you hide your meaning in jargon—language that combines the pretentiousness of "big" words and the deadliness of cliché with a degree of abstraction that isolates what's said from the world of living beings:

One of the prominent factors in marital discord is economic.

If the writer of that sentence stopped to ask himself what he really had to say, he might come up with "Many husbands and wives fight over money"—a sentence with its feet on the ground.

Abstract terms are essential in all kinds of writing, and language that's predominantly abstract is capable of great precision. But it's annoying when it's substituted unnecessarily for concrete expression, and it can cripple communication by forcing readers to guess at the meaning. The literature of the social sciences often suffers from a lack of clarity because of its fondness for impersonal constructions ("It is generally agreed that . . .") and for abstract and general terms that deny the reader images of human activity:

Conflict within and between groups in a society can prevent accommodation and habitual relations from progressively impoverishing creativity.

Here, from an article on jargon, a jargon-ridden passage is followed by an attempt to reduce it to plain, clear prose:

It has been observed that the offspring of familial units in the lower economic brackets demonstrate a frequent tendency to sublimate status-anxiety by means of organized aggression against societal mores, such aggression taking the form of vandalistic assaults upon institutional properties.

. . . the children of poor parents often try to smother their sense of inferiority by throwing rocks at the schoolroom windows.—Robert Gordon, AAUP *Bulletin*

The original passage creates no images at all; it is only when the abstract terms are replaced by concrete ones and the general terms are made more specific that we "see" what the writer is talking about. Notice that one abstraction remains, and properly so: the concept of insecurity. Yet here, too, the change from jargon—"status-anxiety" —to the normal English of "sense of inferiority" is an improvement.

Just as the use of cliché expressions can lead to cliché ideas, so the application of laboratory jargon to human affairs can lead to a kind of thinking that ignores people. The children of poor parents just about disappear in "the offspring of familial units in the lower economic brackets." Many other collectives hide the particulars they stand for. *Doublespeak* is a handy term for language that obscures meaning rather than communicates it. "Urban renewal" that means "removal of blacks," "inner city" for "slums," "correctional institutions" for "prisons" are examples.

Jargon is hard to avoid. All of us are exposed to it constantly. Daily, on radio and television, in newspapers and magazines, we hear and read the jargons of politics and economics, the arts and sciences, the professions and the academic disciplines. In every college classroom words are regularly used for which simpler, more direct, more concrete, often more honest substitutes could be found. Indeed, for college students jargon presents a unique problem. Their instructors use the specialized vocabularies of the various disciplines and defend them as necessary:

Developing an adequate terminology for sociological concepts in an exacting—and sometimes exasperating—task. It is complicated not only by the fact that almost all of the concepts in the field are undergoing continuous revision and refinement but also by the fact that many of them deal with aspects of social behavior already understood in part by the lay person. Often a new name must be invented to symbolize some newly discovered property of a familiar societal phenomenon, or a term already in popular use must be assigned a new meaning so that it can be used to signify properties of social events which have not previously been studied. Thus, in their search for adequate tools of conceptualization, social scientists often find it necessary to manipulate language in ways that are puzzling or even irritating to members of the general public, some of whom charge that sociological terminology is a hopeless jargon that obscures communication instead of clarifying it. Sociologists are aware of this difficulty, but they rightly insist on the need for using the symbols of language in whatever way is necessary to define the concepts they need as tools for systematically exploring the nature of social reality.—Melvin L. DeFleur, William V. D'Antonio, and Lois B. DeFleur, *Sociology: Human Society*

The style of the following tongue-in-cheek "college essay," a combination of sociologese and educationese, is meant to reflect unfortunate parental influence:

First, let me say that I understand why you want to know as much as you can about me before your institution decides whether to enter into a commitment situation with respect to my enrollment. You prefer healthy, well-rounded individuals as students. I believe that, thanks to nurturing and careful parenting by my father, a sociologist, and my mother, a high-school curriculum expert, combined with an innovative education in which all subjects were taught as a cohesive, interrelated whole, I am such an individual. So, indeed, are my siblings.

I do have a special interest, based on what I hope is a creative self-perception. It is to upgrade my potential. When I prioritize my goal/objectives, that comes first. I have other goal/objectives, of course, and my view of my development perspective is not rigidized. Far from it. Members of my peer group say that I have a propensity for exuding enthusiasm, and I know that at times I may overdo it, so that my ambitions appear to lack integration. Nonetheless, with me, the core programmatical element is upgrading my potential, and in realizing that goal/objective, I am sure that I will not require achievement motivation. I need only the academic tool concepts that will enable me eventually to achieve and attain at my full potential.

How would I acquire these concepts within the normal university temporal sequence? How would I choose among the multifaceted services your institution offers to those to whom it grants studenthood? It would be my hope, in planning for my career and life style, to participate in structured dialogues dealing with communication relationships at work, and so to optimize my interpersonal communication skills.

That done, I would hope to study the ecology of the leadership phenomenon, for the country needs leaders, and we young people, after all, must be the leaders of tomorrow. I hope that this does not sound self-delusive: I don't envision myself as President of the United States. But I believe that with suitable preplanning, I can make a meaningful contribution. I believe that I can articulate a constructive input to manipulative interaction and problem solving in the community by functioning positively and learning to look critically at the present so as to influence the future as it emerges. My social-studies teachers have impressed on me that this can be taught best by multidisciplinary faculty working at interdisciplinary interfaces. I know that in this field, your university has broken new ground.

To sum up: The energizing principle of my application is a quest for a quality educational experience that will complete the task of making my self whole. I believe that the thrust of this application is reality-oriented and that your ongoing placement service would be able to help me find a professional context in which my expertise could be doubly impactful in our increasingly techno-humanistic society.—Edwin Newman, *New York Times Magazine*

Some students are able to switch from jargon to jargon as they shift from class to class. They recognize the changing rhetorical situations and speak and write accordingly. But many students lack the versatility to match jargons to audiences. They use the jargon of the sociology lecture hall in an English course, or the jargon of literary criticism in a course in economics, or the jargon of economics in a course in education. And they often suffer for it. While some terms—*entropy* is one example—break out of the discipline they start in and travel the circuit, many are rejected with horror outside their field of origin. For most students the best advice is to learn the essential vocabulary of each discipline—what's shoptalk in the discipline but jargon outside it—and, beyond that, to stick to the vocabulary of general English.

Finding the right substitute for jargon isn't always a workable solution. In reading over the first draft of a paper you've written, you're likely to come upon some "big" words you can't translate. They sound right in the context. You have a general notion of what they mean. You think most readers will understand what you intend. But in fact you don't know exactly what you're saying. The right thing to do in such a situation is to ask yourself, "What am I talking about, and what do I want to say?" Then, using words you *can* define, say it as clearly as you can, no matter how many ordinary words it takes.

■ *For Writing*

Rewrite each of the following sentences to make it clearer and more direct. This may mean using more than one sentence.

a. Among the many alterations in life-style that require adjustment on the part of the freshman the most important are environmental changes, which range from a lessening of restrictions in socializing to greatly extended opportunities for intellectual development.

b. The artificiality of the collective conscience has so dehumanized society that nobody has guilt feelings about the difference between his conduct and the principles he professes allegiance to.

c. Governmental mandatory regulation of wages and prices cannot be implemented without consequent disaffection of powerful voting interests.

d. The cost reduction campaign was the most prominent factor in the decision not to augment the work force.

e. Doomed by a poor field position situation and an intimidating opposition that defensed with unremitting savagery and zeal, the Zips found themselves incapable of achieving the momentum that might have muffled the expressions of frustration and discontent to which the occupants of the stands were giving vent with increasing volume and unanimity.

Euphemism and Overkill

You throw up a barrier to communication when you use words to hide or distort the truth — either pale euphemisms chosen to disguise injustice and brutality and stupidity, or invective intended to insult or incite without regard for fairness or reason.

A euphemism is a substitute for a word that is direct and explicit — the *departed* for the *corpse*. The substitute is milder, less disturbing, more neutral in connotation, perhaps less harsh in sound, usually less precise in meaning than the term it displaces. Many euphemisms have their origin in prudishness, as substitutes for the vigorous monosyllabic names of physical functions: *perspire* for *sweat, expectorate* for *spit, odor* for *stink* and *smell*, and so on. Others originate in a desire to gloss over social situations or facts of life that might be regarded as distressing. Old age becomes *golden years;* the poor and oppressed are the *underprivileged,* the *culturally deprived,* or *disadvantaged.* Some of these terms are so firmly established in current usage that you'll find it hard to avoid using them in your writing, but you should never lose sight — or let your reader lose sight — of the reality behind the label.

Euphemism, like the language it supplants, is a relative matter: whether a word sounds genteel or neutral or blunt depends on the ear that hears it. And people differ in their attitudes toward specific euphemisms. Though *senior citizens* is widely deplored by those who are not so labeled, many old people prefer it to *old people*. Deciding whether to use or to avoid euphemism therefore calls for attention to the rhetorical situation. In everyday life the motive for euphemism is usually tact or consideration for the feelings of others. Euphemism is also used in public situations (sometimes justifiably, sometimes not) to dilute the audience's emotional response to a potentially explosive situation — as when a riot is reported as a "disturbance." But it can backfire. Many people prefer *slum* or *ghetto* to the euphemistic *ethnic neighborhood,* especially if they think the euphemism is being used to mask an ugly reality. So there are two sides to the relation between euphemism and good taste: even a well-intentioned attempt to avoid giving offense can itself be offensive.

Because a responsible writer faces facts, he doesn't seek out euphemism in a deliberate attempt to hide the truth. But neither does he use verbal overkill, bludgeoning readers with language that exaggerates where euphemism minimizes. The usual motive for overkill is to blind the audience to all but the emotional aspects of an issue. Besides being irrational, verbal violence, including the use of obscenities, is often ineffective. An overkill expression quickly becomes a cliché and, like every cliché, loses most of its original force.

Renewing Words

Word choice poses a dilemma. If you always use words in just the way everyone is accustomed to seeing and hearing them used, you'll sound like an echo. Yet if you strain for original turns of phrase, you'll sound affected or odd. So you need to look for ways of expressing yourself that fall somewhere between the thoroughly conventional and the idiosyncratic. Try to make familiar words take on freshness.

Giving words new life is partly a matter of perception, of how you see what you see, and partly a matter of controlling the context so that a word is freed from its routine associations. You can use metaphor and allusion to make a new reading of experience, to reinforce or sharpen meaning, or simply to give the reader the pleasure that comes from finding words used in fresh and distinctive ways. Or—and this is worth remembering—to give yourself the fun of capturing on paper the odd connections that pop into your mind. For all kinds of writers, from poets to sports columnists, word play is sometimes a private game that brings some pleasure into the hard work of composing:

MICHIGAN CHOKES ON BOILERMAKER (title of an article about a football upset of the University of Michigan by Purdue)—
Sports Illustrated

We aren't out of the woods yet. The wage-price crunch is fueling inflation, there are eight million Americans without jobs and the stock market is as nervous as a pregnant cat.—Judd Arnett, *Detroit Free Press*

I took the precaution of draping a poncho over myself and the entire ensemble and then wobbled off toward the frontier looking like a greenish-brown lump of ambulatory Jell-O.—Robert Pilpel, *Harper's*

On the constitutional principle that anything we enjoy that much must be evil, we have begun gobbling up exposés like health food—book upon relentless book proving the essential rottenness of coaches, players, hot-dog purveyors, and even us fans. . . . Each of these books contains one possible magazine article surrounded by more padding than an offensive linesman.—Wilfred Sheed, *New York Times Book Review*

Many of the splashy new shows have already gurgled down the unclogged drains of their own commercials.—Robert Mayer, *Newsweek*

While awful puns and outrageous exaggerations won't often be appropriate in your college papers, write down any that occur to you. Sooner or later the right rhetorical situation may come along, and meanwhile you'll have something to turn to when you need a laugh.

Metaphor

There are many different kinds of figures of speech, each with its own label. But since naming them is a lot less important than putting them to work, we'll use the term *metaphor* here for any nonliteral use of words.

Metaphors have greatly extended the meanings of many words. *Head* still has its old literal denotation as part of the body, but it's also applied to the top or principal part of a wide variety of things—of a nail, pin, screw, bay, news story, stalk of grain, bed, golf club, beer, boil, barrel— not to mention parts of a number of machines, the leaders in all sorts of institutions and governments and movements, the users of addictive and nonaddictive drugs, and a ship's toilet. *Head* for the head of a nail has become one of the senses of *head:* there's no other word for it, and it's one of the regular definitions listed in dictionaries. The language is full of such petrified, or dead, figures of speech. What we're interested in here is live figures, extensions of words to new referents.

Functions of Metaphor. Metaphor can be used to please or to persuade or to explain. The simplest of its functions is to enliven style: "Into even a newspaper paragraph phrases are flung the way a teen-ager flings socks into a closet, and half of them inside out" (Hugh Kenner, *New York Times Book Review*). But because it relates an abstraction to a physical process, metaphor can also make an idea more interesting, more amusing, easier to understand, as in these passages:

It's a sobering experience to learn that for years your mind has been blocking out something that should be obvious. It's like realizing there's been a blown fuse in part of your upstairs wiring. — Thomas H. Middleton, *Saturday Review*

The teachers of modernism, having commended extreme subjectivity to their students, were appalled to learn that it was like commending your daughter to a sex maniac. — John Leonard, *New York Times Book Review*

Great luck and catastrophe are equal dawdlers. Good news comes down the road like a herd of snails, and disaster wheezes and coughs along and finally arrives when you are sick of waiting for it. — William A. Emerson, Jr., *Newsweek*

Advertisers should realize that forcing us to waddle through their puddle of sex appeal insults the intelligence of every one of us.

I never felt that studying was a natural and pleasurable activity until I took botany. When I began to learn about the hundreds of different types of trees, I felt that sap had begun to run through the rusting pipes of my mind.

And metaphor can make an idea memorable, as in this comparison of the correspondence between Thomas Jefferson and John Adams to an instrumental duet,

an eighteenth-century music of the mind, in which the two men trade off themes, challenge and echo each other, swell and fade in the give and take of ideas and memories. If Jefferson prefers trim little violin tunes, while Adams more often chuckles or grumbles along on the bass, the marvel is their final mutual deference. — Garry Wills, *New York Review of Books*

Metaphor can become the means of investigating a subject. Analogies to natural objects or processes are often used to trace movements or to analyze intangibles. Following out the implications of a metaphor—if the stirrings of an independence movement are compared to germinating seeds, what caused the germination? how will the plants develop?—may provide new insights into the subject. If using clichés can lead to thinking trite thoughts, using original metaphors can lead to making discoveries. The following passage introduces an analogy that supplies the basis for the author's subsequent discussion:

If you look closely, you will see that every student on campus is playing "The University Game." To qualify for the game, pay a wad of money to the bursar and register for classes. Play begins as you proceed from class to class, fulfilling requirements and striving for an education. It ends when, four years later, you clutch the diploma that indicates you have played and won.

Metaphor provides us with ways to express what we couldn't otherwise express or, at least, couldn't express as well—not only feelings but ideas and concepts. The wave theory of light in physics and the concept of the watershed in the history of ideas—these represent more than ways of describing a subject or investigating it; they represent ways of knowing it. Good metaphors open doors to perception and understanding.

Controlling Metaphor. The figures you use in your papers should represent *your* way of perceiving your subject. If a borrowed figure fits the context, it's usually so general and time-worn that it can't contribute much. Now and then the homely comparisons of everyday speech—"fresh as a daisy," "cold as ice"—can be used effectively in writing, but only now and then. The strength of metaphor lies in its power to evoke images and emotions, to make the reader experience and not just comprehend. And a stale or trite figure—including the pseudo-literary cliché (see p. 299)—simply doesn't stir the reader's imagination.

The risks in using metaphor are greatest when you're working too hard at enlivening your prose. If a figure doesn't represent a way of thinking about the subject that's natural to you, you may lose control of it and produce a conspicuously mixed metaphor. Probably the most common variety results from the meeting of two figurative expressions that have lost most of their metaphorical life. In one context a worn-out figure calls no attention to itself, except as a cliché:

The voters made it clear they didn't want to switch horses in midstream.

In another context it will show just enough life to clash with a similarly enfeebled neighbor. Here the mixture of horses, stream, and limb encourages a mental picture of cowboy acrobatics:

If we switch horses in the middle of a stream, we'll find ourselves out on a limb.

"Her face froze into a mask of indifference" is conventionally trite. When fire is joined with the ice, the effect in ordinary prose is ludicrous:

Once seated, her face froze into a mask of smoldering irritability.—Chicago *Sun-Times*

Here, two metaphors that relate to the same referent are permitted to collide:

She was more sheepdog than chaperone, herding us onto the bus. When, at last, all her chicks were counted, she clucked contentedly.

But the dangers of mixing metaphors can be exaggerated. While the transformation of a metaphorical sheepdog into a metaphorical mother hen is too incongruous to go unnoticed, many good writers slide rather easily from one figure to another, each one yielding pleasure for the reader without calling attention to the company it's keeping:

Accountability has arrived. No longer will flowering fields of congressional alibis be watered by executive branchwater. The Democrats are in charge, and since the buck can no longer be passed, perhaps the dollar will be treated with more respect.— William Safire, syndicated columnist

Whether or not a figure works depends in part on the rhetorical situation. The better you know your audience, the less likely you'll be to stumble into an inappropriate metaphor. And to be sure a figure fits your subject, you need to be aware of all the connotations of the term you're using metaphorically. "Game plans," with connotations of sport, might be acceptable when used in connection with political campaigning but objectionable in the context of the nation's military or economic policies.

Allusion

Sometimes you can add interest or clarity or emphasis to what you're discussing by alluding to something outside your topic. A brief reference to literature, to history, to a public figure can contribute to your meaning and also have a distinct stylistic effect.

An allusion leaves the reader some work to do. Instead of referring directly to an event, the writer refers to the place where it occurred. (Hundreds of political writers have used "Munich" to allude to the attempt to appease Nazi Germany that was made by French and British statesmen at a conference in that city in 1938.) Instead of quoting and naming the source of his quotation, he refers to the source indirectly. Often he incorporates familiar phrases from the Bible or from Shakespeare or suggests such phrases, as "We all know that Britain is awash in a sea of adversity" (Roland Gelatt, *Saturday Review*) suggests Shakespeare's "sea of troubles" (*Hamlet*, III.i.59). Thus a literary or historical allusion may be no more than a word or two (*summer soldier, honorable men*), a place name (*Hiroshima, Times Square, Gethsemane*), or a name (*Pocahontas, Canute*). By summoning up in the reader's mind the context in which the phrase or name originally appeared, an allusion of this kind can add a new level of meaning to the discussion. This reference to Diogenes, the Greek philosopher who supposedly searched Athens for an honest man, makes a very strong claim for the function of news analysts:

We are not in the business of winning popularity, and we are not in the entertainment business. It is not our job to please anyone except Diogenes. — Walter Cronkite, *Saturday Review*

Unless the rhetorical situation demands formality, you can sometimes draw allusions from advertising slogans, popular songs, gag lines. A well-chosen topical allusion may convince the reader that the writer knows what's going on; but the topical allusion quickly becomes a cliché. On the other hand, the obscure, esoteric allusion may be taken as a sign of the show-off — and may baffle the reader completely. Allusions, then, should be appropriate to the rhetorical situation, giving the reader the pleasure of recognition, adding richness to the idea, and at the same time expressing something of the writer's personality.

Some allusions have made themselves so much at home in the language of every day that we no longer think of them as allusive; but recalling that what hangs over the head is the sword of Damocles can give a little more zest to both writing the phrase and reading it:

Drawing a daily comic strip is not unlike having an English theme hanging over your head every day for the rest of your life. — Charles M. Schulz, *Saturday Review*

■ *For Analysis and Writing*

1. Make a list of things, experiences, and activities that interest, amuse, please, or annoy you. Then write a brief figurative passage that shows how you perceive each item in the list and (perhaps) how you feel about it. Sample list: walking, skiing, sunrises, beagles, birthday celebrations, word play, Chinese food.

2. Examine each of these excerpts (those unidentified are by students) and explain why you do or do not find it an effective expression of the idea. Try your hand at rewriting the figurative passages that you consider weak, incongruous, overdone, or otherwise unsatisfactory.

a. This is a blowfish of a novel. It tries to swim the depths, only to puff itself up with false vanity and empty rhetoric, rising pathetically to the shallows to show itself off as the bloated creature it is. — *Newsweek*

b. I loved the freshmen dearly, as one loves a docile child who takes all one's time and love. They were like puppies. They swirled and barked around me like the hellhounds of remorse. — Helen Bevington, *The House Was Quiet and the World Was Calm*

c. Last night I sang like an angel for three hours. You don't even hear yourself when it really gets going. Only the sensation of rushing vibration all through the head and chest everywhere. As if the body were a jet engine taking in air at supersonic speeds then filtering the air into melody. The pitch isn't heard; it's felt.

d. Away from the cities and their parroted chatter of Christmas, which would fail to fool any self-regarding child, the world rolls to the brink of the solstice, where life lives banked in burrows and the earth is a surface of storm tracks: wide miss, near miss, direct hit, and snowbound. — L. E. Sissman, *Atlantic*

e. Man at his best is a sort of caricature of himself, and even when we are eulogizing him for his finer attributes, there has to be a minor theme of depreciation, much as a vein of comedy weaves in and out of a great tragedy. — Richard M. Weaver, *The Ethics of Rhetoric*

f. The lurid, greenish glow of the streetlight showed a woman covered with blood. Thick, ropy blood oozed slowly from angry abrasions on the side of her head, and a stream of bright gore spouted like a geyser from a cut on the bridge of her nose.

g. The island, shielded from the throb of Kowloon by the harbor and Victoria Peak, is necklaced by a road that vistas down over fishing villages like Aberdeen, with its famed double-decker floating restaurants — sweet and sour upstairs, mahjong below decks — and shifting water carpets of sampans. — Carol Wright, *Providence Journal*

h. Children have a tendency to take adult pronouncements as true merely because they are uttered by a source cloaked with mysterious power.

i. As I started on my second pack of cigarettes, I could see my cell membranes laughing at me.

j. I oppose the plan for reorganizing the college because its sponsors have not given enough thought to the effects it will have. We are told by architects that form should follow function. We need to know what functions, what needs, what ends, what values we should be pursuing before we form new structures. We have too often erected buildings and created organizational structures without making a careful analysis of educational goals and ends. Once created, they tend to freeze existing value orientations and severely limit flexibility.

k. In his first few years with the Bureau, he climbed right to the top of the pecking order. His colleagues, all busy in their own affluent ant hills, scarcely realized what was happening.

l. The only opium available to him is that hallucinogenic agent the layman calls "memory" – a drug of the most awful and powerful properties, one that may ravish the psyche even while nurturing the soul. Stiff penalties should be affixed to its possession, for its dangerous components include disappointing inventories, blocked punts, lumpy batters, and iron buckets of burden. It is habit-forming, near-to-maddening in large doses, and may even grow hair on the palms. – Larry L. King, *Harper's*

m. It is a situation which puts the film people in a particularly awkward position. They let TV have their movies but at the same time they object when they find that most stations regard a movie as simply the thread on which to string as many profitable beads as possible. The more commercials, the more money. The movies and TV are, it seems, destined for a shotgun marriage – two spheres locked in combat, yet each realizing in the other the fattening of its pocketbook.

n. The ultimatum was issued in the wake of a rash of outbreaks of violence.

o. He crossed the street and resumed his walk in the comfort of a solid barrier of traffic separating us from him.

p. To call out the National Guard at the first hint of trouble means inflicting a permanent wound on the fabric of our national life.

q. I found I had only nibbled at the vast edifice of sociology.

r. "You failed the test." His words hit me with the impact of a wet snowball.

s. Most students seem to feel, as I did, that the selection of a major field of study is a miraculous phenomenon similar to falling in love. This expectation accounts for the feelings of guilt and anxiety that many of us experience when we realize we have made a wrong choice. It's like feeling unfaithful. In choosing a career it would be better to consider some fields more appropriate than others but no field supernaturally perfect.

t. Every time we get a firm footing, Barthelme pulls the rug out from under us.

u. The rewriter is as one who packs his thought for a long journey. Having packed the garment, he does not merely straighten out the folds and close the paragraph. Instead, he unpacks completely and repacks again. And again; and again and again. Each time, he tucks just one more thought into this or that pocket. When he quits, there are more of them than of words. So many labors of love on a single sentence, that many rewards for the rereader. On the surface, one teasing half-reward; others at successively greater and greater depths, so that each reading finds one more. . . .
Conceivably those successive depths might be achieved in one writing; but more probably the genius is simply the man who can do the repacking inside his skull. In any case, there must be repacking with more ideas insinuated into the wording. The rewards will lie at successive depths only if they were packed into the text in successive repackings. That is simply the kind of wits we have. – Martin Joos, *The Five Clocks*

Chapter Ten
Doing a Close Reading

For one or more papers in your writing course, you may be asked to do a "close reading" (or explication) of a literary work. For such an assignment you're expected to write a paper explaining the work in detail and sometimes — depending on the instructions you receive — evaluating it as well. As the term "close reading" indicates, this project tests your ability both as a reader and as a writer. During the prewriting stage you'll be working out ways to report the understanding you achieved through concentrated study of the poem or short story, the essay, novel, or play.

Reading the Work

Your first step in writing a critical paper about a literary work is to read the work, and read it, and read it again. Begin by getting a sense of the work as a unified whole. Study what the author set down on paper until you know what he *said.* If you're reading a short story or a novel or a play — or a poem with a narrative line — find out what happens, who does what. If you're reading an essay, find the line of logic or emotion that runs through it and follow where that leads, so that you can infer and can demonstrate how the author reaches his conclusion. Once you've done that, you're ready to look at individual sentences, phrases, words — to listen to rhythms and sounds — and see what they contribute to the total effect.

You can't jump into a literary work and achieve instant understanding. Fight against a temptation to skim, to race through the work, and then to leap to an explanation and evaluation of it. And fight down any urge to quit — to struggle through it once and decide then and there that you'll never be able to figure out what the author is talking about. Read carefully, and concentrate on what you're reading. Make notes, ask yourself questions, circle words (and look up those you're not sure of), underline sentences.

Just as you should read your own papers aloud to see if

they sound the way you want them to, so you should read aloud any literary work you're going to write about. A literary work is more than a plot line or a train of thought; it's also a work of art—or an attempt to be one—and you need to take its style into account when you set out to understand it and judge it. Reading poetry aloud is absolutely essential. Unless you can hear what a poet says and describe what you hear, you don't really know a poem.

Each time you read a work, you become more conscious of its elements, the way its author put them together, and the reasons he put them together the way he did. From knowing what happened in a story, you'll move on to why it happened and begin to wonder about its significance. Is the author saying no more than "John and Mary loved each other," or is he saying something about the relationships between men and women, or about the nature of love? Is the poet writing about springtime, the four seasons, a flower, a dead animal, or about a kind of immortality? What's the generalization, the theme, the comment about life or some phase of life that the work embodies?

Deciding what the author's purpose was—what he set out to do—is necessary because only after you've decided what that was can you judge whether he failed or succeeded. In reaching your decision, rely on the work itself. Some students develop an ability to come up with interpretations that are remarkably clever and imaginative but, when tested, prove to have little basis in the text—that is, in what the author wrote. Often such interpretations are built instead on what the reader suggests is a web of images or a pattern of symbols. Images and symbols are important devices that writers use to communicate their meaning; and sometimes a writer will underline a symbol to make its significance unmistakable. The bursting buds of spring, for example, is a popular symbol of rebirth. But remember: A bursting bud may be no more than a bursting bud.

Writing the Paper

When you've done all you can to understand what the author wrote, when you've decided (or at least done your best to decide) what he wanted to accomplish, and when you've arrived at a judgment of his work, then remind yourself of what you've learned about writing as you've moved through this book. All the time you were reading and rereading the literary work, you should have been engaging in the prewriting process. The rhetorical situation suggests a rather formal approach, unless you're writing on a work that itself makes formality seem out of place. Whatever method of development you use, generalizations and details will make up the bulk of your explication. Support, discovery, and pro-and-con are all possible organizational patterns; pro-and-con would be particularly appropriate if you should find yourself torn between two possible interpretations of the work.

A critical essay has to meet the criteria for any piece of good persuasive writing. To convince your readers that your interpretation is justified and your evaluation sound, you must do more than assert. You must demonstrate. Fortunately, your evidence is the work itself. You have that to draw on to make your case. In doing so, remember what's been said about building paragraphs, shaping sentences, choosing words. Strive for continuity, clarity, precision. The labels we all toss around so freely in conversation—"beautiful," "wonderful," "great"—can be an embarrassment when they're attached to quotations that most readers don't find particularly impressive.

Writing a good critical paper demands time, concentration, and hard thought. But as you're writing the paper, don't be concerned primarily about having the "right" answer. While some close readings are unquestionably more valid, more acceptable, than others, it can be argued that for many works there is no single "right" reading. Be careful not to confuse the writer's intention with your own experience ("I grew up on the Plains and know what a tornado does to a community") or bias ("Poems about death are morbid") or personal needs or private emotions. Say what the work means to you, but keep your emphasis on the *work*, not the *you*. Your interpretation may not be the one generally accepted by literary scholars. It may not be what the author has announced as his intended meaning. But if you support it with adequate evidence from the work itself, and if your paper shows that you've read the work thoroughly, thought about it long and hard, and then written about it to the best of your ability, you will have earned a fair hearing.

■ *For Analysis*

Read the poem printed below. First read it silently; then read it aloud three or four times. In these readings, try to do two things simultaneously or nearly so. Put your main effort into grasping the plain sense of the poem—what the poet is saying to you—but at the same time listen *to what you're reading as you'd listen to a piece of music.*

The Explosion

On the day of the explosion
Shadows pointed towards the pithead:
In the sun the slagheap slept.

Down the lane came men in pitboots
Coughing oath-edged talk and pipe-smoke,   5
Shouldering off the freshened silence.

One chased rabbits; lost them;
Came back with a nest of lark's eggs;
Showed them; lodged them in the grasses.

So they passed in beards and moleskins,   10
Fathers, brothers, nicknames, laughter,
Through the tall gates standing open.

At noon, there came a tremor; cows
Stopped chewing for a second; sun,
Scarfed as in a heat-haze, dimmed.   15

The dead go on before us, they
Are sitting in God's house in comfort,
We shall see them face to face—

Plain as lettering in the chapels
It was said, and for a second   20
Wives saw men of the explosion

Larger than in life they managed—
Gold as on a coin, or walking
Somehow from the sun towards them,

One showing the eggs unbroken.   25

—Philip Larkin, *High Windows*

A Close Reading

Here's a paper that a student wrote in response to this assignment: "Do a close reading of Philip Larkin's 'The Explosion.' Quote freely from the poem to support the assertions you make as you explicate the poem and advance your interpretation of it. Directly or indirectly express your own opinion of 'The Explosion.' Your analysis of the poem should warrant your evaluation of it."

"The Explosion" by Philip Larkin

"The Explosion" is a short, extremely powerful poem that deals with an explosion in a mine. The language is simple and direct, the poetic images few. There are no unnecessary words, no frills. The result is a haunting work of great emotional impact.

Larkin isn't coy with us. He begins matter-of-factly with "On the day of the explosion" (line 1), and we therefore know (as we do also from his title) what is going to happen. At the scene, however, there are no warning signs. Although we can read something ominous into the shadows that "pointed towards the pithead" (line 2) or something sinister into the slagheap that slept in the sun (line 3), in fact the shadows and the slagheap are doing what they always do. All appears to be normal.

The three short lines of the second stanza offer some fine examples of Larkin's power with words. He captures the gruff, masculine world of the miners: "Down the lane came men in pitboots" (line 4). The harshness of the sounds they make—"Coughing oath-edged talk and pipe-smoke" (line 5)—reminds us of the stale, dead, dust-filled air they must breathe in the mine and of the brutal lives they lead. But as we hear the early morning quiet broken by the rough voices of the men heading for the pit, we are also reminded of their comradeship: "Shouldering off the freshened silence" (line 6).

The third stanza is important on several levels. It reemphasizes the absence of any threat of impending catastrophe. The miners walk to work in early morning innocence: "One chased rabbits" (line 7). It demonstrates the reverence for life that they share: "Came back with a nest of lark's eggs;/Showed them; lodged them in the grasses" (lines 8–9). The eggs are not dropped or tossed away but are set down gently. The stanza also lays the groundwork for what I feel is the theme of the poem. "The Explosion" is not a poem of death but rather a poem of life. More explicitly, it is a poem about the cycle of life celebrated and made complete by the event of death. The concept of the egg as the symbol of life will be echoed in the last line.

The warm feeling of brotherhood that is so evident in the fourth stanza adds to the positive tone: "So they passed in beards and moleskins,/Fathers, brothers, nicknames, laughter" (lines 10–11). Larkin shows us the tight-knit fellowship of men bound both by the blood of kinship and by the bonds of shared labor and shared danger. Every day they pass together "Through the tall gates standing open" (line 12). Today they will pass together through the gates of death.

The description of the explosion in stanza five is subdued and almost casual. The world above the mine is barely affected: "At noon, there came a tremor; cows/Stopped chewing for a second" (lines 13–14). Death, symbolized by the explosion, is only a tiny interruption in the day's (life's) events. Down below all may be fire and pain and death, but above there is only slight evidence that something out of the ordinary is taking place: "sun,/Scarfed as in a heat-haze, dimmed" (lines 14–15).

When people live as close to death as miners and their families do, they must have an easy, trusting relationship with their God, one that will make death less fearful. The people in Larkin's poem have such a faith, as is demonstrated by the litany of the sixth stanza. Belief in a tangible afterlife is present in the words,

"The dead go on before us, they/Are sitting in God's house in comfort" (lines 16–17). Death does not mean permanent loss. It is only a transition from one life to another: *"We shall see them face to face"* (line 18). Although Larkin's poem is about a catastrophe, there are no scenes of horror, no blood and gore. The dead men have gone home to God. Life will go on.

The last three stanzas describe a transcendental vision experienced by the widows of the dead miners. At the moment of the explosion, the images of the dead men, "Plain as lettering in the chapels" (line 19), are seen. By using this particular example, Larkin emphasizes that this is a spiritual experience. The "men of the explosion" (line 21) have made the transition from this life. They have achieved immortality and become like gods, "Larger than in life . . . /Gold as on a coin, or walking/Somehow from the sun" (lines 22–24).

The dead appear to the living, and their message is one of life: "One showing the eggs unbroken" (line 25). We sense the wonder at life in that last line, the childlike awe, and the acknowledgment that life will continue in spite of this horrible interruption. The last line is a beautiful affirmation of life. The egg, the universal symbol of life, is fragile yet somehow durable. Life continues, life survives to bring forth new life, in spite of its fragility and the ever present threat of death.

"The Explosion" uses the occasion of death to emphasize life — survival, continuity, and order in the face of chaos. The poet's stress is on the "eggs unbroken" — life uninterrupted in its cycle.

In producing this close reading of the poem by Philip Larkin, the student first offers an evaluation of the poem in a brief opening paragraph, then leads his audience through "The Explosion," stanza by stanza. He explains what happens in the poem, discussing the action in his own words but keeping in close touch with the poem by citing lines that illustrate and justify his commentary. He's not simply giving a prose paraphrase but providing interpretation ("it is a poem about the cycle of life") and critical reaction ("fine examples," "beautiful affirmation"). He finds a symbol ("the egg, the universal symbol of life") and assigns it a central position in the meaning of the poem. This "discovery" is announced in the discussion of the third stanza and supported with evidence thereafter.

A major strength of the paper is the student's obvious familiarity with Larkin's poem; this does a good deal to win our confidence and hold our attention. A serious weakness of the paper is its failure to deal with the sound of the poem and the effect of sound on meaning. The student makes no mention, for example, of the way Larkin controls the tempo — the single pauses in the first and second stanzas; the rhythmic tread of the miners in the second stanza; then the jagged movement in the third, with four punctuation breaks to mark the activity of the lively miner; and so on. And doesn't the *sound* of "In the sun the slagheap slept" invite reading something sinister into the line? The student gives every evidence of knowing the work except the evidence that only his ear could provide.

■ *For Analysis and Writing*

1. Reread "The Explosion." Do you disagree with any of the assertions made about it in the paper, either interpretations or judgments? Are there ways in which you would have handled the assignment differently? If so, write a short paper stating specifically where and why you disagree and explaining what you would do instead. Or rewrite the student's paper according to your own ideas of what it should say and how the content should be expressed and organized.

2. Choose a poem or a short story and, once it's been approved, do a close reading of it. Your instructor will tell you whether to limit yourself to analysis or go on to evaluate the work.

Chapter Eleven
Writing the Research Paper

Although in college you can't learn everything about everything, you should learn how to find out about almost anything. You should know where to look and how to find what you want quickly and efficiently. This chapter deals with a special form of expository writing, the research paper, which grows out of the writer's efforts to find information, reclaim it, and use it for his special purpose. As such, the research paper—sometimes called the reference paper, library paper, term paper, or source paper—has a place in many college courses. To write a satisfactory one calls for resourcefulness in using the library and other facilities of scholarship, critical judgment in transforming a collection of data into cogent support of a thesis, and skill in organizing and writing a paper of some length.

Preparing a research paper in your writing course will give you practice in finding material, taking notes on it, evaluating its reliability and its relevance to your topic or your thesis, ordering it, and presenting it. Advanced study, especially in literature, history, and the social sciences, depends on this sort of work, and in the physical sciences a laboratory experiment is often supplemented by research in records of previous experiments. These same methods, more elaborately developed, are used in writing monographs, theses, and dissertations in graduate school and in preparing many business reports and industrial studies. Your reference paper, then, is an introduction to scholarly activity and practice for the research that you may do later.

The Nature of the Research Paper

A research paper is an ambitious and complicated undertaking; every stage takes time, patience, and judgment.

At first your personal contribution may seem negligible. Most of the material will come from sources outside your immediate experience, the style you write in will probably be more impersonal and formal than you normally use, and your primary objective will be to inform and interpret rather than to express your feelings. But serious work on the project will show that the range and direction of your research offer considerable scope for originality. And though the methods of gathering material have been worked out by thousands of researchers before you and the form of the manuscript has been standardized, the actual content, organization, and style of your paper will be the product of your thought and judgment and imagination.

It would be wrong, then, to regard the research paper as totally unlike other kinds of writing we've discussed. While following the conventions of proper footnote form is an indispensable obligation in writing a research paper, meeting that obligation doesn't guarantee that the paper will be worth reading. To produce a really effective paper, you must first find a subject that stirs your curiosity, one that you'd like to know more about. Beginning with such curiosity can turn what might be a tiresome canvassing of sources into an investigation that interests you and will ultimately interest your readers. Your research may simply turn up information you can add to your own store of knowledge as well as pass on to your audience in an expository paper—for example, "The Growth of Evangelicalism in the 1970s." Or you may undertake to explain why evangelicalism grew in the period: "Causes of the Growth of Evangelicalism in the Seventies." Or investigating explanations of religious phenomena (or interpretations of literary works or evaluations of technical developments or solutions to social problems) may lead you to support a particular point of view in a persuasive paper. Regardless of the topic or the approach, your paper is not likely to be satisfactory unless it gives the impression that in writing it you found out something *you* consider worth knowing.

Research and Writing Procedures

If you're to produce a good research paper, your intelligence and your intellectual curiosity must dominate your research. Wearied by long hours in the library and confronted by a stack of notecards, you may find yourself losing both your confidence and your enthusiasm (they're related), and you may be tempted to fit together mechanically the bits of information you've collected. A paper composed in this way is bound to be unsatisfactory—the proportions bad, the continuity rough and awkward, the focus unclear or nonexistent. What your readers are mainly interested in is what your research led you to—the store of information or the interpretation that's the outcome of your inquiry. Only if they see clearly how you move toward that goal can they judge the pertinence and value of the facts you present.

One note of caution about the methodology outlined in the following pages. During the time you spend on the project, you'll need to strike a balance between your interest in the subject for its own sake and your interest in the procedures of research. Exclusive absorption in either is costly and unwise. At first you may feel a certain impatience at having to follow a rather rigid pattern in preparing and documenting your paper, particularly if you begin by simply wanting to know more about the subject. Meticulousness in recording bibliographical data and taking notes may seem to be a waste of good hours. But in the long run what you learn about the procedures and standards of scholarship will probably be more valuable to you than the paper itself.

This is not to say that the writing of the paper can be treated lightly. It's as unwise to concentrate solely on method as it is to slight it. In the end, converting material gathered from many sources into a paper that has its own integrity presents more challenges and offers more rewards than hunting for the material. If you become absorbed in the details of preparing extensive bibliographies and taking full notes, you may exhaust your interest and enthusiasm as well as your time before you begin to cope with the central task of the whole project—writing a paper that reflects discriminating use of a variety of sources to arrive at a point worth making.

The Focus of the Research

You begin work on a research paper by gathering material —looking up references, examining books and articles, taking notes. In most cases you're not entirely sure where your research will take you. You think you know what you want to write about, but until you've done some reading and collected some notes on what you've read, you can't know what you're going to say. Even if you know what you *want* to say, your research may make you change your mind.

Still, you'll probably find it helpful to make an outline – a *tentative* outline – fairly early in the note-taking stage. In the first few days of looking for material, you'll no doubt have in mind a few points you want to develop or some problems you want to solve; but if you let them control your note-taking, you may overlook many interesting alternative approaches to your topic. On the other hand, if you have only the haziest notion of your subject – if you haven't begun to ask questions of it – you can hardly take notes intelligently or economically. And because your full notes will represent a sizable investment in time and energy, you may later find yourself struggling to incorporate in your paper a miscellany of information. Some notes are bound to be wasted; every researcher duplicates information and jots down some irrelevancies. But you can reduce the duplications and irrelevancies if you keep a tentative outline beside you as you take notes and if you revise it regularly. After every lengthy session of reading, while your notes are fresh in your mind, spend some time studying, modifying, and developing your outline, trying always to arrive at what will be the justification for writing the paper, its *statement of purpose* or *thesis sentence.*

In a research paper, with its considerable length and numerous details, an exact formulation of the thesis or purpose is especially important. Often writing the paper calls for a good deal of juggling and testing of ideas. The point is to force yourself, as soon as your research permits, to define the purpose of your paper to *yourself.* It may help to conceive of the thesis sentence or statement of purpose as a response to a question – for example, "Does our correctional system do a better job in discouraging crime or in reforming criminals?"

Possible response and thesis sentence:

Since the crime rate continues to rise and most prison inmates return to prison at least once, our correctional system is failing either to discourage crime or to rehabilitate criminals.

You may never use this sentence in your paper, but it will serve its purpose in focusing your ideas and your source materials during the preliminary stages of your research and writing. Without it your selection of material would be aimless and your organization would be diffuse, with innumerable supporting details in search of something to support.

■ *For Writing*

1. The subjects in the following list are too broad or too general for successful treatment in a reference paper of moderate length. Select two that interest you, and make up for each of them at least three topics that could be treated adequately in papers of the length assigned for your course. You may see a possibility at the point where one topic intersects with another—for example, George Bernard Shaw and the Salvation Army.

Acid rock
Anarchism
Astrology
Ballet on campus
Blood banks
Capital punishment
Censorship
Chinook Jargon
Civil rights
Computer culture
Detective stories
Electoral college
Eskimos
Feminism
Folk sayings
Game laws
George Bernard Shaw
Harpsichords
IWW
Individual ethics
Insanity in modern poetry
Kung-fu
Lasers
Lewis and Clark
Libel laws
Linguistics
Male liberation
Marine Corps

Mass media
Meditation
Modern productions of
   Hamlet
Music in industry
National health insurance
Nonobjective painting
Nuclear power plants
Pan-African movement
Peer counseling
Peyote cults
Poetry readings
Pollution
Primitive peoples
Prison conditions
Radar
Rights of the dying
Rural poverty
Salvation Army
Satellites
Solar heating
Stereophonic sound
Styles of parenting
Televised political debates
Third World
Utopias
Vonnegut's novels
Witchcraft

2. From the topics you've selected and narrowed for 1 above, choose a subject for your research paper; then prepare brief statements on the following:

a. Your reason for choosing the subject and your purpose in writing the paper.

b. Your present knowledge about the subject and the gaps you have to fill.

c. The audience you have in mind and the information you assume this audience already has about the topic.

d. Some sources that you plan to include in your bibliography —the list of books and articles you'll draw on in writing your paper.

e. The main points you now think you'll make and the methods you'll use to develop them.

Gathering Material

Reading and learning more about your subject, searching out sources in the library, discovering the most useful references for your subject, selecting data that support the points you want to make, and recording the data in properly documented notes—these are the important early steps in preparing your research paper.

Sources of References

Almost everyone begins compiling references for a research paper with some sources in mind—a discussion in a textbook, a magazine article, the name of a writer, the title of a book. Very often, preliminary reading furnishes references to other works, and these make a natural starting point for the working bibliography. But to assemble a fairly comprehensive list of possible sources, you must make informed use of the resources of the library. There are several aids planned specifically to direct you to books and periodicals. No matter what your choice of topic, you'll want to consult your library's card catalog, its periodical indexes and special bibliographies, and its other general and special reference works.

The Card Catalog. The library card catalog lists all the books in the library by author and usually by title and subject as well (sometimes under more than one subject heading). This means that most books in the library can be located in three ways. If you know the name of the author of a book you think will be useful to you, look it up in the card catalog. If you know the title of a book dealing with your topic, look up the title. And if you don't yet know of specific books or authors, look up the subject you're interested in.

Besides finding books listed under the subject heading, you may also find cross-reference cards that will give you clues to other places to look. There are two kinds of cross-reference cards, *see* and *see also*. For example, if you looked up scuba diving in the card catalog, you might find a card reading "SCUBA DIVING, see SKIN DIVING." This would tell you that all books in the library dealing with scuba or skin diving are listed under SKIN DIVING. If you looked under SKIN DIVING you might find several cards for books on that subject and perhaps also a card reading "SKIN DIVING, see also UNDERWATER EXPLORATION." "See also" suggests a closely related subject that may provide further useful information.

If you don't find anything under the first topic you look for, try to think of synonymous or related subject headings. Since no card catalog can possibly have every imaginable cross-reference, you may have to try two or three alternatives before you find the right one. Don't assume the library has nothing on the subject just because you don't find sources listed under the first heading that comes to mind.

The library subject card below illustrates the information given about a book. In preparing your working bibliography (see p. 339), you would transfer items 2, 3, 4, and 5 to a bibliography card (pp. 340–42). The entry on the bibliography card should follow the form prescribed for the final bibliography (pp. 359–61) so that making the bibliography will be simply a matter of arranging the cards alphabetically and copying the entries, inserting conventional punctuation.

Library Subject Card

```
②E169.1      ① UNITED STATES--SOCIAL LIFE AND CUSTOMS.
  N92
     ③ Nye, Russel Blaine, 1913-
          The unembarrassed muse: the popular arts in America, by
     ④ Russel Nye.  New York, Dial Press, 1970. ⑤
          497 p.  illus., facsims., ports.  24 cm.  (Two centuries of American life)
     ⑥  12.50
          Includes bibliographical references.


     ⑦      1. United States  Civilization.  2. United States—Social life and customs.
            I. Title.
     ⑧  E169.1.N92              917.3'03           70-111449
                                                    MARC
          Library of Congress          70[70]
```

1. Card catalog subject heading
2. Library call number
3. Author
4. Title
5. Facts of publication
6. Relevant facts about the book
7. Subject index
8. Information for librarians

Periodical Indexes. Next to the card catalog, your most useful source of references will probably be *Readers' Guide to Periodical Literature* and other periodical indexes. *Readers' Guide* indexes more than 150 current magazines of general interest, giving references to articles by author and subject. (See illustration below.) It appears twice a month from September through June, and monthly in July and August; these indexes are published in quarterly cumulative issues and annual volumes. Some libraries have cumulative volumes going back as far as 1900. The following is an excerpt from the May 10, 1977, quarterly issue of the *Guide:*

DIRIGIBLES. See Airships
DIRKS, Raymond
    High cost of whistling. T. Nicholson and others.
        pors Newsweek 89:75+ F 14 '77 •
DIRTY linen & New-found-land; drama. See
        Stoppard, T.
DISARMAMENT
    Assembly to hold special session on disarma-
        ment questions next year; with text of resolu-
        tions. UN Chron 14:21, 102-4; 115-16 Ja '77
    Stonewalling on the arms control impact state-
        ments. B. R. Schneider. Bull Atom Sci 33:5 Ja
        '77
    United States discusses disarmament issues in
        U.N. General Assembly debate; statements,
        with text of resolution. November 1, 18 and
        December 10, 1976. F. C. Iklé; J. Martin, Jr.
        Dept State Bull 76:17-29 Ja 10 '77
    What lies ahead in arms control? address.
        November 12, 1976. F. C. Ikle. Vital Speeches
        43:166-8 Ja 1 '77
            See also
    Atomic weapons and disarmament
    United Nations—Committee on Disarmament
    United States—Defenses
                        Conferences
            See also
    Strategic Arms Limitation Talks

Readers' Guide uses abbreviations, explained at the beginning of each issue, for titles of magazines indexed, for
the months, and for various facts about the articles. In
the references the number before the colon refers to the
volume, and the numbers after the colon refer to the pages
of the articles (89:75+ means volume 89, page 75 and
continued). When using *Readers' Guide*, write out all
important words on your bibliography card in order to
avoid confusion later and to have the data in correct form.

A number of other magazine indexes list articles from
specialized periodicals not covered by *Readers' Guide*.
Many appear annually, some more frequently than that.
The list below – by no means complete – is intended to introduce you to some of the widely used indexes and to
show you that other, more specialized subject indexes
exist. The titles marked with a † are the most generally
useful. Consult one or more of these titles first. If you don't
find enough information try a more specialized index, or
ask the librarian for help.

† *Applied Science and Technology Index*, 1958–date (that is,
from 1958 to the present). Subject index to a selected list of
engineering and trade periodicals. Before 1958 see *Industrial
Arts Index*.

Art Index, 1929–date. Author and subject index to fine arts
periodicals and museum bulletins.

Bibliographic Index, 1937–date. Subject index to bibliographies in books and periodicals.

† *Biography Index*, 1946–date. Subject index to biographical
material in books and periodicals.

Biological and Agricultural Index, 1964–date. Subject index to a selected list of periodicals, bulletins, documents. Before 1964 see *Agricultural Index.*

† *Book Review Digest,* 1905–date. Author, subject, and title index to published book reviews. Gives extracts from reviews and exact references to sources.

† *Business Periodicals Index,* 1958–date. Subject index to a selected list of business periodicals. Before 1958 see *Industrial Arts Index.*

Catholic Periodical and Literature Index, 1968–date. Author and subject index to a selected list of Catholic periodicals. Before 1968 see *Catholic Periodical Index.*

† *Education Index,* 1929–date. Subject index to educational periodicals, books, and pamphlets.

Engineering Index, 1884–date. Subject index to technical periodicals; transactions and journals of engineering and other technical societies; reports of government bureaus, engineering colleges, research laboratories.

Guide to the Performing Arts, 1957–date. Annual index to articles and illustrations pertaining to the performing arts in selected American and foreign periodicals.

† *Humanities Index,* 1973–date. Author and subject index to periodicals in the humanities. Issued as part of *Social Sciences and Humanities Index* from 1965 to 1973. Before 1965 see *International Index to Periodicals.*

Music Index, 1949–date. An index to music periodicals arranged by author, composer, subject, and country.

Philosopher's Index, 1957–date. An international index to philosophical periodicals. Abstracts about 150 journals, including many foreign-language as well as English-language publications.

Public Affairs Information Service Bulletin, 1915–date. Subject index to books, periodicals, pamphlets, and other materials on economics, government, and other public affairs.

† *Social Sciences Index,* 1973–date. Author and subject index to periodicals in the social sciences. Issued as part of *Social Sciences and Humanities Index* from 1965 to 1973. Before 1965 see *International Index to Periodicals.*

United States Government Publications, Monthly Catalog, 1895–date. A bibliography of publications issued by all branches of the government.

Ulrich's International Periodicals Directory (16th ed., 1975) lists approximately 57,000 foreign and domestic periodicals by title and also by the subjects they treat, answering the question: What periodicals are there in this field?

The Wall Street Journal, The Christian Science Monitor, and some metropolitan daily newspapers have indexes. Most of these go back only a few years, but *The New*

York Times Index, which appears semimonthly, runs back to 1913. Although it indexes only *The New York Times,* it can be used as a rough general index to material in other newspapers, since the dates indicate when news stories were breaking. Through this index you can find many speeches and important documents as well as news stories of significant events.

Indexes to Books, Pamphlets, and Collections.　A few of the periodical indexes listed above cover material published in books, pamphlets, and collections as well as in periodicals. Miscellaneous indexes that concentrate specifically on books, pamphlets, or collections include the following:

Books in Print, 1948–date. Author and title index to books currently in print in the United States.

Cumulative Book Index, 1898–date. An author, subject, and title index to books printed in English.

Essay and General Literature Index, 1900–1933. Supplements, 1934–date. Author and subject index to essays and articles in collections and miscellaneous works.

Granger's Index to Poetry, 6th ed., 1973. Author, title, and first-line index to poetry in collections.

Play Index, 1949–52, 1953–60, 1961–67, 1968–72. Author, title, and subject index to plays in collections. Brief information about each play is also included.

Ottemiller's Index to Plays in Collections, 6th ed., 1976. Author and title index to plays in collections from 1900 to 1975.

Popular Song Index, 1975. Index to 301 songbooks published between 1940 and 1972.

Short Story Index, 1953. Supplements, 1950–54; 1955–58; 1959–63; 1964–68; 1969–73. Author, title, and, in many cases, subject index to stories in collections.

Vertical File Index, 1932–date. Subject and title index of pamphlets, booklets, leaflets, and mimeographed materials.

General Reference Works.　General reference works offer a good starting point for compiling a bibliography because they almost always refer you to authoritative specialized works. Comprehensive guides to reference works of all kinds include:

Finding Facts Fast (Todd), 1972.

Guide to Reference Books (Winchell, rev. Sheehy), 9th ed., 1976.

How and Where to Look It Up: A Guide to Standard Sources of Information (Murphey), 1958.

Reference Books: A Brief Guide for Students and Other Users of the Library (Barton and Bell), 7th ed., 1970.

Reference Books: How to Select and Use Them (Galin and Spielberg), 1969.

General encyclopedias are helpful in early stages of research, offering basic information in a given subject area and often referring you to more complete specialized sources. The major American encyclopedias vary in size from the single-volume *Columbia* to the multivolume *Britannica* and *Americana*. Though by no means infallible and always in need of revision (the larger ones revise some articles for each new printing), they contain information on a vast number of subjects.

Dictionaries and books of quotations are other standbys of the general reference section of the library. For dictionaries of the language, see pp. 280–85. For books of quotations, the following are generally helpful:

Familiar Quotations (Bartlett), 14th ed., 1968.

The Home Book of Bible Quotations (Stevenson), 1949.

The Home Book of Quotations, Classical and Modern (Stevenson), 10th ed., 1967.

The Home Book of Shakespeare Quotations (Stevenson), 1937.

The Oxford Dictionary of Quotations, 2nd ed., 1953.

Special Reference Works. Even more important for college papers than general reference books are the reference works in specific fields. The following list includes useful books in art and architecture, biography, education, literature, music and drama, philosophy, psychology, religion, science and technology, and the social sciences.

Art and Architecture

Art Books: A Basic Bibliography on the Fine Arts (Lucas), 1968.

Art-Kunst: International Bibliography of Art Books. Annual.

Art and Architecture: Including Archaeology (Besterman), 1971.

Britannica Encyclopedia of American Art, 1973.

Encyclopedia of the Arts (Read), 1966.

Encyclopedia of Modern Architecture (Pehnt), 1964.

Encyclopedia of World Art, 1959–68, 15 vols.

Guide to Art Reference Books (Chamberlin), 1959.

A History of Architecture on the Comparative Method (Fletcher), 18th ed., 1975.

Index to Reproductions of American Paintings (Monro and Monro), 1948; supplement, 1964.

Index to Reproductions of European Paintings (Monro and Monro), 1956, 3 vols.

McGraw-Hill Dictionary of Art (Myers and Myers), 1969, 5 vols.

Mallett's Index of Artists, 1940; supplement, 1948.

Oxford Companion to Art (Osborne), 1970.

Who's Who in American Art, 1936–date.

Biography (General)
Chambers's Biographical Dictionary, rev. ed., 1969.

Current Biography, monthly since 1940, with annual cumulative volume.

Index to Women of the World from Ancient to Modern Times (Ireland), 1970.

International Who's Who, 1935–date.

McGraw-Hill Encyclopedia of World Biography, 1973.

Twentieth Century Authors (Kunitz and Haycraft), 1942; supplement, 1955.

Webster's Biographical Dictionary, rev. ed., 1972.

Who's Who in the World, 1971–date.

Biography (American)
Dictionary of American Biography, 1927–72, 14 vols.

Encyclopedia of American Biography (Garraty), 1974.

National Cyclopaedia of American Biography, 1967, 50 vols.

Notable American Women, 1607–1950 (James), 1971, 3 vols.

Webster's American Biographies, 1974.

Who Was Who in America (since 1897), 5 vols., 1951–73. Historical volume, 1943, covers the years 1607–1896.

Who's Who in America, 1899–date.

Who's Who of American Women, 1958–date.

Who's Who Among Black Americans (Matney), 1976.

Biography (British)
Dictionary of National Biography, 22 vols., 1885–1901; supplements through 1960.

Who Was Who, 6 vols., 1952–62.

Who's Who, 1849–date.

Education
Dictionary of Education (Good), 3rd ed., 1973.

The Encyclopedia of Education (Deighton), 1971, 9 vols.

Encyclopedia of Educational Research (Ebel), 4th ed., 1969.

Literature (General)

Cassell's Encyclopedia of World Literature (Buchanan-Brown), new rev. ed., 1973, 3 vols.

Columbia Dictionary of Modern European Literature (Smith), 1947.

A Concise Bibliography for Students of English (Kennedy and Sands, rev. Colburn), 5th ed., 1972.

Contemporary Authors, 1962–date.

Dictionary of World Literature (Shipley), rev. ed., 1968.

A Handbook to Literature (Thrall, Hibbard, and Holman), 3rd ed., 1972.

Reader's Guide to English and American Literature (Wright), 1970.

Selective Bibliography for the Study of English and American Literature (Altick and Wright), 4th ed., 1971.

Literature (American)

American Authors, 1600–1900 (Kunitz and Haycraft), 1938.

Articles on American Literature, 1900–1950 (Leary), 1954; *1950–67* (Leary et al.), 1970.

Bibliography of American Literature (Blanck), 1955–73, 6 vols.

Contemporary American Authors (Millett), 1940; reprint, 1970.

Literary History of the United States (Spiller et al.), 4th ed., 1974, 2 vols.

The Oxford Companion to American Literature (Hart), 4th ed., 1965.

The Reader's Encyclopedia of American Literature (Herzberg), 1962.

Twentieth Century Authors (Kunitz and Haycraft), 1942. Supplement (Kunitz, Haycraft, and Colby), 1955.

Literature (Black)

Afro-American Writers (Turner), 1970.

Black American Fiction Since 1952 (Deodene and French), 1970.

Black American Literature (Whitlow), 1973.

Encyclopedia of Black Folklore and Humor (Spalding), 1972.

From the Dark Tower: Afro-American Writers from 1900 to 1960 (Davis), 1974.

Literature (British)

British Authors Before 1800 (Kunitz and Haycraft), 1952.

British Authors of the Nineteenth Century (Kunitz and Haycraft), 1936.

The Cambridge History of English Literature (Ward and Waller), 1907–33, 15 vols.

The Concise Cambridge Bibliography of English Literature, 600–1950 (Watson), 2nd ed., 1965.

The Concise Cambridge History of English Literature (Sampson), 3rd ed., 1970.

A Literary History of England (Baugh), 2nd ed., 1967, 4 vols.

The New Cambridge Bibliography of English Literature (Watson), 1969–76, 5 vols.

The Oxford Companion to English Literature (Harvey, rev. Eagle), 4th ed., 1967.

Twentieth Century British Literature (Temple and Tucker), 1968.

Literature (Mythology and Classics)

Larousse Encyclopedia of Mythology, 1959.

Mythology of All Races (Gray et al.), 1916–32, 13 vols.

The Oxford Classical Dictionary (Hammond and Scullard), 2nd ed., 1970.

The Oxford Companion to Classical Literature (Harvey and Heseltine), 2nd ed., 1937.

Music and Drama

Black Image on the American Stage: A Bibliography of Plays and Musicals 1770–1970 (Hatch), 1970.

A Concise Oxford Dictionary of Music (Scholes), 2nd ed., 1964.

The Dance Encyclopedia (Chujoy and Manchester), rev. and enl. ed., 1967.

Dictionary of Music and Musicians (Grove), 5th ed., 1954–61, 10 vols.

Harvard Dictionary of Music (Apel), 2nd rev. ed., 1969.

A History of English Drama 1660–1900 (Nicoll), 1959, 6 vols.

The International Cyclopedia of Music and Musicians (Thompson, rev. Bohle), 10th ed., 1975.

McGraw-Hill Encyclopedia of World Drama, 1972, 4 vols.

Music and Drama (Besterman), 1971.

New Oxford History of Music (Westrup et al.), 10 vols. In progress.

Reader's Encyclopedia of World Drama (Gassner and Quinn), 1969.

Theater Dictionary: British and American Terms in the Drama, Opera, and Ballet (Granville), 1974.

The Theatre: Three Thousand Years of Drama, Acting, and Stagecraft (Cheney), 1972.

Voices of the Black Theatre (Mitchell), 1974.

Philosophy

The Concise Encyclopedia of Western Philosophy and Philosophers (Urmson), 1960.

The Dictionary of Philosophy (Runes), 1960.

The Encyclopedia of Philosophy (Edwards), 1973, 4 vols.

Guide to Philosophical Bibliography and Research (DeGeorge), 1971.

A History of Philosophy (Copleston), 1946–48, 8 vols.

Psychology

A Comprehensive Dictionary of Psychological and Psychoanalytical Terms (English and English), 1952.

Dictionary of Psychology and Related Fields (Beigel), 1974.

Encyclopedia of Psychology (Eysenck), 1972.

Encyclopedia of Human Behavior (Goldenson), 1974, 2 vols.

Psychological Research: An Introduction (Bachrach), 3rd ed., 1974.

Religion

The Concise Encyclopedia of Living Faiths (Zaehner), 1959.

Dictionary of the Bible (Hastings), rev. ed., 1963.

Dictionary of Comparative Religion (Brandon), 1970.

A Dictionary of Non-Christian Religions (Parrinder), 1973.

Encyclopaedia Judaica (Roth and Wigoder), 1971, 16 vols.

Encyclopedia of Religion and Ethics (Hastings), 2nd ed., 1908–27, 12 vols.

The Exhaustive Concordance of the Bible (Strong), 1894; reprint, 1958.

The Interpreter's Bible (Buttrick), 1951–57, 12 vols.

New Catholic Encyclopedia, 1967, 15 vols. and index. Volume 16, 1974.

The New Schaff-Herzog Encyclopedia of Religious Knowledge, 1908–12, 12 vols. and index; reprint, 1949–50, 13 vols.

The Oxford Dictionary of the Christian Church (Cross and Livingstone), 2nd ed., 1974.

Shorter Encyclopedia of Islam (Gibb and Kramers), 1953.

Twentieth-Century Encyclopedia of Religious Knowledge (Loetscher), 1955, 2 vols.

Science and Technology (General)

American Men and Women of Science, 13th ed., 1976, 7 vols.

Dictionary of Science Terms (Speck and Jaffe), 1965.

Dictionary of Scientific Biography (Gillispie), 1970–75, 14 vols.

Harper Encyclopedia of Science (Newman), rev. ed., 1967.

McGraw-Hill Encyclopedia of Science and Technology, 3rd ed., 1971, 15 vols.

The New Space Encyclopedia, 2nd ed., 1973.

Reference Sources in Science and Technology (Lasworth), 1972.

Technology (Besterman), 1971, 2 vols.

Understanding Technology (Susskind), 1973.

Van Nostrand's Scientific Encyclopedia, 4th ed., 1968.

Science and Technology (Biology)
Biological Sciences (Besterman), 1971.

A Dictionary of Biological Terms (Henderson and Henderson), 8th ed., 1963.

Encyclopedia of the Biological Sciences (Gray), 2nd ed., 1970.

Student Dictionary of Biology (Gray), 1973.

Science and Technology (Chemistry)
The Encyclopedia of Chemistry (Hampel and Hawley), 3rd ed., 1973.

Hackh's Chemical Dictionary (Grant), 4th ed., 1969.

How to Find Out in Chemistry (Burman), 2nd ed., 1966.

Lange's Handbook of Chemistry (Dean), 11th ed., 1973.

Thorpe's Dictionary of Applied Chemistry (Thorpe and Whitely), 4th ed., 1937–56, 12 vols.

Science and Technology (Engineering)
Dictionary of Modern Engineering (Oppermann), 3rd ed., 1972–73, 2 vols.

Engineering Encyclopedia (Jones and Schubert), 3rd ed., 1963.

How to Find Out About Engineering (Parsons), 1972.

Science and Engineering Reference Sources (Malinowsky), 1967.

Science and Technology (Geology)
A Dictionary of Geology (Challinor), 4th ed., 1974.

Geologic Reference Sources (Ward and Wheeler), 1972.

Science and Technology (Mathematics)
How to Find Out in Mathematics (Pemberton), 2nd ed., 1970.

Mathematics Dictionary (James and James), 3rd ed., 1968.

Universal Encyclopedia of Mathematics, 1964.

Science and Technology (Physics)
Encyclopaedic Dictionary of Physics (Thewlis), 1961–64, 9 vols.; supplement, 1966–71, 4 vols.

Encyclopedia of Physics (Besancon), 2nd ed., 1974.

How to Find Out About Physics (Yates), 1965.

New Dictionary of Physics (Isaacs and Gray), 2nd ed., 1974.

Social Sciences (General)
Encyclopedia of the Social Sciences (Seligman and Johnson), 1930–35, 15 vols.

How to Find Out in the Social Sciences (Burrington), 1975.

International Encyclopedia of the Social Sciences (Sills), 1968, 17 vols.

Sources of Information in the Social Sciences (White et al.), 2nd ed., 1973.

Worldmark Encyclopedia of Nations, 5th ed., 1976, 5 vols.

Social Sciences (Black Studies)
A Bibliography of the Negro in Africa and America (Work), 1965.

Black American Reference Book (Smythe), 1976.

Black Studies (Irwin), 1973.

Index to Periodical Articles By and About Negroes, 1960–date.

International Library of Negro Life and History, 1970, 10 vols.

The Negro in America: A Bibliography (Miller and Fisher), rev. ed., 1970.

Social Sciences (Economics)
Dictionary of Economics and Business (Nemmers), 3rd ed., 1974.

Encyclopedia of Banking and Finance (Munn; rev. Garcia), 7th ed., 1973.

How to Find Out About Economics (Parsons), 1972.

The McGraw-Hill Dictionary of Modern Economics (Greenwood), 2nd ed., 1973.

Social Sciences (Geography)
Goode's World Atlas, 14th ed., 1974.

How to Find Out in Geography (Minto), 1967.

Webster's New Geographical Dictionary, 1972.

Social Sciences (American History)
Dictionary of American History (Adams), rev. ed., 1976, 7 vols.

Encyclopedia of American History (Morris and Morris), 5th ed., 1976.

Harvard Guide to American History (Handlin et al.), 1954.

Historical Statistics of the United States, Colonial Times to 1970, Bicentennial ed., 1975, 2 vols.

The Oxford Companion to American History (Johnson), 1966.

Social Sciences (General History)

The Cambridge Ancient History (Bury et al.), 2nd ed., 1923–39, 17 vols.

The Cambridge Medieval History (Bury et al.), 1911–36, 8 vols.

The Cambridge Modern History (Ward et al.), 1902–26, 13 vols. and atlas.

Encyclopedia of World History (Langer), 5th ed., 1972.

How to Find Out in History (Hepworth), 1966.

Guide to Historical Literature (Howe et al.), 1961.

The New Cambridge Modern History, 1957–75, 14 vols.

Rand McNally Atlas of World History (Palmer), 1965.

Research Guide in History (Wilson), 1974.

Shepherd's Historical Atlas, 9th ed., 1964.

Social Sciences (Political Science)

American Political Terms (Sperber and Trittschuh), 1962.

The New Language of Politics (Safire), 1968.

Political Handbook of the World (Banks et al.), 1928–date. Annual.

Political Science: A Bibliographic Guide to the Literature (Harmon), 1965; supplements, 1968–74.

Research Guide in Political Science (Kavelage and Segal), 1976.

United States Government Manual, 1935–date. Annual.

Social Sciences (Sociology)

Dictionary of Sociology and Related Sciences (Fairchild), 1970.

Encyclopedia of Social Work (Morris), 1965–date.

Handbook of Modern Sociology (Faris), 1964.

A Modern Dictionary of Sociology (Theodorson and Theodorson), 1969.

The Uses of Sociology (Lazarsfeld et al.), 1967.

Yearbooks and Almanacs.   Various publications can direct you to the facts you need:

The Americana Annual, 1923–date. Annual supplement to the *Encyclopedia Americana.*

The Annual Register of World Events, 1758–date. Summary of events which emphasizes Great Britain and the Commonwealth.

Britannica Book of the Year, 1938–date. Annual supplement of *Encyclopaedia Britannica.*

Facts on File, 1940–date. Weekly digest of world and domestic news, with index.

Information Please Almanac, 1947–date.

McGraw-Hill Yearbook of Science and Technology, 1962–date.

Reference Shelf, 1922–date. Reprints of articles, bibliographies, and debates on topics of current interest.

The Statesman's Year Book, 1864–date. Descriptive and statistical information about world governments.

Statistical Abstract of the United States, 1878–date. Summary of statistics on the industrial, social, political, and economic organization of the United States.

Women's Rights Almanac, 1974–date.

United Nations Demographic Yearbook, 1948–date.

United Nations Statistical Yearbook, 1948–date.

University Debater's Annual, 1915–date. Annual survey of debates in American colleges.

The World Almanac and Book of Facts, 1868–date.

You'll always find some important references indirectly, unexpectedly, by hunch or by chance. Almost every article or book will refer to some other source or give you a clue to follow up. (Check the bibliographies you'll find at the end of many of the books you consult.) Your instructor and specialists in the field will offer suggestions. If you combine orderly work habits with a certain alertness and ingenuity in following up clues, the sources of material on your topic will begin to spread out before you like a river system, with one stream leading into another.

Since one of the values in undertaking a research paper is to become self-reliant in the use of research methods, you should do as much as possible on your own. The library has trained reference librarians, and you should ask their help when you're stumped, but you'll learn most by not asking for help until you've exhausted your own resources.

The Working Bibliography

Before you concentrate on gathering material for your topic, you should compile a *working bibliography* of sources you expect to consult. Check reference works of the kind described in the preceding section, and consult the appropriate subject headings in the card catalog and the periodical indexes. To make sure that enough material on your subject is available in the library, compile the working bibliography before you start to take notes. This preliminary survey of materials will save you time and worry when you begin reading and will help you make an intelligent selection of books and articles.

Everyone should have a consistent method for keeping track of references and for taking notes. For casual study, notebooks and odd sheets of paper may do, but for large projects standard filing cards, either 3″ × 5″ or 4″ × 6″, are most efficient. To begin with, you should prepare a separate bibliography card for each reference. Later you'll add note cards on the content of the reference.

The bibliography card records all the facts you need to identify a book or an article, to find it in the library when you want it, and to make the formal bibliography that will appear at the end of the paper. Each card should carry these facts:

For the formal bibliography:

1. The *author's or editor's name,* last name first, *ed.* after editor's name. If no author or editor is given, omit this item and start with 2.

2. The *title* of the article (in quotation marks) or of the book (underlined to represent italics).

3. *The facts of publication:*

    a. Of a book, the city, the name of the publisher, and the date.

    b. Of a magazine, the name of the magazine (underlined), the volume, the date, the pages on which the article appears.

    c. Of a newspaper story, the name of the paper (underlined), the date, the section if the pages are numbered by sections, and the page. You may also include the edition and the column number.

For your own use:

4. *The library call number* or location of the source — "Per." for Periodical Room, for instance — preferably in the upper left corner, as it is in the card catalog. If you're working in two or more libraries, put an identifying symbol before the call number.

5. *Any other facts* that relate to the use of the reference, such as the pages that treat your subject or the value of the source — preferably at the bottom of the card.

6. *A subject heading,* a phrase for the particular part of your topic that the reference pertains to, at the top center of the card. This label is known as a *slug.*

7. *A code reference* in the upper right corner. This reference may be a number, a letter, or the author's last name. Using it instead of a full citation on each note card taken from this source will save a great deal of needless copying.

The form and arrangement of bibliography cards are illustrated on the next page. Numbers on the cards correspond to the items in the preceding list.

Keep your bibliography cards in alphabetical order according to author or, if no author is given, according to title.

The number of references depends on the nature of the topic. An undergraduate paper should represent adequate coverage of the subject; that is, the writer should locate and consult the most important and influential commentary, especially by modern authorities, and not merely use the first three books he comes across, regardless of their dates or their quality. On the other hand, most undergraduate research projects, by their nature, impose a limit of some sort: there comes a time when sleuthing must give way to the critical job of reading, evaluating, and note-taking.

Evaluating Sources

Sources are classed as *primary* (or *original*) and *secondary*. A primary source is a first record of facts or the closest a person now writing can come to the subject he's discussing. A secondary source is something written by someone else using original sources. In a paper on an author, for example, the primary sources are the works written by the person you're discussing and the letters, diaries, and so on written by him and by others who knew him. The secondary sources are what critics and historians have written about this author on the basis of these materials. In a science, primary sources are records of observations or experiments; secondary sources are discussions and analyses of such records. In history, primary sources are records and artifacts of all sorts; secondary sources are historians' accounts based on this evidence. Most textbooks and reference works are secondary sources. Don't go beyond secondary sources to *tertiary sources* — that is, to material that is itself drawn entirely from secondary sources, as in popular magazines and newspaper supplements. Any information that is third-hand is obviously of limited use and value.

Particularly in research papers on works of literature, you should try to come to grips with the major primary sources before immersing yourself in commentary. A study of the theme of corruption in language in George Orwell's *1984* and *Animal Farm* should begin with a reading of these books. Without this informing experience

④ E 169.1   ⑥ Authenticity in   ⑦ Nye
    N 92   Western Fiction

① Nye, Russel
② The Unembarrassed Muse: The Popular
      Arts in America
③ New York: Dial Press, 1970
⑤ pp. 288-9 · The cowboy, "a useful
      fictional myth," was first romanticized
      in Owen Wister's The Virginian (1902).

Bibliography Card for a Book

④ Per.   ⑥ Women's Rights   ⑦ ERA
② "The Unmaking of an Amendment"
③ Time, 109 (April 25, 1977), 89-90

⑤ Analysis of Florida's failure to
      ratify the Equal Rights Amendment.

Bibliography Card for a Magazine Article

④ Per.   ⑥ Prison Drug Ring   ⑦ New York Times
② "Heroin Trafficking and Bribery Found at
      Jail in Brooklyn"
③ New York Times, April 25, 1977, p. 1, col. 4

⑤ At least twenty guards and civilian
      employees will be charged with heroin
      trafficking and taking bribes at
      Brooklyn House of Detention.

Bibliography Card for a Newspaper

you'll have no way to evaluate the critics' views when you take up the substantial body of Orwell criticism. Scholarly interpretations are sometimes more authoritative in style than substantial in content. The danger in reading criticism before you've really engaged the subject of the criticism is that you may be taken in by argument that's well written but ill-founded.

Because preparing a reference paper is largely an exercise in critical judgment, you must evaluate the sources you use. "I found a book in the library that said . . ." is a confession of uncritical work. Some sources are better — more comprehensive, more accurate, more penetrating — than others. Your aim should be to find the best books and articles, the most recent and most reliable material on your subject. When you come on contradictions or differing estimates in two sources, you should investigate to determine which is more accurate or more probable. At first you'll have to rely on the judgment of others. In your reading you may find that the author of one of your sources is generally accepted as the authority in the field but that the scholarship or the fairness of another has been questioned. You should note judgments like these and, if possible, substantiate or disprove them through further investigation.

For recent books it's often possible to find reviews that give some indication of their quality. The best sources of reviews of scholarly works are the learned journals of the various academic disciplines. *Book Review Digest* will lead you to reviews of less specialized works.

After you've worked on a subject for a while, you can evaluate a good deal of the material yourself, and your informed judgment should guide your further choice of materials. If you're impressed by a psychologist's report on a study of high-school students, you may decide to examine his book on adolescent behavior.

Taking Notes on Reading

Good notes are crucial in the preparation of a reference paper. Illegible handwriting, meaningless phrases (clear when the note was taken but not when it's cold), and inadequate labeling of the source may send you back to the library when you should be settling down to write. As you become experienced in note-taking and comfortable with your topic, you'll learn to evaluate the importance of a source quickly and to vary the kind, length, and number of your notes accordingly. From some sources you may need only a few facts or statistics; from others you'll want not only direct quotations but careful summaries of whole paragraphs, sections, or even chapters; for a few you may simply jot down a sentence or two describing and briefly evaluating the content. In the beginning, of course, you'll be taking notes partly on faith, feeling your way note by note toward a thesis. Once you've defined your thesis, it will determine what material should be recorded.

Form of Notes. Notes on 3″ × 5″ or 4″ × 6″ cards are easy to sort, discard, and rearrange; they can be accumulated indefinitely and kept in good order in an indexed file box. (Notes may also be taken on the pages of a loose-leaf notebook.) The three essential parts of a note card are: (1) the *material*—the facts and opinions to be recorded; (2) the exact *source*—title and page from which the material is taken; and (3) a *subject label*, or slug, for the card, showing what it treats.

Sample Note Card

Label / Note with page reference

> Truth in presidential memoirs
>
> Brodie, "Hidden Presidents." (*Harper's*)
>
> 76 Presidential diaries and memoirs leave out details that don't reveal their authors in the best light. Like most autobiographers, "Presidents write not to conceal the truth but to reveal the best."

The sample note card above shows a convenient form. In the upper right-hand corner put the author's name and the source—just enough to make reference to the full bibliography card easy and sure. Before writing the note, set down the exact page on which the material was found. Inclusive pages (such as 87–92) should not be used unless the note actually describes or summarizes what those pages say. Put the slug in the upper left corner; these labels should identify the subject matter of each card in specific terms, so that you can sort the cards when you get ready to outline and write. Avoid weak, general headings like "causes" and "cures."

A single card should contain only one point or a few facts that bear on one point. If unrelated bits of information are included (the temptation is always strong), you'll find when you sort the cards that one bit belongs here and another there. One hundred items of information on one hundred cards can be organized and reorganized speedily and efficiently; fifty items on ten cards will lead to confusion, exasperation, and error.

It's good practice to use only one side of each card. If only a few words remain at the end of a statement, they can be written on the back, but the signal OVER should be put on the front as a reminder.

Not all notes need be taken in full sentences. Words, phrases, and topics are enough if you're not quoting directly and if you're sure the note will be meaningful after you've laid it aside for a while. Take notes in ink as you do the reading, but don't bother to recopy them except for some very good reason. They're only means to an end—a good paper.

Suggestions for Note-Taking. It's impossible to give exact rules for taking notes. As you gain experience, your judgment will improve, and you'll probably formulate your own special rules as you go along. But it's wise to begin by reading through the article or chapter rapidly to see what it contains for your purpose. Then go over it again, this time taking notes. From your first few sources you'll probably take a good many, but after you've accumulated material covering the major points of your topic, a new reference may give only a few additional facts.

In taking notes, distinguish between the author's facts and his opinions. If there's any chance of confusion, label the opinions "So-and-so thinks . . . ." In general, pay most attention to the *facts* presented, unless you're writing on a topic for which the sources are chiefly expressions of critical opinion. You'll need facts as the basis of your own interpretations and as evidence to support them in the paper.

You should also distinguish carefully between direct quotation and summary. Anything you quote should be taken down exactly as it appears in the original and enclosed in quotation marks. If you omit a word or more in a direct quotation, indicate the omission with three spaced periods (. . .) called an ellipsis. After an obvious error in the source, write *sic* (meaning "thus") in brackets to indicate that the error was in the original.

In the early stages of note-taking, before you have a clear perspective on your subject, you may want to quote rather fully. Many of these quotations won't appear in the final draft, but having a quotation before you as you write can help you work the summary of it into your discussion more smoothly. (It can also prevent unintended plagiarism.) In the later stages of note-taking, quotations should be copied out only for good reason: material that's crucial for your paper; controversial or difficult material that you want to think about; a striking statement that you want to quote for its pithiness or its authority.

Finally, distinguish between what you take from a source and comments of your own. Either bracket your own comments or circle them and write your initials alongside. "Notes to myself" often prove very valuable when you begin to write. Indeed, as you take notes, it's a good idea to keep a running log of questions, notions, and leads on a separate pad.

Taking notes on literary works may require some changes in method. As each work is a developing whole, it can't be broken down into "main points" as an article or chapter can; so you may find it best to take running notes (on paper) of your impressions and questions while you read and then go back over these comments to find out what lines of interpretation are worth pursuing in detail.

The Summarizing Note. You use the summarizing note when an argument or explanation in one of your sources seems crucial to your project. Doing a good summary tests your ability to read critically. Read the material several times. Watch for the main ideas and see how each is developed. Move from the general to the specific. Try to determine the overall meaning or purpose, then the main points, and then the subdivisions supporting each main point. The author's transitional expressions give clues to the pattern of his ideas. As in any other note-taking, you must be sure you understand and record the author's ideas, not your own, even when you disagree violently with his point of view. Don't interrupt or distort a summary by including your personal opinions. They'll come into play later.

Your success in producing a good summary will depend partly on the care with which you read the original and partly on your skill in cutting unnecessary passages and in condensing. A good summary reproduces as faithfully as possible the ideas and the emphasis of the original—and if incorporated in the final paper must credit the original. Condense by eliminating nonessentials—anecdotes, descriptive details, digressions, illustrations, and all kinds of repetition—and by using appositives, series, and verbals to make the phrasing more compact.

Original Passages	Summarizing Notes
At the top of agricultural society are the minority of corporation farms and big farm owners. For them, the technological revolution has meant enormous profits and fantastic feats of production. In 1954, some 12 per cent of the operators controlled more than 40 per cent of the land and grossed almost 60 per cent of the farm sales. These were the dramatic beneficiaries of the advance in the fields. — Michael Harrington, *The Other America*	The technological revolution in farming benefited most dramatically a small minority of big operators.
As the nuclear reactor program expands, its wastes will also increase, and the burden of radioactivity in our surroundings will rise, and go on rising. At some point the deleterious effects of this radiation will become unacceptable even to a nation which is able to tolerate 50,000 deaths on its roads each year. Because the effects of radiation go on making themselves felt decades after the first damage is done, it would be well to anticipate the eventual saturation of our surroundings. For the environment which supports us has only a limited capacity for radiation, and that capacity can only be used once. — Sheldon Novick, *The Careless Atom*	Radioactivity produced by wastes from our nuclear reactor program will ultimately saturate our environment.

Many words from the original necessarily appear in a summary. But if you deliberately use a phrase exactly as it appears in the original, enclose it in quotation marks and cite the page number in parentheses.

■ For Analysis and Writing

The writing of précis—formal condensed paraphrases of someone else's writing—is excellent practice for writing summary notes. Moreover, it's instructive for the challenge it offers to the writer's vocabulary and command of sentence structure. The précis calls for a scrupulous condensation of the passage

—a condensation that keeps the proportions, tone, emphasis, and point of view of the original. In the formal précis the final version is from one third to one fifth as long as the original passage. To accomplish all this and still maintain readability is a large order—but it can be done, and it gets easier with practice. Write précis of two of the following:

a. "The Rhetorical Situation," pp. 2–3.

b. The first two paragraphs of the Declaration of Independence.

c. George Orwell's essay, "Politics and the English Language."

d. An article you plan to use in your paper, or a chapter from a book you intend to refer to.

Writing the Paper

Writing a research paper doesn't differ essentially from writing other papers in which the purpose is to explain or persuade, interpret or criticize, but some of the procedures discussed in earlier chapters have special pertinence. For one thing, it's imperative to budget your time and to work systematically at every stage of the project. However thorough your research and however lucid your report on your findings, your paper won't be satisfactory if the footnoting is inconsistent and the proofreading careless. And however elegant the footnoting, shoddy basic research will undermine its effect. A good reference paper shows deliberate care in all its aspects—enough evidence of care that the reader feels he can take the accuracy of text, documentation, and mechanics for granted and concentrate on the thesis, the evidence, and the movement of ideas through well-constructed sentences, paragraphs, and sections.

Planning and Writing

Although the quantity of material and the length of the paper make it advisable to have your outline on paper before you begin writing, consider several possibilities before you commit yourself to one plan. Your material will fall into blocks, probably from five to eight. The order of these blocks, which turn out to be paragraph sequences as you write, should grow logically out of your material, your approach, and your purpose.

The Outline. When you survey the notes you've taken, you'll probably revise the tentative outline you've used as a guide in gathering material. For your final outline you'll sort your facts into those that must be used, those that will probably be used, those of incidental interest that may be used, and those that clearly don't belong. To avoid wasting time in planning and writing, you may want to sort your cards into four groups: *Must, Probably, Maybe,* and *No.* Throw out *No.* Once you've done that, you can draw up an outline in standard form so that your instructor can examine it and offer suggestions.

The Writing Process.   Perhaps because it's long, some of the typical problems of writing any paper occur in more exaggerated form in the research project. Many writers waste an alarming amount of time making a beginning. The usual advice holds: Pull yourself out of a bogged-down introduction and get on with the rest of the paper. After the whole paper has begun to take shape, go back and compose an introductory passage. This advice assumes that you're in command of a workable thesis. Sometimes floundering at the outset is caused by vagueness of purpose. If you're in that predicament, the thing to do is admit the problem and think through the material again, working toward a thesis that you believe in and find manageable.

As you write, you'll almost certainly encounter unexpected problems. What seemed like intersecting avenues of meaning will become blind alleys. Authorities you took to be unshakable will totter and fall. But as you struggle with a deskload of material, you'll often surprise yourself by coming up with new connections between ideas, new alignments of facts, new interpretations of evidence. The important thing is to cultivate an attitude of openness to such possibilities as you write — and to proceed with the deliberateness of a writer to whom each sentence and paragraph is a matter of rhetorical calculation. Given the nature of the subject, the audience, and your own intentions, what strategies of language, method, organization, and argument will produce the most clarity and persuasiveness?

Even when you're well launched into the writing and feel thoroughly at home with your material, it's wise to review all your notes periodically. Much of your paper will be a digest of sources in your own words, and you need to have a good grasp of the ideas and facts so that you won't rely too heavily on what you wrote on the cards. A great deal of rephrasing of even your best summaries will be necessary if they're to fit comfortably into the paper and harmonize with your own style.

Use of Quotation and Paraphrase.   You'll need to decide
when it's better to paraphrase and when to quote directly
from your sources, and how you can best integrate the
material you're citing. Use direct quotation rather sparingly—keeping it within, say, 10 percent of your final
manuscript. A research paper shouldn't be a string of
quotations knotted together with transitional sentences;
too many quotations betray an overdependence on sources
and reveal a failure to assimilate the material into your
own thinking. What you are expected to do is give the
material a form and a thrust of meaning of its own.

Quote directly from sources when the exact words in the
passage illustrate or support your point more effectively
than a restatement of the idea could. A short quotation—
of a sentence, a phrase, key words—should be run into
your text in quotation marks and footnoted (see p. 370).
If what you quote contains quotation marks, change the
double quotes of the original to single ones, since they
now indicate a quotation within a quotation. A quoted
passage that's more than four lines long when you type it
out should be set off from the rest of the manuscript. Unless your instructor wants you to double-space, type it
single-spaced. Indent each line five spaces from the left-
hand margin, using an additional five-space indention for
new paragraphs (at the opening or within the passage).
Don't use quotation marks around passages set off in this
way. Place the footnote number at the end of the last word
of the passage. This procedure is illustrated in the sample
research paper, on the pages numbered 6, 7, and 9. (See
pp. 371, 372, and 376.)

As you write, you'll paraphrase many of the facts and interpretations you've recorded in your notes. In restating
the idea in your own words and fitting it into the context of
your paper, recheck your notes to be certain that in using
the material you're remaining true to the sense of the original, that it provides the support you want in developing
your subject, and that you're crediting it properly.

Often you'll mix paraphrase with brief quotations—integrating ideas and key words from your sources into the
pattern of your own presentation. Go over these portions
of your paper to achieve a smooth blending of elements,
and be sure to give proper credit to your sources. (See pp.
5 and 6 of the sample research paper for examples of paraphrase, brief quotation, and a longer quotation.)

Because the finished paper gives credit in footnotes to
the sources used, you'll want to indicate these sources in
your first draft. You can put an abbreviated reference to

the source in parentheses after a statement (see the draft reproduced on p. 375) or in the margin. Either method enables you to transfer the data to a footnote when you make your final copy.

Type your rough draft triple-spaced or write it with wide margins to leave room for revisions.

■ For Analysis and Writing

1. Write a rough draft of the first four or five paragraphs of your paper. Don't try to write an introduction to the whole paper; just begin with the substance of your discussion. Submit the draft to your instructor with a trial sentence outline.

2. Read the following passage on academic hiring and determine which ways of incorporating that material in a paper (items a to m) are satisfactory and which are unsatisfactory. A superior number means that the writer intends to footnote.

Original Passage

When we examine the specific procedures of hiring in the American university, they turn out to be almost unbelievably elaborate. The average salary of an assistant professor is approximately that of a bakery truck driver, and his occupancy of a job is likely to be less permanent. Yet it may require a large part of the time of twenty highly-skilled men for a full year to hire him. —Theodore Caplow and Reece J. McGee, *The Academic Marketplace*

Uses Made of the Passage

a. Hiring university teachers is so elaborate nowadays that twenty professors will spend a good deal of their time for a whole year hiring one assistant professor.[7]

b. Most assistant professors get about the same salary as bakery truck drivers, but the driver is likely to hold his job longer.

c. When we look at the specific procedures of hiring in U.S. colleges, they turn out to be incredibly complex. The pay of an assistant professor is approximately the same as that of a bakery truck driver, and his tenure in the job will probably be less permanent. Yet it might take much of the time of twenty highly trained men for a whole year to appoint him.[6]

d. Hiring teachers, even at the lower ranks, is a complicated process.

e. Hiring methods in our universities are "almost unbelievably elaborate." Though an assistant professor makes about the same salary as a bakery truck driver, and though the driver will probably hold his job longer, "yet it may require a large part of the time of twenty highly-skilled men for a full year to hire" the teacher.[8]

f. The average salary of an assistant professor is approximately that of a bakery truck driver.

g. The hiring methods in American colleges are almost unbelievably elaborate.

h. The hiring methods in American colleges are "almost unbelievably elaborate."

i. The average salary of an assistant professor is approximately that of a bakery truck driver.[11]

j. "Hiring teachers, even at the lower ranks, is a complicated process," according to Caplow and McGee.

k. The salaries of assistant professors and bakery truck drivers are about the same: they are about equally underpaid, that is.[9]

l. According to Caplow and McGee, "The average salary of an assistant professor is that of a bakery truck driver, and yet it may require a large part of the time of twenty men for a full year to hire him." [17]

m. The main point of Caplow and McGee's discussion of hiring in *The Academic Marketplace* is that hiring procedures in the colleges should be more like those used in the business world.[6]

Style and Point of View. The conventional style of research papers is formal and impersonal. Usually the writer doesn't refer to himself extensively – though there's no good rhetorical reason why the first person pronoun shouldn't be used for special emphasis (it's certainly preferable to the stuffy "the present writer" or the editorial "we"). Writing that strives for accuracy and objectivity in its treatment of a subject doesn't have to be dull, nor does it require total self-effacement. Just keep in mind that your reader will be more interested in what you've done with your material than in what it's done to you – and try to write prose that's concise, specific, readable, and calculated to reach your audience.

What assumptions to make about your reader? This question, like others about rhetorical strategy, should be discussed with your instructor. A safe general rule is to pitch your essay at the brightest members of your class – intelligent, critical readers who know little about your subject but want to know more. Assume that you'll be asked to read parts of the paper aloud to them.

Beginning and Ending the Paper. Although there's more reason for a research paper to have formal introductory and concluding sections than for a short essay to have them, most professionals studiously avoid the kind of beginning that self-consciously announces what is going to be said and the kind of ending that solemnly sums up point by point what *has* been said. Instead, the best practice involves finding a provocative angle in the research material and building an introduction around that – one that succeeds in stirring interest and at the same time defines the nature of the inquiry. An essay on ideas about the political significance of language in George Orwell's novels might, for instance, begin with the image a friend has given of Orwell propped up in bed in his final illness, happily cutting out newspaper articles confirming his fears about the general decline of English through political misuse and propaganda.

As for the conclusion, a skilled writer will generally resist the urge to grandly recapitulate his argument one more time, choosing instead to end the paper with a final, clinching point that grows directly out of the body of the paper. If he offers a summary at all, it will be brief and straightforward, a final demonstration that the paper's argument speaks for itself.

Proofreading.   Proofreading is not just a matter of striving to please your instructor—"profreading" one student called it. It's essential in all writing and particularly crucial in the writing of a research paper. The attention you give to it is a courtesy to your readers and a basic way of serving your paper's best interests. What would you think of the authority and dependability of an essay on, say, pollution in Lake Ontario that spelled *effluent* three different ways, omitted several footnotes, put Chart I where Chart III should have gone and vice versa, and added three zeros to the 1970 population of Rochester, New York? You might not be especially impressed to find all such errors *avoided* in a paper, to be sure; but the positive virtues of an essay rest in part on such negative virtues, the result of careful proofreading.

Footnotes

Any paper based on the writings of others should acknowledge the sources used. Common courtesy and honesty require that credit be given where credit is due, and a scrupulously documented source allows the reader to judge for himself the evidence an assertion is based on. It also allows the reader to turn to the sources for further information. College students are expected to draw their materials from various sources, but they are also expected to make a frank acknowledgment of these sources.

In formal academic papers it's conventional to give exact references in footnotes. The forms differ slightly, but the purpose is the same—to record in some brief and consistent form the author, title, facts of publication, and exact page from which each quotation and each fact or opinion is taken. Your instructor will prescribe the style of documentation you should follow. The style of footnotes and bibliography suggested in this section follows the recommendations of *The MLA Style Sheet,* second edition. (One exception is in the listing of publishers. The *Style Sheet* approves shortened forms of publishers' names, like those in the bibliography on pp. 384–85.)

Footnotes are needed for all direct quotations, except for lines from the Bible, proverbs, and other familiar sayings, and for all important statements of fact, interpretations, opinions, and conclusions that you've derived from the work of other writers. You need to give the source for all statistics, descriptions of situations, scientific data, and the like that are neither common knowledge nor the product of your own investigation. (Common knowledge includes not just facts like the location of San Francisco but undisputed matters—the dates of Theodore Roosevelt's birth, marriage, and death, for example—that anyone can find out without difficulty.)

Presenting the work of others as your own is a serious intellectual offense—first of all against your own neglected capabilities. You must acknowledge your source not only when you reproduce verbatim a paragraph, a sentence, or even a significant phrase but also when you reword or summarize. Whenever you use in a paper information and ideas you've obtained through research, it's up to you to credit the authors and the works the information and ideas came from. Any question about what to footnote that's not resolved by these guidelines should be raised with your instructor.

Placing Footnotes. To footnote a quotation or a statement in your paper, follow it with a number placed slightly above the line. Then use that number to introduce your footnote. Type footnotes at the foot of the page—single-spaced with a triple space between the text and the first note—and number them consecutively throughout the paper. (An alternative way of handling the notes is to group them together at the end of the paper, either single- or double-spaced, as your instructor recommends.) Indent the first line of a footnote five spaces. The footnote number should be slightly raised and should be separated from the note by one space.

Form for the First Reference. The first time a source is identified in a footnote, the documentation must be complete. As you'll see in the examples below, you'll need to vary the form according to the kind of source you're citing—books, compilations, translations, articles in journals or newspapers, unpublished dissertations, and so on. Examine each form carefully to see what elements are included, in what order they appear, and how they're punctuated.

A book by a single author:

1 Jerrold J. Katz, The Philosophy of Language (New York: Harper & Row, 1966), p. 42.

A book by more than one author:

2 James E. Brady and Gerard E. Humiston, General Chemistry: Principles and Structure (New York: Wiley, 1975), p. 42.

(If there are more than three authors, substitute "et al." for all but the first: Shirley Gorenstein et al.)

A work in more than one volume:

3 Richard B. Sewall, The Life of Emily Dickinson (New York: Farrar, Straus & Giroux, 1974), II, 251-58.

(The roman numeral is the volume number. When the volume number is given, page numbers are not preceded by "pp.")

An edition other than the first:

4 Lewis A. McArthur, Oregon Geographic Names, 4th ed. (Portland: Oregon Historical Society, 1974), p. 664.

An edition revised by someone other than the author:

5 Stuart Robertson, The Development of Modern English, 2nd ed., rev. Frederic G. Cassidy (Englewood Cliffs, N.J.: Prentice-Hall, 1954), pp. 36-52.

An edited work:

6 S. Y. Agnon, Twenty-one Stories, ed. Nahum N. Glatzer (New York: Schocken Books, 1970), p. 27.

A compilation by an author:

7 Joan C. Baratz and Roger W. Shuy, eds., Teaching Black Children to Read (Washington, D.C.: Center for Applied Linguistics, 1969), pp. 3-7.

A selection, chapter, or other part of a compilation:

8 Richard McKeon, "Rhetoric in the Middle Ages," in Critics and Criticism, ed. R. S. Crane (Chicago: Univ. of Chicago Press, 1952), p. 271.

A translation:

9 Maurice Merleau-Ponty, Phenomenology of Perception, trans. Colin Smith (London: Routledge, 1962), pp. 88-90.

A book that is part of a series:

[10] Carl N. Degler, <u>Affluence and Anxiety,</u> 2nd ed., The Scott, Foresman American History Series (Glenview, Ill.: Scott, Foresman, 1975), p. 125.

A reprinted book:

[11] Alfred North Whitehead, <u>Modes of Thought</u> (1938; rpt. New York: Putnam, Capricorn Books, 1958), pp. 26-27.

A signed article in a newspaper:

[12] Steve Cady, "Dreams Grow from Asphalt," <u>New York Times</u>, 13 July 1975, Sec. 5, p. 3, cols. 6-7.

An unsigned article in a weekly newsmagazine:

[13] "Nixon's Fight for Life," <u>Newsweek</u>, 11 Nov. 1974, p. 27.

An article in a monthly magazine:

[14] Walter Litten, "The Most Poisonous Mushrooms," <u>Scientific American</u>, March 1975, pp. 90-91.

A journal article:

[15] Walter J. Ong, "The Writer's Audience Is Always a Fiction," <u>PMLA</u>, 90 (1975), 19.

(Because this journal is paged continuously throughout the calendar year, the volume number is given and only the year of publication is provided.)

A journal article with corporate authorship:

[16] NCTE Commission on Composition, "Teaching Composition: A Position Statement," <u>College English</u>, 36 (October 1974), 219.

(In this case, because the volume does not coincide with the calendar year, the month is included. See the previous example.)

A signed encyclopedia article:

[17] S[tanley] We[intraub], "George Bernard Shaw," <u>Encyclopaedia Britannica</u>, Macropaedia 16, 1974.

A book review:

[18] Michael Wood, "Incomparable Empson," rev. of <u>William Empson: The Man and His Work</u>, ed. Roma Gill, <u>New York Review of Books</u>, 23 Jan. 1975, p. 30.

An unpublished dissertation:

[19] Frances Nicol Teague, "Ben Jonson's Stagecraft in His Four Major Comedies," Diss. Univ. of Texas, 1975, p. 71.

The citation of an unusual source that doesn't fit any

of the conventional forms (a phonograph record, mimeographed pamphlet, or personal letter, for example) should resemble as closely as possible the style used for other footnotes:

[20] W. S. Merwin, letter to the author, June 24, 1977.

Form for Later Reference. Subsequent references to a source you've already cited in full should be no longer than is necessary to identify the work. For example, a second reference to Michael Wood's review of the book on Empson should be reduced to "Wood" and the page number: Wood, p. 31. If more than one work by the same author is footnoted, then a subsequent reference to one of them must include at least the key word in the title. If two or more authors with the same last name appear in footnotes, a second reference to any one of them must include enough additional detail—first name or initials—for identification.

For reference to the footnote immediately preceding, *ibid.*, meaning "in the same place," can be used; but it saves very little space and if used inaccurately can cause serious confusion.

When a single work is quoted frequently—as, for example, in an analysis of an article or book—the first footnote to it can state that all subsequent page references will be made in parentheses immediately following the quotations, as here:

Of his "defensibles," Follett says that *aggravate* "is perhaps the one least entitled to mercy" (p. 125).

Split Note. If the author's name is given in full in the text, it can be omitted from the footnote. This does not apply to the title of a work, however. If title and author both appear in the text, the title should still begin the note.

Informational Footnote. In some scholarly publications, an additional fact, a statement of a different opinion, a quotation, or a reference to other sources is sometimes given in a footnote. In college writing you may occasionally want to use an informational footnote for useful material not directly pertinent to the discussion; but be careful not to use the device for digressions that, however interesting, are irrelevant to the discussion.

You can also use informational footnotes to explain special documentation and thus save footnotes. For example, a paragraph containing a number of statistics from a single source interspersed among the writer's own comments would need only a single footnote if the footnote explained that it applied solely to the statistics.

Common Abbreviations. The following abbreviations are commonly used in footnotes. Although you're not likely to use more than a few of them, you should know what they mean. *The MLA Style Sheet* notes that practice varies in italicizing abbreviations of Latin words. Of the following only *sic* is italicized in *A Manual of Style*, 12th ed. (Chicago: Univ. of Chicago Press, 1969).

art.	article.
c. or ca.	for *circa:* around a given date (ca. 1480).
ch. or chap.; chs. or chaps.	chapter; chapters.
col., cols.	column, columns.
comp.	compiler, compiled by.
ed.	editor, edition (2nd ed.), edited by.
e.g. (set off by commas)	for *exempli gratia:* for example.
et al.	for *et alii:* and others (used in MLA style when there are more than three authors; but the English words are also widely used: Walter S. Avis and others).
f., ff.	and the following page (386f.), and the following pages (286ff.). Exact references are preferable: pp. 286–87, pp. 286–91 (MLA style); or pp. 286–287, pp. 286–291.
ibid.	for *ibidem:* in the same place.
l., ll.	line, lines.
MS, MSS	manuscript, manuscripts.
n., nn.	note (to refer to a footnote in a source: p. 135, n. 2), notes.
n.d.	no date of publication.
n.p.	no place of publication.
NS or N.S.	new series of a periodical.
OS or O.S.	old series of a periodical.
p., pp.	page, pages.
passim	throughout the work.
sic	thus, so (used to indicate that erroneous or doubtful information has been quoted exactly).

trans. or tr.

vol., vols.

translator, translation, or translated by.

volume, volumes (vol. and p. are not used when figures for both are given: Vol. III *or* p. 176; but III, 176).

If you're writing your research paper from a casebook, source book, or "controlled research" text, footnote your references to sources in the book as if you had found them in the library. Most casebooks provide full bibliographical information and original pagination (indicated in the text itself by numbers in brackets or slashes); document according to this information instead of citing the case-book each time. Your instructor will probably ask you to provide an identifying footnote for the casebook, too.

The Final Bibliography

The bibliography of the sources actually used in the preparation of a reference paper comes at its end. It contains not all the sources consulted but only those that have actually furnished material. (Your instructor may, how-ever, ask you to supply a supplementary list, "Other Works Consulted.") Its purpose is to enable a reader to see at a glance the range of works cited in the footnotes; there-fore authors' names that begin entries are inverted for alphabetizing. When no author is given, the first important word of the title is used as the key word for alphabetizing.

The first line of each entry in a bibliography is begun at the left margin, and succeeding lines are indented five spaces. The sample entries that follow are single-spaced, but double spacing—as illustrated in the sample research paper on p. 378—may also be used, if your instructor pre-fers. The sample entries here are for the same works used earlier to illustrate footnote form. Comparison will make clear how the two differ.

A book by a single author and a second book by the same author:

Katz, Jerrold J. The Philosophy of Language. New York: Harper & Row, 1966.
————. Semantic Theory. New York: Harper & Row, 1972.

(Instead of repeating the author's name, use a ten-space line.)

A book by more than one author:

Brady, James E., and Gerard E. Humiston. General Chemistry: Principles and Structure. New York: Wiley, 1975.

(Do not reverse the names of co-authors following the first author's name: Bryant, Barbara, William Jensen, and Ann Wagner. If there are more than three authors, substitute "et al." for all but the first: Gorenstein, Shirley, et al.)

A work in more than one volume:

Sewall, Richard B.   The Life of Emily Dickinson.   2 vols.
    New York: Farrar, Straus & Giroux, 1974.

(If the books in a multivolume work are published over a period of years, give the full span: 1909–49.)

An edition other than the first:

McArthur, Lewis A.   Oregon Geographic Names.   4th ed.
    Portland: Oregon Historical Society, 1974.

An edition revised by someone other than the author:

Robertson, Stuart.   The Development of Modern English.   2nd
    ed. Rev. by Frederic G. Cassidy.   Englewood Cliffs,
    N.J.: Prentice-Hall, 1954.

An edited work:

Agnon, S. Y.   Twenty-one Stories.   Ed. Nahum N. Glatzer.
    New York: Schocken Books, 1970.

A compilation by an editor:

Baratz, Joan C., and Roger W. Shuy, eds.   Teaching Black
    Children to Read.   Washington, D.C.: Center for
    Applied Linguistics, 1969.

A selection, chapter, or other part of a compilation:

McKeon, Richard.   "Rhetoric in the Middle Ages."   Critics
    and Criticism.   Ed. R. S. Crane. Chicago: Univ. of
    Chicago Press, 1952.

A translation:

Merleau-Ponty, Maurice.   Phenomenology of Perception.   Trans.
    Colin Smith. London: Routledge, 1962.

A book that is part of a series:

Degler, Carl N.   Affluence and Anxiety: America Since 1945.
    2nd ed. The Scott, Foresman American History Series.
    Glenview, Ill.: Scott, Foresman, 1975.

A reprinted book:

Whitehead, Alfred North.   Modes of Thought.   1938; rpt.
    New York: Putnam, Capricorn Books, 1958.

A signed article in a newspaper:

Cady, Steve.   "Dreams Grow from Asphalt."   New York Times,
    13 July 1975, Sec. 5, p. 3, cols. 6-7.

An unsigned article in a weekly newsmagazine:

"Nixon's Fight for Life."   Newsweek, 11 Nov. 1974, pp. 26-29.

An article in a monthly magazine:

```
Litten, Walter.  "The Most Poisonous Mushrooms."  Scientific
    American, March 1975, pp. 90-101.
```

A journal article:

```
Ong, Walter J.  "The Writer's Audience Is Always a Fiction."
    PMLA, 90 (1975), 9-21.
```

(*PMLA* is the title of the journal, and 90 is the volume number. Because the journal—unlike most newspapers and magazines—is paged continuously throughout the calendar year, only the year is given, in parentheses, after the volume number. But if the volume does not coincide with the calendar year, as in the following example, the month is included. Note that when the volume number is given—without "Vol."—page numbers are not preceded by "pp.")

A journal article with corporate authorship:

```
NCTE Commission on Composition, "Teaching Composition: A
    Position Statement," College English, 36 (October
    1974), 219-20.
```

A signed encyclopedia article:

```
We[intraub], S[tanley].  "George Bernard Shaw."  Encyclopaedia
    Britannica.  Macropaedia 16, 1974.
```

A book review:

```
Wood, Michael.  "Incomparable Empson."  Review of William
    Empson:  The Man and His Work, ed. Roma Gill.  New
    York Review of Books, 23 Jan. 1975, pp. 30-33.
```

An unpublished dissertation:

```
Teague, Frances Nicol.  "Ben Jonson's Stagecraft in His Four
    Major Comedies."  Diss. Univ. of Texas, 1975.
```

■ *For Analysis*

1. Put the following references to source material in consistent footnote form as they would appear in a reference paper. Keep them in the present order.

a. To page 225 of this book.

b. To an editorial in The Christian Science Monitor of January 19, 1977, entitled No More Executions.

c. To pages 139 and 140 in the second volume of a book by George Philip Krapp called The English Language in America. The book was published by the Century Company of New York and the date on the title page reads MCMXXV.

d. To pages 228 to 231 inclusive of the book mentioned in *a.*

e. To an unsigned article called Black Shopping Centers on pages 43, 45–47, and 49 of the magazine Black Enterprise for September 1972.

f. To page xvii in the Introduction of a book called Burke's Politics. The book has a subtitle, Selected writings and speeches of Edmund Burke on Reform, revolution and war. It was edited by Ross J. S. Hoffman and Paul Levack, and was published in 1949 by Alfred A. Knopf in New York.

g. To an article entitled Report from Greece: Under the Junta, written by two men, Nicholas Gage and Elias Kulukundis, and printed in the American Scholar for Summer 1970, pages 475 to 497. This issue was part of volume 39.

h. To the same pages of the article mentioned in *g.*

i. To a passage by Joseph Alsop in The New York Times Magazine of December 14, 1975, quoted by Saul Bellow on pages 98–99 of To Jerusalem and Back: A Personal Account, published in 1976 by the Viking Press, New York.

j. To an unsigned article called Equatorial Current in the Encyclopedia Americana, a thirty-volume work published in New York in 1973 by Americana Corporation. This article appeared on page 532 of volume 10.

2. Put the items above in proper form and order for a bibliography.

In short bibliographies like those you'll prepare for most of your college papers, all the items are run in one list, alphabetically arranged. Very long bibliographies are sometimes grouped by type of material: primary sources, secondary sources; works by an author, works about him; and so on. They should not be grouped according to type of publication, such as books and periodicals, except in a list of the works of a single writer.

Typically the completed paper comprises the following units:

1. *Title page.* Give the title of the paper, the writer's name, the date submitted, and any other required information, such as course and section number.

2. *Outline and table of contents.* Make the type of outline assigned. Be sure it conforms to the order of material in the finished paper. Check its form by referring to the models on pp. 127–28. The outline can serve as a table of contents if you give at the right of each main topic the page on which it begins.

3. *Text of the paper.* This is the final copy of the paper, complete with footnotes and diagrams or any other illustrative material used. Put the title at the top of the first page, and follow the manuscript form required by your instructor. Before making this final copy, go through pp. 354–57 of this chapter and the sample paper on pp. 366–77 to make sure your footnotes follow the suggested form.

4. *Bibliography.* On a separate page, list in the form suggested on pp. 359–61 the books and articles you actually used in writing your paper.

[*Appendix.* Occasionally a paper needs a table of statistics too long to work into the body of the essay, or it may require a long quotation, such as part of a treaty or other document that much of the paper is based on. Such material can be placed in an appendix, but in student research papers it generally should be abridged and included in the text.]

Sample Research Paper

The sample research paper beginning with the sentence outline on the next page follows the guidelines for research and writing set forth in this chapter and the style of documentation described on pp. 353–59. Comments in the margin and questions are designed to help you identify particular details of form to be followed and alert you to specific problems that you may encounter in writing your paper.

For comparison with the final typed version, samples are included of material from the early stages of preparing the paper: preliminary version of the outline (p. 365), note cards (p. 373), rough draft (p. 375), and bibliography cards (p. 379).

Sentence Outline

EXPLORING THE LAND OF THE STICKS

Compare with
preliminary
outline on
facing page.

The familiar expression "out in the sticks"
evolved from explorers' and loggers' use of the
Chinook Jargon word for <u>forest</u> and may have originated
in an Indian word, <u>stiyakha</u>, meaning "a forest
spirit," known to white men as a "stick Indian."

I. Many words and expressions become detached from
their origins, and change their meanings.

II. The expression has been widely current since the
nineteenth century and has come to have special
professional meanings, generally unfavorable.
   A. Uses in the nineteenth century are on record.
   B. Baseball players speak of farm clubs "in the
   sticks," and actors use the expression to
   denote uncultured regions.
   C. Hoboes speak of their jungles as "sticks."

III. Speculation that the word is a corruption of
"Styx" is unfounded.

IV. Western loggers borrowed the Chinook Jargon word
<u>stick</u>, meaning everything relating to wood, to
describe "woods."

V. Indians told about a wild race of "stick
Indians" living in the forest.
   A. Henry Gibbs understood that these were simply
   less civilized Indians.
   B. Reports by C. B. Bagley and others suggest on
   the contrary that they were spirits.

VI. The expression may derive from an Indian word for
"spirit" sounding like <u>stick</u>, rather than from
the Jargon word itself.
   A. The Jargon and dialect word for "goblin,"
   <u>tsiatko</u>, sounds like <u>stick</u>.
   B. Shitike Creek in Oregon is another possible
   form of the word.
   C. Warm Springs Indians tell of "stick Indians,"
   mountain spirits who lived around Shitike
   Creek and were called <u>stiyakha</u>, or spirits.

VII. If this origin were confirmed, the connotations
of "out in the sticks" might change from
unfavorable to favorable.

Preliminary Version

Out in the Sticks

Our expression "out in the sticks" probably comes from an Indian word having to do with forest spirits.

I. Introduction
II. Words and sayings often change their meanings
III. The expression's widespread use
   A. 19th century
IV. Specific professional meanings
   A. Theater
   B. Baseball
   C. Joggers
   D. Hoboes
V. Confusion with "Styx"
VI. Meaning of _stick_
   A. In Chinook Jargon
   B. Western loggers' meaning
VII. Indians told about "stick Indians" who lived in the sticks
   A. Henry Gibbs' report
VIII. Essay by C.B. Bagley makes it clear that Indians believed "stick Indians" were spirits
IX. Indian words for spirit
   A. goblin
   B. Shitike Creek in Oregon
X. Warm Springs Indians' belief in "styakha"
XI. Conclusion

■ For Analysis and Writing

1. Compare the sentence outline with the preliminary version and analyze the differences. What changes were made in the revision to regularize the form? Why is the revised thesis sentence more satisfactory? Why has the order of topics been changed? Which sections of the preliminary version overlap?

2. Convert the sentence outline to a topic outline.

EXPLORING THE LAND OF THE STICKS

One of the rewards of acquiring more than a speaking acquaintance with the English language lies in the discovery of words and sayings whose popular usage has wandered far from their original sources. Thus, many of our words--bloomers, macadam, guillotine--are unsuspected memorials to people whose names somehow or other got attached to new items and eventually became, in uncapitalized form, common currency. The process by which the origins of new words are forgotten and the words become literally nonsense can be surprisingly rapid. For example, everyone has heard and probably used the word boondocks, meaning "the sticks," the "backwoods," and so on--but who remembers now that this odd-looking word came into English in the Second World War, when American soldiers picked up the Philippine Tagalog word bunduk, which means "mountains"?[1]

And what about "the sticks" itself? We use the expression to refer to back country, hillbilly territory, or, as Webster's Third New International Dictionary puts it, "wooded lands, rural districts,

---

In a citation of a book by two authors, both names are given.

[1] William Morris and Mary Morris, A Dictionary of Word and Phrase Origins (New York: Harper & Row, 1962), I, 43.

2

sections of a country remote from or held to be little
touched by centers of civilization." The dictionary
definition is connotatively neutral; but in fact,
although we Americans tend to be sentimental about
"country . . . little touched by centers of
civilization," we generally use "out in the sticks"
(like "boondocks") somewhat contemptuously. Does the
current usage bear any relation to its origins?

The phrase apparently entered American popular
speech in the nineteenth century,[2] and it seems to
carry with it a generally Western flavor, although it
has come to have a Southern usage too.[3] In addition
to its general application, the phrase has been
appropriated by a number of professions in which a
sharp distinction is drawn between "bigtime" status
and lower levels of fame and glory. Baseball players,
for example, shudder at the prospect of a career on a
farm club somewhere "in the sticks," and actors
traditionally would do almost anything rather than go
on an extended tour "back in stick country"--that is,

[2] C. Merton Babcock, "The Social Significance of
the Language of the American Frontier," American
Speech, 24 (1949), 256.

[3] A Dictionary of Americanisms on Historical
Principles, ed. Mitford M. Mathews (Chicago: Univ. of
Chicago Press, 1951), II, 1649.

out of New York City!⁴ In a rather different kind of
profession, hoboes sometimes refer to their camps or
"jungles" as "the sticks."⁵

But if the expression has a clear currency in
American speech and writing, <u>how</u> did it come to make
its small enrichment of our vocabulary? And would its
original users recognize the way we use it today? The
answers are strange ones, proving again that the
meaning of a familiar idiom sometimes rests on
unexpected and romantic foundations.

The educated guess might be made that <u>sticks</u> is
only a corruption of <u>Styx</u>, the mythological river of
Hades. But if by stretching things a little the
connotations of the two words seem to match up (our
unsuccessful baseball player might feel that he is
being sent down to a kind of Hades, perhaps), in more
particular terms "the sticks" has apparently never
denoted "river" or "river-country," or anything
especially suggestive of the Underworld; and in fact
no modern dictionary offers this explanation of the

Two sources that
supply informa-
tion for the
same sentence
are cited in one
footnote and
separated by a
semicolon.

⁴ Lester V. Berrey and Melvin Van den Bark, <u>The
American Thesaurus of Slang</u> (New York: Crowell, 1942),
p. 576; <u>Dictionary of American Slang</u>, comp. and ed.
Harold Wentworth and Stuart Berg Flexner (New York:
Crowell, 1967), p. 519.

⁵ <u>Dictionary of American Slang</u>, p. 520.

4

expression's etymology.

In their <u>Dictionary of Word and Phrase Origins</u>,
William and Mary Morris offer some clues. "The phrase
was originally used . . . by loggers to designate
timberlands. Gradually it has come to mean any rural
district, especially, but not necessarily, a backwoods
area."[6] Now it is a fact that Western loggers still
sometimes refer jovially to the huge evergreens they
cut as "sticks"[7] (perhaps this is what Theodore
Roosevelt had in mind when he proposed to "speak
softly and carry a big stick"), so, logically, "out in
the sticks" would be where the big trees grow, out in
the tall timber. But the true origins of the saying
are not so simple: <u>Why</u> did Western loggers start
calling their trees "sticks" in the first place?

Our expression is current in Canada, too, and <u>A</u>
<u>Dictionary of Canadianisms</u> points out that in the
Chinook Jargon (the famous <u>lingua franca</u> through which
Western Indians communicated with each other inter-
tribally and with the first white explorers and
settlers) the word <u>stick</u>, according to the simplifying

> Is the transition clear at the beginning of this paragraph?

[6] Morris and Morris, p. 338.

[7] In his <u>Woods Words</u>: <u>A Comprehensive Dictionary</u>
<u>of Loggers' Terms</u> (Portland: Binfords, 1952), p. 182,
Walter F. McCormick notes that loggers also use the
word to specify tall spars used as booms.

> An informational footnote.

diction of the Jargon, denoted literally everything made of wood--from spears to ships' masts, from twigs to whole forests of pine and fir.[8] A standard dictionary of the Jargon notes that "The word 'stick' is used to denote 'tree' or wood of any kind; anything made of wood"[9]--thus, tree bark was known as stick-skin, a wooden eating bowl was a stickpan, and a forest was simply sticks. So it seems logical that early settlers, loggers, and traders would turn this all-purpose Jargon word into our metaphorical expression. At this point, however, our search takes a very odd turn. We must ask why the Indians themselves (whose own words from many dialects make up the great bulk of the Jargon) used this particular word.

Many early Western explorers (before the rise of the logging industry and the development of trade generally) report that Indians told them about other, wilder natives who lived back in the forest and were called "stick Indians." In Canada, for example, Indians on the Pacific Coast reported having dealings

In a citation of a work with more than three editors or authors, only the first is named, followed by "et al."

[8] A Dictionary of Canadianisms, ed. Walter S. Avis et al. (Toronto: Gage, 1967), p. 752.

[9] W. S. Phillips, The Chinook Book (Seattle: privately printed, 1913), p. 91.

6

with "the interior, or 'stick' Indian, as he was
known, because he came from the land of forests, or
'sticks.'"[10]   In his "Account of Indian Mythology in
Oregon and Washington Territory" (1865), the explorer
and anthropologist George Gibbs observes that

> the foreign medicine men are apt among the
> Indians, as among some other peoples, to enjoy a
> greater reputation than their own, those of the
> wilder tribes, the "stick Indians" in particular,
> being supposed to have the most potent spirits at
> their command.

The date of Gibbs'
essay is included
to make it clear
that this is an
early firsthand
account.

In a footnote Gibbs explains that

> a race of tall Indians, called "wild" or "stick"
> Indians, was said to wander through the forest.
> . . . Their homes were hollowed out like the
> sleeping places of animals. . . . It is because
> of this lack of any houses or villages that they
> were characterized as "wild." A young Quinault-
> Chehalis told me that they were called "Stick
> Indians" simply because they lived in the
> woods.[11]

Ellipses are used
to indicate that
words have been
omitted.

Now the more one reads about these "tall," "wild"
Indians who lived in the deep forest and who were
somehow never directly encountered by white explorers,

[10] A Dictionary of Canadianisms, p. 752.

[11] "Account of Indian Mythology in Oregon and
Washington Territory," ed. Ella E. Clark, Oregon
Historical Quarterly, 57 (1956), 133-34.

Because the two
citations appeared
on the same
page in Gibbs'
original account,
one footnote
is sufficient.

the more one suspects that to the Indian informants
they were something more than human, not mere figments
of the imagination or jokes played upon gullible
whites but supernatural beings, perhaps too important,
too sacred for ordinary Indians to identify exactly to
unbelieving or evangelizing white foreigners.
Confirmation of this hunch is found in C. B. Bagley's
Indian Myths of the Northwest, a collection of
stories and tales which includes the following from
the state of Washington:

Compare with
note cards on
facing page.

> When a boy, the Yakima Indians told me of the
> "Eliquas Tein" (Stick Indians), a wild race of
> people who inhabited the high craggy peaks along
> both sides of the summit of the Cascade Mountains
> around the headwaters of the Chelan and Skagit
> Rivers. They were held in superstitious awe by
> many who believed that they were the spirits of
> departed warriors.[12]

Bagley goes on to note that, because these
creatures were usually glimpsed just as they
disappeared over a crag or leaped into a mountain
abyss, the Indians believed that they had wings.[13]

---

[12] Indian Myths of the Northwest (Seattle: Lowman,
1930), p. 118.

[13] On p. 3 of the magazine section of the
Portland Oregonian for April 28, 1940, Robert L.
Sicade describes similar beliefs: "The Indians Have
Bogey-Men Too: Old Legends Tell of the Tsiatko Who
Roamed the Woods at Night."

Note Cards

Stick Indians   Bagley, <u>Indian Myths of the Northwest</u>

118 "When a boy, the Yakima Indians told me of the 'Eliquas Tein' (Stick Indians), a wild race of people who inhabited the high craggy peaks along both sides of the summit of the Cascade Mountains around the headwaters of the Chelan and Skagit Rivers. They were held in superstitious awe by many who believed that they were the spirits of departed warriors."

Stick Indians   Bagley, <u>Indian Myths of the Northwest</u>

119 - Notes that because S.I.'s were seen only around precipices and peaks, Indians thought they were winged.

Some Indian hunters claim to have talked to the spirit chief, who told them to kill all the game they needed, for his people had plenty.

- Legend of the young squaw who was kidnapped by a Stick Indian.

Several notes were taken on the same card because they were meant to be used at the same point in the paper. The last two items were not used. Should they have been?

Compare with
rough draft on
facing page.

So, it seems clear, the original denizens of "the

sticks" were not uncultured hillbillies, not white

loggers, but a race of elusive nature spirits,

haunting lonely areas of the West where the Indians

themselves were not inclined to travel. Is it

possible that our expression actually derives from an

Indian word for spirit or supernatural being then,

perhaps in a particular dialect rather than the

Jargon, and that it does not come from the Indian-

English Jargon word for wood, as is generally

accepted?

Throughout the
paper Indian
words are under-
lined to indicate
that they are
foreign.

In the Chinook Jargon, a strong evil spirit was a

skookum, and a great spirit was a tahmuhnawis. More

suggestively, a goblin was a tsiatko in many

individual dialects as well as in the Jargon, and this

word might be twisted into something sounding like

The three page
references to
Thomas' book are
for the three
Indian words.
Since they appear
in sequence, only
one footnote is
needed.

"stick."[14] In central Oregon on the Warm Springs

Indian Reservation, there is a large tributary of the

Deschutes River known as Shitike Creek,[15] which,

again, could easily be corrupted into our word: the

name is thought to be a Wasco term, but its meaning is

---

[14] Edward Harper Thomas, Chinook: A History and
Dictionary (Portland: Gill, 1935), pp. 102, 104,
106.

[15] Lewis A. McArthur, Oregon Geographic Names, 4th ed.
(Portland: Oregon Historical Society, 1974), p. 664.

Rough Draft

So, ~~it appears to be a safe speculation that the first~~ *it seems clear, the original denizens of*

~~Stick dwellers~~ *"the sticks"* were not, *uncultured hillbillies, not white loggers, but* ~~backwoodsmen but Indian~~ nature *a race of*

spirits, haunting lonely areas of the West. ~~Whether~~ *where the Indians themselves were not, elusive inclined to travel*

~~they were tall or short, malevolent or good-hearted~~

~~seems to vary with the informant; the important thing~~

~~is that, disguise their belief as they might (Gibbs~~

~~was probably misinformed by his informant), the~~

~~Indians did believe in their existence.~~ *Is it* ~~It appears to~~

~~be~~ possible, ~~then,~~ that our expression actually ~~was~~ *derives*

~~developed~~ from, *an Indian word for spirit or supernatural* ~~a dialect word meaning spirit, rather~~ *being* ~~than from the Jargon word for wood.~~ *then, perhaps in a particular dialect rather than the Jargon, and that it does not come from the Indian-English*

In the Chinook Jargon, a strong evil spirit was a *Jargon word for wood, as is generally accepted?*

skookum, and ~~Indians called~~ a great spirit, *was* a

tahmuhnawis. *More suggestively,* ~~However,~~ a goblin was a <u>tsiatko</u> in many

individual dialects as well as in the Jargon, and this

word, *might be twisted into something sounding like* ~~rather sounds like~~ "stick." (Thomas, pp. 102, 104, 106)

A brief citation
in parentheses re-
cords the source.
Footnotes at the bot-
tom of the page
could be overlooked
if the draft and final
copy didn't cor-
respond page for
page.

9

unrecorded. And a recently published Indian myth from

this area seems to give strong support if not

confirmation to our etymological hunch. It is worth

quoting in full:

> When an Indian is traveling up in the mountains
> in a lonely place and hears a certain bird
> singing, he knows it is probably a "stick"
> Indian. The stick Indians are spirits who live
> in high gloomy places, like Grizzly Flats (in the
> Cascades south of Mt. Jefferson) and upper
> Shitike Creek (southwest of Warm Springs Agency),
> and their favorite trick is to sing like a bird
> in the evening when birds don't sing. If you
> follow the song, the stick Indians will lead you
> deeper and deeper into the woods--and you just
> won't come out, maybe you will lose your mind in
> there. Some Indians when they're out huckle-
> berry-picking or hunting scatter matches all
> around their camp at night--they say the stick
> Indians like matches best of all, living in the
> dark.[16]

If you underline for emphasis, acknowledge that the underlining is yours and does not represent italics in the source.

The word "stick," according to the Indian informant,

is a white man's corruption of a Wasco-Warm Springs

word, stiyakha, meaning "a kind of mountain spirit."

It should be acknowledged that no other instance

of this Indian word has yet found its way into print;

and it is barely possible, of course, that stiyakha

might represent a late corruption of the Jargon word

---

[16] Jarold Ramsey, "Three Wasco-Warm Springs
Texts," Western Folklore, 29 (Winter 1970), 97.
Italics added.

10

stick in the Wasco dialect! But at least we have
traced our familiar saying back to the real "forest
primeval" where it began its journey into the American
vocabulary, and we have uncovered the possibility that
the first inhabitants of "stick country, stickdom, the
sticks, the stix"[17] were supernatural beings who gave
their magical name to the wild woods where they lived
and thence, through who knows what process, to the
language at large.

The irony is that if this etymology were
confirmed, instead of using "out in the sticks" with
an unfavorable twist, we might use it with positive,
even reverent connotations in mind. The growing
number of Americans who long nostalgically for
untouched wilderness frontiers and for the supposed
simplicity of Indian life would find themselves
expressing an urge to retreat to "Stiyakha
Country." But as the popular usage now stands, cut
off from its romantic origins, most of us don't crave
to be that deep in the sticks.

Should the writer
acknowledge the
limits of his theory
here at the end as
he does? Should he
be more emphatic
in his claim to
have discovered
the true etymol-
ogy of the saying?
Would the paper
be improved sub-
stantially if the
crucial material
about the *stiyakha*
was introduced at
the beginning of
the paper, rather
than built up to
and disclosed
near the end?

[17] Berrey and Van den Bark, p. 576.

Bibliography

See sample bibli-
ography cards on
facing page.

Babcock, C. Merton. "The Social Significance of the

Language of the American Frontier." American

Speech, 24 (1949), 256.

Bagley, C. B. Indian Myths of the Northwest. Seattle:

Lowman, 1930.

Berrey, Lester V., and Melvin Van den Bark. The

American Thesaurus of Slang. New York: Crowell,

1942.

Dictionary of American Slang. Comp. and ed. Harold

Wentworth and Stuart Berg Flexner. New York:

Crowell, 1967.

A Dictionary of Americanisms on Historical

Principles. Ed. Mitford M. Mathews. 2 vols.

Chicago: Univ. of Chicago Press, 1951.

A Dictionary of Canadianisms. Ed. Walter S. Avis et

al. Toronto: Gage, 1967.

Gibbs, George. "Account of Indian Mythology in Oregon

and Washington Territory," ed. Ella E.

Clark. Oregon Historical Quarterly, 57 (1956),

128-56.

McArthur, Lewis A. Oregon Geographic Names. 4th ed.

Portland: Oregon Historical Society, 1974.

McCormick, Walter F. Woods Words: A Comprehensive

Dictionary of Loggers' Terms. Portland:

Binfords, 1952.

Bibliography Cards

Location   Slug   Code

Per   "Sticks" - first uses   Babcock

Babcock, C. Merton   Author

"The Social Significance of the
Language of the American Frontier"   Title

American Speech   Publication data
24 (1949), 256

"in the sticks" - 19th century usage   Comment

Call number   Slug   Code

L 970.62   Stick Indians   Bagley
B146   as Spirits

Bagley, C. B.   Author
Indian Myths of the Northwest   Title
Seattle : Lowman, 1930   Publication data

Yakimas believed Stick Indians   Comment
were mountain spirits — pp. 118-19

Morris, William, and Mary Morris. A Dictionary of

   Word and Phrase Origins. 3 vols. New York:

   Harper & Row, 1962.

Phillips, W. S. The Chinook Books. Seattle: privately

   printed, 1913.

Ramsey, Jarold. "Three Wasco-Warm Springs Texts."

   Western Folklore, 29 (Winter 1970), 95-97.

Sicade, Robert. "The Indians Have Bogey-Men Too: Old

   Legends Tell of the Tsiatko Who Roamed the Woods

   at Night." Portland Oregonian, April 28, 1940,

   Magazine section, p. 3.

Thomas, Edward Harper. Chinook: A History and

   Dictionary. Portland: Gill, 1935.

■ *For Analysis and Writing*

1. Write a summary or précis of this sample paper.

2. Evaluate "Out in the Sticks" as a piece of writing. Pay particular attention to the organization, to the development of the thesis, and to the quality of the prose. What would you have done differently?

3. Write a brief report on one of the following topics:

  a. Different methods by which you could have developed your paper, and why you chose the one you did.

  b. The sources you found most useful, and why.

  c. Some problems you encountered in organizing your paper, and how you solved them.

  d. Some by-products of your research—what you've learned about finding material, about the subject itself, or about areas for further investigation.

4. Write a summary or précis of your paper, giving its essential ideas and emphasis.

Index
to
English

Introduction

Index to English applies the principles of style discussed in *Writer's Guide*. Because it deals with English as it exists – in publications addressed to moderately educated and to well-educated audiences, as well as in student essays – many of its articles don't offer a simple Right and Wrong, Do and Don't. Often they give both the formal choice and the general choice, sometimes the informal choice as well. When you have a particular job of writing to do, with a particular audience in mind, the relevance of the choices will come clear.

The articles in the *Index* are alphabetically arranged. They fall roughly into six categories:

1. Articles on particular words and constructions, like *among, between; definitely; like, as; not about to; who, whom.* Information about the standing of a locution in current usage is often supported by examples quoted from newspapers, popular magazines, scholarly journals, and books. (The fact that something is printed doesn't mean that it's recommended; bad writing may appear in respectable publications.) Read the article to see where the locution is placed among the varieties of English, and then decide whether it fits your style in the particular rhetorical situation. The entry titles for articles on words and phrases are the only ones that are not capitalized.

2. Articles to be used in correcting and revising papers. Accompanied by longhand correction symbols, these articles are listed in the correction chart on the inside back cover of this book. They offer straightforward advice – practical *do*s and *don't*s. Go to them when your corrected papers have been returned to you, but also get in the habit of consulting them *before* you submit your essays, while you're in the process of revising your first drafts. Checking what you've written against their instructions and illustrations will help you decide whether you've punctuated a sentence correctly, used the expected case of a pronoun, made clear what a modifier relates to.

3. Articles on composition, rhetoric, and style. Prewriting, Beginning an essay, Thesis statement, Organization, Outline form, Paragraphs, Coherence, Transition, Emphasis, Unity, and Concluding an essay – these and other articles carry you through the stages of writing a paper. Some articles deal with specific topics in rhetoric – Argument, Cause and effect, Classification and division, Comparison and contrast, Definition, Deduction, Fallacies, Induction, Logical thinking. Style is treated more directly in such articles as Abstract language, Diction, Doublespeak, Figurative language, Nominalization, Parallelism, and Periodic sentence.

4. Articles offering information and advice on a range of topics that are useful in special writing situations, such as Research papers (and the related articles Bibliographical form and Footnote form), Business letters, and Technical writing.

5. Articles on grammar, offering definitions and discussions of standard grammatical terms and concepts – Collective nouns, for example, and Parts of speech, Relative clauses, Subjunctive mood.

6. Articles about language and language study, such as British English, English language, Linguistics, Sexist language, and Usage.

Refer to the *Index* when you're faced with a writing assignment (see Prewriting), as you write, as you revise what you've written, and when your corrected essay is returned to you for further revision. Besides following up the cross references that most articles contain, look up any term you come upon that is new or unclear to you – *modal auxiliaries,* for example, or *deep structure.* Most such terms are explained in articles of their own.

Index to English is intended to be more than a reference work for college writers. It's meant to be browsed in and annotated. By updating the slang and vogue words and by noting changes in usage, fresh figures of speech, allusions, and turns of phrase, you can keep the *Index* alive at the same time that you keep yourself in touch with your language.

Many articles include references to books and journals where you can find further discussion. In the references, the titles of the journals *American Speech* and *College Composition and Communication* have been abbreviated to *AS* and *CCC.*

Books to which frequent reference is made are cited by author's name only:

Atwood, E. Bagby. *A Survey of Verb Forms in the Eastern United States.* Ann Arbor: Univ. of Michigan Press, 1953.

Bolinger, Dwight. *Aspects of Language.* 2nd ed. New York: Harcourt, 1975.

Bryant, Margaret M. *Current American Usage.* New York: Funk, 1962.

Christensen, Francis. *Notes Toward a New Rhetoric.* New York: Harper, 1967.

Copperud, Roy H. *American Usage: The Consensus.* New York: Van Nostrand, 1970.

Evans, Bergen, and Cornelia Evans. *A Dictionary of Contemporary American Usage.* New York: Random, 1957.

Follett, Wilson. *Modern American Usage: A Guide.* Ed. and compl. by Jacques Barzun. New York: Hill, 1966.

Fowler, H. W. *A Dictionary of Modern English Usage.* 2nd ed. Rev. by Sir Ernest Gowers. New York: Oxford Univ. Press, 1965.

Francis, W. Nelson. *The Structure of American English.* New York: Ronald, 1958.

Fries, Charles Carpenter. *American English Grammar.* New York: Appleton, 1940.

Hungerford, Harold, Jay Robinson, and James Sledd, eds. *English Linguistics: An Introductory Reader.* Glenview, Ill.: Scott, 1970.

Jacobs, Roderick A., and Peter S. Rosenbaum. *English Transformational Grammar.* Waltham, Mass.: Blaisdell, 1968.

Jespersen, Otto. *Essentials of English Grammar.* 1933; rpt. University, Ala.: Univ. of Alabama Press, 1964.

Joos, Martin. *The English Verb.* Madison: Univ. of Wisconsin Press, 1964.

Long, Ralph B. *The Sentence and Its Parts.* Chicago: Univ. of Chicago Press, 1961.

————, and Dorothy R. Long. *The System of English Grammar.* Glenview, Ill.: Scott, 1971.

Mencken, H. L. *The American Language.* Abridged 4th ed. Ed. Raven I. McDavid, Jr. New York: Knopf, 1963.

Pooley, Robert C. *The Teaching of English Usage.* Urbana, Ill.: National Council of Teachers of English, 1974.

Pyles, Thomas. *The Origins and Development of the English Language.* 2nd ed. New York: Harcourt, 1971.

Quirk, Randolph, et al. *A Grammar of Contemporary English.* New York: Seminar, 1972.

Roberts, Paul. *Understanding Grammar.* New York: Harper, 1954.

Sledd, James. *A Short Introduction to English Grammar.* Glenview, Ill.: Scott, 1959.

Summey, George, Jr. *American Punctuation.* New York: Ronald, 1959.

Whitehall, Harold. *Structural Essentials of English.* New York: Harcourt, 1956.

Williams, Joseph M. *The New English.* New York: Free Press, 1970.

Two stylebooks are frequently referred to: *A Manual of Style*, 12th ed. (Chicago: Univ. of Chicago Press, 1969), and *United States Government Printing Office Style Manual*, rev. ed. (Washington, D.C.: Government Printing Office, 1967), cited as *U.S. Style Manual*.

A word about editorial procedure: In order to keep the topic of each article in sharp focus, unnecessary material has been deleted from illustrative quotations; and when what remains is grammatically a complete sentence, it is printed without opening or closing ellipses.

A

a, an

The choice between *a* and *an* depends on the initial sound, not on the initial letter, of the word that follows. *A* is used before all words beginning with a consonant sound: a business, a European trip, a D, a usage. *An* is used before all words beginning with a vowel sound, including words spelled with initial silent *h*: an apple, an F, an honor, an hour, an uncle.

In words beginning with *h* but not accented on the first syllable, like *histo'rian, hyster'ical, h* was formerly not pronounced, so *an* was used. Although the *h* is now often pronounced, some people continue to say and write *an histor'ical event* (but *a his'tory*). In contemporary usage *a* is more common in such locutions, but *an* also occurs: "an habitual set of choices" (Josephine Miles, *CCC*).

Repeating *a* or *an* before each noun of a series keeps the various words distinct: a pen, a sheet of paper, and an envelope.

See *awhile, a while; half; kind, sort* 2.

ab Abbreviations

Write in full the word or words inappropriately abbreviated. Or use the correct form of the abbreviation marked.

1. Appropriateness. Abbreviations are appropriate in manuals, reference books, business and legal documents, scholarly footnotes, and other works in which they are conventionally used in order to save space. They are also suitable in informal writing — notes for your own use, letters to friends. Otherwise, use only those abbreviations that are fully established in standard usage (see 2) or those that regularly occur in discussions of a particular subject.

2. Standard abbreviations. *Dr., Mr., Mrs., Messrs.* are always abbreviated when used with names. (A comparable term of address, *Ms.*, is technically not an abbreviation but a combination of *Miss* and *Mrs.*) A number of abbreviations, such as *St.* (see *saint*), *B.C.* and *A.D., a.m.* and *p.m., Jr.* for *Junior*, and abbreviations for government agencies like *CIA* and *SEC*, are standard. In formal writing, titles like Reverend, Professor, President, and Senator and naval and military ranks are not abbreviated. In general writing they may be abbreviated when initials or given names are used: Professor Hylander *or* Prof. G. W. Hylander (*but not* Prof. Hylander).

Scholarly writing still uses some abbreviations of Latin words. The following are no longer customarily italicized:

cf. *(confer)*	compare (for which *see* may be used)
e.g. *(exempli gratia)*	for example
ibid. *(ibidem)*	the same (used in footnotes)
i.e. *(id est)*	that is

Abbreviations less commonly used are often italicized: *c.* or *ca.* (*circa,* "about," used with uncertain dates), *seq. (sequentes* or *sequentia,* "following").

Dictionaries give abbreviations either in the main alphabetical list of words or in a special list.

3. Period with abbreviations. Where standard practice requires the period, its omission (as in *eg*) is a careless slip. Only one period is used after an abbreviation at the end of a sentence.

Periods are increasingly omitted from the abbreviations of names of government agencies *(CIA, FBI, HEW)* and of other terms if the abbreviation is generally used instead of the name *(AFL-CIO, CBS, GNP, ID, IQ),* and from abbreviations like *mph, hp, kwh, rpm* in scientific contexts or when used with figures (780 rpm). They are not used with the two-letter abbreviations for states adopted by the United States Postal Service *(PA, TX).*

Abbreviations that are pronounced as words *(WASP, UNESCO)* are called acronyms. Dozens of acronyms entered the language during World War II *(Nazi, Gestapo, radar, sonar, Wac, Wave),* and thousands have been created since that time *(NATO, SALT, laser).* A recent example is *Candu,* from Canadian deuterium-uranium reactor.

For abbreviation of dates, see Months. Compare Contractions, Numbers, Origin of words 3d.

ability to

The accepted idiom is *ability* plus a *to*-infinitive (ability *to do,* not *of doing*): He has the ability to design beautiful buildings. The idea is often better expressed by an adjective or verb: He is able to [He can] design beautiful buildings; He designs beautiful buildings.

able to

Able to followed by a passive infinitive (like *to be done* or *to be ended*) sounds awkward: This was not able to be done because of lack of time. *Revised:* This could not be done because of lack of time. *Or* They were not able to do this because of lack of time. Though *can* or *could* can sometimes replace *be able to,* in standard English they do not combine with another modal auxiliary as *be able to* does: *will* be able to attend, *might* be able to come. See Modal auxiliaries.

about

About has a variety of uses. Check these for trouble spots.

1. about–around. In describing physical position these are nearly interchangeable, though *around* is the more common (about the barn – around the barn). In the sense of "nearly" or "approximately," *about* is more common (about 70°), but both are standard American usage. In telling time, *around* (around two o'clock) is considered more informal. Reference: Copperud, p. 21.

2. *about–almost.* In the sense of "almost" (about finished), *about* is standard but mainly informal.

3. *at about.* In formal English *at about* is avoided on the grounds that something must be either *at* or *about.* But *about* is being used here as an adverb, and the preposition-adverb pattern is well established: at approximately noon; in about ten minutes. Reference: Bryant, pp. 31–32.

4. *about* followed by an infinitive is a convenient general idiom for "on the point of": He was about to make a third try. The negative *not about to* (an emphatic "not going to") is more informal.

above
Above is primarily a preposition (above the clouds) and an adverb (dark above and light below). Its adverbial use in such phrases as "the evidence cited above" and its use as an adjective (the above prices) and as a noun (the above is confirmed) are fully established if not universally accepted. For example, *above* as an adjective is avoided by some careful writers but not by others: "for a comment on the above use of the word 'claims' . . ." (Theodore Bernstein, *Watch Your Language*). References: Bryant, pp. 3–4; Copperud, p. 2; Pooley, pp. 120–22.

Abridged clauses
In an abridged clause, the subject and a form of *be* are deleted: When [she was] first hired, she made little impression. See Clauses 2b.

Absolute phrases
An absolute phrase (sometimes called a nominative absolute or an absolute clause) is a sentence modifier—that is, it modifies the sentence as a whole, not just a part of it. The most common type of absolute phrase consists of a participle or an adjective modifying a noun that has no grammatical connection with the rest of the sentence:

The battle lost, the army surrendered.
She begins to scream, *her face white with terror.*

1. Structure. An absolute phrase is sometimes explained as the result of deleting a form of *be* (or of *have* or of both *be* and *have*) from an underlying sentence: The battle *was [had been]* lost; Her face *is* white with terror. Because the underlying sentence does not have the same subject as the main clause, its subject is not deleted in the absolute phrase. In this respect it differs from a participial phrase; the subject of the sentence underlying a participial phrase is deleted because that subject is identical with the subject of the main clause: *Losing the battle,* the army surrendered. (It is the army that loses the battle and the army that surrenders.)

2. Absolute phrases as formulas. Some absolute phrases have been used so frequently that they have become fixed formulas or idioms: all things considered, other things being equal, this being the case, God willing.

3. Absolute phrases and style. Absolute phrases are economical, offering a compact way of singling out details of a scene or relating parts of a whole:

He entered the room, *eyes bloodshot, tie askew.*

The curtain rises on a dark stage, *its horizon lit by a full moon.* — Arlene Croce, *New Yorker*

It was about four of a winter afternoon, *the sky about thirty feet up, the flats looking like a testing ground for biological warfare, the horizon smoking away.* — Theodore Solotaroff, *The Red Hot Vacuum*

Suddenly the President leans forward, and with a vigor far surpassing any I have previously seen him show, *his voice rising almost to a shout, his forefinger pounding on the edge of the desk,* he adjures the Secretary to get the Navy going on the Elk Hills petroleum reserve. — John Hersey, *New York Times Magazine*

But the somewhat formal quality of absolute phrases makes them out of place in casual writing: *Camp made,* the kids went to bed. And absolute phrases that contain auxiliaries (*being, having, having been*) may be heavy and clumsy-sounding: *The description of the scene having been completed,* the stage is set for the crucial action. A dependent clause is often smoother and, in situations where relationships of time or cause are important, more precise.

Absolute phrase: The dry falls were formed by the erosive glacial waters, *the ice cap having changed the course of the Columbia.*

Clause: . . . *after the ice cap had changed the course of the Columbia.*

See Dangling modifiers. References: Christensen, Ch. 2; Dorothy Petitt, *CCC*, Feb. 1969, pp. 29–34; Martha Solomon, *CCC*, Dec. 1975, pp. 356–61.

Absolutes, comparison of

Logically, absolutes like *perfect* and *final* can't be more or most, less or least. But see Comparison of adjectives and adverbs 4.

abst Abstract language

Make this word or passage more concrete or more specific.

Abstract words refer to emotions, qualities, concepts, relationships: *love, courage, square root, symmetry.* They contrast with concrete words like *kiss, lion, computer,* and *hoop,* which refer to things we can see or touch or otherwise perceive with our senses.

Abstract terms are essential in communicating ideas, and abstract language can be just as precise as concrete language. But writing that relies heavily on an abstract vocabulary sometimes seems to lose contact with the world of human experience.

If your writing is criticized as too abstract, try these remedies:

1. Provide concrete examples. If you're writing about courage, describe a courageous action or contrast a brave act with a cowardly one. The shift from the concept to the example will make it natural to use concrete terms. Or supplement an abstract statement with a concrete expression of the same idea:

The survey's assumption that the bodily symptoms in question are indicators of psychological distress leads to the conclusion that the working class tends to somatize its emotional troubles, whereas the middle class experiences them more directly. In other words, clammy hands and upset stomach are apt to be the poor man's substitute for angst. – Charles J. Rolo, *Atlantic*

2. Replace general terms with specific ones. *General* and *abstract* are sometimes used interchangeably, and so are *specific* and *concrete;* but the pairs are not identical. Although we can easily classify a word as concrete or abstract, we can say that a term is specific or general only if we compare it with a related term. In the series *Volvo, car, vehicle,* all the words are concrete; but judged in relation to each other, *car* is more general than *Volvo* and more specific than *vehicle.* In the series *emotion, love, lust,* all the words are abstract; but *love* is more specific than *emotion* and more general than *lust.* Thus a concrete term is not always specific, nor is an abstract term always general.

Prose that strikes the reader as "abstract" often contains a high proportion of general terms, both concrete and abstract. Instead of using the general, abstract term *immorality*, specify the kind of immoral act you have in mind *(adultery, bribery, robbery)*. Instead of the general, concrete term *lawbreakers,* use *muggers, vandals, burglars, rapists, speeders* – naming the kind of lawbreakers you're actually writing about. It's the specifics of a subject just as much as concrete language that make a style concrete.

3. Choose your abstract terms with care. What often causes trouble is not the use of abstract terms but the particular ones chosen. If you find that every sixth or seventh word you write is a noun ending in *-ence, -ity, -ment,* or *-tion (permanence, responsibility, management, utilization),* your style will be abstract and heavy. Many abstract nouns are related to verbs or adjectives: *intention (intend), goodness (good), refusal (refuse), stupidity (stupid), response (respond).* Given a choice between representing an action in an abstract noun or in a full verb, you will generally write a livelier, clearer sentence if you choose the verb:

The achievement of clarity of thought has a clear dependence on the correctness of the formulation of the problem.

To think clearly, you need to formulate your problem correctly.

Although neither sentence contains any concrete words, the second is decidedly more direct and easier to read than the first. Its style is more concrete.

See Description, Details, Nominalization.

Accent marks

Accent marks and other diacritical marks placed over, under, or through letters are used, most commonly in dictionaries, to indicate pronunciation. Now that the dieresis to mark the syllable break in words like *cooperate* and *reentry* has largely disappeared, virtually the only accent marks in English are those retained on words taken from foreign languages:

Acute ('): attaché, resumé, détente
Cedilla (‿): français, garçon
Grave (`): cortège, derrière
Circumflex (^): crêpe, rôle
Dieresis (¨): naïve
Tilde (˜): cañon, piñon
Umlaut (¨): doppelgänger

In general writing, accent marks are usually dropped; newspapers rarely use them. An accent mark is sometimes used in English words to show that a syllable is pronounced, especially in verse: "blessèd artifacts" (John Hall Wheelock, "There Is a Place"). See Foreign words in English.

accept, except

Accept means "receive" or "say yes to"; *except*, as a verb, means "leave out" or "exclude." See *except, accept*.

Accusative case

In English six distinctive pronoun forms are often called accusative (or objective) forms and usually occur in the object function: *me, her, him, us, them, whom.* See Case 2; Gerunds 2; Infinitives 4b; *it's me;* Objects; *who, whom.*

Acronyms

Abbreviations pronounced as words are called acronyms (*WASP, WHO*). See Abbreviations 3.

Active voice

All verbs except those consisting of a form of the verb *be* and a past participle (*is cooked*) are in the active voice. See Voice. Compare Passive voice.

actually

Actually, like *basically* and *definitely*, is overused in speech. It is seldom necessary in writing even when meant literally: "My nomination for the 'most neglected book' is actually a trilogy" (Carlos Baker, *American Scholar*).

ad

Ad, the clipped form of *advertisement*, has no period. Like other clipped words it belongs to general and informal speech and writing.

A.D.

Since *A.D.* stands for *anno Domini* and means "in the year of our Lord," it precedes the date: 240 B.C. to A.D. 107. Logically, a century can't be labeled *A.D.;* and though some writers use the abbreviation as if it meant "after Christ" (the second century A.D.), the practice is not appropriate in scholarly or other formal writing.

ad hoc, ad hominem

Most Latin phrases beginning with the preposition *ad* are italicized in English, especially formal English. The most common exceptions are *ad hoc* and *ad hominem.* The first is most frequently used to describe committees established for a special purpose (ad hoc committees), as opposed to standing committees; the second describes arguments attacking a man's character instead of his reasoning (arguments ad hominem).

Adjectival clauses

Adjectival, or adjective, clauses modify nouns and pronouns: The man *who is speaking* is my uncle. See Adjectives 5, Relative clauses, Restrictive and nonrestrictive.

Adjectives

The function of an adjective is to modify—that is, to restrict or limit—a subject, object, or indirect object.

1. Position. We recognize adjectives in sentences chiefly by their position in relation to the nouns they modify, especially by the fact that they can stand between an article *(a/an, the)* and a noun or between a word like *our, this, some* and a noun: an *old* parka, their *youngest* son, this *characteristic* gesture, some *favorable* opportunity.

According to its position in a sentence, an adjective is either attributive or predicate. Attributive adjectives are placed next to their nouns, usually preceding (as in *tiny* brook, *horseless* carriages) but occasionally following (as in time *available*). Predicate adjectives come after a form of the verb *be* or some other linking verb, stated or implied *(taste, feel, turn):* The day is *warm;* That pie smells *good.* They precede the verb only in inverted sentence order: *Silent* was the night.

2. Forms. We also recognize some adjectives by their form. While many adjectives do not have a form that sets them off from other parts of speech *(high, civil),* others consist of a noun or verb plus a derivational ending or suffix. Some suffixes that are still being used to create adjectives are *-able* and *-ible (translatable, edible), -al (critical, hypothetical), -ed (sugared, four-footed), -ful (playful, soulful), -ish (darkish, childish), -less (harmless, fearless), -ous (callous, ferrous),* and *-y (cranky, dreamy, corny).*

Many adjectives are compared by adding *-er* or *-est* to the positive (or base) form or by preceding the positive form with *more* or *most: warm, warmer* or *more warm, warmest* or *most warm; talkative, more talkative, most talkative.* See Comparison of adjectives and adverbs.

3. Types. Traditionally, adjectives have been given three labels:

a. *Descriptive* adjectives are said to modify the noun by naming a quality or condition of the object named: a *gray* shutter, *vivid* colors, *difficult* words. They are ordinarily compared and may themselves be modified by qualifiers, words like *almost, very, quite.* Because new members are constantly being added, this class of words is said to be open.

b. *Limiting* adjectives point to, locate, or number: *her* book, *this* car, *third* period. See 5b.

c. *Proper* adjectives, derived from proper nouns, originally are limiting (French possessions) but also become descriptive (French culture). Sometimes they mingle both functions, as *Elizabethan* in "the Elizabethan drama" both limits drama to a period and brings to mind qualities of a group of plays. Proper adjectives are also an open class and may even be compared: He is *Frencher* than the French.

A proper adjective may be used so frequently in a merely descriptive sense that it becomes a simple adjective, written without a capital: *bacchanalian, pasteurized, diesel, india* ink.

4. Adjectives as subjects and objects. Preceded by an article, words that are ordinarily adjectives occur in the functions of nouns: the *just,* the *rich,* a new *low.* Though most such words don't have genitive or plural forms, some do (new *lows*).

5. Adjectival function. Since phrases, clauses, and words that are usually other parts of speech may, like adjectives, restrict or limit a subject, object, or indirect object, we can speak of an *adjectival* function.

a. Phrases and clauses used in adjectival function:

The man *with his hat on* is Harry.
I like the one *on the end* best.
Everyone *who approves* will raise his right hand.
That was the summer *we went to Bermuda.*
He asked the first man *he met.*

b. Other parts of speech in adjectival function. Participles are verbals that function as adjectivals: a *coming* attraction, a *deserved* tribute. They may combine with regular adjectives: a *long-billed* bird. They are not normally compared.

One of the most characteristic traits of English is the use of nouns in the adjectival function: a *glass* jar, the *Roosevelt* administration, *adjective* modifier, *high-school mathematics* test. In form, such words are nouns: they all may be inflected for plural and genitive. In context, because they occur in the same position adjectives occur in, we may call them adjectivals. Thus in isolation they are nouns; in context they may be either adjectivals (*home* cooking), adverbials (He went *home*), or nominals (My *home* is your *home*).

Traditionally, *this, that, his, other, former, two, second, both,* etc., have been called limiting adjectives. (*This, that, these,* and *those* have also been called demonstrative adjectives. See Demonstrative adjectives and pronouns.) Some grammarians find it clearer to classify all these words as determiners that usually perform adjectival functions. Unlike regular adjectives, they cannot be compared, they ordinarily do not occur as predicates, they are lexically empty, and they belong to a closed class – new ones are not added. See Determiners.

See Parts of speech. References: Francis, pp. 268–81; Quirk et al., pp. 231–67; Roberts, Chs. 4, 14; Sledd, pp. 79–80, 92–93.

adj Adjectives and style

Reconsider your choice of the adjective marked.

The adjectives you use should make your statements more precise or more forceful.

1. Adjectives that fail. Some adjectives are redundant. In *briny ocean, briny* adds nothing because all oceans are briny; *stark* adds nothing to *tragedy* or *madness* because most tragedies and madnesses are stark. All emergencies are sudden, so *sudden emergency* is redundant. Very general adjectives are often weak: *good, bad, beautiful, wonderful, terrific, fantastic, incredible, awful,* and so on communicate an attitude toward something, rarely any of its characteristics. The reader wants to know the particular sort of *good* – generous? virtuous? affable? delicious? efficient? Many adjectives that are exact enough have been used so frequently with certain nouns (*fond* farewell, *beady* black eyes) that they have become trite. Though most of us use inexact adjectives in conversation, in writing we should think twice before using any combination of adjective and noun that comes automatically to mind. See Triteness.

2. Adjectives that clutter. If you try too hard to paint a picture, you may pile up too many adjectives. Deleting most of them from this passage would improve the style:

In a hotel dining room there is not the clamorous, raucous bedlam of its immediate surroundings, but a refined, subdued atmosphere, pervaded by distinct, faintly audible sounds. The orchestra, with a barely perceptible diminuendo, concludes the melodic, slow-tempo arrangement, climaxed by the beautiful strains of the "Merry Widow" waltz – rising, falling, fading with plaintive supplication.

The stylistic effect is even worse when the words in adjectival position are nouns. Piling nouns in front of nouns produces prose that is heavy and hard to understand: The chairman selection committee progress report date has been changed = The date for the progress report of the committee on selecting a chairman has been changed. If a string of prepositional phrases is not very graceful, a string of nouns is less so.

3. Adjectives that work. Used sensibly and sensitively, adjectives reinforce meaning and improve style. As Herbert Read puts it, "Appropriate epithets may be either exact or happy." In most factual writing the first requirement of adjectives is exactness; they must answer the needs of the material. And in writing that makes a definite attempt to capture the feelings and sensations of the reader, the adjectives must also deserve the epithet "happy"; that is, they must seem to fit, as in this account:

He had a quick impression of hard-faced men with gray eyes burning some transparent fuel for flame, and said, "I won't go back. If you don't arrest me, I'm going on to the Pentagon," and knew he meant it, some absolute certainty had come to him, and then two of them leaped at him at once in the cold clammy murderous fury of all cops at the existential moment of making their bust . . . and a surprising force came to his voice, and he roared to his own distant pleasure in new achievement and new authority – "Take your hands off me, can't you see? I'm not resisting arrest. . . ." – Norman Mailer, *Harper's*

According to E. B. White, "The adjective hasn't been built that can pull a weak or inaccurate noun out of a tight place." True enough. And Carl Sandburg is said to have warned a writer, "Think twice before you use an adjective." This is probably sound advice for anyone who automatically attaches an adjective to every noun and so produces what a critic of the works of H. P. Lovecraft called "adjective-benumbed prose." But adjectives can help a writer describe his subject as he has seen it, and if he chooses the right ones – adjectives that are happy as well as exact – they will help the reader see it too.

See Description. Compare Adverbs and style.

Adverbial clauses
Adverbial clauses, so named because they function like adverbs, are dependent clauses that may be introduced by a variety of subordinators, including *as, as if, because, since, when, where*: He walks *as if his shoes are too tight; When they finally arrived*, all the tickets were sold. See Adverbs 2, 3.

Adverbs
Traditionally, the adverb as a grammatical category has been a ragbag, including a variety of words that modify verbs, adjectives, other adverbs, and whole clauses and sentences. Some words in the category, like *almost, very, quite, yes, no*, obviously differ in certain respects from more typical adverbs – they cannot be compared – and could be set off as different parts of speech; but because some of their functions resemble those of adverbs, they can also be regarded as adverbial and assigned to appropriate subgroups. Grammarians continue to experiment with new classifications.

1. Forms. Most adverbs are formed by adding *-ly* to adjectives or participles: *badly, deservedly, laughingly, surely*. Some adverbs have developed from Old English forms without a special adverbial sign: *now, then, here, there*.

A number of adverbs have the same forms as adjectives, including these:

bad	doubtless	hard	much	slow
better	early	high	near	smooth
bright	even	late	new	straight
cheap	fair	loose	right	tight
close	fast	loud	rough	well
deep	first	low	sharp	wrong

Most of these unchanged adverbs are matched by forms in -ly, with which they may or may not be interchangeable. See Adverbs and style.

Most adverbs are compared, either by adding -er and -est or by preceding them with more and most. See Comparison of adjectives and adverbs.

2. Functions. Adverbs are typically used in two functions:

a. To modify single words, phrases, and clauses: He came early (*early* modifies *came*); They were practically in the street (*practically* modifies *in the street*); Fortunately, no one was home (*Fortunately* modifies all of *no one was home*). In direct and indirect questions, *when, where, why,* and *how* perform adverbial functions even though they are not in the adverbial position at the end of a statement:

When did he leave? (*Compare* He left yesterday.)
Do you know why he left? (*Compare* He left because he was tired.)

As in all information questions, the item being questioned – in this case a time, place, reason, or degree question-word – is shifted to the beginning of its clause.

b. To connect separate sentences or the independent clauses of a compound sentence (see Conjunctive adverbs):

We found the dormitories empty, the classrooms silent and deserted. *Consequently* we returned to the city.

They agreed to call the matter closed; *however,* they were by no means convinced.

Phrases and clauses may also have the function of adverbs (see Phrases) and thus be classed as adverbials: He came *in the morning; After the exam* he quit; *When it was time to go,* she didn't know what to do.

Is *home* in "He went home" or *days* in "He works days" an adverb or a noun? The simplest solution is to define such words formally as nouns but functionally as adverbials. In most contexts and by most tests, *home* and *day* would be nouns: they occur in all noun contexts and with all noun inflections. But since they may also occur in positions normally occupied by adverbs, we can say that in such sentences they are nouns in adverbial functions or adverbials. The -al of *adverbial* indicates that we are defining these words by their syntactic function in the context, not by their form.

3. Position. Different subclasses of adverbs occupy different positions in sentences, and often a single subclass can occupy more than one position. Among the one-word adverbs, for example, qualifiers (like *very* and *extremely*) precede the words they qualify, different negatives (like *never* and *not*) occupy different positions with respect to the verb, and adverbs of manner (like *worse, keenly, openly*) often may stand initially, medially, or finally:

The air was *extremely* clear.
Tom had *never* liked pizza. Tom *never* had liked pizza.
Patiently she replied. She replied *patiently*. She *patiently* replied.

Some adverbial phrases and clauses have comparable mobility. In "When the tide turned, all the boats headed for the channel," the opening clause could be shifted to the end or, enclosed by commas, could be inserted between *boats* and *headed*. Whether its position should be changed is a matter of style.

See Parts of speech. References: Stanley Greenbaum, *Studies in English Adverbial Usage* (Coral Gables: Univ. of Miami Press, 1970); Long and Long, Ch. 38; Quirk et al., pp. 267–84, 743–56.

adv Adverbs and style

Correct the form of the adverb marked, change its position, or reconsider your choice of adverb.

1. Use the standard form of the adverb. You can say "He sang loud" or "He sang loudly"; both are standard. The short form is often preferred in general and informal English, the *-ly* in formal English. The choice is a matter of style. Problems arise when you fail to recognize the situations in which standard English does *not* offer a choice.

a. Omitting the *-ly* ending: Some adverbs have the same form as adjectives (see Adverbs 1). But most adverbs are formed by adding *-ly* to the adjective (*considerably, regularly, suddenly*). In such instances, the form without *-ly* is nonstandard: It hurt *considerable;* He did it *regular.* Use the *-ly* ending unless your dictionary recognizes its omission as standard.

b. Adding an unnecessary *-ly:* Even when an adverb has two forms, they are not always interchangeable. Although you can say "Drive slow" or "Drive slowly," you can't replace *close* with *closely* in "That shot came too close."

After a linking verb, a predicate adjective is called for, not an adverb: The breeze smelled sweet (*not* sweetly). Compare *bad, badly.*

Adding *-ly* to a word that already ends in *-ly* (*kindlily* for *kindly*) is a blunder. To make an adverbial from an adjective ending in *-ly* (*leisurely, orderly, worldly*), put the adjective in a prepositional phrase headed by a noun like *manner* or *way:* He approached us in a friendly way; she handled the subject in a scholarly manner. Adjectives in *-ly* that indicate time may function as adverbs unchanged: The train departed hourly.

2. Placing adverbs for clarity and style. Many adverbs can occupy different positions in a sentence (see Adverbs 3). When you have a choice, first of all place the adverb so that it makes the meaning clear: not "She answered the questions that the students asked patiently" but "She patiently answered the questions that the students asked" — if it was the answers and not the questions that were patient. Other considerations are rhythm and emphasis. Some writers hesitate to insert an adverb into a phrasal verb: instead of *have easily seen,* they write *have seen easily.* But *have easily seen* is smoother and more idiomatic. Normally an adverb should not be placed between a verb and its object. "He expects employees to obey promptly all his orders" should be revised to "He expects employees to obey all his orders promptly." See *only,* Split infinitive.

3. Making adverbs count. The use of adverbs, like the use of adjectives, should be at least precise and if possible happy. Adverbs are used unhappily when they are used unnecessarily and redundantly (Shrill horns scream *threateningly;* automobiles careen *wildly;* giant buses lumber *heavily* along), when they qualify excessively (the *seemingly* difficult problem of race relations), and when they set up a flutter of unstressed syllables (as in the first part of this sentence). Sometimes writers use an adverb to shore up an imprecise adjective or verb when an exact adjective or verb would be neater and at least as expressive:

Scholarships should be kept *for those who are academically industrious* [for the studious].

When no one was looking, I took the goggles and *swiftly made my way* [hurried] out of the store.

Many of the adverbs regularly used in conversation are better omitted in writing: *continue* [*on*], *refer* [*back*].

References: Copperud, pp. 6–7; Follett, pp. 50–55.

adverse, averse
Adverse is an adjective meaning "unfavorable" or "hostile" (adverse conditions). *Averse,* also an adjective, means "opposed" (I would not be averse to a short vacation).

advise
Besides meaning "to give advice," *to advise* is used to mean "to inform, to give information." In this sense the verb is commonly used for information that is rather formally given: Reporters were advised by an administration spokesman that. . . . In other situations simple *tell* is more appropriate: Peter tells us he won't be back next year.

affect, effect
Affect is usually a transitive verb meaning "influence" (This will affect the lives of thousands) or "put on" (He affected a stern manner). The noun *affect* is a technical term in psychology. *Effect* is most common as a noun, meaning "result": The effects will be felt by thousands. But it is also a formal verb meaning "bring about": The change was effected peaceably.

aggravate

In general and informal usage *aggravate* ordinarily means "annoy" or "irritate": The higher he turned the volume, the more aggravated I got. Formal writing still limits *aggravate* to the sense "make worse," as to aggravate a wound or a situation: Friction between faculty and administration was aggravated by cuts in the budget. The same division occurs in the use of the noun *aggravation*. References: Copperud, p. 8; Pooley, pp. 122–24.

agr Agreement

Make the verb or pronoun marked agree in form with the word to which it is related — its subject if it is a verb, its antecedent if it is a pronoun.

When used together, certain parts of speech "agree," or correspond in form in such a way as to express relationships of number, person, or gender. Several instances of agreement are illustrated in this pair of sentences:

This habit, which in *itself is* harmless, *is* likely to lead to *others* that *are* decidedly harmful.

These habits, which in *themselves are* harmless, *are* likely to lead to *another* that *is* decidedly harmful.

In English, agreement is largely a matter of linguistic etiquette. There are not many situations in which a change in grammatical form buttresses a difference in meaning. But when these situations occur, they are important: making your meaning clear — especially in writing — may hinge on your choosing the right form of a pronoun or the correct number of a verb.

1. Subject and verb agree in number (Those birds *were* seen; that bird *was* seen). There are four main causes of problems in subject-verb agreement: (a) phrases and clauses between subject and verb; (b) collective nouns as subjects; (c) compound subjects; and (d) dialect differences in verb inflection.

a. Most mistakes in agreement occur when a writer makes the verb agree with a word that is not the subject and that differs from the subject in number. The word is often a noun ending a clause or phrase that intervenes between subject and verb: An *analysis* of the extent to which audio-visual aids are used in schools *make* me conclude that books are no longer the chief means of education. The singular subject *analysis* calls for the corresponding verb form *makes*, but the writer has been misled by the plural noun *schools* immediately preceding the verb and perhaps also by *aids*.

b. The problem with collective nouns is, first of all, whether to treat the subject as singular or plural. If you're thinking of the group as a unit, make the verb singular (The first *couple* on the floor *was* Tom and Jane). If you're thinking of the individuals that make up the group, use a plural verb (When we found ourselves near where the old *couple were* living . . .). Once this problem has been solved, you simply need to make sure that the verb and any related pronoun are used consistently. If the team *was* very much on edge, the reason was that *its* (not *their*) big game was only a week away. Sometimes the pronoun will determine the verb form: When we found ourselves near where the old couple *were* living, we dropped in to see *them*. "We dropped in to see *it*" (even after *was living*) would be impossible; hence the *were-them* combination. See Collective nouns.

c. Problems with compound subjects usually arise either because a compound subject is felt to be singular or because the writer is uncertain about the conventions governing the use of correlative conjunctions. Some compound subjects designate a unit that calls for a singular verb: Bacon and eggs is my favorite breakfast. Other compound subjects may represent a unit to one writer, separate things to another:

Her loyalty and patriotism *was* unparalleled in the history of her people.

Her loyalty and [her] patriotism *were* unparalleled in the history of her people.

Before deciding to use a singular verb with a compound subject, be sure your audience will not only recognize your intention but accept the logic behind it. Only subjects that are closely allied (*loyalty* and *patriotism*) can reasonably be construed as a unit. This principle rules out "Her beauty and duplicity *was* apparent even to me," which would be taken as an error in agreement.

When both elements of a compound subject connected by the correlative conjunctions *either . . . or* or *neither . . . nor* are plural, the verb is naturally plural; and when both elements are singular, the verb is usually singular. When one of the subjects is singular and the other plural, the traditional rule is that the verb should agree with the nearer subject (Neither the ideas nor the style *is* satisfactory; Neither the style nor the ideas *are* satisfactory). Although actual usage varies, this is a sensible rule to follow. See Compound subject, Correlative conjunctions.

d. Some American dialects, notably Black English, lack an ending in the third-person singular, so that *do* and *see*, for example, are treated like standard English *can* (he can, he do, he see). Writers for whom this is the natural grammatical pattern feel the standard forms (he does, he sees) to be unreal and superfluous. When writing in a variety of standard English, they have the double problem of adding the ending to most present-tense, third-person-singular verbs (*starts, stops, sees*) and of not adding it elsewhere, as in plural verbs and past-tense forms. See Principal parts of verbs 2.

2. A third-person pronoun agrees with its antecedent in number and gender. If the antecedent (the noun to which it refers) is plural, the pronoun is *they, their(s),* or *them,* depending on its use in the sentence. If the antecedent is singular, the choice of pronoun is more complicated because gender enters in. Generally, if the noun refers to a male, we use *he, his,* or *him,* and if to a female, *she, hers,* or *her.* Otherwise, including situations where the sex is unknown or irrelevant, we use *it(s)*: The baby dropped *its* rattle; The dog was looking for *its* master.

Problems sometimes arise when the antecedent is a noun referring to a member of a group containing both sexes or a group of uncertain composition (each member of the class), or when it is one of the so-called indefinite pronouns, such as *one, anyone, everyone, no one, anybody, everybody,* or *nobody,* which, like *person,* are best regarded as indefinite nouns. When one of these words has a sphere of reference which includes only one sex, that sex generally determines the pronoun used: No one in the Girl Scout troop looked forward to *her* test [though *their* might be used here if everyone was taking the same test]. More often the reference includes both sexes, either actually or potentially. The problem then is that the common-gender *they* — because it developed rather indeterminately out of the plural *they* — is frequently looked upon as plural. In spite of the parallel with *you,* which also has both singular and plural functions, with the singular having likewise developed out of specialized uses of an original plural, many fail to recognize or acknowledge that *they* in indefinite reference is usually a singular pronoun. A form of *they* to refer to words like *everyone* (Everyone in the class turned in their paper [*or* papers] Tuesday) is now firmly established in informal English, is increasingly accepted in general, but is strongly resisted in formal. See Sexist language, *they.*

3. A demonstrative adjective, or determiner (*this, that, these, those*), usually agrees in number with the noun it modifies: *That coat* is expensive; *These shoes* cost more than my old pair did. See *kind, sort.*

agree to, agree with
One person agrees *to* a plan and agrees *with* another person. One thing agrees *with* another. Other idioms: I agree *in* principle; we agreed *on* a plan of attack; he agreed *to* fly or *on* flying or *that he would* fly.

ain't
Though in speech millions of Americans regularly use *ain't* as a contraction for *am not, is not, are not, has not,* and *have not,* it is never used in formal writing or in ordinary expository prose. When *ain't* does appear in general writing, it is almost always a deliberate attempt to suggest informality or down-to-earth common sense:

It will never reach the audience Welles might have and should have reached, because there just ain't no way. — Pauline Kael, *New Republic*

Those tiresome people with their tiresome quotes from Socrates about the fact that youth is going to the dogs are just trying to reassure themselves that it's all just a little bit more of the same. It ain't. — John M. Culkin, *New York Times*

See Divided usage. References: Bryant, pp. 16–17; Copperud, p. 9; Evans and Evans, p. 23.

all

Note the spelling of these words and phrases:

1. *all ready* (adjective phrase): At last they were all ready to begin.

2. *already* (adverb of time): They had already begun.

3. *all together* (adjective phrase): We found them all together in an old trunk.

4. *altogether* (adverb, equivalent to *wholly*): That's another matter altogether.

5. *all right* (adjective phrase): The seats seemed all right to me.

Alright now appears frequently enough to be accepted as a variant spelling by some dictionaries. Others specifically label it a misspelling, and many authorities consider it nonstandard. Reference: Copperud, p. 11.

Alliteration

Alliteration is repetition of the same sound, usually at the beginnings of several words in a series or at the beginnings of stressed syllables within several words. Besides possibly appealing to the reader's or listener's ear, alliteration serves to bind the phrase, or sometimes a whole series of phrases, into a unit: "the crowded, cloistered colleges of Oxford" (Paul Elmer More); "carried by wind and water and soil and seed" (John F. Kennedy).

Alliteration is one of the figures of sound that contribute to the musical effect of poetry. It is appropriate in formal prose that has oratorical or poetic overtones, and it occurs in some passages of description that are deliberately evocative: "like strange sea shells, their silken-nacreous lining welcoming the wind" (*New York Times*). But conspicuous alliteration is out of place in ordinary expository prose unless it helps reinforce meaning, as in "those crunching, nut-cracking Soviet consonants" (Alfred Kazin, *Starting Out in the Thirties*); otherwise it tends to attract attention to the expression at the expense of the idea. In writing of any kind, unconscious alliteration is likely to be distracting and may be disastrous. Check your first draft to get rid of unintentional alliteration that results from one combination of sounds summoning up another.

Compare Assonance.

all of

In general and informal usage *all* is followed by *of* in many constructions: All of the milk was spilled; They passed all of the candidates; You can't fool all of the people all of the time. In formal usage the unnecessary *of* is often omitted: all the milk, all the candidates, all the time. With personal pronouns and the relatives *who* and *which*, *all* may follow the pronoun (we all), or *all of* may precede it (all of us). *All of which* and *all of whom*, as subjects of relative clauses (four attempts, all of which failed),

are especially common and are more formal than their alternatives, *who all* and *which all* (four attempts, which all failed).

all that

"It didn't seem all that important," "It wasn't all that bad," and
similar uses of *all that* work well enough in conversation and in
informal writing but are likely to be criticized for imprecision in
more formal contexts.

all the farther

Although in some parts of the country *all the farther* is heard in
informal and general speech (This is all the farther I'm going),
standard written English uses an *as . . . as* construction: This is
as far as I'm going. Reference: Bryant, pp. 19–20.

Allusion

Loosely, an allusion is a brief reference to an event, person, or
place, real or fictional, that is not a part of the subject under discussion. Strictly, an allusion differs from a reference in that it
does not name the event, person, or place but mentions it indirectly. "This latter-day Paul Revere calls on us to arm against
our home-grown revolutionaries" is a reference to Revere. "His
signal is always a single lantern in the church steeple" alludes to
Revere, leaving it to the reader to make the connection through
his knowledge of Longfellow's poem.

In more elaborately contrived prose, a writer may incorporate
well-known phrases from a literary work, as in this sentence
with its deliberate echoes of *Hamlet* and *Macbeth:*

There is nothing new in heaven or hell not dreamt of in our laboratories;
and we should be amazed indeed if tomorrow and tomorrow and tomorrow failed to offer us something new to challenge our capacity for read-
justment. — Carl L. Becker, *The Heavenly City of the Eighteenth Century Philosophers*

By stimulating memory of a context — a historical event, the career of a celebrity, a scene in a play — a pertinent allusion enrich-
es the passage in which it appears and at the same time gives
the reader the pleasure of recognition. But the writer needs to
know his audience: an obscure or esoteric allusion will not only
be wasted but may be resented as pretentious. Like other aspects
of style, allusions should fit the rhetorical situation.

Reference: Follett, p. 58.

allusion, illusion

Allusion, discussed in the preceding article, should not be confused with *illusion,* a misapprehension or a misleading appearance (Smoking a pipe can create an illusion of wisdom).

almost

Most for *almost* is informal. See *most, almost.*

also

Also as an adverb ordinarily stands within a sentence, not at its beginning (They also serve who only stand and wait), but inversion may shift an *also* to initial position: Also defeated was the party's candidate for mayor. As a loose conjunction meaning "and," *also* is a weak sentence opener: He subscribed to eight magazines. Also he belonged to the Book-of-the-Month Club.

In many cases the information introduced with initial *also* should have been included in the preceding sentence: He subscribed to eight magazines and belonged to the Book-of-the-Month Club.

See Conjunctive adverbs. Reference: Copperud, p. 13.

alternative

Alternative comes from the Latin *alter,* "the second of two." Some formal writers, in deference to the word's origin, confine its meaning to "one of two possibilities," but it is regularly used to mean one of several possibilities and is so defined in dictionaries.

although, though

Although and *though* connect with the main clause an adverbial clause of concession—that is, a statement that qualifies the main statement but does not contradict it.

Although [Though] the rain kept up for almost three weeks, we managed to have a good time.

We managed to have a good time, though [although] the rain kept up for almost three weeks.

Here there is no distinction in meaning; the choice between the two may be based on sentence rhythm. *Although* is slightly more formal.

Often one of two clauses connected by *but* can be turned into an *although* clause for a slight change of emphasis:

We had rehearsed the act time and time again, but we all missed our cues the first night.

Although we had rehearsed the act time and time again, we all missed our cues the first night.

Although can't be substituted for *though* in a sentence like "He did it, though."

See *but.* References: Bryant, pp. 216–18; Follett, pp. 60–62.

alumnus, alumna

A male graduate is an *alumnus,* a female graduate an *alumna.* Two or more male graduates are *alumni,* two or more female graduates *alumnae.* The graduates of coeducational schools— males and females together—have traditionally been called *alumni;* but *graduates* itself is a sound, and sexless, alternative. Also sexless is *alums,* the plural of the clipped word, *alum.* See Sexist language.

a.m. and p.m.

These abbreviations (for *ante meridiem,* "before noon," and *post meridiem,* "after noon") are most useful in tables and lists of times but are also used in general writing for specific hours, usually with figures: from 2 to 4 p.m. (*not* I went there in the p.m.). Though *m.* is the abbreviation for noon (12 m.), *12 noon* is more common; midnight is *12 p.m.* See Hours.

amb ## Ambiguity
_____

Make your meaning unmistakable.

A word or phrase or sentence that is ambiguous is one that can be interpreted in two or more ways. Though the context usually shows which of the possible meanings is intended, the reader is momentarily confused and occasionally remains so. The most common sources of confusion are:

1. Inexact reference of pronoun, especially in indirect discourse: He *told* his father he had been talking too much. Rewrite as: He admitted to his father that he had been talking too much; or as: He criticized his father for talking too much. Or recast as direct speech. See Indirect discourse, Reference of pronouns 1.

2. Modifiers that can be misinterpreted.
a. Squinting modifiers may refer to either of two words or constructions: The governor penalized those officeholders who had opposed him *for good reason.* Rewrite as: The governor had good reason for penalizing those who had opposed him; or as: The governor penalized those who had had good reason to oppose him. The sentence "Some people I *know* would go there anyway" could not be misinterpreted if it began, "Some people *whom I know,*" or if it read, "Some people would go there anyway, *I know.*"
b. Modifiers should be clearly identified as restrictive or nonrestrictive. "Out-of-state students who were delayed by the blizzard will not be penalized for late registration" seems to mean that only the out-of-state students who were held up by the storm will be excused; but if the meaning intended is that all out-of-state students are home free, then commas are needed after *students* and *blizzard.* See Restrictive and nonrestrictive.
c. Modifiers should not mislead even momentarily. In revising a first draft, be on the lookout for puzzlers like the headline "Police Repair Man Killed by Car." See Hyphen 5.

3. Incomplete idioms, especially in comparisons: "I like Alice as well as Will" might mean "I like Alice as well as Will does," "I like Alice as well as I do Will," or "I like both Alice and Will."

4. Changing meanings.   Many words are undergoing changes in meaning. Sometimes the shift can be completed without risk of ambiguous communication because the context makes the intention clear. Before *car* came to apply primarily to an automobile, such restricting labels as *motor, railroad,* or *street* prevented misunderstanding. But when such safeguards are not present, serious misunderstanding may occur. See *censor, censure; disinterested, uninterested; imply, infer; incredible, incredulous; rhetoric; transpire.*

5. Intentional ambiguity. The literary artist may deliberately suggest multiple meanings, inviting the reader to draw inferences, to understand more than is said. Sleepy readers will see only what's on the page.

See Comma 6.

American

Because there is no simple adjective that corresponds to the United States of America (as *Italian,* for example, corresponds to Italy), *American* is ordinarily used. It is obviously inexact, since Canadians and Mexicans and Brazilians and others are as American (in the continental sense) as we are; and many Latins refer to themselves as Americans. But it is no more inexact than many other words, and the usage is standard. Use *American* as the adjective and the name of an inhabitant. Reference: Copperud, p. 14.

Americanism

Americanism, as a usage term, means a word or construction originating in the United States *(hydrant, zipper, realtor)* or first borrowed here, as from an African language *(goober, juke, okra),* an Indian language *(hominy, caucus, mugwump),* or from Spanish *(canyon, rodeo, lariat).* It also refers to a sense of a word added in the United States *(campus, carpetbagger, creek).* A *Dictionary of Americanisms,* edited by Mitford M. Mathews (Chicago: Univ. of Chicago Press, 1951), lists such vocabulary.

Americanism may be extended to include words continued in the United States after becoming obsolete in England *(loan* as a verb, *gotten)* or any item of usage characteristic of the United States and not of other areas of the English-speaking world. The label *American* or *chiefly U.S.* in dictionaries records such facts of usage. Americanisms in this extended sense are included in *A Dictionary of American English,* edited by Sir William A. Craigie and James R. Hulbert (Chicago: Univ. of Chicago Press, 1938–1944).

among, between

Between is used with two, *among* with more than two. But see *between, among.*

amount, number

Number is used only of countable things: a number of mistakes, a number of apples. *Amount* is preferred with mass nouns (a small amount of money, a certain amount of humor). Distinguishing between the two words often improves clarity and is therefore recommended. See Mass nouns. Compare *fewer, less.*

Ampersand

Ampersand is the name for the & sign (originally a linking of the letters of Latin *et*), called also *short and*. Because its primary use is to save space, it belongs only where abbreviations are appropriate. Otherwise, write out *and*.

Analogy

Analogies may be either figurative or literal. A figurative analogy suggests a resemblance between things or situations that on the surface are totally unlike: a mathematical equation and a Mozart quintet, for example, or a football team and an epidemic. There are no actual resemblances between an undefeated team and the Black Death; what they have in common is the capacity to mow down everything in their paths. This shared characteristic can be expressed in terms of the proportion a:b::c:d — the team figuratively slaughters its opponents as the Black Death killed its victims in the fourteenth century.

Literal analogies uncover relationships between two members of the same class, often revealing unexpected correspondences between widely separated historical events or persons. The attitude of young people toward marijuana laws in the 1960s has been analogized to the attitude of their grandparents toward liquor laws in the 1920s.

Whether compressed into a metaphor (the Muhammad Ali of the political ring) or elaborated through an entire essay, an apt analogy throws new light on the subject. Presenting the unfamiliar in terms of the familiar (the earth's strata in terms of the layers of an onion) is a common method of exposition. Here a writer relies on analogy to introduce his interpretation of recent changes in international relations:

There has been a radical transformation of power. In traditional conflicts, states were like boiled eggs: War — the minute of truth — would reveal whether they were hard or soft. Today interdependence breaks all national eggs into a vast omelet. Power is more difficult to measure than ever before. — Stanley Hoffman, *New York Times*

Analogy becomes the basis for argument when a writer tries to persuade his audience that because two situations are alike in some respects (current proposals for gun registration in the United States and gun registration in Nazi Germany), they are alike in still another (if enacted into law, the current proposals will result in government seizure of all civilian-owned guns). Although analogies are seldom sufficient to carry the full burden of proof, they can induce strong conviction; and if the likenesses cited have real bearing on the point at issue and the differences are not fundamental, analogies have logical force as well.

Whether used to explain or to persuade, an analogy can stir the imagination and stimulate thought. For both writer and reader, a good analogy opens the door to a fresh, inventive approach.

See Comparison and contrast, Figurative language.

Analogy in language

In linguistics *analogy* is the name for the natural tendency in users of a language to make their speech more regular by forming new words on the pattern of existing ones, bringing old words closer together in form, or bringing less common constructions into line with more familiar patterns. It results from the fact that, in general, the patterns of a language form a consistent though complex system (most English noun plurals end in -*s*, past tenses in -*ed*, and so on). It is easiest to observe analogy in the attempts of children to master their language. Before they learn the irregular conventional forms used by grownups, they regularize on the basis of the patterns they are familiar with, saying *mans*, perhaps, for *men* or *singed* for *sung*.

Analogy has removed many irregularities in the body of the language. Of various plural forms used in Old English, -*s* has won in all but a few words, and analogy is still bringing more words to that form, like *formula, formulas*. Occasionally the spelling of words is changed by analogy, as -*b* was rather recently added to *crumb* and *thumb* from analogy with *comb* and *dumb* – showing that analogy does not always result in a simpler form. Other words are in the process of changing: *cole slaw* is often replaced by *cold slaw*, and *alright* is slowly making its way from analogy with *already*. New words are formed on analogy with old ones, like *astronaut, telecast*.

The extension of *was* to the plural – a common form in nonstandard English, based on the analogy of most English verbs in the past tense (I did, we did; he went, they went) – illustrates not only the force of analogy but also the fact that the result, however logical and consistent, is not necessarily acceptable. To become standard English the analogical form must be frequently used by educated writers and speakers – and "we was" is not.

See *due to*. References: Raimo Anttila, *An Introduction to Historical and Comparative Linguistics* (New York: Macmillan, 1972), Ch. 5; Leonard Bloomfield, *Language* (1933; rpt. New York: Holt, 1961), Ch. 23; Bolinger, pp. 403–405; E. H. Sturtevant, *Linguistic Change* (Chicago: Univ. of Chicago Press, Phoenix Books, 1961), Chs. 2, 6.

Analysis

Analysis is the term applied to a wide range of intellectual undertakings – attempts to grasp the nature of a thing or concept, to separate a whole into its parts, to discover the similarities and differences between two or more things, to investigate origins, to attribute effects. The aim of analysis is to increase one's understanding of a subject. A writer may also use analysis as a guide to action; that is, he may analyze a rhetorical situation in order to decide how best to arrange his material or what details to include or what arguments to advance. See Cause and effect, Classification and division, Comparison and contrast, Definition, Logical thinking.

and

1. Appropriate uses. *And,* the most frequently used connective, joins two or more elements of equal grammatical rank:

Adjectives: a *pink* and *white* apron; a *blue, green,* and *white* flag
Adverbs: He drove *very fast* and *rather carelessly.*
Nouns: trees and *shrubs; trees, shrubs,* and *plants*
Verbs: I *found* the book and *opened* it at the exact place.
Phrases: in one ear and *out the other*
Dependent clauses: While the boys were swimming and [*while*] *the older folks were resting,* I was reading.
Independent clauses: The first generation makes the money and *the second spends it.*

2. Inappropriate uses. In careless writing, elements of unequal grammatical value are sometimes connected by an unnecessary *and:*

Main verbs and participles: Three or four men *sat* on the edge of the lake with their backs to the road, [and] apparently *watching* the ducks.

Independent and dependent clauses: A contract has been let to install new copper work on the Post Office [and] *which will give it the facelifting it needs.*

And sometimes appears where no connective is needed or where some other connective would show more clearly the logical relation: "Shah was a founding member of the Club of Rome and [but?] while he retains his membership, he did not attend last fall's gathering in Berlin" (Elizabeth Hall, *Psychology Today*). See Coordination 2.

3. To begin sentences. In current writing of all varieties, *and* may stand at the beginning of a sentence. Used with restraint, it can contribute to movement and emphasis. Overused, it can be damaging to both, as well as boring for the reader.

4. Omitted or repeated. *And* may be omitted in a series (Cousins, uncles, aunts – all the relatives were there), but if repeated again and again this omission contributes to a telegraphic style inappropriate in general writing. *And* may also be used between the items in a series as an effective way of giving emphasis to each: "I do not mean to imply that the South is simple and homogeneous and monolithic" (Robert Penn Warren, *Southern Review*).

and etc.

Etc. is the abbreviation for *et cetera,* in which *et* means "and." Therefore *and* before *etc.* is redundant. See *etc.*

and/or

Though *and/or* is used primarily in legal and business writing, it may be useful when three alternatives exist (*both* items mentioned or *either* one of the two): *fruit and/or vegetables* means "fruit" or "vegetables" or "fruit and vegetables." Its use in general writing is objected to by many readers both because *and/or* looks odd and because *and* or *or* alone is very often sufficient. Reference: Copperud, p. 16.

angle

Angle meaning "point of view" or "aspect" (from an economic angle) is general but carries a strong suggestion of jargon. In the sense of "scheme" or "plan" (What's his angle?), *angle* is slang.

Antecedent

An antecedent is the word, clause, or sentence that a pronoun or pronominal adjective refers to. It usually stands before the word that refers to it, but not always: We did not hear their call again, and when we found the Thompsons, they were almost exhausted. (*The Thompsons* is the antecedent of the pronominal adjective *their* and of the pronoun *they.*) For relations between antecedents and their pronouns, see Agreement 2, Reference of pronouns.

Anticipatory subject

In sentences like "It was Ann who found the food stamps" and "There are more important things than graduating," *it* and *there* are anticipatory subjects. See *it; there is, there are.*

Anticlimax

An anticlimax ends a series with an element much weaker than what precedes it. It may be intentional, as a form either of serious irony or of humor, or unintentional, a lapse of judgment on the writer's part: She had a warm and sympathetic personality, a quick and perceptive intelligence, beautiful features, and real skill at bowling.

Antithesis

The stylistic device of using neighboring statements that contrast sharply in meaning is called antithesis. Often the statements are presented in parallel form: He is shamed for being backward; he is scolded for being forward.

Antonyms

An antonym is a word that means approximately the opposite of another word: *hot, stingy, boring* are antonyms of *cold, generous, entertaining.* Most books of synonyms also give antonyms, as do the synonym entries in dictionaries. Reference: Bolinger, pp. 211 – 15.

any

1. Uses. *Any* is used primarily as an adjective (Any dog is a good dog) but also as a pronoun (Any will do).

In comparisons of things of the same class, idiom calls for *any other:* This book is better than any other on the subject. But *any* alone is used when different classes are compared: I like a movie better than any book.

2. Compounds with *any*. Anybody, anyhow, anything, and *anywhere* are always written as single words. *Any rate* is always two words: at any rate. *Anyone* is written as one word when the stress is on the *any* (Anyone would know that) and as two when the stress is on the *one* (I'd like any one of them). *Anyway* is one word when the *any* is stressed (I can't do it anyway) and two when the stress is about equal (Any way I try, it comes out wrong). If the word *whatever* can be substituted for the *any* (Whatever way I try, it comes out wrong), *any way* should be written as two words.

3. Pronouns referring to *anybody, anyone.* *Anybody* and *anyone* are singular in form and take singular verbs: anybody [or anyone] feels bad at times. They are referred to by *he, his, him* (Anybody knows what *he* deserves) or, since they often apply to a person of either sex, by a form of *they* with the meaning "he or she," "his or her," "him or her": "It is not usually possible to achieve intimacy with anybody in the back seat of a car; you have to live with them in every sense of the phrase" (Edgar Z. Friedenberg, *New York Review of Books*). Formal usage insists on a singular pronoun. See Agreement 2, *he or she, they.* Compare *every*. References: Evans and Evans, p. 36; Fries, p. 50.

4. Other forms. *Anyways* is regional for the generally used *anyway*, and *anywheres* is nonstandard for *anywhere*. Though objected to by many, *any more* now frequently appears in print as one word: "They want to protect all those traditional events whether or not they mean something anymore" (Herbert Warren Wind, *New Yorker*). *Any more* (or *anymore*) in a strictly affirmative context (Any more I do that) is a regional idiom.

Anyplace (now usually written as one word) has become a general synonym for "anywhere": "Life can be as good and rich there as anyplace else" (Granville Hicks, *Saturday Review*).

Reference: Copperud, p. 18.

Aphorisms

An aphorism gives good advice or expresses a general truth in concise form. See Epigrams and aphorisms.

Apostrophe

Insert an apostrophe where it belongs in the word marked; or take out an apostrophe that is incorrectly used.

Typical mistakes in the use of the apostrophe are *mans* for *man's*, *mens'* for *men's*, *it's* for *its*, and *their's* for *theirs*. Review these uses of the apostrophe:

1. In genitives. The most common use of the apostrophe is in spelling the genitive (possessive) case of nouns and of the words traditionally labeled indefinite pronouns (*anyone, nobody, someone* . . . .): Dorothy's first picture; the companies' original charters; everybody's business is nobody's business; the boys' dogs. It should be used in singular genitives of time and value even though they carry no idea of possession: a day's hike, this month's quota, a dollar's worth. In formal writing it is also pre-ferred in plural genitives of this kind (two weeks' work), but usage is divided (teachers college). For special examples of pos-sessive form, see Genitive case. Reference: Follett, pp. 434–35.

2. In contractions. The apostrophe shows the omission of one or more letters in contractions: *can't, I'm, I'll, it's (it is).*

3. In plurals. An apostrophe has ordinarily been used in plurals of figures, letters of the alphabet, and words being discussed as words: the 1920's, three *e*'s, the first of the two *that*'s. But cur-rent usage is divided, and the plurals of figures in particular are often made with no apostrophe: "In the mid-1950s, Hoffa was scratching to take over the union" *(Newsweek).*

4. In representing speech. An apostrophe may be used to show that certain sounds represented in the usual spelling were not spoken: "He turned to someone else on the landing outside and said, 'Paddy, 'ere, 'e doesn't want 'is duff,' and went to walk on" (Brendan Behan, *Borstal Boy).* This is a legitimate use, but too many apostrophes distract the reader. It is better to suggest oc-casional pronunciations of this sort than to try to represent all of them.

Apostrophes are not used in the genitive of the personal pro-nouns: *his, hers, its, ours, theirs, yours;* and they should not be introduced into words that do not have them. *Till* is not *'till* or *'til.*

Apposition, appositives

Beside a noun or noun-equivalent in a sentence, we may place another nominal expression called an appositive: My aunts, *Mary and Agnes,* moved to Boulder in 1969. The noun headword, or head, and its appositive refer to the same person or thing. Typ-ically, the appositive is set off by commas, but sometimes no punctuation is needed (He caught so many fish that we called him Jim *the fisherman*).

An appositive agrees in case with its head; the case of the head is determined by its relation to the rest of the sentence: The win-ners [subject as head], Al and *I*, will lend bus fare to the losers [object as head], you and *him.* See Headword.

Don't insult your readers by using appositives unnecessarily. For example, in referring to the President of the United States, either the President's name or "the President" is sufficient iden-tification.

References: Jespersen, pp. 93–95; Quirk et al., pp. 620–48.

Arabic numerals

Arabic numerals are the ones we normally use: 1, 2, 3, etc. See Numbers 3.

Archaic words

When words drop out of all spoken and written use, they are said to be obsolete. When they are old-fashioned but still used occasionally or in special circumstances, they are called archaic. Examples are *anon* for *at once* or *soon*, *betimes* for *quickly*, *parlous* for *dangerous*, *doth* for *does*, and the *thou* and *saith* of some church services. Archaic words should be used only for very good stylistic reasons. They seldom fit in general writing.

Argument

Aside from its everyday meaning of "disagreement" or "dispute," *argument* is used in three distinct ways. It refers to an entire speech or essay that is designed to produce conviction. Or it refers to the line of thinking, the string of key propositions that runs through a piece — "the argument" of a book or a poem. Or it designates a reason for believing what might otherwise seem doubtful; in this sense "an argument" can be a single sentence. Thus in presenting his argument (first sense) to Congress, a legislator may use as his argument (second sense) the thesis that wiretapping should be discontinued, and he may offer as one of his arguments (third sense) the proposition that wiretapping is an illegal invasion of privacy.

Argument in the first sense may make appeals that are primarily intellectual or primarily emotional. Either kind of appeal can be used well or badly, for good purposes or bad.

Sometimes argument is distinguished from persuasion on the basis of purpose: argument is designed to change the mind of an audience; persuasion is designed to make an audience act. Normally both purposes are included when argument is classed as one of the four forms of discourse.

See Analogy, Deduction, Fallacies, Forms of discourse, Induction, Logical thinking, Rhetoric, Syllogisms.

arise

Arise is the formal word for *get up*. See *rise, arise, get up*.

around

Around, like *about*, can be used to mean "approximately." See *round, around*.

Articles

Traditionally *a* and *an* are known as indefinite articles, *the* as the definite article. Traditional grammars call articles adjectives; structural grammars call them function words; transformational grammars group them under determiners. See *a, an;* Nouns 3c; Parts of speech.

as

Among the meanings of *as* are "while" (As we walked along, he told us stories) and "because" (His speed is amazing, particularly as he weighs 260 pounds). *While* is preferable to *as* if the emphasis is on the time of the action (While we were walking along, he told us stories). And though *as* is used to mean "because" (or "since") in all varieties of English, many readers dislike the usage, which can easily be ambiguous: As we have continued responding to erratic change in Asia, our position has inevitably become more complex. (Does *as* mean "because" or "while"?) Reference: Copperud, p. 22.

For the growing tendency to use *as* where *like* would be expected, see *like, as*.

as . . . as

1. *As I* or *as me*. In a sentence like "He dislikes her as much as I/me," meaning determines whether the nominative *I* or the accusative *me* is used. The nominative implies the sense "as much as I dislike her"; the accusative, "as much as he dislikes me."

In a sentence like "They sent for someone as big as I/me," the choice of *I* or *me* does not affect the meaning. Both the nominative and the accusative are good English.

For a third type of sentence – "He is as big as I/me" – in which there is no preceding noun or pronoun in the accusative position, usage has always been divided. The nominative *I* is preferred in formal contexts and is insisted upon by many stylists.

2. Omitted *as*. Writers frequently omit the second *as* in a comparison of equality (as big as) when it is joined by *or* or *if not* to a comparison of inequality (bigger than): It was as large or larger than last year's crowd. But many readers and writers regard the omission as inelegant and prefer the complete form: It was as large as, or larger than, last year's crowd. Sometimes the second comparison can be moved to the end of the sentence: It was as large as last year's crowd, if not larger. Reference: Bryant, p. 57.

3. *As . . . as* and *so . . . as*. *As . . . as* is much more common than *so . . . as* in simple comparisons of degree (as big as that, as late as you like). Unlike *so . . . as*, it is suitable for both affirmative and negative statements. Many handbooks have urged that *as . . . as* be used only in affirmative statements (She's as clever as any of them) and *so . . . as* in negative statements (She's not so clever as she thinks); but the distinction has never become established in practice. Reference: Bryant, pp. 26–27.

as if, as though

In formal English the subjunctive is commonly used after *as if* and *as though:* He acted as if [*or* as though] he *were* losing his temper. In general English the indicative is usual: He acted as if [*or* as though] he *was* losing his temper. See Subjunctive mood.

as, like

As is the conjunction (He voted as he was expected to); *like* is the preposition (He voted like the rest). See *like, as*.

Assonance

Assonance is the repetition of vowel sounds in words having different consonant sounds *(brave–vain, lone–show)*. It is characteristic of verse and also occurs in prose, especially in heightened style: "that ideal country, of green, deep lanes and high green banks" (Osbert Sitwell). Like unintentional alliteration, unintentional assonance can be distracting.

as though

As though is commonly followed by the subjunctive in formal English but not in general English. See *as if, as though.*

as to

As to is often a clumsy substitute for a single preposition, usually *of* or *about:* Practice is the best teacher as to [in, for, of] the use of organ stops. In some locutions it is completely unnecessary: [As to] whether college is worthwhile is a question we must all try to answer. But in specifying a subject initially, it is preferable to more cumbersome expressions like *as regards, as concerns, with respect to:* As to the economic value of going to college, the effect on earning power is clearly established.

as well as

When an *as well as* phrase between subject and verb gives a strong impression of adding to the subject, some writers treat it as part of the subject and let it influence the number of the verb: The singer as well as four of the band members *were* arrested. In such cases the phrase is not set off by commas. According to traditional grammarians, however, the phrase is parenthetical, is usually set off by commas, and has no bearing on the verb: "This volume, as well as others, consists of a collection of basic articles" (Robert R. Wilson, *ISIS*). Reference: Pooley, p. 80.

at about

At about can be reduced to either *at* or *about*. But see *about* 3.

athletics

When the collective noun *athletics* refers to sports and games, it usually takes a plural verb and pronoun: Our athletics *include* football, basketball, and baseball. When *athletics* refers to a skill or activity, it usually takes a singular verb and pronoun: Athletics *is* recommended for every student.

author

An author writes a book. Does a writer author a book? *Author* as a verb is widely used (by publishers, among others) but also widely disapproved. It may be most defensible in referring to publication by a group (the report was authored by the President's Commission on Campus Unrest) and to autobiographies of celebrities "as told to" professional writers. Reference: Copperud, p. 27.

Auxiliaries

A verb used with another verb to form a phrasal tense or, in the case of *be,* to change the active voice to the passive is called an auxiliary verb or helping verb. The most common auxiliaries, *be* and *have,* are used in forming the progressive and perfect tenses and the passive voice: I am going; He has gone; They were shot. The modal auxiliaries — *can, may, shall, will, must, ought to, should, would,* and *might* — are used to refer to future time and to suggest possibility, necessity, or obligation: He will go; You should reply; He must leave.

As a group, the auxiliaries play a major role in the structure of sentences, not only in questions (Does he know?) but also in negatives (He has not left), in emphatic affirmatives (They *are* working), and in substitutes for verb phrases: Jo could not have enjoyed the evening, and neither could Mary [have enjoyed the evening]. When no *be,* auxiliary *have,* or modal auxiliary is available for a question, negation, or affirmation, the meaningless *do* fills the structural position.

He works late.
Question: Does he work late?
Negation: He does not work late.
Affirmation: He *does* work late.
Substitution: If anyone works late, he does.

A few other verbs, such as *get,* resemble these structurally defined auxiliaries in some respects *(was arrested, got arrested)* but do not participate in the basic syntactic patterns (instead of "Got he arrested?" we say, "Did he get arrested?"). See Modal auxiliaries, Parts of speech, Tenses of verbs, and entries on the individual verbs. References: Jacobs and Rosenbaum, Chs. 14–15; W. Freeman Twaddell, *The English Verb Auxiliaries,* 2nd ed. (Providence: Brown Univ. Press, 1965).

awful

In formal English *awful* means "inspiring with awe." In informal English it is a convenient utility word of disapproval — "ugly, shocking, ludicrous" (awful manners). General writing avoids the confusion by seldom using the word except to intensify meaning: " . . . delusions that are being chosen by an awful lot of people in preference to standard, orthodox explanations" (Elizabeth Janeway, *Atlantic*). This use of either *awful* or *awfully* (an awfully long wait) is deplored by some authorities. References: Copperud, p. 28; Pooley, p. 127.

awhile, a while

Awhile is an adverb (They talked awhile). Strictly, a prepositional phrase in which *while* is a noun should be in three words (for a while, in a while), but *awhile* is increasingly common: "It had been found that many nonimmigrants, after they had been here for awhile, decided that they would like to stay" (Marion I. Bennett, *Annals*).

awk Awkward

R **Rewrite the passage to make the phrasing smoother and more effective.**

Awkward is a general word of disapproval sometimes used in correcting essays. It may refer to unnecessary repetition of a sound or word, unsuccessful alteration of normal word order, overloading of a sentence, or any phrasing that attracts unfavorable attention or handicaps a reader. Several kinds of awkwardness occur in this passage:

Primarily an agricultural country, New Zealand's dairy products are of a quality unknown to pollution-threatened, chemical-saturated America. As high as anywhere in the world are New Zealand's sanitation standards, and rigid animal inspection procedures are, even in the sparsely populated areas, rigidly enforced. These facts, combined with cattle and sheep which graze all year round on natural grass pasture lands, produce products with a uniquely wonderful fresh-tasting flavor.

The way to correct a phrase or sentence marked *awkward* is to rewrite. *Index* articles that deal with and illustrate specific weaknesses that may be labeled *awkward* include Coordination, Nominalization, Passive voice, Reference of pronouns, Repetition, Shifted constructions, Subordination, Wordiness, Word order.

B

bad, badly

Bad is ordinarily used as the adjective (a bad apple) and *badly* as the adverb (He speaks badly). Because the position after a linking verb is usually filled by a predicate adjective, we would expect "I feel bad about it," as well as "He looks bad" and "It tastes bad." But after *feel, badly* is widely used to modify the subject, particularly in speech. In formal written usage, *bad* is preferred. In general writing, the choice often depends on which form fits the rhythm of the sentence.

Bad as an adverb (I played bad all day) is informal.

Badly meaning "very much" (He wanted it badly) is standard, and *badly off* is general as a group adjective: "But we are not Satan. Fallen though we are, we are not that badly off" (John Morris, *American Scholar*).

References: Bryant, pp. 35–36; Copperud, p. 102.

Bad grammar

Bad grammar is used as a term of reproach and is applied to all sorts of locutions, from "I ain't got none" to imaginary confusions in the use of *shall* and *will*. It is too vague and emotional a term to be useful. See *grammatical, ungrammatical*.

Balanced sentence

When parallelism in a sentence produces structures that are noticeably alike in length and movement, the sentence is said to be balanced: "But we must go on or we will go under" (Douglas MacArthur, *Centennial Review*). Though associated with ornate style, balance can make any statement emphatic, often by bringing out likenesses or differences: "Grammar maps out the possible; rhetoric narrows the possible down to the desirable and effective" (Francis Christensen, *Notes Toward a New Rhetoric*). See Parallelism.

be

1. Forms. The forms of *be* are more numerous and more varied than those of any other English verb:

Present: I am, you are, he is; we, you, they are
Past: I was, you were, he was; we, you, they were
Infinitive: be
Present participle: being
Past participle: been

Sometimes *be* (in all persons) is used as a present subjunctive and *were* (both singular and plural) as a past subjunctive.

Some old forms survive in stock phrases (the powers that be) and in the nonstandard "You ain't [sometimes "be'n't"] going, be you?" Nonstandard also uses *was* in the plural (Was the Adamses there?), leveling the past tense to one form *(was)*, like the past of other English verbs.

2. As a linking verb. *Be* is the most common linking verb, joining a subject and a predicate noun (Jerome was the secretary) or predicate adjective (She is sick). When it joins a subject and a pronoun, the pronoun is in the nominative case in formal written English (It was *he*), in the accusative in informal (It was *him*). "It's I" is formal for the general "It's me." See *it's me*.

When the infinitive *be* has a subject and complement, both are in the accusative form: I wanted *him* to be *me*. When the infinitive has no subject, formal usage has a nominative as the complement (I wanted to be *he*); general usage more often has an accusative (I wanted to be *him*).

3. As an auxiliary verb. Forms of *be* are used with the present participles of other verbs to make the progressive tense: I *am* asking; he *was* asking; you *will be* asking. Forms of *be* with past participles form the passive voice: I *am* asked; you *will be* asked; he *was* asked. In general English a form of *be* may be omitted in the second of two clauses with subjects of different number: One was killed and six wounded. Formal style would have "were wounded."

4. As a verb of independent meaning. *Be* is sometimes considered a verb of independent meaning when indicating states or positions: He was at home anywhere; The fire was just across the street. In its unmistakable use as an independent verb with the sense "exist," "live" (Hamlet's "To be, or not to be"; Can such things be?), *be* is now rare.

See *ain't,* Subjunctive mood.

because

Because introduces an adverbial clause giving the reason for the statement in the main clause: *Because* we were getting hungry, we began to look for a convenient restaurant. *Since* and *as* can be used in such clauses, but they are less definite, more casual.

Because also finds some use in informal contexts where a more formal style would insist on *for*—that is, where *because* introduces the premise for a conclusion, not the cause of an effect:

Informal: Komarov clearly had some control over his ship, because he was able to orient it well enough to accomplish re-entry.

More formal: Komarov clearly had some control over his ship, for he was able to orient it well enough to accomplish re-entry. *—Newsweek*

See *as, for, reason is because.* For *because of,* see *due to.*

Begging the question

Begging the question is the logical fallacy of assuming a conclusion that needs to be proved. The debater who bases his argument for reform on the assertion "This unfair method of voting must be changed" begs the question of the method's fairness. Though in a broad sense we all beg questions all the time—"Use enough evidence to prove your point" begs the question of how much is enough—as a deliberate tactic in argument, begging the question is notably unfair. See Fallacies.

Beginning an essay

Revise the opening of your essay to make it lead more directly and smoothly into your subject or to arouse your reader's interest.

The best advice for beginning a short paper is "Get on with it." An elaborate windup is silly when the pitch is to be no more than a straight throw in a backyard game of catch. And an opening that indulges in philosophizing ("Since the days of Plato's Academy, violence and learning have been alien entities") or announces a grand strategy ("In the paragraphs that follow, I shall attempt, first by analyzing and then by synthesizing, . . .") is equally silly in a two-page paper on a campus controversy.

Ordinarily, the first step is to let your reader know what you are writing about—not by telling him what you are going to discuss but by discussing it: "We think of the drug addict as unwilling or unable to work, but he works harder to get his dope than most of us do to get our daily bread" ("Addicts in the Wonderland of Work," *Psychology Today*). This does not rule out a personal approach; there may be good reason for you to tell why you have chosen your topic or how you are qualified to discuss it. It does rule out beginnings that fail to begin.

In addition to getting the essay under way, the opening paragraph or two should interest a reader enough to make him want to continue. But straining for humor or excitement or cuteness or sentiment is no way to go about it. Such attempts often distract or mislead. And as imitations of the techniques used by some professional journalists, they are likely to fail: the humor doesn't amuse; the excitement doesn't stir; and so on. Instead of trying out gimmicks, move into your topic and treat it with the interest *you* feel. If it doesn't interest you, your chances of making it interest your readers are slim. If it does interest you, and if you write about it as honestly and directly as you know how, your readers will keep reading.

For long papers – from five to ten pages, say – somewhat more elaborate beginnings are justified and perhaps necessary. But getting on with the discussion remains fundamental. If you sketch the historical background of a problem, make sure that this material contributes to solving the problem.

beside, besides

Beside is used chiefly as a preposition meaning "by the side of," as in "beside the road," "beside her"; it is used figuratively in a few rather formal idioms like "beside the point," "beside himself with rage." *Besides* is used as an adverb meaning "in addition" (We tried two other ways besides), as a preposition meaning "in addition to" (Besides ourselves, no one was interested), and as a conjunctive adverb (He didn't think he ought to get into the quarrel; besides, he had come to enjoy himself).

between, among

Among implies more than two objects: They distributed the provisions among the survivors. *Between* is most strictly used of only two: They divided the prize between Kincaid and Thomas. But attempts to limit *between* to use with only two items have failed. When the relationship is between individual items, *between* is the word to use no matter how many items there are:

There are often two or more possible arrangements between which a choice must be consciously made. – H. W. Fowler, *Modern English Usage*

This is so . . . of some part of the debate between Einstein, Bohr, Wolfgang Pauli, and Max Born. – George Steiner, *Atlantic*

When treating a group as a collective unit, use *among:* Divide the books among the poor. References: Bryant, pp. 38 – 40; Copperud, p. 32; Pooley, pp. 129 – 31.

between you and me

Although *you and I* as the object of a preposition or a verb is frequently heard and has a long history in written English, anyone who uses it now is apt to be thought only half-educated. *Between you and me* is always correct. See Hypercorrectness.

bi-

Although *bicentennial* offered no problem, there is much confusion about some time words beginning with *bi-*. *Bimonthly* and *biweekly*, for example, may mean either "every two . . ." or "twice a. . . ." And *biennial* means "every two years" whereas *biannual* means "twice a year." Where the context does not distinguish exactly the time meant, it is safest to use phrases like "every two months," "twice a day," "twice a year."

Bible, bible

When referring to the Christian Scriptures, the word is capitalized but not italicized: You will find all that in the Bible. In the sense of an authoritative book, the word is not capitalized: *Gray's Manual* is the botanist's bible.

These are the usual forms of particular references to parts of the Bible: the Old Testament, the New Testament, the Ten Commandments, Exodus 20 (or Exodus XX), Exodus 20:3-17, I Corinthians 4:6. The adjective *biblical* is seldom capitalized.

Bibliographical form

The details of bibliographical form in a research paper may differ from author to author, from publication to publication, and especially from discipline to discipline. In some sciences, for example, a list of the references cited replaces the full bibliography of the humanities, only the first word of a book title is capitalized, the title of a journal article is omitted entirely, and the name of a journal is abbreviated. Whatever the style your instructor recommends, remember that the first rule for bibliographical form, as for footnote form, is consistency. Follow one style of documentation throughout.

The entries in a bibliography are listed alphabetically, according to the last name of each author. When no author is given, the first important word of the title—whether of a book, of a chapter or selection in a book, or of an article in a magazine, newspaper, or encyclopedia—serves as the key word for alphabetizing (*Manual* for *A Manual of Style*). Each entry begins at the left margin. Subsequent lines are indented five spaces.

The entries that follow conform closely to recommendations in *The MLA Style Sheet*, second edition. (There, short forms of the names of publishers are approved. If your instructor wants you to use short forms, examples can be found in the list on pages 384–85.) Examine each entry carefully to see what elements are included, what order they appear in, and how they are punctuated. Entries may be double-spaced, if your instructor prefers.

A book by a single author and a second book by the same author

```
Katz, Jerrold J.  The Philosophy of Language.  New York:
      Harper & Row, 1966.
            .  Semantic Theory.  New York: Harper & Row,
      1972.
```

Instead of repeating the author's name, use a ten-space line.

A book by more than one author

Brady, James E., and Gerard E. Humiston. <u>General Chemistry</u>:
    <u>Principles and Structure</u>. New York: Wiley, 1975.

Do not reverse the names of co-authors following the first author's name:
Bryant, Barbara, William Jensen, and Ann Wagner. If there are more
than three authors, substitute *et al.* for all but the first: Gorenstein,
Shirley, et al.

A work in more than one volume

Sewall, Richard B. <u>The Life of Emily Dickinson</u>. 2 vols.
    New York: Farrar, Straus & Giroux, 1974.

If the books in a multivolume work are published over a period of years,
the full span is given: 1909-49.

An edition other than the first

McArthur, Lewis A. <u>Oregon Geographic Names</u>. 3rd ed.
    Portland: Binfords, 1952.

An edition revised by someone other than the author

Robertson, Stuart. <u>The Development of Modern English</u>. 2nd
    ed. Rev. by Frederic G. Cassidy. Englewood Cliffs,
    N.J.: Prentice-Hall, 1954.

An edited work

Agnon, S. Y. <u>Twenty-one Stories</u>. Ed. Nahum N. Glatzer.
    New York: Schocken Books, 1970.

A compilation by an editor

Baratz, Joan C., and Roger W. Shuy, eds. <u>Teaching Black
    Children to Read</u>. Washington, D.C.: Center for
    Applied Linguistics, 1969.

A selection, chapter, or other part of a compilation

McKeon, Richard. "Rhetoric in the Middle Ages." <u>Critics
    and Criticism</u>. Ed. R. S. Crane. Chicago: Univ. of
    Chicago Press, 1952.

A translation

Merleau-Ponty, Maurice. <u>Phenomenology of Perception</u>. Trans.
    Colin Smith. London: Routledge, 1962.

A book that is part of a series

Degler, Carl N. <u>Affluence and Anxiety: America Since 1945</u>.
    2nd ed. The Scott, Foresman American History Series.
    Glenview, Ill.: Scott, Foresman, 1975.

A reprinted book

Whitehead, Alfred North. <u>Modes of Thought</u>. 1938; rpt.
    New York: Putnam, Capricorn Books, 1958.

A signed article in a newspaper

Cady, Steve. "Dreams Grow from Asphalt." <u>New York Times</u>,
    13 July 1975, Sec. 5, p. 3, cols. 6-7.

An unsigned article in a weekly newsmagazine

"Nixon's Fight for Life." <u>Newsweek</u>, 11 Nov. 1974, pp. 26-29.

An article in a monthly magazine

Litten, Walter. "The Most Poisonous Mushrooms." <u>Scientific
    American</u>, March 1975, pp. 90-101.

A journal article

```
Ong, Walter J.   "The Writer's Audience Is Always a Fiction."
    PMLA, 90 (1975), 9-21.
```

PMLA is the title of the journal, and 90 is the volume number. Because this journal (unlike most newspapers and magazines) is paged continuously throughout the calendar year, only the year is given, in parentheses, after the volume number. But if the volume does not coincide with the calendar year, as in the following example, the month is included. Note that when the volume number is given—without "Vol."—page numbers are not preceded by "pp."

A journal article with corporate authorship

```
NCTE Commission on Composition, "Teaching Composition: A
    Position Statement," College English, 36 (October
    1974), 219-20.
```

A signed encyclopedia article

```
We[intraub], S[tanley].   "George Bernard Shaw."   Encyclopaedia
    Britannica.   Macropaedia 16, 1974.
```

A book review

```
Wood, Michael.   "Incomparable Empson."   Review of William
    Empson:  The Man and His Work, ed. Roma Gill.   New
    York Review of Books, 23 Jan. 1975, pp. 30-33.
```

An unpublished dissertation

```
Teague, Frances Nicol.   "Ben Jonson's Stagecraft in His Four
    Major Comedies."   Diss. Univ. of Texas, 1975.
```

See Footnote form, Research papers. References: James D. Lester, *Writing Research Papers*, 2nd ed. (Glenview, Ill.: Scott, 1976); *The MLA Style Sheet*, 2nd ed. (New York: Modern Language Association, 1970).

"Big" words
A word is "big" if it is too heavy or too formal for the subject. See Diction 2.

black
Since the 1960s the term *Negro* has been replaced in a great deal of writing by *black*, usually not capitalized. *Afro-American* is also used.

born, borne
In most senses the past participle of *bear* is spelled with a final *-e:* The tax burden was borne by the middle class; The conclusion was borne out by the evidence; The ewes had borne many more lambs. But the spelling *born* is used in the senses "brought into being," "determined by birth," in the passive voice: A child was born; Corruption is born of public apathy; He was born to be hanged. Thus "She has borne three children," but "Three children were born to her." Both *borne* and *born* are used as modifiers: an airborne soldier, a born soldier.

both

Both is a favorite way of emphasizing two-ness: The twins were both there; Both Harry and his brother went. Though neither is necessary, each of the *both*s gives a legitimate emphasis. In "They were both alike," on the other hand, *both* awkwardly duplicates the meaning of *alike*. "The both of them," a fairly common spoken idiom, should be avoided in writing.

both . . . and

When used as a pair (both the tire and the tube), the coordinating conjunctions *both* and *and* are called correlative conjunctions. See Correlative conjunctions.

Bound modifiers

A bound modifier is a restrictive modifier: The horse *that I picked* came in third. See Restrictive and nonrestrictive.

Brackets

Brackets have specific uses in academic writing. Their main function is to enclose editorial interpolations within quoted material. Here they are used to clarify references: "The story answers precisely . . . to that told in the third paragraph of Curll's *Key:* 'But when he [Thomas Swift] had not yet gone half way, his Companion [Jonathan Swift] borrowed the Manuscript to peruse' " (Robert Martin Adams, *Modern Philology*).

In quoted material, *sic* in brackets indicates that an error in the original is being reproduced exactly: New Haven, Connecicut [sic]. Brackets may also be used to insert a correction: Cramer writes, "In April 1943 [the month was July], Jones published his first novel." And brackets function as parentheses within parentheses, particularly in legal documents and scholarly footnotes.

If your typewriter keyboard does not have brackets, you can make them with diagonals and underscores ($/\overline{}\ \overline{}/$) or put them in by hand.

In this *Index* brackets are used in examples to enclose words or marks of punctuation that might better be left out (In [the course of] the next year I read such books as . . .), to suggest improvements (The contraption made a noise similar to [like] a concrete mixer), and to indicate alternatives (He has proved [*or* proven] his case).

bring, take

Bring implies motion toward the speaker (Bring it with you when you come); *take* implies motion away from him (Take it with you when you go). When the speaker (or writer) is doing the moving, he is glad he *brought* his camera along; when he has returned, he is glad he *took* the camera and *brought* it back. In situations in which the point of view is of no significance, either form is used: Potatoes were brought [*or* taken] from Ireland to France.

bring up

Bring up (like *raise*) is general usage (That's the way I was brought up) for the more formal *rear* or *nurture*. It also means "to introduce" a subject: Having brought it up, he couldn't stop talking about it. See *raise, rear*.

British English

In the written language there are noticeable differences between British and American English in spelling. The British still prefer *-re* to *-er* in ending words like *center* and *theater*, though they use both forms; they still keep *-our* in a number of words where Americans use *-or;* they use *x* in a few words like *inflexion* where Americans use *ct;* they double more consonants, as in *traveller, waggon;* and they spell some individual words differently, such as automobile *tyre* for U.S. *tire*. They use hyphens more freely than we do (*no-one* and *hand-book*) and single rather than double quotation marks. Differences such as these are just pervasive enough to show that a book is of British or American origin but certainly not enough to interfere with comprehension.

The grammar of the popular levels of British and American English differs somewhat—contrast the speech of ordinary people in novels and movies of the two countries—though less than vocabulary. Collective nouns are more likely to be plural in British usage (the government intend); British writers differ in small matters like the position of *only,* the proper preposition with *different,* the use of *shall,* and various idioms (see *different*). A fairly long catalog of such minor differences could be drawn up, but their importance should not be exaggerated nor their occurrence allowed to obscure the fact that the resemblances far outnumber the differences and that the speech of the two countries represents two strands of the same language.

References: W. H. Mittins et al., *Attitudes to English Usage* (London: Oxford Univ. Press, 1970); Randolph Quirk, *The English Language and Images of Matter* (London: Oxford Univ. Press, 1972), Chs. 1–4.

Broad reference

A pronoun referring to a preceding idea rather than to a particular antecedent is said to have a broad reference. See Reference of pronouns 2.

bug

Both as a noun for an electronic listening device and as a verb for the planting of such a device (They bugged his home phone), *bug* has become established in general English.

bunch

In formal English, *bunch* is limited to objects that grow together like grapes or can be fastened together like carrots or keys. Used of people, *bunch* is moving into the general vocabulary: ". . . another monumental American myth—that Washington is run by a bunch of cynical, untrustworthy fools" (Nona B. Brown, *New York Times Book Review*).

burglar, robber, thief

All three take what is not theirs; but the robber uses violence or threats, and the burglar breaks into a building. See *rob*.

burst, bust

Burst is the unchanged past tense and past participle of the verb *burst. Bust* (with *bust* or *busted* as past tense and participle) is a nonstandard variant of *burst* in its literal meanings: dams and balloons burst (*not* bust).

But in contexts where the meaning is figurative, *bust* (frequently with the adverbs *up* and *out*) is now common, though still somewhat informal (The game was busted wide open). And of broncos and trusts and noncommissioned officers, *bust* is general; *burst* cannot be substituted in these senses. Nor can *burst* be substituted when *arrested* is meant, as in "He was busted for possession of marijuana."

Business letters

Business letters include not only the correspondence sent out by companies and corporations but also the letters of individuals to business firms, colleges, government agencies, newspapers, civic organizations, and so forth. When you write a letter to apply for a job or a scholarship, to obtain information, to request assistance, or to register a complaint, the recipient is most likely to give it serious attention if you have done your best with the packaging as well as the content.

1. Materials and appearance. Use good-quality white paper measuring 8½ by 11 inches. If at all possible, type your final draft. Keep a carbon of every business letter you write.

Most business letters are now written in block style without indentions, as shown in the sample. Convention calls for one line of space between inside address and salutation, between salutation and body, and between body and close. Three lines of space are usually left for the written signature. Other spacing depends on the length of your letter. In your drafts – and you may need to write several – work for an attractive, balanced page, with generous margins and plenty of white space at top and bottom.

If you can sensibly do so, limit your letter to a single page. When you must write more than one page, number the additional pages.

2. Heading. Give your full address and the date. Unless you use the abbreviations adopted by the Postal Service (which are not followed by periods), write out the names of states. Note that there is no comma between state and ZIP code and no punctuation at the ends of lines. If you use stationery with a letterhead that provides the address, type the date beneath it.

3. Inside address. Give the name and full address of the recipient, just as it will appear on the envelope, beginning each line at the left margin. How far down the page you begin the inside address will depend on the length of your letter. For good balance, a short letter should naturally begin lower than a longer one.

Whenever possible, direct your letter to an individual or at least to an office (Personnel Director) or a department (Personnel Department).

4. Salutation. When you are writing to a person you can name, the best greeting is the simplest:

Dear Ms. Nash:
Dear Mr. Mahoney:

Note that a colon follows the name. When the circumstances call for special formality, "Dear Sir" or "Dear Madam" is the right choice. If you are addressing an organization or an anonymous individual, the traditional greeting is "Dear Sirs" (or "Gentlemen") or "Dear Sir."

5. Body. Your first paragraph should make the subject of your letter clear. Let your reader know immediately the circumstances of your writing. If you're replying to a letter, answering an advertisement, or writing at the suggestion of someone known to your reader, say so. By making clear from the outset why you're writing, you help your reader concentrate immediately on what you have to say.

Your paragraphs will usually be much shorter than in an essay — often no more than two or three sentences. Use a new paragraph for each item or each subdivision of your message, so that your reader can swiftly identify the specific requests you're making or the information you're providing and can refer to them in his response.

The style of a business letter should be clear, direct, and as brief as is consistent with clarity and completeness. The tone should be brisk without being brusque. You don't want to waste your reader's time, but neither do you want to insult him. And while being concise, be careful not to mystify him. Provide all relevant information, especially if you are complaining about defective merchandise, outlining a proposal, or seeking a job.

Finding a suitable voice for your letter may require some effort, since you will often have little notion what sort of person your reader is. Under such conditions, attempting to make your writing seem personal may instead make it sound artificial and insincere. On the other hand, if you make no attempt to approach the reader as an individual, your writing may sound cold and aloof. The best technique, then, is to address the reader as a stranger but as an intelligent, respected stranger, who is probably short of time.

Don't make the mistake of trying to write in what you may think of as business style. The good business writer of today uses general English, avoiding both the clichés of commerce *(contact, finalize, angle, and/or)* and pretentious words like *ameliorate* for *improve*, *terminate* for *end*.

6. Close and signature. Begin the close at the left margin, in the middle of the page, or aligned with the heading—depending on overall balance—and follow it with a comma. For most business letters, "Sincerely," or "Sincerely yours," is appropriate. If you're writing as an official—as purchasing agent of a campus co-op, for example—give your title under your typed name:

```
              Leslie Archer
              Purchasing Agent
```

In typing her name, a woman may or may not choose to indicate her marital status: Dorothy Olson

```
              (Miss) Dorothy Olson

              (Mrs.) Dorothy Olson

              Dorothy Olson
              (Mrs. Henry Olson)
```

7. Mailing. An envelope measuring 4 by 10 inches is best for business letters, but a smaller envelope ($3\frac{1}{2}$ by $6\frac{1}{2}$ inches) may also be used. Repeat the inside address on the envelope, and give your own name and address in the upper left corner.

Heading	431 University Place Madison, Wisconsin 53706 November 12, 1976
Inside address	Mr. Dwight Morrison Program Director WSTR Television 546 Main Street Madison, Wisconsin 53703
Salutation	Dear Mr. Morrison:
Body	Members of the Sociology Club at the University of Wisconsin have been examining the influence of the University on the surrounding community, and we believe that some of our findings may be of interest to your viewers. In order to assess the importance of the University to local business, we have talked with many shop owners about the products they carry to attract student customers. We have looked into the way political opinions in some Madison neighborhoods have changed since students began taking an active role in local elections. And we have found that a tutorial project started by students has begun to change some people's attitudes toward the University. Members of the Sociology Club would like very much to discuss with you the possibility of using our study as the basis of a special program. Two or three of us could arrange to meet with you at your convenience.
Close	Sincerely yours,
Signature	*Marilyn Thompson* Marilyn Thompson President Sociology Club University of Wisconsin

but

But is the natural coordinating conjunction to connect two contrasted statements of equal grammatical rank. It is lighter than *however*, less formal than *yet*, and, unlike *although*, does not subordinate the clause that follows it.

1. Connecting equals. The locutions connected by *but* should be of equal grammatical rank:

Adjectives: not *blue* but *green*
Adverbs: He worked *quickly* but *accurately.*
Phrases: He finally arrived, not *at lunch time* but *in the early evening.*
Clauses: The first day we rested, but *the second we got down to work.*
Sentences: The Rio Grande defied the best engineering minds of two countries for a century; but *$10,000,000 in flood-control work harnessed the treacherous stream.*

See *which* 4 for comments on *but which.*

2. Connecting statements in opposition. The statements connected by *but* should be clearly opposed: "He knows vaguely that the nation is not much good any more; he has read that the crust of the earth is shrinking alarmingly and that the universe is growing steadily colder; but he does not believe that any of the three is in half as bad shape as he is" (James Thurber, *My Life and Hard Times*). In "Our view was limited to about twenty yards down Tuckerman Ravine, but beyond that everything was in clouds," the statements are not genuinely opposed because "was limited" includes the idea of "only." So *but* should be deleted. The two clauses can better stand side by side as partial statements of a complex fact, an effect and its cause.

3. Minor uses.
a. As a subordinating conjunction, after some negative constructions and in some questions:

Nothing would do but I must spend the night with them.

I never go by a hospital and smell anesthetic, but I know we die. – Harvey Breit, *Esquire*

Who knows but everything will come out right?

b. As a preposition, equivalent to *except* (no comma preceding):

They asked none of the family but her.

A New Englander talks about everyone's income but his own.

c. As a formal adverb, equivalent to *only:* In that village there was but one light on after midnight.
d. As a relative pronoun in formal constructions like "There was no one in town but knew [who did not know] the whole story."

4. At beginning of sentences. *But*, like *and*, often stands at the beginning of sentences, especially if the sentences are short. The separation emphasizes the contrast with the preceding clause. But when a clause beginning with *but* (or *nevertheless* or a similar word) is followed by another clause beginning with *but*, both the contrast and the logic break down.

5. Punctuation. Two clauses connected by *but* should ordinarily be separated by a comma. The contrast in ideas makes punctuation desirable even when the clauses are relatively short: I couldn't get the whole license number, but it began with AOK. One of the most common punctuation errors is the use of a comma after an initial *but:* But [,] it was too late for the aging man to regain his lost skill. No punctuation should separate *but* from the clause it introduces.

References: Copperud, p. 39; Fowler, pp. 68–69.

but that, but what

Although formal style avoids *but that* as a subordinating conjunction after a negative (I do not doubt [but] that he will come), it is common in general and informal. In the same construction *but what* sometimes appears. Here, too, *that* can be substituted. References: Bryant, pp. 46–47; Copperud, pp. 38–39.

but which

If you write a clause that begins "but which," be sure it's preceded in the sentence by a *which* clause. See *which* 4.

C

c.

Often italicized, both *c.* and *ca.* are abbreviations for the Latin *circa*, "about," and are used to indicate that a date is approximate or uncertain. "Geoffrey Chaucer (c. 1340–1400)" means that Chaucer was born about 1340. The same uncertainty may be signaled by a question mark: (1340? to 1400).

can, may (could, might)

1. To express possibility, both *can* and *may* are used. *Can* is reserved for simple ability ("I can swim" meaning "I am able to swim") and for feasibility ("I can swim today" meaning "There is nothing to prevent me from swimming today"). *May* is also used to express feasibility, particularly in formal writing: "The Introduction only hints at the many paths the reader may follow" (Anna Benjamin, *Classical Philology*). Stylistically, habitual use of *may* in this sense can create an excessively tentative tone.

2. In requesting permission, *may* has a cool politeness appropriate to formal occasions: May I add one further point? Informally, *can* requests permission.

In granting or denying permission, *may* is also formal: "The Board adhered to the view that an employer . . . may not lawfully refuse recognition" (Howard Lesnick, *Michigan Law Review*). But except in institutional contexts, where the notion of authority is central, the more democratic *can* is apt to be chosen: "After forbidding the Colonel to speak of love to her, she . . . tells him he can" (Henry Hewes, *Saturday Review*).

3. Might and could, originally the past of *may* and *can*, are now used chiefly to convey a shade of doubt, or a smaller degree of possibility than *can* and *may:* He could be here by Sunday; I might have left it in my room. *Might could* is regional for *might be able to:* I might could borrow a car.

See Divided usage. References: Bryant, pp. 48–49; Copperud, p. 41; Long, pp. 138–42.

cannot, can not

Usage is divided; *cannot* is more common.

can't hardly

Since *hardly* means "probably not," *can't* (or *cannot*) *hardly* should be changed to *can hardly.* See Double negative.

can't help but, can't seem to

Can't (or *cannot*) *help but* and *can't* (or *cannot*) *seem to* are established general idioms:

The reader cannot help but question whether they, indeed, were so universally excellent. — Peter Wall, *Annals*

What they can't seem to tolerate is unemployment, the feeling of being useless. — Alfred Kazin, *Saturday Review*

Even so, *cannot help but* is avoided by many conservative stylists (who may prefer *cannot but,* or *cannot help* followed by a gerund: cannot help saying); and formal usage would have *seems unable to* rather than *cannot seem to.* See *seem.* References: Bryant, pp. 49–50; Copperud, pp. 41, 42.

cap Capital letters

Capitalize the word marked.

Certain uses of capitals, as at the beginning of sentences, for proper names, and for *I,* are conventions that almost everyone observes. Other uses of capitals are matters of taste. Formal English uses more capitals than general English, and newspaper style cuts them to a minimum. The best policy is to follow convention that is well established and not to capitalize in other situations without good reason.

1. Sentence capitals. Capitalize the first word of a sentence.
a. Capitalize the first word in a complete sentence that you enclose in parentheses and place between two other sentences. But don't capitalize it if you insert it in parentheses within a sentence or set it off with a dash or dashes.
b. Capitalize the first word in a sentence following a colon if you want to emphasize it (He promised this: The moment agreement was reached, the trucks would roll).
c. In dialog capitalize the first word of any quoted utterance but

not the second part of an interrupted quoted sentence: "Well," he said, "it was nice to see you again." Except in dialog, don't capitalize parts of sentences that are quoted: "Stressing that legal restrictions on surveillance are few, he rallied the assembled with the intelligence that 'the challenge is wide open'" (David M. Rorvik, *Playboy*).

2. Proper names. Capitalize proper names and abbreviations of proper names: names of people and places, months, days of the week, historical events (the Civil War, the Council of Trent, the New Deal), documents (the Treaty of Paris), companies and organizations, trade names, religious denominations, holidays, races and ethnic groups (but see *black*), languages, ships, named trains and planes, and nicknames. See Course names.

a. Capitalize *north, south,* and so on when they denote particular regions (She was much more familiar with the Southwest than with the East) but not when they indicate direction (They started west in 1849).

b. Capitalize *army, navy,* and so on when they appear in full titles (the United States Army, the British Navy) and when they stand for the teams of the service academies. In other cases usage is divided: the American army (or Army), their navy (or Navy).

c. Capitalize *college* as part of a full title (He went to Beloit College) but not as a level of schooling (Neither of them went to college).

d. Don't capitalize proper nouns that have become common nouns (*tweed, sandwich, bohemian, diesel engine, plaster of paris*). Many proper adjectives in senses that no longer suggest their origins are not capitalized (*india ink*) but other such adjectives usually are (*French cuffs, Bessemer process, Bordeaux mixture*).

e. Don't capitalize the names of the seasons except in *Fall term, Spring semester,* and so on, or for stylistic reasons.

3. Titles of books, articles, etc. Capitalize the first word and last word (and the first word after a colon), all nouns, pronouns, verbs, adjectives, and adverbs, and all prepositions of more than five letters: *With Malice Toward Some; Socialist Humanism: An International Symposium; Now Don't Try to Reason with Me;* "Biological Clocks of the Tidal Zone"; "Computer Control of Electric-Power Systems."

4. Titles, positions, relatives.

a. Capitalize personal titles before proper names: President Taft, Ambassador Clark, Senator Lodge, Sergeant York. When the title alone is used to refer to an individual (the Colonel was there), usage is divided, though "the President" for the President of the United States is still customary.

b. Capitalize the names for family members used as proper nouns: We had to get Father's consent. Do not capitalize when they are used as common nouns: My sister and two brothers are older than I am.

5. Deity. Capitalize *God, Jesus,* and nouns such as *Savior.* With pronouns referring to them, practice is divided: *He, Him, His,* or *he, him, his.*

6. *Street, river, park,* and so on. Capitalize such words as *street, river, park, hotel,* and *church* when they follow a proper name (Fifth Avenue, Missouri River). Abbreviations too should be capitalized: 2319 E. 100th St.

7. Abstract nouns. Usage is divided. Abstract nouns are likely to be capitalized in formal writing (less often in general) when the concept they refer to is personified or when they refer to ideals or institutions: The State has nothing to do with the Church, nor the Church with the State.

8. Quoted lines of verse. Follow the poet's capitalization exactly.

9. Stylistic capitals. Some writers use capitals as a form of emphasis, to lead the reader to stress certain words or give them more attention: "And a woman is only a woman, but a good Cigar is a Smoke" (Rudyard Kipling, "The Betrothed"). The effect is sometimes amusing, but unless you're feeling confident, avoid this practice.

References: *A Manual of Style;* Copperud, p. 42; *U.S. Style Manual.*

✗ Careless mistakes

Correct the obvious and apparently careless mistake marked.

Careless lapses are inevitable in hurried work. But an essay is not expected to be hurried work. Comma faults and fragments, mistakes in the forms of verbs and pronouns (*broke* for *broken, it's* for *its*), missing words, and scores of other slips are likely to occur if you give too little time or too little attention to the final stages of preparing a paper.

Train yourself to proofread carefully. Check your manuscript for such elementary mistakes as these:

letters omitted (the *n* of *an,* the *d* of *used to,* a final *y*)

end punctuation omitted, including the closing quotation marks after a quoted passage

words run together (*a/lot,* in *a/while*)

words confused that are closely related in sound or spelling (*affect, effect; principal, principle; quite, quiet; than, then; there, their; to, too; whether, weather; who's, whose*)

Check for the unnecessary repetition of a preposition or a conjunction: It is only natural *that* with the sudden change in the administration *that* people are worrying about what new policies might be instituted.

If you are uncertain about the spelling of a word, consult your dictionary. If you are unsure what word, word form, construction, or punctuation to use, consult this *Index.*

Caret

This inverted *v* points to the place in a line of manuscript where something written above the line or in the margin should be inserted:

```
                                                    because
There was no reason for them not to get good grades,∧all
they did was study.
```

This is an acceptable way to revise papers so long as the revisions are few in number and are completely clear.

A caret used by an instructor as a correction mark indicates an omission.

Case Case

Correct the mistake in case.

The case of a noun or pronoun is one indication of its relationship to other elements in the sentence. (The second indication is word order.) The subject of a verb and the complement of a linking verb are in the subjective or nominative case *(Who is she?)*; the object of a verb or preposition is in the objective or accusative case (I introduced *him* to *her*); certain modifiers of a noun (*his* hat, the *dog's* bone) are in the possessive or genitive case.

Except for the spelling differences in the genitive singular *(cat's)*, the genitive plural *(cats')*, and the common plural *(cats)*, the case of nouns presents no problems: the same form is used in both subject and object positions (Your *cat* chased my *cat*). Pronouns have more forms—especially those pronouns we use most often. And because we may be in the habit of using a few nonstandard forms in speech, the case of these pronouns causes some problems in writing. Most of the problems relate to the six pronouns that change form to indicate all three cases: *I, he, she, we, they, who* (and its variant *whoever*). Thus: *She* sings (nominative); The song pleased *her* (accusative); It's *his* song, not *hers* (genitive). Note that four of these pronouns have a second form of the genitive, used when the pronoun does not stand before a noun: *mine, hers, ours, theirs*. The pronouns *it* and *you* change their form only in the genitive *(its; your, yours)*. These pronouns, as well as the indefinites, have the same form whether they are subjects or objects.

Here are the basic conventions to observe in standard written English:

1. Use the forms *I, he, she, we, they, who(ever)*

a. In subject position: *She* and *I* played on the same team; *He* asked *who* wrote the play (*who* is the subject of *wrote*, not the object of *asked*); *Whoever* wrote it had a good ear for dialog.

b. In apposition to a noun or pronoun in subject position: The winning couple, Phil and *I*, got a trip to Disneyland; We, Phil and *I*, got a trip. . . .

c. After a linking verb: It is *he* who should pay the bill. (But see *it's me*.)

2. Use the forms *me, him, her, us, them*
a. In object position: The song reminded Jack and *me* (object of verb) of our high-school graduation; College is harder for *him* than for *me* (object of preposition—see also *between you and me*). The object of the infinitive is often in the accusative case (I wanted to be *him*) in general writing and always in informal; the nominative (I always wanted to be *he*) is the rule in formal writing.
b. In apposition to a noun or pronoun in object position: Prizes went to the top students, Mary and *me*; The prizes went to us, Mary and *me*.

3. The special problem of *whom(ever).* The object form *whom(ever)* is regularly used after a preposition: To whom was the remark addressed? But speakers and writers sometimes deliberately use *who* for the object of a verb when it stands at the beginning of a sentence, especially in questions. Although "Whom do we turn to for advice?" is the choice of some formal stylists, others would use *who*, which has become widespread in general usage: Who do we turn to for advice? See *who, whom.*

4. Use the genitive case of nouns and pronouns to indicate possession and the other relationships discussed in Genitive case 2, except when the *of* phrase is customary (the end of the street, the roof of the house): It was the other *man's* hat, not *his*; the mixup resulted from *their* putting them on the same hook. *"Their* putting" illustrates the standard form for a pronoun that is the subject of the gerund. When a noun is the subject of the gerund, the accusative is common in informal and general English and is the choice of some formal writers: He complained of the *book* (more formal: *book's*) going out of print. See Gerunds 2.
 Avoid the nonstandard forms *hisself* (for *himself*) and *theirself* or *theirselves* (for *themselves*).
 See Pronouns 1, 4; Genitive case.

case
In case for *if* (In case you're driving east, I'd like a ride) is a general idiom that is avoided in formal writing. *In any case* appears in formal usage but is objected to by some as vague and ambiguous. And the group preposition *in the case of* is frequently deadwood: In [the case of] television commercials, stereotypes are as inescapable as they are deplorable. Reference: Copperud, p. 43.

catholic, Catholic
Written with a small letter, *catholic* is a rather formal synonym for "universal or broad in sympathies or interests." In general American usage, *Catholic* written with a capital is taken as equivalent to *Roman Catholic*, both as a noun (She is a Catholic) and as an adjective (Catholic labor unions).

Cause and effect

Why something occurred (cause) or *what* will result from it
(effect) often interests us as much as *what* happened.

1. Signals of cause-effect relations. Causal connections are conveyed by explicit statements (*A* caused *B*; *B* is the effect of *A*),
by many familiar transitional words and phrases (*because* or
since, so that or *in order that, thus* or *as a result*), and sometimes by the simple device of juxtaposing statements (In March
he was told he had cancer; three months later he shot himself).

2. Discovering causes. Essays that investigate cause range
from discussions of historical events and scientific experiments
to arguments that attribute responsibility or predict the consequences of a policy. Almost all causal analysis has an argumentative edge to it, for the writer is always attempting to win acceptance for a *probable* interpretation of facts. He therefore has to
do more than simply state his conclusion; he must justify and
support it by demonstrating, offering specific information, knit-
ting probable cause to known effect or probable results to an existing situation.

Because we have a habit of leaping to the most obvious answer, anyone analyzing causes and effects must discipline himself to keep an open mind until he has collected enough evidence
to make a convincing case. But he needs to keep in check another tendency, too—the tendency to keep searching out causes that
are more and more remote. There is no need to go back to Genesis to explain the genesis of an event of current, local interest.
Finally, he should resist the tendency to end up showing not that
something happened *because of* something else—the whole
purpose of causal analysis—but merely that something happened *after* something else. Confusing temporal sequence with
cause results in the logical fallacy of *post hoc, ergo propter hoc,*
"after this, therefore because of this." See Fallacies, Logical
thinking.

2. Testing causes. John Stuart Mill formulated five methods or
canons for testing causal relationships. Outside the laboratory
they have practical limitations, for they assume that all circumstances can be known, that controlled experiments can be repeated, and that only a single cause is operating. Even so, they
are valuable in stressing the need for rigor in any causal inquiry.
Here, followed by very simple examples, are Mill's canons, with
punctuation modernized:
a. *The method of agreement.* If two or more instances of the
phenomenon under investigation have only one circumstance in
common, the circumstance in which alone all the instances
agree is the cause (or effect) of the given phenomenon. (If several people have an attack of food poisoning after eating lunch
in the same cafeteria, and if it is learned that the one item their
meals had in common is smoked fish, it is probable—but not certain—that the smoked fish caused the food poisoning.)

b. *The method of difference.* If an instance in which the phenomenon under investigation occurs, and an instance in which it does not occur, have every circumstance in common save one, that one occurring only in the former, the circumstance in which alone the two instances differ is the effect, or the cause, or an indispensable part of the cause of the phenomenon. (If two people had exactly the same menu except that one added smoked fish, and if he became sick while his companion did not, the fish was probably – but not certainly – the cause of his illness.)

c. *The joint method of agreement and difference.* If two or more instances in which the phenomenon occurs have only one circumstance in common, while two or more instances in which it does not occur have nothing in common save the absence of that circumstance, the circumstance in which alone the two sets of instances differ is the effect, or the cause, or an indispensable part of the cause of the phenomenon. (This method combines the first two; it suggests the process of testing over an extended period of time used by doctors to isolate, through elimination of various possibilities, the cause of an allergy.)

d. *The method of residues.* Subduct from any phenomenon such part as is known by previous inductions to be the effect of certain antecedents, and the residue of the phenomenon is the effect of the remaining antecedents. (If only four people could have committed a crime and three can be proved not to have done it, then the fourth is presumed guilty.)

e. *The method of concomitant variation.* Whatever phenomenon varies in any manner whenever another phenomenon varies in some particular manner is either a cause or an effect of that phenomenon, or is connected with it through some fact of causation. (If a field which is heavily fertilized yields a better crop than one which has received half as much fertilizer and a much better crop than one which has received none at all, the farmer concludes that there is probably a connection between the amount of fertilizer he uses and the yield of the crop.)

Reference: Irving M. Copi, *Introduction to Logic*, 4th ed. (New York: Macmillan, 1972), Ch. 12.

censor, censure

When we *censure*, we condemn or disapprove. When we *censor*, we delete or suppress. But *censorious* refers to censuring.

center around

Although some condemn it as illogical, *center around* (The story centers around the theft of a necklace) is standard idiom:

We could sometimes look out on shooting and fights that seemed to center around this saloon. – Edmund Wilson, *New Yorker*

. . . accompanied by a propaganda war centered around her rightness and fitness for the throne. – Kerby Neil, *Modern Philology*

In formal styles precisionists may substitute *on* or *upon* for *around* or use *revolve* instead of *center*.

Centuries

The first century A.D. ran from the beginning of the year 1 to the end of the year 100, the nineteenth century from January 1, 1801, through December 31, 1900. Thus, to name the century correctly, add one to the number of its hundred except in the last year, when the number of the hundred is the number of the century, too. We live in the twentieth century.

For clarity, the hundred can be named, even in formal writing: Dr. Johnson lived in the seventeen hundreds. Similar practice – with and without the century – is standard in naming decades: the nineteen twenties, the thirties.

cf.

Cf., an abbreviation of the Latin *confer*, means "compare." See Abbreviations 2.

Chronology

One of the ways a good narrative achieves coherence is through chronology – what happened next. Because what happens goes on in a temporal sequence, a narrative finds its chief organizing principle and its momentum in *then* and all the related indicators of time – *later, next, after that, meanwhile, the following day, finally*, and so on. See Narration, Transition.

Circumlocution

A circumlocution is a roundabout way of saying what could be expressed concisely. See Wordiness.

claim

Used in the sense of "say" or "declare," *claim* suggests to many readers that the assertion should be regarded skeptically or scornfully: He claims to be opposed to thought control. Using it as a mere variant of *say* (He claimed he was taking Chemistry 301) can therefore be misleading.

Classification and division

Classification and division are related methods of investigating and writing about a subject. Division is the process of separating a single object (a car) or institution (a college) or concept (communism) into its parts or constituent elements. Classification is the process of bringing together objects, institutions, or concepts that have something in common: cars, colleges, political philosophies can be sorted into groups on the basis of their resemblances. Division reveals internal structure; classification identifies family likenesses. In writing an essay on college life, you might draw on both methods, analyzing the curriculum or campus social life and classifying students on the basis of their attitudes toward their courses or the ways they use their leisure time or some other principle.

As the example suggests, one group can be classified in many different ways, and the same object can be divided into different collections of parts, depending on the writer's purpose or interest. That interest will determine whether the division or classification should meet strict requirements of completeness (all parts or items accounted for) and consistency (no overlapping of parts or of groups). Some groupings are deliberately alogical, making no attempt to be either complete or consistent ("Some Nuts on a Knotty Family Tree"); their purpose is simply to entertain. But a writer interested in trying to organize his experience – the real purpose of classifying or dividing – will work hard to make his analysis reasonably complete and consistent. And if he has selected an original basis for dividing or classifying, he may offer his readers a new way of looking at the world.

See Logical thinking.

Clauses

Each combination of a complete subject with a complete predicate is traditionally called a clause. "He came home" is an independent clause; grammatically it can stand alone. "When he came home" is a dependent clause. In ordinary prose it does not stand alone as a sentence; it is preceded or followed by an independent clause (When he came in, he looked for the cat).

1. The clause structure of sentences. The sentences in *a, b, c,* and *d* both define and illustrate. Simple subjects and simple predicates are italicized. *IC* in brackets introduces an independent clause, *DC* a dependent one.

a. [IC] A simple *sentence* (like this one) *consists* of a single independent subject-predicate combination.

b. [IC] A compound *sentence has* two or more clauses of grammatically equal value; [IC] these *clauses are joined* by a coordinating conjunction, a conjunctive adverb, or (as in this sentence) by a semicolon. [IC] A *writer may decide,* for reasons of emphasis or rhythm, to break his compound sentence into two separate simple sentences, and [IC] in such cases the only *difference* between the compound sentence and the separate sentences *is* punctuation.

c. [IC begun] A complex *sentence,* like the one [DC] [that] *you are* now reading, [IC continued] *has* at least one independent clause and one or more dependent, or subordinate, clauses, [DC] *which function* as nominals, adjectivals, or adverbials.

d. [DC] As the hyphenated *term indicates,* [IC] a compound-complex *sentence* (again illustrated by the sentence [DC] *you are reading*) *combines* the features of both compound and complex sentences: [IC] *it contains* two or more independent clauses and one or more dependent clauses.

See Adjectives 5, Adverbial clauses, Noun clauses, Relative clauses.

2. Reduced clauses. Though the typical clause as traditionally defined has an expressed subject and a predicate with a full finite verb, many constructions lack one or the other of these elements and yet function in sentences much as typical clauses do. These are accounted for in transformational grammars by a transformation that deletes either a repeated verb or a form of *be* and a repeated subject. Reduced clauses are of two types:

a. Elliptical clauses, in which a full verb can be reconstructed because it occurs earlier in the sentence:

I don't *believe it* any more than you [*believe it*].
They can *speak Russian* and so can Bill [*speak Russian*].

b. Abridged clauses, in which a subject and form of *be* are deleted:

While [*I was*] waiting, *I* read the newspaper.
When [*he was*]sixteen, *he* went to work.
Though [*he was*] a rapid reader, *he* disliked books.
After [*I had been*] standing in line for an hour, *I* left.
Though [*she was*] tired, *she* continued to work.

When the deleted subject is not the same as the subject of the main clause, the result is often a dangling modifier.

See Complex sentence, Compound sentence, Dangling modifiers, Elliptical constructions, Restrictive and nonrestrictive. References: Jerrold J. Katz, *The Philosophy of Language* (New York: Harper, 1966), pp. 119–51; Long and Long, pp. 143–58; Quirk et al., pp. 720–65.

Cliché

A cliché is a worn-out word or phrase (white as snow). See Triteness.

Clipped words

Ad [*vertisement*] and [*tele*]*phone* are clipped words. See Origin of words 3d.

coh Coherence

Make clear the relation between the parts of this sentence or between these sentences or paragraphs.

Coherence – the traditional name for relationship, connection, consecutiveness – is an essential virtue in expository writing. It is essential because the reader's mind differs from yours; you must provide guidance from one idea, from one sentence, to another. To make a coherent presentation you have to arrange your ideas so that others can understand them.

Though careful planning in the prewriting stage will help to make clear the relationship of consecutive ideas, for the most part coherence must be tested after writing. To see if what you've written hangs together not only for you but for those who will read it, go over it as if you were encountering its content for the first time. Ask yourself, "Is the relation between these statements clear? Can a reader move from this sentence or from this paragraph to the next without losing the thread?"

A natural arrangement of material is not enough; you often need to signal the relationship between sentences and paragraphs. These signs, with suggestions for establishing coherence, are discussed in Conjunctions and style, Prepositions, Reference of pronouns, Transition. Reference: E. K. Lybbert and D. W. Cummings, *CCC*, Feb. 1969, pp. 35–38.

Collective nouns

A collective noun is a noun whose singular form names a group of objects or persons or acts. Here are some familiar examples:

army	contents	gang	number
athletics	couple	group	offspring
audience	crowd	herd	politics
class	dozen	jury	public
committee	faculty	majority	remainder

Some collectives have regular plural forms (*army-armies*); some (*athletics, offspring*) do not. The plural of a collective noun signifies different groups: The *audiences* of New York and Chicago differed in their reception of the play.

Some collectives are typically used in the singular (*committee is*) and some typically in the plural (*police are*). Most, however, are singular in one context, plural in a different one, depending on the way the writer is thinking about the group. When the group as a whole is intended, the collective noun takes a singular verb and a singular pronoun:

During the performance a *series* of barges covered with scenery *chugs* silently into place. – Edwin Wilson, *Wall Street Journal*

When the individual units of the group are intended, the noun takes a plural verb and plural pronoun:

Psychologists asked a *group* of young men and women what sex *they* wanted *their* first child to be. – *Psychology Today*

With this example, compare "Now that John is back, the *group has its* old solidarity."

Trouble occurs when a collective noun is treated inconsistently. The usual cause is that the writer has come to no firm decision about the group it names. He begins by treating the word as a singular, and as long as the verb follows it closely, he makes the verb singular: The inner *circle has* great influence. But if a plural modifier comes between the collective noun and the verb, he thinks of the members of the group rather than of the group as a unit, and he shifts to a plural verb: This inner *circle* of ambitious men *pose* a serious threat.

Inconsistency is also likely to occur when the writer's initial way of thinking about the collective and the meaning of a subsequent sentence come into conflict. He may want to keep a collective noun singular, but if the meaning calls for a plural construction, he is likely to make the shift unconsciously, sometimes in mid-sentence:

The entire *congregation troops* into the church, *seats itself,* and *remains* for a good two hours, while an aged curé berates *them* [consistency demands *it*] for *their* [*its*] sins.

In making constructions consistent, you will often find that, as in the example just given, it is the collective subject rather than its pronouns that needs to be changed. Beginning with "All members of the congregation troop into the church, seat themselves . . ." would avoid the problem.

Casual shifts in number are common in speech, but they may attract unfavorable attention in general writing, and they are almost certain to in formal prose. When reading over what you've written, be sure you haven't treated the same collective noun as both singular and plural.

See Agreement 1b, *each, every.* References: Bryant, pp. 6–7; Copperud, p. 50; Fries, pp. 48–50, 54, 57–59; Jespersen, pp. 210–12; Pooley, pp. 80–81.

Colloquial English

Usage that is characteristic of speech is colloquial. One familiar class of examples is made up of words that strive for emphasis, like *actually, really* (or *real*), *awful, terrible, terrific, fabulous, incredible, unbelievable.* In current writing the division between what is spoken and what is written is not nearly so sharp as it once was, though some spoken usages may be inappropriate in all but the most informal writing, just as some features of written English are inappropriate in all but the most formal speech.

Dictionaries sometimes mark words *Colloq.* to suggest that in the editors' judgment they are more common in speech than in writing. Many people mistakenly take the label to mean that the dictionary frowns upon their use, when in fact colloquial words are often accurate, expressive words that are used freely in good general writing. Because this misinterpretation of *colloquial* is so common, the label is less used in recent dictionaries and is generally avoided in this book. If a usage is more common in speech than in writing, that fact is stated; if the word or expression is standard English but is rarely found in general or formal writing, it is labeled informal.

See Spoken and written English.

Colon

Use a colon here. Or reconsider the use of this colon.

The colon is a mark of anticipation, indicating that what follows the mark will supplement what preceded it.

1. Introductory uses. Use a colon before a series of words, phrases, or clauses when they are not preceded by an introductory word or phrase or when they are formally introduced by a set phrase like *as follows* or *including the following.*

Two "parallel economies" have now emerged in India: the "white economy," involving taxes, salaries, receipts . . . and the "black economy," involving bribes, unrecorded cash transactions, hidden inventories. . . .
—Ved Mehta, *New Yorker*

Classifying the poetry written from 1500 to 1900 in accordance with this distinction, we discover a sequence which runs as follows: predicative, then balanced; predicative, then balanced.—Josephine Miles, *PMLA*

Don't use a colon after less formal introductory words (*like, such as*) that make what follows a part of the clause: The shop carried a lot of ethnic recordings, like [:] West African, Moorish, Egyptian, and Arabian. And don't use a colon between a verb and its object or complement: The reason I went broke freshman week was that I had to buy [:] books, furniture, and tickets to a lot of things I knew I'd never go to; My three immediate goals are [:] to survive midyear exams, to get to Colorado, and to ski until my legs wear out.

When appropriate, use a colon to introduce quotations in factual writing, especially if they run to more than one sentence. The colon is more common in formal than in general and informal writing, and its suitability depends in part on the way you introduce the quotation. If it's built closely into the sentence, a comma is usual; if it's more formally introduced, a colon:

For example, the report cannot say, "It was a wonderful car," but must say something like this: "It has been driven 50,000 miles and has never required any repairs."—S. I. Hayakawa, *Language in Thought and Action*

2. Between clauses. Particularly in a formal essay, you may sometimes want to use a colon between the clauses of a compound sentence when the second clause is an illustration, a restatement, or an amplification of the first:

The supposition that words are used principally to convey thoughts is one of the most elementary of possible errors: they are used mainly to proclaim emotional effects on the hearers or attitudes that will lead to practical results.—H. R. Huse, *The Illiteracy of the Literate*

In less formal writing a semicolon or a period is common in this position. It is the one use in which the colon and the semicolon are sometimes interchangeable. (A semicolon should never be used to introduce a series or a quotation.)

3. Conventional uses.
a. After the salutation of formal letters: Dear Sir:
b. Between hours and minutes expressed in figures: 11:30 a.m.
c. In formal bibliographies and formal citations of books:

Sometimes between volume and page: *The Mt. Adams Review,* 160: 129–40 (A comma, however, is now more common.)

Between title and subtitle: *The Great Tradition: An Interpretation of American Literature Since the Civil War*

Between place of publication and publisher: Austin: Univ. of Texas Press

Between Bible chapter and verse: Genesis 9:3–5

d. In ratios and proportions when the numbers are written as numerals: concrete mixed 5:3:1. Two colons are used instead of an equals sign in a full proportion: 1:2::3:6.

4. Stylistic use. You may sometimes choose a construction that requires a colon in order to spotlight what the colon introduces: "It is a common dream: To stand beneath sun and blue sky, harvesting your own . . . fruits and vegetables" *(New York Times).* The more common order, "To stand . . . is a common dream," is much less emphatic.

Sometimes, for stylistic effect, an experienced writer will use colons where other writers would use commas, dashes, semicolons, or periods. James Agee's *Let Us Now Praise Famous Men* contains many examples.

5. Capitals following. After a colon either a capital (as in the last quoted sentence) or a small letter may be used; but a small letter is much more common, as in the example in 2. Use a capital after a colon only when what follows it is long or complicated, with internal punctuation, or when you want to give it special prominence: "Beneath the surface, however, is the less tangible question of values: Are the old truths true?" *(Newsweek).*

For other uses of the colon, see *A Manual of Style* and the *U.S. Style Manual.*

comma Comma

Insert or remove a comma at the place marked.

The most common question about punctuation is "Should there be a comma here?" The general advice of this book is to use commas wherever they are considered obligatory and to use them elsewhere if they contribute to understanding. When choice is possible, the decision depends on appropriateness: the complex syntax and deliberate pace of much formal writing call for more commas than the simpler, brisker sentences of general English.

1. To separate independent clauses.
a. Use a comma before the coordinating conjunction when the clauses are rather long and when you want to emphasize their distinctness, as when they have different subjects:

For all its impressiveness, Monks Mound is only a part of the even more impressive Cahokia group, and Cahokia in turn is only one, albeit the largest, of 10 large and small population centers and 50-odd farming villages. —Marvin L. Fowler, *Scientific American*

When the independent clauses are short and closely related in meaning, the comma is often omitted:

Two years ago, the Dallas Cowboys had become dangerously long of tooth and the team's decline and fall seemed imminent. —Anson Mount, *Playboy*

But there is no rule that forbids using a comma to separate the clauses in a compound sentence, no matter what their length or relationship. Many experienced writers automatically place a comma before the conjunction, and so guard against the momentary confusion that a sentence like this one invites: A crowd

Uses of the comma
The following list of uses of the comma outlines the treatment in this article. The numbers and letters refer to sections and subsections.

1. **To separate independent clauses**
   a. Between clauses connected by a coordinating conjunction
   b. Between clauses connected by *but*
   c. Between clauses connected by *for*
   d. Between clauses not connected by a coordinating conjunction

2. **With preceding and following elements**
   a. After a dependent clause or long phrase preceding the main clause
   b. Before a dependent clause or long phrase following the main clause and not essential to its meaning

3. **To set off nonrestrictive modifiers**

4. **To enclose interrupting and parenthetical elements**
   a. Around interrupting elements
   b. Around conjunctive adverbs within clauses

5. **In lists and series**
   a. Between units in lists and series
   b. Between coordinate adjectives

6. **For clarity**

7. **For emphasis and contrast**

8. **With main sentence elements**
   a. Subject and verb
   b. Verb and object
   c. Compound predicates

9. **In conventional uses**
   a. In dates
   b. In addresses
   c. After salutations in all but formal letters
   d. After names in direct address
   e. In figures
   f. With degrees and titles
   g. With weak exclamations
   h. To show omission

10. **With other marks of punctuation**
    a. With parentheses
    b. With dash
    c. With quotation marks (Quotation marks 4b, 4c)

of spectators lined the walkway to see him [ ] and the President, in standard fashion, passed along the crowd *(New York Times)*.

b. Use a comma between two independent clauses joined by *but*, regardless of their length, to emphasize the contrast: "His achievements in office have been difficult to assess, but they have been formidable" (John David Hamilton, *Atlantic*).

c. Use a comma between independent clauses connected by the conjunction *for* to avoid confusion with the preposition *for:* They were obviously mistaken, for intercollegiate sports are always competitive.

d. Use a comma in place of a coordinating conjunction when you have good reason for doing so and when you can do so without inconveniencing or outraging your readers. In the great majority of cases such punctuation represents a comma fault (see Comma fault); but under certain circumstances a comma can appropriately stand between independent clauses that are not joined by a coordinating conjunction:

The intellect gets busy, means and methods are studied, purposes are assessed. – Gerald Warner Brace, *The Stuff of Fiction*

This writer is not merely good, she is *wickedly* good. – John Updike, *New Yorker*

The clauses here are short, parallel in form, and closely bound together in meaning. Semicolons, the most likely alternative punctuation, would slow the pace and add formality. In the following example the comma reinforces a contrast:

Both colloquial styles – consultative and casual – routinely deal in a public sort of information, though differently: casual style takes it for granted and at most alludes to it, consultative style states it as fast as it is needed. – Martin Joos, *The Five Clocks*

Sentences punctuated like these are increasingly common in print. Not all are successful. If the clauses are neither short nor closely related in form, and if one or more of them contains internal punctuation, the reader may have a hard time grasping the meaning: "The strongest and luckiest private constituencies win, social needs get pushed aside, as in the 50s, to explode a decade later" (Bill Moyers, *Newsweek*). Here, a reader who assumes that the writer is building a series is brought up short and forced to reread the sentence.

The choice of a comma alone instead of a coordinating conjunction (with or without a comma), a subordinating conjunction, or a semicolon is a matter of style. But convention needs to be taken into account. Before using the comma alone, consider your audience. Some very conservative readers look on such punctuation as invariably incorrect. If you can assume that your audience will not automatically condemn the practice, then be sure you are using a comma for a purpose. And, most important, be sure that your use of a comma won't make your readers' task more difficult.

See Fused sentence, Semicolon 1.

2. With preceding and following elements.

C2 **a.** Use a comma after an introductory dependent clause or a long introductory phrase:

Since encouraging women to spend money was the main point of magazines directed at us, they had distinctive characteristics. – *Ms.*

Far from being a neutral instrument, the law belongs to those who have the power to define and use it. – Michael Parenti, *Democracy for the Few*

Often when the preceding phrase is short or when the dependent clause has the same subject as the independent clause, the comma is omitted:

During my convalescence [ ] I will meditate on a few items. – Goodman Ace, *Saturday Review* (short phrase)

Although Grant ignores such details [ ] he is shrewd not only about his colleagues but about his former colleagues. – Gore Vidal, *New York Review of Books* (subjects the same)

But some professional writers make a practice of putting commas after all introductory clauses and after all introductory phrases that contain verb forms. By doing so they establish a consistent pattern and avoid risking the confusion that sometimes results from lack of punctuation.

b. Use a comma before a dependent clause or a long phrase that follows the main clause if the subordinate element is not essential to the meaning of the main clause:

In addition, most of these men have just spent years in the regimented, choiceless life of prison, which makes a life of freedom and responsibility a frightening prospect. – Sol Chaneles, *Psychology Today*

Again and again they tried to start the engine, with the breeze freshening and the tide beginning to turn.

3. To set off nonrestrictive modifiers.

C3 Use a comma to set off word groups that do not restrict the meaning of the noun or verb or clause they modify. The italicized word groups in the following sentences are nonrestrictive:

From where I was standing, *almost directly above the trunk*, I could see many of the articles that had been lost.

Pigeons breed in the spring and the hen lays two eggs, *one of which usually hatches into a hen and the other into a cock*.

A modifier that restricts the reference of the word it modifies (as "that had been lost" restricts "articles" in the first of the illustrative sentences above) is essential to correct understanding and is therefore not set off by commas. Out of context, many modifiers could be either restrictive or nonrestrictive. The word groups in italics in the following sentences might or might not be set off, depending on the writer's meaning:

A winding road *which seemed to lead nowhere in particular* passed through the village.

The man *who was carrying a gun* walked across the campus and into the administration building.

See Restrictive and nonrestrictive.

C4

4. To enclose interrupting and parenthetical elements.

a. Use commas around a word, phrase, or clause that interrupts the main structure of the sentence:

Next summer, no matter what happens, I intend to go to Africa.

The prank, I suppose, seemed amusing at the time.

My uncle, as was his habit, stopped for a drink on his way home from work.

Forgetting to complete the enclosure with a second comma can result in a confused sentence: "If factory workers and farmers became more efficient, Soviet citizens were told this week [ ] they would get more domestic goods, food, housing, hospitals and schools" *(Newport Daily News)*.

Usage is divided over setting off short parenthetical expressions like *of course*. Enclosing them in commas is more characteristic of formal than of general writing. There is often a difference in emphasis as well as tone according to whether or not commas are used:

And of course there are those who talk about the hair of the dog. —*Providence Sunday Journal*

The question, of course, is not whether the family will "survive." —*Time*

b. Use commas around a conjunctive adverb that stands after the first phrase of its clause: It was this ridiculous proposal, however, that won majority approval. At the beginning of a sentence such adverbs may or may not be set off: Therefore [,] I have decided to withdraw my application.

But and other coordinating conjunctions are a part of the clauses in which they appear and should not be set off: But a solution must be found. Nor should *however* be set off when it modifies an adverb or adjective: However strongly you feel. . . . However tired you are. . . .

C5

5. In lists and series.

a. Use commas to separate the units in lists and series: "He has read everything he could lay his hands on, manuscript and printed, that was written during the period: plays, sermons, ballads, broadsides, letters, diaries, and, above all, court records" (Edmund S. Morgan, *New York Review of Books*). See Semicolon 2.

Usage is divided over the use of a comma before the conjunction in a series: "letters, diaries, and records" or "letters, diaries and records." The comma is a safeguard against ambiguity: "He had small shoulders, a thick chest holding a strong heart [ ] and heavy thighs" (Richard Mandell, *Sports Illustrated*). See Series.

b. Use a comma between adjectives modifying the same noun. In the sentence "Though it was a hot, sticky, miserable day, Mrs. Marston looked cool in her fresh gingham dress," there are commas between *hot* and *sticky* and between *sticky* and *miserable* because each stands in the same relation to the noun *day*. "Hot *and* sticky *and* miserable" would make sense. There is no comma between *fresh* and *gingham* because *fresh* modifies *gingham dress*, not just *dress*. "Fresh *and* gingham" would not make sense.

Frequently in current writing, when only two adjectives modify the noun, no comma is used: a hot sticky day; the tall dark woman. There is no loss of clarity, but if you follow this style consistently, you deprive yourself of a rhetorical resource. By separating, a comma provides emphasis. Compare these two versions:

His long, greasy hair hung down to the shoulders of his worn, faded jacket.

His long greasy hair hung down to the shoulders of his worn faded jacket.

In the first, *greasy* and *faded* stand out as separate modifiers of their nouns.

6. For clarity. Use a comma to guide a reader in interpreting a sentence and to make it unnecessary for him to go back over it for meaning. A comma between clauses joined by *for* makes it clear that the word is functioning as a conjunction rather than as a preposition. Similarly, a comma can prevent the subject of one verb from being mistaken even momentarily for the object of another:

When the boll weevil struck, the credit system collapsed and ruined both landowners and tenants. *Not* When the boll weevil struck the credit system. . . .

Soon after the inspector left, the room was crowded with curious onlookers. *Not* Soon after the inspector left the room. . . .

A comma can also make immediately clear whether a modifier goes with what precedes or with what follows: A great crowd of shoppers milled around inside, and outside hundreds more were storming the doors. *Not* . . . milled around inside and outside. . . .

And a comma helps when a word is used twice in a row: What he does, does not concern me.

7. For emphasis and contrast. When two words or phrases are connected by *and*, they are not usually punctuated; but because a comma tends to keep distinct the elements it separates and to emphasize slightly the element that follows it, writers may use commas for these purposes alone: My brother was delighted with the prestige of his new position, and with the increase in pay.

Here a comma is used for emphasis, and irony: "Midge Decter is disappointed, again" (Jane O'Reilly, *New York Times Book Review*).

8. With main sentence elements.
a. Subject and verb. Though it sometimes occurs in old-fashioned formal usage, don't use a comma between a subject and its verb.

b. Verb and object. Don't use a comma between a verb and its object. (Words or phrases that must be set off by pairs of commas may, of course, intervene between subject and verb and between verb and object. See 4.)

c. Compound predicates. Use a comma between the verbs of a compound predicate only when the sentence is so long and involved that reading it is difficult or when you feel the need for special emphasis or contrast. This is a sensible rule and one that is insisted upon by many writers, teachers, and editors, though in published prose the verbs in a compound predicate are frequently separated by a comma without obvious cause:

> Works by other writers in the past few months have reflected this fascination with language, but have delved deeper into the mysterious origins of words. – *Time*

9. In conventional uses.

a. In dates, to separate the day of the month from the year: May 26, 1971. When the day of the month is not given, a comma may or may not be used: In September 1846 *or* In September, 1846. If a comma precedes the year, punctuation should also follow: In September, 1846, the government fell.

b. In addresses, to separate smaller from larger units: Washington, D.C.; Chicago, Illinois; Hamilton, Madison County, New York; Berne, Switzerland.

c. After salutations in all but formal letters: Dear John,

d. After names in direct address: Jim, try that one again.

e. In figures, to separate thousands, millions, etc.: 4,672,342. In some styles no comma is used in figures with four digits: 2750.

f. To separate degrees and following titles from names: George Emmett, M.A.; Charles Evans Hughes, Jr. (this comma is now sometimes omitted); Elihu Root, Esq.

g. After a weak exclamation like *well, why, oh:* Oh, what's the use?

h. Sometimes to show the omission of a word that is required to fill out a construction: He took the right-hand turn; I, the left.

10. With other marks of punctuation.

a. When parentheses come within a phrase or clause that is followed by a comma, put the comma after the closing parenthesis.

b. Use a comma or a dash, not both.

c. For the use of commas with quotation marks, see Quotation marks 4b, 4c.

References: Summey, index entries; Whitehall, pp. 126–29.

Comma fault

Revise the sentence marked by changing the comma to a semicolon or a period, or by inserting an appropriate conjunction, or by rephrasing to make a more satisfactory sentence.

A comma fault (comma blunder, comma splice) occurs when a comma alone is used to separate the independent clauses of a compound or a compound-complex sentence: He stared at his visitor, it was too dark to see who it was. Occasionally such sentences are deliberately constructed for an intended effect: "I was awed by this system, I believed in it, I respected its force" (Alfred Kazin, *A Walker in the City*). The term *comma fault* marks uses of the comma that are not justified either by the structural similarity of the clauses or by the close relationship of their content.

There are various remedies for a comma fault:

1. Replace the comma with a semicolon or a period.

He stared at his visitor, it was too dark to see who it was.
Revised: He stared at his visitor. It was too dark to see who it was.

This is the simplest remedy but not always the best one. Sometimes inserting a period simply produces two weak sentences in place of one.

I think Americans should read this book, they would get a more accurate picture of problems in the Middle East.
Revised: I think Americans should read this book; they would get a more accurate picture of problems in the Middle East. [A period would produce two weak sentences. For a better revision, see 3.]

2. Join statements that belong together with a conjunction that makes their relationship clear. When the choice is a coordinating conjunction, the comma is ordinarily retained (see Comma 1a); when the choice is a conjunctive adverb, the comma is replaced by a semicolon (see Semicolon 1b).

An increase in student fees would enable us to balance the budget, this is clearly not the time for it.
Revised: An increase in student fees would enable us to balance the budget, but this [*or* budget; however, this] is clearly not the time for it.

3. Rewrite the sentence, perhaps subordinating one of the clauses, perhaps making a single independent clause. Work to produce a satisfactory sentence, not just to eliminate the comma fault.

I think Americans should read this book, they would get a more accurate picture of problems in the Middle East.
Revised: I think Americans should read this book because it would give them a more accurate picture of problems in the Middle East.

One part receives the stimulus from outside and transmits the impulse to the cell, this is known as the dendrite.
Revised: One part, known as the dendrite, receives the stimulus from outside and transmits the impulse to the cell.

If you can make a sure distinction between an independent clause and a dependent clause, you should find it easy to spot any comma faults in your sentences. Look first to see how many independent subject-verb combinations you have in each group of words punctuated as a single sentence. If there are two independent clauses, see if you have a connective between them. If there is no connective but only a comma, you have probably produced a comma fault. For exceptions, see Comma 1d. Compare Fused sentence.

Commands and requests

Direct commands, also called imperatives, are expressed by the simple (infinitive) form of the verb:

Hurry up!
Shut the door, please.
Fill out the coupon and mail it today.

In speech, the force of the command or request is shown by the stress and tone of voice, which are hard to represent on paper. Emphatic commands are punctuated with an exclamation mark, less emphatic ones with a period. Negative commands are expressed with *not* and the *do* form of the verb: Don't go yet.

Commands and requests can be made less abrupt through phrasing and the use of auxiliaries or adverbs of courtesy. Often in the pattern of a question, they are punctuated with either a period or a question mark, depending on the intonation intended.

Try to get them in on time.
Please think no more of it.
Would you be willing to take part in this program?
Would [*or* Will] you please close the window.
Let's go around and see what we can do with him.
Suppose we say nothing more about it.

In indirect discourse a command becomes an infinitive with *to* or a clause with *should:* He told us to write a 5000-word paper. *Or* He said that we should write a 5000-word paper.

References: Long, pp. 76–79; Quirk et al., pp. 402–405.

committee

Committee is a collective noun, usually construed as singular. When the writer is thinking of the several individuals who compose it, *the members of the committee* is preferable.

compare, contrast

Compare with *to* points out likenesses: He compared my stories to Maupassant's [said they were like his]. *Compare* followed by *with* finds likenesses and differences: He compared my stories with Maupassant's [pointed out like and unlike traits]. *Contrast* always points out differences.

When the things compared are of different classes, *to* is used: He compared my stories to a sack of beans. In the common construction with the past participle, either *to* or *with* is used: Compared with [*or* to] Maupassant's, mine are feeble. *In comparison* is followed by *with:* In comparison with Maupassant's, mine are feeble. *Contrast* ordinarily takes *with:* He contrasted my work with [*sometimes* to] Maupassant's. *In contrast,* however, usually takes *to:* In contrast to Maupassant's, my stories are feeble.

Comparison and contrast

To compare and contrast is to establish the similarities and the differences between two or more objects, people, places, institutions, ideas, and the like. Comparing is a natural way of communicating information. You can acquaint a reader with a subject that is unfamiliar to him by telling him how it is like and how it is unlike something he knows well. And you use contrast automatically in arguments when you set out to prove that one thing is better than another.

To make a comparison, first select the points that are significant for the purpose you have in mind. (Is cost a significant factor in deciding what make of car you want to buy? Is safety? Speed? Color?) Then find out how your subjects are alike and how they differ in each of these respects. In organizing your discussion, you may treat one of the subjects (A) fully before taking up the corresponding points in the other (B); or you may compare A and B point by point; or you may set out all the likenesses between A and B and then all the differences (or the reverse). In any case, it is not enough to offer a mass of details about each of the subjects under discussion. You must work out the comparison, relating details about one to the corresponding details about the other, so that the reader understands the ways in which the subjects differ and the ways in which they are alike.

See Logical thinking.

comp Comparison of adjectives and adverbs

Correct the fault in comparing the adjective or adverb marked. To express degrees of what is named, adjectives and adverbs are compared—that is, their forms are changed by adding -*er* or -*est* to the root, or base, form (*long, longer, longest*) or by preceding it with *more* or *most* (*beautiful, more beautiful, most beautiful*).

1. Choosing the form. We say "a longer walk," not "a more long walk"; we say "a more beautiful picture," not "a beautifuller picture."
a. Some adjectives and adverbs add -*er*, -*est* to the root form (the positive degree).

	Positive	*Comparative*	*Superlative*
Adjective	early	earlier	earliest
	hoarse	hoarser	hoarsest
	unhappy	unhappier	unhappiest
Adverb	fast	faster	fastest
	soon	sooner	soonest

b. Other adjectives and adverbs precede the root form with *more, most.*

	Positive	*Comparative*	*Superlative*
Adjective	exquisite	more exquisite	most exquisite
	afraid	more afraid	most afraid
	pleasing	more pleasing	most pleasing
Adverb	comfortable	more comfortable	most comfortable
	hotly	more hotly	most hotly

Three-syllable adjectives and adverbs are ordinarily compared with *more* and *most*, those of one syllable with -*er* and -*est*. Two-syllable modifiers are usually compared with *more* and *most*, but many can take either form: *able – abler, more able – ablest, most able; empty – emptier, more empty – emptiest, most empty.* When you're in doubt, *more* and *most* are the safer choices. It was once possible to use both methods of comparison in one lo- cution, as in Shakespeare's "most unkindest cut of all," but dou- ble comparatives and double superlatives are no longer standard English.

Some points of usage that arise with irregular forms of com- parison are discussed in *former, first – latter, last;* and *last, lat- est.* Reference: Fries, pp. 96– 101.

2. Using the comparative. The comparative expresses a greater degree (It is *warmer* now) or makes specific comparison between two units (He was *kinder* [*more kind*] than his wife). The two terms of a comparison should be actually comparable:

Comparable: His salary was lower than a shoe clerk's. *Or* than that of a shoe clerk. *Not comparable:* than a shoe clerk.

(This rule holds when the root form of the adjective is used: His salary was low, like a beginner's. *Not . . .* a beginner.)

Logic calls for *other* with *any* in comparisons between a thing and the group to which it belongs: She is a better dancer than *any* of the *other* girls. The comparative is, however, frequently used absolutely, with no actual comparison involved (*higher education, the lower depths, older people*). In much adver- tising copy the task of supplying a comparison is left to the reader (*cooler, fresher, stronger, faster, more economical*).

3. Using the superlative. In formal and most general writing, the superlative is used to indicate the greatest degree of a quality among three or more people or things (He was the *jolliest* of the whole group; This is the *brightest* tie in the showcase). Infor- mally, the superlative of two objects is common, and it is not rare in general writing: Roy and Joe did pushups to see who was strongest; Russia and China compete to see which can be most critical of the other's policies. Use of the superlative as a form of emphasis is also informal (She has the loveliest flowers; We saw the best show). The form with *most* is now largely restricted to formal social correspondence (You are most kind; She is most clever) in which no specific comparison is intended.

Superlatives are not completed by *other:* The Egyptians had obtained the highest degree of cultivation in medicine that had up to that time been obtained by any [*not* any other] nation.

References: Bryant, pp. 201– 202; Fries, pp. 99– 101; Pooley, pp. 112– 14.

4. Comparing absolutes. Purists raise objections to the compari- son of *black, dead, excellent, fatal, final, impossible, perfect, unique* on the grounds that there can be no degrees of *deadness* or *blackness* or *impossibility.* But in fact these words are fre- quently compared: a more equal society, a more complete victo- ry, a more impossible situation; and the Constitution has "to form a more perfect union." Many absolutes are used figuratively with meanings that naturally admit comparison: This is the *deadest* town I was ever in. See Divided usage. References: Bryant, pp. 58–59; Pooley, pp. 112–14.

Complement

Complement often refers to the noun or adjective completing the meaning of a linking verb and modifying the subject: He was *busy;* He became *the real head of the business.* In some grammars *complement* is used to include direct and indirect objects. See Linking verbs, Predicate adjectives.

complement, compliment

As a noun, *complement* means "that which completes or is called for" (a full complement); as a verb, it means "to make complete" or – of two things – "to fill out each other's lacks" (the scarf and blouse complemented each other perfectly). *Compliment* is the noun (He received many compliments for his work) and verb (He complimented her on her victory) having to do with praise and congratulations.

Complex sentence

A complex sentence has one independent, or main, clause and one or more dependent clauses, ordinarily introduced by relative pronouns or subordinating conjunctions: She married the man *who* picked her up *when* she fell. See Clauses.

Compound-complex sentence

When one or more of the independent clauses of a compound sentence are modified by dependent clauses, the sentence is called compound-complex. Here the opening dependent clause modifies the first independent clause: "When its facilities were offered to Kansas State Teachers College, they were refused, for enrollment at that institution had already declined 500 below capacity" (John R. Silber, *Atlantic*). See Clauses.

Compound predicate

Two or more verbs with the same subject, together with their modifiers, form a compound predicate: Ruth *wrote* and *mailed* three letters.

Compound predicates help make writing economical. Note how far removed this sentence is from the type that gives only one small idea to a sentence:

The case is made more interesting if the great daily has, among other things, distorted political news, reported its political opponents with miserable unfairness and glaring prejudice, tried to goad the government into declaring war on Cuba, lowered the mental level of life in the community, debased the language, filled its pages with vast ads for pork butts, storm windows, under-garments, dollar sales, antiperspirants, failed to inform the public on matters of great importance, fought medical care for the aged, and so forth. – Saul Bellow, *Atlantic*

See Comma 8c.

Compound sentence

A compound sentence coordinates two or more independent clauses.

1. With coordinating conjunction. Usually the clauses of a compound sentence are connected by one of the coordinating conjunctions: "Lavin's stories are centered almost entirely on the lives of women, and they are informative in the most humane way" (Rosellen Brown, *Ms.*).

2. Without connective. A compound sentence may have a semicolon instead of a connective between the clauses: "They are generous-minded; they hate shams and enjoy being indignant about them; they are valuable social reformers; they have no notion of confining books to a library shelf" (E. M. Forster, *Aspects of the Novel*). Since each of these clauses could also be written as a separate sentence, it is apparent that the traditional definition of *sentence* is somewhat arbitrary. For the use of a comma instead of a connective, see Comma 1d.

3. With conjunctive adverb. The clauses of a compound sentence may be connected by a conjunctive adverb *(however, moreover, whereas, consequently, therefore . . .)* preceded by a semicolon: The FBI had proved themselves expert in publicizing their solution of crimes; consequently, some local police gave them only grudging support.

See Clauses, Conjunctive adverbs.

Compound subject

Two or more elements standing as subjects of one verb make a compound subject: "Capitalists, militarists, and ecclesiastics cooperate in education" (Bertrand Russell, *What I Believe*). The verb following a compound subject is usually plural: Christianity and humanity have gone hand in hand through history. See Agreement 1c.

Compound words

Compound words in written English are combinations of two or more words that are usually written as one word or hyphenated: *doorknob, notwithstanding, quarter-hour, father-in-law, drugstore.* Some compounds — especially those that express more than the sum of their parts — continue to be written as separate words: *the White House, high school, post office.* In speech these are usually distinguished by the stronger stress on the first words: compare *a white house* and *the White House.* See Group words, Hyphen, Plurals of nouns 5. For the spelling of particular compound words, consult your dictionary.

comprise

Traditionally, *comprise* means "consist of" or "include": The whole comprises its parts. In current usage the nearly opposite senses of "constitute," "compose," and "make up" are very common: "The four states that at one time comprised French Equatorial Africa . . ." (Harold G. Marcus, *American Historical Review*). But many writers, editors, and teachers insist that *comprise* be used only in its traditional sense. Since it is a relatively formal word, the more general *make up* is a better choice in most contexts.

concept

Concept as a vogue word is often used where *idea* would be more appropriate: "Research tests . . . whether concepts for [TV] shows are promising" (Jeff Greenfield, *New York Times Magazine*). See Vogue words.

concl Concluding an essay

Revise the ending of your paper to round out the discussion.

When you reach the end of your discussion, wrap it up. Don't simply stop, so that your reader wonders if the last page is missing. And don't keep rambling on until your reader is missing.

If your paper is a long one, you may need to review the ground you have covered, preferably in fresh phrasing. If the material is complex, you may need to pull together the points you have made and show how they add up and what they add up to. Short papers, like long ones, must add up to something.

When the reader of an essay finishes the last sentence and thinks "So what?" the writer has produced an essay that has no point, or—more likely—he has failed to make clear what that point is. A conclusion can't save a pointless essay by simply announcing a point; but by clarifying a fundamental causal relationship, by restating the essential argument, by bringing out an implication, the final paragraph or two can greatly strengthen an essay.

If your essay has been a voyage of discovery in which you've tried to define your own attitudes, you may end up with something like, "What I feel now is that my parents gave too much to me without thinking enough about me." Whether or not such a conclusion works depends on what has gone before. If that point has been gradually emerging throughout the essay, fine. If it hasn't—if, for example, you have only told about the size of your allowance, your charge accounts, the gifts on birthdays and at Christmas—then your ending will leave the reader perplexed and dissatisfied.

Final sentences should avoid tag ends and anticlimax as well as irrelevance. They should build to a firm conclusion, not trail away to a dying fall. They should wrap up the essay in such a way that the reader not only recognizes its completeness but feels satisfied that the last words were the right ones.

Concrete words

Concrete words name things that can be seen and touched: *box, building*. See Abstract language.

Conditional clauses

A conditional clause states a condition or action necessary for the truth or occurrence of what is expressed in the independent clause that the conditional clause modifies. *If, if not, unless,* and *whether* are the most common conjunctions for conditional clauses. Somewhat more formal words and phrases introducing conditions are *in case, provided, provided that, in the event that.*

1. For real or open conditions—statements of actual or reasonable conditions under which the main statement will hold—use the indicative verb forms:

If the red light is on, you know a train is in that block of track.
He will be there *unless something happens to his car.*
Whether he comes or not, I shall go just the same.

An older type of condition survives in some proverbs: Spare the rod and spoil the child. (*If you spare the rod,* you will spoil the child.)

2. For hypothetical conditions—theoretical but still possible—use *should . . . would* or the past tense: *If he should offer another $100,* I would take it. Or *If he raised his offer,* I would take it.

3. For contrary-to-fact conditions—those that cannot be met or that are untrue—use in general English the past tense of the verb in a present or future sense (If he *was* here, we would have seen him by now). In formal English, the plural form of the past tense is not uncommon in the third-person singular, usually called a subjunctive (If he *were* here . . .) and is firmly established in the first person (If I were you). Formal literary English may use inversion (Were he here . . .).

See *if, whether;* Subjunctive mood. References: Fries, pp. 104–107; Long, pp. 130–36; Quirk et al., pp. 745–49.

Conjunctions

Conjunction is the traditional term for a limited group of words without distinctive formal traits, which join words, phrases, clauses, or sentences. In this *Index* conjunctions are further defined and discussed according to their conventional classification:

Coordinating conjunctions (*and, but, for,* etc.)
Correlative conjunctions (*either . . . or, not only . . . but,* etc.)
Conjunctive adverbs (*however, therefore, consequently,* etc.)
Subordinating conjunctions (*as, because, since, so that, when,* etc.)

Since most conjunctions are also used as other parts of speech, especially as prepositions and adverbs (*as, for, so . . .*), the exact application of the term is not always possible, nor is the distinction between coordinating and subordinating conjunctions always apparent. Though relative pronouns (*who, which, that . . .*) also have a connective function, they are not classed as conjunctions. See Parts of speech.

conj Conjunctions and style

Make the conjunction marked more accurate or more appropriate to the style of the passage.

1. Conjunctions and meaning. In everyday speech we get along with a relatively small number of conjunctions—*and, as, but, so, when,* and a few others—because we can emphasize shades of meaning and exact relationships by pauses, tones, gestures. In writing, we lack these means of relating ideas, and a more thoughtful choice of connectives is essential.

Choose your conjunctions carefully. Don't toss in *but* when there is no contrast between statements (see *but* 2). Decide whether your meaning can be better conveyed by a coordinating conjunction or by a construction that uses the corresponding subordinating conjunction (*but* versus *though,* for example). And note distinctions between subordinating conjunctions. *As* means "because," but it is a weak *because* (see *as*); *while* may mean "although" or "whereas," but the core of its meaning relates to time. Sometimes, if a writer's thinking has been truly consecutive, the most satisfactory linkage will be implicit; a *therefore* or an *accordingly* will be unnecessary and unwelcome. See Transition and the articles on the particular conjunctions.

2. Conjunctions and style. Conjunctions should be appropriate to other traits of style. Often simple *but* is a better choice than *however: The trail is easy walking as far as the canyon; from there on, however, it's no route for Sunday strollers. Better:* . . . *canyon, but from there on.* . . . See Conjunctive adverbs 1.

Repeating a conjunction at the beginning of each element of a series makes each element distinct, avoids possible confusion, and achieves the advantages of strong rhythm and clear-cut parallelism:

I took an old shutter and fixed a sort of porch roof on it, and nailed it to a locust tree nearby, and set the nest with the eggs carefully on it.—Wendell Berry, *The Long-Legged House*

The tribal chants echoing from the seats were always fitting accompaniments to Mick's grunts and wails and hoots.—Robert Mazzocco, *New York Review of Books*

In contrast, omitting *and* before the last member of a short series may build an emphatic climax: "The most important of these, the most characteristic, the most misleading, is called *Some Glances at Current Linguistics*" (William H. Gass, *New Republic*). Or it may suggest that the series is only a sample, not a complete enumeration: "Many were the Northerners who, during and after the Civil War, went South to train, to educate, to rehabilitate Negro refugees and freedmen" (William H. Pease, *Journal of Southern History*).

See Conjunctive adverbs, Coordinating conjunctions, Correlative conjunctions, Subordinating conjunctions. See also Coordination, Subordination.

Conjunctive adverbs

A number of words that are primarily adverbs are used also as connectives. They are called conjunctive adverbs (or transitional adverbs or adverbial connectors or sentence connectors or sentence adverbials). Because their adverbial meaning remains rather prominent, their connective force is relatively weak. They are used after a semicolon between independent clauses and also after a period to introduce a new sentence. The most common conjunctive adverbs are:

accordingly	furthermore	namely
also (see *too*)	hence	nevertheless
anyhow	however	otherwise
anyway (informal)	indeed	still
besides	likewise	then
consequently	moreover	therefore

Adverb: No campaign, *however* violent, could make him vote.
Conjunction: The results were poor; *however*, we were not surprised.

1. Style. Because conjunctive adverbs are relatively heavy connectives, they are most appropriate in formal writing and in sentences of some length and complexity. In general writing they are more likely to serve as transitional devices between sentences than to connect clauses within a sentence. Excessive use of conjunctive adverbs is a major barrier to simple, straightforward writing.

Note these appropriate and inappropriate uses:

The armored saurians, the dodo, and a few other extinct creatures are supposed to have become unviable through their exaggerated specialties; usually, however, such excesses are not reached. [Appropriate with the formal sentence structure.] – Susanne K. Langer, *Philosophical Sketches*

In the morning I still felt sick; *nevertheless,* when the bugle sounded, I got up. [Inappropriately heavy in this context. Could substitute *but.* Better to rewrite as a complex sentence: Though I still felt sick the next morning, I got up when the bugle sounded.]

2. Position. Placing conjunctive adverbs inside their clauses instead of at the beginning gives the initial stress to more important words. When they are so placed, they are usually set off by commas, as in the first example in 1.

3. Punctuation. When used to introduce the second independent clause in a compound sentence, a conjunctive adverb is preceded by a semicolon, as in the second example in 1.

Connotation

Connotation means the associations a word or phrase carries, as distinguished from its denotation – what it refers to. It is connotation that makes the difference between *house* and *home*, between a *dutiful* child and an *obedient* one. See Denotation.

A writer needs to be conscious of what words connote as well as of what they signify. Although *flush* (in the sense "turn red") and *blush* are so close in meaning that they can often be substituted for each other, the overlap of the two words is not complete. We say "He flushed with anger" but not "He blushed with anger."

Although dictionaries give some information about the shades of difference among words, context tells more. The situation in which a word has regularly occurred, the variety of usage to which it belongs, the prevailing social attitude toward what it refers to and toward the people who use it (politicians, salesmen, children) all contribute to the public connotations of a word. Beyond that are the private connotations that stem from an individual's personal experiences. For one student, *school* has connotations of confinement, for another intellectual excitement, for still another sociability.

Heavily connotative words are sometimes called slanted, loaded, or evaluative; and writers are sometimes urged to replace them with words that are more nearly neutral. The advice is not always sound. We use words not only to give information about things but to express our own feelings about them and to influence the attitudes of others. It is natural to describe an action we admire as *courageous,* one we deplore as *foolhardy.* Neutral terms are preferable only when we are in fact neutral or when we are striving to give that impression.

Construction

A construction is a group of words which stand in some grammatical relationship to each other, as that of modifier and headword (black cat), preposition and object (to the roof), or subject and predicate (They walked slowly). Any grammatical pattern may therefore be spoken of as a construction.

contact

The verb *contact,* meaning "get in touch with, communicate with" (Will you contact Mr. Hubble?), is more acceptable in nonbusiness contexts today than it was a generation ago, though it remains rare in formal usage. Its popularity in general English may be explained by its inclusiveness, embracing as it does the notions of "call," "write," "visit," and even communication through intermediaries: "He contacted a leading American corporation, but the corporation heads were skeptical" (Grace M. Spruch, *Saturday Review*). See Divided usage. References: Bryant, pp. 60–61; Copperud, pp. 59–60.

Context

The word *context* is used in different ways.

1. **Verbal context.** In writing, the context is the discourse that surrounds and limits a word or passage. The context is tremendously important in revealing the particular meanings of words. The word *check,* for example, has forty or so dictionary senses. Yet in actual use, in definite contexts, it gives no trouble:

They were able to *check* the fire at the highway.
The treasurer's books *check* with the vouchers.
He drew a *check* for the entire amount.
The tablecloth had a red and white *check*.
He moved his bishop and shouted *"Check!"*
With difficulty he held his temper in *check*.
He had the *check* list on the desk in front of him.

And so on. Though *check* has more senses than most, a great many English words have more than one sense, so a particular meaning must be gathered from the context—and ordinarily can be. Context gives clues not only to the particular denotative sense of a word, as illustrated with *check*, but also to its connotative value. This fact is recognized whenever someone says, "By itself that might seem insulting, but in the context it couldn't possibly give offense." See Parts of speech 2c.

2. The context of allusions and quotations. An honest writer takes care that allusions and quotations are true to the context in which they occur, that they really represent the ideas of their authors. The complaints of politicians and government officials that their words have been quoted "out of context" are often justified.

3. Rhetorical context. Every piece of writing occurs in a rhetorical situation or context, which includes the writer, the subject, the writer's purpose, and the audience. The choice of material, the organization, and the style of a good essay all reflect the writer's sense of the rhetorical context. See Rhetoric.

continual(ly), continuous(ly)
In the sense "uninterrupted," with reference to time, formal stylists prefer *continuous(ly)*, but *continual(ly)* is also used: For weeks we observed an almost continuous eruption of the volcano. In the sense "recurring rapidly and often," the situation is reversed—conservatives insist on *continual(ly)*, but *continuous(ly)* is also standard: The governor broke his promises, not just repeatedly but continually.

Contractions
In writing, contractions like *can't* are forms that show pronunciation, usually by substituting an apostrophe for one or more letters of the standard spelling. They occur regularly in informal usage but are notably rare in formal. In general usage a writer will favor or avoid them just as he makes other rhetorical choices, considering the rhythm of the particular sentence, how much distance he wants between himself and his readers, and whether the subject and the occasion call for a relaxed or a restrained style. Contractions are necessary, of course, in actual representations of speech, as in dialog. See *have* 3.

contrast, compare
Contrast points out differences; *compare to* points out likenesses; *compare with* does both. See *compare, contrast*.

controversial

Controversial (a controversial book, a controversial person) labels the subject a source of disagreement, of argument. Unfortunately the word has acquired a connotation of warning: Better watch out for this one – some people disapprove! If the subject you are writing about has caused significant controversy, tell what the controversy is and why it's significant.

Conversion

When a word that usually functions as one part of speech is used as another part of speech, it is said to have undergone conversion or functional shift: a *must* book; a good *read;* in the *know;* the experience of *parenting;* I wouldn't *fault* him. The principle of functional shift is well established, but a writer should be cautious in experimenting with new conversions. The student who wrote the following sentence was experimenting – unsuccessfully: She stooped as if to *negative* her height.

convince, persuade

For a long time some uses of *convince* and *persuade* have overlapped: He persuaded (convinced) me of the necessity for action; He convinced (persuaded) me that I should act. *Convince* is now common in still a third context, where *persuade* is traditional: "Advisers to President Ford have apparently convinced him to avoid a meeting with the exiled Russian author, Alexander I. Solzhenitsyn" (*New York Times*). The use of "convince . . . to " instead of "persuade . . . to" (persuaded him to avoid) is deplored by conservative stylists. Reference: Copperud, p. 61.

Coordinate

Two or more grammatically equivalent words, phrases, or clauses are said to be coordinate: *bread* and *butter; in the sink* or *on the stove; dancing, singing, laughing; When he lectured* and *when he prayed*, everyone listened; *He wrenched his back,* and *she broke her leg.*

Coordinating conjunctions

The coordinating conjunctions, *and, but, for, nor, or, so,* and *yet,* are used to connect two or more elements of equal grammatical rank:

Words: books *and* papers; books, pamphlets, *or* magazines

Phrases: in one ear *and* out the other

Dependent clauses: She . . . wrote to young Lewis Rutherford cheerfully enough that his sister looked lovely and that the new baby was delightful. – R. W. B. Lewis, *Edith Wharton*

Independent clauses: At present the common cause between eccentric and hippie is proper hatred of the way things are, and the common inclination is for personal justice. – Jerome Lettvin, *Natural History*

Sentences: Perhaps I should wish that I had liked him better. But I do not wish it. – Renata Adler, *New Yorker*

See Conjunctions and style, Coordination, Series.

Coord Coordination

Correct the faulty coordination.

Faulty coordination is not a lapse in grammar or usage; it is a failure to make logical relationships clear. Faulty coordination means that in the particular context the material calls for a relationship or emphasis different from the one reflected in the writer's use or arrangement of independent clauses.

1. Some examples of faulty coordination result from joining two statements that don't belong together: The condition of the house is deplorable, and the dining nook seats six comfortably. Revision should take the two statements out of the coordinate relationship by putting them in separate – and separated – sentences.

2. Sometimes faulty coordination can be corrected by turning one of the independent clauses into a dependent clause. "He went to France for the summer, and his novel was published" suggests that there is an obvious causal relationship between his going to France and the publication of his novel. In some contexts, this might make sense. But if the only relationship that can be established is a temporal one – two events happening at about the same time but not otherwise related – the sentence needs to be revised: "When he was spending the summer in France, his novel was published," or "At the time his novel was published, he was spending the summer in France," or in some other way.

3. In the example above, coordination might be confusing or misleading. Sometimes it is simply ineffective:

When I reached the intersection, I found a group of people gathered around a wrecked car. The left front tire had had a blowout, and the car had gone out of control and rolled over, and the driver was obviously dead.

The independent clause "the driver was obviously dead" needs to be taken out of the coordinate relationship it is in; to gain its proper effect, it should be made a separate sentence. Left in the series, it implies that the death of the driver had no more importance than the blowout and the crash.

See Subordination. Reference: Sledd, pp. 275 – 81.

Correlative conjunctions

Some coordinating conjunctions are used in pairs: *both . . . and, either . . . or, neither . . . nor, not only . . . but [also], whether . . . or.* Of these correlatives, *neither . . . nor* and *not only . . . but [also]* are slightly formal, showing a more conscious planning than is common in informal or general English: "Neither the gold drain nor the beautification of America deters them from going abroad" (Thomas L. Hughes, *Foreign Affairs*).

Like coordinating conjunctions, correlatives normally join expressions of the same grammatical rank:

Nouns: He said that both *the novel* and *the play* were badly written.

Adjectives: He must have been either *drunk* or *crazy.*

Prepositional phrases: They can be had not only *in the usual sizes* but also *in the outsizes.*

Verb phrases: The wind scoop not only *caught the cool breezes* but also *picked up the captain's conversation.*

Clauses: Whether *Mitch thumbed a ride through the mountains* or *Jenny made the long bus trip,* they were determined to be together during the vacation.

Like similar rules, the rule that constructions built on correlative conjunctions must be strictly parallel should be broken when it gets in the way of natural, rhythmic expression.

See Shifted constructions. Reference: Pooley, pp. 91–92.

could(n't) care less

Formerly (and too frequently) a lack of concern was expressed by "I couldn't care less." Recently the negative has been dropped; now "I could care less" is used to mean the same thing: "kids who never heard of Little Richard and could care less" (Ellen Willis, *New Yorker*). Neither form is suited to college writing, except perhaps to point up triteness in dialog.

Count nouns

Count nouns name things that can be counted as separate units. See Mass nouns, Noun 3c.

Counter words

Counter words are usually words of general approval or disapproval or else rather abstract words that are overused. Like slang, they are popular and current; unlike slang, they are ordinary words, used with no spark of originality. In Elizabethan times, *fair* as in "fair maid" was a counter word. In modern speech *fine, great, lovely, nice, pretty, poor* are samples. Some counter words do no harm in informal writing, but they are no substitute for more precise terms. See Vogue words.

couple

The primary meaning of the collective noun *couple* is "two persons or things associated in some way," as in "a married couple." In general and informal usage it is equivalent to the numeral *two* (a couple of pencils) or to *a few* (a couple of minutes). The *of* is frequently omitted in speech and informal writing and sometimes in general: "Yet some of his classmates do not sleep through the night, and live happily on a couple hours sleep" (Gay Gaer Luce and Julius Segal, *Insomnia*); but this use offends many readers. See Collective nouns.

Course names

In general discussions, only the names of college subjects that are proper adjectives (the languages) are capitalized. In writing a list of courses including one or more of these proper adjectives, it is possible to capitalize them all for consistency (and courtesy), though the distinction is usually kept: I am taking biology, chemistry, European history, English composition, and French. Names of departments are capitalized (the Department of History), and so are names of subjects when accompanied by a course number (History 347).

credibility

In journalese, *credibility* was joined to the vogue word *gap* to refer to public loss of faith in President Johnson's statements about the Vietnam War. In the Nixon administration the gap became a gulf, and *gap* went out of vogue. But *credibility* moved into officialese and flourished. Readers should remember that *honesty* and *credibility* (what will be believed) are by no means synonymous. Writers should shun *credibility* as a vogue word that has some of the connotations of *image*.

Cumulative sentence

A cumulative sentence makes its main statement at or near the beginning, usually in a short independent clause, and then goes on to add details in modifiers that are free or detachable. The modifiers may be parallel to each other:

Ragtime is a unique and beautiful work of art about American destiny, built of fact and logical fantasy, governed by music heard and sensed, responsive to cinema both as method and historical datum, shaken by a continental pulse. — Stanley Kauffmann, *Saturday Review*

Recognized and greeted by restaurant personnel, Zero becomes manic, draping hat and coat onto the headwaiter, wrapping his arms and one leg around the manager, then bellowing his way into the main room. — Robert Alan Arthur, *Esquire*

Or they may be built onto each other:

The cars have been piling into the infield by the hundreds, parking in there on the clay and the grass, every whichway, angled down and angled up, this way and that, where the ground is uneven, these beautiful blazing brand-new cars with the sun exploding off the windshields and the baked enamel and the glassy lacquer, hundreds, thousands of cars stacked this way and that in the infield with the sun bolting down and no shade, none at all, just a couple of Coca-Cola stands out there. — Tom Wolfe, *Esquire*

As the last example shows, the cumulative sentence offers a way of clustering or massing details; Wolfe's one sentence does the work of a dozen on the subject-verb-object pattern. Because it observes the natural order of speech — main statement first, then qualifications and particulars — a cumulative sentence can and often does give the impression of ease and naturalness. But unless the modifiers add strength or richness or support the initial assertion, the sentence may wander off into insignificant or irrelevant detail. In itself, a cumulative sentence is neither good nor bad. What counts is the skill with which it is constructed and the effect that it produces.

Compare Periodic sentence. Reference: Christensen, Ch. 1.

cupfuls, cupsful

Cupfuls is usual. See *-ful, full*.

curriculum

Curriculum has the Latin plural *curricula* and the English *curriculums*. The adjective is *curricular;* the compound adjective with *extra* is usually written as one word: *extracurricular*.

D

 Dangling modifiers

Revise the sentence so that the expression marked is clearly related to the word it is intended to modify.

A phrase is said to dangle (or to be misrelated) if its position makes it seem to relate to a word that can only make nonsense of the meaning or if, in a context that demands an explicit relationship, it has no clear relation to any word in the sentence.

In the sentence "Looking farther to the left, we saw the spire of a church," *looking* obviously modifies *we;* if the subject of the verb *look* were reconstructed, it would be *we:* [*We* were] looking farther to the left, *we* saw the spire of a church. In the sentence "Defined in psychological terms, a fanatic is a man who consciously overcompensates a secret doubt" (Aldous Huxley, *Proper Studies*), it is clear that *defined* modifies *fanatic*, for the same reason. The subject of *defined* must be *fanatic:* [*A fanatic* is] defined in psychological terms, *a fanatic* is a man who consciously overcompensates a secret doubt.

When the phrase does not refer to the subject — that is, when it has a different subject from the subject of the main clause — then the modifier dangles. In the sentence "To get the most out of a sport, the equipment must be in perfect condition," the reconstructed subject of the introductory phrase would be something like "[For *someone*] to get the most out of a sport, *the equipment* must be in perfect condition." But since *someone* is different from *equipment*, *someone* should not be dropped. If the sentence "At eleven, my family moved to Denver" is reconstructed, it reads "[When *I* was] eleven, *my family* moved to Denver." *I* does not equal *family*, so *I* should not be deleted. In the following examples, try to reconstruct the subject of the introductory phrase:

Upon telling my story to my adviser, he stopped and thought.

Born in England in 1853, John MacDowell's seafaring activities began after he had migrated to this country. [This type of dangling modifier, in which the phrase refers to a noun — *MacDowell* — represented only by its genitive form modifying the subject, sometimes appears in edited prose.]

Modifiers that dangle may also follow the independent clause:

Many signs read "Visit Our Snake Farm," driving toward the city.

Dangling modifiers are to be avoided chiefly because educated readers do not expect to find them. As a rule there is no real question of the intended meaning of the sentence, and in context the dangling phrases are not apt to be conspicuously awkward or as nonsensical as they seem in isolation. But they are distracting in any writing that is meant to be read attentively. By forcing the reader to search for (or guess at) the related noun, they can make a piece of writing needlessly difficult.

Such dangling constructions should not be confused with absolute phrases, in which the phrase has its own subject. Compare an absolute phrase, a correct modifier, and a dangling modifier:

Absolute phrase: The car paid for with my last dollar, I was at last out of debt.

Correct modifier: Paid for with my last dollar, the car became my first piece of personal property.

Dangling modifier: Paid for with my last dollar, I drove the car away elated.

In revising what you write, examine carefully every introductory verbal phrase, for the phrases most likely to dangle are those that begin with participles or infinitives or that contain gerunds. If you continue to have trouble relating them to the words they should modify, you might try giving them up and using clauses instead.

See Absolute phrases, Gerunds, Infinitives, Participles. References: Byrant, pp. 64–65; Copperud, pp. 64–66; William H. Pixton, *CCC*, May 1973, pp. 193–99; Roberts, pp. 351–52, 358–59, 366–67.

Dash

The dash—typed as two hyphens not spaced away from the words they separate—can be used singly to link a following word or word group to the main structure of a sentence or in pairs to enclose a word or word group that interrupts the main structure. Enclosing dashes indicate greater separation from the core context than enclosing commas, less separation—or less formality—than parentheses.

If used sparingly, the dash suggests a definite tone, often a note of surprise or an emotional emphasis equivalent to a mild exclamation. If used regularly in place of commas, colons, and semicolons, it loses all its distinctiveness and becomes merely a sloppy substitute for conventional punctuation. At its best the dash is an abrupt, emphatic mark.

1. Before a kicker. The single dash is often used to throw emphasis on what follows, which may be dramatic, ironic, humorous:

The old nations still live in the hearts of men, and love of the European nation is not yet born—if it ever will be.—Raymond Aron, *Daedalus*

We do not question the right of an author to spell, capitalize, and punctuate as he wishes—provided he follows consistently a recognizable system.—John Benbow, *Manuscript and Proof*

2. Before a summary or illustration. The dash is used singly or in pairs with word groups that summarize what has just been said or provide details or examples:

It takes a cataclysm—an invasion, a plague, or some other communal disaster—to open their eyes to the transitoriness of the "eternal order."—Eric Hoffer, *The True Believer*

He was strongly in favor of peace—that is to say, he liked his wars to be fought at a distance and, if possible, in the name of God.—George Dangerfield, *The Death of Liberal England*

3. Between independent clauses. A dash is sometimes used to link independent clauses when the second expands, develops, completes, or makes a surprising addition to the first. In this function, it is less formal than a colon:

And yet they had a thing in common, this oddest of odd couples—they both cared about the social graces.—George Frazier, *Esquire*

In one respect, Welles was unique among the Cabinet members—he did not think himself a better man than the President.—Margaret Leech, *Reveille in Washington*

4. Enclosing interrupting elements. Dashes are used to set off words and word groups, including complete sentences, that break with the main structure of a sentence:

Fitzgerald's people believed in their world—it really mattered who won the Princeton-Harvard game, it really meant something to appear at the theatre or the opera—and because they believed in their world they owned it.—Frank Conroy, *Esquire*

References: Summey, pp. 101-104; Whitehall, pp. 123, 129.

data

Formal usage follows the Latin, treating *datum* as singular and *data* as plural. In general usage *datum* is rare, and *data* is treated as a collective noun, taking a singular verb to emphasize the whole—"Data so far available makes it seem doubtful" (John Mecklin, *Fortune*)—and a plural verb to emphasize the parts—"There were still a good many data in the 33-page report" (William H. Honan, *New York Times Magazine*). References: Bryant, pp. 66–67; Copperud, pp. 66–67; Pooley, pp. 59–60.

Dates

The typical American form for writing dates is "August 19, 1976." The form "19 August 1976" prevails in British usage and in American military usage and is gaining popularity in the United States. If the full date is given within a sentence, the year is usually set off by commas; and if the day of the week is also given, full comma treatment is used: The legislature met on Wednesday, December 13, 1905. When only month and year are given (in August 1976 he died), no commas are necessary, though they are often used in formal styles.

The year is not written out in words except in formal social announcements, invitations, wills, and some other ceremonial situations and at the beginning of a sentence—and most writers manage to avoid beginning sentences with the year. Expressions like "January in the year 1885" are wasteful: "January 1885" is enough. In business writing and references, months having more than four (or five) letters are often abbreviated: Jan. 3, 1970.

In writing dates in figures only, American practice is month-day-year: 9/17/76; European practice is day-month-year, some-times with the month in roman numerals: 17-IX-76.

Deadwood
Words or phrases that add nothing at all to the meaning or effec-tiveness of a statement are deadwood. See Wordiness.

Declension
Declension means the list or listing of the forms of nouns and pronouns (and in many languages the forms of adjectives and participles also) to show number (singular, dual, plural), gender (masculine, feminine, neuter), and case (nominative, genitive, accusative, and others in different languages). The English noun has two regular forms: the form ending in *s*, which serves as genitive and plural, though these are written differently (*sister's, sisters', sisters*), and the form without an ending, which is used for all other relationships. Personal pronouns in English have from two forms (*it, its*) to four (*I, my, mine, me*). Adjectives and adverbs are compared but not declined.

Deduction
Deduction is the process of drawing a conclusion from proposi-tions known to be true, or accepted as true, or assumed to be true. You are reasoning deductively when you notice a ring around the moon and say, "We're in for some bad weather." Your unspoken premise, based on your own experience or perhaps on what you've read somewhere or heard from someone, is that the ap-pearance of a ring around the moon means that bad weather is bound to follow. The essence of the deductive process is the *must* – drawing an inevitable conclusion (the weather will be bad) from two related propositions: (1) a ring around the moon forecasts bad weather and (2) there's a ring around the moon.

For the conclusion of a deductive train of reasoning to be valid and true, correct inferences must be made from true premises. See Fallacies, Logical thinking, Syllogisms. Compare Induction.

Deep structure
Generative-transformational grammarians distinguish between the surface form of a sentence and the more abstract relation-ships in its deep structure. In the five sentences "Bill bought Jane a stereo," "Bill bought a stereo for Jane," "Jane was bought a stereo by Bill," "A stereo was bought for Jane by Bill," and "It was a stereo that Bill bought for Jane," the surface sub-jects are *Bill, Bill, Jane, a stereo,* and *it;* but at a deeper level all the sentences have the same subject or agent – Bill – since he did

the buying regardless of the form the expression of the fact is given. Yet this deep-structure subject *(Bill)* is the object of the preposition in the third and fourth sentences, and the deep-structure or underlying object *(a stereo)* is the subject on the surface of the fourth sentence.

Such a concept of sentences may enlarge your view of the sentences you write. You can experiment with ways of expressing the same deep grammatical relationships through different surface structures, noting the varying rhetorical effects of each. Our sentences about Bill and Jane and the stereo are an example. And each of these could also be embedded in a larger structure in various ways:

When Bill bought Jane a stereo, he surprised her.
Bill's buying Jane a stereo surprised her.
Jane was surprised by Bill's buying her a stereo.
That Bill bought Jane a stereo surprised her.
For Bill to have bought Jane a stereo surprised her.
The buying of a stereo for her by Bill surprised Jane.

These are only a few of the possibilities. Usually such considerations as focus, tone, transition from one sentence to another, and the rhythm of the sentence in its context will help you choose, often intuitively, between one surface structure and another.

This view of sentences can also sharpen your awareness of ambiguity and its sources. Although some sentences are ambiguous because a particular word can be interpreted in more than one way, others are ambiguous because the same surface structure may derive from two different deep structures. "Visting relatives can be boring" is ambiguous because *visiting relatives* may be derived from a deep structure with *relatives* as object (someone visits relatives) or from one with *relatives* as subject (relatives visit someone). Such ambiguity can be resolved by providing a surface structure to which only one deep structure can be related: To visit relatives can be boring.

See Clauses 2, Grammar 3c, Transformation. References: Noam Chomsky in Hungerford, Robinson, and Sledd, pp. 108–50; Paul Postal in *Language and Learning,* ed. Janet Emig, James T. Fleming, and Helen M. Popp (New York: Harcourt, 1965), pp. 153–75.

definitely

Definitely has been overused as a counter word to give emphasis or in the sense of "certainly" (I will not do it, definitely; He was definitely worse than usual; She definitely uses those methods; But definitely!) instead of in its more limited sense of "clear-cut, in a definite manner."

Definition

1. Types of definition. Definitions are of two main kinds:
a. A lexical or dictionary definition tells how a word is used in different contexts. Lexical definitions that appear in everyday

prose often use the verb *means* or *expresses* or, when connotations are foremost, *suggests: expectorate* means "spit"; *hooked,* applied to drug use, suggests hopeless addiction.

b. A real or logical definition (sometimes called a philosophical definition) identifies the essential characteristics of the thing that is the referent of the word. It joins subject and predicate with a form of the verb *be* on the model of the equation

term-to-be-defined	=	genus	+	differentia(e)
A ballad	is	a song		that tells a story

Thus, in "Logic is a specialized language dealing with the relationship of truth and falsity within a language" (Dwight Bolinger), *language* is the genus, and the two differentiae are *specialized* and *dealing with the relationship of truth and falsity within a language.*

Logicians have formulated rules for real definitions. One is that the definition must include all things designated by the term but exclude anything to which the term does not properly apply. Thus "A bachelor is a person who is unmarried" is unsatisfactory because the genus is too broad. In "A shoe is a leather covering for the foot," one of the differentiae—*leather*—is too restrictive.

Other traditional rules are these: A definition should not be circular (Hostility is the state of being hostile). Except when loss or lack is a distinguishing characteristic (as in *baldhead* and *bastard*), a term should not be defined negatively (Liberty is the absence of restraint). A term should not be defined metaphorically (Television is the opiate of the people), nor should a term be defined by a synonym (A pail is a bucket).

These rules have all been laid down in the interest of precision, and they should be observed when rigor is required (in answering examination questions on the special terms of a subject matter, for instance). But for some purposes the pattern of the logical definition is too confining or smacks too much of textbook style. Not all our definitions require the rigor of formal logic, and normally we want to say more about a term than can be compressed into the genus + differentiae formula.

2. Definition in exposition and argument. As a writer, you will have occasion to use both lexical and real definitions. When you do, you should make clear which kind you are using.

a. In the stipulative definition, a variety of lexical definition, the writer gives a word a special, limited sense that is necessary for his specific purpose:

I do not use the word "myth" to imply something entirely false. Rather, I use it to connote a complex of profoundly held attitudes and values which condition the way men view the world and understand their experience.—Richard Weiss, *The American Myth of Success*

A stipulative definition shouldn't be so remote from ordinary usage that it won't be taken seriously. Most readers will go along with the writer who says, "In this paper I will use the word *teen-*

ager to include twenty-year-olds," but will probably stop reading if they find, "In this paper *teenager* means everybody who knows what's really going on."

b. An extended definition gives information about the essential nature of a thing, like the one-sentence logical definition, but it is not restricted to the processes of classification and division that yield the genus and differentiae. It may use *description*, telling what the thing looks like; *chronology*, giving its genesis and development; *example*, giving instances of it; *comparison*, saying what it is like; *contrast*, saying what it is not; *causal analysis*, indicating what circumstances produced it and what consequences it has; and *testimony*, telling what authorities have said about it. Etymologies and synonyms may also be used to develop a definition. What the central elements in a definition are depends on what is being defined and also on where the writer's interest lies. A psychologist and a biologist define *man* in different ways.

An extended definition may be simply explanatory, with the aim of giving information about the subject in a readable, interesting essay. Or it may pave the way for further analysis: once he has established his definition of *tragedy*, a writer can go on to show that a new play is, or is not, a tragedy. Defining is also one way of conducting an argument. When opponents of legalized abortion argue that abortion is murder and its proponents argue that it is not, the issue is one of definition. Defining is often geared not to the purpose of explaining but to proving that a belief is sound or a policy wise.

3. Phrasing a definition. When a definition is given the prominence of a separate sentence, subject and complement—whether joined by *is* or by *means*—should normally be the same part of speech: noun matched by noun, adjective by adjective, and so on. Consider the sentence "Defining is to locate a thing in its class and then separate it from other members of the class." The meaning is clear, but the sentence would be easier to read if the two parts matched: "To define is to locate . . ." or "Defining is locating . . . and then separating. . . ."

Definitions that begin with *where* or *when* (Erosion is when rain washes away the topsoil) are common but are objected to in formal contexts. They occasionally occur—in this example metaphorically—in literary works of established reputation: "Morning is when I am awake and there is a dawn in me" (Henry David Thoreau, *Walden*). See *when, where*.

Degree of comparison

Smaller, smallest, more handsome, most handsome are expressions of degree. See Comparison of adjectives and adverbs.

Degrees

Ordinarily, academic degrees are not given with a person's name except in college publications, reference works, and articles and

letters where the degrees indicate competence in a particular
field, as in a doctor's comment on a medical matter. When used,
the names of the degrees are abbreviated, and the abbreviations
are separated from the person's name by a comma; in alumni
publications they are often followed by the year in which the
degrees were granted:

Harvey J. Preble, A.B. [or B.A.]   Harvey J. Preble, A.B. '08
Jane Thomson, Ph.D.   Jane Thomson, Ph.D. '61
Royce Walton, B. Arch., was master of ceremonies.

As a rule, except in reference lists, only the highest degree in an
academic professional field is mentioned.

If the institution granting the degree is named, the following
form is usual:

George H. Cook, A.B. (Grinnell), A.M. (Indiana), Ph.D. (Chicago)

Demonstrative adjectives and pronouns
The determiners *this, that, these, those* have traditionally been
called demonstrative adjectives or demonstrative pronouns,
according to their use in a sentence:

Adjectives: This car is fast. *Those* people never think of anyone else.
Pronouns: These cost more than *those. That*'s a good idea.

See Determiners; *kind, sort;* Pronouns 6; *that; this.*

Denotation
The denotation of a word is what the word refers to, as described
in a dictionary definition: fuel = a substance that is burned to
produce heat or power. When heating oil is in short supply or
gasoline doubles in price, *fuel* takes on additional overtones, or
shades of meaning, that go far beyond this literal definition. See
Connotation.

Dependent clauses
A dependent, or subordinate, clause has a subject and verb but
can't stand as a sentence: If he comes today. See Clauses.

Description
Description normally deals with the visible and tangible, telling
how a thing looks or feels or tastes or smells. Abstractions can be
described, too, but a writer who undertakes to produce a word
picture of grief or pride or chaos is likely to find that he can best
present them in terms of physical sensations. Description feeds
on the concrete.

Although most common in narration, description is used in all
types of writing. Discussions of all subjects, except perhaps the
most theoretical, include patches of description, for only description can help the reader visualize a subject or know the truth
about it through sensory experience.

1. Kinds of description. In describing an object or a scene, the
writer may try to present what any impartial observer would

see—to come as close as he can to putting into words the image a camera would record. Or he may try to present a scene as it appears to an observer whose perception is highly colored by emotion—for' example, a fire in which he was temporarily trapped or a fire as he imagines it appeared to someone who was trapped in it. Thus descriptions range from the precise, informative reports of technical writing to impressionistic sketches.

2. The function of details. Most descriptive passages fall somewhere between factual reporting and poetic evocation; the writer tries to provide a picture of reality so clear that the actual scene or object would be immediately recognizable and, in addition, to make the reader aware of how the writer (or the writer's imagined observer) feels about it and understand why he feels as he does.

Such description, if successful, will make the subject particular and individual. Second Beach in Middletown, Rhode Island, will not be described in details that apply equally well to every beach on the Atlantic coast. Instead, the writer will search out the details that give the beach its special character and convey them in words that communicate what he feels as well as what he perceives. It is always best to make the details evoke the feeling. Outright statements of emotions (I was excited by the big surf) or judgments (The beach is best in late September) are singularly unconvincing in the absence of the stimulus that gave rise to them. If the details are authentic, such assertions become unnecessary, for the appropriate generalization will have formed in the reader's mind. Good description shows; it doesn't need to tell.

3. The selection and organization of details. When an observer who has looked long and hard at his subject (even in memory) begins to write about it, he has far more details than he can use. Selection is vital. A profusion of unrelated details will only bewilder the reader. The beachcomber will not name all the shore birds any more than he will number the grains of sand. Which birds? What details about the sand? Leo Rockas gives a clue: "The night club in Mozambique need only be plainly presented; the corner supermarket had better be invested with novelty." As in every writing situation, then, the audience must be taken into account. What is commonplace to one group of readers will be exotic to another.

Organization of the details in a description should be determined by the subject and the writer's purpose. Does the reader need to understand the spatial relations in order to picture the scene? The directions must be clear, with the writer making use of indicators such as *here, there, on top, in the middle, below, to the left, on the right, beyond, in the distance, on the horizon.*

4. The language of description. Again, selection counts. A rush of adjectives may call attention away from the scene to the writing. Descriptive prose should be neither flat nor overexcited; it should suit the subject and the feeling the subject is intended to evoke. Details can be conveyed most directly and compellingly in language that is concrete and specific. Concrete diction gives things color, shape, and texture; specific terms give them particularity and individuality.

See Abstract language, Adjectives and style, Details, Point of view. Reference: Leo Rockas, *Modes of Rhetoric* (New York: St. Martin's Press, 1964), pp. 29–54.

det Details

Develop the passage or the topic more fully by giving pertinent details.

The symbol *det* is shorthand for "Give an example" or "What's your evidence?" or "Make this specific" or "Don't just *say* the house is in bad condition; make me *see* that it is." In revising a paper so marked, you need to supply particulars that will make your ideas or your impressions clearer, your argument more convincing, or your essay more readable.

The details of a physical object are its parts (the *webbed feet* of a duck) or its attributes or qualities (*scorching* wind, *smooth* leather). The details of an abstraction like pride are the words and attitudes and actions that justify our saying that someone is proud. The details of a novel are specifics of plot, character, style, and so on. Thus the details of any subject are its particulars. In a good paper they fit together, making a pattern, leading to a generalization, or inviting the reader to draw an inference. Besides giving substance to an essay, details enliven writing, capturing and holding the reader's interest. See Description, Induction. Reference: Christensen, Ch. 2.

Determiners

Determiner is a general term for several types of words, other than adjectives, that precede nouns in English. Chosen usually to fit the semantic context, determiners may be subclassified as articles (*a/an, the*), prearticles (*none, all, half, most, much,* etc.), and postarticles (*two, three; first, second; first, last; former, latter;* etc.). The three subclasses are illustrated in "*half* of *the last* installment."

The prearticles can serve as transitional devices between sentences when the noun has been deleted:

Several boys walked in. A *few* were wearing black leather jackets.

Demonstrative articles and the postarticles can serve the same function:

These were the last ones. The *first* were more interesting.

Genitive, or possessive, forms can also function as determiners. "George's book was very interesting" becomes in some contexts "*George's* was very interesting"; and "My father is a teacher" becomes in some contexts "*Mine* is a teacher." In "George's book" and "My father" the genitive form occurs where the definite article *the* would occur. Since they occur in identical positions in the noun phrase, the definite article and the genitives belong to the same class of words.

See Parts of speech. References: Copperud, pp. 70–71; Arthur Norman in *Readings in Applied English Linguistics*, ed. Harold B. Allen, 2nd ed. (New York: Appleton, 1964), pp. 156–63.

Dialects

A dialect is the speech (sounds, forms, meanings) characteristic of a fairly definite region or group. It is speech that does not attract attention to itself among the inhabitants of a region (regional dialect) or among members of a group (group or class dialect) but that would be recognizably different to an outsider. Because the educated middle class is the dominant group in the United States, its dialect is called standard English.

The term *dialect* is also applied to written expression: there are writing dialects as well as speech dialects. Standard written English is the appropriate form for college work. But this does not mean that a college student should set out to purge his writing of all the words and word forms and phrases from a regional dialect or another group dialect. The guiding principle should be appropriateness: What are you writing about? Who is your audience? If you are reminiscing about your childhood or describing your homesickness, don't resist the natural impulse to use dialectal expressions. If your instructor and your classmates are familiar with the dialect you grew up using, you may also use it effectively in other essays. The more formal and impersonal your topic and the broader your audience, the less appropriate dialectal usages will be. In any circumstances avoid those that are likely to mystify your readers or strike them as simply ungrammatical (see *grammatical, ungrammatical*).

See English language 3. References: Hungerford, Robinson, and Sledd, Part II; Raven I. McDavid, Jr., *PMLA*, May 1966, pp. 7–17.

d Diction

Replace the word marked with one that is more exact, more appropriate, or more effective.

Diction means choice of words. Good diction is exact, appropriate, and effective. Faulty diction either fails to convey the writer's meaning fully or accurately or in some other way disappoints the expectations of the reader.

1. Choose the exact word. The exact word is the one that conveys better than any other the meaning you intend. Some mistakes in word choice result from confusing two words that resemble each other in some way (*delusion* for *illusion*, *predominate* for *predominant*). Others result from confusing two words that, although similar in basic meaning, are not interchangeable in all contexts. We can speak of a *durable* friendship or a *lasting* friendship; but though we describe shoes as *durable,* we do not say shoes are *lasting.* Idiom allows "the oldest existing manuscript" but not "the oldest living manuscript." In some instances, finding the exact word means searching for a more specific one, as *complained* is more specific and may be a better choice than *remarked.* Often it means settling for simpler expression. If you reach for a fancy phrase, you may come up with one that has nothing to do with your meaning: Because of pressure to do well on examinations, a *disquieting aura pervades* me even when I am relaxing. See Connotation, Dictionaries, Idiom, Meaning, Wrong word.

2. Choose the appropriate word. The words should fit both the subject and the relation between writer and audience. If your subject is technical, complex, serious, and if you are addressing readers who know something about it and want to learn more, you will probably use a rather formal vocabulary. If your subject is light or humorous and if you know your readers well or want to establish a sense of intimacy with them, you'll express yourself more informally.

Though a style can err on the side of excessive informality, probably the more common fault in college papers is inappropriate formality—"big" words selected more to impress an audience than to express meaning. "Big" words need not be long—*deem* (for *think*) is as "big" as *domicile* (for *house*); they are "big" in the sense of "pretentious." *Ignominious, cantankerous, lachrymose, florid, inscrutable, mortified, chronicled*—these words may be "big" in one context but not in another. You can catch the "big" words in what you write by reading your essays aloud. If you have used words that you would be unlikely to speak in or out of the classroom, reconsider them. See if you can't substitute words that are just as precise but more natural to you.

Although formal, general, and informal English overlap and are frequently mixed in current prose, you can seriously weaken what you write if you mix the varieties of usage carelessly. When informal name-calling interrupts a thoughtful paper on welfare, when high-flown poetic clichés break the mood of an honest piece of nature description, when *know-how* is applied to a painter's technique or *finalize* to a composer's efforts, readers will be distracted and disturbed. If you mix usage deliberately, have a good reason for doing so—to amuse or startle your readers, perhaps, or to emphasize the point you're making. Keep your audience in mind, and avoid overkill. If you find yourself being criticized for mixing usage, read and reread your essays before turning them in, and maybe ask a friend to read them as well, with an eye open for sore thumbs and an ear cocked for sour notes.

See Dialects, Fine writing, Formal English, Informal English.

3. Choose the effective word. If your words convey your meaning accurately and if they are appropriate to the rhetorical context, your diction will be competent, and it may be effective too.

But you will probably move beyond competence only if you pay very close attention to your style. Effectiveness nearly always means choosing words that convey your meaning directly and economically. It may mean deliberately repeating a word, or turning a familiar word to a new use, or choosing a word for its sound as well as its sense. In short, effective diction often requires the imaginative use of words; it calls for finding a middle course between diction that is commonplace and trite and diction that turns the reader's attention from what is being said to the way it is being said. See Abstract language, Adjectives and style, Adverbs and style, Conjunctions and style, Counter words, Euphemisms, Figurative language, Imagery, Nominalization, Repetition, Style, Triteness, Vogue words, Wordiness. See also articles on individual words: *claim, contact, drunk, finalize, hopefully, however, massive, relate, viable,* and so on.

Dictionaries

Next to a well-stocked mind and a good ear, your dictionary is your chief resource in writing papers. Refer to it to check spelling and word division; consult it when you are trying to choose the word that conveys your meaning most precisely; browse in it to increase your own word hoard.

A good dictionary tells what a word denotes in various contexts (see the several meanings of *office, cast, culture, critical* in your dictionary). It gives linguistic information about the word (its part or parts of speech, its inflections), something of its history, its synonyms and its antonyms, and the idioms in which it occurs. It may also suggest some of the connotations of a word. Watch for the labels that indicate limitations on the use of a word or of some sense of it—subject labels like *chemistry,* temporal labels like *archaic,* geographic labels like *British,* and usage labels like *nonstandard.* And be sure you know what the labels mean. Some dictionaries use *colloquial* to mark words that are characteristically used in conversation and in informal writing; some use *informal* for the same words.

Because dictionaries differ in the labels they apply and in the amount of labeling they do, determining the status of a word is not always easy. You may be told that *plenty,* as in "plenty hot," is *informal* or *colloquial* and therefore inappropriate for a formal essay, but you will not be warned that *adumbrate* is too formal and literary for general writing. Although a dictionary can give you a great deal of information, it can't substitute for a good ear and good judgment.

The following desk dictionaries, listed alphabetically, are recommended for college work:

American Heritage Dictionary of the English Language (Houghton)

Funk & Wagnalls Standard College Dictionary (Funk)

Random House College Dictionary (Random)

Webster's New Collegiate Dictionary (Merriam)

Webster's New World Dictionary (Collins and World)

Each of these dictionaries has its own policies, procedures, abbreviations, restrictive labels, and order of definitions. To use your dictionary well, become familiar with the explanatory notes in the opening pages.

Your college library will have unabridged dictionaries – the three most recent are *Webster's Third New International Dictionary of the English Language* (Merriam), the *Funk & Wagnalls New Standard Dictionary of the English Language* (Funk), and the *Random House Dictionary of the English Language* (Random) – as well as dictionaries in a variety of special subjects such as law, business, psychology, and economics.

See Connotation, Definition 1a, Denotation, Diction. References: Bolinger, pp. 582–89; James Sledd and Wilma R. Ebbitt, *Dictionaries and* That *Dictionary* (Chicago: Scott, 1962).

different

Formal usage prefers *different from:* The rich are different from you and me. General usage is divided between *different from* and *different than:* "The young TV generation has a completely different sensory life than the adult generation which grew up on hot radio and hot print" *(Newsweek). Different than* is particularly common when the object is a clause: "The story would be different for an investigator who accepts the verdict of the court than for one who doesn't" (Meyer Shapiro, *New York Review of Books*). The formal alternative would be the longer, wordy expression: . . . verdict of the court from what it would be for one who doesn't.

Different to is a British idiom, rare in American usage.

References: Bryant, pp. 69–70; Copperud, p. 72; Evans and Evans, pp. 135–36; Pooley, pp. 163–67.

Direct address

In direct address the audience being spoken to is named:

My friends, I wish you would forget this night.
What do you think, *Doctor,* about his going home now?

Words in direct address are usually set off by commas. See Indirect discourse.

Direct objects

In "Dogs chase cats," *cats* is the direct object of the transitive verb *chase.* See Objects 1, Transitive and intransitive verbs.

disinterested, uninterested

From its first recorded uses in the seventeenth century, *disinterested* has had two senses: "indifferent, uninterested" and "impartial, not influenced by personal interest." But the first meaning gradually disappeared from educated writing, and its revival in this century has met strong opposition – in part, at least, because assigning the two different meanings to two different words set up a distinction that prevented ambiguity. Even

though *disinterested* in the sense "uninterested" is established
in general usage, a writer who uses it should know that he risks
being thought semiliterate: "I began to hate someone once who
habitually said 'disinterested' when he should have said 'uninterested' " (Alexander Cockburn, *New Statesman*). Reference:
Copperud, pp. 73–74.

Divided usage

Usage is said to be *divided* when two or more forms exist in the
language, both of them in reputable use in the same dialect or
variety. *Divided usage* doesn't apply to localisms, like *poke* for
sack or *bag*, or to differences like *ain't* and *isn't*, which belong to
separate varieties of the language. It applies to spellings, pronunciations, or grammatical forms in which those of similar
education follow different practices.

Most of us have no idea how many of these divided usages exist within standard English. In addition to hundreds of instances
of divided usage in pronunciation, most dictionaries record
forms like these:

In spelling: *buses, busses; millionaire, millionnaire; catalog, catalogue*

In verb forms: past tense of *sing: sang* or *sung;* past tense of *ring: rang*
or *rung;* past participle of *show: shown* or *showed;* past participle of
prove: proved or *proven*

The point about divided usage is that both alternatives are
acceptable. A person who has learned to say "It's I" does not
need to change to "It's me," and one who says "It's me" need not
change to "It's I." When there is a choice between variants of
equal standing, choose the one that you use naturally, that is
appropriate to your style, or, if you are taking pains to be tactful,
the one that is customary among the audience you want to
reach. Before criticizing another person's usage, make sure that
it's not a variant that is as reputable as the one you prefer.

The entries in this *Index* include divided usages. When one or
the other of two acceptable usages is likely to disturb many readers or listeners and arouse emotional attitudes, evidence is usually presented: there's security in knowing what is dangerous
ground. For examples, see *can, may; different; disinterested,
uninterested; dove, dived; due to; enthuse; farther, further;
like, as;* Principal parts of verbs; *reason is because;* Sexist language; *slow, slowly.*

Division of words

Break the word at the end of this line between syllables.

To keep the right-hand margin of a manuscript fairly even, you
must divide some words at the end of a line with a hyphen. The
following words are divided to show typical syllables: *mar gin,
ca ter, hy phen, chil dren, long ing, hi lar i ous, cat ty, ac com
plished, ad min is trate.* When you are not sure how to divide a
word, consult a dictionary. Here are the basic rules:

1. Both the divided parts should be pronounceable: the break should come between conventionally recognized syllables. Words of one syllable, like *matched, said, thought,* should not be divided at all.

2. Double consonant letters are usually separable (*ef fi cient, com mit tee, daz zling, bat ted*); but they are kept together if there is no syllable break (*im pelled*) or if both belong to a root to which a suffix has been added (*stiff ly,* not *stif fly; yell ing,* not *yel ling*).

3. A single letter is never allowed to stand by itself: do not divide words like *enough* or *many.*

4. Words spelled with a hyphen (*half-brother, well-disposed*) should be divided only at the point of the hyphen to avoid the awkwardness of two hyphens in the same word.

Fuller directions will be found in the stylebooks of publishing houses, like *A Manual of Style.*

do

Do may be considered two verbs, one of which is a meaningless but structurally important auxiliary verb. The other *do* is synonymous in some of its uses with *perform.* In "Do they do the job well?" the first *do* is the auxiliary verb, the second a main verb. The forms of both are the same and quite irregular: *do, does, did, done.*

Do has many idiomatic meanings and is part of many idiomatic phrases: *do for, do away with, do in, do over, do up.*

See Auxiliaries, Tenses of verbs 2. References: Evans and Evans, p. 140; Quirk et al., pp. 684–98.

doctoral, doctor's, doctorate

Doctoral is an adjective, *doctorate* a noun: a man who has earned his doctorate has earned his doctor's degree (his Ph.D.) in a doctoral program.

don't

Don't is the contraction of *do not,* universally used in conversation and often in writing when *do not* would seem too emphatic or when the rhythm seems more comfortable with the shorter form. Until about 1900 *don't* was the usual third-person singular (*he don't, it don't, that don't*) in informal speech, but the usage is now regarded as nonstandard. References: Atwood, p. 28; Bryant, pp. 73–74; Fries, pp. 52–53.

Double negative

1. In standard English. Two negative words in the same construction are not used in standard English to express a single negation: not "He couldn't find it nowhere," but "He couldn't find it anywhere" or "He could find it nowhere." But two negatives may be used in general English to make an emphatic affirmative: "Its re-emergences into view, out of covering buildings, never are not dramatic" (Elizabeth Bowen, *A Time in Rome*). And in a few constructions one negative statement modifies another negative statement to give a qualified meaning or a meaning with some special emphasis: I wouldn't be surprised if he never spoke to us again; He isn't sure he won't be able to afford it; Don't think he isn't clever. The negated negative, or *litotes*, is used in some formal styles (a not unattractive young woman). See Negatives and style.

2. Hardly, scarcely. A concealed double negative sometimes occurs with *hardly* or *scarcely*. Since *hardly* means "almost not" or "probably not" and *scarcely* means the same a little more emphatically, a sentence like "The campus paper contains hardly nothing" should read "contains hardly anything," and "For a while we couldn't scarcely see a thing" should read "could scarcely." Reference: Bryant, pp. 106–107.

3. In nonstandard English. Two or more negatives are very often used in nonstandard English to express a simple negation: Ain't nobody there; Couldn't nobody find the body; I don't have nothing to lose. Such double negatives are not a backsliding from the current idiom of standard English; the form survives from an older period. In early English two negatives were used in all varieties of language. The objection to a double negative is not that "two negatives always make an affirmative," for they do not. The objection is simply that the double negative is not now in fashion among educated people. References: Bryant, pp. 75–76; Copperud, p. 75; Fries, p. 35.

Double prepositions
The *of* in double prepositions like *off of* and *outside of* is unnecessary. See Prepositions and style 2.

Doublespeak
Doublespeak is the use of language not to express but to obscure, disguise, or deny the truth. Dwight Bolinger has suggested that the label be applied to "jargon that is a sophisticated form of lying." Doublespeak is common in the pronouncements of governments and government agencies, corporations, and special interest groups of all kinds. In some cases doublespeak in the form of euphemisms is used to protect the feelings of the old, the poor, the mentally retarded, the crippled, or the criminal; but the inaction encouraged by bland doublespeak does more harm than hurt feelings. Deliberate manipulation of the language by the government during the Vietnam War and Watergate led to the formation of the Committee on Public Doublespeak by members of the National Council of Teachers of English. See Euphemisms, Gobbledygook. Reference: *Language and Public Policy*, ed. Hugh Rank (Urbana, Ill.: NCTE, 1974).

doubt

The word used to introduce a clause after a statement with the verb *doubt* (or *it is doubtful*) depends on whether the statement is negative or positive.

1. Negative (when there is no real doubt), *doubt that:* I do not doubt that he meant well. (For *doubt but,* see *but that, but what.*)

2. Positive (when doubt exists), *that, whether,* less often *if:*

But there is reason to doubt that this is so. – Wayne F. LaFave, *Supreme Court Review.*

A couple of days ago, Walter Heller . . . said that he doubted whether that level could be reached. – Richard H. Rovere, *New Yorker*

I doubt if this was ever a really important reason for his leaving London. – George Woodcock, *Esquire*

dove, dived

Dove as well as *dived* is acceptable as the past tense of *dive.* References: Copperud, pp. 75–76; Pooley, pp. 134–35.

drunk

It seems to take courage to use this general word. We either go formal–*intoxicated;* or grasp at respectability through euphemisms–*under the influence of liquor, indulged to excess;* or make a weak attempt at humor with one of the dozens of slang expressions like *looped, bombed, stoned.* But *drunk* is the word.

due to

No one complains when *due* (followed by *to*) is used as an adjective firmly modifying a noun: "The failure was due to a conceptual oversight" (William Jaffé, *Journal of Political Economy*). But there has been strong objection to the use of *due to* in the sense "because of" to introduce prepositional phrases functioning as adverbs: "Cooperative self-regulatory efforts among newspapers in a locality have become rare, partly due to the tradition of independence in the field" (*Harvard Law Review*). The objection – on the grounds that *due to* is adjectival only – ignores the fact that the change of a word from one part of speech to another is commonplace in English. And though the distinguished lexicographer John S. Kenyon presented evidence in 1930 that this use of *due to* had become standard, the prejudice (which he shared) remains widespread. As a result, some writers are afraid to use *due to* in any context. References: John S. Kenyon, *AS*, Oct. 1930, pp. 61–70; Bryant, p. 81; Copperud, p. 77; Pooley, pp. 135–38.

E

each

1. Though the pronoun *each* is singular (To each his own), we use it to individualize members of a group. As a result, it inevitably attracts plural forms. In informal and increasingly in general usage, *each* is treated as a collective when the plural idea is uppermost (compare *every*):

Each of the stages in child development produce typical conflicts. – Selma Fraiberg, *New York Review of Books*

Each of these peoples undoubtedly modified Latin in accordance with their own speech habits. – Albert C. Baugh, *A History of the English Language*

But in formal usage *each* is ordinarily singular: "Each of them was asserting its own individuality" (John Higham, *American Historical Review*).

Sometimes when *each* refers to both men and women, a writer will use *they* rather than *his* as one way of avoiding sexist language: Each of the weekend guests brought their own climbing gear. See Agreement 2, Sexist language.

2. As an adjective, *each* does not affect the number of the verb or related pronoun. When the subject modified by *each* is plural, the verb and related pronoun are also plural: "The editions that have appeared since World War I each have their weak and strong points" (James McManaway, *PMLA*).

References: Bryant, pp. 8–9; Copperud, p. 78.

each other, one another

Although some textbooks have insisted that *each other* refers to two only and *one another* to more than two, writers ignore the distinction. See Pronouns 3. References: Bryant, pp. 82–83; Copperud, pp. 78–79; Pooley, pp. 138–39.

Echo phrases

An echo phrase calls to mind a passage in literature or a popular saying. See Allusion.

Editorial we

Traditionally the anonymous writers of editorials use *we* and *our* (We believe that . . . ; It is our recommendation that . . .) rather than *I* and *my*. The practice makes sense because editorials supposedly speak for the group that publishes the periodical. See *I, we*.

effect, affect

The common noun is *effect*, meaning "result." As verbs, *effect* means "bring about"; *affect* means "influence" or "put on" (She affected a Southern accent). See *affect, effect*.

e.g.

E.g. stands for the Latin words meaning "for example." The best way to avoid possible confusion with *i.e.* is to use *for example*. See Abbreviations 2, *i.e.*

either

The pronoun *either* normally takes a singular verb: "Welsh and Irish are closer to each other than either is to English" (William W. Heist, *Speculum*). Reference: Copperud, p. 81.

either . . . or, neither . . . nor

When one element of a compound subject connected by *either . . . or* or *neither . . . nor* is singular and the other is plural, make the verb agree with the nearer subject. See Agreement 1c.

elder, eldest

These forms of *old* survive in references to the order of birth of members of a family—"the elder brother," "our eldest daughter"—and in some honorific senses like "elder statesmen."

Ellipsis

A punctuation mark of three spaced periods in a quotation, indicating the omission of one or more words, is called an ellipsis: "Four score and seven years ago our fathers brought forth . . . a new nation . . . dedicated to the proposition that all men are created equal." When the last words in a sentence are omitted, the end punctuation precedes the ellipsis, just as it does when the omission follows the sentence: "Four score and seven years ago our fathers brought forth on this continent a new nation. . . ."

The omission of a line or more of poetry is generally indicated by a full line of spaced periods. The omission of a paragraph or more of prose is traditionally indicated in the same way; but current practice often uses only an ellipsis at the end of the paragraph preceding the omission.

No ellipsis should be used when a quotation is just a phrase: It is worth asking whether we continue to be "dedicated to the proposition." (Not ". . . dedicated to the proposition. . . .")

In dialog, an ellipsis indicates hesitation in speech. It is also used as an end stop for a statement that is left unfinished or allowed to die away: "The town was poor then. And like so many who grew up in the Depression, we never expected we would have real jobs. There was no place for us in the world. It was depressing . . ." (John Thompson, *Harper's*).

References: *A Manual of Style; The MLA Style Sheet*, 2nd ed. (New York: Modern Language Association, 1970); *U.S. Style Manual*.

Elliptical constructions

An elliptical construction omits a word or two that can somehow be supplied, usually from a neighboring construction: I work much harder than you [work]. Grammarians differ in the extent to which they use ellipsis as a means of explanation. In the sentence "We had the same experience you did," some grammarians would say that the relative pronoun *that* has been omitted after *experience*, some that it is present in zero position, still others that no relative occurs, even implicitly. Constructions like "The more, the merrier" and "First come, first served" are commonly accepted as established idioms, not elliptical.

The choice between longer and shorter forms is a matter of style. Formal English tends to be explicit and uses relatively few ellipses. General and informal English use the shorter constructions freely. Compare Clauses 2a. References: Long and Long, pp. 143–53; Quirk et al., pp. 536–50.

else

In phrases with pronouns like *anyone, nobody,* and *someone, else* (not the preceding pronoun) takes the sign of the possessive: The package was left at somebody else's house.

emp Emphasis

Strengthen the emphasis of this passage.

Rightly used, emphasis indicates the relative importance of the points you are making, so that your reader recognizes the most important as most important, the less important as less important, the incidental as incidental. A lack of emphasis means a failure in guidance; misplaced emphasis means serious confusion.

1. Proportion. Give the point you want to emphasize the space and development its importance calls for. Ordinarily, mass is evidence of significance; we allot space on the basis of importance. When you finish a paper in a hurry, you may leave the major point undeveloped and therefore unemphatic. Sometimes you must lay a good deal of groundwork before you can present the central issue in an essay, but one of your jobs in revising is to see that you have not given preliminaries so much space as to mislead the reader.

2. Position. Generally speaking, the most emphatic position in a sentence, a paragraph, or a full essay is the end (hence the danger of leaving the final point undeveloped). The second most important is the beginning. Don't waste these natural positions of emphasis. In an essay you will often want to use both – stating your thesis in the opening paragraph and, after presenting the arguments that support it, restating it in your conclusion. In any case, don't let your major point get lost somewhere in between, and don't announce it at the beginning and then fail to get back to it. See Beginning an essay, Concluding an essay.

3. Separation. Use a comma, a colon, or a dash to set off part of a sentence and thereby emphasize it, lightly or heavily. Or begin a separate sentence or a new paragraph to achieve the same purpose. See Colon 4, Comma 7, Dash 1.

4. Repetition. As long as you don't overdo it, you can gain emphasis by repeating significant words and by repeating ideas in different words, perhaps in figurative expressions. Repeating a structural pattern, especially in a series that builds to a climax, is an excellent device for emphasizing. See Parallelism, Repetition, Series.

5. Economy. In the condensing that is a regular part of revision, pay special attention to the expression of the ideas that deserve major emphasis. Strip the sentences of any verbiage that blurs their clarity and blunts their impact. Emphatic statement need not be brusque, but it must be direct and uncluttered. See Wordiness.

6. Mechanical devices. Using underlinings, capitals, and exclamation marks for emphasis is likely to bore, annoy, or amuse the reader. Telling him that he should be interested ("It is interesting to note") or impressed ("Here is the really important point that we should all recognize") is likely to irritate him. Pretentious or portentous word choice has the same effect, and the intensifiers used in speech—*very, terribly, extremely, incredibly*—are almost uniformly ineffective in writing. On paper, "a very shocking incident" turns out to be less, not more, emphatic than "a shocking incident." So avoid mechanical devices as a means for achieving emphasis. They demand the reader's attention instead of earning it.

End stop
An end stop is a mark of punctuation—usually a period, exclamation mark, or question mark—used at the end of a sentence. In writing dialog, a double dash may be used as an end stop when a speech is interrupted. An ellipsis may be used as an end stop for a sentence that is intentionally left unfinished.

When two end stops would fall together at the close of a sentence, only one mark, the more emphatic or more necessary for meaning, is used. Here a question comes at the end of a sentence that would normally close with a period; only the question mark is used: "When we say, for example, that Miss A plays well, only an irredeemable outsider would reply, 'Plays what?'" (C. Alphonso Smith, *Studies in English Syntax*).

English language
To the linguistic historian there is no real beginning for any language. The earliest records of English date from the seventh century A.D., two centuries after invading Germanic tribesmen from northwestern Europe—Angles, Saxons, Jutes, and Frisians—had made their homes in the British Isles, bringing with them the differing but mutually intelligible dialects which are the direct ancestors of the English language. But through those dialects, English is connected to a prehistoric past—to an unrecorded language called Germanic, parent of the Low and High German languages, the Scandinavian languages, and English.

Through Germanic, English is connected to a still more ancient and unrecorded language called Indo-European, the parent of several language groups besides Germanic: Indo-Iranian, Armenian, Celtic, Albanian, Balto-Slavic, Italic, Hellenic, and the ancient tongues Hittite and Tocharian.

The history of English is often divided, somewhat arbitrarily, into three main periods: Old English (OE), c. 450–1100; Middle English (ME), c. 1100–1450; Modern English or New English (MnE or NE), c. 1450–, with this latter period sometimes subdivided into Early Modern English (EMnE), c. 1450–1700, and Modern English, c. 1700–. Some knowledge of the history of English can help a writer understand the richness and complexity of the medium he uses.

1. Vocabulary. Of all aspects of language, vocabulary is the surest index to cultural change. English is no exception to this rule, since its lexicon reflects ever-widening contacts with foreign speakers and foreign cultures as well as the inevitable expansion of word stock which goes hand in hand with an increase in cultural complexity. Throughout history, English speakers have borrowed words from foreign tongues; but they have also met their needs for new words by relying on native processes of word formation.

Latin, Scandinavian, and French have contributed most to the common vocabulary of English. Latin makes its mark early— first before the English-to-be had left their continental homes, next when Roman missionaries converted the English to Christianity in the OE period. Scandinavian influences strike still more deeply into the core of English vocabulary. Danish and Norwegian armies invaded England in the ninth century; in the tenth, colonists followed to establish permanent settlements in north and east; by the eleventh, Danish kings ruled England. Because Englishmen and Norsemen lived side by side, and because the languages were similar, many Scandinavian words entered English. French influence, resulting from the Norman conquest and occupation, is still more pervasive. For almost three hundred years, French replaced English as the tongue of law, learning, politics, and influence. One scholar has calculated that during the ME period alone over ten thousand French words were borrowed and that, of these, 75 percent survive.

Loan words from the modern period reflect the ever-widening circle of contacts. Terms from Low German (particularly Dutch and Flemish) result from late medieval trade across the channel; Italian and Spanish terms show English movements into the Mediterranean. Excursions to more distant lands provided English with loans from Turkish, Arabic, Persian, Indo-Aryan, Chinese, Japanese, Malayo-Polynesian, Australian, African, and Amerindian languages. Some words from exotic sources have entered the general English vocabulary *(apricot, caravan, coffee, taboo, tulip)*; others belong to the common vocabulary of only one national variety of English (e.g., Amerindian loans in

American English); still others retain their exotic flavor and are used only in reference to foreign locales (*gaucho, amboyna, parang, punkah*).

Many words have made their way into English through books. Latin and Greek have contributed most to the learned vocabulary. The Christian missionaries to the earliest English brought terms related to learning and to church activities: *school, gloss, grammatic(al), master, verse* alongside *abbot, alms, cleric, hymn, priest*. OE borrowings of animal terms show that the world of books is opening: *dragon* (OE *draca*), *elephant* (OE *elpend*), *basilisk, camel, phoenix*. The language of English learning is predominantly Latin through the EMnE period, joined then by Greek as a complementary source. The scholarly, scientific, and technical vocabulary of the twentieth century reflects the persistent influence of the classical tongues: *aerospace, allobar, antibiotic, astrophysics, astronaut, biochemistry, chronograph, ecology, isotope, positron, spectroscope, telemetry*.

Of the native processes for forming new words, two have been most productive: compounding and word composition (see Origin of words). English vocabulary is rich in its collection of noun, adjective, verb, and adverb compound terms. OE *scops* (bards, poets) relied heavily on compounds to meet the demands of alliterative verse; OE prose writers used compounds almost as frequently, often preferring native formations to borrowed terms: e.g., *ānhorn, allmihtig, gōdspell* (literally, "good tidings"), instead of *unicorn* (L. *unicornus*), *omnipotent* (L. *omnipotens*), *evangel* (L. *ēvangelium*). Compounding has continued as a productive process throughout the history of English; examples abound in modern colloquial English: *highbrow, egghead, hotbed, deadbeat, lowbrow;* in the vocabularies of occupations, sports, and hobbies; and in technical vocabularies — *countdown, earthshine*.

History has worked changes in English word composition, but has never restricted its productivity. Over the centuries, some native affixes have disappeared altogether; some survive only as fossils (e.g., *for-* in *forbear*); still others have become restricted in use (e.g., *-dom, -hood, -th* as in *width*). But to its dwindling stock of natives affixes, English has added others, principally from Latin, Greek, and French. How completely English has assimilated foreign elements may be seen in the freedom with which it combines foreign and native word elements: to native bases are added foreign affixes — *goddess, endearment, mileage, hindrance, murderous, heathenism, womanize;* to foreign bases, native affixes — *graceful, faintness, courtship, unconscious, forbearance, martyrdom;* foreign elements from two sources are mixed — *postal, socialist, jurist, communism*. With its borrowings and its still flourishing native supply, English possesses a rich and precise system of formatives.

In spite of its cosmopolitan quality, the English lexicon remains fixed to its origins. Perhaps a quarter of the present English vocabulary goes back to the words of Old English, and many of these are the most frequently used of all. The modern descendants of OE words are changed almost always in pronunciation and nearly as often in meaning, as are borrowed words which have long been in common use. As objects change in shape or in the uses to which they are put, the meanings of the terms naming them change: *ship, car, weapon* are obvious examples; *atom* has a long history in English, but scientists change its definition each time they discover more about its structure. Words naming specific things can be generalized in application (*thing* was once a legal term); general terms can become specific (*deer* once meant "wild animal"); words can slide up and down an evaluational scale with the fortunes of the referents (*lust* once meant "pleasure," harmless as well as otherwise; a *marshall* was once a horse-servant, a *steward*, a pig-keeper). Writers must be on their guard for fluctuations in denotation and nuance but quick to seize potentialities in their rich lexical heritage. English offers an everyday vocabulary rich in its synonyms, an exotic vocabulary redolent of distant countries, a learned vocabulary precise in denotation and partially preserved by its literary character from rapid semantic change. The effective writer learns to exploit the nuances of synonymous terms, to respond to the demands of occasion on vocabulary level, and to recognize that the English lexicon is not a closed book.

2. Grammar. Although a modern student needs assistance in learning to read Old English, he will recognize more similarities than differences in the grammatical systems of Old and Modern English. The inflectional system of OE has been extensively simplified by historical changes, but in syntax the two stages show fundamental likenesses.

Space permits only hints of the inflectional complexity of OE. The OE noun, for example, had distinctive forms for singular and plural and for four cases (nominative, genitive, dative, accusative) and exhibited grammatical gender (nouns fell into one of several declensions, mainly according to gender). Articles, demonstratives, and adjectives agreed with nouns in gender, number, and case. Thus, where MnE has only the form *the*, OE had separate inflections for masculine, neuter, and feminine forms, for singular and plural, and for the various cases. Where MnE has an invariant form of the adjective, OE possessed a full array of endings for number, gender, and case.

From the complex of forms in OE comes the sparse inflectional machinery of MnE: *the* and *that* are remnants from an OE demonstrative article; *this, these,* and *those* come from a second demonstrative; *a, an* come from the OE word *ān* (one), separately inflected in OE. Adjective inflections disappeared entirely by the end of the ME period. The noun endings that remain in MnE trace back to OE origins: the *-s* of plural to *-as* in the masculine declension (*cyningas* "kings"); the *-s* of genitive to the OE genitive of the same declension (*cyning-es*). From other noun declensions, MnE retains only fossils: the *-en* of *oxen;* the *-ren* of *children* (a double plural); the vowel gradation of *man, men; goose, geese.* Verb inflections underwent similar processes of decay, particularly of personal endings, and in the conversion of strong (irregular) verbs to the weak pattern. This last change is reflected in the variations of past and past participle forms in British and American dialects: *dived* vs. *dove, climbed* vs. *clomb, blowed* vs. *blew, heaved* vs. *hove.*

Some syntactic changes have occurred. The MnE use of *do* in interrogatives (Do you dance?) and emphatics (You *do* dance) is an EMnE addition to the auxiliary system of English (cf. Chaucer's question form, "Lady myn, Criseyde, lyve ye yet?"). The auxiliary *be* in progressive forms first appeared in OE, and only slowly made its way into the English auxiliary system. Forms like "He is laughing" were not common until the sixteenth century; passive progressive (The house is being painted) does not develop until the end of the eighteenth. The full participation of progressive forms in the auxiliary system will be reached when a sentence like "The runner could have been being trained during that time" no longer strikes us with its rarity. But significant innovations are rare in the history of the English grammatical system. To look at deep rather than superficial features of English grammar is to convince oneself of how slowly they alter, no matter what happens to vocabulary and pronunciation, or to surface inflections. Purists sometimes maintain that changes in usage will render the language chaotic and unintelligible. As a consequence, writers are urged to cling to the *whom* in "Whom did you see?" Historical perspective helps us to see that English preserves its basic form, its semantically significant categories and relations, through many superficial changes.

3. Standardization and the spread of English. In modern times, English has undergone two developments which may at first glance seem contradictory. On the one hand, large groups of English speakers have migrated from England in apparent imitation of their continental Germanic ancestors, whose migrations resulted in the split of Germanic into separate languages. In North America, Australia, New Zealand, India, and Africa, new national varieties of English have arisen, but none has diverged far enough from its parent or its siblings to be considered a separate tongue. The failure of history to repeat itself may be attributed to the second major development in Modern English — standardization. In England after the ME period, a relatively uniform and powerfully dominant form of English spread to all parts of the island kingdom; in other English-speaking nations, similar tendencies toward standardization have kept the separate national varieties basically alike.

Dialect differences have always existed in English. The major varieties of OE — Kentish, West Saxon, Anglian (sometimes divided into Mercian and Northumbrian) — derive from differences among the dialects brought by Germanic invaders and lead in turn to the major varieties of ME. In the ME period conditions favored localism in the use of English—particularly the replacement of English with French in official documents, in Parliament, in law courts and schools, and in the literature intended for the upper classes. Although English emerged from its subservience in the thirteenth century and became common in official use in the fourteenth, the three major English poets of the fourteenth century—Chaucer, Langland, and the Pearl Poet—all wrote their separate native dialects.

Sixteenth-century poets, however, used a uniform written standard based on a late ME form of London English. Thus what is later known as standard English began as a regional dialect—the dialect of England's capital, naturally prestigious because it was the dialect of powerful and influential men. Early in the fifteenth century the standard spread into official documents written outside London, later in the century into private documents such as letters and journals. Printers felt a particular need for uniformity, especially in spelling and choice of word forms, and helped spread written standard by putting it before the eyes of a growing number of readers. Renaissance scholars and schoolmasters pushed standardization almost as actively, seeking to demonstrate that English was as proper a medium of learning as the classical tongues, pressing their claims by working for spelling reform and by providing English with grammars and dictionaries. What the Renaissance left untidy, eighteenth-century schoolmen sought to regularize and fix. Prescriptive grammarians labored to settle cases of disputed usage: to unravel the uses of *between* and *among,* to decide what case properly follows *than* and *as,* to explicate the differences between *shall* and *will.* Uniformity and correctness were cardinal linguistic virtues.

The benefits of standardization are many: learning to read is made easier as the number of variant spellings and forms is reduced; communication is facilitated; the growth of a national literature is undoubtedly encouraged when writers and audience share a common tongue. But there are disadvantages and dangers when standards are asserted so stringently that no room is left for variations introduced by the natural processes of linguistic change; greater dangers when, as has happened in the history of English, the standard dialect becomes a class dialect invested with the status of its speakers. The process began early in England with the feeling that one kind of pronunciation must be correct. Sir Thomas Elyot urged sixteenth-century nurses, if they could not teach a nobleman's son pure and elegant Latin, at least to teach "none englisshe but that which is cleane, polite, perfectly and articulately pronounced, omittinge no lettre or sillable." Such pronunciation was soon equated with the speech of "the better sort": educated and influential people who hovered about the seats of power. After the eighteenth century—a great age of snobbism, when aristocrats looked down their noses at the lower classes and lower classes did all they could to imitate their betters—spoken standard English became firmly established as a class standard, carefully maintained as an outward sign of status. Those who could not adapt betrayed their origins merely by opening their mouths.

Although most traces of provincial dialects disappeared from English writing after the fifteenth century, the dialects themselves continued to be spoken. Earlier dialect differences are, of course, the bases of modern British dialects, and also of differences between British English, American English, Australian English, etc. But American English has never diverged far from the parent language, partly because of cultural contacts, partly because standardizing processes in American English have retarded linguistic change. British and American usage remained close during the colonial period—the differences consisting mainly of vocabulary items. Growing nationalism after the Revolution led Americans to predict, and eagerly expect, a new American language, "as different from the future language of England, as the modern Dutch, Danish and Swedish are from the German, or from one another" (Noah Webster, 1789). But concern for preserving national unity suggested that American dialects must not be allowed to develop unchecked lest they become so different from one another as to make communication difficult: "a national language is a band of national union," wrote Webster, and as textbook writer for the new nation he pushed a standard of general (that is, national) custom:

. . . general custom must be the rule of speaking, and every derivation from this must be wrong. The dialect of one state is as ridiculous as that of another; each is authorized by local custom; and neither is supported by any superior excellence.

But American prescriptivism has tended to concentrate on the written word. Webster's "general custom" is easily translated into marks on a printed page, and general custom in pronunciation must inevitably be abstract as long as differences in speech exist. America has never had an official standard of pronunciation, based on the speech of a single locale or class. And American prescriptivism has paid more attention to grammar than to pronunciation. Southern, Northern, and Western speakers may sound different but still speak standard American English; the same is not true of Southerner, Northerner, or Westerner who utters "He don't never do that."

Class dialects do exist in the United States. When we use the terms *standard* and *nonstandard* English, we refer to the social status of the speakers of each, not to good or bad qualities inherent in the dialects themselves. And while it is true that standard English in the United States has been flexible and tolerant of regional variation and of importations from nonstandard, dialect conflict has emerged in our century. Massive migration to Northern cities, particularly from the South and South-Midlands, has brought Northern and Southern speakers into close contact. Because many of the migrants have been poor and ill-educated, their speech—regional in its origins—has been taken as indicative of their class. Thus in many Northern cities, Southern

speech is equated with nonstandard speech. The new migrant –
particularly if he is black – does not find the city welcoming him.
Hostility toward him, toward his class or race, attaches easily
to his language; in return, the migrant may see in Webster's
"general custom" only the values of an oppressive class.

Dialects are not merely collections of sounds, forms, words.
They are powerful social and psychological symbols – expressive
of who one is, what groups he belongs to, what values he shares
with others. Standardized languages have vital functions to perform in breaking down intense regionalism and in facilitating
international communication: Englishmen, Americans, Canadians, Australians, New Zealanders can talk to one another; they
can also talk to English speakers in India, Pakistan, Ceylon,
Malaysia, Nepal, the Philippines, Nigeria, Rhodesia, Sierra
Leone, Ghana, Kenya, the British West Indies, to name only a
few of the nations where English holds some official status.
Standardization has helped make English available as a com-
municative medium for educated people in Africa, Asia, and the
Western world, as a potential link between peoples of diverse
cultures. The link, however, can be easily broken by an over-
zealous commitment to inflexible standards that take no account of the personal, social, and cultural validity of dialect difference. West Indian poets and novelists insist that their own
English is the proper medium for their works; African writers do
the same; some black authors in the United States insist that
they write in Black English – a dialect symbolizing the values
and attitudes of black people in coexistence with or rebellion
against white society. If standard American English is defined
too narrowly and without reference to the usage of social minorities – if it is identified too closely with the usage of the white
middle class – we invite the division of America into fixed castes.

References: Histories: Albert C. Baugh, *A History of the En-
glish Language,* 2nd ed. (New York: Appleton, 1957); Thomas
Pyles, *The Origins and Development of the English Language,*
2nd ed. (New York: Harcourt, 1971); Joseph M. Williams, *Ori-
gins of the English Language* (New York: Free Press, 1975).
American English: G. P. Krapp, *The English Language in
America,* 2 vols. (New York: Ungar, 1960); A. L. Marckwardt,
American English (New York: Oxford Univ. Press, 1958); H. L.
Mencken, *The American Language,* abridged 4th ed., ed. Raven
I. McDavid, Jr. (New York: Knopf, 1963); Thomas Pyles, *Words
and Ways of American English* (New York: Random, 1952).
English words: George H. McKnight, *English Words and Their
Background* (New York: Appleton, 1923); Mary S. Serjeantson,
A History of Foreign Words in English (London: Routledge,
1935); J. A. Sheard, *The Words We Use* (New York: Praeger,
1954). Dialects: G. L. Brook, *English Dialects* (New York:
Oxford Univ. Press, 1963); Raven I. McDavid, Jr., in Francis;
Carroll E. Reed, *Dialects of American English* (Cleveland:
World, 1967); Harold B. Allen and Gary N. Underwood, eds.,
Readings in American Dialectology (New York: Appleton,

1971). A survey of British dialects is in process of publication by Leeds University under the editorship of Harold Orton and Wilfred J. Halliday. Many publications have resulted from the survey of American dialects called *The Linguistic Atlas of the United States and Canada*. Bibliographical references may be found in the books by Reed and by Allen and Underwood.

Jay Robinson

enormity, enormousness

Because *enormity* looks like a more compact way of expressing the idea of "enormousness," it is often used in that sense, as most dictionaries indicate. But this use is deplored by those who restrict *enormity* to the meaning "enormously evil" or "great wickedness," as in "the enormity of the crime."

enthuse

Enthuse is a back formation (see Origin of words 3e) from *enthusiasm*. Although widely used in general and informal writing, it is still not established in formal usage, and many readers object to it. The only other locutions we have for the idea are the longer *be enthusiastic over* or *be enthusiastic about*. Reference: Copperud, p. 87.

Epigrams and aphorisms

An epigram is a short, pithy statement, in verse or prose, usually with a touch of wit. In prose this means a detached or detachable and quotable sentence. In consecutive prose, epigrams sometimes become too prominent, attract too much attention to themselves, or give the impression of straining for effect. But they can focus attention and phrase an idea so that it will be remembered: "Conscience is the inner voice that warns us that someone may be looking" (H. L. Mencken).

Closely related to epigrams are aphorisms—pithy statements that are more likely to be abstract and are not necessarily witty. The essays of Francis Bacon are packed with aphorisms:

To spend too much time in studies is sloth; to use them too much for ornament is affectation; to make judgment wholly by their rules is the humor of a scholar. . . . Read not to contradict and confute; nor to believe and take for granted; nor to find talk and discourse; but to weigh and consider. . . . Reading maketh a full man; conference a ready man; and writing an exact man.—Francis Bacon, "Of Studies"

A special type of epigram is the paradox, which makes a statement that as it stands contradicts fact or common sense or itself and yet suggests a truth or at least a half-truth: All generalizations are false, including this one.

equally as

Although *equally as* is an established idiom (Color is equally as important as design), one of the words is always redundant. With that in mind, use *equally* or *as*, not both: *Either* Color is as important as design *or* Color and design are equally important. References: Bryant, p. 85; Copperud, p. 88.

-ese

The suffix -*ese* is used to make new nouns, such as *Brooklynese, journalese, educationese, Pentagonese,* which have the disparaging sense of "lingo, jargon, or dialect": His mastery of sociologese left us impressed if uninformed.

Establishment

In the 1960s *Establishment* (sometimes not capitalized) became a vogue word for the powers-that-be: "In the intellectuals' lexicon 'the Establishment' now seems to include federal, state, and local government, business corporations, foundations and other philanthropic organizations, Big Labor, Big Science, and the administrators of universities" (Max Ways, *Fortune*). While sometimes simply descriptive, it is more often a term of abuse, expressing discontent with the ins and sympathy with the outs.

In *The New Yorker*, October 19, 1968, Henry Fairlie tells of launching the term in its present sense in the British *Spectator* of September 23, 1955. At that time Fairlie wrote: "By the 'Establishment,' I do not mean only the centres of official power — though they are certainly part of it — but rather the whole matrix of official and social relations within which power is exercised." *Establishment* has remained anything but precise but continues to refer to often sinister inner circles: "John O'Hara was underrated by the critical-academic axis sometimes called The Literary Establishment" (Matthew J. Bruccoli, *The O'Hara Concern*).

et al.

Et al. is the abbreviation for the Latin words meaning "and others." A footnote style may call for reducing a list of four or more authors to the first author named and *et al.* (See Footnote form.) In ordinary writing, and in some footnote styles, use "and others."

etc.

Though sometimes a convenient way to end an incomplete list, *etc.,* the abbreviation for the Latin phrase *et cetera* ("and the rest"), belongs primarily to business and reference usage: This case is suitable for large photographs, maps, blueprints, etc. In most writing *and so forth* or *and so on* is preferable when the reference is to things, and *and others* is preferable with lists of people. The incompleteness of a list can also be marked by an introductory phrase like *such as* after the category the list exemplifies: This case is suitable for large papers such as photographs, maps, and blueprints.

Ethnic labels

American English has more than its share of slang terms for members of racial and ethnic groups. While these may at times be used with no hostile intent — may even be used by members of the groups they name — our vocabularies would be healthier without them. Besides the labels for peoples of European, African, and Latin American origins, these terms should be avoided: *Asiatic* (for *Asian*), *Jap* (*Japanese*), *Chinamen* or *Chink* (*Chinese*), as well as words like *gook*.

Etymology
Etymology is the study of word origins. See Origin of words.

Euphemisms
A euphemism is a word used in place of one that names more explicitly something unpleasant or something regarded as not quite nice: *perspire* for *sweat*, *passed on* for *died*, *senior citizens* for *old people*, *lavatory* or *powder room* or even *comfort facility* for *toilet*. Political, military, and promotional vocabularies offer countless examples. Occasionally euphemisms are warranted, to avoid causing pain or embarrassment, but ordinarily honesty is better—and makes for better writing—than evasion. The persistent substitution of *attacked* and *assaulted* for *raped* in news stories succeeded chiefly in making the substitutes ambiguous.

every

1. *Every, everybody, everyone* were originally singular and are still so to the extent that they nearly always take a singular verb: *Every man on the team did well; Everybody loathes the mayor; Everyone takes the freeway.* Usage is divided, however, for related pronouns that come later in the sentence. The singular is perhaps more common in formal writing, but the plural appears in all varieties: "Everybody who has praised the inaugural address cannot possibly be as enthusiastic as they sound, unless they are merely reacting to its music" (James Reston, *New York Times*). The plural is reasonable, since the reference is to a number of people. Instead of substituting a *he* for each *they*, formal written usage might replace *Everybody* with an explicit plural: All those who have praised. . . .

A plural pronoun is also used for clarity when the *every* phrase is the object of a verb with a singular subject: "The traditional leader then comes forward and thanks everyone for their attendance and invites them to lunch" (John A. Woodward, *Ethnology*). Treating the *every* words as collectives can sometimes prevent confusion and also avoid the awkward he-or-she problem. But some conservatives continue to insist that, in writing, related pronouns be singular. See *he or she*. References: Bryant, pp. 8–10; Fries, p. 50.

2. *Everybody* is always written as one word; *everyone* is usually written as one word, but when the *one* is stressed, it is written as two:

Everyone knew what the end would be.
Every one of us knew what the end would be.

3. *Every so often,* meaning "occasionally," should not be confused with *ever so often,* meaning "very frequently":

Every so often we have to get away from the city.
We go to the country ever so often in the summer.

One way to avoid confusing the two is to avoid using the exclamatory *ever so often.*

4. *Everyplace,* meaning "everywhere," is avoided in formal usage. *Everywheres* is nonstandard.

Examples

Examples are instances that illustrate general statements. They clarify explanations, confirm assertions, and provide support for arguments. See Details, Induction.

except, accept

Except as a verb means "leave out, exclude": He excepted those who had made an honest effort. It is decidedly formal. *Excused* would be more appropriate for the same meaning in general writing.

Accept means "receive" or "respond to affirmatively" and is slightly formal: I accept with pleasure; He accepted the position (as contrasted with "He took the job").

Exclamation mark

An exclamation mark (or point) is used after an emphatic interjection, after a phrase, clause, or sentence that is genuinely exclamatory, and after forceful commands. Clear-cut exclamations are no problem:

Oh! Ouch! No, no, no!
Damn those mosquitoes!
It was the chance of a lifetime!

But many interjections are mild and deserve no more than a comma or a period: "Well, well, so you're in college now." Often sentences cast in exclamatory patterns are simply statements (What a memorable experience that was), and the type of punctuation is optional.

In deciding whether or not to use an exclamation mark, you should first ask yourself whether you intend an exclamation. Are you in fact expressing strong feeling or saying something that you want to give special emphasis to? Walt Kelly said, "Using the exclamation point is like wearing padded shoulders." But when used sparingly, to signal genuine emotion, the mark can serve the writer as the raised voice or dramatic gesture serves the speaker:

The Sun Also Rises is a major work, brilliantly constructed and colored —
though last year I was taken aback to hear some students complain that
Jake Barnes indulges himself in too much self-pity. How imperious the
young can be when judging the victims of disasters they don't even trouble to learn about! — Irving Howe, *Harper's*

Exclamations

What distinguishes an exclamation from other kinds of utterance is its purpose: emphatic expression. In form, an exclamation may be a declarative sentence (She's late again!), a question (Can she be late again!), a command or request (Be ready when I call! Please be on time!), a verbless sentence (How terrible for you!), or an interjection (Ouch!). See Exclamation mark.

expect

In general and formal writing, *expect* is ordinarily limited to the senses "anticipate" (He expects to be a great success) and "require as reasonable" (Winsock, Inc., expects its employees to arrive on time). In American usage the sense "to suppose, presume, believe" in reference to past and present events (I expect there were times when Lincoln was heartily fed up) is likely to be limited to informal contexts. Reference: Copperud, p. 95.

Exposition

Most of the writing required in college courses is explanatory — writing that is intended primarily to inform and enlighten the reader. *Exposition* (or *expository writing*) is the traditional term for writing of this kind. When it is extended to include argument, *exposition* refers to all factual prose, in contrast to fiction. See Argument, Forms of discourse, Rhetoric.

F

fact

The fact is often deadwood that can simply be omitted: The study demonstrates [the fact] that workers can become affluent. Sometimes phrases with *fact* can be replaced by single words: In spite of the fact=*although;* due to the fact that=*because.* In the redundant *true fact, fact* alone should be retained.

factor

Windy phrases with *factor* should be deleted: Determination and imagination [were the factors that] brought the program its popularity. *Factor* itself, which means "something that helps produce a result," can often be replaced by a more precise, expressive word: A major factor [stimulus? influence? resource?] in creating the system was the artisan class.

Fallacies

As the term is used in logic, a fallacy is an error in reasoning. If a college announces that it awards scholarships only to students who are needy, then we are reasoning correctly when we assume that a particular student who receives a scholarship at that institution is needy. But it would be fallacious to say, on the basis of the same announcement, that every needy student in the college is receiving scholarship aid. Similarly, a person who acts on the premise that no X-rated movie is fit to see can't confidently assume that any movie not so rated *is* fit to see. *Non sequitur* ("it does not follow") is a comprehensive category covering all those errors in reasoning in which the stated conclusion does not follow from the premises or starting points.

Popularly, *fallacy* is extended to include all misleading statements and errors in interpretation, intentional or unintentional. In this sense, a speaker or writer who deliberately withholds facts, slants evidence, draws an unjustified inference, or argues beside the point commits a fallacy. So does the speaker or writer whose attempt to reach a sound conclusion is thwarted because he doesn't know enough about a situation or because he makes a mistake in interpreting his information.

The common fallacies go by names that are almost self-explanatory. *Hasty generalizing* means jumping to a conclusion before sufficient evidence has been gathered: The fact that two of every three students in my physics class are interested in a career in engineering indicates that engineering is the first choice of science majors these days. *Faulty generalizing,* which is based on weak or unrepresentative instances, may take the form of *card-stacking* (deliberately suppressing data that contradicts the conclusion) or *stereotyping* (applying labels to an entire group—calling all Scots stingy, for example).

Ignoring the question is the fallacy of shifting the grounds of the argument from the real issue to one that is not under debate. An *argumentum ad hominem* attacks not the issue itself but the character of those who support it. Setting up a *straw man* is arguing not against the opposing point of view but against a caricature of it. And using a *red herring* is introducing an issue that shifts the argument from its proper course. *Name-calling* is the irresponsible use of epithets and labels chosen for their connotations for particular audiences (for some audiences, *liberal* is inflammatory; for others, *conservative* is). *Hypostatization* is the appeal to an abstraction as an authority: "Science tells us" instead of "Heisenberg tells us in *Physics and Beyond. . . .*"

For other fallacies, see Begging the question, Cause and effect 2. See also Logical thinking.

farther, further

Some careful writers make a distinction between *farther*, referring to physical distance (Farther north there was heavy snow), and *further*, referring to more abstract relations of degree or extent (Nothing could be further removed from experience). But the distinction is not consistently maintained, even in formal English. References: Bryant, p. 87; Pooley, pp. 141–43.

feel

Although one of the accepted meanings of *feel* is "think" or "believe" (I feel that Barnum was right), *feel* should not be allowed to replace those verbs. Readers need to be reminded now and then that a writer thinks and has convictions.

fellow

Fellow is general and informal when used to mean "person, man, or boy" but formal in the sense "associate." It is most commonly used in writing in the function of an adjective: his fellow sufferers, a fellow feeling ("a similar feeling" or "sympathy").

female

In current usage the noun *female* seems most appropriate in somewhat formal or technical contexts in which the designation of sex is significant: "Each female is assigned a number of social security quarters at the beginning of the simulation" (James H. Schulz, *Yale Economic Essays*). As an adjective *female* has more general usefulness but does not entirely escape its pejorative or technical connotations. See Sexist language.

fewer, less

The rule is that *fewer* refers to number among things that are counted (fewer particles) and *less* to amount or quantity among things that are measured (less energy). Formal usage ordinarily observes the distinction; and though *less* is applied to countables fairly often in general writing—"I suggest they sell two less tickets to the public" (Dwight Macdonald, *Esquire*)—it grates on some readers' ears. References: Bryant, pp. 129–30; Copperud, p. 103.

field

The phrase "the field of" can almost always be omitted: He has long been interested in [the field of] psychiatry.

Figurative language

We use figurative language when we transfer a word from a context in which it is normally used (a smelly cheese) to one in which it is not (a smelly scandal). The moment we begin to look for figures of speech, we find them everywhere: we *play ball* when we cooperate, *chime in* when we join in a conversation, *tax* someone's patience when we talk too much. Many of these word transfers have been around so long that they have lost all their figurative, or image-making, power. (Who pictures an animal when he hears that someone has *weaseled* out of a situation?) Although *foot* continues to serve as the name for a part of the body, its reference has been extended to include the bottom or lowest part of a tree, a bed, a path, and a mountain, among many other things. In these uses, *foot* is a petrified, or dead, figure. (*Dead* is used here figuratively.)

A live figure is created when a word is extended to a new referent. We speak routinely of peeling an apple or a potato; Paul Auster, writing of the poet Laura Riding, speaks of her "trying somehow to peel back the skin of the world" (*New York Review of*

Books). The yoking of things not ordinarily thought of as alike or the phrasing of a perception in a fresh way may serve the double function of seizing the attention and of informing or persuading. Both functions are served by these figurative descriptions of musical performances, the first by a rock group, the second by a jazz pianist:

Aston Barrett's pounding bass line kicks you in the guts and Al Anderson's . . . guitar lead cuts through the air like a knife. — Michael Goodwin, *Rolling Stone*

He uses his considerable technique beautifully: His arpeggios, which whip and coil, have logic and continuity; his double-time dashes are parenthetical and light up what they interrupt; his single-note passages continually pause and breathe; no tempo rattles the clarity of his articulation, which has a private, singing quality. — Whitney Balliett, *New Yorker*

Traditionally, distinctions among figures of speech are made on the basis of the way the meaning of the word or phrase is transferred. In a metaphor it is often made directly: the bass line *kicks* you. In a simile it is made through *like* or *as:* the guitar lead cuts through the air *like a knife.* In other common figures the part stands for the whole (*wheel* for bicycle) or the whole for the part (*Navy* for a team at the Naval Academy) or the author for the works (*Shakespeare* for his plays). Hyperbole uses extravagant language for emphasis (a *thousand* apologies); understatement seeks the same effect by the opposite means (Enthusiasm for the draft was *not overwhelming*).

Personification gives life to abstractions and inanimate objects. In this elaborate figure General Motors, Chrysler, and Ford, losing sales to foreign automakers, are pictured as pompous aristocrats being hard pressed by snapping dogs:

The Auto Lords of Michigan continue to stride about the interior, making gruff and manly sounds, but their legs are beset with Saabs and Volvos, their ankles nibbled at by Datsuns and Volkswagens. — Michael J. Arlen, *New Yorker*

For other figures of speech, see Analogy, Imagery, Irony, Metaphor, Oxymoron. For figures of sound, see Alliteration, Assonance, Onomatopoeia, Puns. See also Figures of speech. Reference: Lawrence Perrine, *College English,* Nov. 1971, pp. 125–38.

Figures

Figures are the symbols for numbers. See Numbers.

fig Figures of speech

This figure of speech is trite, inconsistent, or inappropriate. Revise the passage.

A good figure of speech can add color, humor, interest, and information and may convey meaning more economically than its literal equivalent. But literal expression is always preferable to figures that are overused or carelessly chosen.

1. Replace trite figures. Use fresh ones that represent your own perceptions. Many figures that once were fresh and vivid are now clichés: *cool as a cucumber, a ribbon of concrete, Old Man Winter.* The writer who thinks about what he is setting down on paper either avoids them or at least tries to give them a new look. "A cucumber-cool manner" might get by where "cool as a cucumber" would bore the reader. But there are dangers in trying to disguise clichés. Although "A lot of water has flowed under the bridge" takes on some new life in "all the water, and war, that had flowed under the bridge" (Karl Miller, *New York Review of Books*), some readers may feel that water and war don't mix. Whenever possible, offer the reader an original figure, like James Thurber's road "which seemed to be paved with old typewriters." If you can neither freshen an old figure successfully nor invent a new one that works, stick to a literal statement of your meaning.

2. Untangle mixed figures. Sometimes, instead of coming up with no images at all, you may find yourself with too many:

The noise, like an enthusiastic roar from a distant sports stadium, yet as insistent as the surge of distant surf, grew till it was galloping up the quadrangle in massive waves.

Here sports fans, the ocean, and horses create a catastrophe. To catch such incongruous mixtures before the final draft, read what you've written as objectively as you possibly can. More difficult to spot are the mixed figures that involve dead metaphors. Keep in mind that a figure that is dead in most contexts may revive in some relationships, with ridiculous results. In the first of the following sentences, the student invents a figure that is apt. In the second, the word *faces,* which is regularly used to stand for "people," simply won't work with *sitting* or with suiting up:

As we dressed, comments were tossed about the room as casually as the rolls of tape we were using to tape our ankles. The familiar faces, sitting in their usual corners, were all getting into their uniforms.

Don't just read what you've written before you turn a paper in. Think about what it *says.* When your figures call up pictures of physical impossibilities or other absurdities because you have mixed images, they are bound to distract your readers from the point you're trying to make. If in speaking figuratively you seem to be speaking foolishly, your figurative language needs to be overhauled.

3. Replace inappropriate figures. A figure of speech may be inappropriate to the audience, to the subject, or to you as the writer. Whether used to explain or to amuse, similes, metaphors, and analogies drawn from biology or trout fishing or from the folklore of your home town won't work with an audience that knows nothing about those things. Describing bluegrass music with figures appropriate to a discussion of Beethoven's symphonies, or vice versa, makes sense only if you are trying, rather desperately, to be funny. And using figures that don't match your own attitudes or temperament—poetic figures, for example, when your natural style is down-to-earth, or hard-boiled ones when your approach is gentle and thoughtful—gives them an off-key prominence that will disturb readers.

A figure of speech can be judged good or not good only in a context, a rhetorical situation. When you write your final draft, judge each of your figures by its appropriateness to the audience, the subject, and your prevailing tone. If you decide that a figure doesn't fit, replace it with a suitable figure or with the literal equivalent. But don't discard a figure simply because it startles you when you read over what you've written. In the context of your essay "the moon crashed through the clouds" may be just right. See Figurative language.

finalize

Finalize has been in widespread use for more than a generation. Its near-synonyms, *finish, conclude,* and *complete,* lack the connotation "to make official" that give *finalize* its usefulness in some contexts: "Before they finalize new guidelines they will consult listeners in East Europe to make sure the proposed changes are having the right effect" (Mary Hornaday, *Christian Science Monitor*). But no writer can afford to be ignorant of the great prejudice against *finalize*. It was included in Maury Maverick's original list of gobbledygook in 1942, and some consider it gobbledygook today. Reference: Copperud, p. 104.

"Fine" writing

"Fine" writing is generally a term of dispraise, applied to writing that is too pretentious for the material or purpose. "Fine" writing betrays itself chiefly in the use of "big" words and in strained, artificial figures of speech. If you write more to impress an audience than to express an idea, you are likely to produce "fine" writing. See Diction, Figures of speech.

Finite verbs

A finite verb is one that is limited in number (singular or plural) and in person (first, second, or third), as contrasted with the nonfinite forms—the infinitives *(to drive, drive),* the participles *(driving, driven),* and the verbal nouns or gerunds *(driving).* Only finite forms can be the verbs of sentences and unreduced clauses.

fix

In formal usage *fix* means "fasten in place"; in general usage it means "repair" or "put in shape": The TV had to be fixed. As a noun meaning "predicament," *fix* has passed from informal to general: "In some respects economic theory is in the same fix as biology was years ago" (Henry M. Boettinger, *Harvard Business Review*).

flaunt, flout

Flaunt, to "wave, display boastfully," is frequently used with the sense "treat with contempt, scorn," the meaning traditionally assigned to *flout*. Readers aware of the traditional distinction deplore the confusion.

flounder, founder

Flounder means "stumble about, wallow." *Founder* is applied literally to horses ("go lame") and to ships ("sink"); in an extended sense it means "fail." *Flounder* is frequently used in this sense, but for the flounderer there's still hope.

Folk etymology

When people are puzzled by an unfamiliar word or phrase, they sometimes try to make it more regular or more meaningful by reshaping it from familiar elements: from *aeroplane* they made *airplane;* from Spanish *cucuracha,* English *cockroach;* from *saler,* "a salt-holder," first the redundant *salt-saler* and then *saltcellar,* which has no more to do with a cellar than the *sir-* in *sirloin* has to do with a knight (the *sir-* in the steak is *sur,* "above").

folk, folks

In formal writing, *folks* is uncommon. *Folk* is used in the senses "the common people" (usually of a certain region) and "people" (of a specified type). In general writing, *folks* for "people," often with the connotation "ordinary, everyday," and for "relatives, parents" is carried over from informal.

Footnote form

In any paper based on the words of others, the writer has an obligation to acknowledge the sources. This is primarily a matter of honesty and courtesy. In addition, documentation in the form of footnotes and bibliography invites the reader to judge for himself the evidence an assertion is based on and, if he wishes, to turn to the sources for further information.

You must acknowledge your sources not only when you reproduce a paragraph, a sentence, or even a significant phrase exactly but also when you reword or summarize. Whether you use direct quotations or not, you need to give the source of all facts, interpretations, and conclusions that are not common knowledge and that you have not arrived at through independent thought, experiment, or investigation. If you name in the text the original source of a quotation that you obtained from a secondary source, you should cite that secondary source in a footnote. To neglect to credit the authors and the works that the information and the ideas came from is plagiarism. See Plagiarism.

1. Placing footnotes. Each footnote is keyed to a number in the text that is placed slightly above the line after the statement or quotation. The footnotes, numbered consecutively throughout the paper, appear at the foot of the page (single-spaced with a triple space between the text and the first note and with a double space between notes) or, if the instructor so recommends, on separate sheets at the end, either single-spaced or double-spaced. Whatever the position, the form of the note is identical. The number is slightly raised and is separated from the note by one space; the first line of the note is indented five spaces.

2. Form for the first reference. The first time a source is identified in a footnote, the documentation is complete. In general, the form given here is that recommended in *The MLA Style Sheet,* second edition. (One exception is in the listing of publishers. The *Style Sheet* approves shortened forms of publishers' names, like those in the bibliography on pp. 384–85 of this text.) Other footnote styles used in the humanities differ in details, and those used in most of the sciences are fundamentally different from the form described in this article.

In the examples given below, examine each footnote carefully to see what elements are included, in what order they appear, and how they are punctuated.

A book by a single author

[1] Jerrold J. Katz, The Philosophy of Language (New York: Harper & Row, 1966), p. 42.

A book by more than one author

[2] James E. Brady and Gerard E. Humiston, General Chemistry: Principles and Structure (New York: Wiley, 1975), p. 42.

If there are more than three authors, substitute "et al." for all but the first: Shirley Gorenstein et al.

A work in more than one volume

[3] Richard B. Sewall, The Life of Emily Dickinson (New York: Farrar, Straus & Giroux, 1974), II, 251-58.

The roman numeral is the volume number. When the volume number is given, page numbers are not preceded by "pp."

An edition other than the first

[4] Lewis A. McArthur, Oregon Geographic Names, 4th ed. (Portland: Oregon Historical Society, 1974), p. 664.

An edition revised by someone other than the author

[5] Stuart Robertson, The Development of Modern English, 2nd ed., rev. Frederic G. Cassidy (Englewood Cliffs, N.J.: Prentice-Hall, 1954), pp. 36-52.

An edited work

[6] S. Y. Agnon, Twenty-one Stories, ed. Nahum N. Glatzer (New York: Schocken Books, 1970), p. 27.

A compilation by an author

[7] Joan C. Baratz and Roger W. Shuy, eds., Teaching Black Children to Read (Washington, D.C.: Center for Applied Linguistics, 1969), pp. 3-7.

A selection, chapter, or other part of a compilation

[8] Richard McKeon, "Rhetoric in the Middle Ages," in Critics and Criticism, ed. R. S. Crane (Chicago: Univ. of Chicago Press, 1952), p. 271.

A translation

[9] Maurice Merleau-Ponty, Phenomenology of Perception, trans. Colin Smith (London: Routledge, 1962), pp. 88-90.

A book that is part of a series

[10] Carl N. Degler, Affluence and Anxiety, 2nd ed., The Scott, Foresman American History Series (Glenview, Ill.: Scott, Foresman, 1975), p. 125.

A reprinted book

[11] Alfred North Whitehead, Modes of Thought (1938; rpt. New York: Putnam, Capricorn Books, 1958), pp. 26-27.

A signed article in a newspaper

[12] Steve Cady, "Dreams Grow from Asphalt," New York Times, 13 July 1975, Sec. 5, p. 3, cols. 6-7.

An unsigned article in a weekly newsmagazine

[13] "Nixon's Fight for Life," Newsweek, 11 Nov. 1974, p. 27.

An article in a monthly magazine

[14] Walter Litten, "The Most Poisonous Mushrooms," Scientific American, March 1975, pp. 90-91.

A journal article

[15] Walter J. Ong, "The Writer's Audience Is Always a Fiction," PMLA, 90 (1975), 19.

Because the journal (unlike most newspapers and magazines) is paged continuously throughout the calendar year, the volume number is given and only the year of publication is provided.

A journal article with corporate authorship

[16] NCTE Commission on Composition, "Teaching Composition: A Position Statement," College English, 36 (October 1974), 219.

In this case, because the volume does not coincide with the calendar year, the month is included. See the previous example.

A signed encyclopedia article

[17] S[tanley] We[intraub], "George Bernard Shaw," Encyclopaedia Britannica, Macropaedia 16, 1974.

A book review

18 Michael Wood, "Incomparable Empson," rev. of
William Empson: The Man and His Work, ed. Roma Gill, New
York Review of Books, 23 Jan. 1975, p. 30.

An unpublished dissertation

19 Frances Nicol Teague, "Ben Jonson's Stagecraft in
His Four Major Comedies," Diss. Univ. of Texas, 1975, p. 71.

3. Form for later reference.
a. Subsequent references to a source you have already cited in
full should be no longer than is necessary to identify the work.
For example, a second reference to Michael Wood's review of the
book on Empson should be reduced to "Wood" and the page
number: Wood, p. 31. If more than one work by the same author
is footnoted, then a subsequent reference to one of them must
include at least the key word in the title. If two or more authors
with the same last name appear in footnotes, a second reference
to any one of them must include enough additional detail – first
name or initials – for identification.

For reference to the footnote immediately preceding, *ibid.*,
meaning "in the same place," can be used; but it saves very little
space and if used inaccurately can cause serious confusion. See
ibid.
b. When a single work is quoted frequently – as, for example, in
an analysis of an article or book – the first footnote to it can state
that all subsequent page references will be made in parentheses
immediately following the quotations. For example:

Of his "defensibles," Follett says that *aggravate* "is perhaps the one
least entitled to mercy" (p. 125).

4. Split note. If the author's name is given in full in the text, it
can be omitted from the footnote. This does not apply to the title
of a work, however. If title and author both appear in the text,
the title should still begin the note.

See Bibliographical form, Research papers. References: James
D. Lester, *Writing Research Papers,* 2nd ed. (Glenview, Ill.:
Scott, 1976); *The MLA Style Sheet,* 2nd ed. (New York: Modern
Language Association, 1970).

for
Since *for* always comes between the clauses it joins, it is classified as a coordinating conjunction, but coordinating *for* may
mean the same as subordinating *because:* He was exhausted,
for he had gone two nights without sleep. A comma is usually
needed between clauses joined by *for* to keep it from being read
as a preposition: The tutors must love the work, for the pay,
which is only $300 a year plus room and board, can't be very at-
tractive. The comma prevents the misreading: The tutors must
love the work for the pay. See *because.*

Foreign words in English

1. Anglicizing foreign words. English has always borrowed words and roots freely from other languages and is still borrowing, especially from Greek and French. Words usually cross the threshold of English with their foreign spelling, perhaps with un-English plurals or other forms, and with no established English pronunciation. The process of anglicizing brings them more or less in line with English usage, but they may keep some of their foreign quality, like the *i* of *machine,* the silent *s* in *debris,* the *t* where we are tempted to put a *d* in *kindergarten.*

The speed and degree of anglicizing depends on how frequently the word is used, the circumstances in which it is used, and the people who use it. Formal writers and conservative editors keep the foreign spelling longer than writers and editors of general English. If the words come in through the spoken language, like those of the automobile vocabulary, they are anglicized sooner than if they come in by way of literature: *chassis, chauffeur, garage, detour.* Words that come in through and remain in literary, scholarly, or socially elite circles change more slowly, in both spelling and pronunciation: *tête-à-tête, faux pas, nouveau riche, laissez-faire.*

2. Using borrowed words.

a. Italics. Words which have not been completely anglicized are usually printed in italics in magazines and books and should be underlined in copy. Words on the borderline will be found sometimes in italics, sometimes not. Formal writers use italics more than general writers.

b. Accents and other marks. In books and magazines, words recently taken in from other languages are usually written with accent marks if they were so written in the language of their origin. After a time the accents are dropped unless they are needed to indicate pronunciation. Publications for the general public are more likely to drop accent marks *(expose, detente)* than are those for limited, scholarly audiences *(exposé, détente).* See Accent marks.

c. Plurals. English usually brings borrowed words into its own system of conjugation and declension *(campuses),* though some words change slowly, especially words used mainly in formal writing *(syllabi* or *syllabuses).* See Plurals of nouns 4.

See English language, Origin of words. References: Albert C. Baugh, *A History of the English Language,* 2nd ed. (New York: Appleton, 1957); Mencken; Pyles; Thomas Pyles, *Words and Ways of American English* (New York: Random, 1952); Mary Serjeantson, *A History of Foreign Words in English* (London: Routledge, 1935).

form ## Formal English

The word or passage marked is too formal for the subject or for the style of the rest of the essay. Revise, making it more appropriate.

Formal written English is appropriate (though not mandatory) in discussions of ideas, in research papers and other scholarly works, in addresses to be delivered on ceremonial occasions, and in literary essays intended for well-educated readers. It is usually not appropriate in accounts of personal experience, in papers about campus issues, in comments on current books, movies, TV shows, or popular records, or in other writing intended for general readers.

The vocabulary of formal style includes many words not used in general written English. *Form* in the margin of your paper may refer to a word that is too formal for the context: For a while it looked as though the bad habits he had picked up were irremediable [*Better:* could never be corrected]. Or it may point to a sentence pattern that suggests the deliberate pace of formal English and therefore mixes poorly with sentences that suggest the spontaneity of speech:

In addition to being younger than my classmates, I had retained, along with the babyish habit of sucking my thumb, a tendency to cry when I was not allowed to have my own way, thereby turning them against me. *Possible revision:* Besides being younger than my classmates, I still sucked my thumb. This irritated them, and I made things worse by crying when I didn't get my own way.

For discussion, see *Writer's Guide,* pp. 291–93.

Form-class words

These are the nouns, verbs, adjectives, and adverbs that function words bind together in sentences. See Parts of speech.

former, first — latter, last

Traditionally, *former* and *latter* refer only to two units—"the former called the latter 'little prig'" (Ralph Waldo Emerson)—and though, in fact, the use of *latter* with more than two is common enough to be standard, conservative readers would prefer "the last named" in references like this one: "The list of products . . . could include potassium, bromine, chlorine, caustic, and magnesium. The latter might become a very important lightweight metal" (Glenn T. Seaborg, *Bulletin of the Atomic Scientists*). *Former* should be used only with two. Reference: Copperud, p. 109.

First and *last* refer to items in a series, usually more than two:

The first president had set up a very informal organization.
His last act was to advise his family on their future.

Latest refers to a series that is still continuing (the latest fashions). *Last* refers either to the final item of a completed series (their last attempt was successful) or to the most recent item of a continuing series (the last election). See *last, latest.*

Forms of discourse

For the last century or so it has been conventional to divide writing into four forms of discourse—narration, description, exposition, and argument. The classification is useful because it emphasizes purpose as the controlling element in a piece of writing, and studying the forms one by one allows concentration on certain traits of content, organization, and style peculiar to each type. The categories are not, however, sharply distinct—description contributes to all, notably to narration; many essays which are primarily argumentative include stretches of exposition; and so on.

Formulas

Every language has some fixed phrases that have become customary in certain situations: Once upon a time, Ladies and gentlemen, Good morning, Best wishes, Dear Sir, Yours truly, How do you do? Occasionally fresh substitutes can be found, but more often the attempt merely calls attention to itself. Such phrases, though stereotyped, are too useful to be called trite, and they are not, as most trite expressions are, substitutes for some simpler locution. When called for, they should be used without apology and without embarrassment. See Idiom, Subjunctive mood 2a.

Fractions

Fractions are written in figures when they are attached to other figures ($72\frac{3}{4}$) or are in a series that is in figures ($\frac{1}{2}$, $\frac{2}{3}$, 1, 2, 4) or are in tables or reference matter. In most running text they are written in words: In the local newspaper three fourths of the space was given to advertising, one eighth to news, and one eighth to miscellaneous matters. Hyphens may be used between the numerator and denominator if neither part itself contains a hyphen (*seven-tenths*), and they should be used to avoid confusion: though *twenty seven eighths* probably means "twenty-seven eighths," it could mean "twenty seven-eighths." But hyphens are less used than formerly and are not used at all when the numerator has the value of an adjective, as in "He sold one half and kept the other."

Decimals are increasingly used in place of fractions in factual writing, since they are more flexible and may be more accurate: .7; .42; 3.14159.

See Numbers.

Fragment

The construction marked is not a satisfactory sentence. Revise by joining it to a neighboring sentence, by making it grammatically complete, or by rewriting the passage.

A sentence fragment is a part of a sentence—usually a phrase or dependent clause—that is carelessly or ineffectively punctuated as a whole sentence. You can usually correct a fragment by joining it to the preceding or following sentence or by otherwise making it grammatically complete. But sometimes you'll find that rewriting is the best solution.

Below, with suggested revisions, are three common types of fragments.

1. A prepositional phrase punctuated as a sentence

The northern part of the city is mainly residential. On the eastern outskirts are the oil refining plants. And to the south beaches and parks.
Revision: The northern part of the city is mainly residential. On the eastern outskirts are the oil refining plants and to the south beaches and parks.

2. A participial phrase punctuated as a sentence

For sixteen years I did pretty much what I wanted. Being distrustful and avoiding anyone in authority.
Revision: For sixteen years I did pretty much what I wanted to, distrusting and avoiding anyone in authority.

3. A dependent clause punctuated as a sentence

I still remember him as the best teacher I ever had. Because right then he sat down and helped me work all the problems.
Revision: I still remember him as the best teacher I ever had, because right then he sat down and helped me work all the problems.

In an unexpectedly heavy turnout, over 80 percent of the citizens voted. A fact that shows how strongly they felt about the issue.
Revision: . . . the citizens voted—a fact that shows. . . . *Or* . . . the citizens voted. This fact shows. . . .

The deliberate setting off of a phrase or dependent clause for rhetorical effect is common in print. Unfortunately, it has become a cliché of heavy-breathing advertising copy (The magic of a coral atoll; Discovering the real you). But it can do good service as an organizational road sign that briskly points the reader toward the next topic—"But first, the new troops" (Lucian K. Truscott IV, *Harper's*)—or provides informal notice of the progress of the discussion—"Which brings us back to the absurdity of the backlash accusations" (Letty Cottin Pogrebin, *Ms.*). And fragments of some length can sometimes be used effectively to pile up details in descriptive writing:

Prairie wool blue-green, spring wheat bright as new lawn, winter wheat gray-green at rest and slaty when the wind flaws it, roadside primroses as shy as prairie flowers are supposed to be, and as gentle to the eye as when in my boyhood we used to call them wild tulips, and by their coming date the beginning of summer.—Wallace Stegner, *Wolf Willow*

See Clauses, Phrases.

Free modifiers

A free modifier is a nonrestrictive modifier. See Restrictive and nonrestrictive.

freshman, freshmen

The modifier is *freshman,* not only before nouns with an obviously singular reference (a freshman dorm) but before plural and abstract nouns (freshman courses, freshman orientation).

-ful, full

When the adjective *full* is used as a suffix to nouns of measure (*basketful, spoonful*) or of feeling or quality (*peaceful, sorrowful, soulful*), it has only one *l*. In the separate word, both *l*'s are kept (a basket full of apples).

The plural of nouns ending in *-ful* is usually made with *-s: spoonfuls, basketfuls.* When *full* is written as a separate word, the preceding noun is made plural: *spoons full, baskets full.*

fulsome

The *ful-* in *fulsome* misleads some readers and writers into thinking the word means "generous" or "hearty," but *fulsome praise* (a rather formal cliché) actually means praise that is overdone and insincere and therefore offensive. Because of possible ambiguity, *fulsome* is a good word to avoid.

Function words

Function words are the auxiliaries, conjunctions, determiners, and so forth that bind together form-class words. See Parts of speech.

further, farther

Both *farther* and *further* are used in referring to distance. See *farther, further.*

Fused sentence

Fused or *run-on sentence* is the name sometimes given to two grammatically complete sentences written with no mark of punctuation between them: If you ask me why I did it, I can only say that at the time it seemed the right thing to do [ ] that is my only explanation. To correct the error, begin a new sentence or insert a semicolon. Compare Comma fault.

Future time

English verbs do not inflect, or change their form, to express future time. Some of the means we use to refer to the future are illustrated in these sentences: I am leaving next week; He sails tomorrow; She is to speak on Saturday; He is about to resign; When I am elected, I will make an investigation; They will try to be on time; She is going to refuse. See Tenses of verbs.

Gender

Modern English does not have regular and distinctive endings for masculine, feminine, and neuter nouns, for articles and adjectives modifying them, or for many pronouns referring to them—grammatical gender. Instead, we call nouns masculine, feminine, or neuter according to the sex or lack of sex of their referents, using *he, she,* or *it* as their pronouns. We use *who* mainly for human beings, *which* and *what* for inanimate objects. Usually, then, in speaking of gender in English, we are talking about the choice of pronouns and about the meaning of the words that govern that choice.

Some English nouns refer to living things of either sex *(parent)*, some to one sex *(father)*, some to the other *(mother)*. Some names for animate beings imply no sex distinction *(friend)*, though compounds allow the distinction to be made *(girl friend)*. When we ignore the sex of an animal, we use *it* to refer to the noun that names the beast, just as we sometimes use *it* of a child. We have no pronoun meaning "either-he-or-she." Traditionally, *he* has been used, but that usage is rejected by opponents of sexist language, who prefer *he or she, he/she,* or *they.* Though a fair number of nouns have endings that distinguish gender *(actor, actress; alumnus, alumna; comedian, comedienne)*, they remain an unsystematized minority. Here, too, feminists call for sex-free labels.

In rather old-fashioned formal styles, the sun may be *he,* the moon *she.* In informal English, *she* sometimes replaces *it,* especially where affection or intimate concern is involved, as when a driver speaks of his car. See *he or she,* Sexist language.

General English

General English is the core of standard English. Spoken general English is what we hear in most talks for general audiences, in news broadcasts, and in the ordinary conversation of educated people. Written, edited general English is what we read in newspapers, magazines, and most books. The main focus of this *Index* is on written general English. See *Writer's Guide,* pp. 295–96.

Genitive case

1. Signs of the genitive. The genitive (or possessive) function in English is shown in four ways:

a. Apostrophe-*s* or apostrophe alone. Singular nouns that do not end in the sound of *s* as in *chess* or of *z* as in *breeze* and plural nouns that do not end in the letter *s* add apostrophe-*s: boy's, one's, England's, men's, children's, freshmen's.* After plural nouns ending in -*s,* only an apostrophe is used: *workers' incomes, dogs' teeth, coaches' rules.*

For singular nouns ending in the *s* or *z* sound, practice varies, as do the recommendations of the stylebooks that encourage systematic rules for the sake of consistency. The system proposed by the *Manual of Style* calls for an apostrophe-*s* after all singular nouns except *Jesus, Moses,* classical names ending in -*es* *(Socrates, Xerxes),* and words like *conscience* and *goodness* before *sake;* these exceptions take an apostrophe only.

To indicate joint possession, the apostrophe is added only to the second of two coordinate nouns: "Martha and George's son."

In "Mary's and Tom's bicycles," separate objects are possessed, and an apostrophe-*s* is needed for each noun. References: *A Manual of Style,* pp. 129–30; Margaret Nicholson, *A Practical Style Guide for Authors and Editors* (New York: Holt, 1967), pp. 93–97; *U.S. Style Manual,* pp. 70–71.

b. The *of* genitive. Any genitive formed with an apostrophe or apostrophe-*s* can also be formed with an *of* phrase (the dancer's performance, the performance of the dancer). The choice between the two will usually depend on considerations of rhythm, idiom, and the syntactical pressures of neighboring phrases and clauses. Idiom calls for "the roof of the house," not "the house's roof." The *of* genitive is easier to work with when the noun in the genitive is to be modified by clauses or by other genitives. For example, both "the car's tires" and "the tires of the car" are acceptable, but if *car* is to be modified by the clause "that John used to drive," the *of* genitive is clearer: the tires of the car that John used to drive (*not* the car that John used to drive's tires). If we want to indicate that the car is John's, the *of* genitive avoids a perplexing succession of apostrophes: the tires of John's car (*not* John's car's tires).

There is also a possible difference in meaning between the two forms. "Jane's picture" probably means a picture belonging to Jane, but it might mean a picture of Jane. "A picture of Jane" can only mean that Jane is represented in the picture.

c. Double genitive. Using the *of* genitive and apostrophe-*s* together is an English idiom of long and respectable standing. It is especially common in locutions beginning with *that* or *this* and usually has an informal flavor: that boy of Henry's; friends of my father's; hobbies of Anne's. It is useful in avoiding the ambiguity mentioned above: "Jane's picture" is resolved as either "that picture of Jane" or "that picture of Jane's."

d. Genitive of the personal pronouns. The personal and relative pronouns have genitive forms without an apostrophe: *my, your, his, her, its, our, their, whose.* It is as important not to put apostrophes in these pronouns (and in the forms used without nouns: *ours, yours, theirs, hers*) as it is to put one in a noun in the genitive. See *its, it's;* Pronouns 1; *which* 2.

2. Uses of the genitive. The most common function of the genitive is to indicate possession: the professor's house, Al's dog, my daughter. It also indicates a number of other relationships:

Description: a man's job, children's toys, suit of wool

Doer of an act (the "subjective genitive"): the wind's force, the force of the wind; John Knowles's second novel; with the dean's permission, with the permission of the dean; the doctor's arrival, the arrival of the doctor

Recipient of an act (the "objective genitive"): the policeman's murderer, the murderer of the policeman; the bill's defeat, the defeat of the bill

Adverb: He drops in of an evening.

See Case, Gerunds 2. References: Bryant, pp. 50–51, 74–75, 93–94; Copperud, pp. 215–16; Fries, pp. 72–88; Jespersen, pp. 138–46; Quirk et al., pp. 192–203.

Gerunds

1. Form and function. A gerund – also called a verbal noun – is the *-ing* form of a verb used as a noun. It can serve in any noun function: as subject or complement of a verb (*Seeing* is *believing*) or as object of a verb or preposition (He taught *dancing;* The odds are against your *winning*). Like a noun, a gerund can be modified by an adjective (Good *boxing* was rare) or used as a modifier (a *fishing* boat, a *living* wage). Yet, like a verb, it can take a subject and an object and can be modified by an adverb: One despairs of the author [subject] ever [adverb] *constructing* a really forceful play [object].

A gerund may be in the present or the perfect tense and in the active or passive voice: *seeing, having seen; being seen, having been seen.*

Though the gerund has the same form as the present participle, it is used differently:

Gerund: Running a hotel appealed to him. (*Running* is the subject.)
Participle: He was busy running a hotel. (*Running* modifies *he.*)

2. Subject of a gerund. The subject of a gerund is sometimes in the genitive and sometimes in the accusative or objective (in nouns, the "common") case. Formal writing uses the genitive more than general writing does: "Such a view leads to the metaphor's becoming a brief poem in itself" (Alex Page, *Modern Philology*). General is likely to use the common case: "The Vice President's humorous remarks about Hofstra not picking up this ball are somewhat offset . . . by the record" (Clifford Lord, *College Board Review*).

In both formal and general, the circumstances in which the subject of a gerund occurs make one choice more probable than the other:

a. When the subject is a personal pronoun or a proper noun, the genitive is more usual than the common case: They wanted to discuss *my going* AWOL; We overlooked *Joe's swearing.* When the subject is a personal pronoun and begins the sentence, the genitive is required: *Our* [not *Us*] *worrying* won't solve anything; *His* [not *Him*] *lying* deceived nobody.

b. If the subject is a plural noun, it is likely to be in the common case even if it refers to persons: I don't approve of *men drinking* or *women smoking.*

c. If the subject is abstract or the name of an inanimate object, it is most often in the common case: It was an instance of *imagination getting* out of hand; The city was seized without a *shell being fired.*

References: Copperud, pp. 113–14; Evans and Evans, pp. 245–48; Pooley, pp. 107–12.

3. Phrases with gerunds. Gerunds are often used in phrases that function somewhat like dependent clauses: *In coming to an agreement*, they had compromised on all points; *By refusing to sing*, he embarrassed his father. The relation of ˙the gerund phrase to the word it modifies should be immediately apparent; the reader should not have to pause to make sure just what the writer intended:

Dangling: In coming to an agreement, campaign promises were ignored.
Revision: In coming to an agreement, both sides ignored their campaign promises.

Dangling: After sleeping sixteen hours, my headache was finally gone.
Revision: After sleeping sixteen hours, I was finally rid of my headache.

See Dangling modifiers.

4. Idioms with gerunds. Some words are characteristically followed by gerunds, others by infinitives. For example:

Gerunds	*Infinitives*
can't help *doing*	compelled *to do*
capable of *painting*	able *to paint*
the habit of *giving*	the tendency *to give*
an idea of *selling*	a wish *to sell*
enjoys *playing*	likes *to play*

With many common words, either is used: the way *of doing* something, the way *to do* something.

Compare Infinitives, Participles. References: Jespersen, Ch. 31; Long and Long, pp. 192–96.

get up
In general English you get up when you stand up or get out of bed. See *rise, arise, get up.*

go
Go in the sense "become" is used as a linking verb in a number of idioms. While some *(go broke, go native, go straight)* are informal to general, others *(go blind, go lame)* are fully established in all varieties. *Go and,* as an intensive with no actual motion implied, is common in speech and turns up in some general writing: "He has gone and made a genuine commercial film" (Joseph Morgenstern, *Newsweek*). *Going for* in the sense "working to the advantage of" is general: "when women in England didn't have much going for them" (Emily Hahn, *New York Times Book Review*). Neither *go and* nor *going for* in these senses is appropriate in formal writing.

Gobbledygook
Maury Maverick, a congressman from Texas, coined the term *gobbledygook* for wordy, pompous, overweight prose that confuses and irritates more than it informs. Although government bureaus have produced their full share of examples, business, the military, the social sciences, and the humanities have shown an equal weakness for inflated jargon. Frequently gobbledygook serves the purpose of disguising the truth. See Diction 2, Doublespeak, Jargon. Reference: Copperud, pp. 118–19.

good, well
Good is usually an adjective in standard English; *well* is either an adjective or an adverb. "I feel good" and "I feel well" (adjectives) are both usual but have different meanings, *good* implying actual bodily sensation, *well* referring merely to a state, "not ill." In nonstandard usage, *good* takes the place of *well:* He played good; She sings good. Adverbial *good* is also heard in informal speech and frequently appears in printed representations of speech: "She's running good now," the mechanic said. Reference: Copperud, p. 119.

got, gotten
Either *got* or *gotten* is acceptable as the past participle of *get* except in the following senses:

Got (not *gotten*) is often added to *has* or *have* to emphasize the notion of "possess" (I haven't got a cent) or of "must" (You've got to lend me a dollar). Though seldom used in formal writing, the emphatic *got* is fairly common in general: "A lot of adults are bored by Bach because they haven't got the faintest idea of what music is about" (Marya Mannes, *TV Guide*). References: Bryant, pp. 95–98; Copperud, pp. 119–20; Pooley, pp. 144–47.

gourmet
A gourmet is a connoisseur of food and drink. As a vogue word, the adjective *gourmet* is regularly applied to food, restaurants, and cooking that a gourmet could not stomach. If you mean "foreign," "expensive," or "fancy," use those words. To express general approval, *good* is available.

graduate
The idiom *to be graduated from* an institution has generally gone out of use except in formal and somewhat archaic writing and has been replaced by *graduated from:* He graduated from Yale in 1850. Omitting the *from* – He graduated high school in 1976 – is a common usage that many still consider nonstandard. References: Bryant, pp. 102–103; Copperud, p. 120.

Grammar
Grammar has several different senses. Just as *history* can mean a field of study, events in the past, or the book that describes those events, so *grammar* can refer to a field of study, a set of abilities in our brains, or the book that describes those abilities.

1. As a field of study, grammar is as old as intellectual inquiry itself. The pre-Socratic philosophers in Greece in the sixth century b.c. had begun speculating about language and words (*grammar* comes from *grammatikos*, "one who understands the use of letters") long before the Stoics in 300 b.c. singled grammar out as a field separate from rhetoric and poetics. Since then scholars have continued to study the structure of language, not only because language is the central defining characteristic of

humankind but because it seems possible that the very foundations of our knowledge and thought—perhaps even perception itself—are shaped by the grammatical structures of our language. Grammar thus becomes an entry to the study of mind.

2. *Grammar* may also refer to this capacity of mind, the ability every normal human being possesses to speak and understand sentences. Thus we all have a grammar in our heads. Every human being understands an indefinite number of new sentences he has never heard before. He can recognize grammatical and ungrammatical sentences (see *grammatical, ungrammatical* 1). He can recognize sentences which are ambiguous in several different ways. He also understands that some sentences relate to others, as this one does to the next two.

That some sentences relate to others is also understood by him. It is also understood by him that some sentences relate to others.

The goal of a linguist, a scholar who studies grammatical structure, is to describe in a written grammar this tacit knowledge, this internalized grammar, that all of us share.

3. Though the formal aspects of language have been studied for over 2500 years, linguists are debating more strenuously than ever before both what questions they should concern themselves with and how their answers should be formulated in written grammars. At the risk of gross overgeneralization, it can be said that the history of linguistic study in the last hundred years falls into three schools.
a. Traditional. Although this label is applied to a great variety of approaches, most traditional grammars start with semantic definitions for parts of speech and the inflections that are associated with them: nouns are names of persons, places, and things, and so on. Once the parts of speech have been described, the grammar describes functions: subjects, verbs, objects, modifiers, etc. The definitions are illustrated by examples. The reader of the grammar is expected to understand the labeling through the descriptions and examples and then to use his native knowledge of the language to apply the label in any new sentence that might contain the pattern. For example:

A sentence adverb modifies a whole sentence rather than any individual word or construction. It usually stands at the beginning of the sentence, though it may occur elsewhere: *Fortunately,* he left; He is *allegedly* still here; No one cares, *obviously.*

Confronted with the sentence "*Apparently,* she left," you could identify *apparently* as a sentence adverb on the basis of the explanation and examples. Such descriptions—semantically based as they are—require the ability of a native speaker to make them work. References: George Oliver Curme, *Parts of Speech and Accidence* (Boston: Heath, 1935), and *Syntax* (Boston: Heath, 1931); Otto Jespersen, *A Modern English Grammar on Historical Principles,* 7 vols. (1909–49; rpt. New York: Barnes, 1954); Long; Quirk et al.

b. Structural. When, in the early part of this century, anthropologists began to deal more and more with languages that had no written form and were totally unrelated to the Indo-European languages already well known, a new approach to grammatical description emerged in this country. Structural linguists tried to devise objective techniques for discovering the structure of a language without relying on semantics. They began by cataloging the sounds produced by native speakers, then identifying the smallest units that seemed to have meaning (morphemes), and then arranging these units into larger classes, not according to their lexical content but according to their customary relationships with other units. Once the parts of speech were classified, higher-order syntactic sequences were identified (noun–verb, verb–noun, preposition–noun, adjective–noun, etc.) and then further described functionally (subject–predicate, verb–object, modifier–head, etc.). A rough approximation of this technique can be found in Parts of speech. References: Francis; Fries; Sledd.

c. Generative-transformational. Through the 1940s and most of the 1950s, structural grammars were thought to be the new wave in English language education. Then in 1957 Noam Chomsky, a linguist at the Massachusetts Institute of Technology, published *Syntactic Structures* and revolutionized the study of language. Chomsky turned linguists away from formal discovery procedures, which he claimed were largely useless, and toward a model of language that tries to account in a formal set of rules for the ability of native speakers to produce and understand an infinite range of new sentences. Grammarians of the generative-transformational school assume the existence of a grammar in the mind of the native speaker. They seek to account for what all languages have in common, as well as for the peculiarities which distinguish English, say, from German; and they attempt to deal with the full range of language, from sounds to meaning, in an integrated theory.

Chomsky's initial formulations of generative theory have been considerably modified and revised in recent work, which has assigned more importance to semantics than to syntax (generative semantics and case grammar are the most important examples). And there are adherents of theories of language description other than generative—tagmemic grammars, stratificational grammars, dependency grammars, and others. But the dominant models for research into the structure of English and other languages have been generative-transformational. References: Adrian Akmajian and Frank Heny, *An Introduction to the Principles of Transformational Syntax* (Cambridge, Mass.: MIT Press, 1975); Noam Chomsky, *Language and Mind,* enl. ed. (New York: Harcourt, 1972); Charles J. Fillmore and D. Terence Langendoen, *Studies in Linguistic Semantics* (New York: Holt, 1971); Jacobs and Rosenbaum; Robert P. Stockwell, Paul Schachter, and Barbara Hall Partee, *The Major Syntactic Structures of English* (New York: Holt, 1973).

4. So far, we have ignored what may be the most common meaning of *grammar*. This is grammar in the sense of "good grammar"—making the "right" choice between *who* and *whom*, avoiding prepositions at the ends of sentences, not splitting infinitives, and so on. This is *grammar* in its normative sense. It concentrates only on those areas where usage varies from one social class to another or from the way English teachers think educated people speak to the way their students actually speak.

How we communicate depends on our social class, our geographical roots, the social situation we happen to be in, and our mode of communication—speaking or writing. What most schools teach as grammar are those features that allegedly distinguish written, fairly formal, supposedly upper-middle-class usage from all other varieties. It is a serious mistake to assume that this form of usage alone defines "correct" usage.

Thus when you use the word *grammar*, you have to distinguish a variety of senses:

Grammar is a field of scholarly inquiry dating back beyond Aristotle.

A grammar of a language is in the mind of every speaker of that language. Its "real" nature is entirely inaccessible to direct observation.

A grammar of a language is that set of rules which can be written down and which will generate the sentences of that language along with a description of each sentence. The object of this grammar is to "model" or explain grammar in sense 2.

Grammar in the sense of "He uses good grammar" is the ability we have acquired that allows us to demonstrate that we can observe certain usages that allegedly characterize the practice of upper-middle-class speakers and writers. A grammar of good usage consists of the prescriptions found in grammar books—usually fewer than twenty or thirty—that allow someone aspiring to membership in the "educated" community to speak and write as those already in that community allegedly speak and write.

This last sense of *grammar* is, unfortunately, the sense most familiar to American students. The associations that cluster about this sense make it very difficult for linguists to communicate the excitement of discovering something about grammar (sense 2) that he can write down in a grammar (sense 3) that reveals the elegantly complex organization of human linguistic knowledge.

Reference: Quirk et al., pp. 7–12.

grammatical, ungrammatical

Sentences can be grammatical in two senses:

1. Sentences are grammatical when they meet the structural requirements of the grammar used by an individual speaker. "Can't nobody tell me what to do" is ungrammatical for some speakers, but it is grammatical for others, if the grammar they have incorporated into their nervous systems allows them to construct that sentence for ordinary conversation (see Grammar 2). "Nobody can tell me what to do" might, conversely, be ungrammatical for those speakers who habitually put the modal auxiliary and negative first ("Can't nobody tell me what to do") but grammatical for those who do not. In this sense, *grammatical* simply describes the structure of a sentence that is normal for use by a particular speaker in his ordinary discourse. And in this sense nobody, except by mistake or by intention, utters an ungrammatical sentence. For example, the made-up sentence "I know the man who and the woman left" is ungrammatical for all speakers of English.

2. In common and school usage, sentences are said to be "grammatical" when they meet the requirements set by those who are in a position to enforce standards of usage. In this looser sense, "Can't nobody tell me what to do" is said to be "ungrammatical" for everyone, and a person to whom the construction is normal and systematic with reference to an internalized grammar (see Grammar 2) is said to be speaking "ungrammatical" English. In such cases the terms *grammatical* and *ungrammatical* are judgmental rather than descriptive: they name social behaviors acceptable or unacceptable to those whose judgments often carry the most weight in our stratified society. Such usages would be more accurately termed "socially acceptable" and "socially unacceptable." In many cases, advice based on this sense of *grammatical* can be quite accurate: most educated people in this country do not say "Can't nobody tell me what to do"; in writing, most make their subjects and verbs agree; most avoid *ain't* in all but relatively informal situations. On the other hand, rules for sociologically grammatical usage also involve a good deal of folklore, as many of the articles in this *Index* make clear.

See Usage. References: Harold B. Allen, ed., *Readings in Applied Linguistics,* 2nd ed. (New York: Appleton, 1964), Part IV; Noam Chomsky in *The Structure of Language*, ed. Jerry A. Fodor and Jerrold J. Katz (Englewood Cliffs, N.J.: Prentice-Hall, 1964), pp. 384–89; William Labov, *Language in the Inner City* (Philadelphia: Univ. of Pennsylvania Press, 1972), Ch. 5.

Group words

In English many groups of two or more words (that is, phrases) function like single words. Examples:

Nouns: hay fever, back door, holding company, home run, safety razor, baby blue, school year, sacrifice hit

Verbs: dig in, hold off, look into, flare up, follow through, follow up, close up, show up, blow up, back water

Prepositions: according to, in spite of, in consequence of, previous to, due to, in opposition to

In this book we ignore the superficial difference between a part of speech written as a single word and one that is written as a group of words. *Noun* (sometimes *noun phrase*) or *verb* or *preposition* refers both to single words and to group words functioning as noun or verb or preposition.

guess

Formal usage limits *guess* to its sense of "conjecture, estimate, surmise": "The employers can only guess whom the victims will choose to sue" (Henry L. Woodward, *Yale Law Journal*). But in general and informal usage *guess* is common in its looser senses of "think, suppose, believe": "They were foolish, I guess, in trying to hold history still for one more hour" (Larry L. King, *Atlantic*).

H

had better, had rather

Had better is the usual idiom in giving advice or an indirect command: You had better take care of that cold; You'd better go. The assimilation of the *d* in *you'd* to the *b* of *better* has given rise to the informal construction without either *had* or *'d:* "But I better get with it if I'm going to be a TV viewer" (Goodman Ace, *Saturday Review*). Reference: Copperud, p. 32.

   Had rather and *would rather* are both used to express preference: He would rather ski than eat; He had rather ski than eat. Use whichever seems more natural. In speech both *had* and *would* contract to *'d:* He'd rather ski than eat. Reference: Bryant, pp. 104–105.

half

Though *a half* is traditionally considered the more elegant of the two idioms, little distinction can be found between *a half* and *half a* in current formal and general usage. For example, both "a half century earlier" and "nearly half a century removed" occur in a single issue of the *American Historical Review. A half a* (a half an hour) is an informal redundancy.

   The number of the noun accompanying *half* or *half of* in a subject determines the number of the verb: Half of the book is . . . ; Half the men are. . . .

hanged, hung

In formal English people are hanged, pictures are hung. General and informal usage often ignores this distinction, using *hang, hung, hung* in all senses: "Of course, McCarthy hung himself at the hearing" (Isidore Silver, *New Republic*). Reference: Copperud, p. 133.

hardly

Hardly means "probably not," so don't add another *not.* See Double negative 2.

have

1. Independent meaning. As a verb of independent meaning *have* means "own, possess" in a literal sense (have a car) or a transferred sense (have the measles). Because *have* occurs so frequently as an "empty" auxiliary word, its meaning as an independent word is often reinforced by *got* (see *got, gotten*).

2. Auxiliary. *Have* plus a past participle makes the perfect tense (They have come); *shall have* or *will have* plus a past participle makes the future perfect tense (They will have gone by then); *had* plus a past participle makes the past perfect (They had gone to the beach before we arrived). In this use *have* is a function word — a signal of tense. See Tenses of verbs 2.

3. Contractions. *He, she, it has* contract to *he's, she's, it's* (He's not tried to in years; It's rained for a week). Contractions with *has* and *is* are indistinguishable: *He's gone* may be *He has gone* or *He is gone. I, you, we, they have* contract to *I've, you've, we've, they've.* Both *had* and *would* contract to *'d* (They'd already spoken; She'd already be waiting).

Would have, wouldn't have are sometimes written would of, wouldn't of, a nonstandard transcription of what is spoken as would've, wouldn't've.

4. *Had ought, hadn't ought.* *Had ought* (He had ought to take better care of himself) is a common nonstandard idiom, sometimes heard in informal speech. *Hadn't ought* (He hadn't ought to lie like that) is regional and informal. Reference: Atwood, pp. 38–41.

5. *Have to.* *Have to* and *must* are nearly synonymous in the affirmative (I *have to* [or *must*] go now), but in the negative there is a difference (I don't have to go; I mustn't go). *Have to* has the advantage that it can be conjugated in all tenses.

6. Other idioms. For *have got*, see *got, gotten*. See also *had better, had rather.*

Headword

A headword, or head, is a word modified by another word, especially a noun modified by one or more adjectives (his first long *sleep*), a verb modified by one or more adverbs (*walk* carefully), or an adjective or adverb modified by qualifiers (very *old*, more *intelligently*). The term is used differently by different linguists but always to mean the word around which the rest of the construction is built: *men*, old *men*, very old *men*, very old *men* in raincoats, very old *men* in raincoats who had been waiting outside. References: Paul Roberts, *Patterns of English* (New York: Harcourt, 1956), pp. 77–105; Long, p. 490; Sledd, pp. 226–27; Whitehall, pp. 9–18.

healthful, healthy

The distinction between *healthful* "conducive to health" (places and foods are healthful) and *healthy* "having good health" (persons and animals are healthy) is maintained in formal and some general writing, but by and large *healthy* is now used for both meanings.

help but

Conservative stylists avoid using *can't* (or *cannot*) *help but*. See *can't help but, can't seem to*.

hence

Hence is primarily an adverb but it is also used as a rather formal connective. See Conjunctive adverbs.

he or she

The pronoun *they* does not indicate sex, but *he, she,* and *it* are masculine, feminine, and neuter. Traditionally, *he* is used with indefinite pronouns like *anyone* and *everyone* and with noun antecedents that may refer to either men or women: Every student must accept responsibility for his acts. But feminists find this usage a prime example of sexist language and prefer *he or she* (or *he/she* or *s/he*) and *his or her*. Sometimes antecedents make a masculine pronoun inappropriate and the double pronoun convenient: "In enabling a young man or woman to prepare for life in a shorter period of time, we direct his or her attention to other values" (Edward H. Litchfield, *Saturday Review*).

For writers and readers to whom avoiding *he* and *his* after a sexually indefinite antecedent is not a matter of principle, *he or she* and its variants often seem unnecessarily awkward: "Any individual who is a candidate for promotion or tenure should her/himself make sure that records are complete" (Committee recommendation). When *he* or *his* is inappropriate, *they* is a frequent choice in general writing: In helping a young man or woman to prepare for life, we must direct their attention to other values. See Agreement 2, Sexist language. References: Evans and Evans, pp. 221, 239–40, 509; Thomas H. Middleton, *Saturday Review*, June 29, 1974, p. 40.

himself, herself

Himself and *herself* are used in two ways:

1. As reflexive pronouns, referring to the subject of the sentence: George has always taken himself too seriously; She looked at herself in the window.

2. As qualifiers, for emphasis: He told me so himself; I looked up, and there was the captain himself.

historic, historical

Unlike many pairs of adjectives ending in *-ic* and *-ical, historic* and *historical* ordinarily have quite different meanings. *Historic* usually has the sense "important in history, noteworthy, famous": "a historic act: the toast to the French fleet by which the archbishop . . . urged French Catholics to abandon royalist opposition" (James E. Ward, *American Historical Review*). *Historical* is much more neutral, meaning "based on the facts of history," "having occurred in the past," "suitable for study by historians or using their methods": "This autobiography . . . provides a wide range of historical persons and events" (Heinz E. Ellersieck, ibid.).

hopefully

From an adverb with the established meaning "in a hopeful way, full of hope" (The dog waited hopefully for a handout), *hopefully* became a vogue word meaning "it is hoped": "Hopefully, they will reveal the thickness of the planet's polar ice cap" (Jonathan Spivak, *Wall Street Journal*). Sometimes it means no more than "I hope": Hopefully she'll be down in a minute. So long as it is kept away from the verb and set off by commas, there is little chance of real ambiguity; but strong prejudice against the usage continues. Reference: Copperud, p. 131.

Hours

In consecutive formal writing, hours are often written in words: at four o'clock; around five-fifteen. In newspapers and in much general writing, figures are used, especially if several times are mentioned and always in designations of time with *a.m.* and *p.m.*: at 4 p.m., just after 9 a.m., around 4:30 p.m., from 10 to 12. The twenty-four hour system used in Europe and by the U.S. military makes *a.m.* and *p.m.* redundant: 9 a.m. = 0900; 9 p.m. = 2100.

however

Though particularly appropriate as a connective in the fully developed sentences of formal style, *however* is also the most common conjunctive adverb in general writing. There it typically serves to relate a sentence to what has gone before rather than to connect main clauses within the same sentence:

Murder is usually reported, and 86 per cent of all reported murders lead to arrests. Among those arrested, however, only 64 per cent are prosecuted. – Ramsey Clark, *Saturday Review*

However is more maneuverable than *but;* it can either introduce the clause it modifies ("However, among those arrested . . .) or, as in the example, follow the words the writer wants to emphasize ("Among those arrested"). To open a clause the simpler *but* is often the better choice.

See Conjunctive adverbs. Reference: Copperud, pp. 132–33.

hung, hanged

In formal English, pictures are hung, people are hanged. See *hanged, hung.*

Hyperbole

This very common figure of speech – obvious and extravagant overstatement – is a staple of humor; but we also use hyperbole regularly in ordinary conversation when we describe our troubles as *incredible*, our embarrassments as *horrible*, our vacations as *fabulous*. Such efforts to dramatize and intensify rapidly cease to have any effect, including the hyperbolic. They are particularly tiresome in writing. See Figurative language.

Hypercorrectness

Hypercorrect forms are used by speakers and writers who extend the patterns of supposed correctness beyond their established limits. Perhaps the most common example of hypercorrectness is the use of *I* for *me* in a compound object: It is a wonderful moment for my wife and I; They invited Jack and I; between you and I. Other common hypercorrect forms include *whom* for *who* (He is critical of the other members of the committee, whom he feels spend more time making accusations than solving problems), *as* for *like* (She, as any other normal person, wanted to be well thought of), the ending *-ly* where it doesn't belong (Slice thinly), some verb forms (*lie* for *lay*, *shall* for *will*), and many pronunciations. Hypercorrect forms are also called hyperurbanisms. References: Theodore M. Bernstein, *The Careful Writer* (New York: Atheneum, 1968), pp. 322–23; Margaret Schlauch, *The Gift of Language* (New York: Dover, 1955), pp. 264–68.

Hyphen

In *Manuscript and Proof*, stylebook of the Oxford University Press, John Benbow wrote, "If you take the hyphen seriously, you will surely go mad." To ward off madness, adopt a recent dictionary or stylebook as your guide and follow it consistently.

1. Word division. The hyphen is always used to mark the division of a word at the end of a line (see Division of words). Other uses are in part a matter of style.

2. Compound words. Some compound words are written as two words (*post office*), some as one (*notebook*), and some as a combination of words joined by hyphens (*mother-in-law*). The trend is away from hyphenation, toward one-word spelling. Even when a prefix ends and a root word begins with the same vowel, the current tendency is to write the word solid: *cooperate, reelect, preeminent.*

A number of compound adjective forms are conventionally hyphenated when they precede a noun: *clear-eyed, able-bodied, first-class.* Compounds consisting of an adverb plus a verbal are hyphenated when the adverb does not end in *-ly:* a well-marked trail (*but* a plainly marked trail).

3. Noun phrases. Usage is divided on hyphenating noun phrases used as modifiers, as in "seventeenth century philosophy." A hyphen is more likely in formal styles: seventeenth-century philosophy.

4. Miscellaneous uses. A numeral as part of a modifier (5-cent cigar, nine-inch boards) is hyphenated, and a hyphen is used between a prefix and a proper name: pre-Sputnik, pro-Doonesbury.

A "suspension" hyphen may be used to carry the force of a modifier to a later noun: the third-, fourth-, and fifth-grade rooms; both thirteenth- and fourteenth-century texts.

5. To avoid ambiguity. Occasionally a pair of modifiers is ambiguous without a hyphen. "A light yellow scarf" may be either a scarf that is light yellow or a light scarf that is yellow. *Light-yellow* makes the first meaning clear; *light, yellow* the second. Similarly, "new car-owner" and "new-car owner" prevent misunderstanding.

References: Copperud, pp. 133–36; Regina Hoover, *CCC*, May 1971, pp. 156–60; *A Manual of Style; U.S. Style Manual;* Summey, Ch. 10.

I

I

The pronoun *I* is still written as a capital simply because in the old manuscripts a small *i* might have been lost or attached to a neighboring word; the capital helped keep it distinct. The notion that *I* should not be the first word in a sentence is groundless. *I* should be used wherever it is needed. Circumlocutions to avoid the natural use of *I* are usually awkward and are likely to attract attention to themselves: "My present thinking is that relief projects are unsound" is a clumsy way of saying "I think now   [or "I think" or "I have come to think" or "At the moment I think"] that relief projects are unsound." See *it's me, myself, we.*

ibid.

Ibid., an abbreviation of the Latin *ibidem* ("in the same place"), is still used, though less often than formerly, in footnotes of scholarly books, articles, and research papers. When it stands alone (² Ibid.), it refers the reader to the preceding citation. When it is followed by a page number (² Ibid., p. 37), it refers to a different page of the work just cited. With or without a page number, it always refers to the citation *immediately* preceding. If a reference to a different work has intervened, the new footnote gives the author's name followed by *op. cit.,* an abbreviation of *opere citato* ("in the work already cited"), and the page number or, more commonly now, simply gives the author's name and the page number.

In modern styles of documentation, *ibid.* has been widely replaced by the author's name or by his name followed by a shortened version of the title of his work. Even when *ibid.* appears, its use is often restricted to a second reference on the *same page* of the manuscript or publication.

See Footnote form 3.

id **Idiom**

The expression marked is not standard idiom. Revise it, referring to an article in this *Index* or to a dictionary if you are not sure of the correct form.

Idioms are certain phrases that are established in the language but are not easy to explain grammatically or logically. Some examples are "in good stead," "come in handy," "strike a bargain," "look up an old friend," "many's the time," "make good," "in respect to." We learn these phrases as individual units, and if we are native speakers, most of them cause us no trouble. No native speaker is likely to say "the time is many" or "hit a bargain" or "look down an old friend" (though "track down" – another idiom – might be a satisfactory substitute). Many idioms are completely frozen: you can use thousands of words as subjects and verbs of sentences, but you can't substitute any other adjective in the phrase "in good stead."

We have trouble with idioms we have not learned, and most commonly the error is in the choice of preposition. Because we know *conform to,* we may speak of a policy that is "in conformity to public opinion"; but the idiom is "in conformity with." In using the formal word *arise,* we might attach the preposition *off* instead of the *from* idiom demands. Because logic is no help, the prepositions must be learned in the phrases that determine their usage. Dictionaries generally show the preposition that is conventionally used with a particular word.

See *agree to, agree with; compare, contrast; different;* Gerunds 4; *it;* Prepositions and style 1; Subjunctive mood 2a; Verb-adverb combinations. References: Copperud, p. 138; Fowler, p. 261.

i.e.

I.e. is the abbreviation for the Latin words meaning "that is." It is appropriate only in scholarly writing. See Abbreviations 2.

if, whether

Writers have a choice between *if* and *whether* before interrogative clauses (indirect questions) and clauses expressing doubt or uncertainty. *Whether* is almost always chosen in formal contexts: "It is appropriate to ask whether these decisions are to be considered a victory for those who champion individual rights" (Wayne F. LaFave, *Supreme Court Review*). Both words are used in general writing, but *if* is more common: "The survey first asked people if TV made them feel more opposed to the war or not" (*Newsweek*).

Whether is required when the clause begins a sentence (Whether it rains or shines . . .), is the object of a preposition (The question of whether . . .), modifies a noun (The question whether . . .), or follows *be* (The question is whether . . .).

Reference: Pooley, pp. 147–49.

illiterate

Illiterate and *literate* are used to refer both to the ability to read and write (There were few schools, and most of the peasants were completely illiterate) and to familiarity with what has been written (Any literate person should know the name Kafka). Usage called nonstandard in this book is often loosely referred to as illiterate in the second sense—that is, uneducated.

ill, sick

Ill is the less common, more formal word. See *sick, ill.*

illusion, allusion

An illusion misleads, an allusion refers. See *allusion, illusion.*

image

Image meaning a public conception or impression—"Ford . . . said he hopes to project the image of a president rather than a campaigner" (Associated Press story)—has moved from the jargon of the public relations man and the advertiser into general use. It can also be found in scholarly writing, applied at times to persons whose lives antedated the usage, if not the attitude behind it: "Even in France, where Franklin was widely admired and loved, he still remained self-consciously aware of his image" (Melvin Buxbaum, *Benjamin Franklin and the Zealous Presbyterians*). For some readers, the connotations of *image* in this sense are distasteful.

Imagery

An image is a word or group of words that makes an appeal to one of the senses: sight (*shiny, ghostly, mist, slime, green, thick brown hair*), hearing (*creaking, faraway shouts, the pounding of surf*), taste (*salty, dry, a pickled pear*), smell (*jasmine, fresh paint, a blown-out candle*), touch (*smooth, glassy, razor sharp, a stubbly beard*), and the muscular tension known as the kinesthetic sense (*squirm, jerky, jogging heavily along*). Though an image may appeal to more than one sense (*a rough, angry sea*), in a specific context one sense is usually dominant.

Imagery is especially characteristic of poetry, in which the content or activity of the mind is often rendered concretely—thought manifested in things. But most writers of expository prose also use imagery to keep in close touch with the visible and tangible world:

The first attempt of men to live collectively under the rule of reason ended in the bloodletting of the French Revolution. This was a sorry disappointment to liberals, but they accommodated it to their thesis by arguing that rational behavior could not be expected to sprout overnight from soil that had for centuries been eroded and poisoned by injustice and oppression.—Reinhold Niebuhr, *The Search for America*

Studying the images in a writer's work will usually show what has impressed him in his experience, what appeals to him—colors, lines, odors, sounds. Your own writing will be richer and stronger if it includes images drawn from your own experience. A borrowed image is likely to be a dead one. An image drawn from experience is a live image; and a live image is like a good photograph: it reveals something of the photographer as well as showing what he has photographed.

See Figurative language.

Imperative mood

The form of the verb that is used for direct commands and requests is said to be in the imperative mood: Bring the tapes when you come; Run! Imperatives have no overt ending and usually no expressed subject. See Commands and requests.

implement

The catchall bureaucratic verb *implement*, meaning to "give effect" to policies or ideas (It's a great scenario, but who's going to implement it?), might often be replaced by *fulfill, execute, put into practice*, and *carry out*, if only for variety. See Gobble-dygook.

imply, infer

Careful users of English make a distinction between *imply* and *infer:* a writer or speaker *implies* something in his words or manner, suggesting a conclusion without stating it; a reader or listener *infers* something from what he reads or hears, drawing a conclusion from the available information. Indeed, both implying and inferring can be wordless: The dean implied by his half smile that he doubted my story; They inferred from his silence that he disapproved of the new policy.

Having a word for each of these acts contributes to clear communication. But for centuries *infer* has also been used to mean "imply," and today many dictionaries recognize this meaning (as well as the traditional meaning) of *infer* as standard. Thus when clarity is essential, the safe course is not simply to distinguish between *imply* and *infer* but to provide a context that underlines your meaning: From the President's words, I infer that he. . . .

References: Copperud, p. 141; Follett, pp. 175–76; Fowler, p. 282.

Incoherence

Writing is incoherent when the relationship between parts (of a sentence, of a paragraph, of a whole paper) is not made clear. The cause may be that there actually is no relationship between the parts, or it may be that the writer has failed to indicate the relationship that he perceives. See Coherence, Transition.

Incomplete sentence

Punctuating a phrase or a dependent clause as if it were a complete sentence is often the result of carelessness. See Fragment.

incredible, incredulous

A story or situation is incredible ("unbelievable"); a person is incredulous ("unbelieving"). One way to avoid confusing the two is to refrain from using *incredible,* an example of trite hyperbole in current vogue.

Indention

To indent in manuscript or printed copy is to begin the first line of a paragraph some distance to the right of the left-hand margin – about an inch in longhand copy, about five spaces in typewritten copy. Hanging indention is indention of all lines below the first line, as in bibliographies and in many newspaper headlines, outlines, headings, and addresses of letters. If a line of verse is too long to stand on one line, the part brought over to the second line should be indented. For indenting quotations, see Quotation marks 1d.

Independent clauses

An independent clause (like this one) can stand alone as a simple sentence. See Clauses.

Indicative mood

Verb forms that make assertions or ask questions are said to be indicative or in the indicative mood. The indicative is the mood of most verbs in English sentences: They *sat* on the porch even though it *was* late October; *Will* you *come* if you *are* invited? Compare Imperative mood, Subjunctive mood.

Indirect discourse (indirect quotation)

When someone's words are reported in paraphrase or summary instead of being quoted exactly, they are in indirect discourse:

Direct: He said, "I won't take it if they give it to me."
Indirect: He said he wouldn't take it if they gave it to him.

An indirect question restates a question at second hand:

Direct: "Is everyone all right?" he asked.
Indirect: He asked if everyone was all right.

See Commands and requests, Questions, Quotation marks 2b, Tense 3b.

Indirect objects

An indirect object names the person or thing to which something is given, said, or shown: She gave *him* a prize. See Objects 2.

Induction

The process of reasoning known as induction originates in curiosity and ends in conviction. You are reasoning inductively when, after asking your friends how they feel about a proposed change in the pass-fail policy and after listening to what's being said on the subject around campus, you decide that the student body is strongly opposed to the change. Note that you haven't polled the student body; that would be nose-counting, not inductive reasoning. Instead, at some point in your gathering of information, you have made the "inductive leap," assuming that what is true of the people you have talked to and listened to is true of the whole group.

You can't be certain that it's true. But you can have confidence in your conclusion—you can assume that it is highly probable—if the evidence you have examined has been adequate, representative, and related to the issue.

In serious argument, induction usually takes the form of example after example offered in support of a generalization. As used in everyday life, inductive reasoning may seem to be little more than a hunch or an informed guess. But it is nonetheless important, for only by using induction can we spot trends, make predictions, and discover causal relations.

See Cause and effect, Deduction, Fallacies, Logical thinking.

infer, imply

The writer or speaker implies; the reader or listener infers. See *imply, infer*.

Infinitives

Infinitive is a Latin grammatical term for a verb form expressing the general sense of the verb without restriction as to person, number, or tense. In Old English the infinitive had a distinctive form, but in Modern English the root form of the verb is used, often with *to* before it.

1. The *to* infinitive and the bare infinitive. More often than not, an infinitive is used with the preposition *to*: He is the man *to see;* He was glad *to come;* He likes *to be visited*. But *to* is seldom or never used after the modal auxiliary verbs or after some full verbs: I can *see;* He must *carry* it; We let him *go*.

With or without *to*, the infinitive may be in the active voice (*to ask, to have asked*) or in the passive (*to be asked, to have been asked*). As the examples show, there are two tenses. The present infinitive indicates a time that is the same as, or subsequent to, the time of the main verb: He is here *to help;* They expected *to be asked*. The perfect infinitive indicates action previous to the time of the main verb: I am glad *to have been* one of his friends.

2. Functions of infinitives. Infinitives serve as subjects, as objects, as complements, and as modifiers. They in turn may have subjects, objects, complements, or modifiers.

Subject: To sit and read was his idea of a holiday. For you *to do* that again would be a serious mistake.

Object: He prefers *to wait* until Tuesday. The police attempted *to hold back* the crowd.

Complement: He seems *to be* happy.

Modifier: My friend is the man *to see*. Jane is the person *to do* that. He was happy *to stay* longer. The police are trying *to find out* what happened. *To avoid* colds, stay out of crowds.

3. Subject of the infinitive. When *for* + nominal precedes the infinitive, the subject of the infinitive is the nominal: For Tom to say that shocked us. When it does not, the subject is either the indefinite *someone* or *anyone* (To ignore the suffering in the world is criminal = For anyone to ignore the suffering in the world is criminal) or a referent expressed elsewhere in the sentence (To ignore the suffering in the world is criminal of them = For them to ignore the suffering in the world is criminal).

4. Infinitives and style.

a. Infinitives in a series. In a short, unemphatic series, *to* is not repeated: He decided to shower, shave, and dress. When the series is complex or when separate verbs deserve emphasis, *to* is repeated: These were his goals – to escape the city, to avoid routine, and to find contentment.

b. Case of pronoun. For the pronoun after the infinitive of a linking verb that has no expressed subject, general English usually has the accusative: I always wanted to be him. Formal favors the nominative: I always wanted to be he. But that locution makes the pronoun prominent, and another phrasing might be preferable: He was the one I always wanted to be.

c. Dangling infinitives. Infinitives that function as absolute phrases (to tell the truth, to be sure) are sentence modifiers and as such present no problems. But an infinitive, like a participle or a gerund, will dangle if it seems to relate to a word that it cannot sensibly modify or if, in a context that demands an explicit relationship, it has no clear relation to any word in the sentence.

Dangling: To swim well, fear of the water must be overcome.
Revised: To swim well, the learner must overcome fear of the water.

See Absolute phrases, Dangling modifiers.

d. Split infinitive. In a split infinitive, a word or phrase (usually an adverb) comes between *to* and the verb: to actively pursue. Some infinitives should not be split; some should be. In still other contexts, it is a matter of choice, with more splits occurring in general English than in formal. See Split infinitive.

References: Jespersen, Ch. 32; Roberts, pp. 359–67.

Inflection

In grammar *inflection* refers to the change of form that some words undergo to indicate certain grammatical relationships, like singular and plural number for nouns or past and present tense for verbs. See Case, Comparison of adjectives and adverbs, Plurals of nouns, Pronouns, Verbs.

inf

Informal English

The word or passage marked is too informal for the subject or for the style of the rest of the paper. Revise, making it more appropriate.

Informal written English is appropriate (though not mandatory) in letters to your close friends and to members of your family and may be the style you use in a diary or journal. Its casual, intimate tone makes it unsuitable for most college writing, though informal usages and locutions may be successfully introduced into papers written in general English if they are chosen with taste and judgment.

You'd be unlikely to use the informal *pretty* (pretty big, pretty soon, pretty old) in a chemistry report or a psychology examination, and you probably wouldn't describe Robert Frost as a "pretty good poet" in a paper for a literature course. But in writing about a local hero for an audience of classmates, you might call him a "pretty good quarterback." Whether or not *inf* should appear in the margin of your paper would depend on the context. If your style was generally relaxed and conversational, *pretty* would be appropriate. If your style placed some distance between you and your readers, *fairly* would be a better choice.

As applied to sections of papers or whole papers, *informal* usually implies sloppiness—rambling, loose-jointed sentences, vague references, trite slang, counter words, repetition, incoherence. If something you've written has been so marked, the best solution is to rethink what you wanted to say and rewrite the passage, aiming for clarity and precision.

For discussion, see *Writer's Guide*, pp. 293–95. See also Agreement, Counter words, Repetition, Slang, Spoken and written English, Triteness.

in, into, in to

In usually shows location, literal or figurative: He was in the house; He was in a stupor. *Into* usually shows direction: He came into the house; He fell into a stupor. But in general and informal usage, *in* is common when direction is meant: "Twice a week we get in the car, and drive down the Parkway" (Richard Rose, *St. Louis Post-Dispatch*). Reference: Copperud, p. 141.

The *in* of *in to* is an adverb and the *to* a preposition (They went in to dinner) or sign of the infinitive (They went in to eat).

Intensifiers

Qualifiers like *very, greatly, terribly, much* intensify the meaning of adjectives: He is much older than she. See Qualifiers.

Intensive pronouns

Reflexive pronouns—the personal pronouns plus *-self* or *-selves*—may be used as intensives: We ourselves are responsible. See *myself*, Pronouns 2.

Interjections

Interjections are expressions of emotion like *oh, ow, ouch, ah*. See Exclamations, Parts of speech.

Interrogative pronouns

Who, whom, whose, which, what are interrogative pronouns. See Pronouns 5.

Intransitive verbs

An intransitive verb takes no object: The money vanished. See Transitive and intransitive verbs.

Introductions

Don't "introduce" any paper you write unless such a beginning is absolutely necessary. See Beginning an essay.

Inversion

Inversion means placing the verb, or some part of the verb phrase, before its subject. This is the regular syntactical pattern in questions: Will she go? Did they enjoy it? Inversion is also used with expletive *there* and *it* (There was a man at the door) and in a few other situations: What a fool he is; Long may it wave; Here comes the thunder. Occasionally a declarative sentence may be inverted for emphasis: Down he went; This I know; That she was brilliant he had no doubt.

Irony

Irony implies something markedly different, sometimes even the opposite, from what is actually said. Light irony is humorous, as in the greeting "Lovely day!" in pouring rain. Heavy irony is usually a form of sarcasm or satire.

irregardless

Irregardless is redundant: both the prefix *ir-* and the suffix *-less* are negative. The standard word is *regardless*.

Irregular verbs

Verbs that do not form their past tense and past participle by adding *-ed* are irregular. See Principal parts of verbs.

it

It is the neuter third-person singular pronoun, used most commonly to refer to inanimates but sometimes to living things. Typically, it replaces preceding neuter noun phrases: Have you seen *the neighbors' new car?* — Yes, isn't *it* a mess? The antecedent may be a clause or a sentence: Some people say *that more money will solve the problem of our schools*, but I don't believe *it*. But sometimes *it* has no antecedent, as in impersonal statements about the weather, time, distance, or events in general, and in numerous idioms:

It's three hours since *it* began to rain, and *it's* still five miles to camp.
It isn't pleasant to live in Washington these days.
Damn *it*, we'll have to talk *it* out with the dean.

Though typically neuter, the antecedent of *it* may be an animal or a small child whose sex is unknown or irrelevant. *It* is also used with reference to collective nouns denoting persons (The faculty must decide for itself) and in sentences where individuals are identified (I'm not sure who the violinist was, but it could have been Oistrakh).

The more important uses of *it*, stylistically, are those where it fills the position of a subject or object fully expressed later in the sentence. In such sentences, "expletive" *it* is called the "formal" or "provisional" or "anticipatory" subject or object:

It is doubtful *that he should be given so much freedom.*
He found *it* painful *living in the same house with a person whose racial attitudes he detested.*
It was *Wordsworth* who called his gun a "thundering tube."

The advantages of such constructions are that they offer an alternative to lengthy separation of sentence parts that belong together (He found living in the same house with a person whose racial attitudes he detested painful) and a means of assigning emphasis: "It was Wordsworth who . . ." emphasizes *Wordsworth;* "Wordsworth called his gun a 'thundering tube'" emphasizes *thundering tube.*

See *its, it's; it's me; there is, there are.* References: Copperud, p. 154; Long, pp. 211–12, 342–45; Pooley, pp. 115–17.

ital   ## Italics

In longhand and typewritten copy, underline words or passages to correspond to the conventions of using italic type.

Words or statements that would be printed in italics are underlined in manuscript. Although newspapers have generally abandoned italic type, most magazines and books use it, and in academic writing—course papers, articles in learned journals, dissertations, reference books—italics have standardized uses:

1. To indicate titles of books, plays, motion pictures, and other complete works, and to indicate titles of periodicals and newspapers. See Titles 2.

2. To mark words and expressions considered as words rather than for their meaning: There is a shade of difference between *because* and *for* used as conjunctions.

3. To mark unanglicized words from foreign languages: Good clothes were a *sine qua non.* See Foreign words in English 2a.

4. To indicate words that would be stressed if spoken. This easily abused device is more appropriate in dialog than in exposition.

5. To indicate key words, phrases, or sentences in an argument or explanation. Here also italics must be used sparingly if they are not to lose their force. See Emphasis 6.

References: *A Manual of Style; The MLA Style Sheet,* 2nd ed. (New York: Modern Language Association, 1970).

its, it's

Its is a possessive pronoun and, like the possessive pronouns *his, her, our, your,* and *their,* has no apostrophe: A car is judged by its performance. *It's* is the contraction for "it is" or "it has": It's a long road; It's been said before. Like other contractions, *it's* is more appropriate to informal and general than to formal styles.

it's me

The argument over "it's me" illustrates a conflict between theory and practice. The theory—that after a finite form of the verb *be* the nominative or subjective case should always be used—is consistently contradicted by the usage of good writers and speakers (see *be* 2). We tend to use the nominative form of a pronoun when it is the subject and stands alone directly before the verb, but we are likely to use the accusative in most other positions, especially when it comes after the verb—in "object territory," as it has been called. (Compare *who, whom.*) All the large grammars of English regard "it's me" as acceptable. References: Bryant, pp. 120–21; Copperud, p. 155.

-ize

The formation of verbs from non-Greek nouns or adjectives by adding the Greek ending *-ize* (often *-ise* in British usage) has been going on since the sixteenth century. Some readers object to recent extensions of the verbs in *-ize*, either because the new verbs duplicate in meaning verbs in common use (*fantasized, fantasied; formularize, formulate*) or because the proliferation adds to the stock of advertising jargon (*customize, personalize*), much of which is virtually meaningless. See *finalize*. Reference: Copperud, p. 155.

J

Jargon

1. Sir Arthur Quiller-Couch popularized *jargon* as the name for verbal fuzziness of various sorts—wordiness, a high proportion of abstract words, "big" words, and words that add nothing to the meaning. *Jargon* and *gobbledygook* are sometimes used interchangeably. Reference: Sir Arthur Quiller-Couch, *On the Art of Writing* (1916; rpt. New York: Putnam, Capricorn Books, 1961), pp. 100–26.

2. *Jargon* is also used for shoptalk or the specialized language of a group—doctors, printers, sociologists, photographers, chicken farmers, and so on. So defined, jargon is appropriate in certain circumstances, as when a physicist writes for fellow physicists, but not in others, as when he writes for a general audience.

In many groups and many situations there is a tendency to go beyond the necessary technical jargon and create a jargon in the first sense. Examples of the use of language to impress more than to inform include sociologese, psychologese, educationese, journalese, and bureaucratese.

See Doublespeak, Shoptalk.

job, position

Job is general for the formal *position:* He got a job at the oil re-finery. The word *position* has more dignity, and what it refers to is usually thought of as better paid; but because *position* can sound pompous, many writers use *job* for all levels of employment.

Journalese

Journalese, once limited in meaning to a kind of writing found in newspapers, can be applied as well to a kind of prose read by radio and television news broadcasters. At its best it is slick and smooth; but smooth or rough, it is loaded with jargon and lacking in character and conviction. The sensational personal reporting of earlier times has been replaced in large part by a bland "communicating" of whatever the newsmakers—politicians, bureaucrats, celebrities—have to say, no matter how meaning-less or untrue. Whether based on handouts or on observation, journalese is full of clichés, vogue words, gobbledygook, and doublespeak. Yet for all their fondness for the in phrase from Washington, New York, or Las Vegas, the writers cling to such hoary headline words as *slay, flee, vow,* and *ailing* (ailing Joanne Starr). And there are reminders of the old journalistic love of violence, not only in the trite hyperbole of the sports pages but in the "firestorms" of protest and in the "firefights" and "shoot-outs" that journalese has transported from distant wars and the Hollywood West to urban liquor stores and rural gas stations.

As a result of the shortcomings of current journalese, the columnist or commentator who expresses himself with some originality is almost as welcome as one who has something original to say. Journalese provides evidence that even professional, grammatical writing can be awful.

Reference: Edwin Newman, *Atlantic,* October 1974, pp. 84–89.

just

The qualifier *just* is redundant in expressions like *just exactly* and *just perfect.* The locution "just may [might]" or "may [might] just"—"Mr. Kilpatrick may just be right" (*Centre Daily Times*)—in which *just* means "just possibly," is a cliché.

K

kid

The noun *kid* for "child" and the verb *kid* for "tease" are now so widely used in serious contexts that they should be regarded as established in general, though not in formal, usage. A problem with *kid* as a noun is that it now may mean not only someone past puberty but someone past adolescence (the kids in graduate school). In many contexts a more specific term is needed.

kind, sort

The words *kind* and *sort* are involved in three different problems for writers.

1. Agreement. *Kind* and *sort* are singular pronouns with regular plurals. A problem arises only when singular *kind* or *sort* is followed by *of* and a plural noun. Then there is a strong tendency to treat the plural object of *of*, rather than *kind* or *sort*, as the head of the construction and to use plural demonstratives and verbs: These sort of books are harmless; "Those kind of overhead expenses" (Lewis H. Lapham, *Harper's*).

The construction is common in speech, and there are numerous examples of its use by esteemed writers—"these kind of marks have not been left by any other animal than man" (T. H. Huxley, "The Method of Scientific Investigation")—but strong objection to it continues. For one kind (or sort), then: *That kind of book is.* . . . For more than one: *Those kinds* of books *are.* . . . References: Bryant, pp. 124–25; Copperud, p. 160; Fries, p. 58; Jespersen, p. 202.

2. *Kind (sort) of a(n).* Although shunned in formal writing, *kind of a(n)* and *sort of a(n)* are general idioms: "People just didn't trust that kind of an approach" (Charles Mohr, *Esquire*). Formal style would have "kind of approach." Reference: Copperud, pp. 160–61.

3. *Kind (sort) of.* As adverbs equivalent to imprecise qualifiers like *rather* and *somewhat* in more formal usage, *kind of* and *sort of* are informal to general: "She was kind of plump" (Claude Brown, *Commentary*); "Everything just sort of limped along" (E. J. Kahn, Jr., *New Yorker*).

know-how

Although *know-how* occurs in every variety of writing, for many readers its connotations remain commercial and technical. To speak of the know-how of a great violinist, for example, would be inappropriate.

L

lab

The clipped form of *laboratory* is now common in all but the most formal usage.

last, latest

Both *last* and *latest* are used as superlatives of *late* (his last book; his latest book). But to avoid ambiguity, formal English uses *last* for the final item in a series and *latest* for the most recent of a series that may or may not be continued: "Mao Tsetung's latest battle is almost certainly his last" (Mark Gayn, *Foreign Affairs*).

latter

The use of *latter* in referring to the last of more than two items is standard, but conservative stylists prefer "the last named." See *former, first — latter, last*.

lay, lie

In standard English *lie (lay, lain)* is intransitive: He let it lie there; She lay down for a nap; The boards had lain there for months. *Lay (laid, laid)* is transitive: You can lay it on the table; They laid the keel; She had laid it away for future reference. In much spoken English *lay* does the work of both verbs, but in most writing they are kept distinct. The *-ing* forms sometimes give trouble, with *laying* appearing where *lying* is meant: I spent the summer laying around the house. Reference: Copperud, pp. 165 – 66.

learn, teach

Nonstandard English often uses *learn* in the sense of *teach*: He learned me how to tie knots. Standard usage makes the distinction: He taught me how to tie knots; I learned how to tie knots from him.

leave, let

Let, not *leave*, is standard English for "permit" or "allow." See *let, leave*.

lend, loan

In referring to material wealth, *lend* and *lends* are preferred to *loan* and *loans* in formal writing, but the past tense and past participle *loaned* is preferred to *lent* in all varieties: "About $4 billion have been loaned" (Adolf A. Berle, *The American Economic Republic*); "those who wished to lend" (George V. Taylor, *American Historical Review*). In general contexts, *loan* and *loans* are as common as *lend* and *lends* and are entirely reputable.

In the sense "grant, impart, furnish" or "adapt or accommodate (itself)," *lend* and *lent* are always preferred: "America always lent itself to personification" (Norman Mailer, *Harper's*). Reference: Copperud, p. 170.

less, fewer

Use *fewer* for things that can be counted, *less* for things that can't. See *fewer, less*.

let, leave

A common nonstandard idiom is the use of *leave* for "permit" or "allow," meanings that standard English assigns to *let*. Both uses are shown in this sentence by a writer making a transition between the two varieties: "In high school I was cured of the practice of leaving [nonstandard] notebooks go, but I fell into the habit of letting [standard] homework slide."

Only with *alone* and the meaning "refrain from disturbing" are the two verbs interchangeable in standard English: Leave [*or* Let] me alone; Americans like to be let [*or* left] alone. References: Bryant, pp. 127–29; Copperud, p. 164.

Lexical meaning

In linguistics a distinction is often made between grammatical or structural meaning and lexical meaning. In "Birds were killed," the information that *bird* and *kill* give us is of the sort regularly provided by a dictionary or lexicon—hence, lexical meaning. The information given by the *-s* of *birds* (plural), *were* (past tense, passive voice), and the *-ed* of *killed* (past participle in this position) is of the sort provided by our awareness of the structure or grammar of the language—hence, grammatical or structural meaning. When we fully understand the sentence, we have grasped its total meaning.

liable

In formal and most general writing, *liable*, when followed by an infinitive, is restricted to predictions of undesirable results (The effects are liable to be disastrous). *Liable* plus infinitive to predict desirable results occurs most often in informal and casual general contexts: "Walleyes are year-round sport and . . . they're liable to hit any time of the day or night" (Roger Latham, *Field and Stream*). *Likely* and *apt* are not restricted in this way. Reference: Copperud, pp. 19–20.

lie

The transitive verb *lay* should not be substituted for the intransitive *lie*: you *lie*, not *lay*, down when you're tired; you *lay*, not *laid*, down yesterday. See *lay, lie*.

like, as

1. As prepositions. In all varieties of English, *like* is used as a preposition introducing a comparison: The description fits him like a plaster cast; Habit grips a person like an octopus; She took to selling like a bee to clover. *As* seems to be increasing as a hypercorrect form: "The University of Texas, as so many American campuses during the Kennedy years, has exploded with vitality" (Willie Morris, *North Toward Home*).

2. As conjunctions. In all varieties of English, *as*, *as if*, and *as though* are used as conjunctions introducing clauses of comparison: Habit grips a person as an octopus does; He walked as though he was hurt. *Like* as a conjunction is common in speech and appears frequently in informal and general writing: "It looks now like it will take us years of John Cage, Godard, Burroughs, *et al.*, to absorb it" (Theodore Solotaroff, *The Red Hot Vacuum*). But many people remain strongly opposed to *like* as a conjunction, and it is avoided in formal and much general writing. References: Bryant, pp. 133–35; Copperud, pp. 166–67; Fries, pp. 225, 239; Pooley, pp. 149–52.

3. The way. *The way* provides an escape from the *like–as* thicket for writers who shy from *like* and find *as* prissy: "Hemingway once told Callaghan, 'Dostoevski writes like Harry Greb fights.' Unfortunately, Callaghan writes the way Hemingway fights" *(Time).*

Linguistics
Linguistics is a broad discipline incorporating several perspectives from which language may be studied systematically. Linguists study the structures of languages and the universal structure of language; they study language history and the variations of language as correlated with geographical and social distance; they study how language is acquired and how it is used.

Linguistics differs from other disciplines devoted to the study of language by having at its center a theory of language derived from the study of formal, regular, and recurrent patterns in the structures of human languages. While theories of language differ and hence schools of linguistics exist, all linguists are empiricists, sharing a desire to be as objective and "scientific" as possible, rejecting conclusions not based in consistent theory and verified by significant data.

For some linguists, especially those termed structuralists or descriptivists (see Grammar 3b), significant data consist only of those features of language they can directly perceive either as marks on a page (writing) or as vibrations in the air (speech); consistent theory, for these same linguists, consists of a set of generalizations derived inductively from the data through means of formal discovery procedures. For other linguists, particularly those termed generative-transformational or generative (see Grammar 3c), significant data also include what the native speaker (including the linguist himself) senses or intuits about the structures of sentences, the relations of those structures to one another, and the correlation between structured sound and meaning. The structuralist's goal is to write grammars that will *describe* the surface regularities of sentences in particular languages. The generativist's goal is to *predict* the sentences that will occur in a particular language, given the set of rules for sentence construction that native speakers have internalized. The generativist is more interested in explanation than he is in description, and seeks deeper relations between surface structures and meanings in the organization of human cognitive capacities as these are revealed through a study of rules that all human languages have in common.

In addition to describing the grammatical, phonological, and semantic structures of modern languages, linguists are interested in other linguistic phenomena. *Dialectology* examines the characteristic linguistic patterns that distinguish groups of speakers of the same language. Geographical dialects have been most thoroughly studied; but in recent years social dialects have drawn increasing attention as higher education has encompassed all classes of speakers, forcing teachers to reconsider their own attitudes toward the variety of English spoken by those not part of the white, Anglo-Saxon, upper-middle-class community. *Historical linguistics* attempts to reconstruct the grammars of earlier forms of a current or dead language and to account for change in language. *Comparative linguistics* studies the relationship between languages that are genetically related to a parent language or between languages that differ or resemble each other structurally, without regard to their historical sources. Specialists in child language investigate the development of linguistic competence among infants and young children.

Other areas of linguistics are often termed *applied,* to emphasize that they touch on practical concerns as well as theory. In *lexicography* the findings of semanticists and dialectologists are being used in compiling dictionaries. In *foreign-language teaching,* the findings of comparative and contrastive linguistics have helped pinpoint those differences between a native language and a target language that would make learning the new language particularly difficult. In *machine translation* the findings of syntactic studies and semantics have been used in attempts, so far largely fruitless, to program machines to translate from one language to another. In *literary studies* transformational grammars have been used to analyze the syntactic, metaphorical, and prosodic structure of poems and the styles of various prose writers. In *composition courses* transformational grammars have been used to analyze the characteristics of mature sentence structure to help students write better. In *reading,* phonological studies have shown how the apparently chaotic system of English spelling is in reality a regular system that, far from preventing a child from learning to read, may actually help him. The findings of phonology have also been used to construct better communications systems. And the scientific attitudes of linguists have forced those concerned with usage to look at language as it really is used rather than as they would like it to be used.

As linguistics has developed theoretically and in its practical applications, a number of related fields have developed. *Psycholinguistics* studies the correlation between linguistic structures and experimentally describable behavior. *Stylistics* studies the linguistic characteristics of literary language. One kind of *linguistic philosophy* studies the nature of meaning in sentences from the point of view of deep and surface structures. *Linguistic anthropology* uses the semantic structures of individual languages and the verbal interaction of their speakers to discover distinctive patterns of culture. Related to this field is *sociolinguistics*, the specific study of the verbal interaction between and among social classes and linguistic variation as it correlates with the behaviors of definable social groups.

References: Bolinger; Francis P. Dinneen, *An Introduction to General Linguistics* (New York: Holt, 1967); Ronald W. Langacker, *Fundamentals of Linguistic Analysis* (New York: Harcourt, 1972); Archibald A. Hill, *Linguistics Today* (New York: Basic Books, 1969); Hungerford, Robinson, and Sledd; R. H. Robins, *A Short History of Linguistics* (Bloomington: Indiana Univ. Press, 1968).

Linking verbs

When a verb like *be* functions chiefly as a structural bridge between a subject and another noun or a modifier, it is called a copulative or linking verb. It is followed by elements that function as adjectives or nouns (single words, phrases, or clauses) and are traditionally known as predicate adjectives (This bottle was *full*) and predicate nouns or predicate nominatives (The man was a *carpenter*). Some grammarians prefer to call them complements, or subjective complements.

Many verbs besides *be* are used as linking verbs; one grammarian has counted about sixty. For example, instead of having a verb of full meaning like *colden*, English uses the verb *turn* or *get* and the adjective *cold* (which carries the chief part of the meaning) in such a sentence as "The weather turned cold." Many verbs are used both with full meaning of their own (The tree *fell* into the water) and as linking verbs (She *fell* silent; He *fell* ill). Other linking verbs are italicized in the following sentences:

He *became* a doctor. The butter *tastes* rancid. She *felt* sad. He *acts* old. The ground *sounds* hollow. He *grew* moody. He *appeared* to be recovering. This *looks* first-rate. His story *seemed* incredible.

Because many speakers have been taught that verbs are modified by adverbs, and because they are unaware that the same verb can function either as a linking verb or as a transitive verb, they correct correctness by substituting an adverb for the correct adjective: "He felt sadly" for "He felt sad." Such hypercorrectness sometimes appears in writing.

For the most common source of difficulty in using the linking-verb pattern, see Predicate adjectives. See also *bad, badly; be* 2; *it's me; look.* References: A. S. Hornby, *A Guide to Patterns and Usages in English* (London: Oxford Univ. Press, 1954), pp. 62–72; Gustave Scheurweghs, *Present-Day English Syntax* (London: Longmans, 1959), pp. 19–32.

literally

Literally means "actually, without deviating from the facts," but it is so often used to support metaphors that its literal meaning may be reversed. In statements like the following, *literally* means "figuratively" and *literal* means "figurative":

The Village in the twenties [was] a literal hotbed of political, artistic, and sexual radicalism. —Louise Bernikow, *New York Times Book Review*

In this struggle, women's bodies became a literal battleground. —Martin Duberman, ibid.

[New York City is] literally hanging by its fingernails. —Walter Cronkite, *CBS News*

Literal-minded readers find such locutions absurd.

literate

Literate is used to mean both "capable of reading and writing" and "acquainted with what has been written—educated." See *illiterate*.

loan

In referring to possessions, *lend* is more formal in the present tense. For the past tense, *loaned* is preferred in all varieties of English. See *lend, loan*.

Loan words

Loan words in English are words borrowed from other languages. See Foreign words in English, Origin of words 2b.

Localisms

A localism is a word or other expression in regular use only in a certain region, like the "baby cab" used in western Pennsylvania for "baby carriage." Though appropriate in conversation and informal writing, localisms are out of place in general and formal writing except to give a regional flavor. See Dialects.

locate

Locate is in general use for "find" (I can't locate the letter now). Although avoided by many stylists in the sense "settle" (The family located near Nashua), it may be useful when it refers to considered placement: "Thus the small department store is probably wise to locate close to its competition" (Richard H. Holton, in *Competition, Cartels and Their Regulation*, ed. J. P. Miller).

Locution

Locution is a handy term for referring to a word or a group of related words; that is, it may be applied to a single word or to a phrase or clause considered as a unit. In the preceding sentence, "a handy term," "that is," and "phrase" are locutions.

logic Logical thinking

Reconsider the logical relationship that is expressed or implied.

At some time or other everyone has protested, "That doesn't make sense," or "That doesn't follow from what you just said." Everyone, that is, has some notion of the difference between logical and illogical thinking, and when something doesn't make sense or fails to show a logical progression, everyone's impulse is to dismiss it.

In an essay illogical thinking is revealed in irrelevant material, faulty organization, incoherent sentences, words that blur or skew the meaning of what's being said. More narrowly, it shows up in faulty relationships between ideas. Often the seeming breakdown in logic is simply the result of careless writing. In taking issue with the statement, "The true university is a collection of books," a student wrote, "If I were to agree that a true university is no more than a collection of books, I would graduate well-read but not socially mature." This makes no sense, because simply agreeing or not agreeing with the statement about a true university could not determine the kind of education a particular student would receive at a particular school.

Presumably the student meant, "If a true university is no more than a collection of books, and if this is a true university, then I can expect to be well-read when I graduate but not necessarily socially mature." If the student intended to base an *if . . . then* relationship on his agreement with the statement, the logical conclusion would be something like, "then I would spend all my time in the library."

You can avoid such apparent lapses in logic by carefully reading what you write — seeing what you have said rather than what you meant to say — and revising your sentences before making a final draft. Much more serious are the kinds of illogical thinking that undercut a whole essay. When you write a paper to express an opinion, defend a point of view, argue for or against something, persuade or convince your readers, keep these recommendations in mind:

Limit your generalizations to what you can support with evidence.

Make sure that what you offer as evidence is authoritative and that it bears on the issue.

Make sure that you have attacked the actual issue instead of skirmishing around the edges or wandering off into another battle.

Make sure that no links are missing in the chain of reasoning that leads to your conclusion.

In reading over what you've written, take a hard look at your generalizations. Are they sound enough to support your argument? Are they based on fact and justifiable inferences, or are they little more than unexamined assumptions or expressions of prejudice?

When you find yourself saying that *A* caused *B* or that *B* is the result of *A*, think over your reasons for saying so. Are they convincing? Are there reasons for *not* saying so that you have deliberately omitted? Are your comparisons justifiable and your analogies plausible?

After enjoying the violent language you've used in condemning those who hold an opposing point of view, or admiring the moving words you've used in supporting those whose side you're upholding, ask yourself whether the faults of the former group or the virtues of the latter have anything to do with the issue itself. If they haven't, don't confuse your comments on them with logical thinking.

See Cause and effect, Classification and division, Deduction, Fallacies, Induction, Syllogisms.

Logic and language

Sometimes items of usage are objected to as being "illogical"— for example, "he don't," "the reason is because." But the real trouble with "he don't" is simply that it has become nonstandard. And when the objection to "the reason is because" is elaborated, it is usually that an adverbial clause (*because* . . .) is equated with a noun (*reason*)—a criticism that has to do with grammar rather than with logic. Logic proper is not involved in either objection.

Idiom illustrates particularly well the lack of correspondence between logic and usage. The meanings of many idioms are not the sum of the meaning of their separate words: hard to come by, a little water, many's the time, out of order. These show, more clearly than the general patterns and rules of English, that language is a human development, the result of millions of speech situations, not a preplanned system; it is not illogical but simply alogical.

Probably arguments from logic had an influence in establishing the double negative as nonstandard English; in Old and Middle English, the more negatives there were, the more forceful the negation. But arguments from logic have had few such successes, and the term *logical* can be applied to language only in its most general popular sense of "more or less systematic."

See Double negative, Idiom, *reason is because.*

Long variants

Some writers are tempted to add an extra prefix or suffix to a word that already carries the meaning they intend. They write *irregardless,* though *regardless* already means "without regard to," or they write *doubtlessly* for *doubtless.* Some like to use sonorous suffixes that add nothing to the meaning, like the *-ation* in *analyzation,* which means no more than *analysis.* Some other long variants that it is wise to avoid are *certificated* for *certified, confliction* for *conflict, emotionality* when only *emotion* is meant, *hotness* for *heat, intermingle* for *mingle, orientate* for *orient, ruination* for *ruin, subsidization* for *subsidizing,* and *utilize* when *use* is entirely adequate.

Occasionally a long form acquires a special sense: a *certificated* teacher is one who has a certificate from the state, licensing him to teach. But in general the more compact form is the right choice. See Diction 2, Gobbledygook, Jargon. Reference: Fowler, pp. 342–43.

look

When used as an intransitive verb meaning "use the eyes, gaze," *look* is modified by an adverb: look longingly, look searchingly. As a linking verb, equivalent to *appear*, *look* is followed by an adjective which modifies the subject: He looks well [*or* healthy *or* tired *or* bad]. See Linking verbs.

lot, lots

In the senses "much," "many," "a great deal," the various expressions *a lot*, *a lot of*, *lots*, and *lots of* have an informal flavor but are established in general (though not in formal) usage:

He tells Celine to make herself attractive and buys her a lot of new clothes. – Edmund Wilson, *New Yorker*

There is lots of talk. – *Fortune*

Reference: Copperud, p. 171.

lc Lowercase

Use a lowercase (small) letter instead of a capital.

As an alternative or supplement to *lc*, the correction may be indicated by a slant line through the capitals:

```
It was a Øreat Øxperience.
```

Such unconventional use of capitals may work occasionally to indicate emphasis, but an exclamation mark is the safer choice. For the conventional uses of capitals, see Capital letters.

M

m.

Lowercase *m.* is the abbreviation for noon: 12 m. But see *a.m. and p.m.*

Main clauses

Main clauses (like this one and the next) are independent clauses. They can stand alone as sentences. See Clauses.

majority, plurality

Technically, a majority in an election is more than half the total number of votes cast, while a plurality is the largest number of votes cast for any one candidate but not more than half the total. Though the distinction is sometimes neglected, it is worth preserving for clarity.

In formal usage, *majority* is applied only to groups of at least three things that can be counted. In informal and general usage it is sometimes used also of the larger part of a single thing or mass: "A majority of the LP is taken up with bouncy dance tunes" (Robert Palmer, *New York Times*). *Most* is preferable.

Malapropisms

A malapropism is a ludicrous confusion of two words that sound somewhat alike but differ in meaning: *prodigy, progeny; contiguous, contagious.* The humor of malapropisms has faded since the eighteenth-century playwright Richard Brinsley Sheridan used them in the speeches of Mrs. Malaprop, a character in *The Rivals.*

Manuscript form

Your manuscript is not in the proper form. Revise or rewrite as directed.

Instructors usually establish their own specifications for manuscript form at the beginning of the course. Whatever the details, the goal is a clean, legible copy that can be read easily. Use regulation paper, leave adequate margins, number the pages, make corrections neatly, and observe your instructor's directions for endorsing the paper. See Division of words, Typewritten copy.

massive

Used with abstract nouns, *massive* has been a vogue word since the 1960s: massive retaliation, massive resistance, massive inequality, massive unemployment. Applying it only to icebergs would be a step in the right direction.

Mass nouns

Mass nouns denote masses that can be divided but not numbered as aggregates of separate units: *dirt, oxygen, wealth.* They are used with *the* (not *a* or *an*) or without an article in the singular, and ordinarily they have no plural. Mass nouns are opposed to count nouns, which can be counted as separate units, are used with both *a(n)* and *the* but not without an article in the singular, and have plurals: *a boy, the stick, horses.* See Nouns 3c. References: Jespersen, pp. 206–209; Sledd, p. 225; Williams, pp. 71–73.

may, can

In requesting or granting permission or expressing feasibility, *may* is the formal choice. *Can* expresses ability and is commonly used in place of *may* in general English. See *can, may.*

Meaning

The word, phrase, or sentence marked does not make sense in this context. Replace it with one that communicates the meaning you intend.

For a reader to question the meaning of what you have written indicates a serious failure in communication. Ordinarily the problem is not simply the use of one word for another that is reasonably close to it in sound or meaning—*comprehension* for *comprehensibility,* for instance. This would be marked *ww* (wrong word): the reader knows the word is wrong because he knows what the right one is. But *mng*, often followed by a question mark, means that the reader can't, or won't, make a guess at what you were trying to say. Rethinking and rewriting are in order. Compare Ambiguity, Coherence, Wrong word.

media, medium(s)

Medium and *media,* the Latin singular and plural forms, were taken directly into English, and formal usage consistently maintains the distinction in number, while recognizing the alternate plural *mediums:* "the moral possibilities of the mediums themselves" (Robert J. Reilly, *American Literature*). But *media,* like many other Latin plurals, has tended to become singular in American usage and is frequently so used in general writing, with *medias* sometimes as its plural. Word watchers find these usages highly objectionable: "Nomination for the most common error among men who should know better: 'The media is . . .'" (*Columbia Journalism Review*). Reference: Copperud, p. 176.

Metaphor

Metaphor, now widely applied to any nonliteral use of language, traditionally refers to the figure of speech that implies an identity or resemblance between two unlike things. When we are talking literally, we say that it is people or machines that *polish,* flags that *unfurl,* liquids that *stream,* and flowers that *bloom.* Yet a writer can, through metaphor, put these words to new uses and so make a description of even the simplest things both fresh and pleasing:

The wind continued to polish the grasses. And a purple finch unfurled his song. Twice, and now three times, its last sure note streamed into the sun-bloom. — Sally Carrighar, *One Day on Beetle Rock*

The power of metaphor goes beyond its capacity to please: it can provide a new view of things and so shape attitudes and change minds. It may create a sharp image with a single verb (White House action *defused* the demands of Congress), or it may call up a sequence of analogous situations:

Before prose rhythm can be sensibly considered, one must redefine reading. It cannot be a jet flight coast-to-coast. It must be a slow walk in the country, taken, as all walks should be, partly for the walking itself. — Richard A. Lanham, *Style: An Anti-Textbook*

And metaphor may amuse with what, put literally, would be insulting:

In "Execution Eve: And Other Contemporary Ballads," William F. Buckley Jr. slithers venomously across the usual broad terrain of sacred and secular topics. — Steven R. Weisman, *New York Times Book Review*

See Figurative language, Figures of speech, Mixed metaphors.

Metonymy

Metonymy is a figure of speech in which the thing named suggests the thing meant, as in "guns [war] or butter [peace]." See Figurative language.

might, could

These two words express a slighter degree of possibility than *may* or *can:* I might go; They could turn up. See *can, may.*

Misrelated modifiers

A misrelated modifier is so placed that it relates to the wrong word in the sentence. See Dangling modifiers.

Mixed metaphors

Speakers frequently run two inconsistent metaphors together: The new measure has taken a firm foothold in the eye of the public; If they are to win in November, they need a fresh face on the ticket — one that has not been straddling the economic issue. Writers, who can reconsider their words, have less excuse for such blunders and — since what they allow to stand can be read again and again — more reason for avoiding them. See Figures of speech 2.

Mixed usage

Indiscriminate, thoughtless mixing of vocabularies — formal with informal, poetic with technical — weakens writing. See Diction 2.

Modal auxiliaries

Can, could; may, might; must; ought; shall, should; will, would are called modal auxiliaries. They differ from other verbs in having no -*s* in the third-person singular, no infinitive, no participle, and therefore no compound or phrasal forms; instead, they themselves always occur as part of verb phrases, complete or elliptical. The generally similar *dare* and *need* are also sometimes treated as modal auxiliaries. See Elliptical constructions.

Modifiers

Typically, a modifier limits the meaning of its headword and makes it more exact (a *green* apple). Modification has never been satisfactorily defined, however, and for the present, students of English grammar must be satisfied with examples. In the following illustrations the words in italics modify the words in small capitals: A *cold windy* DAY; He FAILED *miserably;* She was *truly* SUPERB; *Undoubtedly* IT WAS THE CAT WHO STOLE THE BUTTERMILK; *Coming around the corner,* WE met him head on. See Absolute phrases, Adjectives, Adverbs, Dangling modifiers, Gerunds 1, Infinitives 4, Participles 2, Phrases, Restrictive and nonrestrictive.

Money

1. Exact sums of money are usually written in figures: 72¢, $4.98, $168.75, $42,810. Though round sums are likely to be written in words (two hundred dollars, a million dollars), figures may be used for them, too, when several sums are mentioned.

2. In consecutive writing, amounts are usually written out when they are used as modifiers: a million-dollar project. Informally, figures are often used: a $2 seat.

3. For amounts in millions and billions, the dollar sign followed by the number followed by the word is most common: $50 billion. Instead of "three and a half million dollars" or "$3,500,000," "$3.5 million" is increasingly used.

4. A sum of money is usually thought of as a single unit: More than $9 million *was* invested in paintings.

Months

In reference matter and informal writing, the names of months with more than four or more than five letters are often abbreviated in dates: Jan. 21, 1972; Dec. 2, 1904; *but* May (June, July) 12, 1904. In formal writing the names of months are not abbreviated. When only the month is given, or the month and year, abbreviation is rare in any style: He was born in January 1959; Every September he tries again. See Dates.

Mood

The mood of a verb, indicated by its form, tells whether the writer or speaker regards what he is saying as a statement of fact or a question concerning fact (indicative mood), as a wish or an expression of possibility or doubt (subjunctive mood), or as a command (imperative mood). See Commands and requests, Imperative mood, Indicative mood, Subjunctive mood.

more, most

Preceding the base forms of adjectives and adverbs with *more* and *most* is one way of expressing their comparative and superlative degrees. See Comparison of adjectives and adverbs 1.

most, almost

In speech, *almost* is often reduced to *most: A* drop in prices would appeal to most anybody. *Most,* used thus, is occasionally seen in factual prose ("Most everybody is gaining on us" – Paul A. Samuelson, *Newsweek*); but in all formal and most general writing, if you can substitute *almost* for *most* in a sentence (almost always, almost everywhere), *almost* is the word to use.

Ms.

Ms. is a substitute for both *Miss* and *Mrs.* Its use is favored by those who believe that a woman should not be labeled unmarried or married any more than a man is. If a first name is used after *Ms.* for a married woman, the name is hers, of course, not her husband's: Mrs. John Doe becomes Ms. Jane Doe.

In writing for college courses a choice between *Ms.* and *Miss* or *Mrs.* is most often necessary when the topic is a biographical or critical essay about a woman or her work – for example, a review of the poetry of Sylvia Plath. Sylvia Plath can be called Ms.

Plath or Miss Plath as the writer chooses. (As a poet, she remained Sylvia Plath during her marriage.) She can also be called Sylvia Plath or simply Plath. The latter usage is becoming increasingly common in published writing about women.

MS

MS, usually in caps, is the conventional abbreviation for *manuscript*. The plural is *MSS*. Though usage is divided, the *Manual of Style* and the *MLA Style Sheet* recommend that in most contexts the abbreviation be used without a following period.

must

In general English (but not in formal) *must* has become a noun meaning "necessity" ("It has never been a must" — Henry Brandon, *Saturday Review*) and an adjective modifier meaning "essential": ("This book is a must assignment for reporters" — Robert O. Blanchard, *Columbia Journalism Review*).

myself

Myself is a reflexive or an intensive pronoun referring back to *I*: I shave myself (reflexive); I saw the whole thing myself (intensive). In addition, *myself* and the other *-self* pronouns are now used, in some grammatical environments, in the same way as the corresponding personal pronouns:

The writing was then done by myself, taking perhaps fifteen days. — Hollis Alpert, *Saturday Review*

Then the two of us, President Johnson and myself, walked out. — Malcolm Kilduff, *Columbia Journalism Review*

For the *-self* forms, most conservative stylists would substitute the regular nominative or accusative (*me* in the first example above, *I* in the second). See *himself, herself;* Pronouns 2; *self*. References: Bryant, pp. 141–43; Copperud, pp. 184–85; Pooley, pp. 153–56.

N

namely and other introductory words

The beginning of wisdom with introductory words like *namely, that is, for example* is to use them as seldom as possible. Very often they can be omitted altogether in compact general writing: His topic was a particularly unpleasant one — [namely] rising prices.

Narration

Stories (factual as well as fictional), autobiographies, biographies, and histories are all narratives. Like accounts of natural or mechanical processes and reports of laboratory experiments, they relate a sequence of events. In college papers you will frequently be called on to narrate such sequences.

1. Chronological order. As a writer of narrative, you may have reasons for altering actual chronological order. To arouse interest, you may decide to begin in the middle, making the reader ask how a character got into a certain situation. Or you may give the ending first, so that the reader will see how each step contributes to the final outcome. Or you may use a flashback ("Six years ago we had had a similar experience") to explain antecedent causes or to draw a parallel.

Although the events in a narrative can be told in any order, the reader must finally be able to understand the actual order in which they occurred. To make that order clear, you must use appropriate indicators of time (*then, later, after that,* and so on) and the right verb tenses (*had said* instead of *said* in a flashback, perhaps). And you need to use indicators of causal relationships (*in order to, because, as a result*) if the reader is to understand why an event took place or what effects it had.

2. Pace. In narration you can compress the events of a decade into a single sentence or extend the happenings of an hour through ten pages. You may slow your narrative with patches of description so that the reader can visualize the scene or gain a vivid sense of what's taking place. Or you may vary the pace by using dialog to dramatize a crucial action. You can make similar changes of pace in objective, factual reporting – of an industrial process, for example, or of a traffic accident – speeding up simpler stages and slowing down complex ones for clarity. Varying the pace is one of the ways you can direct the attention of your audience and control its responses.

3. Distance and point of view. How the reader sees and interprets the events depends on the distance you establish between yourself and your subject and between yourself and your reader. You may be close to your subject, taking part in the action, even motivating it; or you may be a remote observer, reporting and analyzing. You can present yourself as a learner and invite the reader to share that perspective, or you can assume the role of a professional – someone who knows much more than the reader does. The prevailing point of view will help define the tone of what you write. See Point of view.

4. The point of the narrative. A good narrative relates a sequence of events in such a way that a point emerges: the reader grasps not only what took place but the significance of what took place. In an expository narrative the significance may be clearly stated. In other narratives – personal reminiscences, for example – a brief comment on the significance of the action may be justified; but the better the storytelling, the less need there will be for spelling out the so-what.

nauseous, nauseated

Nauseated usually means "sickened, disgusted" (I felt nauseated at the sight); *nauseous* usually means "causing sickness or disgust" (The food looked nauseous). But speakers, and some writers, frequently use "feeling nauseous" and "getting nauseous." The ambiguity involved (sickened/sickening) suggests the wisdom of retaining the distinction between the two words. Reference: Copperud, p. 186.

Negation

In mathematics, -3 is as much less than 0 as $+3$ is more than 0 and $-(-3) = +3$ because the only mathematical alternative to minus is plus. In language a contrary is likely to be stated by another positive (good–evil, short–tall); the negative usually means "less than" or "different from": *not good* is "less than good" but not necessarily "evil," and *not short* is "taller than short" but not necessarily "tall." In *not uncommon,* we get a reduced reduction: *uncommon* is "less than common"; *not uncommon* is "less than less than common" or "not quite common"–an unemphatic or understated affirmative.

On the other hand, when *not* negates the verb, and one or two additional negatives modify either the verb or some other sentence element (as in "He can't never do no work"), the multiple negatives may actually reinforce the negation. But this cumulative effect is no longer used in standard English. See Double negative.

Sometimes the negative form shows unexpected variation from the affirmative: "must go" and "have to go" are nearly synonymous; "mustn't go" and "don't have to go" are not.

See Negatives and style.

Negatives and style

When you use both negative and positive words in the same sentence, be sure the combination says clearly what you intend: "The vocational counseling office will try to increase their clients' inability to support themselves" should be rephrased either as "to increase their ability" or as "to remedy their inability."

Poor sentences often result from stating negatively what might better be put positively:

This mob violence does not reflect the sentiment of an overwhelming majority of the students.
Better: This mob violence reflects the sentiments of only a small minority of the students.

Some writers are fond of tricky negative constructions, including litotes, a variety of understatement in which an affirmative is expressed by the negative of its contrary: "Marquand is not unfond of poor Apley" (Alfred Kazin, *Saturday Review*). Litotes can be effective, but when overused it makes the writer sound coy, evasive, or simply tiresome. See Double negative.

Negro

Negro has been replaced by *black* in much general usage since the 1960s. See *black*.

neither

As a pronoun, *neither* is ordinarily construed as singular and followed by a singular verb. When the verb is separated from *neither* by a prepositional phrase with a plural object, a plural verb frequently appears in informal writing and sometimes in general: "Marx and Trotsky, neither of whom were notably gentle or vegetarian" (Dwight Macdonald, *Esquire*); but in these cases, too, grammatical convention calls for a singular verb.

As an adjective, *neither* modifies a singular noun (neither man), and by grammatical convention a pronoun referring to the noun should be singular (Neither man lost *his* temper).

References: Bryant, pp. 8–10; Copperud, p. 188; Fries, p. 50.

Newspaper English

Today, newspaper English is only one form of journalese. See Journalese.

nice

Nice, a counter word indicating mild approval, is useful in speech but so imprecise that it is out of place in most writing. In formal prose *nice* is usually restricted to meanings like "subtle" or "discriminating": Kirk raises a nice point in his article on Camus.

nobody, no one

The pronouns *nobody* and *no one* take singular verbs, and, strictly speaking, a pronoun referring to either of them should be singular: No one lowered his voice. But sometimes meaning demands a plural pronoun: "No one sings; they simply listen reverently" (Ray Jenkins, *New York Times Magazine*). In formal writing the sentence might be recast: No one sings; everyone simply listens reverently.

nom Nominalization

Change the abstract nominalization into a concrete verb.

For most purposes the best writing is direct writing—writing that avoids three words where two will do, writing that represents an action in a verb and the agent of that action as its subject. The difference between indirect and direct writing is the difference between these two sentences:

It seems to be the case that certain individuals in attendance at this institution of higher education are in a state of anger over recent announcements on the part of the dean in regard to a necessity for greater restrictions where demonstrations are concerned.

Some students here are angry because the dean announced that he would not let them demonstrate as freely as they had.

Probably the most common source of indirect writing is the abstract nominalization, a noun that, according to transformational theory, has been derived from a full subject + verb in the deep structure of a sentence:

Tom *paid* the money   → Tom's *payment* of the money
The monks *reject* wealth   → The monks' *rejection* of wealth
The students *are responsible* → The students' *responsibility*

The direct subject-verb-object or subject-*be*-adjective construction is here made indirect and accordingly less vivid and forceful. If this kind of construction occurs often in your writing (about once every seven or eight words), readers are likely to find your style heavy, abstract, even pretentious, and possibly dishonest.

To improve such a style, first look for nouns made out of verbs: An investigation is being made of the causes for the decline in wheat production. When you find them (*investigation, causes, decline, production*), ask whether the crucial action is in the main verb or in one of these abstract nouns. If it is in the noun (*investigation*), change the noun to a verb (*are investigating*), find a subject for it (*they*, referring to a specific antecedent? *scientists? agricultural chemists?*), and rewrite the sentence around the new subject-verb:

An investigation is being made of the causes for the decline in wheat production.
Agricultural chemists are investigating what has caused wheat production to decline.
Agricultural chemists are investigating why farmers are producing less wheat.

See Deep structure, Passive voice 1, Subjects, Verbs 3. References: Roderick A. Jacobs, *CCC*, Oct. 1969, pp. 187–90; Sledd, pp. 300–301; Rulon Wells in *Style in Language*, ed. Thomas A. Sebeok (Cambridge, Mass.: MIT Press, 1960), pp. 213–20; Williams, pp. 311–21.

Nominative case

A noun or pronoun that is the subject of a finite verb, the complement of a linking verb, or an appositive to either is said to be in the nominative (or subjective) case. The form of the nominative singular is the common form of the noun, the form to which, typically, the endings for the genitive and for the plural are added. The pronouns with distinctive nominative forms are the personals — *I, you, he, she, it, we, you, they* — and the relative *who*. Though these are the usual forms for the nominative functions, see *it's me; who, whom.* See also Case 1, Subjects.

none

The use of *none* with a plural verb has often been condemned, usually on the grounds that *none* means "no one" or "not one" and so must be singular. Actual usage is divided. Plural *none* would be ungrammatical as a substitute for an uncountable (He talks nonsense, but none of it matters), but when the reference is to countables, *none* has long been used as a plural in the most reputable writing:

Almost none [of the letters] are either thoughtful in their approach or deliberative in their style. — Louis J. Halle, *New Republic*

None have been older than this sacramental alliance. — Sidney Hook, *New York Times Book Review*

None of these documents afford any solid support for those historians who have viewed Pike as a tool or accomplice in the Wilkinson-Burr schemes. — Harvey L. Carter, *American Historical Review*

References: Bryant, p. 8; Copperud, p. 190; Follett, pp. 227–28.

Nonrestrictive

A nonrestrictive modifier does not provide essential identification of the word modified and should therefore be set off by commas. See Restrictive and nonrestrictive.

ns Nonstandard English

Change the nonstandard word, form, or idiom to one in standard use.

He do, they is, theirself, nobody ain't got nothing: these are nonstandard. Among the articles that treat nonstandard words or forms are Adverbs and style; Double negative; *lay, lie; learn, teach;* Principal parts of verbs. See also *Writer's Guide,* pp. 290–91; English language 3.

no place

Although *anyplace, everyplace,* and *someplace* for "anywhere," "everywhere," and "somewhere" have become common in general writing, *no place* for "nowhere" is still mainly informal. It is sometimes spelled as one word.

nor

By itself, *nor* is an emphatic negative conjunction, most commonly used at the beginning of a sentence in the sense "and . . . not": Nor was Paris the only place he visited. Before the last member of a negative series, *nor* gives an added distinctness and emphasis: "I did not see him or hear him" is less emphatic than "I did not see him nor hear him."

As a correlative conjunction, *nor* is paired with *neither.* See Correlative conjunctions.

not about to

Not about to is not the simple negative of *about to* but an idiom that stresses the remoteness of the suggested possibility: I'm not about to go along with their weird schemes. It occurs mainly in speech but also in writing, where it quickly becomes tiresome.

not hardly, not scarcely

When *hardly* and *scarcely* mean "almost not," an additional *not* is redundant. See Double negative 2.

Noun clauses

A noun clause is a dependent clause that fills a nominal position: *What I can do in society* [subject] depends on *what my neighbors will tolerate* [object of a preposition]. Many noun clauses are introduced by *that* or *whether*, some by *what, which, who, whoever, whatever, why, when*, and other interrogatives.

Subject: That anyone could raise his grades by studying has never occurred to him. *Whether or not he should go* had bothered him for days. *Why sociology has been growing so rapidly* is a complicated question. (A noun clause as subject suggests a formal style.)

Object: He knew [*that*] *it would never happen again.* (When the noun clause is object of the verb, introductory *that* is often omitted in general English.)

Complement: His favorites were *whoever flattered him.*

Appositive: The doctrine *that we must avoid entangling alliances* was first stated by Washington.

Compare *that* in a noun clause (I know *that he loves me*) with *that* in a relative clause (The man *that I love* left town). In the noun clause *that* has no syntactic function. In the relative clause *that* is the direct object.

See Relative clauses.

Nouns

Nouns are best identified by their forms and by the positions they fill in sentences.

1. Forms. English nouns may be inflected for number and case. Many have a plural ending in -s or -es: *hats, kindnesses, lecturers.* These and other forms of the plural are discussed in Plurals of nouns.

The ending of the genitive singular is written with an apostrophe and an s: *boy's, manufacturer's.* The genitive plural adds an apostrophe to the regular plural spelling (*boys', manufacturers'*) and apostrophe-s to plurals not ending in -s (*men's, sheep's*). See Genitive case.

A few distinctive endings make nouns from other parts of speech. They include -er or -or, -ness, -th, -tion: *buyer, advisor, darkness, warmth, inflation.*

Some nouns in English have different forms for masculine and feminine: *actor–actress, confidant–confidante, executor–executrix.* See Gender, Sexist language.

Nouns may be single words or compound words written solid, as two words, or hyphenated: *bathroom, bookcase, stickup, hub cap, go-getter.* See Group words, Hyphen.

2. Position and function. *Dog* and *day* are nouns by their forms: they occur with plural and genitive inflections (a dog's leash, two days' work). But since they can occur in positions normally filled by adjectives (*dog* days) and adverbs (He works *days*), they can be called, in context only, adjectiv*als* or adverbi*als*. Thus if we call them *nouns*, we define them by formal characteristics; if *adjectivals* or *adverbials*, by syntactic function. If they also function as nouns syntactically, as in "The *dog* is man's best friend" or in "*Day* will come eventually," then they are nouns in *nominal* function.

Within noun phrases, nouns may be preceded by determiners and adjectives and followed by appositives, prepositional phrases, and relative clauses. Here are examples of the chief syntactic uses of noun phrases and hence of nouns:

Subject of a verb: A high wind from the east blew for three days.
Object of a verb: The wind damaged *the trees, which were loaded with ice.*
Object of a preposition: In *the night,* on *a frozen pond,* fishing is no sport for *a feeble spirit.*
Complement: He has become *president of the firm.*
Attributive: The young woman's partner had the grace of a *baby* hippo.
Apposition: The first settler, *Thomas Sanborn,* came in 1780.
Modifier of a verb: He came *two months ago.*

3. Classes of nouns. In the traditional grouping of nouns that follows, many nouns clearly fall into more than one group:
a. Proper nouns, names of particular people and places, written with capitals and usually without *the* or *a:* Anne, Dale A. Robb, London, Georgia, France, the Bay of Naples. All other nouns are called common.
b. Concrete nouns, names of things that can be perceived by the senses: *leaf, leaves, road, trousers, intellectuals.* Concrete nouns are opposed to abstract nouns, names of qualities, actions, types, ideas, and so on: *goodness, theft, beauty, heroism.*
c. Mass nouns, names of material aggregates, masses, or other units not defined by their discrete parts and their shape: *food, money, health, water, chaos, intelligence.* Mass nouns are syntactically distinguished by the fact that they cannot be preceded by indefinite articles: *Intelligence* depends on *environment* and *heredity.* (When *environment* can be preceded by *an,* it is not being used as a mass noun.) Mass nouns are opposed to count nouns, which refer to things that are conceived of as discrete units: *car, book, street, machine, horse.* Count nouns require *a/an* to mark their indefiniteness: a car, a book, a street, a machine, a horse. Some words can be either mass or count nouns: Wood is used in building—Mahogany is a valuable wood; Steak is expensive—I ate a steak.
d. Collective nouns, names of groups of things regarded as units: *fleet, army, committee, trio.* See Collective nouns.

See Parts of speech. References: Francis, pp. 237–52, 298–312; Quirk et al., pp. 127–203; Sledd, pp. 68–73; Williams, pp. 70–79.

nowhere near

Though in general use, *nowhere near* has an informal tone: It was a good score but nowhere near as large as we'd hoped for. Formal usage would substitute "not nearly so large as." Reference: Bryant, pp. 148–49.

Number

Number in English grammar is the singular and plural aspect of nouns and pronouns and verbs. Number in nouns is most important, since it controls the number of verbs and pronouns. In verbs, overt indication of number is limited to the present tense except in the pair *was–were*. See Plurals of nouns, Reference of pronouns, Subjects.

number

Number is a collective noun, taking a singular verb when the group as a group is meant and a plural verb when the individual units are the concern. Ordinarily "a number of" takes the plural (A number of tickets have been sold) and "the number of" takes the singular (The number of tickets left to sell is discouraging).

Numbers

1. Figures. Figures are conventionally used for the following:
a. Dates (June 29, 1918; 6/29/18), except in formal social correspondence and some ceremonial contexts.
b. Hours with *a.m.* or *p.m.*: 5 p.m. (*but* five o'clock).
c. Street addresses and highway numbers: 2841 Washington Avenue, Route 99.
d. Pages and other references: p. 761; Act III, scene iv, line 28 (III.iv.28) *or* act 3, scene 4, line 28 (3.4.28).
e. Exact sums of money: $4.98, 75¢.
f. Measures expressed in the conventional abbreviations: 15 cc., 3 km, 6″, 10 lbs., 32° F.

The plural of a figure is formed by adding either -*s* or, somewhat more formally, apostrophe-*s* (six 5s or six 5's; the 1970s or the 1970's). For the genitive, the apostrophe is not usual with figures: They imported $12,000 worth of equipment.

Except in dates, street numbers, zip codes, telephone numbers, and a few other regular series, a comma is used to separate thousands, millions, etc., though it may be omitted in four-digit numbers: 2,736 (*or* 2736) bushels; $4,682,981.

2. Figures or words. Words are conventionally used for round numbers and indefinite numbers: ten million, hundreds, a dozen, a score. Words are also customary for numbers that begin sentences—"Nineteen-eighteen did not usher in the millennium" (Henry Steele Commager, *Saturday Review*)—and for ordinal numbers (*first, second, third*).

As a rule, newspapers use figures for numbers over ten, words for smaller numbers; magazine and book styles (most general writing) ordinarily use figures for numbers over one hundred except when the numbers can be written in two words: *four, ten, ninety-two, two thousand.*

This passage illustrates a typical book style in handling numbers:

Stage coaches reached new top speeds as their horses galloped over the improved roads. It had taken four and a half days to travel the 160 miles from London to Manchester in 1754; thirty-four years later the journey had been shortened to twenty-eight hours. – T. Walter Wallbank et al., *Civilization Past and Present*

Words and figures should not be mixed in a series of numbers applying to the same units. If one of the numbers is conventionally written in figures, use figures for all: from 9 (*not* nine) to 125 days. But large numbers are increasingly written in a combination of figures and words: "$3 billion" is quicker to grasp than "$3,000,000,000."

Numbers in two words between twenty-one and ninety-nine are usually hyphenated, though the practice is declining: *forty-two* or *forty two*. A hyphen is used between figures to indicate a range: The prediction was based on 40–50 personal interviews and 200–300 telephone calls. It should not be used if the numbers are preceded by *from* or *between*: from 40 to 50 (*not* from 40–50).

3. Arabic and Roman numerals. Arabic numerals (1, 2, 146) are used in almost all places where numbers are not expressed in words. Roman numerals, either lowercase (i, ii, cxlvi) or capitals (I, II, CXLVI), are occasionally used to number units in a rather short series, as in outlines, chapters of a book, acts of a play, though now less often than formerly. The preliminary pages of books are almost always given Roman numerals; the body of a book begins a new pagination with Arabic numerals. Sometimes Roman numerals are used for the date on title pages and in formal inscriptions.

See Fractions, Hyphen 4, Money. References: Copperud, pp. 193–94; *A Manual of Style; U.S. Style Manual.*

O

Objective case

The object forms of pronouns are said to be in the objective, or accusative, case. See Accusative case.

Objects

1. Direct objects. In the simplest kind of sentence, the direct object is a noun phrase that follows a transitive verb to which the object is related as one of the primary elements of the predicate: Grammar puzzles *normal people;* Alice saw *the white rabbit;* The man was building *a fence.* In more complicated sentences a variety of elements, which do not always follow their verbs, can stand as direct objects; and, of course, pronouns can replace noun phrases in the object relation: Everybody enjoys *eating steak;* Somebody said *that porpoises are smart; What he meant* I never knew; John met *them* earlier.

Often the direct object of an active verb can be made the subject of a synonymous sentence in the passive: *Normal people* are puzzled by grammar; *The white rabbit* was seen by Alice. See Passive voice.

Traditionally, direct objects are said to name what is affected or effected by the actions of their verbs, but this description appears incorrect for "He received a wound in the war" or "They experienced many humiliations." On a deeper level, however, what appear to be subjects (*he* and *they*) may be objects (Someone wounded him; Someone humiliated them). See Deep structure.

2. Indirect objects. What is called the indirect object names the person or thing to which something is given, said, or shown – the person or thing affected, not directly but indirectly, by the verbal action: He gave *the church* a memorial window; She showed *him* the snapshot. Like direct objects, indirect objects are noun phrases or their equivalents. They follow a special set of transitive verbs, precede direct objects, and are synonymous, in corresponding sentences, with prepositional phrases introduced by *to* or *for*: He gave a memorial window *to the church*.

3. Objects of prepositions. The object of a preposition is the noun phrase, or equivalent, that follows the preposition and bears to some other element in the sentence a relation which the preposition indicates: here, "some other element in the sentence" is the object of *to*. A relative or interrogative pronoun as object may precede the preposition: *What* are you talking *about*?

4. Other objects. Different grammarians use *object* in different ways. Noun phrases or adjectives that follow direct objects after a special set of transitive verbs and that are related to the direct objects as if they were joined to them by the verb *to be* are sometimes called object complements: They considered his behavior *a threat to the school's welfare*.

When a direct or indirect object is made the subject of a passive sentence and the other object or object complement remains after the verb, that remaining object is called a retained object: His behavior was considered *a threat*.

Many linguists reject as direct objects words in a sentence that can't be made the subject of a passive version of the same sentence: He resembles his father – His father is resembled by him; I have a cold – A cold is had by me; It cost a nickel – A nickel was cost by it.

References: Sledd, pp. 126–36; Jacobs and Rosenbaum, Ch. 18.

Obscenity

Although the vulgar terms for the sexual and the excretory body parts and functions – the so-called four-letter words – are used much more freely in print, as well as in speech, than they were a decade ago, they ordinarily serve either as counter words or as expressions of generalized emotion—for example, disgust. In either case, they don't belong in college writing. See Profanity.

of course

Of course should be used sparingly and fairly. It should not be used as a substitute for evidence: Of course, we all know the administration is corrupt. Nor should it be used to suggest that, for the writer, the esoteric is the everyday: Old English had, of course, no inflected passive. Reference: Copperud, p. 196.

off of

The double prepositions *inside of, outside of, off of* are heard regularly and are in general use in writing. Many formal stylists reject the *of*, particularly with *off*.

OK, O.K., okay

OK or *O.K.* or *okay* is informal and commercial English for "approval" (The foreman put his OK on the shipment), for "all right, correct" (It's OK with me), and for "endorse, approve" (If you'll OK my time sheet, I can get paid). As a verb the forms are *OK, OK'ed* or *OK'd, OK'ing* and *okay, okayed, okaying*. Reference: For the most extensive treatment of the history of *OK*, see the series of studies by Allen Walker Read, *AS*, 1963–1964. Mencken, pp. 169–71, summarizes some of Read's findings.

Old English

Old English is the form of English in use from about 450 to 1100. See English language.

one

1. The use of the impersonal *one*, referring to people in general or to an average or typical person, is formal in tone, especially if it is repeated: "the victories and defeats of one's children, the passing of elders, one's own and one's mate's" (Benjamin De-Mott, *Atlantic*); One can't be too careful, can one? Many writers consider a series of *one*'s pretentious and refer back to *one* with forms of *he*—"One can determine his own life" (J. A. Ward, *Journal of English*)—but some readers would regard *his* in this context as offensively sexist.

A shift from *one* to impersonal *they* is avoided in writing, and while a shift from *one* to impersonal *you* is not rare, it would be inappropriate in formal contexts and disapproved by many readers. The *you . . . you* pattern is most common in general English. See *they, you.*

2. The use of *one* for *I*—"One hopes he will enter a primary campaign" (William F. Buckley, Jr., syndicated columnist)—is a stylistic eccentricity.

3. *One* may be used to avoid repeating a noun in the second of two compound elements: Fred took the new copy, and I took the old one. The plural *ones* is often so used, and logically enough, since *one* is not only a number but an indefinite pronoun: She had a yellow poncho and two red ones. But *one* as a noun substitute is often deadwood, taking emphasis away from the adjective that carries the real meaning: The plan was certainly [an] original [one].

Reference: Jespersen, pp. 83–85.

one another

The reciprocal pronoun *one another* is used to refer to two as well as to more than two. See *each other, one another;* Pronouns 3.

one of those who

In formal English the clause following *one of those who* and similar locutions is usually plural because the relative pronoun refers to a plural antecedent:

He is one of those people who believe in the perfectibility of man. *(Who refers to people.)*

This is one of the books that make you change your ideas. *(That refers to books.)*

But because there is a strong tendency to regard *one* as the antecedent, a singular verb is common:

Leslie Fiedler is one of those literary personalities who has the effect of polarizing his readers. — Peter Michelson, *New Republic*

. . . one of those crucial questions that comes up again and again. — David Garnett, *American Scholar*

The more formal your context, the more necessary a plural verb.

Reference: Copperud, p. 199.

only

According to the conventions of formal English, a single-word modifier should stand immediately before the element modified: I need only six more to have a full hundred. But usage often favors placing *only* before the verb: I only need six more to have a full hundred. The meaning is equally clear, and placing *only* with the verb is an established English idiom.

Even so, precise placement of *only* may be more satisfying to both writer and reader: "In this bicentennial year, let us only praise [*better:* let us praise only] famous men" (Gore Vidal, *New York Review of Books*). And so long as it isn't insisted on where it sounds stilted and unnatural, it can at least prevent silly statements like "He only had a face that [*better:* He had a face that only] a mother could love."

In this respect, *even, ever, nearly, just, exactly,* and other such limiting adverbs are similar to *only.* They can be placed so that they spoil the emphasis: I'm tolerant about such things, but his conduct even surprises me [*for* surprises even me].

References: Bryant, pp. 155–56; Pooley, pp. 87–90.

Onomatopoeia

By their pronunciations some words suggest particular sounds: *buzz, bang, clank, swish, splash, whir, pop, clatter.* Such imitative words are well established in the English vocabulary. Using sounds that match the sense of a passage in order to intensify its meaning is a stylistic device known as onomatopoeia. Ordinarily the writer works with existing words, sometimes adapting them in the process: "The wire is cut into bullet sizes, the slippery bullets slide from the chopping block on a gangway of grease, they are slithering, skiddering, and slippering into one another" (John Sack, *Esquire*). Onomatopoeia may also inspire outright imitation of sound, as in Tom Wolfe's description of stunting motorcycles: "thraaagggh." Conscious striving for words like *thraaagggh* can produce embarrassing results unless the writer's tongue is visibly in his cheek. See Alliteration, Assonance, Figurative language.

on, onto, on to

When *on* is an adverb and *to* a preposition in a separate phrase, they should be written as two words: The rest of us drove on to the city. The test is that *city* cannot be the object of *on*. Used as a preposition, they are written solid: The team trotted onto the floor; They looked out onto the park. Both *floor* and *park* are objects of the compound *onto*.

In the sense "to a place on" – The evangelist leaped up on(to) the platform – *onto* and *on* are sometimes used interchangeably.

Reference: Bryant, p. 152.

on the part of

On the part of is often wordy for "by," "among," "for," and the like: The new law resulted in less wild driving on the part of [by] young people; There has been a growing awareness of political change on the part of [among] scholars.

or

Or is a coordinating conjunction and, like *and, but,* and *for,* should connect words, phrases, or clauses of equal value. According to conventional rules, two subjects joined by *or* take a singular verb if each is singular, a plural verb if both are plural or if the one nearer the verb is plural:

Cod-liver oil or halibut oil is often prescribed.
Cod-liver oil or cod-liver oil capsules are often prescribed.
Cod-liver oil capsules or cod-liver oil is often prescribed.

Sometimes, writers use a plural verb after singular subjects joined by *or,* suggesting "either and perhaps both" rather than "not both but one or the other": "There is no evidence that Mao or Castro are taking advantage of their young fans" (Andrew Kopkind, *New Republic*). The lack of agreement would be condemned by most formal stylists. See Correlative conjunctions.

oral, verbal

Literally, *verbal* means "pertaining to words" and *oral* means "pertaining to the mouth." Insisting on the etymological distinction, some writers maintain that *oral* is the one true opposite of *written;* but *verbal* is used in the sense "unwritten" in all varieties of English: "Though written contracts were fairly often produced, a large proportion of the agreements seem to have been verbal" (Robert Sabatino Lopez, *Speculum*).

org Organization

Improve the organization of your essay by arranging the parts in an orderly sequence, or by making the movement clear through the use of appropriate signals and transitions, or both.

The main cause of poor organization is failure to get clear in your own mind the natural or logical divisions of your subject and the right relation of the parts of your discourse. Every essay should have a definable structure. In writing your paper, you should arrange the parts in an order that makes sense in terms of your purpose; and as you develop each part, you should take into account its place and importance in the whole scheme.

A poorly organized essay lacks direction – a logical movement from beginning to end. Or it lacks shape – proportions that do justice to the relative significance of the ideas. Or it lacks unity, with irrelevant material diverting attention from the main thread of the discussion. The best way to pinpoint such structural weaknesses is to outline your essay, reducing it to a skeleton of key statements. Then set about reorganizing and rewriting.

If rereading your essay and studying your outline leaves you convinced that the organization is basically sound, examine the ways you have introduced topics and linked up paragraph sequences. Even though you can justify the order of the parts of the essay, you may find that you've neglected to give the reader guidance in seeing the relationships you intend. If this is so, relatively simple repair work – improving connections and supplying transitions – should give the essay the direction, shape, and unity it *seems* to lack. The remedy is not drastic reworking of the entire structure but adding or rewriting sentences, particularly those at the structural joints that connect the main blocks of material. See Coherence, Outline form, Paragraph indention, Transition, Unity.

Originality

Original is applied to writing in two different senses. Content is original when it is gathered by the writer from his experience, from his observation of people, events, or places, or from documents like letters and newspapers. Most college papers should contain some original material. Merely rewriting a magazine article is certainly not a profitable exercise in composition. Putting together ideas taken from several such secondary sources has some value, since it requires selection and comparison. But the most useful work for growth in writing is composing papers in which a good deal of the content is original. The writing is more fun and the gain is much greater than in simply working over what others have done. (See Plagiarism.)

Originality in expression, in style, is a different matter. The English language has been used a long time, and absolutely new words and phrases are rare. You can, however, avoid the more threadbare figures and locutions—like "threadbare figures"—and an honest attempt to tell exactly what you see and believe will ordinarily result in straightforward, readable writing that has some freshness of expression. Trying too hard for originality will result in strained writing or "fine" writing, uncomfortable to writer and reader alike. When a style deserving the label *original* appears, it is usually the by-product of an active and independent mind, not the result of a deliberate search for novelty. See Figurative language, Figures of speech.

Origin of words

1. The study of the sources of words. Every word has a history. Some words, like *chauffeur, mores, television, parapsychology,* are relatively new in English; some, like *home, candle, go, kitchen,* have been in the language for centuries; others have recently acquired new meanings, like *satellite* (from a Latin word for "attendant," a term in astronomy which probably now means for most people either a dependent nation or a man-made object which orbits the earth, moon, or other celestial body). Etymology, the study of word origins, traces the changes of forms and combinations of word elements (as in *dis/service, wild/ness, bath/room, room/mate*) and pursues the word or its component parts to Old English, or to the foreign language from which it came into English, and so on back to the earliest discoverable forms. Of some words, especially informal words like *dude, stooge, rumpus,* earlier forms are unknown; of others, like *OK* or *blizzard,* the sources are debated. But the efforts of generations of scholars have discovered fairly full histories for most words. These are given briefly in most dictionaries and more fully in the *Oxford English Dictionary* and in special works.

Many of our everyday words come down directly from Old English *(brother, go, house, tell)* or, if they are of foreign origin, were borrowed many centuries ago *(candle, debt, pay, travel).* Many French words, of both early and recent borrowing, entered the vocabulary by way of high society *(debutante, fiancée).* The vocabulary of philosophy and abstract thought has a large Latin element *(concept, fallacy, rational, idealism),* and the vocabulary of science has many Greek elements *(atom, hemoglobin, seismograph).*

The sources of words will often reveal something about our history, as the many Norman French and Latin words in law *(fine, tort, certiorari, subpoena)* remind us of the time, following 1066, when the government of England was in the hands of the Norman French. But it is more interesting to discover what meanings the words have had in their earlier career in English and in the foreign languages from which they have come. *Supercilium* in Latin meant "eyebrow"; *rehearse* is from a French word meaning to "harrow again"; *sarcophagus* is, according to its Greek originals, "a flesh eater," referring to the limestone coffins that hastened the disintegration of bodies; *profane* (Latin) meant "outside the temple" and gathered the meaning of "against religion, the opposite of sacred"; *alcohol* goes back to an Arabic word for a finely ground powder, used for painting eyelids, and came to be applied, in Spanish, to specially distilled spirits, and so to our alcohol. See English language.

Words have arrived and are still arriving in English through two general processes – the making of new words, by either creating or borrowing them, and the compounding or clipping of words and parts of words that are already in the language. Then the usefulness of this new stock of words is increased as the words undergo changes in form.

2. New words.

a. Creation of words. Coinage, or outright creation, is rare. Even *gas*, first used by Van Helmont (1578–1644), a Belgian scientist, probably had the Greek *chaos* as well as a Dutch or Flemish word behind it. *Kodak* is an actual creation, as are a good many other trade names, some familiar from advertising. Informal words like *dud* and *burble* were also creations, good-sounding words someone made up. F. Gelett Burgess invented *blurb*, defining it as "self-praise; to make a noise like a publisher." Imitative words like *buzz, honk, swish, whiz* are attempts to translate the sounds of nature into the sounds of language. Various exclamations of surprise, pain, scorn, may have started as emotional noises – *ow, ouch, fie, phooey* – and then became regular words. A word that is coined for a special occasion is a nonce word – *steakola*, for example, used in Illinois in 1961 to mean meat given by a butcher as a bribe to an inspector of weights and measures. As a rule, arbitrary coinages do not stick. Outright creation is a very minor source of new words.

b. Borrowed words. English has always borrowed words freely, from Latin, German, French and from other languages with which English-speaking people have come in contact. It has assimilated words of quite un-English form: *khaki* (Hindi), *tycoon* (Japanese), *ski* (Norwegian), *hors d'oeuvres* (French), *intelligentsia* (Russian). The various words for *porch*, itself Norman French but the oldest and the most English-seeming of the group, come from various languages: *piazza* (Italian), *stoop* (Dutch), *veranda* (Hindi).

Borrowing is still going on, though perhaps more slowly than at some periods. Some words come into formal English and remain formal words: *intelligentsia, bourgeois, chef d'oeuvre, objet d'art, Zeitgeist,* and many others of political, philosophical, scientific, or literary bearing. *Sphygmograph* and many other scientific words are recent compoundings of Latin and especially of Greek words which are not otherwise in English usage, so that they may be regarded as borrowings as well as compounds. Others come in as general words, especially when large numbers of people go abroad, as during a war (*blitzkrieg, camouflage*) or when a foreign invention becomes suddenly popular, as in *chauffeur, garage, chassis* of the automobile vocabulary. Some words brought by immigrants have stuck: *sauerkraut, kohlrabi, pronto, pizza, kosher, goulash, zombie.*

Many borrowed words are dropped before they gain any general currency. The useful words are more or less adapted to English spelling and pronunciation and become true English words. (See English language and, for suggestions about the use of recently borrowed words, Foreign words in English 2.)

3. Changes in form of words.

a. Word composition. Most new words are made by putting together two or more elements to create a different meaning or function, as *un-* added to *interesting* gives a word of the opposite meaning, *uninteresting,* or *-ize* added to the noun *canal* gives a verb, *canalize.* The fact that dictionaries separate words formed with prefixes into two groups, those that need to be defined and those that are self-explanatory, shows how deceptive affixes can be. The elements may be a prefix placed before the root word (*mis-related*), or a suffix added (*foolish-ness*), or a combining element like *mono-* (*mono-syllable, mono-rail*), or two independent words built together (*book-case, basket-ball, gentle-man*). Group words like *high school, out of town,* though not written as single words, could be included as a type of word composition.

A list of prefixes and suffixes that are still active in English would take several pages. Here are a few of the more common prefixes:

a- (not): asymmetrical, amoral, atypical
ante- (before): anteprohibition era
anti- (against): antiprohibition
bi- (two): bivalve, biplane, bicycle
dis- (not): disinterested, dispraise
in- (not): inelegant, independent
mis- (wrong): mistake, misnomer
pre- (before): preview, prenatal, preempt
re- (again): revise, redecorate

A few suffixes are:

-en (to form a verb): heighten, lighten, weaken
-ful (full): playful, spoonful
-fy (to make): electrify, horrify
-ish (to form an adjective): dryish, foolish, smallish
-ize (to form a verb): circularize

Combining elements include a number of words or roots, many of them Greek:

-graph- (writing): biography, photograph
micro- (small): microcosm, micrometer, microphone, microbiology

mono- (one): monotone, monorail
-phil- (loving): philanthropy, philately, Anglophile
tele- (distant): television, telemeter
-trop- (turning): geotropic, heliotropic

At first a compound has no more than the meaning to be expected from its elements: *unable = not able.* But often it will develop an independent sense which can hardly be guessed at from the meanings of its elements: *cupboard, loudspeaker.*

Several pairs of prefixes and suffixes have the same meaning, and often two words with the same meaning but somewhat different forms exist side by side, especially words with *in-* (not) and *un-* and nouns with *-ness, -ity,* or *-tion:*

aridness, aridity	indistinguishable, undistinguishable
completeness, completion	precocity, precociousness
corruption, corruptness	torridness, torridity
ferociousness, ferocity	unobliging, disobliging

b. Phonetic alterations. For a variety of reasons, one word may have two or more developments in its pronunciation, each form emphasizing a different shade of the older word's meaning. Here are four of the many Anglo-Saxon words that have had such double developments: from *ān* we get *one* and *a, an;* from *of* come *off* and *of;* from *thurh, through* and *thorough;* and from *ūtera, utter* and *outer.* In many such doublets the spellings do not differ, though the pronunciations, functions, and meanings do: *con'duct,* noun; *con duct',* verb.

c. Blends. Informal English has a number of words that show the liberties that the users of language have always taken with their words and always will take. Some of their experiments have been added to the main English vocabulary.

One common type is blends, or portmanteau words, made by telescoping two words into one, often making a letter or syllable do double duty. *Squish* is probably a blend of *squirt* and *swish; electrocute,* of *electro-* and *execute; smog,* of *smoke* and *fog.* Blends are common in the names of many firms and products. Other examples include *motel, paratroops, cinemactress* (*Time* magazine was once obsessed with such blends), and a good many folksy efforts like *absogoshdarnlutely.*

d. Clipped words. One of the commonest types of word change is clipping, dropping one or more syllables to make a briefer form: *ad* from *advertisement, bus* from *omnibus, taxi* from *taxicab* (earlier, from *taximeter cabriolet*), *quote* from *quotation, hifi* from *high fidelity* (a blend of clips), *mob* (an eighteenth-century clip from *mobile vulgus*), *auto, movie, plane, phone,* and so on. Shoptalk has many clips — *mike* for *microphone* or *micrometer.* The speech of any closely related group is full of clips; campus vocabulary shows a full line: *econ, home ec, phys ed, grad, dorm, ad building, lab, exam, gym, prof, premed,* and scores more. Clipped words are written (when they are appropriate to the context) without apostrophe or period.

e. Back formations. *Back formation* refers to the derivation of a new word (for example, *orate*) from an older word assumed to be its derivative *(oration)*. The new word usually serves as a different part of speech, like *baby-sit* from *baby-sitter, opt* from *option, peddle* from *peddler, typewrite* from *typewriter*. Some back formations are long established *(beg, diagnose, browse, edit);* some are still avoided by conservative writers *(emote, enthuse, sculpt);* some are mostly for fun *(buttle, revolute)*.

f. Common nouns from proper names. Some words have come into general use because of an association with a person or place: *boycott,* from the name of an Irish land agent, Captain Boycott, who was so treated; *macadam,* from the inventor of the road surface, John L. MacAdam; *sandwich,* from the Earl of Sandwich; *jersey,* from the island of Jersey; *pasteurize,* from Louis Pasteur, who developed the process.

g. Playful formations. Blends and back formations are likely to have a playful note, and so do some other word shifts that can't be classified. Some become quite generally used: *dingus, doodad, beanery, jalopy.*

References: The authority on the history of English words is the *Oxford English Dictionary;* the *Dictionary of American English* and the *Dictionary of Americanisms* supplement it for words peculiar to the United States. Besides general books on English, the following pay special attention to origin of words: Valerie Adams, *An Introduction to Modern English Word Formation* (London: Longmans, 1973); W. Nelson Francis, *The English Language* (New York: Norton, 1963); Pyles; Margaret Schlauch, *The English Language in Modern Times,* 2nd ed. (London: Oxford Univ. Press, 1964); Joseph M. Williams, *Origins of the English Language* (New York: Free Press, 1975).

other

In comparing things of the same class, add *other* to *any:* That movie scared me more than any *other* I've seen. See *any* 1.

outl Outline form

Revise the form of your outline to observe the conventions given below.

1. The title. The title of the essay should stand three spaces above the outline. The heads should carry their full meaning and not refer back to the title by pronouns. See Titles 1.

2. Thesis statement. An optional practice – but a good one – is to put a sentence stating the subject and scope of the whole paper between the title and the first main head.

3. Numbering systems. The most widely used numbering alternates letters and figures, as shown in the examples in 7. Avoid intricate or confusing schemes of numbering.

4. Indention. Write the main heads flush with the left margin and indent subheads two or three spaces from the left – enough to place them clearly in a different column. Heads that run over a single line should be further indented.

5. Punctuation and capitalization. Don't use punctuation at the ends of lines in a topic outline. In a sentence outline the punctuation should follow regular sentence practice. Capitalize only the first word of a head and proper names; an outline head is not a title.

6. Heads.
a. Meaningful heads. Each head should be understandable by itself, especially if the outline is to be shown to someone for criticism or is to be submitted with the essay. The following would do as a scratch outline but would not be satisfactory for other purposes:

My Vocation

    I. The work I am interested in
    II. Why I prefer this type of work
III. What my responsibilities would be
IV. The chances for success

b. Heads of equal importance. The main heads of an outline, those usually marked by Roman numerals, should show the several main divisions of the material. Similarly, the immediate subdivisions of these heads, those usually marked by capital letters, should designate logical divisions of one phase of the subject. The same principle applies to further divisions under any subhead.

Unequal headings	*Equal headings*
Books I Have Enjoyed	Books I Have Enjoyed
I. Adventure stories	I. Adventure stories
II. Historical novels	II. Historical novels
III. *Walden*	III. Science fiction
IV. Autobiographies	IV. Autobiographies
V. What I like most	V. Books on mysticism

c. Headings in parallel form. Equivalent heads and subheads are expressed in parallel grammatical form. In a sentence outline, use complete sentences throughout; in a topic outline, use phrase heads only. Make all heads of the same rank parallel; that is, make the heads in one series all nouns or all adjectives or all phrases, or whatever is most appropriate.

Heads not parallel	*Parallel heads*
The Art of Putting	The Art of Putting
I. The stance is fundamental	I. The stance
II. The grip	II. The grip
III. Watch the backswing	III. The backswing
IV. Stroking the ball	IV. The stroke
V. Follow through with care	V. The follow-through

7. Division of main points. Since a topic is not "divided" unless there are at least two parts, a formal outline should have at least two subheads under any main head—or none at all. For every heading marked *I* there should be at least a *II*, for every *A* there should be a *B*, and so on.

Illogical single heads	*Logical subdivision*
The Tripartite System	The Tripartite System

I. The executive branch
   A. President and Cabinet

II. The legislative branch
   A. The House
   B. The Senate
      1. Functions

III. The judicial branch
   A. The Supreme Court

I. The executive branch
   A. President
   B. Cabinet

II. The legislative branch
   A. The House of Representatives
   B. The Senate
      1. Special functions
      2. Special privileges

III. The judicial branch
   A. The Supreme Court
   B. Lower courts

When a main point cannot be divided, include any necessary detail in the head. For an organization in which the whole executive power lies in the president, this heading would be satisfactory:

I. The executive branch (the president)

8. Introduction and conclusion. Ordinarily an essay has a beginning, a middle, and an ending (or an introduction, a body, and a conclusion), but don't use such labels in the outline. They are too general to reflect specific content. Besides, the beginning and ending can rarely be represented by heads that are coordinate with the others. The first and last topics in the outline are from the main body of material, chosen with a special view to their fitness for starting and concluding the discussion.

Oxymoron

An oxymoron is a contradiction in terms used as a figure of speech—for example, "sweet bitterness," "loving hate," "mildly fatal," "making haste slowly," "literary illiterates" (Aleksandr Solzhenitsyn). *Oxymoron* is occasionally used with the extended meaning "a compound of incongruous elements": "He was that religious oxymoron, a gentle Calvinist" (George P. Elliott, *Commentary*).

P

pair

When not preceded by a number or other plural indicator, *pairs* is the preferred plural of *pair*: Pairs of figures were common in the design. Otherwise usage is divided:

These hypotheses are confounded in two pairs.—Roselle and Campbell, *Psychological Bulletin*

He found a car with one too many pair of skis.—*Time*

Paradox

A paradox is a statement that seems to contradict common sense. See Epigrams and aphorisms.

¶ Paragraph indention

Indent here for a new paragraph.

no ¶ No paragraph indention

Join this paragraph to the preceding one.

1. Indent for a new paragraph. A paragraph symbol in the margin of your paper means that you have failed to meet your readers' expectations. From their experience with books and magazines, they are in the habit of regarding a paragraph as a series of related statements, all bearing on the scene being described or the argument being advanced; and they expect to be forewarned by a paragraph break of any shift in focus or any turn in the course of reasoning. When they come to a stretch of prose that drifts or leaps from one topic to another, they are confused and distracted by the lack of unity and cohesion.

Your instructor may have other reasons for recommending indention. A single sentence or short sequence of sentences that makes a significant point may demand the emphasis it will gain by being set apart. Or a brief passage that marks a transition from one stage of the discussion to another may be more helpful to the reader if it is detached from the end of a long paragraph to stand on its own. And sometimes, even if there are close enough connections in the material to justify a very long paragraph, you may be advised to break it up simply to give the reader a mental breathing spell. Although it's not uncommon to find an 800-word paragraph in a scholarly journal where a closely reasoned argument is addressed to interested readers, most exposition and argument receives nothing like such close attention. Indention helps break a discussion into manageable units or (to use a familiar food metaphor) into digestible bites. In using indention this way, be sure to take advantage of natural subdivisions within the long paragraph. Don't divide the paragraph at a point that will separate two closely related sentences.

In general, the development of your topic should determine the length of your paragraphs. But take into account what your subject is: narrative and descriptive paragraphs are likely to be shorter than paragraphs of criticism or philosophy. And take into account the probable interest and attention span of your readers.

2. Join separate paragraphs. A succession of very short paragraphs, like a succession of very long ones, makes reading difficult. An unjustified paragraph break throws the reader off the track so that he loses the connection between one idea and another. In revising an essay, combine paragraphs in which the details or ideas are so closely related that they form a single stage in the development of the essay. In the process, make sure that you provide whatever transitional words or phrases may be needed to emphasize the unity.

While a transitional passage that sums up one substantial section of an essay and forecasts the next may be a very short paragraph—perhaps just one sentence—most paragraphs are from four to ten sentences long. If you have more than two paragraphs on a typed page of expository prose, look closely to be sure you can justify the breaks. A sequence of very short paragraphs may indicate that you are not developing your points adequately, not providing enough examples or details or comparisons. Or it may be that you have failed to recognize the close logical connections that pull your ideas together into larger units. In either case, a reader is likely to consider short, choppy paragraphs a collection of random observations rather than the unified development of a central idea. See Coherence, Transition.

par Paragraphs

Revise or rewrite this unsatisfactory paragraph.

A paragraph is a group of related statements that a writer presents as a unit in the development of his subject. It strikes the eye as a unit because it is physically set off by indention or spacing. It should also strike the mind as a unit because the statements in it are closely related, representing a stage in the flow of the writer's thought.

Here are the most common faults in paragraphs, with suggested remedies:

1. Lack of development. Rewrite the paragraph, including details and illustrations that will lead the reader to understand and accept its central point. See Details.

2. Lack of unity. Rewrite, deleting any material that fails to contribute to the central idea, or core of meaning, that is the focus of the paragraph and that justifies its inclusion in the paper. See Unity 2.

3. Lack of continuity. Revise or rewrite to make clear the relation between the statements that make up the paragraph. Occasionally you will find that you can improve the continuity by simply altering the order of the sentences. Sometimes you need to supply a transition between sentences. And sometimes you need to rethink and then rewrite. See Coherence, Logical thinking, Transition.

4. Lack of transition. Begin the paragraph with a word, phrase, or sentence that will integrate it firmly with the material that precedes it. See Transition.

5. Lack of a required topic sentence. Provide a topic sentence to strengthen the unity of the paragraph or to make clearer to the reader the direction your essay is taking. Not all paragraphs need topic sentences. But some do, either to announce the generalization that subsequent details will support, or to pull details together in a generalization, or to introduce or sum up a stage of the discussion. See Topic sentence.

Parallelism

When two words or groups of words are alike grammatically and structurally, they are said to be parallel. Parallel constructions range from matching pairs of adjectives (*cold and wet*) to series of phrases or clauses – "Some metaphors are harmless, some are useful, some are beautiful, and some are stumbling blocks to clear thinking" (Thomas H. Middleton, *Saturday Review*) – to sequences of elaborately balanced sentences. The extent to which a writer should deliberately employ parallelism depends on the context. The simple parallelism that contributes to clarity and efficiency is appropriate in all varieties of English. The exact, sustained, intricate parallelism of some balanced and periodic sentences is at home only in formal prose. See Balanced sentence, Cumulative sentence, Periodic sentence.

Parallelism and style

Use parallel structures for elements that should logically be performing the same grammatical function.

Parallelism is one of the simplest, neatest, and most economical ways of achieving clarity. The sentence you have just read illustrates what it says. The three sentences that follow express the same idea without taking advantage of parallelism:

Parallelism is one of the simplest ways of achieving clarity. Neatness is a major contribution made by parallelism. A sentence that uses parallel structures is more economical than one that does not.

Parallelism is a mode of coordination. This means that as a general rule *and, but, nor,* and *yet* should match noun (or noun equivalent) to noun, adjective to adjective, infinitive to infinitive, dependent clause to dependent clause, and so on.

1. Put into the same grammatical forms and structures those words, phrases, and clauses that are alike in purpose and related in meaning (complementary or contrasting). "He was *brilliant* but *unstable*" (predicate adjectives modifying *he*) and "He was a *brilliant* but *unstable* person" (adjectives modifying *person*) both make use of parallelism. "He was *brilliant* but an *unstable* person" does not, though the purpose of *brilliant* and *unstable* remains the same: they are still describing the subject of the sentence.

Here are some sentences that use parallelism, followed in each case by a version that does not:

Parallel participles: Expanding the dimensions of the individual, or *contracting* them, continues to be the ultimate occupation of art in our time. – Harold Rosenberg, *New Yorker*
Not parallel (participle mismatched with infinitive): Expanding the dimensions of the individual, or *to contract* them, continues to be. . . .

Parallel nouns: Rational thought and rational behavior rarely govern either the *formation* or the *operation* of policy. – Barbara W. Tuchman, *Newsweek*
Not parallel (noun mismatched with dependent clause): Rational thought and rational behavior rarely govern either the *formation* of policy or *how it operates.*

Parallel gerunds: Sir Percy was given to *sniffing* snuff and *prattling* foolishly as a cover for the daring Pimpernel. — Thomas H. Middleton, *Saturday Review*
Not parallel (gerund mismatched with independent clause): Sir Percy was given to *sniffing* snuff and *he also prattled foolishly as a cover for the daring Pimpernel.*

Failure to use matching grammatical structures is particularly noticeable with the correlative conjunctions *both . . . and, either . . . or, neither . . . nor, not only . . . but (also)*. A simple example is given in the second rewritten version on the preceding page. Here is an equally common type:

The rule is *not only* ignored by those it is directed at *but* those who are supposed to enforce it ignore it too.

It seems clear that the writer wants to emphasize how thoroughly the rule is being ignored. In revising, then, a good first step would be to place the verb before *not only:* The rule is being ignored. Who is ignoring it? Those who . . . and those who. . . . Then, with the correlative conjunctions added, the phrasing falls naturally into parallel form:

The rule is being ignored *not only by those who are supposed to* observe it *but also by those who are supposed to* enforce it.

2. Do *not* make structures parallel unless the relationship of the ideas or details they express justifies parallelism. If parallelism in structure fails to represent the logic of the material, the reader will be misled. The three grammatical elements that end the next sentence are not parallel:

My year abroad taught me a lot about the way Venezuelans earn a living, spend their leisure time, and their attitudes toward Americans.

To make the elements parallel (. . . and feel about Americans) would produce a smoother sentence, but so far as meaning goes, it would be a mistake. In the context, the way Venezuelans feel about Americans is not logically related to the way they earn their living or spend their leisure time. The best revision, then, would be to retain the first two elements in the series but turn the third into a separate sentence. How the new sentence would be phrased would depend on whether the writer was making a casual addition or introducing a significant topic:

My year abroad taught me a lot about the way Venezuelans earn a living and spend their leisure time. It also taught me a lot about their attitudes toward Americans. *Or* More important, I learned a lot. . . .

See Parallelism, Phrases 2, Shifted constructions. For further examples of the effective use of parallelism, see Periodic sentence.

Paraphrase

A paraphrase is a restatement of a writer's ideas in different words. The term *paraphrasing* is now usually applied to digesting the contents of a passage in one's own words, as in taking notes. Difficulties may arise in the next step: using the paraphrase in a paper of one's own. First of all, the source of the materials must be acknowledged. Second, if phrases or sentences from the original are included in the paraphrase, they must be enclosed in quotation marks and either footnoted or otherwise identified as the original author's. See Plagiarism, Research papers.

Parentheses

Like commas and dashes, parentheses are used to enclose words and word groups that break away from the main structure of the sentence. Of the three types of enclosing marks, parentheses indicate the greatest degree of removal.

1. For additions. Within sentences parentheses are used to enclose words and word groups that add facts to a statement without essentially altering its meaning. They allow such additions to stand outside the frame of the principal sentence. The additions may be illustrations (as in this book), definitions, or information thrown in for good measure:

The few verb endings that English now retains (-s, -ed, -ing) are being still further reduced in ordinary speech.

Gresham's Law (that bad money drives out good) applies as usual in this case.

His concerts were well received in most cities (Cleveland was an exception), but he was still dissatisfied.

Like dashes, parentheses can become a bad stylistic habit. If the information they enclose is as unimportant as parentheses usually suggest, it probably should be omitted. If it is worth including, work it into the structure of the sentence in which it appears, or make it a separate sentence.

2. With other marks. When a complete sentence in parentheses comes within a sentence (notice the punctuation of this one), it needs neither a capital letter nor a period. Commas and other marks of punctuation in the main sentence always *follow* the parenthesis (as here and in the preceding sentence). (Parenthesized sentences, like this one, that do not stand within other sentences have the period before the closing parenthesis.)

3. To enclose numbers or letters in an enumeration. Parentheses are sometimes used to enclose letters or figures that mark items in an enumeration: The additions may be (1) illustrations, (2) definitions, or (3) information thrown in for good measure. Parentheses make the listed items more conspicuous.

See Brackets, Dash.

Participles

Participles are derived from verbs but do not stand as independent predicates.

1. Forms. The present participle adds *-ing* to the base form of the verb: *asking, singing.* The past participle of regular verbs adds *-ed* to the base *(asked),* and the perfect participle adds *having* to the past participle *(having asked).* In the passive, the *-ed* form is preceded by *being (being asked)* and *having been (having been asked).* Many irregular verbs have special past participle forms: *sung, having sung, being sung, having been sung.*

2. Functions.

a. In verb phrases. Participles enter into many verb phrases: I am asking, I am being asked, I have asked, I have been asked. Although participles are referred to as present and past, they do not themselves indicate definite time but time in relation to the context in which they are used. See Tenses of verbs.

b. As modifiers. When not part of verb phrases, participles are most commonly adjectivals. They are like adjectives in that they modify nouns (a *coming* era, a *frightened* cat). They are like verbs in that they may take an object *(Following these clues,* he soon found her). They are like both in that they may be modified by adverbs *(rolling crazily).* Generative-transformational grammars derive them from full underlying clauses:

The car [the car was rolling crazily] crashed into a bus.
The car, rolling crazily, crashed into a bus.

When used as an adjective, a participle should refer clearly to some particular noun or pronoun: Having opened the envelope, he began to read the letter *(Having opened* modifies *he).* A modifying participle is said to dangle when it seems to refer to a word the writer does not mean it to refer to: Kissing his wife good-bye, the door slammed behind him. Errors like this occur when the subject of the participle and the subject of the main clause differ. In "[*He* was] kissing his wife good-bye, *the door* slammed behind him," *He* and *the door* are not the same. Compare a correct modifier: [*He* was] kissing his wife good-bye, *he* let the door slam behind him. *He* in "[He was] kissing" and *he* in "he let the door slam" are the same. The first subject can be deleted. See Dangling modifiers.

c. In absolute phrases. The participle-as-adjective should not be confused with the participle in a phrase that relates to the whole sentence — to the situation — rather than to a particular word. Some such phrases have become formulas: Judging from her looks, she isn't under fifty. See Absolute phrases.

3. Stylistically objectionable participles. Unskilled writers sometimes use a participle or a gerund where a subordinate clause would read more smoothly: The train was on time, necessitating our hurrying. *Better:* . . . so we had to hurry. Clumsy nominative absolutes should especially be avoided: The plane arriving then, we boarded it.

For *very* with participles, see *very* 2. Compare Gerunds. References: Donald W. Emery and R. W. Pence, *Grammar of Present-Day English,* 2nd ed. (New York: Macmillan, 1963), pp. 305–15; Roberts, pp. 345–55.

Particles

Of the eight traditional parts of speech, four have no inflected forms in English – adverbs, prepositions, conjunctions, interjections – and can be discussed only in terms of function and position. They are sometimes lumped under the label *particles*.

Parts of speech

Parts of speech are the categories a linguist sets up in order to describe structures in sentences and finally sentences themselves. Since it would be pointless to list all the words in English, indicating for each one whether it can serve as a subject or object or modifier, linguists group words into categories and subcategories and then describe where these categories may occur in various patterns and how they form larger structures. The "correctness" of these categories, however, depends on how the linguist wants to describe sentence structure – even on what his notion of "structure" is. Linguists working with different grammatical theories will create different sets of definitions. Thus one linguist will classify a word like *some* as an indefinite pronoun and another will classify it as a prearticle. The different names are not just terminological quibbles. They may reflect different theories that determine the definitions.

1. Three approaches. Traditional schoolroom grammarians, using a system much like that developed for describing classical languages, cite eight parts of speech: nouns, verbs, adjectives, adverbs, pronouns, prepositions, conjunctions, and interjections. Nouns and verbs are defined semantically: a noun is the name of a person, place, or thing; verbs show action. The other parts of speech are defined functionally: adjectives modify nouns; adverbs modify verbs, adjectives, and other adverbs; pronouns replace nouns; and prepositions relate a noun or pronoun to some other part of the sentence.

Because semantic definitions are imprecise (it is hard to say what the noun *lack* refers to in "There is a lack of time") and because the functional definitions are much too broad (the definition of *preposition* would, for example, cover *is* in "John is a friend"), structural linguists reject them in favor of purely formal definitions: Nouns, they say, are those words that can occur with plural and genitive endings or in positions after *the* and before a verb; verbs are those words that can occur with third-person singular -*s* endings, with past-tense inflections, with perfect inflections, and with progressive -*ing* endings; adjectives are those words that can occur with comparative or superlative endings, after *more* or *most*, and in the position "The [noun] is very _____"; adverbs are those words made up of an adjective and an -*ly* ending. The residue of words such as *and, in, can, very, the, not, all, therefore, because, please,* and *hello* are put into a large category of "indeclinable" words, or function words, which is subcategorized according to where these words occur in a sentence relative to the parts of speech already identified.

Transformational grammarians, or generativists, are much less concerned than structuralists with devising formal tests to classify parts of speech and more concerned with the most economical and general overall description. The labels for individual words are judged "correct" only if they are necessary to describe how the words behave in the context of a sentence. Generativists assume that one part of speech may derive from another, as the verb *discover* in a deep structure like "Tom *discovered* gold" becomes, in a surface structure, the noun *discovery*, "Tom's *discovery* of gold." For transformational grammarians, it is impossible to talk about parts of speech without explaining the whole grammar of a language and without distinguishing between deep and surface structures. See Deep structure.

Because structural grammars emphasize the careful and logical classification of parts of speech, we will rely chiefly on their methods here.

2. Form-class words and function words. The structuralist approach suggests that English words are of two general types: (1) form-class words, which express the primary lexical or semantic meaning of a sentence and can usually be inflected for number, tense, or comparison; and (2) function words, which perform the grammatical or structural function of connecting, relating, and qualifying the form-class words. These function words usually cannot be inflected. The form-class words are commonly called nouns, verbs, adjectives, and adverbs, with certain pronouns fitting into subgroups under the category *noun*. All other words are function (or structure) words.

a. Form-class words. In addition to expressing lexical meaning, form-class words share other characteristics. They can be inflected to indicate specific semantic meanings and grammatical relationships. Nouns (and the personal pronouns) inflect to show plural number and possession: *girl, girls, girl's, girls'; I, we, my, mine; she, her, hers; they, their, theirs.* Verbs inflect to indicate present third-person singular, past tense, present participle, and past participle: *walks, walked, walking, walked; sings, sang, singing, sung.* Adjectives and most adverbs add *-er* or *-est* (or *more, most; less, least*) to indicate comparison: *tall, taller, tallest; more fully, most fully; less difficult, least difficult.*

Form-class words are an "open" class. Borrowed words and coined words, such as *astronaut, hippie, telecast, video, stereo,* are still being added. See Origin of words 2.

b. Function words. Function words (also called structure words) have less specific lexical meanings than form-class words. (Consider the various meanings of *green* or *run* in comparison with the meaning of *by* or *the*.) Only a few groups of function words (if we choose to so classify them) can be inflected: the demonstrative, relative, and interrogative pronouns and the modal-auxiliary verbs. In contrast to form-class groups, which include hundreds of thousands of different words, most groups of function words contain a very small number; some, like *not* and *do,* contain only one. And function words are members of closed groups. The idiomatic use of certain prepositions may vary or change, but English has borrowed or developed very few new prepositions or conjunctions over the seven hundred years since it was interpenetrated by French borrowings after the Norman Conquest. In that time it has lost pronouns and has added no articles.

The most detailed description of function words from a structural point of view is that by C. C. Fries in *The Structure of English.* Fries points out that such words as *yes* and *no* (or their colloquial equivalents), *please, not,* and *let's* are used in limited contexts. He also shows that *very, extremely, considerably,* and others are quite different from such words as *quietly, thoroughly, angrily.* For example, the sentence "He collected the materials quickly" is meaningful; the sentence "He collected the materials very" is not. A structural linguist is thus forced to classify these two groups of words in two different categories—the first, qualifiers; the second, adverbs (or, in Fries' more esoteric terminology, Class 4 words).

c. Words in context. The respective grammatical roles of form-class words—to express the primary lexical meaning of communication—and of function words—to relate and give understandable structure to combinations of form-class words—can be illustrated either with regular English sentences or with nonsense sentences. Consider, for example, the sentence used by Fries: The mother of the boy will arrive tomorrow. The basic lexical information can be expressed telegraphically with the four form-class words: Boy's mother arrives tomorrow. The function words, *the* and *of,* signal the grammar of the message; *will* indicates that the arriving will occur in the future.

Or consider the nonsense sentence "The slithy toves will gyre and gimble very gluggily in the wabes." The sentence possesses only such meaning as grammatical structure (that is, word order, word forms, and function words) gives to it. The "nouns" *toves* and *wabes,* the "verbs" *gyre* and *gimble,* the "adjective" *slithy,* and the "adverb" *gluggily* can be replaced with meaningful words or with other nonsense words. But the function words *the, will, very, in* cannot be replaced if this is to be an English "sentence."

Both sentences indicate the distinctive features of the two general types of words. Form-class words can be inflected and are members of open classes: we recognize them by their forms and their position in the sentence and by the function words used to connect and relate them. Function words have almost no inflected forms (except for *will–would, this–these,* etc.); they are in closed groups; they occupy regular positions or slots in syntactic structures.

As the two illustrative sentences also indicate, we classify parts of speech according to their context in a sentence or according to their inflections. Certain words, like *walk, burn, run,* are used as either nouns or verbs. Other words, like *bomb, radio, dust,* are used not just as nouns or verbs but also, without change in form, as modifiers: bomb shelter, radio station, dust belt. The conjunction *after* (We will leave after we have eaten) may also serve as a preposition: After dinner, the group dispersed. How a word is classified in a specific instance depends upon the context in which it is used. That is why, in the chart of form-class words, we list the usual function of each part of speech.

The chart of function words lists the types that occur most frequently, along with examples and usual functions. The same words may either serve as different kinds of function words or (like some prearticles, *some, many, all*) serve as both form-class words (nouns) and function words (prearticles). See Determiners.

FORM-CLASS WORDS

PART OF SPEECH	INFLECTED FORMS	FUNCTIONS
Nouns *(boy, house, city, truth)*	Plural: *-s (boys)* and a few anomalous forms: *oxen, deer, teeth,* etc. Genitive (or possessive): *-'s, -s' (boy's, boys')*	Serve as subject; complement; object of verbs, of verbals, of prepositions.
Personal pronouns *(I, you, he, she, it)*	Plural: *we, they* Genitive: *my, mine, his, her, its* Objective: *me, him, them*	Same function as nouns.
Indefinite nouns *(everybody, everything, everyone, no one)*		Serve in many but not all of the positions nouns do.

Other pronouns, such as *who* and *that,* are listed under function words, because they do not possess a full set of noun inflections and cannot be used in all the positions filled by nouns or personal pronouns.

Verbs *(walk, play, breathe)*	Present participle: *-ing* Past participle: *-ed* Third-person singular, present tense: *-s* past tense: *-ed* (For irregular verbs, see *be*, Principal parts of verbs.)	Assert an action or express a state or condition.
Adjectives *(tall, green, poor)*	Comparative: *-er* (or *more, less*) Superlative: *-est* (or *most, least*)	Modify nouns or pronouns.
Adverbs *(slow, quickly)*	Comparative: *-er* (or *more, less*) Superlative: *-est* (or *most, least*) (Some adverbs—like *here, tomorrow, everywhere*—are not compared.)	Modify verbs, adverbs, phrases, and clauses, usually indicating place, time, or manner.

FUNCTION WORDS

PART OF SPEECH	USUAL FUNCTIONS
Auxiliaries (usually called modal auxiliaries): *can, could, will, shall, may, must, get, used (to),* etc.	Precede, point to, and qualify predicating verbs or serve as substitutes for verbs.
Determiners (also called noun determiners) are subdivided into prearticles, articles, and postarticles.	
Prearticles: *some, few, several, much, many, each, both, all, neither, half, two,* etc.	Precede and enumerate nouns; they stand alone when the nouns are deleted: Several [boys] were here.
Articles: *a/an, the, some; this, that, these, those*	Specify definiteness of reference. The words traditionally defined as demonstrative pronouns—*this, that, these, those*—can be classed as a variety of article. The absence of an article indicates indefiniteness before noncount nouns and plurals: Food is expensive; Carrots are cheap.
Postarticles: *several, many, few; first, second, third,* etc.; *one, two, three,* etc.; *former, latter, next, first, last,* etc.	Follow articles and precede adjectives: the few old men, the second young woman, the three pretty girls. *Several, few,* and *many* are identical to the prearticles *some, few,* and *many:* Few of the several sick children, several of the many brave soldiers. Postarticles usually quantify or indicate an order to the head noun.
Qualifiers: *very, rather, fairly, mighty, less, least, more, most, too, quite, much,* etc.	Qualify or limit adjectives, usually by indicating degree or extent. Some qualifiers are intensifiers.
Conjunctions or connectors	
Coordinating conjunctions: *and, but, nor, yet, for, or, so,* and sometimes *not, rather,* etc.	Connect like or equal grammatical components (words, phrases, clauses, sentences).
Correlative conjunctions: *both . . . and, either . . . or, so . . . as, not only . . . but (also),* etc.	Used in pairs to connect clauses within a sentence.
Conjunctive adverbs (also called sentence connectors): *accordingly, also, consequently, hence, however, therefore,* etc.	Connect either independent clauses within a sentence or sentences within or between paragraphs.
Subordinating conjunctions: *after, as, if, since, when, until,* etc.	Join and subordinate, as a structure expressing modification or qualification, a dependent clause to another clause in the sentence. Usually the dependent clause modifies a verb, a clause, or an entire sentence.
Noun substitutes	
Interrogative pronouns: *who, which, what, whoever,* etc.	Serve as subjects, objects, or single-word modifiers in interrogative sentences or dependent noun clauses.

Relative pronouns: *who, whose, whom, which, that, when,* and also *where, wherever,* etc.	Serve as subjects, complements, objects, or single-word modifiers to link independent noun and adjective clauses to other clauses within a sentence.
Prepositions: *at, about, by, in, on, under, underneath, back of, due to, in front of, on account of,* etc.	Precede and connect object, consisting of a noun or pronoun, with or without modifiers, to other constituents of the sentence. Usually the phrase can be identified as either adjectival or adverbial.

Miscellaneous

do (did, does, done)	Used to form *yes – no* questions, to give emphasis, and as a substitute verb.
Exclamations (including interjections): *oh, ouch, no, yes, hey, never, really,* etc.	Used to show feeling or – in some instances – to indicate that the speaker is listening.
Interrogators: *when, why, where, how,* etc.	Used alone or as introductory word for a phrase or clause asking a question.
Negatives: *no, not, never*	Show negation.
Yes – no words: *yes, yeah, uh-huh; no, not at all, maybe,* etc.	Give responses or – in some instances – indicate that the speaker is listening.

See Grammar, Linguistics. References: Charles Carpenter Fries, *The Structure of English* (New York: Harcourt, 1952), Ch. 5; Francis, Ch. 5; Sledd, Ch. 2.

pass Passive voice

Change the verb or verbs to active voice.

1. Avoiding the passive. Using the passive voice without good reason will tend to make your sentences awkward and wordy, place emphasis where it doesn't belong, and at times leave your readers wondering who did what.

a. Don't use the passive to avoid using *I.*

Between Laredo and Austin the driving was done by me.
Revision: Between Laredo and Austin I drove. *Or . . .* I did the driving.

b. Don't use the passive in an attempt to sound weighty or scientific.

The proposals that were made by the administration have been received negatively by the student body.
Revision: Students disliked the administration's proposals.

c. Don't use the passive to hide or obscure the identity of the source of an action.

My roommate and I were summoned by the dean because of the waterbags that had been thrown from our windows.
Revision: The dean summoned my roommate and me for throwing waterbags from our windows. *Or (depending on the facts)* The dean summoned my roommate and me because he thought, wrongly, that we were the ones who had thrown the waterbags.

d. Don't use the passive to vary the pattern just for the sake of varying the pattern.

After finding our way through the woods, we reached the campsite. A half-dozen trips were made to bring in our supplies. By sunset we were more than ready for a hot meal.

The shifts from active to passive are unjustified and distracting. Revising the second sentence (We had to make . . .) would keep the focus clear and so make the passage easier to read.

2. Appropriate uses of the passive. The passive voice is appropriately used in at least three rhetorical contexts.
a. Passives are appropriate when the agent of the action is either unknown, unimportant, or better left unidentified:

As many as a hundred notices of teaching jobs are printed each month in a newsletter best described as a "whole education" catalogue. — Jean Collins, *Change*

The grammars could not be dismissed as inferior or crude; they were simply different. — J. J. Lamberts, *A Short Introduction to English Usage*

Postal rates are to be increased.

b. Passives can be used (as in this sentence) when the subject of the discourse would otherwise be the direct object. Because passives are the subject of this section, it's natural that the noun phrase referring to them be the subject-topic of most sentences in these paragraphs.
c. Passives allow a writer to focus on the agent of an action by shifting the agent to the end of the sentence, where it will be stressed. This is especially desirable when the agent is represented by a fairly long and complicated noun phrase:

Active: A team bigger and tougher than any you would find outside professional football defeated us.
Passive: We were defeated by a team bigger and tougher than any you would find outside professional football.

Such a shift often makes it possible for the writer to build a tighter transition from one sentence to another. The element ending one sentence leads into the subject of the sentence that follows.
　　See Voice.

Past tense
For past tense, regular verbs add *-ed* to the base form: *ask, asked; answer, answered.* See Principal parts of verbs, Tenses of verbs.

people, persons
People has long been used as a collective noun referring to a group, but as recently as the early part of this century, it was regarded as nonstandard when used with numerical quantifiers as the plural of *person,* as in "Five people are here." Though formal usage still tends to prefer *persons, people* is now thoroughly established in such contexts. *Person* and *persons* are frequently resorted to by writers who object to using *man* or *men* to represent both sexes. See Sexist language.

per

Per (Latin, "through, by, among," etc.) is most appropriate in phrases that are still close to their Latin originals (per capita, per diem), in commercial expressions ($125 per week, $3.00 per yard), and in some technical phrases (revolutions per minute). In less specialized contexts, *a* or *every* is preferable (a dime a dozen, a thousand words every day).

percent

In informal and general writing (but not formal) *percent* is often used instead of *percentage* or even *proportion:* Only a small percent of the class was [*or* were] present. So used, it is treated as a collective noun, sometimes taking a singular verb, sometimes a plural. With figures, *percent* (97.6 percent) is preferred to the percent sign (97.6%) except in technical and statistical material. *Percent* is also written as two words. It is not an abbreviation and should not be followed by a period.

Perfect tense

Tenses formed with *have* and a past participle are traditionally called perfect tenses: present perfect, *has laughed;* past perfect, *had laughed;* future perfect, *will have laughed.* See Tenses of verbs.

Period

1. At the end of statements. A period is used to mark the end of every completed sentence that is not a question or an exclamation. Sometimes if he is not really inquiring or exclaiming, a writer will use a period at the end of a sentence in the form of a question or an exclamation: Would you be so good as to return the book at your earliest convenience. What a day. See Rhetorical questions.

2. Miscellaneous conventional uses.
a. After abbreviations: Oct.; etc.; Mr. W. Fraser, Jr.
b. Between dollars and cents: $5.66; $0.66 (*but* 66 cents *or* 66¢)
c. Before decimals: .6, 3.14159, 44.6 percent
d. Sometimes between hours and minutes in giving precise time, though a colon is more usual: 2.36 p.m.

3. With quotation marks. When a quotation ends a sentence, most American publishers place the period inside the quotation marks whether the quotation is a complete sentence or a single word:

"The longer you put it off," he said, "the harder it's going to be."
He glared at me as he said "harder."

Periodic sentence

A periodic sentence withholds its complete meaning until its last word (as in the first sentence below) or until its last clause (as in the second and third):

Exhaustive in its scholarship, discerning in its literary judgments, sensible in its theorizing, it merits the adjective all biographies aspire to: *definitive* – Robert F. Moss, *Saturday Review*

Not so long before he died, still receiving carloads of honors as he always had, and still receiving, as also he always had, from Right or Left in turn, fanatic attacks on his social views, Mann remarked that he was a "great, unloved name." – John Thompson, *Harper's*

The importance of disciplinary studies, the value of humanistic thinking and illumination, the urgency of facing the public with the best that the humanities can do, the clear need of bringing together the best humanists (which includes some social and natural scientists) as well as other figures such as journalists, labor leaders, businessmen, and politicians, all argue for an institution devoted to such and other ends. – Morton W. Bloomfield, *PMLA*

A great many short and simple sentences have their base structures at the end and therefore fit the definition of a periodic sentence; but rhetoricians reserve the term for sentences of some length and complexity. Because such a sentence keeps the reader in a mild or an acute state of suspense, its resolution creates a sense of satisfaction. A long periodic sentence almost always lends a passage a distinct touch of formality, for it is necessarily an artful and studied production, often using, as in the examples above, sustained parallelism. Remaining airborne through clause and phrase as it does, it can achieve unusual dramatic emphasis when it finally returns to earth – or, if poorly done, it can end with the thud of anticlimax. In appropriate contexts the periodic sentence can contribute to a variety of rhetorical purposes; but a succession of periodic sentences is tiring to read and creates a style too elaborate for everyday topics.

The prime example of the periodic sentence as cliche is the nominating speech. Here, a very long series of clauses beginning "a man who," or "a woman who," precedes the name of the nominee, which usually comes as a surprise to no one.

See Parallelism. Compare Cumulative sentence.

Person

Person as a grammatical term refers to both pronoun classification and verb inflection. Personal pronouns are in the first person, the one(s) speaking (*I, my, me, we, our, us*); second person, the one(s) spoken to (*you, your, yours*); third person, anyone or anything else (*he, his, him, she, her, hers, it, its, they, their, them*). Nouns are regarded as third person, as are most other pronouns (the relative *who* and its derivatives take their persons from their antecedents).

Except in the verb *be* (*I am, you are, he is* . . .), English verbs indicate person only for the third singular of the present and perfect tenses: I see, you see, he *sees;* we see, you see, they see; I have seen, you have seen, he *has* seen; etc.

Personal pronouns

The personal pronouns are *I, we, you, he, she, it,* and *they.* See Case, Person, Pronouns 1.

Personification

Personification is a figure of speech in which an object or animal or quality or ideal is given some attributes of a human being:

There has been, after all, something in the talk of American innocence. No doubt it is a false innocence, fabricated by a myth-charged education: the lady who was "once a beauty of magnificence unparalleled" nourished her complexion on genocide and slavery. Yet her beauty existed in the eyes of her children, especially her adopted, immigrant children. – Conor Cruise O'Brien, *New York Review of Books*

It is less common today than formerly, and less common in prose than in verse. Flat and unnecessary personification is likely to sound amateurish: No steam engine can brag of such efficiency. See Figurative language, Gender, Pathetic fallacy.

persons

With numerical quantifiers, *persons* is preferred to *people* in formal usage: five persons. See *people, persons*.

phenomenon, phenomena

Phenomenon is the singular and *phenomena* (sometimes *phenomenons*) the plural: phenomena of the mind. Originally, *phenomenon* meant "any observable event," but now it also means "something remarkable," and *phenomenal* is almost always used in that sense. See Hyperbole.

Phrasal verbs

A main verb preceded by one or more auxiliaries (will go, has left, was thinking, is considered, must have been punished) is called a phrasal verb or a periphrastic verb. A verb-adverb combination is also currently called a phrasal verb. See Verbs.

Phrases

A phrase is a group of words that functions as a unit in a sentence, a clause, or another phrase. In "The man in the car under the tree yelled," *the man in the car under the tree* is a noun phrase made up of an article, *the*, a noun, *man*, and a prepositional phrase, *in the car under the tree*. The prepositional phrase, in turn, is made up of the preposition *in* and another phrase, *the car under the tree*. This noun phrase is made up of the article *the* and the noun *car* and the prepositional phrase *under the tree*, which, in turn, is made up of the preposition *under* and the noun phrase *the tree*. Thus phrases can be contained in phrases ad infinitum.

Noun phrase: the *plumber*
Verb phrase: have *gone* to the store
Adjective phrase: old enough to be my father
Adverbial phrase: more *quickly* than usual
Prepositional phrase: in the house
Participial phrase: walking down the street
Infinitive phrase: to go faster

1. Function. Phrases may be further classified by their function in a sentence. *The plumber* is an adjectival noun phrase in the larger noun phrase, *my friend the plumber. Walking down the street* is a nominal participial phrase (traditionally called a gerund) in "Walking down the street was dangerous." *In the morning* is an adverbial prepositional phrase in "He left in the morning," an adjectival prepositional phrase in "Breakfast in the morning," a nominal prepositional phrase in "In the morning will be soon enough."

2. Phrases and style. The style of a passage depends in part on how a writer combines and coordinates phrases:

```
His ideas
            about the need
                        for intellectual renewal
                                    and
                        spiritual reform
indicate the crisis
            faced not only
                        by those
                                    in places
                                                of power
                                    but
                        by those
                                    in all walks
                                                of life.
```

In this sentence, the phrases are balanced and coordinated to create a rhythm that carries the reader along smoothly to the end. In this next sentence, the phrases are merely strung out one after the other, creating a heavy, bumping kind of movement that interferes with the reader's understanding of the writer's idea:

```
Our situation
            in this century
                        of turmoil
                                    in the cities
can only be alleviated
                        by improving the living conditions
                                                in ghettoes
            in the central cities
                        which have decayed
                                    beyond the endurance
                                                of most
to live
            in them.
```

See Absolute phrases, Gerunds, Infinitives, Participles, Prepositional phrases. See also Dangling modifiers, Parallelism.

Plagiarism

Plagiarize is defined in *Webster's New Collegiate Dictionary* as "to steal and pass off (the ideas or words of another) as one's own." Plagiarism occurs in college courses for several different reasons, including panic, dishonesty, and ignorance of what plagiarism is. Sometimes it comes of an unconscious drift from paraphrasing into copying. Whatever the cause, the penalty—a failing mark on the paper and, if the cheating is chronic, a failing mark in the course—is justified. Copying someone else's work is the most complete failure possible.

The student who has not learned how to handle material obtained from reading needs guidance in the fundamentals of scholarship. Anyone using published material has a twofold responsibility: first, to make the ideas part of his own thinking and, second, to give credit to the sources he has consulted. No one is *composing* when he is merely copying. A student should read and digest the material, get it into his own words (except for the brief passages he intends to quote directly). He should be able to talk about what he has read before he writes about it, and when he does write, he should name the sources of his ideas and facts, including ideas and facts he has paraphrased or summarized. This is not only courtesy but a sign of good workmanship, part of the ethics of writing. It is also part of the legality of writing, since the plagiarist who uses copyrighted material is liable to prosecution.

In an informal essay, credit can be given informally, perhaps in a preliminary note saying "This essay is based on. . . ." Or a source may be acknowledged in the body of the essay: "Professor Martin said in a lecture . . ." or "According to an editorial in . . ." or "Here is Jackson's position as presented in last night's debate." Or credit may be given more formally in the footnotes that are a customary part of a research paper.

Plagiarizing is stealing. And besides being unethical, it is unnecessary and unproductive. By giving credit where credit is due, you gain free and legitimate access to everything in print (though if what you write is to be printed, you must secure permission to quote copyrighted material directly); and you learn to integrate the ideas of others with your own ideas. Finally, when you express what you have to say in your own words, you are not copying but composing. See Footnote form, Originality, Paraphrase, Research papers.

plenty

As a qualifier (I was plenty worried; The car is plenty fast) *plenty* is chiefly informal. It is used by some general writers, but others avoid it entirely, using instead such established adverbs as *extremely, amply,* and *quite.* In general writing, an *of* is expected between *plenty* and the following noun: We had plenty of time. Reference: Copperud, p. 213.

plurality, majority

In an election a plurality is the largest number of votes received by any one candidate but less than a majority, which is more than half of all the votes cast. See *majority, plurality.*

Plurals of nouns

The plural of the great majority of English nouns is made by adding -s. Some exceptions and special cases follow.

1. Special groups in -s or -es.
a. Some plurals can be pronounced only by adding a full sylla-ble. The spelling is -s if the noun already ends in silent -e, other-wise -es: *birches, edges, misses, dishes, mazes.*
b. With a few exceptions, common nouns ending in -y preceded by a consonant or *qu* change *y* to *i* and add -es: *beauties, bodies, caddies, cherries, soliloquies.* Words ending in -y preceded by a vowel add -s: *bays, boys, moneys* (but *monies* in the technical economic sense).
c. Nouns ending in -o preceded by a vowel make regular plurals with -s: *cameos, folios, radios, studios.* Some words ending in -o preceded by a consonant always or nearly always take -s: *dyna-mos, Eskimos* (or *Eskimo*), *Filipinos, pianos, solos, sopranos.* Some always or nearly always take -es: *echoes, heroes, potatoes, tomatoes, vetoes.* Some take either: *banjos, banjoes; cargoes, cargos; dominoes, dominos.*
d. Some common nouns ending in -*f* or -*fe* (*calf, half, knife, leaf, loaf, self, shelf, thief*) use -*ves* (*calves, halves, knives,* and so on). Some have two plurals: *elf, elves – elfs; hoof, hoofs – hooves; scarf, scarfs – scarves.* But many nouns ending in -*f*, -*fe*, and -*ff* form regular plurals with -s: *beliefs, fifes, rebuffs.*

2. Same form for both singular and plural. Nouns with the same form for singular and plural include names for some living creatures (*fowl, sheep, fish* — but *fishes* for varieties of fish), all words in -*ics* (*athletics, politics, civics*), and some common measurements (*foot, pair, ton*).

3. Survivals of older English plural forms. Survivals include plu-rals in -*en* (*brother, brethren*, in church use; *child, children; ox, oxen*) and plurals with changed vowels (*foot, feet; goose, geese; louse, lice; man, men; mouse, mice; tooth, teeth; woman, women*).

4. Foreign language plurals. Many nouns taken into English from other languages keep their foreign plurals, at least for a time. Words used chiefly in scientific or formal writing keep the foreign form longer. *Antenna,* for instance, has the plural *an-tennae* in biology but *antennas* in discussions of radio and TV. When the word is in transition, both forms will be found in the same context.
Some common words have two plurals — the foreign (*appen-dices, media, nuclei*) and the English forms (*appendixes, mediums, nucleuses*).

5. Compound and group words. Most compound words and group words add -*s* to the end of the group, whether written as one word or as several: *high schools, cross-examinations, book-cases.* In a few the plural sign is added to the first element: *daughters-in-law* (and other *in-law* words), *passersby, courts-martial* (also *court-martials*).

6. Plurals of figures, words, letters. Usually the plural of a letter

of the alphabet, of a word as a word, or of a figure is written with
-'s: There are two c's and two m's in *accommodate;* Don't use
several *that*'s in a row; three 2's. But usage is divided; the plural
of figures especially is often made with -s: three 2s; no *if*s, *and*s,
or *but*s.

See Apostrophe 3; *-ful, full;* Genitive case 1a. References:
Fries, pp. 40–59; Jespersen, pp. 198–203; Long, pp. 203–27.

plus

Plus is a preposition having the sense "with the addition of." A
phrase introduced by *plus* should not therefore affect the number of the verb, but it is allowed to do so in some general writing,
particularly when the *plus* phrase is not set off by commas: The
committee report plus some newspaper headlines *were* all that
was needed. In more formal writing the *plus* would be changed
to *and* or the verb would be made singular.

Plus as a substitute for the adverb *besides* or *in addition* (The
school has a good engineering department, plus its campus is
beautiful) is informal and is objectionable to many. *Plus* is also
used as a noun (a plus for the new cafeteria is its lighting) and
an adjective (a plus factor). Some writers avoid the word entirely
except in arithmetical and commercial contexts.

p.m.

This abbreviation for *post meridiem,* "after noon," should not be
used as a noun. See *a.m. and p.m.*

Poetry

When verse is quoted, it should be lined off (as well as capitalized and punctuated) exactly as written. If possible, the quoted
lines should be approximately centered on the page, indented
according to the scheme of the original. When so spaced, lines of
verse quoted in a prose passage do not need quotation marks.
Diagonal marks, or virgules, are sometimes used to indicate line
breaks when a short passage is run into the text: It was Marlowe
who wrote, "I walk abroad 'a nights / And kill sick people groaning under walls."

Point of view

**The shift in point of view in the passage marked is illogical or un-
justified.**

Your point of view in a paper is the position from which you view
your subject. The position may be physical—your location in
space and time—or psychological—your attitude toward your
subject. The correction symbol *pv* indicates that, in the context,
your change in point of view is unjustified or unmotivated or
that, in the rhetorical situation, your choice of point of view is
ineffective.

1. Don't make unjustified shifts in physical point of view. When
you write a description of an object, a place, a process, or an inci-

dent, the reader sees it through your eyes; and if he is to grasp what he is looking *at*, he must have a clear idea of where he is looking *from*. In describing a building on the campus, for example, you may begin with a head-on view and then lead the reader in full circuit, using such phrases as "looked at from the left," "the view from the rear," "the Main Street side." Or you may begin with a view from far across the campus or even a bird's-eye view — how the building would look if you approached it in a helicopter. The important thing is to keep the reader oriented. A description that jumps from facade to basement lab to clock tower to classrooms is bound to befuddle.

2. Don't make unmotivated shifts in psychological point of view. If you set out to describe your dormitory, what you show the reader, what you show in greatest detail, and what you don't show at all will differ according to your attitude toward the place. Thus psychological point of view may determine physical point of view. And psychological point of view may also lead to some role-playing. Suppose you hate your dorm and want to convince your reader that it deserves hating. Can you best accomplish your purpose by stating your attitude in the opening sentence? By being sarcastic throughout? Or by adopting an objective, analytical tone and counting on the examples and details you present to win the reader to your side? The strategy is yours to choose; but once you've made your choice, maintain your point of view consistently, or clearly justify any deviation from it. Like an erratic change in physical point of view, an unexplained switch in tone from sympathetic to contemptuous or from hostile to nostalgic will confuse and irritate the reader.

3. Don't make confusing changes in the distance between you and your reader. Point of view — physical or psychological or both — influences your choice between a *personal* mode of narration, description, or argument, in which your presence is clearly felt, and an *impersonal* mode, in which you efface yourself. The pronouns, if any, that you use to refer to yourself will signal to the reader something about the relationship you want to establish. Heavy reliance on the pronoun *I* (or *we*) may suggest casual intimacy; it may suggest restricted but personal knowledge of the subject; it may suggest real authority. Use of *you* may give the impression that you hope to engage your reader in a dialog. Use of the third person ("If one should . . .") may lend objectivity or imply remoteness. A completely impersonal approach focuses on what is being discussed without calling attention to either the writer or the audience. Once you have established yourself in one relation to your audience, it is unwise to adopt another without good reason.

Many problems in word choice and syntax stem from failure to maintain a consistent point of view. For related grammatical problems, see Passive voice, Reference of pronouns, Shifted constructions, Tense, *you*. See also Description, Details.

politics

Politics in the usual sense is treated as a singular: In almost any group, politics *is* a controversial subject. But when used in the sense of "principles," "activities," or "tactics," it may be treated as a plural: Republican politics *were* offensive to the Federalists. Avoid treating the word both ways in the same passage.

position, job

Position is the formal word for *job.* See *job, position.*

Positive degree

The positive degree of adjectives and adverbs is the base, or root, form of the adjective *(poor, high, golden)* or adverb *(slow, slowly, bitterly).* See Comparison of adjectives and adverbs.

Possessive adjectives

See Possessive pronouns, possessive adjectives.

Possessive case

The possessive, or genitive, case is indicated by the apostrophe, with or without -*s;* by *of;* by the genitive form of the personal pronouns; and by the relative *whose.* See Genitive case.

Possessive pronouns, possessive adjectives

The personal pronouns have the following possessive forms: *my, mine; your, yours; his; her, hers; our, ours; their, theirs;* and the relative *who* has *whose. Its* is the only one that regularly tempts writers to use an apostrophe, through confusion with *it's,* the contraction for "it is."

My, your, her, his, our, their are used as adjectives (and sometimes called possessive adjectives) in the attributive position: my car. *Mine, yours, his, hers, its, ours, theirs* are used without a noun: Ours is better than yours.

Précis

A précis is a paraphrase of someone else's writing that condenses the original but retains its information, emphasis, and point of view. Rules for the formal précis prohibit direct quotation and call for a final version that is between one third and one fifth the length of the original. Condensation is achieved through the substitution of appositives, verbals, and series for more expansive statement and through the elimination of nonessential material. To produce a précis that accomplishes all this and is also well written calls for practice, hard work, and considerable skill.

Predicate

Almost all English sentences divide into two main elements— subject and predicate. The predicate of a clause or sentence is the verb with its modifiers and objects or complements. The predicate may be a single verb (The bell *tolled*), a transitive verb and its object (He *landed the big fish*), or a linking verb and its complement (The oldest member of the family *is usually the first to go*). Two verbs depending on one subject are known as a compound predicate: The three of them *washed* and *wiped* the dishes in fifteen minutes.

 Predicate adjectives

Use an adjective here, since the verb is a linking verb.

Loudly in "The music sounds loudly" should be revised to *loud*.

The use of an adverb instead of a predicate adjective results from the habit of thinking that only adverbs follow the verb. But adjectives fill that position whenever the verb is a linking verb. In addition to *be*, about sixty verbs (*become, feel, turn, look, taste,* and so on) can perform this linking function. What follows the verb relates to or qualifies the subject, not the verb. Accordingly, an adjective – known as a predicate adjective or an adjective in the predicative position – is required, even though in its other functions the same verb is followed by an adverb. Compare: He felt *tired* (adjective, relates to subject); He felt the edge of the knife *carefully* (adverb, relates to verb).

Adjective: She acts *tired.*　　*Adverb:* She acts *brilliantly.*
Adjective: She looks *cold.*　　*Adverb:* She looked at him *coldly.*

The test for a linking verb is that the appropriate form of *be* can replace it: "The story rings true" is structurally the same as "The story is true." When you have identified the verb as linking, use an adjective after it.

See *bad, badly;* Linking verbs; *look.* See also Adjectives 1.

Predicate nominative

Words and word groups that follow linking verbs and function as nouns are called predicate nominatives or complements. They include nouns, pronouns, phrases, and clauses. See Linking verbs.

predominant, predominate

Predominant is the adjective: a predominant sentiment, a sentiment predominant in the state. *Predominate* is the verb: The Muslims predominate there. Although increasingly common and recognized by dictionaries, the spelling *predominate* for the adjective and *predominately* for the adverb is offensive to many readers.

prefer

To is ordinarily used with *prefer:* I prefer Ireland to Spain; He preferred going by train to flying. But when an infinitive is used instead of a noun or gerund, *to* is impossible, and *than* or *rather than* is used: He preferred to take the train rather than to fly [or rather than a plane]. Reference: Copperud, pp. 217–18.

Prefix

A prefix is a form that can be placed before a word or root to change its meaning or function: un*tie*, im*mobilize*. See Origin of words 3a. See also Hyphen 4, Long variants.

Prepositional phrases

A prepositional phrase consists of a preposition and its object: *without hope, in a hurry, toward a more abundant life*. Prepositional phrases are modifiers, used in the functions of adverbs or adjectives:

Adverbial modifier: She arrived *at just the right time*.
Adjectival modifier: The man *in the black coat* has left.

See Phrases.

Prepositions

A preposition connects a noun phrase or a pronoun or a clause to some other part of the sentence. The whole phrase is usually adverbial or adjectival in its function: He showed her *to her room;* He was old *in experience;* He was surprised *at what he saw;* the click *of flying wheels*. What follows a preposition is called its object or, by some grammarians, its complement. Prepositions may be word groups (in regard to, according to) as well as single words. And many words that serve as prepositions, such as *after, but, since,* also serve as adverbs and conjunctions.

In some contexts, prepositions signal purely grammatical functions. *By* can signal the agent of an action: The window was broken by Mike. *Of* can signal either agent or object: The destruction of the city shocked everyone; The discussions of the committee were kept secret. *With* can signal instrumentality: He cut the bread with a knife. But *by, with,* and *of* can also indicate specific meaning. *By* can be paraphrased as "in a space adjacent to" in "He sat by the river"; *with* means "in the company of" in "I left with Tom"; *of* means "belonging to" in "He is a citizen of France." Even in abstract contexts (under a cloud, with ease) prepositions have meaning.

See Objects 3, Parts of speech, Prepositions and style. References: Follett, pp. 257–59; Fowler, pp. 473–75; Quirk et al., pp. 299–337.

prep Prepositions and style

Change the preposition to one that is idiomatic or less conspicuous; or supply a missing preposition.

1. Use prepositions that are exact or idiomatic. A number of words are accompanied by certain prepositions; we say "contented *with* conditions," "*in* my estimation." Some words take on different meanings with different prepositions: agree *with* (a person), agree *to* (a suggestion), agree *in* (principle).

Selecting the right preposition presents no problem with words that we use often, because we learn the words by hearing or seeing them in their typical combinations. When learning new words, learn their usage as well as their meaning: *acquiesce in* (acquiesce in a decision) rather than just *acquiesce*. Dictionaries usually give the preposition appropriate to particular words. This book treats a few idioms that are occasionally troublesome: *ability to; agree to, agree with; all of; compare, contrast; different.* See also Idiom.

When using together two words that take different prepositions, include both prepositions: The first lesson he learned was obedience *to* and respect *for* others besides his parents. *Not* . . . obedience and respect for others. When both words take the same preposition, there's no need to use it twice: The box office refused to make any allowance [ ] or refund *for* tickets purchased from an agent.

2. Keep your prepositions from bulking too large. English has a number of group prepositions that become conspicuous when they take up too much space for the work they do. A reference to "recent demonstrations on the part of dissatisfied students" is weighed down by "on the part of" where *by* would do the job. Sometimes we carry over from speech the habit of using double prepositions: *(in) back of, outside (of), off (of)*. See *as to; off of; on, onto, on to; prior to.*

3. Don't omit prepositions in general or formal writing. Sometimes prepositions are dropped:

. . . one of the best pieces written about the United States [in] this century. — Arthur Schlesinger, *New Republic*

. . . the mysterious command center beneath the Pentagon [from] where [*or* from which] the ultimate orders go to distant area commanders. — Mark S. Watson, *New York Times Book Review*

Although such omissions as these are increasingly common in general writing, expressions like "a couple [of] days later," "a different type [of] girl," and "outside [of] his interest in boxing" remain decidedly informal.

4. When a preposition falls naturally at the end of a sentence, leave it there. There is an old "rule" that prepositions should not stand at the end of their constructions (What did I do it for?), but postponing the preposition has long been a characteristic English idiom. Both idiom and rhythm often demand the preposition at the end, particularly with compound verbs like *dispose of* and in relative clauses with *that* or with no relative expressed. Attempts to avoid the postponed preposition are often clumsy or ungrammatical: Tell me what it is to which you object [*better:* what you object to]. Reference: Bryant, pp. 162–64.

Placing the preposition at the end is such a firmly fixed habit that in some sentences you must be careful not to repeat one that has already been expressed: He brightened the life of everyone with whom he came in contact [with].

See Phrases 2.

Present tense

The base form of a verb (*ask, answer, buy, say*) is its present tense. In most verbs -*s* is added in the third-person singular. See **Tenses of verbs.**

pretty

Pretty for *rather* or *fairly* gives a sentence an informal tone: "[Archibald Cox] sets pretty straight . . . the real impact of the great case of Marbury v. Madison" (Charles L. Black, Jr., *New York Times Book Review*).

Prewriting

Prewriting is the stage of thinking, worrying, and doodling that you go through before you set down even the rough form of an essay. The process is related to what is known in classical rhetoric as invention and discovery—finding out what you have to say about your subject.

People prewrite in different ways. Some scribble, apparently aimlessly, trying to find their way to a lead-in idea. Some think through the subject again and again, doing their prewriting entirely in their heads. And some look into promising sources, jot down facts, thoughts, and impressions, and try various ways of ordering their ideas to discover the points that need most emphasis.

Whether or not your exploration of your subject involves hunting up information and finding out what others have said, the end product of prewriting is not a collection of notes. It is a sure sense that you have made the subject your own. Making the subject your own means that whatever you write will be motivated by personal concern. Writing that lacks personal concern—intellectual commitment or emotional commitment or both—is very likely to be dull writing, trite and mechanical in both thought and expression. Writing that grows out of personal concern is just as likely to have some drive and freshness; it is the kind of writing that quickly engages the attention of a reader.

Though no rules can be provided that will guarantee successful prewriting, or pump priming, one practice that helps many writers is keeping a daily journal—entering sentences or paragraphs that capture thoughts and opinions, making a note of images that match half-formed ideas. Because his journal proved so rich a source for his public writing, one author called it his savings bank. Certainly keeping a journal is worth a try. You may find that, like other prewriting techniques, it will give you a running start on writing your essays.

Reference: D. Gordon Rohman, *CCC*, May 1965, pp. 106–12.

 ## Principal parts of verbs

Change the verb form to one in standard use.

1. The principal parts of a verb. These are the base form or infinitive (*ask*), the past-tense form (*asked*), the past participle (*asked*).

Most English verbs are "regular" — that is, their past tense and past participle are formed by adding -ed to the base form. A number, most of them descended from Old English strong verbs, make their past-tense and past-participle forms by a change in vowel (*strike, struck, struck*). Some (*let, cost*) remain unchanged; some (*bend, make*) change the final consonant; some have less common irregularities (past forms of *teach: taught, taught*).

The trend has been toward regularity. A few verbs (*broadcast, shine, speed*) have acquired regular forms in addition to their old ones: *broadcasted, shined, speeded*. A few others (*dive, fit, prove, sew*) have reversed the general trend, acquiring irregularities that are either new or a revival of archaic forms: *dove, fit* (past tense), *proven, sewn*. For some verbs (*dream, plead, show, strive, thrive*) variant pairs have long existed side by side: *dreamed, dreamt; pleaded, pled; showed, shown; strived, strove; thrived, throve*.

The following list includes a number of verbs with irregular past-tense or past-participle forms. The forms labeled *NS* (nonstandard) and *D* (dialect) would not ordinarily be written. When doubts arise, a recent dictionary should be consulted for verbs not listed here; but usage is by no means uniform, even among speakers and writers of standard English, and neither this list nor the dictionaries record all variations.

Infinitive	Past tense	Past participle
arise	arose	arisen
bear	bore	borne
bear	bore	born (given birth to)
begin	began (D: begun)	begun
bite	bit	bitten, bit
blow	blew (D: blowed)	blown (D: blowed)
break	broke	broken (NS: broke)
bring	brought (NS: brung)	brought (NS: brung)
catch	caught (chiefly D: catched)	caught (chiefly D: catched)
choose	chose	chosen
come	came (NS: come)	come
dig	dug	dug
dive	dived, dove	dived
do	did (NS: done)	done
drag	dragged (D: drug)	dragged (D: drug)
draw	drew (NS: drawed)	drawn
dream	dreamed, dreamt	dreamed, dreamt
drink	drank (D: drunk)	drunk
eat	ate (D: pronounced et)	eaten (D: pronounced et)
fall	fell	fallen
fly	flew	flown
forget	forgot	forgotten, forgot
freeze	froze (D: friz)	frozen (chiefly D: froze)
get	got	got, gotten
give	gave (NS: give)	given (NS: give)
go	went (D: goed)	gone (NS: went)
grow	grew (D: growed)	grown (D: growed)
hang	hung	hung
hang (execute)	hung, hanged	hung, hanged
hear	heard	heard

know	knew (D: knowed)	known (D: knowed)
lay	laid	laid
lead	led	led
lend (loan)	lent	lent
lie (*see* lay)	lay	lain
lose	lost	lost
prove	proved	proved, proven
ride	rode (D: rid)	ridden (D: rid)
ring	rang, rung	rung
run	ran (NS: run)	run
see	saw (NS: seed)	seen (NS: seed, saw)
shake	shook (chiefly D: shaked)	shaken (chiefly D: shaked)
shine	shone, shined	shone, shined
show	showed	showed, shown
shrink	shrank, shrunk	shrunk
sing	sang, sung	sung
sink	sank, sunk	sunk, sunken
sit	sat (D: set)	sat (D: set)
slide	slid	slid
sneak	sneaked (chiefly D: snuck)	sneaked (chiefly D: snuck)
speak	spoke	spoken
spring	sprang, sprung	sprung
steal	stole	stolen (chiefly D: stole)
swim	swam	swum
take	took (D: taken)	taken (D: took)
tear	tore	torn
throw	threw (D: throwed)	thrown (D: throwed)
wear	wore	worn
write	wrote (D: writ)	written (D: wrote)

2. Nonstandard verbs. Linguists investigating the patterns of some Black English dialects have found a predictable and therefore grammatical structure in sentences that have traditionally been called ungrammatical:

The teacher gone right now, but she be back soon.
He always be playing records late at night.

The lack of a *be* form in the first clause — the teacher [is] gone — and the apparently incorrect form of *be* in the second — she [will] be back — result from a deletion transformation. It regularly and predictably deletes a form of *be* and other auxiliary verbs such as *will, would, have*, etc., where standard English speakers contract their form of *be*. (An exception is *'m*, as in "I'm going.") This sequence represents the process:

The teacher is   gone right now, but she will be back soon.
The teacher's   gone right now, but she'll   be back soon.
The teacher[ ] gone right now, but she[ ] be back soon.

Where standard English speakers cannot contract a form of *be*, neither can speakers of some dialects of Black English delete it:

Standard English: I don't know who he is. *Not* I don't know who's.
Black English: I don't know who he be. *Not* I don't know who he.

The form of *be* in "He always be playing records late at night" is a different problem. It is evidently an invariant verb form that always appears as *be* to indicate a repeated action. When the action is temporary, not repeated, the first variations on *be* are found, as in "He not here right now, but he be back in a minute."

See *born, borne; do; got, gotten; hanged, hung; lay, lie; proved, proven; set, sit.* References: Atwood; Fries, pp. 59–71; Mencken, pp. 527–28; Pyles, pp. 124–30, 194–205; *Webster's Third New International Dictionary.*

principal, principle

Principal is either an adjective or a noun, *principle* a noun only. One way to remember that the adjective is spelled *principal* is to associate it with other adjectives ending in *-al: historical, political, musical.*

Principal as a noun is probably an abbreviation of a phrase in which it was originally an adjective: the principal that draws interest was once the principal sum; the principal of a school, the principal teacher; the principal in a legal action, the principal party; the principals in a play, the principal actors. These are the only common uses of *principal* as a noun.

The noun meaning "a general truth or rule of conduct" is *principle:* the principles of science, a man of high principles.

prior to

Prior to, a rather formal preposition, is most appropriate when it adds to the notion of "before" that of "in anticipation of": "He urged reform leaders to work prior to the convention so as to minimize the influence of Greeley's supporters" (Matthew T. Downey, *Journal of American History*). In most contexts, particularly in general writing, *before* is the better word.

Profanity

Using profanity – that is, referring to sacred beings carelessly or irreverently – is primarily a matter of muscular or emotional release rather than of meaning, and in writing, profanity often attracts more attention to itself than it deserves. Like other kinds of swearing, it has no place in college writing, except perhaps in dialog. See Obscenity.

professor

Write: Professor Moore; Prof. E. W. Moore; E. W. Moore, a professor of chemistry; *or* E. W. Moore, Professor of Chemistry.

The colloquial *prof* (my math prof) is a clipped word, not an abbreviation, and is written without a period.

Strictly speaking, the title *Professor* should be given only to assistant professors, associate professors, and full professors, not to those who have not reached professorial rank. When the title follows the name in an *of* phrase, exact rank is usually indicated: Professor A. B. Plant, *but* A. B. Plant, Assistant Professor of English.

Progressive verb forms

Progressive verb forms are verb phrases made with *be* and the present participle to show continuing action: I *am asking,* he *was asking,* they *have been asking.* See Tenses of verbs, Verbs.

Pronouns

A pronoun is commonly defined as a word that replaces a noun or another word or group of words used as a noun. The word or phrase or clause that it substitutes for, as *it* substitutes for *a pronoun* in the sentence you're reading, is called its antecedent: *it* is said to refer to *a pronoun; a pronoun* is the antecedent of *it*. Not all pronouns have antecedents. The reference of *I* and *you* depends on the identity of the writer or speaker and the audience being addressed, not on the verbal context in which *I* and *you* appear.

Like nouns, pronouns can serve as subjects and objects (though not all pronouns can serve as both). Many have a genitive form, and a few have a separate plural form. Unlike nouns, pronouns do not occur with *the* or *a;* with a few exceptions (*someone* nice, *something* useful) they are not modified by adjectives; and they are a small, closed class of words.

The traditional subclasses of pronouns are listed below. Because these subclasses don't all share the same characteristics, some grammarians assign a number of them to other parts of speech. See, for example, Parts of speech 2.

1. Personal pronouns. The personal pronouns are those words that specifically indicate person (first, second, or third), number, and, in the third-person singular, gender.

		Nominative	*Genitive*	*Accusative*
1st-person	singular	I	my, mine	me
	plural	we	our, ours	us
2nd-person	singular	you	your, yours	you
	plural	you	your, yours	you
3rd-person	singular			
	masculine	he	his, his	him
	feminine	she	her, hers	her
	neuter	it	its, its	it
	genderless	one	one's, one's	one
	plural	they	their, theirs	them

Except for the relative pronoun *who (whose, whom)*, only the personal pronouns, and not all of them, have different forms for the three cases. Some of the most common grammatical mistakes occur because, unlike nouns, *I, we, he, she, they,* and *who* have different forms in subject and object position. See *between you and me;* Case; *it's me; who, whom.*

In some traditional grammars, personal pronouns in the genitive case are classified separately as possessive pronouns.

2. Reflexive pronouns. The reflexives, sometimes called the compound personal pronouns, are formed by adding -*self* or -*selves* to the genitive case of personal pronouns in the first and second persons (*myself, yourself, ourselves, yourselves*) and to the accusative case in the third person (*himself, herself, itself, themselves*). They are used when an object or a subjective complement has the same referent as a preceding noun or noun

phrase in the same sentence and when no other possible antecedent intervenes:

Direct object:	He hurt *himself*
Object of preposition:	The rope was twisted back on *itself.*
	He autographed a dozen pictures of
	himself
Indirect object:	They made *themselves* caftans.
Subjective complement:	Ben is not *himself* today.
Object of infinitive:	Jane wanted Betty to help *herself*

With the last example, compare "Jane wanted Betty to help her,"
in which the antecedent of *her* is *Jane,* not *Betty.* Since a possible antecedent, *Betty,* intervenes, the reflexive is not used.

When they serve as intensives, the reflexive forms are construed as pronouns in apposition: The owner *himself* sold the
car; The owner sold the car *himself.* See Apposition, appositives.

3. Reciprocal pronouns. The reciprocals *each other* and *one
another* substitute in object position for a compound or plural
noun that has the same referent as a compound or plural subject
when the action of the verb is directed by each member of the
subject toward the other members: Tom and Bill looked at *each
other;* the losers kidded *one another.* Compare: Tom and Bill
looked at *themselves;* The losers kidded *themselves.*

Like the personal pronouns, the reciprocals are freely used in
the genitive: They borrowed *one another's* clothes.

4. Relative pronouns. *Who, which,* and *that* are relatives. Like
the personal pronouns, *who* has different forms for the genitive
(whose) and the accusative *(whom).* *Which* and *that* are not inflected for case.

Relative pronouns introduce dependent clauses:

The student *who* submitted this paper has dropped out.
The paper *that* she submitted won an award.
Her decision to leave school, *which* caused some excitement, was never
explained.

When no specific referent for the pronoun is intended, the indefinite, or expanded, form of the relative is used: *whoever,
whomever, whichever, whatever.* Unexpanded *what* is also an
indefinite relative pronoun:

Whoever receives this will be pleased.
I will support *whomever* you nominate.
They will believe *whatever* he says.
They will believe *what* he says.

See Relative clauses.

5. Interrogative pronouns. The interrogatives *who, whose, whom,
which,* and *what* are used to introduce direct and indirect questions: *What* happened? He asked me *what* happened.

6. Demonstrative pronouns. *This, that, these,* and *those* are considered adjectives when they modify nouns (*this* hat, *these*
books), pronouns when they function as nouns: *This* will fix it;
Those are too large; I prefer *these.* The demonstratives discrimi-

nate between referents close at hand (*this, these*) and referents that are more remote (*that, those*).

7. Indefinite pronouns. *Some, any, every,* and *no* compounded with *one* (*someone*), *thing* (*everything*), and *body* (*nobody*), and other words like *all, any, some, each,* and *either,* have traditionally been called indefinite pronouns. When used as subjects, the compounds take singular verbs, and pronouns referring to them are usually in the singular: Everyone *is* expected to do *his* part. Since the indefinite pronouns do not replace noun phrases and generally have no specific referent, some grammarians find it more logical to classify them as indefinite nouns.

Informally, *they* is also used for indefinite reference: They ought to do something about these roads. See *they.*

See Antecedent, Determiners, Parts of speech, Reference of pronouns. References: Archibald A. Hill, *Introduction to Linguistic Structures* (New York: Harcourt, 1958), pp. 145–52; Jespersen, Chs. 14–18; Quirk et al., pp. 203–25; Roberts, pp. 53–89; John Ross in *Modern Studies in English,* ed. David A. Reibel and Sanford A. Schane (Englewood Cliffs, N.J.: Prentice-Hall, 1969), pp. 187–200.

Proofreading
Checking the final copy of an essay for mechanical mistakes that may have slipped into the last draft is an essential part of preparing a manuscript. See Careless mistakes, Caret, Manuscript form, Typewritten copy.

Proper adjectives
Proper nouns that are used like adjectives are capitalized, and so are adjectives that are directly derived from proper names if they still refer to the place or person. After proper adjectives lose the reference to their origins, they become simple adjectives and are no longer capitalized: the Indian service, india ink; the Roman forum, roman type. See Capital letters.

proved, proven
Prove is a regular verb, forming a past tense and past participle with -*ed: proved. Proven* has been used for centuries as an alternative past participle of *prove* and is now established in all varieties of usage. References: Bryant, pp. 165–66; Pooley, pp. 157–58.

provided, providing
Both are in standard use as connectives. Formal writing strongly prefers *provided;* in general writing usage is divided.

You can't even argue, much, with the picture, providing you look at it only as a clever Western. – David R. Slavitt, *Yale Review*

Anyone who can get into M.S.U. can get into Justin Morrill, provided he is willing to work. – Duncan Norton, *Fortune*

Reference: Copperud, p. 223.

Psychologese

Psychologese, a jargon made up of words from the technical vocabulary of psychology, is used enthusiastically if inexactly by many outsiders: *instinctual* for *instinctive, operant* for *operating, motorical* for *motor.* A great many other terms from psychology *(empathy, motivational, neurotic, paranoid, relate, traumatic)* have entered the general language, become vogue words, and lost much of their technical meaning.

public

Meaning "the people as a whole," *public* is a collective noun and can be treated either as a singular or as a plural. A plural construction is more common: The public depend on TV newscasts for most of their information. But in the sense "a group of people with a common interest," *public* is more often singular: "There is a foreign policy public that is considerably smaller than the general public" (Carl N. Degler, *American Historical Review*).

Punctuation

Insert necessary punctuation, or change your punctuation to conform to standard usage.

No punctuation

Delete the unnecessary punctuation.

The basic purpose of punctuation is to mark off sentences and to link, separate, and set off elements within sentences in ways that will make the meaning clear to readers. A good rule to follow is to use all punctuation required by current convention and as much optional punctuation as you consider necessary to help your reader. Don't use unnecessary punctuation, which may make reading more difficult. And don't rely on punctuation to bail out awkwardly constructed sentences. Instead, rewrite.

1. To end sentences. Use periods to end statements. Use question marks to end sentences that ask direct questions. Use exclamation marks to end sentences (or to follow words or phrases) that express strong emotion and demand special emphasis. See Exclamation mark, Period, Question mark.

2. To separate.
a. Use a comma before the conjunction to separate independent clauses joined by *but, for,* or *so.* You may also use a comma before the other coordinating conjunctions in compound sentences. To indicate a stronger separation, use a semicolon. See Comma 1, Semicolon 1c.
b. Use a comma after a long introductory phrase or dependent clause to separate it from the main clause. You may use a comma after all introductory phrases and clauses. Do not use a comma after introductory *but, and,* or other conjunction. See Comma 2a.
c. Use a comma before a nonrestrictive dependent clause or

phrase that follows the main clause. Do not use a comma before a restrictive modifier that follows the main clause. See Comma 2b.

d. Use commas to separate the units in a series and to separate adjectives modifying the same noun. To separate the units in a series that already includes commas, use semicolons. See Comma 5, Semicolon 2.

e. Do not use a comma between subject and verb, between verb and object or complement, or, in most cases, between the verbs in a compound predicate. See Comma 8.

3. To set off.

a. Use paired commas to set off nonrestrictive modifiers.

b. Use paired commas, paired dashes, or parentheses to set off interrupting elements. Commas mark the least separation, parentheses the most. Setting off short interrupters is optional. See Comma 4a.

4. To link.

a. Use a semicolon between main clauses when you want to link them rather than to separate them with a period. See Semicolon 1.

b. Use a colon (*not* a semicolon) to link a series, a quotation, or other material to the sentence element that introduces it. See Colon 1.

c. Use a dash to link to the end of a sentence a word, phrase, or clause you want to emphasize. See Dash 1.

d. Use a hyphen to link syllables and words. See Hyphen.

5. Other uses.

a. Use quotation marks to identify direct quotations. See Quotation marks 2.

b. Use ellipses to indicate omission of words. See Ellipsis.

c. Use apostrophes to indicate possession and to indicate the omission of letters in contractions. See Apostrophe 1, 2.

References: Summey; Whitehall, Ch. 10.

Puns

A pun is a figure of speech in which a word is simultaneously used in two senses or substituted for another word of similar sound but different meaning (effluent society, the whine of sour grapes). Deliberate punning may serve serious purposes as well as humorous ones, but unintentional puns should be weeded out in revision.

Qualifiers

Qualifiers are words used not to convey meaning in themselves but to qualify—usually by intensifying—the meaning of adjectives. They include the first words in the phrases "much older," "very quiet," "too old," "somewhat sick," "rather careless," "quite intelligent" and degree adverbs like *slightly.* Though sometimes effective in speech, qualifiers are more likely to weaken writing than to strengthen it. See Parts of speech.

Question mark

The chief conventions governing the use of the question mark are these:

1. As an end stop. The principal use of the question mark is as the end stop of a direct question: What was the real reason?

A question mark is not used after an indirect question: He wanted to know what the real reason was.

A request that is phrased as a question may or may not be followed by a question mark, depending on the formality of the style:

Formal: Will you please return the book at your earliest convenience?
General: Will you please get the book back as soon as you can.

2. With quotation marks. When a question mark and a closing quotation mark fall together, the question mark belongs outside the quotation mark if the sentence that encloses the quotation is the question (Did you really say, "I thought you were older than that"?), inside if the quotation is the question (He asked, "Did you really say that?"). If both are questions, only the inside question mark is used: Did she ask, "How many are coming?"

3. Within sentences. Usage is divided over a question built into a sentence: Should I quit school now [ ] I ask myself. A question mark after *now* would emphasize the question; a comma would make it less emphatic. If quotation marks were used around the question, a question mark would be appropriate.

4. Miscellaneous uses. A question mark is used to show that dates are approximate or uncertain: Geoffrey Chaucer 1340?– 1400 *or* Geoffrey Chaucer 1340(?)–1400.

A question mark in parentheses to indicate humor or sarcasm is out of date and out of favor: her fashionable (?) outfit.

Questions

1. Signals of questions. A question may be introduced by a pronoun (*Who* was that? *What* can be done?), an adjective (*Which* way did he go?), or an adverb (*Where* shall we eat?). A question may also be indicated by inverted word order, with the verb or part of the verb coming before the subject (Was he there?). Ordinarily a verb phrase is used, with part of it coming before the subject as a sort of compromise inversion: *Do you think* he can do it? (Here the auxiliary *do* is meaningless but allows us to begin the question with one verb while keeping the main verb, *think,* in its normal position after the subject.) A statement may also be turned into a question by adding an inverted clause at the end: He didn't try, *did he?*

2. Direct and indirect questions. A direct question is a question as actually asked, not just reported. It begins with a capital (unless it is introduced parenthetically into another sentence) and ends with a question mark: Who killed Cock Robin?

An indirect question is not a question as actually asked but a question reported as a subordinate element of another sentence. An indirect question does not begin with a capital or end with a question mark, and it is not set off by quotation marks. When a direct question is turned into an indirect one, the tense of the verb in the question is made to match the tense of the verb in the independent clause, and a subordinating conjunction is often introduced:

Direct: "What are our plans for tomorrow?"
Indirect: He asked *what our plans for tomorrow were.*

Direct: He asked, "Do you really understand what you have read?"
Indirect: He asked us *if we really understood what we had read.* He always asks us *whether we understand what we have read.*

3. Leading questions. A leading question is one phrased to suggest the answer desired, like "You wouldn't do that, would you?" (*Compare:* "Would you do that?") See Rhetorical questions.

4. Questions as transitions. Occasionally, but only occasionally, asking a question is a good way to introduce a new topic: What do we mean by *immoral?*

quot Quotation marks

Make the quotation marks conform to conventional usage.

1. Methods of indicating quotations.
a. Double quotes, not single, are the usual marks in the United States.
b. For quotations within quotations, double and single quotes are alternated; single quotes are used inside double quotes and so on: " 'Perry's instinct,' he says, 'soundly chose the point at which to halt the extension of the term "formula" ' " (Joseph Russo, *Yale Classical Studies*).
c. When a quotation is longer than one paragraph, quotation marks are used at the beginning of each paragraph but at the end of the last paragraph only.
d. When long quotations or a series of quotations are indented or are set in smaller type, as in this book, no quotation marks are used. In double-spaced typewritten copy, such block quotations are usually indented and single spaced.

2. Principal uses of quotation marks.
a. Quotation marks are used to indicate all passages taken from another writer, whether a phrase or a page or more (except when the quotation is indented). Any change of language within the quotation should be indicated—omissions by ellipses, additions by brackets. The quoted matter may stand by itself or may be worked into the writer's own sentence. Both methods are shown in this passage, the more formal first:

The most that could be said for Haig was said by Churchill: he "was unequal to the prodigious scale of events, but no one else was discerned as his equal or better." (Lloyd George, more succinctly, said he was "brilliant to the top of his army boots.")—Geoffrey Barraclough, *New York Review of Books*

When brief passages of conversation are introduced not for their own sake but to illustrate a point, they are usually incorporated in the paragraph:

I am having a drink with the manager, Yves Blais. "You don't speak French," he starts off by saying, "but that is all right because you are from Ontario, which is another country. I will speak English with you. But I have no British accent. I have a pea-soup accent." Blais volunteers the obvious—that he is a separatist. "I'm glad to be. I don't care. I refused to accept a Canada Council grant of $8,000. But it has nothing to do with my shows."—Jon Ruddy, *Maclean's*

b. There are no half quotes. A sentence is either an exact quotation and therefore in quotation marks, or else it is not an exact quotation and so is not quoted. By paying scrupulous attention to the exact language of the material to be quoted, you can avoid using quotation marks with pronouns and verb tenses appropriate only to indirect statements: He boasted that he "could do twice as much work as me." The boast must have been, "I can do twice as much work as you." The choice is between—but not halfway between—direct and indirect quotation: He boasted, "I can do twice as much work as you"; *or* He boasted that he could do twice as much work as me.

3. Miscellaneous uses of quotation marks.

a. Quotation marks enclose titles of poems, articles, stories, chapters of books, and, in most newspapers and many magazines, the titles of books themselves. See Titles 2a.

b. Words that are used as words rather than for their meaning usually appear in italics in formal writing, in quotes in general writing. But usage is divided:

There is the ugly and almost universal use of "like" for "as."—Douglas Bush, *American Scholar*

The word *bluff* is old in the English language.—Webb Garrison, *American Legion Magazine*

c. A word from a conspicuously different variety of speech is sometimes put in quotation marks, but this only calls attention to it. If you decide that such a word suits your needs, use it without apology:

He spurns aspirants not of his clique, thereby creating a tyranny of taste that soon will have every center of imaginative expression . . . under its cheesy [not "cheesy"] thrall.—Benjamin DeMott, *New American Review*

d. A word may be put in quotation marks to show that the writer refuses to accept its conventional sense in the context:

In numerous cases it is impossible to maintain on any solid ground that one pronunciation given is "better" than another, as, for example, that one pronunciation of *swamp* is better than the others given.—John S. Kenyon and Thomas A. Knott, *A Pronouncing Dictionary of American English*

But putting a word in quotation marks to signal sarcasm or derision (The "cute" Great Dane had eaten my sweater) is on a par with putting a question mark in parentheses to get a laugh.

e. Directly quoted *yes* and *no* (sometimes capitalized, sometimes not) frequently appear without quotation marks when they are built into the sentence in which they appear: Steve said Yes, so we went to work at once. When they are not actually spoken, they should not be quoted: If he had said no, I was prepared to resign.

4. Quotation marks with other marks.

a. When a question mark or an exclamation mark ends a quotation, it is placed inside the quotes:

"Don't go near that wire!" he shouted.
Later he said, "Aren't you wondering what would have happened?"

When a question mark or exclamation mark belongs to the construction that includes the quotation, it is placed after the quotes: What is an ordinary citizen to do when he hears the words, "This is a stick-up"? See Question mark 2.

b. American practice is to place periods and commas within the quotation marks, colons and semicolons after the closing marks.

c. "He said" and all its variations are normally set off by commas from the quotations they introduce:

"History," it is said, "does not repeat itself. The historians repeat one another."—Max Beerbohm, *Works*

But the quoted phrase may be so closely built into the sentence that no comma is wanted:

Any moron can say "I don't know who done it."—Francis Christensen, *Notes Toward a New Rhetoric*

R

raise, rear
Raise in the sense of bringing up a child has become suitable in all varieties of usage. *Rear* is now somewhat formal. See *bring up*. Reference: Copperud, pp. 227–28.

reaction
Reaction has drifted from the scientific vocabulary into general usage and become a counter word for nearly any response, whether emotional or mental, general or specific. Reference: Copperud, p. 229.

real, really
Ordinarily *real* is the adjective (a real difficulty, in real life), and *really* is the adverb (a really significant improvement; I really thought so). Both are overused as qualifiers; television commer-

cials could barely exist without them. Adverbial *real*, as in sentences like "Write real soon" and "It's real pretty," is informal.

rear, raise

As applied to bringing up children, *rear* is the formal choice. See *raise, rear*.

reason is because

In formal writing there is a strong preference for *reason is that*, on the grounds that *reason is because* is redundant. Even in general writing, *that* is much more common when there are no intervening words (My only reason is that I have to work tonight) or when the intervening words don't constitute a clause with a subject of its own (The reason usually given for such failures in sports is that there was inadequate concentration). But when many words or a clause with a separate subject intervenes, *reason . . . is because* often occurs in both formal and general prose:

One reason why music can stand repetition so much more sturdily than correspondingly good prose is because music, of all the arts, is by its nature least suited to the psychology of information, and has remained closer to the psychology of form. — Kenneth Burke, *Psychology and Form*

And the reason the press isn't a menace, Reston says, is because it has divested itself of so much of its power. — *Newsweek*

Even though *reason is because* has a long history in literature and is regularly used by educated speakers, writers should remind themselves that to some readers *reason is because* is a hobgoblin. References: Bryant, pp. 170–71; Copperud, p. 230; Pooley, pp. 128–29.

Reciprocal pronouns

Each other and *one another* are called reciprocal pronouns. See *each other*, Pronouns 3.

reckon

Used to mean "suppose" or "think," *reckon* is a localism. See Localisms.

Reduced clauses

Constructions that function like clauses but lack a full verb or a subject or both are sometimes called reduced clauses: I'm happy *if you are* [happy]; John will go to the barbecue *if Jan will* [go to the barbecue]; *Although* [he was] *tired*, he agreed to attend. See Clauses 2.

Redundancy

In writing, words and phrases that are repetitive or simply unnecessary are redundant. See Repetition, Wordiness.

ref   Reference of pronouns

Change the pronoun marked (or revise the sentence) so that the reference will be clear and the pronoun appropriate to the context.

In the sentence "Because my brother loves to ski, he spent Christmas vacation in Colorado," the pronoun *he* replaces the nominal *my brother. My brother* is called the antecedent of *he; he* has the same referent as *my brother.* In "He got so frostbitten I scarcely recognized him," the pronoun *I* has a referent (the speaker), but it does not have an antecedent. Both categories of pronouns—those that have antecedents and those that don't—create some problems for writers.

1. Clear reference. If the meaning of a pronoun is completed by reference to an antecedent, the reference must be unmistakable. Clear reference is a matter of meaning, not just the presence or position of certain words. Confusion may arise

a. When the pronoun seems to refer to a nearby noun that it can't sensibly refer to:

The next year he had an attack of appendicitis. *It* burst before the doctor had a chance to operate.
Revision: . . . His appendix burst. . . . (*It* can't sensibly refer to *appendicitis.* Such slips in reference are common when a sentence boundary separates a pronoun and its antecedent.)

b. When there is no noun nearby:

He isn't married yet and doesn't plan on *it.*
Revision: . . . and doesn't plan to marry.

c. When the pronoun refers to a noun used as a possessive or as an adjective:

Bill was skipping stones across the swimming hole. One cut open a young girl's head *who* was swimming under water.
Revision: . . . One cut open the head of a young girl who. . . .

Nancy longed for a chinchilla coat, though she wouldn't have dreamed of killing one.
Revision: . . . of killing a chinchilla to get one.

d. When two or more pronouns are crossed so that the exact reference can't be readily determined:

Businessmen without regard for anyone else have exploited the mass of workers at every point, not caring whether *they* were earning a decent living but only whether *they* were making big profits.
Revision: . . . not caring whether they paid a decent wage but only whether they were making big profits. (The sentence needs a complete rewriting, but this revision at least makes both *they*'s refer to the same antecedent.)

2. Broad reference. General English uses *which, that, this,* and sometimes *it* to refer not to a specific word or phrase but to the idea of a preceding clause. Formal avoids broad reference.

General: Her friend was jealous of her clothes and money and had taken this way of showing *it.*
Formal: . . . and had taken this way of showing her feeling.

General: They have also avoided titling the categories, so that the arrangement gently and effectively forces itself on the reader's consciousness, *which* adds a good deal to the effect of the whole.
Formal: . . . on the reader's consciousness—a fine choice, which adds a good deal to the effect of the whole.—Deborah Austin, *Journal of General Education*

3. Indefinite reference. Often pronouns are used to refer to the readers or to people in general instead of to specifically mentioned individuals. *One* has a severe, formal, sometimes pompous connotation. *We* and *you*, which seem slightly more personal and more expressive, are often preferred. Whether to choose *you, they, we, one,* or *people* or some other noun is a question of style, not grammar.

Keep indefinite pronouns consistent: When you have worked a day here, you have earned your money. With *one*, a shift to *he* is common: When one has worked a day here, he has earned his money. But *not* When one has worked a day here, you have. . . . See *one.*

Don't substitute an indefinite pronoun for a definite personal pronoun: For me there is no fun in reading unless you can put yourself in the position of the characters and feel that you are really in the scene. *Revision:* . . . unless I can put myself in the position of the characters and feel that I am. . . .

As a common-gender pronoun meaning "he or she," *he* is used in formal English, *they* in informal. General usage is divided between these forms, *he* being more conventional, *they* often more practical. See Agreement 2, Sexist language.

4. Avoiding and misusing pronouns. Writers who are uncertain about the reference or agreement of pronouns sometimes try to avoid them by repeating nouns. The result is usually unidiomatic or clumsy: Arrest of the woman yesterday followed several days of observation of the woman's [her] activities by the agents. On the other hand, overuse of *this* and *that* deprives writing of clarity and force: *This* is the first thing the agency has accomplished; *That* is something to be thankful for.

Referent
The referent of a word is the thing it refers to: in a specific context, "Ann Jackson" and "the love of my life," referring to the same person, would have the same referent. Words without referents are called noise by some semanticists.

Reflexive pronouns
Myself, yourself, himself, herself, itself, ourselves, yourselves, and *themselves* are reflexive pronouns. See *myself*, Pronouns 2.

relate
In the shoptalk of psychology the verb *relate* is a convenient term meaning to "have a realistic social or intimate relationship," as in "the patient's inability to relate." This sense of *relate* has passed into everyday usage, but the relationship is usually—

and preferably—specified by a *to* phrase: They find it almost impossible to relate to adults. *Relate* is a vogue word.

Relative clauses

Relative clauses, often referred to as adjective clauses, are introduced by relative pronouns (*that, which,* or *who*) or by relative adverbs (*where, when, why*). A relative clause stands after the noun it modifies:

The rain *that began in the morning* kept on all night.
The coach was abused by alumni *who two years before had cheered him.*
The road to the left, *which looked almost impassable,* was ours.
The first place *where they camped* turned out to be a swamp.

In general usage, when the clause is restrictive, the adverb, or the pronoun if it is not the subject, is often omitted:

He will never forget the time *you tried to cheat him. Formal:* . . . the time *when you tried to cheat him.*

The man *I met that afternoon* became my closest friend. *Formal:* The man *whom I met.* . . .

When relative clauses are introduced by indefinite relatives (*who, what,* and the compounds with *-ever*), they function as nouns:

The stranger at the door wasn't *who we thought he was.*
What actually happened was very different from *what the newspapers reported.*

Several relative clauses in succession make for an awkward house-that-Jack-built sentence: People who buy houses *that* have been built in times *which* had conspicuous traits of architecture *which* have since been abandoned often have to remodel their purchases completely. See Subordination 1.

See Pronouns 4; Restrictive and nonrestrictive; *that; which; who, whom.* Compare Noun clauses. Reference: Randolph Quirk, *Essays on the English Language Medieval and Modern* (Bloomington: Indiana Univ. Press, 1968), Chs. 9–10.

Relative pronouns

The relative pronouns are *who (whose, whom), which (of which, whose), that, what, whatever,* and *whoever (whomever)*:

Somebody *who* was sitting on the other side shouted, "Put 'em out."
The Senator, *whose* term expires next year, is already worrying.
I haven't read the same book *that* you have.

That refers to persons and things, *who* to persons. *Which* in standard English now refers to animals or objects or situations and also to collective nouns, even if they refer to persons:

The army *which* mobilizes first has the advantage.
The Board of Directors, *which* met on Saturday. . . .
The Board of Directors, *who* are all bankers. . . .

In older English—and still in nonstandard—*which* applies also to persons: "Our Father which art in heaven. . . ."

The use of *as* in place of *that* in sentences like "I can't say as I do" is informal and dialectal.

See Pronouns 4: Restrictive and nonrestrictive; *that; which; who, whom.*

rep Repetition

Get rid of the ineffective repetition of word, meaning, sound, or sentence pattern.

Repeating words, meanings, sounds, or sentence patterns is often effective in writing, giving prose both clarity and emphasis. This article reviews some kinds of repetition that ordinarily call for revision.

1. Of words and phrases. You are bound to repeat nouns unnecessarily if you don't use pronouns:

Ann accepted the boy's challenge and proceeded to teach the boy [him] a lesson. When the boy [he] stayed at the base line, Ann [she] ran the boy [him] from one side of the court to the other. When the boy [he] charged the net, Ann [she] beat the boy [him] with passing shots.

If you write hurriedly and don't take the time to read over what you've written, you are likely to end up with some careless repetition:

I'm having financial difficulties and need to *get* out of housing. So the hassle I *got* when I tried to *get* released from my dorm contract upset me.

When you use the same word in two different senses, the result may be worse: After falling only a few *feet* my left *foot* found *footing;* I would like to find a job with a *concern* that shows some *concern* for the environment. In cases like these, the repetition is obvious enough to be caught and corrected with little trouble — either by omitting the unnecessary repetition or by substituting synonyms. But it does call for that little trouble.

Harder for writers to spot but equally conspicuous to readers is the pet word or phrase that pops up three or four times in the course of an essay. If it's a cliché or a vogue expression, as it's likely to be, it may bother some readers on its first appearance and become increasingly irritating thereafter. In going over a first draft, then, keep a cold eye out for expressions that recur. Some of the repeated words and phrases will be unavoidable, some desirable. But you may also spot some pets that you have repeated simply because they are pets. Sacrifice them.

2. Of meaning. In reviewing what you've written, watch for words and phrases that unnecessarily repeat what you've already said. For example, a gift is free and a fact true by definition, so drop the adjective from "free gift" and from "true fact." If the setting of many TV plays is San Francisco, then San Francisco must frequently be the setting of TV plays. Writing "In many TV plays the setting very often is San Francisco" adds words but subtracts sense. So does "at 8 a.m. in the morning."

3. Of sounds. Jingles and rhyming words (hesitate to take the bait, a glance askance at the dance) are distracting in prose because they draw attention from sense to sound. So are noticeable repetitions of unstressed syllables, especially the *-ly* of adverbs and the endings of some abstract nouns, like *-tion*. Reading first drafts aloud is the best way to catch unintentional repetition of sound. See Adverbs and style, Alliteration, Assonance.

4. Of sentence patterns. If you unintentionally use the same pattern in one sentence after another—beginning three sentences in a row with a dependent clause, for example, or writing three successive compound sentences, or using the same coordinating conjunction in a series of sentences for no rhetorical purpose—your reader is likely to begin nodding. Sometimes this sort of repetition sets up a rhythm even more distracting than the repetition of sound within sentences. Sometimes it simply begins to bore the reader; he feels that he is being led over the same path again and again. Deliberate varying of sentence patterns is not often called for, but if you find yourself recycling the same pattern, make an effort to get untracked. See Parallelism.

Requests
Requests are often expressed in the form of questions: Will you please cooperate? Sometimes the question mark is omitted. See Commands and requests.

Research papers
The research paper—sometimes called the reference paper, library paper, investigative paper, or source paper—is the culminating assignment in many college courses, including Freshman English. Done well, it serves as a valuable introduction to scholarship, for preparing a good paper requires resourcefulness in using the library, ingenuity in following up leads, judgment in analyzing data, and skill in organizing and writing an essay of some length and complexity. Because a research project is an ambitious undertaking, often extending over several weeks, it should be planned carefully and worked at methodically. The main steps are these:

1. Choosing a topic. The best topic is one that you know something about but not nearly enough to satisfy you. The motivation to learn more gives point and direction to your research. And the motivation to learn more about something *in particular* will protect you from taking on an impossibly large topic. "Robert E. Lee and the Civil War" is too big; "Lee at Gettysburg" is manageable. But neither title tells enough about what kind of reading, thinking, and writing you will need to do. Decide early whether your essay is to be primarily a report or a thesis paper. A report assembles the material available on the subject, recovering or reclaiming information and perhaps presenting it from a fresh perspective. A thesis paper shapes the evidence into support for a hypothesis; it argues a point. The decision to make the paper primarily expository or primarily argumentative has some bearing on the sources you investigate and more on the use you make of the material.

2. Preparing a working bibliography. In your initial canvassing of sources, move systematically from the card catalog to indexes or periodicals to appropriate reference books and special encyclopedias. For information about reference books in your field of interest, consult Eugene P. Sheehy's *Guide to Reference Books* (9th ed., 1976). For each source that looks promising, make out a bibliography card: copy accurately on a 3" × 5" or 4" × 6" filing card the facts of publication as well as author and title (see Bibliographical form), and note where the source is located in the library. Keep your working bibliography flexible. As you begin your reading, you will discard items that looked promising but turn out to be dead ends, and you will add items from the new sources that keep coming to your attention.

3. Taking notes on sources. In addition to making out bibliography cards that identify your sources, you will need to take notes on what the sources have to say. Record these notes on the same kind of filing cards you use for bibliography notes or, if you prefer, on the pages of a loose-leaf notebook. In either case, restrict yourself to one note – fact, opinion, quotation, or summary – per card or page, with the source and the page number in the upper right corner and, in the upper left corner, an identifying word or phrase to indicate the specific phase of your topic the note bears on.

As you make notes, be sure they distinguish clearly between an author's facts and his opinions, between direct quotation and summary, between what you are taking *from* the source and observations you are making *on* the source (see Paraphrase). You will find it helpful to keep on a separate pad a running log of notes to yourself – comments, questions, hunches that will remind you, when you begin to sift through and arrange your notes, of leads to be followed up, conflicting sources to be weighed, puzzles to be solved, and hypotheses to be tested.

4. Developing an outline. Early in the note-taking stage, sketch a tentative outline for your paper. Keep it fluid. Let it give direction to your thinking, but don't let it channel your ideas too early. Try to divide your material into logical blocks – from five to eight, perhaps – and then keep shifting these units around until you have them in the right order. Once you can discern the shape of the whole, you can write (and rewrite) one section at a time.

5. Writing drafts. Much of a research paper consists of a digest of sources that lead to, support, or elaborate on the researcher's findings or generalizations. In summarizing, interpreting, and analyzing your sources, it is important to represent them accurately and to do so in your own words. But you will not be able to free yourself of the original phrasing unless you first achieve full comprehension of the ideas. Then you can express them in your own words. If you merely tie together a succession of direct quotations from a source, you display no mastery of the material. If you use phrases and clauses from a source without putting them in quotation marks, you leave yourself open to the charge of plagiarism (see Plagiarism).

As you write, keep a close check on the sources you are consulting and summarizing, so that you can give accurate and adequate credit (see Footnote form). Be meticulous in reproducing direct quotations (see Quotation marks 2b). And when you quote, make sure that the passage bears directly on the point you are discussing, that you present it so that its relevance is immediately clear, and that you fit it smoothly into your text.

The style of a research paper should be comparatively formal and impersonal. This does not mean that it should be stilted or dull. Nor does it mean that you need avoid *I;* in some published research, *I* appears regularly. It does mean that you should keep the focus on the subject and what you have managed to find out about it—not on your feelings about it. But since all good research papers reveal the writers' interest in their topics, communicating your own interest will be a natural consequence of engaging yourself fully in your subject.

6. Documenting the paper. Your readers' chief interest will be in the substance of your paper—what you have found out about your subject—and the clarity and force with which you present it. They will also examine the documentation, the footnotes and the bibliography that record your journey of exploration. Check and recheck details of bibliographical form and footnote form for accuracy and consistency.

References: James D. Lester, *Writing Research Papers,* 2nd ed. (Glenview, Ill.: Scott, 1976); Kate L. Turabian, *Student's Guide for Writing College Papers,* 2nd ed., rev. (Chicago: Univ. of Chicago Press, 1970).

rest Restrictive and nonrestrictive

If the modifier marked is restrictive, don't separate it from the word it modifies by a comma. If it is nonrestrictive, set it off by a comma or by two commas.

"Lemmon, who isn't Jewish, plays Jews who aren't Jewish either" (Pauline Kael, *New Yorker*). The first *who* clause in the quoted sentence tells us something about Jack Lemmon, but it doesn't set him apart; it can be dropped from the sentence without destroying the meaning: Lemmon plays Jews who aren't Jewish. But the *who* clause modifying *Jews* is essential to Kael's point: the Jewishness of the characters Lemmon plays is superficial and trivial. Dropping this clause would leave us with "Lemmon plays Jews," which isn't what Kael is saying. Separating the second *who* clause from the main clause with a comma would give us "Lemmon plays Jews, who aren't Jewish," which is nonsense. The first *who* clause is nonrestrictive. The second *who* clause is restrictive.

1. Restrictive modifiers. An adjective (or relative) clause or an adjective phrase is a restrictive (or bound, or limiting) modifier when the information it provides about something in the main clause is essential to the meaning the writer intends.

If you speak a sentence before you write it, or read it aloud after you have written it, you can usually tell whether a clause or phrase is restrictive:

The girl *whose book I borrowed* has dropped the course.
The books *stolen from the library* were found in that locker.

When the modifier is restrictive, there is no pause between the word modified and the clause or phrase that modifies it.

You can be quite sure a clause is restrictive if you begin it with *that:* The year *that I dropped out* is one I'd be glad to forget. And a clause is restrictive if you can omit the relative pronoun: The year [*that*] *I dropped out;* The people [*whom*] *we met;* The plan [*which*] *they came up with.*

2. Nonrestrictive modifiers. An adjective (or relative) clause or adjective phrase that can be dropped from a sentence without changing or blurring the meaning is nonrestrictive and should be set off by a comma or commas. The importance of the information the modifier provides is not the deciding factor. If you write, "The bullet *which came within an inch of my head* smashed my mother's favorite teacup," the content of your adjective clause is certainly dramatic and significant. But unless you are using the clause to specify *this* bullet among a number of bullets, you must set it off with commas.

If *which* were used to launch only nonrestrictive clauses, as *that* is used to launch restrictive clauses, *which* and *that* clauses would cause few problems. But there are times when *which* seems a better choice for starting a restrictive clause: That was the bad news *which we had been given every reason to expect.* (*Which* avoids the repetition of *that.*) And some clauses are restrictive in one context, nonrestrictive in another. In a different context, the clause *whose book I borrowed,* used as an example of a restrictive clause in the preceding section, can be nonrestrictive: The girl, whose book I borrowed, left soon afterward with an older woman. So can the example of a restrictive phrase: The books, stolen from the library, later turned up in a second-hand store.

Your job, then, is to know what you mean. In the modifying clause or phrase, do you mean to say something that the sentence requires for its basic meaning, or do you mean to offer information which—no matter how important—could be omitted from that sentence without detracting from its central message? If the former, the modifier is restrictive—no commas. If the latter, the modifier is nonrestrictive—commas. Say the sentence out loud. Do you make a definite pause before the modifier? Then it's nonrestrictive—commas.

You may find the same advice useful in punctuating other modifiers. Traditionally, the restrictive/nonrestrictive distinction has applied to a dependent clause introduced by a relative pronoun and functioning as an adjective. Some grammarians extend the principle to all adjectival modifiers, to appositives (see Apposition, appositives), and to some adverbial modifiers, including final adverbial clauses (see Comma 2b). References: Christensen, pp. 95–110; Quirk et al., pp. 261–62, 622–25, 638–48, 858–76.

rhetoric

In its classical, neutral sense of "the art of persuasion," *rhetoric* is now used mainly in formal contexts. In textbooks like this one, it is broadened to mean "the study of the making, the qualities, and the effects of verbal discourse." But *rhetoric* has a wide range of other interpretations, some of which stress its baser uses, some its more dignified, as in these quotations from the same issue of the *Shakespeare Quarterly:*

. . . the great Swiss writer, Ferdinand Ramuz, whom no one has ever accused of rhetoric. – Robert Speaight

A lucid, chaste Virgilian rhetoric. . . . – Howard Felperin

In general usage, where derogatory senses of the word prevail, *rhetoric* frequently suggests flamboyant insincerity, unprincipled manipulation of emotion, or empty verbiage. Currently a writer can assume that most audiences will regard *rhetoric* as a term of abuse.

The suggestion of empty verbiage is equally strong in current uses of *rhetorical:* "It will be interesting to see how many men are prepared to give more than rhetorical support today to the sex from which they have, for centuries, demanded and accepted so much" (Adrienne Rich, *Chronicle of Higher Education*).

Rhetoric

Whenever a writer asks anything of his reader – agreement, understanding, belief, action, even just a laugh – he is within the province of rhetoric. As he composes an essay, every decision he makes, from the selection of the material to the choice of a particular word, should be guided by his sense of the rhetorical situation. Some of these decisions he makes intuitively, some out of habit, some after carefully weighing alternatives.

The chief elements in a rhetorical situation are the writer, his subject, his purpose, and his audience. Each of these elements is influenced by the other three; each offers opportunities and imposes limits. As you plan an essay, and especially as you revise it, questions like the following will sharpen your sense of the rhetorical situation:

What do I want to say about this subject?

Do I have enough information and evidence now, or do I need to dig for more?

Who are my readers? How much do they know about the subject, and what is their attitude toward it? What are their tastes, habits, values, fears, hopes, prejudices?

What common ground is there between us, what shared assumptions? What can I take for granted, and what do I have to explain or argue for?

How can I make my readers see what I want them to see, think the way I want them to think, do what I want them to do? Should I start by declaring what my purpose is, or would my readers be more responsive if I invited them to take part in an inquiry with me, if I raised problems that we would try to solve together?

How can I make my readers identify with me, share my feeling about the situation? How can I make them understand and adopt my point of view?

Will this detail, this bit of evidence, have more weight than that one? If so, should it come first or last? How can I phrase this idea so that it will be both clear and compelling? How can I make this sentence say precisely what I mean?

Will *this* word, *this* image, *this* mark of punctuation work with *this* audience? Do I need to make my style simpler, more relaxed, or does my relationship with my readers require increased distance, greater objectivity, a style that is altogether more formal?

What side of my personality do I want to come through in this essay? How do I want my readers to see me?

As these questions suggest, you can assess the appropriateness of what you are saying and how you are saying it only in a specific rhetorical situation. The arguments you advance, the evidence you offer, the organization you adopt, the language you select—all these should be tested, as you revise your essay, for their fitness in communicating to the particular audience your thoughts and feelings about your subject.

See *Writer's Guide*, pp. 289–96. References: Douglas Ehninger, *Contemporary Rhetoric* (Glenview, Ill.: Scott, 1972); Porter G. Perrin in *Perspectives in English*, ed. Robert C. Pooley (New York: Appleton, 1960), pp. 121–32; Joseph Schwartz and John A. Rycenga, eds., *The Province of Rhetoric* (New York: Ronald, 1965); W. Ross Winterowd, *Rhetoric: A Synthesis* (New York: Holt, 1968).

Rhetorical questions

Rhetorical questions are really statements in the form of questions, since no direct answer is expected: "Did not Henry James, in using the family letters, perversely alter William's Old Abe into President Lincoln?" (Lewis Mumford, *New York Review of Books*). As a stylistic device, the rhetorical question will be a flop if the reader rejects the answer the writer intends.

right

In the sense of "very," *right* is a localism, in good standing in the South: We'll be right glad to see you. The use of *right* before phrases of place and time (right across the street, right after the show) is avoided in most formal writing but is established in general usage.

Phrases like *right here, right there, right now,* and *right then* are similarly avoided in formal contexts though commonplace in general. Idioms like *right away* and *right off* ("at once" or "now") and *right along* ("continuously" or "all the time") are slightly more informal.

rise, arise, get up
In referring to standing up or getting out of bed, *arise* is formal and poetic; *rise* is somewhat less formal; the general idiom is *get up*.

rob
A person or place is robbed. What is taken in the robbery is stolen. *Rob* for *steal* (They're the ones who robbed the money) is an old usage considered nonstandard today.

Roman numerals
Roman numerals may be either lowercase (iii, v, x) or capitals (III, V, X). See Numbers 3.

round, around
Round is a preposition and adverb in its own right, often interchangeable with *around:* "an easy irony, good for a laugh the first two or three times round" (Stanley Kaufmann, *New Republic*). It should not be written with an initial apostrophe ('round).

Around for "approximately" (around 1920, a cast of around forty) is now found in all varieties of usage.

The general adjectives *all-round* and *all-around* are overused, particularly with *athlete*.

Run-on sentence
The label *run-on sentence* is applied variously to a sentence in which two independent clauses are run together with no punctuation between, to a sentence in which two independent clauses are joined with only a comma between, and to a sentence in which a series of independent clauses are joined with coordinating conjunctions. As a result, *run-on* is more confusing than useful. See Comma fault, Fused sentence.

said
As a modifier (the said person, the said idea) *said* is legal language. In general writing, *that* or *this* or simple *the* is the right choice.

saint
The abbreviation *St.* is commonly used in names of places (**St. Albans, St. Louis**) and often before the names of saints (**St. Francis, St. Anthony of Padua**), though some stylebooks call for spell-

ing out *Saint* in both cases. The plural of the abbreviation is *SS*. (SS. Peter and Paul). Occasionally the French feminine form, *Sainte,* is used (Sault Sainte Marie); the abbreviation is *Ste*. Spanish forms are common in the West; San Diego, Santa Barbara. In writing a personal name beginning with *Saint* (Camille Saint-Saëns) or *St.* (Louis St. Laurent), the spelling established by the bearer should be followed.

same

Because *same* without *the* suggests legal or commercial jargon (We enclose payment for same), it is obtrusive and inappropriate in normal prose.

say

Say is the usual word for "speaking" and can also be used for what is written: In his journal, Gide says. . . . In dialog the repetition of "he said," "she said" is almost always preferable to the use of strained alternatives like *expostulated, muttered, babbled. State,* which implies a formal "saying," is a poor substitute for *say,* whether in dialog or in ordinary text: "To be able to state this of the new work of an American poet of 50 is, to state the least, unusual" (Aram Saroyan, *New York Times Book Review*). *Assert* and similar substitutes are also unsatisfactory in most contexts. See *claim.* Reference: Copperud, p. 240.

   Say in the sense of "approximately," "for instance," "let us say," is used in all varieties of writing: "the specialist in the literature of, say, the English eighteenth century" (Howard Mumford Jones, *Journal of the History of Ideas*).

scarcely

Since *scarcely* means "probably not," adding a *not* as in "can't scarcely" is redundant. See Double negative 2.

scenario

A vogue word of the 1970s, *scenario* has taken on meanings having little connection with "script" or "synopsis." Often it should be replaced with *plan, prediction,* or *possibility.* The difficulty for the reader is in deciding which: "The scenario isn't as farfetched as it may sound" (Joann S. Lublin, *Wall Street Journal*).

seem

Seem is often used needlessly to qualify a statement: They [seem to] run with a gang that can't [seem to] keep out of trouble. So used, it loses its power to distinguish between appearance and reality. Limit your use of *seem* to situations in which you must be tentative; don't say something *seems to be* when you mean something *is.* See *can't help but, can't seem to.*

self

Self as a suffix forms the reflexive and intensive pronouns: *myself, yourself, himself, herself, itself, oneself, ourselves, your-*

selves, themselves. These are used chiefly for emphasis (I can do that myself) or as objects identical to the subjects of their verbs (I couldn't help myself). See *himself, herself; myself;* Pronouns 2.

As a prefix, *self* is joined to the root word by a hyphen: *self-control, self-explanatory, self-made, self-respect.* When *self* is the root word, there is no hyphen: *selfhood, selfish, selfless.*

semi-

Semi- is a prefix meaning "half or approximately half" (*semicylindrical*), "twice within a certain period" (*semiweekly, semiannual*), or "partially, imperfectly" (*semicivilized, semiprofessional*). It is a live element in forming new words.

Semicolon

Use a semicolon as the link between these sentence elements.

1. To link coordinate clauses.

a. Between clauses without connectives. Use a semicolon, especially in a rather formal context, to link two independent clauses whose relatedness you want to emphasize:

The auto industry has become a state within a state; its activities cannot and should not escape continuing public scrutiny. — *Consumer Reports*

Some years ago, a learned colleague who was old and ill complained to me that he could no longer read German; it made his legs feel queer. I know that feeling well; I have had it while trying to read Henry James. — P. B. Ballard, *Thought and Language*

b. With conjunctive adverbs. Use a semicolon to link clauses connected by a conjunctive adverb such as *however, moreover, therefore:*

His popularity was undiminished; however, he no longer enjoyed the work.

Finally, despite the hopes and prophecies described before, we do not really agree on philosophical and political values; therefore the conference, moved by the same desire for survival and development as the world at large, carefully avoided exposing the ideological differences that remain. — Stanley Hoffman, *Daedalus*

A comma before *however* or *therefore* in these sentences would produce a comma fault. See Conjunctive adverbs.

c. With coordinating conjunctions. Consider using a semicolon between clauses connected by a coordinating conjunction (*and, but, for, or . . .*) if the clauses are long, if they contain commas, or if for some reason—perhaps for contrast—you want to indicate a more definite break than you could show with a comma:

Words that are beautifully written by a scribe seemed to address his eye and mind in a personal way that was obliterated by mechanical type; and a manuscript illuminated by hand-painted miniatures gave him a pleasure that no woodcut could equal. — Edgar Wind, *Harper's*

I do not suggest that as English teachers we stop talking about planning and organization; nor am I saying that logical thought has nothing to do with the organizational process. — Robert Zoellner, *College English*

2. To separate units with internal commas. The units may be figures, scores, verbal items in series, or internally punctuated clauses:

Three things which a social system can provide or withhold are helpful to mental creation: first, technical training; second, liberty to follow the creative impulse; third, at least the possibility of ultimate appreciation of some public, whether large or small. – Bertrand Russell, *Proposed Roads to Freedom*

3. Semicolon and colon. Don't use a semicolon to introduce a quotation or a listing or to perform conventional functions of the colon (see Colon 3). In linking clauses, however, you sometimes have a choice. The colon is more formal and carries a suggestion that the second clause will explain or illustrate the first; but often the choice is chiefly if not solely stylistic.

4. Semicolons and style. Semicolons are more suitable in the longer, more complicated sentences of formal styles than in general and informal writing. Since they slow the pace, they are more common in exposition than in narrative. In general styles commas are often used where semicolons might appear in formal writing, or clauses that could be linked by semicolons are written as separate sentences. The use of a semicolon, then, is often as much a matter of style as of correct punctuation.

Compare Colon, Comma. References: Follett, pp. 418–23; Summey, pp. 97–101; Whitehall, pp. 121–22.

sensual, sensuous

Both *sensual* and *sensuous* refer to the senses, but the connotations of *sensual* are more physical, of *sensuous* more aesthetic. Sensual music and sensuous music are two different things.

Sentence fragment

A sentence fragment is a part of a sentence that is punctuated as if it were a complete sentence. See Fragment.

Sentences

1. Classifying sentences grammatically. On the basis of their clause structure, sentences are classified grammatically as simple, complex, compound, and compound-complex. Each of these types of sentences can be expanded by making subjects, verbs, and objects compound and by using appositives and modifiers. According to transformational theory, all such expansions, as well as all dependent clauses, represent sentences in the deep structure that have been embedded in the surface-structure sentence. Even a grammatically simple sentence is usually the product of some embedding – the normal process of packing meaning into sentences. See Absolute phrases, Clauses, Deep structure.

2. Analyzing sentences rhetorically. A sentence is not only a grammatical unit but also a rhetorical unit. A rhetorical analysis of a sentence takes into account the order of elements, the repetition of grammatical structures, and the appropriateness of such ordering and repeating to the idea expressed. See Balanced sentence, Cumulative sentence, Parallelism, Periodic sentence, Phrases 2.

3. Building sensible sentences. A writer should build his clauses and arrange their parts so as to bring out the natural and logical relationships in his material. Subordination and parallelism, for example, clarify such relationships when they are properly used. Misused, they blur or distort them. If embedding is a way of packing more meaning into a sentence, reversing the process – converting some elements into separate sentences – can unburden an overloaded sentence and improve its unity and clarity. See Coordination, Shifted constructions, Subordination.

Although some structures that lack an independent subject-verb combination are rhetorically effective, most sentences have at least one independent subject-verb combination. Generally, faults in sentence construction result from failure to recognize the difference between a dependent clause and an independent clause or from failure to show the relation between a modifier and what it modifies. See Comma fault, Dangling modifiers, Fragment, Fused sentence.

Sequence of tenses
In some sentences the tense of a verb in one clause is determined by the tense of a verb in another: When he drives, I brace [*not* braced] myself. See Tense 3.

Series
A succession of words, phrases, or clauses that are grammatically coordinate makes a series. Sometimes the units are simply separated by commas – "the people who cared for Eliot – Cross, Lewes, Edith Simcox, Maria Lewis, Sara Hennell" (Michael Wood, *New York Review of Books*) – but usually the last unit is joined to the rest by a coordinating conjunction. Usage is divided over putting a comma before the conjunction:

It was a novel, confusing, and unnecessary argument. – Richard Harris, *New Yorker*

Another patron . . . came to see the go-go boys with her mother, her sister [ ] and her Kodak movie camera. – Jeannette Smyth, *Washington Post*

Though many writers, especially in general and informal styles, omit the comma, its presence helps to indicate that the units are equivalent, and in some instances it prevents misunderstanding (see Comma 5). If the units are long or have commas within them, they are often separated by semicolons (see Semicolons 2).

For the rhetorical effects of a series, see Parallelism, Parallelism and style, Phrases 2.

set, sit

In standard English, people and things *sit* (past: *sat*) or they are *set* (past: *set*) — that is, are "placed":

I like to sit in a hotel lobby.
I have sat in this same seat for three semesters.
She set the soup down with a flourish.
The post was set three feet in the ground.

A hen, however, sets (on her eggs), cement sets, and the sun sets. A large dining room table sits eight, and few city people know how to sit a horse. Reference: Pooley, pp. 160–63.

Sexist language

Since the revival of the movement for equality of the sexes, there has been much criticism of sexism both in current usage and in the grammar of formal English. Examples of usage that patronizes or denigrates women include labels like *working girls, coed, the little woman, the weaker sex, boss lady, woman driver,* and *lady doctor* and the suffixes *-ess* and *-ette: poetess, Jewess, suffragette, usherette.* Similarly offensive to many is the use of first names for women where men's full names or last names are used: Before Robert Browning came to know her, Elizabeth was already considered a rival of Tennyson.

Add to these the words for certain occupations and offices that seem to imply that women are excluded: *policeman, businessman, chairman, Congressman.* And to many most galling of all is the use of *man* and *men* to stand for *men-and-women (manpower, the common man, man-made, free men)* and for the whole human race *(prehistoric man, mankind,* "all men are equal," "the brotherhood of man") and the use of *he (him, his)* as the pronoun referring to a noun that doesn't specify gender or to an indefinite pronoun *(student, citizen, spectator, person, anyone, no one).*

Although some feminists attach relatively little importance to sexist language, others see it as a subtle but powerful conditioner of attitudes toward the sexes from very early childhood. For those who are seriously concerned, the substitution of *-woman* for *-man* in the words for occupations and offices *(policewoman, businesswoman, Congresswoman)* is no solution to the problem. Like *lady doctor* and *woman driver,* it calls attention to gender where gender is not, or should not be, of any significance. (*Male nurse* belongs in the same category. Opponents of sexist language deplore terms that stereotype either men or women.)

Person(s), people, and *humans* are common substitutes for *man, men, mankind* when both sexes are intended. An increasing number of writers now avoid the traditional use of *he* to stand for *he or she* by using the latter in its various forms: Everyone must turn in his or her theme. . . . But because the wordiness is easily compounded and awkwardness is almost inevitable (. . . if he or she wants a passing grade), there is now a growing tendency to write in the plural (All students must turn in their themes . . .) or to treat *they* as an indefinite common-gender singular (Everyone must turn in their theme [*or* themes] . . .). See Agreement 2, *he or she, they.*

If you consider sexism in language an issue of overriding importance, then as a writer you will avoid all the usages described as sexist, including the use of *man* for an individual of either sex and any age and the use of *he* for *he or she*. If you don't believe that sexism exists in the language, or don't care if it does, or applaud the masculine bias, you will ignore the whole matter. But if you belong to neither of these extremes, there are choices to be made. Even if you are mainly satisfied with the language as it is used, you should be aware that your readers may not be. You can easily avoid the more obtrusive sexist usages, such as descriptive terms that classify women physically when their looks have no relevance (the senator's red-headed wife) or that imply a general lack of intelligence and competence (a cute pre-med student). You may also decide to seek substitutes for the *-man* words and to cut down on your use of generic *he* in sentences like "When a young person says he is interested in helping people, his counselor tells him to become a psychiatrist."

How far you go will depend in part on your own sensitivities as writers. If your sense of style causes you to wince at *he or she* (or *he/she*), if the connotations of *artificial* make it impossible for you to accept it as a substitute for *man-made*, if *persons* and *humans* bother you at least as much as generic *man*, then you face much more difficult choices than those who can settle the problem to their own satisfaction with the rhetorical question, "What's more important—syntax or souls?" For those truly torn between the demands of feminist ideology and the demands of stylistic grace and flow, the only solution is a long grind of writing and revising and rewriting until at last the conflicts are resolved and both ideological and aesthetic demands are satisfied.

In this book *he* is used to refer to *student* and *writer* not because of bias or obtuseness but in the interest of economy and style.

shall, will

Since the eighteenth century some grammarians have insisted that in expressing determination, obligation, or prohibition in statements about the future, *will* should be used with first-person subjects and *shall* with second- and third-; but practice has never been uniform. In current American usage either auxiliary occurs with all three persons. *Will* is more common. The same grammarians have sought to keep the single function of indicating the future distinct by urging that *shall* be used with first-person subjects and *will* with second- and third-; but again, in standard usage *will* is much more common than *shall* with all persons. In questions, *shall* is common only in the first person: Shall I go first? Will you come later? See *should, would.* References: Bryant, pp. 182–83; Copperud, pp. 243–44; Fries, pp. 150–67; Pooley, pp. 47–52.

shift Shifted constructions

Avoid the unnecessary shift in construction.

Shifted constructions are needless changes in grammatical form or point of view within a sentence. In speech and in much informal writing, shifted constructions are common, but in general and formal prose they are avoided because they trouble a careful reader. The many types of needless shift include the following:

1. Between adjective and noun: This book is interesting and an informative piece of work. *Revised:* . . . interesting and informative.

2. Between noun and clause: The most important factors are time and temperature, careful control at every point, and the mechanical equipment must be efficient. *Revised:* . . . and efficient mechanical equipment.

3. Between adverb phrase and adjective phrase: Along these walks are the cottages, some of which have stood since the founding but others quite recent. *Revised:* . . . but others for only a short time.

4. Between gerund and infinitive: Carrying four courses and to hold down a job at the same time will either develop my character or kill me. *Revised:* Carrying four courses and holding down a job . . . .

5. Between gerund and finite verb: I have heard complaints about the plot being weak and that the setting is played up too much. *Revised:* . . . and the setting being played up. . . .

6. Between participle and finite verb: You often see a fisherman trying to get quietly to his favorite spot but instead he broadcasts warnings with his rhythmical squeak-splash, squeak-splash. *Revised:* . . . but instead broadcasting warnings. . . .

7. Between transitive verb and copula: Anyone who has persistence or is desperate enough can get a job on a ship. *Revised:* . . . who is persistent or who is desperate enough. . . .

8. Between past and present: The tanks bulled their way through the makeshift barricades and fan out across the enormous plaza. *Revised:* . . . and fanned out. . . .

9. Between active and passive: The committee members disliked each other heartily, and their time was wasted in wrangling. *Revised:* . . . heartily and wasted their time in wrangling.

10. Between personal and impersonal: When one is sick, you make few plans. *Revised:* When one is sick, one [*or* he] makes. . . .

No enumeration of shifted constructions could be complete: there are too many constructions to shift.

See Parallelism and style; Point of view; Reference of pronouns; Tense 2, 3; *when, where.*

Shoptalk

Shoptalk is the words that people in the same occupation use among themselves to refer to the things they regularly concern themselves with in their work: the noun *mud* among bricklayers to mean "mortar," the verb *docket* among lawyers to mean "make an abstract."

No occupation gets along without shoptalk; all have everyday terms that may be unintelligible to outsiders but are indispensable to those who practice the trade or profession. Especially convenient are short, informal substitutes for long technical terms. So a *mike* may be a microphone in a broadcasting studio, a microscope in a laboratory, a micrometer in a shop; a *hypo* is a fixing bath to a photographer, a hypodermic injection to a nurse. Many such words are metaphoric (the television *ghost*) or imitative (the radar *blip*). Much shoptalk is so specialized or colorless that it has never spread to the general vocabulary—printshop words, for example, like *chase, em, pi, quoins.*

Many words and meanings from shoptalk are given in general dictionaries with the names of the occupations they belong to, but most are listed and adequately defined only in more specialized books. So long as they remain narrowly specialized, they are inappropriate in writing for general audiences.

See Jargon. See also Gobbledygook, Psychologese, Slang. References: Mencken, pp. 709–61, and many articles in *American Speech.*

should, would

In indirect discourse, *should* and *would* can function as the past tenses of *shall* and *will.* "We will go" can be reported as "He announced that we would go," and "We shall go" as "He announced that we should go." Since *should* has a connotation of obligation or propriety that may not be intended, *would* is preferred. See *shall, will;* Tense 3. Reference: Pooley, pp. 52–53.

sic

Sic, the Latin word meaning "thus," is properly used to indicate that what precedes it has been quoted correctly. See Brackets.

sick, ill

Ill is the more formal, less common word. In the United States they mean the same thing. In British usage *sick* is usually restricted to mean "nauseated": "The mere touch of the thing would make me sick or ill, or both" (Richard Jones, *The Three Suitors*). In American usage *sick* in that sense is made clear by adding a phrase: It made me sick to [at/in] my stomach.

Simile

A simile compares with *like* or *as:* He swims like a winded walrus; straight as a lodgepole pine. See Figurative language.

Simple sentence

A simple sentence consists of one independent subject-predicate combination. See Clauses 1.

since

As a subordinating conjunction, *since* can have the meaning "because": Since I was already late, I didn't rush. See *because*.

sit, set

People and things *sit* or *are set*. See *set, sit*.

-size

Size is typical of a class of nouns (*age, color, height, shape, width, weight . . .*) that also function as apparent modifiers: *medium-size, standard-size, life-size, outsize, oversize*. The *-size* words are redundant in compound modifiers with adjectives that might modify the head nouns directly: not "small-size box" but "small box," and similarly with "round-shape table," "younger-age students," "dark-color hair," and so on. See Wordiness 1.

Slang

Drawing a line between slang and other sorts of informal English is difficult. Many people use the term *slang* too broadly, applying it to almost any informal word, and dictionaries have been too generous with the label, marking as slang many words that simply suggest spoken rather than written style. In fact, there is no fully accepted criterion for marking off the segment of the vocabulary that constitutes slang, as disagreement among and between dictionaries and handbooks makes clear.

Though some of the words labeled slang in current dictionaries—*lulu, corker, deadbeat*—have been around for generations, the central characteristic of slang comes from the motive in using it: a desire for novelty, for vivid emphasis, for being up with the times or a little ahead; for belonging—either to a particular social group or, more broadly, to an age group or, more broadly still, to the in-group that uses the current slang. These are essentially qualities of style, and the tone and connotation are as important as the meaning of the words. Other varieties of language have ways of expressing the ideas of slang words, but their tone is more conventional. Young people like novelty, as do grown-ups with youthful ideas, and entertainers need it in their trade. In-groups, both legal and illegal, have their slang vocabularies, which often spill over into general English: some of the slang of the drug culture has wide circulation among nonusers.

Slang is made by natural linguistic processes. It abounds in clipped words (*marvy, natch, hood*) and in compounds and derivatives of ordinary words (*screwball, sourpuss, cockeyed, put-on, rip-off*). Many are borrowed from the shoptalk of sports and the popular arts, especially jazz and rock. And a great many are figurative extensions of general words: *nut, dope, egg* (applied to people); *heavy, hung up, spaced out*. Sound often contributes a good deal, as in *barf, booboo, goof, zap, zip, zonk*.

Since many slang words have short lives, any discussion of slang in print is bound to be out of date. *Twenty-three skidoo, vamoose, beat it, scram, hit the trail, take a powder, drag out, shag out, cut out, split* succeeded each other almost within a generation. Words for being drunk (*soused, plastered, bombed*), for girls (*baby, doll, chick, bird, sister*), and words of approval (*tops, neat, the most, cool, groovy, out of sight, baddest*) and disapproval (*all wet, cruddy, gross, a hype*) change from year to year—though some survive and some recur. Many slang words prove permanently useful and become a part of the informal vocabulary (*blind date, boy friend, go steady*) or the general (*highbrow, lowbrow*).

The chief objection to slang in writing, aside from its conspicuousness, is that it elbows out more exact expressions. A slang cliché is at least as boring as a cliché in standard English, and slang that names general impressions instead of specific ones is in no way preferable to comparable words in the general vocabulary, like *nice* and *good*. If slang expressions are appropriate to the subject matter and the audience and if they come naturally to the writer, they should be used without apology (that is, without quotation marks). If they are not appropriate, they should not be used, with or without quotation marks.

References: Mencken, Ch. 11; Harold Wentworth and Stuart Berg Flexner, eds. and comps., *Dictionary of American Slang*, 2nd ed. (New York: Crowell, 1975).

slow, slowly

Both *slow* and *slowly* are used as adverbs. *Slow* is more vigorous and is widely used in speech and in informal writing in place of *slowly*, but in general usage it is restricted to only a few contexts: He drove *slow; but* He drove away *slowly*. See Adverbs and style 1, Divided usage. Compare *bad, badly*. Reference: Copperud, p. 246.

so

1. *So* and *so that*. To introduce clauses of purpose, *so that* is ordinarily expected in formal contexts, but *so* by itself is respectable in general use:

[The ghost of] Patroclus comes to ask Achilles to bury him quickly so that he may pass into the realm of Hades.—Anne Amory, *Yale Classical Studies*

I might have tried . . . to give a clearer idea of the rest of the contents, so readers could gather some notion of whether or not this kind of material might interest them.—John Thompson, *New York Review of Books*

To express consequence or result, both *so* alone and *so that* are found in all varieties of usage. *Speculum: A Journal of Mediaeval Studies* had these two passages in the same issue:

The old bishop was better known as a fighter than as a churchman, so we may reasonably assume that it was prudence and not cowardice which prompted him. — Herbert L. Oerter

He quotes frequently from the Old French, so that the reader gains a very good appreciation of the style. — Alfred Foulet

2. *So* as substitute. *So* can substitute for a whole clause: I think *I will win;* at least I hope *so.*

3. *So* as an intensive. As an intensive, *so* is informal: He's so handsome!

References: Bryant, pp. 190–93; Copperud, pp. 246–47.

so . . . as

So . . . as is sometimes used in negative comparisons of degree: not so wide as a barn door. See *as . . . as* 3.

so-called

If you have to use *so-called,* don't duplicate the idea by putting the name of the so-called object in quotes: the so-called champion, *not* the so-called "champion."

some

1. As a subject. *Some* as a subject takes either a singular verb (Some of the material is difficult) or a plural verb (Some of the tests are easy), depending on the context.

2. As an adverb. *Some* as a qualifier is informal: He is some older than she is. More formal usage would have *somewhat.* Informally, *some* is also used to modify verbs (The springs were squeaking some).

In formal writing the adverb *someplace* is still avoided in favor of *somewhere,* but in the last generation or so *someplace* has moved from informal to general usage: "I began to get some idea of what I came to call the Civilization of the Dialogue, a phrase I am sure I stole someplace" (Robert M. Hutchins, *Saturday Review*). *Somewheres* is nonstandard. Compare *any.*

3. As one word or two. The compounds *somebody, someway, somewhat, somewhere* are written as one word. *Someone* is one word (Someone is coming) unless *one* is stressed (some one of them). *Someday* is written as either one word or two. *Sometime* in "Drop in sometime" means "at some time [two words] in the future."

sort

Sort takes a singular verb even when it is followed by *of* and a plural noun: That sort of men deserves shooting. See *kind, sort.*

Sound

In good writing, sound reinforces sense. In bad writing, sound distracts attention from sense. See Alliteration, Assonance, Repetition 3.

Spelling

Correct the spelling of the word marked, referring to a dictionary if necessary.

Use your dictionary, and when alternative spellings are listed, choose the first. The following *Index* articles deal with spelling:

Apostrophe	Foreign words in English	Plurals of nouns
Capital letters	Hyphen	Principal parts of verbs

See also Analogy in language, British English, Divided usage.

Split infinitive

An infinitive is said to be split when an adverb or an adverbial element separates the *to* from its following verb: The receptionist asked them to kindly sit down.

The split infinitive gets more attention than it deserves. Many people have been taught to avoid it scrupulously; and sometimes there is good reason to do so. Certainly, long intervening elements are awkward and should be moved, often to the end of the sentence: After a while he was able to, although not very accurately, distinguish good customers from disloyal ones.

On principle, moreover, formal writing does rather consistently avoid the split infinitive, even when the adverb cannot be placed at the end of the clause:

We must have sufficient foresight and vision patiently to guide the peoples of the world along the road they have chosen to follow. – Bernard Kiernan, *American Scholar*

The Chinese model . . . never eclipsed the local differences that made Japan always and Korea sometimes so distinct from China as properly to constitute a separate civilization. – William H. McNeill, *The Rise of the West*

But if long intervening elements are awkward, short adverbs that modify the infinitive may fit most smoothly and clearly between the *to* and the verb; and for such reasons split infinitives often occur in unquestionably reputable general writing. The first of the following citations, for example, would be ambiguous if "really" were placed before "to" and unidiomatic if it were placed after "hate." In the second, "precisely to locate" might be ambiguous, and "to locate precisely enough" would invite misreading:

To really hate the old ruling class we would have to live under it in its days of decay. – John K. Fairbank, *New Republic*

The major mission of Apollo 10 was to precisely locate enough lunar landmarks to prevent the crewmen of Apollo 11 from dropping onto terrain for which they would be unprepared. – John Lear, *Saturday Review*

When the prejudice against the split infinitive makes a writer bend over backwards to avoid it, his meaning is often unclear:

She had demonstrated her inability to rear properly numerous other children.

Myrdal replies that it should be the proper function of planning constantly to strengthen nongovernmental structures.

In the first sentence the adverb "properly" can be read as if it modifies "numerous"; in the second, "constantly" might modify "planning." Both sentences can be improved by splitting the infinitives.

References: Bryant, pp. 194–97; Follett, p. 313; Fowler, pp. 579–82; Fries, pp. 132, 144–45; Pooley, pp. 96–101; Quirk et al., p. 725; Roberts, pp. 204–206.

Spoken and written English

Though talking and writing are related, overlapping skills, they differ in several respects. Speech is peppered with expressions that seldom appear in writing other than recorded dialog: "OK," "y'know," "y'see," "Right?" and all the grunts and murmurs that ask for and provide feedback in conversation. When we talk, we pay less attention to the shape of our sentences than when we write. We are more casual about pronoun reference and agreement; we let *and* do most of the work of joining statements; we rarely make the effort to build phrases and clauses in parallel series; and we scarcely ever use the nonrestrictive clause. (We might write, "Picasso, who was born in Spain, never lost his fondness for Barcelona"; but we would probably say, "Picasso was born in Spain, and he always loved Barcelona.")

The number of significant differentiations in sound that all of us use is much larger than the number of symbols in our writing system. In talk, words are always part of a pattern involving pitch and stress, for which the marks of punctuation provide only the barest hints. Writing therefore blurs or overlooks a great many speech signals—including the stance, the gesture, even the slight rise of an eyebrow that may reinforce or modify the messages sent by speech. Whether "more" modifies "competent" or "competent men" in "more competent men" would be shown in speech by stress (heavier stress on the "more" that modifies "competent men"). To make the distinction in writing, rewording might be necessary: more men who are competent, more truly competent men.

But if we can communicate some things more directly in talk than in writing, the reverse is also true. Punctuation indicates quotations efficiently, including quotations within quotations. Spelling distinguishes some homophones that would be ambiguous in speech: We'll halve it; We'll have it. Because writing can be reread, it's a surer means of communicating difficult material—detailed, complicated instructions, for instance. And because writing can be repeatedly revised, it can be more precise, better organized, more economical than talk.

Though language originated as speech and though writing came very late in its history (only some six thousand years ago), it is legitimate to speak of the written language (or at least of the writing styles of a language) as an entity in itself. Most prose literature was written to be communicated through the eye, not the ear; and though reading aloud often increases its effectiveness, the survival of literature depends mainly on its capacity for communicating without the direct use of sound.

Yet in spite of their differences, written English and spoken English have a close relationship. When we say someone "talks like a book," we mean that his talk is uncomfortably elaborate or stiff; it is more often a compliment to say that he "writes the way he talks." For most purposes we value writing that has the colloquial flavor of good talk. But having the flavor of talk and being just like talk—even good talk—are by no means the same. Even informal written English, the written English that comes closest to casual speech, has to be far more coherent, far more selective, far less casual than casual speech if it is to be read with ease and comprehension.

See Colloquial English.

spoonful, spoonfuls

Spoonfuls is the plural of *spoonful*. See *-ful, full.*

Squinting modifier

A squinting modifier looks in two directions: it may refer to the word or phrase that precedes it or to the word or phrase that follows it. See Ambiguity 2a, Split infinitive.

Standard English

Standard American English is the social dialect used by the middle class. Because the educated members of that class use it, they approve it; and because they are the dominant class in the United States, what they approve is standard. Both spoken standard English and written standard English can be divided into formal, general, and informal, as in this book, or into different and more numerous categories. But when used appropriately, all the locutions called standard are supposed to be acceptable to all educated users of the language. In fact, there is disagreement, in dictionaries, English texts, and books on language etiquette, about a good many usages. Nevertheless, there is agreement about the great majority of them, and it is the chief purpose of this book to call attention to the areas of agreement and to encourage the intelligent use of standard English. See *Writer's Guide,* pp. 290–96; Nonstandard English; Usage.

state

When you mean no more than *said*, don't use *stated*. See *say.*

strata

In formal usage *stratum* is singular and *strata* plural. In general English *strata* is sometimes construed as a singular, but readers who know Latin condemn that usage. Reference: Copperud, p. 251.

Style

Style is choice. Style consists of the choices a writer makes — choice of words, choice of sentence patterns, even choice among optional ways of punctuating. If there were not many different ways of expressing ideas, there would be no such thing as style.

Style is character. Or, as the famous aphorism has it, "Style is the man." How a writer attacks a problem, how he arranges his material, the manner in which he makes his assertions, the "voice" he speaks in — all these reveal something about that writer's personality, his values, his *life* style.

There need be no contradiction between these two views of style if we think of style as the sum of choices, *conscious or unconscious,* that a writer makes among the options offered by the language. Such matters as basic word order in sentences and the ways of forming plurals and indicating verb tenses are part of the structure of English and therefore not stylistic. But other matters — the ways sentences are linked, their relative length and complexity, the placing of those elements that are movable, the connotations and figurative values of the words used — give a passage the distinctive features that we call style. Some of these features are the result of unconscious choice, reflecting linguistic habits and ways of thought that the writer is not aware of; some of them are the product of deliberate calculation. To the extent that style is the result of such conscious choice, it can be improved.

A style is good or bad, effective or ineffective, insofar as it achieves or fails to achieve the writer's purpose, wins or fails to win the response he wants from his readers. One of the best ways of improving your style is to analyze the prose of writers you admire, trying to determine how, in their choosing of words and shaping of sentences, they have won your response. The more you know about the choices the language affords, the more likely you are to write with clarity, force, and grace, qualities that are the foundation of all good styles. And through constant experimenting and rewriting, you will, if you have something you want to say, find your own style, your own voice.

Because syntax, usage, rhetoric, and style are all interrelated, the great majority of the articles in this *Index* have a bearing on style.

Subjective case

A noun or pronoun that is the subject of a verb or the complement of a linking verb is in the subjective, or nominative, case.

Subjects

1. Definition. The subject of a sentence can be defined in at least four ways:

a. The subject performs an action or is in a particular state of being. But this does not explain such sentences as "These socks wear out too quickly" or "He received the condemnation of millions." Neither *socks* nor *he* is the performer of any action. On the contrary, both are the objects of an action.

b. The subject is the person, place, or thing that a sentence is about. But this does not explain "I just heard that a car hit the mayor." The sentence is, quite clearly, not "about" the speaker or a car. It is about the mayor.

Both these definitions could be correct for some sentences: The mayor defeated his opponents in three elections. This is "about" the mayor, the performer of the action—*defeated*.

c. The subject is the word, phrase, or clause that usually stands before the verb and determines whether the verb will be singular or plural. Where the first two definitions are based on meaning, this one is based on formal criteria—on position in the sentence or on the relationship between inflections for number in the subject and the verb: The woman is here; The women are here. When a sentence is transformed into an expletive *there* sentence, the subject is the noun following the *be* verb that the number of the verb agrees with: There *is a woman* outside; There *are women* outside.

d. In one form of a transformational grammar, the subject in the deep structure is the first noun phrase before the verb. This deep-structure subject does not always occur as the surface-structure subject:

Deep-structure pattern	*Surface-structure pattern*
Someone witnessed the accident	*The accident* was witnessed.
Bees swarm in the garden	*The garden* swarms with bees.
Someone wears out socks fast	*Socks* wear out fast.
Someone opened the door with a key	*The key* opened the door.

In each case the deep-structure subject has been replaced by another noun phrase that becomes the surface-structure subject. See Deep structure.

The difference between definitions *c* and *d* is now clear: *c* is a surface-structure definition; *d* is a deep-structure definition. And the similarity between *a* and *d* should also be clear. The semantic definition of a subject in *a* seems to correspond to the semantic function of the first noun phrase in the deep structure. It is usually an agent of some kind, an actor, a performer of an action. But in the examples a transformation has changed a deep structure into a surface structure in which the subject is not the actor. Very often, of course, the deep-structure subject and the surface-structure subject are the same: The boy saw the man.

Thus in defining elements in a sentence, it is important to know what grammatical theory we are working with. Different theories will define elements in different ways.

2. Subjects and style. Despite the qualification in definition *b*, the surface-structure subject is very important because the subject is often the *topic* of a paragraph. Continuing the same grammatical subject from sentence to sentence, with variation provided by synonyms and pronouns, helps keep the focus of a paragraph clear. Further, in direct, vigorous writing, the subject and verb usually express the central action in a sentence. See Nominalization, Passive voice.

See Agreement 1, Comma 8, Compound subject. For subjects of gerunds and infinitives, see Gerunds 2, Infinitives 3.

Subjunctive mood

Traditionally, English grammar recognizes three verbal moods: indicative, imperative, and subjunctive. Subjunctive forms were common in the past in nonfactual and indirect expressions, such as wishes, beliefs, contrary-to-fact conditions, and hypothetical statements, in order to contrast them with statements of known fact: Long *live* the queen (vs. the queen *lives* long); *Were* I you (vs. I *am* you); They insisted he *be* there (vs. He *is* there). Such examples are the remnants of a system of verb inflection that has been mostly replaced by special words, such as *would* or *if* followed by an ordinary verb, and by special uses of certain verbs, such as *were* with *I, he, she, it,* or a noun (*Were* John here, he *would* be pleased).

In modern English very few forms can be surely identified as subjunctives, and the use of those few is so inconsistent that definite syntactical criteria are hard to state. Generally, the subjunctive is optional, a means of setting one's language, consciously or unconsciously, a little apart from everyday usage. It is not always a trait of formal style, though there are formal contexts, such as resolutions, that use the subjunctive regularly.

1. Form of subjunctives.
a. Simple subjunctive. The identifiable forms of the subjunctive are *be* throughout the present tense of that verb, *were* in its past-tense singular, and *s*-less forms of the third-person singular of the present tense of other verbs that normally have an -*s*. Some past-tense forms with present or future reference are also subjunctives.
b. Auxiliaries as subjunctives. Some grammarians include as subjunctives all the locutions that can be used in expressing ideas that may also be expressed by the subjunctive and the forms that could be used in translating into English the subjunctives found in other languages. Under this system several auxiliaries—*may, might, should, would, let, have to,* and others—become subjunctives (or subjunctive markers). Because this broad interpretation makes consideration of the subjunctive unduly complicated, only the simple subjunctive is considered here.

2. Uses of the subjunctive.
a. Formulas. The subjunctive is found in numerous formulas, survivals from a time when the subjunctive was used freely.

Today we do not make other sentences on the pattern of "Far be it from me."

Suffice it to say	Heaven forbid	As it were
Long live the king	God bless you	Be that as it may

Some of these formulas are used in all levels of the language; some, like "Come what may," are rather formal.

b. *That* clauses. The subjunctive is relatively frequent in demands, resolutions, recommendations, and the like, usually in formal contexts. Ordinarily, alternative expressions without the subjunctive are available.

Formal: I ask that the interested citizen *watch* closely the movement of these troops.
General: I ask the interested citizen to watch the movement of these troops closely.

Formal: Who gave the order that he *be dropped?*
General: . . . the order to drop him?

Formal: It is necessary that every member *inform* himself of these rules.
General: . . . that every member should inform himself. . . . *Or* . . . for every member to inform himself. . . . *Or* Every member must [should] inform himself. . . .

c. Conditions. The subjunctive may be used in *if* clauses when the fulfillment of the condition is doubtful or impossible: "If one good were really as good as another, no good would be any good" (Irwin Edman, *Four Ways of Philosophy*). The subjunctive *were* is not necessary to convey the meaning, which the past indicative *was* would convey just as well by its contrast between past form and present or future sense.

A large proportion of the conditions with the subjunctive are real or open conditions, not contrary to fact:

We set up standards and then proceed to measure each judge against these standards whether he be a sixteenth or nineteenth or twentieth century judge. — Louis L. Jaffe, *Harvard Law Review*

Stunkard recorded each subject's stomach contractions for four hours, and at 15-minute intervals asked him if he were hungry. — Stanley Schachter, *Psychology Today*

In such conditions a choice is open between the subjunctive and another verb form. There is no special virtue in using the subjunctive, and it should be rejected when it gets in the way of natural, idiomatic expression. See Conditional clauses.

References: Copperud, pp. 252–53; Fowler, pp. 595–98; Fries, pp. 103–107; Jespersen, Ch. 27; Pooley, pp. 53–56; William M. Ryan, *AS*, Feb. 1961, pp. 48–53, and May 1962, pp. 114–22; Richard L. Tobin, *Saturday Review*, Aug. 8, 1970, pp. 45–46.

Subordinate clauses

A dependent, or subordinate, clause (when day is done) has a subject and verb but cannot stand as a sentence. See Clauses, Comma 2.

Subordinating conjunctions

The most common subordinating conjunctions—words that relate dependent clauses to independent clauses—are these:

after	before	since	until
although	how	so that	when (whenever)
as	if	that	where (wherever)
as . . . as	in order that	though	whether
as if, as though	once	till	while
because	provided	unless	why

The relative pronouns (*who, which, that, what*) also function
as subordinating conjunctions. See also *for*.

sub Subordination

Correct the faulty subordination.

Faulty subordination relates to the handling of dependent
clauses—clauses introduced by subordinating conjunctions or
by relatives and used in the grammatical functions of nouns,
adjectives, and adverbs. Three types of faulty subordination are
commonly distinguished:

1. Tandem or excessive subordination occurs when you write a
succession of dependent clauses, each modifying an element in
the clause before it. The weakness is in style, not grammar:

Tandem: For his teachers, he had carefully selected those who taught
classes that had a slant that was specifically directed toward students
who intended to go into business.

Revised: . . . those who slanted their courses toward students intending
to go into business [*or* toward future businessmen].

2. Thwarted subordination occurs when you add *and* or *but* to a
dependent clause that is already connected to the independent
clause by its subordinating conjunction or relative pronoun. It is
a grammatical lapse, most commonly found in the form of *and
which* and *but which* (see *which* 4).

Thwarted: In the first semester of the course we used three textbooks,
and which were continued for the second semester.

Revised: . . . three textbooks, which were continued for the second semester.

Compare the appropriate use of a coordinating conjunction to
join two dependent clauses that are parallel: Tolerance is a virtue [which] all of us praise but [which] few of us practice.

3. Upside-down or inverted subordination occurs when you fail to
use subordination in such a way as to make the relationship
between statements sensible and logical. Since it is not a blunder in grammar or in style, it is harder to discuss in isolated sentences, for often only the context determines whether subordination is upside-down. In one writing situation, "Pearl Harbor was
attacked when Roosevelt was President" would be satisfactory;
in another, "When Pearl Harbor was attacked, Roosevelt was

President" might be much better. Without a context, we can't be sure which statement should be put in the independent clause and which in the dependent clause. But the nature of the statements may make the choice relatively easy. In most contexts this sentence would sound odd: When I was recovering from the accident, fighting broke out in the Middle East. Some such statement as this would be more likely to make sense: I was recovering from the accident during the week when reports of fighting in the Middle East filled the news. Ordinarily, upside-down subordination is corrected by turning the dependent clause into an independent clause and vice versa. Often, as in the example just given, some rewriting is advisable.

See Coordination.

Substantive

Substantive refers to nominals—nouns and pronouns and other words or groups of words used in the functions of nouns.

such

As an intensifier, *such* is somewhat informal (it was such a hot day; I have never seen such energetic people). In formal and most general writing, the construction would usually be completed by a *that* or an *as* clause (It was such a hot day that the tar melted; I have never seen such energetic people as I saw in Ballydavid), or the basis of the comparison would be indicated elsewhere in the passage:

In spite of high winds and raging seas, they were out in their boats before dawn. I have never seen such energetic people.

As a pronoun, *such* is used to refer to the idea of the preceding sentence or clause, particularly in formal styles.

When the Illyrians did achieve victory on the frontier, an invasion followed. Such was the situation in 359 b.c. — Harry J. Dell, *Classical Philology*

This or *that* commonly serves the purpose in general writing.

Formal usage often has *such as* to introduce examples, where general would have *like*. *Such as* is preferable when the example is only loosely or nonrestrictively connected to the preceding noun: "A number of big processors, such as Campbell and Heinz, still make their own cans" (*Fortune*).

When *such* is used to modify a singular, countable noun, an indefinite article precedes the noun: Such a man is needed. But in the negative the article should be omitted: No such man is needed.

Such is used with *that* to introduce result clauses: There was such a crowd that [*not* so that] we couldn't even get to the door. When *such* comes immediately before the *that*, the form is distinctly formal: . . . a crowd such that we couldn't. . . .

Reference: Bryant, pp. 199–201; Copperud, p. 253; Pooley, pp. 92–94.

Suffix

An element that can be placed after a word or root to make a new word of different meaning or function is called a suffix: *-ize* (*criticize*), *-ish* (*foolish*), *-ful* (*playful*), *-th* (*warmth*). See Origin of words 3a.

Superlative degree

Hottest, most pleasant, quickest, and *most surely* are examples of adjectives and adverbs in the superlative degree. See Comparison of adjectives and adverbs 3.

sure

Sure in standard written English is primarily an adjective (sure footing; as sure as fate; Are you sure?). As an adverb meaning "certainly," *sure* is informal to general, while *surely* is general to formal:

It's a novel interpretation, but it sure saves oranges. – Horace Sutton, *Saturday Review*

The Art Commission said it surely did want to honor this splendid son of Italy. – Donovan Bess, *Harper's*

The idiom *sure* (never *surely*) *enough* is in general use: "And sure enough, in all the fearful discussions about computers, the question that inevitably comes up . . ." (Robert Langbaum, *Yale Review*).

Surface structure

According to transformational theory, the surface structure of a sentence – the sentence as it is spoken or written – is arrived at through a series of transformations from the deep structure. See Deep structure.

Syllabication

When you're not sure where to break a word at the end of a line, consult a dictionary. For general rules, see Division of words.

Syllogisms

A syllogism represents deductive reasoning reduced to a pattern consisting of a major premise, a minor premise, and a conclusion. If the rules of inference are observed, the reasoning will be valid. Good arguments must satisfy another condition as well: the premises must be true. The rules of inference are concerned only with validity.

1. Common patterns for syllogisms.
a. Hypothetical syllogisms:

Major premise:	If P, then Q	*or*	If P, then Q
Minor premise:	P		Not Q
Conclusion:	Therefore Q		Therefore not P

Arguments that follow this pattern will not be valid if the minor premise is "Not P" and the conclusion is "Therefore not Q," or if the minor premise is "Q" and the conclusion is "Therefore not P." The major premise gives no grounds for either of these inferences.

b. *Either-or* syllogisms:

	Disjunctive	*Alternative*
Major premise:	Either A or B but not both	Either A or B
Minor premise:	A	Not A
Conclusion:	Therefore not B	Therefore B

Arguments that follow the pattern of the alternative syllogism will not be valid if the minor premise is positive – that is, "A" or "B." The major premise does not exclude the possibility of both A and B; it simply requires one of the two.

c. Categorical syllogisms:

Major premise:	All M are P
Minor premise:	S is an M
Conclusion:	Therefore S is a P

Arguments that follow this pattern will be invalid if they introduce a fourth term (in addition to M, P, and S); if they shift the meaning of a term; if the middle term (M) is not distributed (that is, if one or more of the premises in which it appears fails to affirm or deny something about the whole class the term stands for); or if a term that has not been distributed in a premise is distributed in a conclusion.

2. Testing arguments. Although a syllogism or, more likely, a series of interlocking syllogisms is the underpinning of most solid arguments, writers normally don't construct arguments by first formulating a syllogism and then searching for evidence to support the premises. Nor does a writer set forth his ideas in statements that fall naturally into the pattern of syllogisms. Nevertheless, an elementary acquaintance with the rules of inference can help a writer in two ways.

First, it can make him aware of the premises that underlie his argument. "It's not a poem; it doesn't rhyme." The first clause is the conclusion and the second clause the minor premise of an incomplete syllogism that has as its major premise a proposition something like "If the lines of the passage do not rhyme, the passage is not a poem" or, to put it another way, "All poems rhyme." That unspoken assertion is too controversial to be allowed to go unsupported. If the writer intends to base an argument on it, he had better argue for it.

Acquaintance with the rules of inference can also help a writer check the validity of his line of reasoning.

Why do colleges waste time teaching students material they can understand or skills they can learn on their own? Instead of giving courses in science fiction, they should teach double-entry bookkeeping. *That's* a skill students can't pick up on their own.

This bit of reasoning might be spelled out as three syllogisms, each of which invites the reader to raise questions about the validity of the reasoning as well as about the truth of the premises. To take just one of the syllogisms:

> If students can learn a skill on their own, a college shouldn't teach it. (If P, then Q)
> Students cannot learn double-entry bookkeeping on their own. (Not P)
> Therefore, colleges should teach double-entry bookkeeping. (Not Q)

Quite aside from questions of truth, the reasoning is invalid. The major premise has not asserted that a college should teach *all* the skills a student can't learn on his own.

See Deduction, Fallacies, Logical thinking.

Synecdoche

Synecdoche is a figure of speech in which the whole stands for the part (a nation adopts a policy) or a part stands for the whole (a baseball player's bat wins a game). See Figurative language.

Synonyms

Broadly, synonyms are words that mean the same thing. More strictly, they are words that share at least one cognitive meaning. Very few words are completely interchangeable, since no two are likely to share all their meanings and to have the same connotations. At the very least, they will differ in sound and therefore in stylistic value.

Choosing among synonyms requires consideration of both sense and sound. The chosen word must be exact in meaning and in suggestions, and it must fit the sound pattern. Relying on books of synonyms to improve vocabulary often results in a stilted, pretentious style.

See Connotation. Reference: Bolinger, pp. 211–15.

Syntax

Though the meaning of the term varies from one theory of grammar to another, *syntax* refers in general to the order and relations of the elements of sentences. That the subject of a sentence, for example, ordinarily comes before the predicate is a feature of English syntax.

T

Tandem subordination

Tying a succession of dependent clauses together is called tandem subordination. See Subordination 1.

teach, learn

A teaches *B*, who is taught by *A*. *B* learns from *A*. See *learn, teach*.

Technical writing

Good expository writing conveys information accurately, clearly, and concisely. When such writing is about specialized subject matter – in engineering, for example, or physics or chemistry – it is called technical writing. More particularly, technical writing appears in the reports, articles, and manuals produced by professionals in science and technology.

Whatever the subject matter or the nature of the communication, the first obligation of the technical writer is to present his information so clearly that it can't be misunderstood by his audience. In addition to presenting information, he must often analyze data, weigh alternative solutions to problems, make predictions, argue for a course of action. Always he needs to take into account what his readers already know and what they want to find out.

1. The technical writer and his audience. The technical writer is the expert on his subject. Nobody knows as much about his project as he does. When addressing his peers (professional associates at a convention, for instance), he will naturally use the specialized terms of his profession. When writing reports for his superiors or giving directions to subordinates, however, he has to gauge their probable familiarity with a vocabulary that is second nature to him. (The president of a potash firm may well have been chosen for his managerial ability rather than his knowledge of potash. In reporting to him, the technical writer may have to work as hard at translating shoptalk as he would if he were addressing a general reader.) Even graduate students in Aerospace Engineering might have trouble understanding this announcement of a lecture by an expert in the field:

He will talk about flow visualization experiments of a turbulent water jet in a confined tank modeled to simulate certain flow conditions expected in the Anechoic Chamber/Jet Noise Facility.

Although the gap between general English and technical vocabularies is often large, what blights technical writing for both layman and professional may not be so much vocabulary as the tangled syntax that results when a writer relies heavily on nominalization, passive verbs, and strings of prepositional phrases (four in the sentence quoted above). Some industrial firms and professional societies have recognized the problem. The American Chemical Society, for one, gives short courses in communication skills for chemists and chemical engineers. Notes on a recent course stressed the need for directness, simplicity, and brevity and recommended the use of the active voice and, on occasion, the first-person pronoun.

2. Technical reports. The merit of any technical report lies in its efficiency in communicating its content to its intended audience. Its format should therefore be carefully planned.

Technical reports differ visually from other expository writing. They are divided into sections, which are often numbered. They have no long stretches of consecutive writing. They use subheads, tables, charts, diagrams. Many, though not all, present at the beginning a summary (or abstract) of the findings, results, or recommendations. In this format, everything vital is in the summary. No crucial new information is introduced as the report proceeds through its next three or four or dozen sections. Subsequent headings depend on the nature of the report; the order in which they appear depends on the nature of the audience. One general, adaptable format follows:

I.   Summary—important results, conclusions, recommendations

II. Introduction—background, purpose, problem being addressed, scope

III. Review of previous work—if short, a part of the Introduction

IV. Description of present study—details of apparatus used, if the investigation is experimental; derivation of equations; procedures followed

V.   Presentation (in table or graph form) and discussion of results—comment on salient features of the data

VI. Conclusions and recommendations—interpretation of results; inferences; recommendation of a solution, action, or future investigation

VII. Appendices—supporting data, usually highly specialized

The technical writer who is preparing his report for several different audiences will choose a format that permits him to move from the simple to the complex in content and in vocabulary. He will begin with a summary phrased in nontechnical language and will keep his introduction as uncomplicated as possible. He will then proceed directly to conclusions and recommendations, again presenting them so that the least informed of his readers can follow them. The experimental section, the discussion of results, and subsequent sections will be increasingly technical, and the final sections will supply data likely to be understood only by specialists. The advantage of this format, with its progression from simple to complex, is that each reader can continue until he has satisfied his interest or reached the limit of his understanding. Even the reader who is ignorant of the technicalities of procedures, operations, or calculations will have a grasp of the general purpose, scope, and results of the study.

See Abstract language, Nominalization, Passive voice, Phrases 2, Shoptalk.

tense Tense

Make the tense of the verb conventional in form, or make it consistent with, or in logical sequence with, other verbs in the passage.

1. Use the standard form. In general English, avoid nonstandard forms like *drawed* and *had went* (which signals past time twice) and dialectal forms like *drug* (for *dragged*), *throwed,* and such double auxiliaries as *might could* and *used to could.* See Principal parts of verbs.

2. Make the tense consistent with others that refer to the same time. Consistency does not mean that you must use the same tense for verbs throughout a sentence or a paragraph or an essay. Choose the verb form or verbal phrase that expresses the distinction of time that you intend. In a single sentence you may have occasion to refer to past, present, and future time: When I *was* ten, I *planned to be* a veterinary surgeon; but now I *know* that I *will spend* my working life as an accountant. Through skillful use of verbs you can interweave particular events with habitual action:

Summers we generally *follow* a simple routine. Every day we *travel* the fifteen miles to our lakeside cabin. We *start off* at dawn, Mother driving and the kids rubbing sleep from their eyes, and we seldom *get* home before dark. Once there, we *fall* into bed, tired from a day outdoors. One night last July our simple routine *was wrecked.* Just before we *turned* into the driveway, we *saw* that the lights *were* on all over the house. Since we *knew* we *had left* the lights off and the doors locked, we *were* puzzled and a little frightened. My brother *offered* to reconnoiter. When he *came* back to the car, he *said* he *had seen* . . .

But though it's natural and easy to shift tense, don't make a shift unless it serves a purpose—normally, to mark a change in time. Careless shifts like the following are distracting:

The observers unobtrusively *slipped* in the back door while the children *were* still getting settled at their desks. The class *begins* with the teacher reading a short passage from *Christopher Columbus, Mariner,* at the end of which she *asked* for comments.

To keep the tenses consistent, *begins* should be *began.* Or, if there were a reason for doing so, all the verbs might be put in the historical present: *slips, are, begins, asks.* See Tenses of verbs 3a.

3. Observe the conventional sequence of tenses. In certain contexts, considerations of actual time are subordinated to the conventions of tense sequence, a pattern of adjustment between verbals and verbal phrases.
a. Between independent and dependent clauses. A dependent clause that is the object of a verb in the past tense is usually put in the past tense even though it refers to an existing state of affairs:

What did you say your name *was?*
They didn't tell me you *were looking* for an apartment.

But when the dependent clause describes a timeless state of affairs, the present tense is often used: He told me that I always *remind* him of my father. And when the point of the sentence is the current existence of the state of affairs reported in the dependent clause, the present tense is common:

Simply observing the people and comparing them with those I had seen three decades ago, I was convinced that they are a lot better off materially than their predecessors.—Robert Shaplen, *New Yorker*

b. From direct discourse to indirect discourse. When a dependent clause reports something said, its verb is ordinarily shifted from present to past (He said, "I *am* leaving" *becomes* He said he *was* leaving) or from past to past perfect (He said, "I *did* it" *becomes* He said he *had done* it). But this formal sequence can sometimes be misleading. To report the statement "I am optimistic about the outcome of the election" as "He said that he was optimistic . . ." invites doubt as to whether the optimism persists. "He said that he is optimistic about the outcome of the election" removes that doubt.

c. With infinitives and participles. Infinitives and participles express time in relation to the time of the main verb. Use the present infinitive to indicate time that is the same as that of the main verb or later than that of the main verb:

I plan *to go* to Washington, and I expect *to see* him there.
I planned *to go* last week and expected *to see* him today.
I would have liked *to see* him on his last trip.

Use the perfect infinitive for action prior to that of the main verb:

I would like *to have seen* him on his last trip.

Use the perfect form of the participle to express time that is prior to that of the main verb, the present form to express time that is the same as that of the main verb:

Having driven safely through the worst blizzard in local history, he slid off the edge of his own driveway and, *jamming on* the brakes too fast, overturned the car.

See Tenses of verbs.

Tenses of verbs

1. Time and tense. Time has three divisions: present, past, future. One of the ways we indicate which of these divisions we are referring to is by changing the form of the verb or by adding a modal auxiliary: He runs (present time); he ran (past time); he will run (future time).

It is a mistake to assume that the time indicated is the name of the tense. When we say, "He leaves for New York tomorrow," we are talking about future time, but the inflection *-s* on *leaves* shows we are using present *tense*. When we say "He has left," we are talking about the past, but the inflection *-s* on *has* shows we are again using present *tense*.

It is also a mistake to assume that the only function of tense is to show time. Sometimes *could* is the past tense of *can* (He could swim better last year than he can now), but in other uses the difference between *can* and *could* has nothing to do with time (Can you please come right away; Could you please come right away).

In English, then, there is no simple correspondence between tense and time. The term *tense* refers to inflection, or change in form. English verbs have only two tenses: present (he leaves) and past (he left). There is no single-word verb, no inflection, that applies solely to the future. Nevertheless, we find various ways of referring to future time. We use the present tense accompanied by an adverb (He leaves tomorrow) or an auxiliary before the uninflected verb (He will leave tomorrow). Or we say, "He will be leaving" or "He is going to leave" or "By this time tomorrow he will have left." Some grammarians call *will leave, will be leaving,* and so on, the future tense; others do not.

2. Tense and auxiliaries. If we use no auxiliaries, the only tenses we can form are present and past (or past and nonpast, as some linguists prefer to call them). But because through using auxiliaries we can refer to times in the future as well as the past extending into the present, the past not extending into the present, the past of a certain time already past, some grammarians speak of six tenses, which roughly translate the six of Latin:

Present:	He eats	*Present perfect:*	He has eaten
Past:	He ate	*Past perfect:*	He had eaten
Future:	He will eat	*Future perfect:*	He will have eaten

Still more tenses emerge if we consider the uses of *do* (emphatic: *does eat, did eat*) and *be* (progressive: *is eating, was eating*). If the past of *shall* and *will* is also taken into account, we can speak of a past future *(would eat)* and even a past future perfect *(would have eaten).*

The emphatic tenses—those with the auxiliary *do*—may be analyzed as transformations. *Do* is added to a verb to produce the emphatic transformation, as well as negatives and questions, only when no other auxiliary is present. "He has eaten" can be made emphatic by putting primary stress on the auxiliary: He *has* eaten. To make "He ate" emphatic requires the addition of *do* to carry the stress: He *did* eat. (The past-tense marker has been shifted from *eat* to the first element in the verb phrase.) Likewise, "He ate" can be transformed into a question or the negative only with the addition of *do* (Did he eat? He did not eat.) See Auxiliaries.

3. Special uses of simple present and past.
a. In addition to its basic function of referring to something going on now, the present tense is used to refer to a state of affairs that is generally true, without reference to time (Oil *floats* on water); to habitual action that continues into the present (He *writes* in his journal every day); and, when accompanied by an adverbial, to a time in the future (She *goes* to college in the fall). Other special uses of the present tense are illustrated in

I *hear* you are going to Europe.
He'll come if you *ask* him.
Thoreau *urges* us to do without luxuries.
Skirts *go* up and down with the economy: in the prosperous Twenties *they're* short; in the Depression Thirties *they're* long.

The third example is sometimes known as the *literary present* (Thoreau died in 1862), the fourth as the *historical present.*

b. The simple past tense is normally used to refer to something that took place in the past, either a single occurrence (He *broke* his leg) or a repeated occurrence (He *skied* at Vail every Christmas). But in certain contexts the past tense does not refer to past time. It is regularly used in a dependent clause that is object of the verb in the independent clause when the main verb is in the past (I *heard* that you *were* in town). It is used in the *if* clause that refers to a hypothetical situation (If you *knew* him, you wouldn't be surprised). It is the polite alternative in questions or requests (*Would* you send me the catalog).

See Auxiliaries, Tense, Verbs. References: Jespersen, Chs. 23–26; Joos, Ch. 5; Geoffrey N. Leech, *Meaning and the English Verb* (London: Longman, 1971); Long, Ch. 7; Quirk et al., pp. 84–97.

than

At its simplest level, the choice of case after *than* can be illustrated by the sentences "He is taller than I" and "He is taller than me." Both are used in general writing. Conservatives favor the nominative after an intransitive or linking verb, but many writers use the objective.

When the verb before *than* takes an object, however, the nominative and objective cases after *than* may have different meanings: She likes him more than I [do]; She likes him more than [she likes] me. Hence in standard English the case of the pronoun used with *than* after a transitive verb is what would be used if the dependent clause were written out. Use of the nominative case where the objective case is called for, as in the following example, is considered hypercorrect: Though the jury said we were both guilty, the judge gave my partner a lighter sentence than [he gave] I.

For *different than,* see *different.* References: Copperud, pp. 256–57: Jespersen, pp. 132–33; Pooley, pp. 163–67.

that

1. *That* or *which*. Writers are often urged to use *that* to introduce restrictive clauses and *which* to introduce nonrestrictive clauses; and the advice has value for those who use *which* everywhere, in the belief that it is more elegant than *that.* In general practice, however, the choice between *which* and *that* in restrictive clauses is more likely to depend on rhythm, sound, emphasis, and personal taste than on any rule. If *that* has already been used in the sentence, writers may shift to *which* to avoid repetition. On the other hand, when the restrictive clause is compound, *which* may be chosen as a clearer signal to the reader that the construction is being repeated: "He had an exploratory operation for cancer which the doctors were reluctant to undertake but which he was convinced he needed" (David Halberstam, *Atlantic*). *Which* normally introduces nonrestrictive clauses in all varieties of usage.

2. Redundant *that*. When *that* introduces a noun clause in which a modifying phrase precedes the subject, *that* should not be repeated after the modifier: "It must seem to many outsiders that if there was room for honest argument [that] a reasonable doubt had to exist, but the America's Cup Committee hasn't given house room to a reasonable doubt in 119 years" (Red Smith, syndicated columnist).

3. Clauses without *that*. A complex sentence like "The work [that] he does shows [that] he has talent" is perfectly correct without either *that*. The dependent clauses "he does" and "he has talent" are related to the rest of the sentence clearly enough to need no explicit signs of subordination, like *that*. No writer should handicap himself by thinking a *that* should be inserted wherever it will fit. *That*-less clauses are common:

He thinks that the Italians neither approved of Fascist terror nor were really terrorized by it. He thinks [   ] they became numb, resigned, apathetic, and cynical. — Naomi Bliven, *New Yorker*

The convention [   ] we accept unthinkingly had not as yet established itself. — William Nelson, *Journal of English Literary History*

To use *that* to stress the subordination of short clauses is often to rob them of their force: He knows [that] I'm sorry; I'm glad [that] you're here; Take anything [that] you want.

But *that* is necessary in writing when the clause comes first (That he might be hurt never occurred to us) and when a clause has no other subject (There is a moral standard that has long been accepted). When a modifier stands between two clauses, *that* is sometimes needed to show which clause is being modified: Mr. Wrenn said [   ] after the guests were gone [   ] Mrs. Wrenn should pack her bags. Depending on the intended meaning, *that* is needed either after *said* or after *gone*.

See *this*. References: Copperud, pp. 257–59; Jespersen, pp. 350–51, 360–65.

that is

That is introduces the equivalent of, or the explanation of, what it precedes. It is a rather formal connective and is best kept to introduce series or complete statements. Usually it is preceded by a semicolon and followed by a comma: The men worked continuously for three whole weeks to complete the dam on time; that is, they worked twenty-four hours a day in three shifts, seven days a week. In briefer constructions a comma or a dash would be adequate: They used the safest explosive for the purpose — that is, dynamite. Better yet, *that is* could be omitted: . . . explosive for the purpose — dynamite.

their

Their is the genitive of *they*. *Theirs* is the absolute form: This table is exactly like theirs. Except in formal usage, *their* is often used as a common-gender singular to refer to words like *somebody, anybody, everyone*:

Almost nobody has the words to really talk about their lives. —*Time*

It is necessary to make anyone on the streets think twice before attempting to vent their despair on you. — James Baldwin, *Show*

See Agreement 2.

then
Then is an adverb of time that is frequently used as a connective (conjunctive adverb): The next three hours we spent in sightseeing; then we settled down to the business of being delegates to a convention. Often *and* is used before *then,* with a consequent change in punctuation: He ate a good meal, and then he took a nap before starting home.

Adjectival *then* (the then President) is common in general writing, rare in formal. Some readers dislike the usage.

then, than
Then, the adverb of time, and *than,* the conjunction in clauses of comparison, should not be confused: *Then* the whole crowd went to Louie's; It was better as a movie *than* as a novel.

there is, there are
When *there* is used as an anticipatory subject, the verb ordinarily agrees in number with the "real" subject, which follows the verb: "There is still occasional sniping at the 'supersquad' and there are still lazy, indifferent homicide detectives" (Barbara Gelb, *New York Times Magazine*). When the subject is compound and the first element is singular, usage is divided. Some writers follow the rules of formal agreement and use a plural verb; others find a plural verb awkward before a singular noun:

There are much good history, intelligent analysis of social problems, and good writing. — David Fellman, *American Historical Review*

There is no jargon, few footnotes, some repetition, few insights and little analysis. — Lewis A. Froman, *American Political Science Review*

Like repeated use of *it is* . . . , repeated use of *there is* . . . , *there are* . . . constructions has a deadening effect on style, mainly because it robs sentences of strong subject-verb combinations. See Subjects 2. References: Bryant, pp. 13–14; Copperud, p. 260; Fries, pp. 56–57.

Thesis statement
A thesis statement is the most explicit statement the writer can make of his purpose—what he wants to assert or prove. Whether or not it appears in the essay itself, the thesis statement must be firmly fixed in the writer's mind, at least by the time he prepares his final draft. See Outline form 2, Topic sentence 3.

they
They occurs in all varieties of usage with no explicit antecedent: "One thinks of Tolstoy, and the story that all day long they had to be beating omelets for him in the kitchen" (Louis Kronenberger,

New York Times Book Review). The indefinite reference is troublesome, however, when the pronoun clashes with the suggestion of particular individuals (Around campus they were saying that they had a plan to boycott classes); and often impersonal *there* is preferable: There have been [*instead of* They have had] no serious accidents at that crossing in years.

They, and especially *their*, is frequently used to refer to *everyone* and similar words that are treated as singular in formal English. See Agreement 2, *he or she*. Reference: Bryant, pp. 211 – 12.

thing

Thing often encourages the accumulation of deadwood in writing: [The] first [thing] you [do is to] get a few twigs burning.

this

Though often criticized as a sign of lazy writing, *this*, like *that*, is regularly used to refer to the idea of a preceding clause or sentence: He had always had his own way at home, and this made him a poor roommate. Confusion is caused not when *this* clearly refers to the idea of a clause or sentence but when it refers to only some part of the idea or to an antecedent that is not actually expressed. See Reference of pronouns 2. References: Bryant, pp. 172– 74; Copperud, p. 261; Long, pp. 290–93.

though

After a period of literary disuse, during which it was considered colloquial, *though* in the sense "however, nevertheless, for all that" now appears in all varieties of writing: Two things are clear, though.

thus

Thus at the beginning of participial phrases has a tendency to encourage loose modifiers. In sentences like this one there is no noun or pronoun for the participle to modify: "D. Eldred Rinehart's term on the racing commission also is expiring, thus opening up the chairmanship" (*Washington Post*). See Dangling modifiers.

Thwarted subordination

Subordination is said to be thwarted when a coordinating conjunction precedes the subordinating connective: By the end of the summer he had completed three reports, [and] which were accepted for publication. See Subordination 2.

till, until

In all varieties of writing, *till* and *until* are interchangeable both as prepositions (Wait till/until tomorrow) and as conjunctions (Wait till/until they get here). As a clipped form of *until*, *'til* is sometimes found in informal contexts, but it is not recognized by most dictionaries.

Titles

1. Composing titles. Since it can help stir the reader's interest, a striking and easily remembered title is an advantage for an essay. But titles that strain for originality or impact often fail. If no good title comes to mind, simply name the subject of the essay as precisely as possible in a few words. Because the title is considered a separate part of the essay, it should not be referred to by a pronoun in the opening sentence: not "This is an important issue today" but "The parking problem is an important issue today."

2. Referring to titles.
a. Italics vs. quotation marks. For most purposes there is a simple rule of thumb: Italicize titles of long works (by underlining them) and quote titles of short works. Italics are traditional for titles of books, magazines, pamphlets, long poems, plays, movies, symphonies, and operas. Quotation marks are usual for essays, short stories, short poems, songs, television shows, chapters of books, lectures, paintings, and pieces of sculpture.
b. Capitalizing. General practice is to capitalize the first and last words of titles and all intervening nouns, pronouns, verbs, adjectives, and adverbs; some styles also capitalize prepositions and conjunctions that contain more than five letters: *Wit and Its Relation to the Unconscious; Peace through* [or *Through*] *Meditation;* "Hills like White Elephants"; "Nobody Knows You When You're Down and Out." Capitals are similarly used, without italics or quotation marks, in titles of unpublished works, book series, and books of the Bible and in the words *preface, introduction, table of contents,* and *index* when they are used for parts of a manuscript or published work.

The (or *a*) is capitalized and italicized or set within quotation marks only if it is part of the recognized title: *The Yale Law Review* but the *Harvard Law Review; The American Historical Review* but the *American Sociological Review; The New York Times* but the *Los Angeles Times.* In some styles initial *the* is never treated as part of the title of a newspaper or periodical. Within the pamphlet entitled *The MLA Style Sheet,* that publication is referred to as "the *MLA Style Sheet.*"
c. Consistency. A writer should choose an accepted style for handling titles and stick to it. For example, the name of the city in a newspaper title may be either italicized or not italicized: the *Los Angeles Times,* the Los Angeles *Times.* Similarly, while strict formality may demand that a title be given in full each time it appears, current styles permit the use of short forms and the omission of initial articles when they would cause awkwardness: Hemingway's [A] *Moveable Feast* provides background for his [*The*] *Sun Also Rises.*

Many newspapers and magazines have their own rules for handling titles. Some use quotation marks around book titles and merely capitalize the names of periodicals. For the more rigid and elaborate rules governing very formal writing, as in dissertations and scholarly articles, consult such detailed treatments as Kate L. Turabian, *Manual for Writers of Term Papers, Theses, and Dissertations,* 4th ed. (Chicago: Univ. of Chicago Press, 1973), and the *MLA Style Sheet.*

too, not too

In the sense "also," *too* is sometimes set off by commas, sometimes not. At times commas are necessary for clarity. Without them, the sentence "Bob, too, frequently interrupted rehearsals to give advice" could be taken to mean that Bob interrupted excessively often.

Though *too* is used to modify past participles after linking verbs in all varieties of usage (She was too excited; He was too concerned), conservative stylists prefer another adverb of degree between *too* and the participle (too greatly excited, too much concerned). Objection is strongest when the participle could not be placed before the noun or pronoun as a modifier: He is not too identified with the opposition; Priests are too removed from real life. In such cases, many writers would insist on intervening adverbs — "too closely identified," "too far removed" — particularly in formal contexts.

Some formal stylists would continue to criticize both examples on the grounds that the constructions are incomplete — "not too closely identified" for what? "too far removed" for what? And many would reject the "not too" phrase, a popular informal substitute for "not very" that is always rather vague and sometimes ambiguous.

Topic sentence

Normally, the topic sentence is the broadest, most general statement in a paragraph, the one that expresses most directly the idea that the paragraph as a whole conveys. The other sentences of the paragraph develop the idea, particularize it, illustrate it, or qualify it.

1. Position. The topic sentence has no fixed position in a paragraph. Most often it is the first sentence, as it is in this paragraph, or the second sentence, coming immediately after a transitional sentence. But it sometimes stands at the end of a paragraph, pulling details and observations together into an inclusive statement. And occasionally it occurs midway through a paragraph, introduced by particulars that lead up to it and followed by further particulars that support or qualify it. In textbooks and in other types of explanation and instruction where it is vital that the reader have a firm grasp of each stage of the discussion, the writer sometimes sets forth the central idea at the start of a paragraph and restates it in a somewhat different way at the end.

2. Rhetorical use. Topic sentences keep a reader fully informed of the chief points being made. Phrasing topic sentences keeps the writer on track, too, encouraging him to stick to his subject and so maintain the unity of his essay. But in some situations —

certainly in describing and narrating and also at times in arguing—he may deliberately shun the explicitness of topic sentences, feeling that his purpose is better served if he simply supplies details and impressions and leaves it to the reader to infer a conclusion or generalization. If the writer has done his work well, the reader will come to the right conclusion.

3. Topic sentence, pointer sentence, and thesis statement. If a reader asks what a paragraph adds up to, it probably needs a topic sentence. If he asks why he is suddenly in the middle of a new subject, it probably needs a pointer sentence. If he asks what the upshot of the whole paper is—what it all adds up to—the writer needs to formulate a thesis statement for himself.

A topic sentence sums up what a paragraph or sequence of paragraphs *says*. A pointer sentence tells what the paragraph or sequence of paragraphs will *do* (or, sometimes, what it has done). "There are three kinds of joggers" is a pointer, an organizational signpost indicating that each kind of jogger will now be described. "But what do we mean by *détente*?" is an implied promise to explain the term.

An expository or argumentative essay usually has several topic sentences and perhaps a pointer or two. By contrast, it has just one thesis statement, and that statement may or may not appear in the essay. Whether or not it does, it is the writer's expression of the controlling idea of his entire essay. It is his reason for writing the essay.

See Outline form 2, Paragraph indention, Thesis statement, Unity 2.

toward, towards

These words are identical in meaning, and the choice of one or the other is a matter of taste. *Toward* is more common, but both appear in all varieties of usage. References: Bryant, p. 220; Copperud, pp. 8, 264.

Transformation

In transformational grammar a transformation is a rule that changes the surface structure of a sentence while retaining the meaning of the basic deep structure (see Deep structure). Each of the following groups of sentences has the same deep structure, although the surface structures are different:

Tom gave the money to Bill.
Tom gave Bill the money.

I held the man up.
I held up the man.

I can read German and Bill can read German, too.
I can read German and Bill can, too.
Both Bill and I can read German.

The above sentences illustrate optional transformations. Many others are obligatory. In embedding a relative clause, for example, the substitution of a pronoun for a noun is required:

The man [The man lives next door] is very noisy.
The man   who   lives next door is very noisy.

In elliptical clauses of comparison, deletions are obligatory:

John is older than I am old.
John is older than I (am).

trans Transition

Make the transition between these sentences (or paragraphs) clear and smooth.

Transitions are words or phrases or sentences that show the relation between one statement and another, one paragraph and another, one part of an essay and another. When you write a sentence or paragraph as an isolated unit — as if nothing had preceded it and nothing was to follow it — your reader is bound to be puzzled. A lack of transition between one paragraph and another is sometimes a sign of faulty organization and sometimes simply evidence that you've neglected to provide a signpost that will show the reader where he's been or where he's going. A lack of transition between sentences usually indicates that you haven't thought through the relationship between consecutive statements.

1. Transitions as signals. The most familiar of the markers that indicate relationships and knit a piece of prose together are conjunctions and adverbs — *and, but, still, yet, for, because, then, though, while, in order that, first, second, however, moreover, therefore,* and so on.

Some of the choices available to indicate the common logical relationships are these:

a. Addition. When you want to call attention to the fact that you're adding something, *and* is the usual connector. Others that indicate equivalent, coordinate, or similar ideas are *also, again, once again, too, likewise, moreover, furthermore, then, in addition, by the same token, similarly, analogously.* You can indicate restatements with such phrases as *that is, to clarify, more simply* or by clauses like *what this means is.*

b. Contrast. When the relation is one of contrast, ranging from direct contradiction through various degrees of opposition, qualification, restriction, and concession, some of your choices are *but, yet, however, nevertheless, nonetheless, by contrast, at the same time, instead, in place of, conversely, actually, in fact, to be sure, at any rate, anyway, still, of course, on the other hand, provided that, in case.*

c. Alternatives. You can call attention to an alternative or option by using *or, nor, either, neither, alternatively, on the other hand* (often following *on the one hand*).

d. Causal relations. You can indicate a causal relation with *for, because, since, then, as.* You can point to result or consequence with various words and phrases, among them *so, then, therefore, thus, hence, accordingly, as a result, in consequence.*

e. Illustration. When the relation is inclusive—when what follows illustrates what has come before or particularizes it in some way—some of your choices are *for example, for instance, thus, to illustrate, in particular, namely.*

f. Sequence. When the relation is sequential, your transitions may indicate temporal or spatial relations in the subject itself, or they may point up the organization of the essay. Sample time indicators are *then, soon, after, now, earlier, later, ten years ago.* Sample space indicators are *here, there, on top, in the middle, below, on the left, on the right, beyond.* You can indicate sequence by transitions like *for one thing, for another; first, second, third; to begin with; in short, in brief; finally, to summarize, in conclusion, as we have seen.* Other transitions bring out the relative importance of points—*more important, less important, above and beyond.*

2. Transitions and style. A transition should give an accurate indication of the relationship you intend. Beyond that, the transition should be in keeping with the style and tone of your essay.

a. Accurate markers. *Actually* and *incidentally* are overworked as transitions. Since *actually* often introduces a correction and *incidentally* a digression, both may be signs that revision is needed. (But when a digression is justified, it should be clearly identified as a digression.) An unwarranted transition—for example, a *therefore* when the case has not been made—can be seriously misleading.

b. Apt markers. Though *first, second, third* are preferable to old-fashioned *firstly, secondly, thirdly,* they should be supplied only when the material demands such emphatic division. Overuse of any of the heavier connectives (*however, nevertheless, consequently*) can clog your style. Often you can make a transition that is just as clear, less obtrusive, and stylistically more pleasing by repeating a key word from sentence to sentence, by using a synonym or a pronoun to echo or pick up the key word, and by binding sentences or parts of sentences through parallel structures. Whether overt or subtle, transitions are your chief means for giving a piece of writing coherence.

References: Stanley Greenbaum, *Studies in English Adverbial Usage* (Coral Gables: Univ. of Miami Press, 1970), Ch. 3; W. Ross Winterowd, *College English,* May 1970, pp. 828–35.

Transitive and intransitive verbs

A transitive verb is one that is used with a direct object; an intransitive verb is not so used: The janitor put [transitive] the books on the shelf, but they soon vanished [intransitive]. Some verbs may be transitive in one sense and intransitive in another (He grows corn; The corn grows well), and in the course of time intransitives may become transitives (as *answer* has done) or transitives may become intransitive (some senses of *withdraw*); but at any one time in the history of English, a given verb in a given sense can be classified according to its use with an object or without. We can disappear, but not disappear something, put something somewhere, but not just put. See *lay, lie; set, sit.*

transpire

Long objected to in the sense of "happen" or "occur" because of its literal meaning in botany and its related figurative meaning "to emerge or come to light," *transpire* is regularly used to mean "happen" in general and formal writing and is understood by many people in no other sense. But this usage still has its critics. For that matter, so does the "correct" usage, to mean "become known." Reference: Copperud, p. 265.

trite Triteness

Replace the trite expression with one that is simpler and fresher.

The most troublesome trite expressions, or clichés, are worn-out figures of speech or phrases: the picture of health, the break of day, reign supreme, from the face of the earth, crack of dawn, acid test. What was once fresh and striking has become stale and hackneyed from being used again and again with no sense of its figurativeness. This passage compresses a great number of trite expressions into small space:

The Blushing Bride

I suppose it is natural that I should have been asked to step into the breach on this happy day, if only because I have had the privilege of knowing Geraldine since she was so high. . . . Onlookers see most of the game, you know, and it is easy to be wise after the event, but I thought I could see which way the wind was blowing last August.

They say marriages are made in Heaven, well, be that as it may, these two look as happy as the day is long. It was a great pleasure to me to see Hubert give away his one ewe lamb to such a regular chip off the old block as our friend here. Like father like son, they say, and I think his father deserves a pat on the back. As for Geraldine, bless her, she is a real Trojan, and has been a tower of strength to her dear mother, who doesn't look a day older than when I first set eyes on her, far longer ago than either of us cares to remember.

At moments like this, when family ties are stronger than ever, these young things should remember how much they owe to their parents.

One last word, I must not fail to remind Geraldine that the way to a man's heart is his stomach, and to warn Bertrand that the hand that rocks the cradle rules the world.

Now, I mustn't take up any more of your valuable time, I feel sure you will all join me in drinking the health of the happy couple, and wishing that all their troubles may be little ones.—Georgina Coleridge, *I Know What I Like*

One way to guard against triteness is to recognize figurative language for what it is and to avoid using it unless you mean it — that is, unless the figure conveys an intended extension or nuance of meaning. Remember, too, that triteness is not a matter of age. Yesterday's vogue expression can be as worn a cliché as one handed down for generations. So if you find yourself writing down a phrase without even stopping to think about it, stop and think about it—think twice. Trite expression is the natural vehicle for trite ideas.

But the rhetorical situation should be decisive. Depending on your purpose and your audience, the same words can be either a cliché that you should avoid or a well-established phrase that, with its connotations, expresses your meaning accurately and succinctly. Going out of your way to avoid an expression only because it has been used many times before may force you into awkwardness, incoherence, or absurdly "fine" writing.

See Figures of speech, Vogue words. References: Theodore M. Bernstein, *Miss Thistlebottom's Hobgoblins* (New York: Farrar, 1971), pp. 156–58; Copperud, pp. 48–49.

try and

Though the idiom *try and* – "Neither Congress nor the Court itself seemed prepared to try and force him to resign" *(Newsweek)* – appears regularly in general and informal contexts, formal style usually demands *try to*. References: Copperud, p. 267; Pooley, pp. 124–25.

-type

The use of *-type* in compound modifiers (Polaris-type missile, new-type car, family-type programs) has spread in all varieties of usage, but outside of technical and commercial contexts it arouses strong distaste in conservative stylists. Most writers prefer *type of* (Polaris type of missile) or, where possible, simply omit *type* (new car, family programs). The practice of shortening *type of* and *make of* to *type* (this type letter) and *make* (this make car) is informal. Reference: Copperud, p. 268.

Typewritten copy

Use only one side of the sheet, leave wide margins at both left and right, keep type clean, and change the ribbon regularly. In first drafts, using triple space and leaving extra space between paragraphs will provide room for revision. Double space the final draft.

Indent the first lines of paragraphs five spaces. Long quotations may be indicated in double-spaced copy by indenting each line as in a paragraph indention and single-spacing the quoted matter. No quotation marks are used with block quotations.

For the figure 1, use the small *l*, not capital *I*. For a dash use two hyphens. Leave a space after all other punctuation marks except at the end of sentences, where two spaces should be used.

Transposed letters should be erased and retyped or corrected with a curved line.

Strike̶o̶vers [*not* Strikeʊʊers] are often hard to read.

A few mistakes can be corrected in ink, but any page that contains several should be retyped. See Caret.

U

Underlining

Underlining in manuscripts is used to mark titles that are not quoted, words used as words, foreign expressions that have not been anglicized, and – sparingly – words or word groups that, for one reason or another, you want to emphasize. See Italics.

Understatement

Understating is one means of emphasizing: Income taxes are not universally popular. See Figurative language, Figures of speech.

uninterested

To be uninterested is to lack interest; to be disinterested is to be neutral, which is not the same thing. But see *disinterested, uninterested.*

unique

In strict formal usage *unique* means "single, sole, unequaled" and consequently is not compared. In general usage, *unique,* like so many other words that formerly had an absolute meaning, has become an adjective of degree. As an emphatic *rare* or *remarkable,* it is often found compared with *more* or *most:* "The more unique his nature, the more peculiarly his own will be the colouring of his language" (Otto Jespersen, *Mankind, Nation and Individual from a Linguistic Point of View*). Because of this varied usage, a reader may find the unqualified word ambiguous. The writer of the following sentence may have been guarding against that possibility: "It is a unique festival, and there is nothing like it in the world" (Harold C. Schonberg, *New York Times*). While redundant by formal standards, the second clause is probably practical. See Comparison of adjectives and adverbs 4. References: Copperud, p. 55; Evans and Evans, pp. 528 – 29.

United States

Like many proper nouns, *United States* is often used as an attributive: "There are some who think that the United States attempt to overthrow the Castro government was an act of international immorality" (Richard H. Rovere, *New Yorker*). No apostrophe is needed. Since *United States* has no adjectival form, the construction often sounds awkward; and in most contexts *American* – or, where confusion is possible, *of the United States* – is preferable. See *American.*

un Unity

Unify this passage.

A sentence, a paragraph, or an essay is unified when its parts fit together to make a consistent whole. The major threat to unity is material that, however interesting, stands outside — or seems to stand outside — the core of thought or feeling that the writer intends to communicate.

Your first obligation as a writer is to have a purpose in writing and a controlling idea against which you can test your sentences, your paragraphs, and your complete essay. Your second obligation is to build your sentences and paragraphs in such a way that your train of thought, and ultimately your purpose, will be clear to your audience.

Failures in unity can be real, as when a writer introduces irrelevant material, or apparent, as when a writer doesn't make plain to his audience a relationship that is perfectly plain to him. The first is a failure in thinking (see Logical thinking); the second is a failure in composition, especially in continuity (see Coherence, Transition). A sentence, a paragraph, or an essay may be coherent but not unified; it may also be unified but not coherent. Good prose is both coherent and unified.

Out of context — and here context means both the writer's thinking about his subject and his expression of his thought — it is difficult to decide whether a passage is lacking in unity or in coherence. But some hints can be given about ways of strengthening passages that have been criticized for lacking unity.

1. Unity in sentences. For a sentence that lacks unity, there are three possible remedies:

a. Delete any phrase or clause that is unrelated to the central thought. In the sentence "Parking space on the campus, which is one of the most beautiful in the state, has become completely inadequate, and recently the city council voted to increase bus fares again," delete the *which* clause.

b. Subordinate one statement to another to show the logical relationship. Even if readers of the quoted sentence can figure out a connection between the shortage of parking space and the cost of public transportation, the coordinating *and* obscures the writer's point. A possible revision: At a time when the shortage of parking space makes commuting to campus by car almost impossible, the city council has discouraged the use of public transportation by increasing bus fares once more.

c. Separate seemingly disconnected statements, making two sentences, and bring in material that will provide a logical link between them. Between a sentence about inadequate parking space and a sentence about increased bus fares, this sentence might be introduced: But the commuting student is hardly being encouraged to switch to public transportation. See Coordination, Sentences, Subordination.

2. Unity in paragraphs. As a general rule, a paragraph lacks unity when one or more of its sentences fail to contribute to the central idea of the paragraph. When that idea is expressed in a topic sentence, it is fairly easy for both writer and reader to see exactly where the discussion slides away from the main point. You would be wise to provide topic sentences when dealing with a subject so complex that a reader might need help in following your treatment of it. On the other hand, you can do without topic sentences if the logic of your thought, or the pressure of your emotion, creates a unified topic *idea* that the paragraph transmits to your audience.

Sticking to a subject does not in itself guarantee unity. In a paragraph on Robert Frost, all the sentences may be about the poet, but the paragraph is not likely to be unified if two sentences deal with his current reputation, one with his last public appearance, one with his marriage, and three with his poem "After Apple-Picking." Bringing together several loosely related ideas usually means that no one of them will be adequately developed and that the paragraph will badly lack unity. See Paragraph indention, Topic sentence.

3. Unity in essays. Even when each paragraph in an essay is satisfactorily unified, the essay as a whole may not be. Each paragraph should bear on the writer's intent in writing the essay (whether or not that purpose is expressed in a thesis statement); and the paragraphs should be in such an order and should be so linked that the reader understands the relation of each to the controlling idea.

A useful way of testing an essay for unity is to outline it. Questions of relevance and relatedness can be more easily answered when you have seen through the surface of what you have written to the underlying structure of thought.

Reduce each paragraph to a heading. If your essay is brief—four or five paragraphs, say—each heading may represent a main point; but in a longer paper the paragraphs should fall into logical groups, with each sequence developing a theme. Be on the lookout for a heading that doesn't logically follow another heading or lead into another heading. If you find one, consider dropping the paragraph it stands for. If you find a sequence of paragraphs that strays from your central thesis, rethinking and rewriting are in order. See Organization, Outline form, Thesis statement.

until, till

Until and *till* (not *'til*) are interchangeable. See *till, until.*

up

Up is a member of many typical verb-adverb combinations in general use (*give up, grow up, sit up, use up*). Because they have developed meanings that are not the sum of the meanings of their parts, they are usually entered separately in dictionaries, and they behave like independent verbs. *Up* also appears in a number of other combinations to which it contributes no new element of meaning *(divide up, fill up, raise up, join up)*. These idioms are usually avoided in formal.

Upside-down subordination
Subordination is said to be upside-down when logically the dependent clause of a sentence should be independent and the independent clause dependent. See Subordination 3.

Usage
The study of usage is based on an accumulation of specific instances and depends on wide observation of what people say and write in various situations as a basis for judging the standing of particular words, forms, and constructions. Works on usage include scholarly studies of the ways the language is used, and has been used, in speech, in print, in letters, and so on; polls to determine attitudes toward particular usages; and guides to usage based in large part on the authors' taste. Both the polls and the guides focus on disputed usages, and it is this area of usage study that has most interested the general public. J. Lesslie Hall dealt with disputed usages in his pioneering *English Usage* of 1917. Sterling A. Leonard used the polling technique to investigate cultivated usage for his *Current English Usage* of 1932. In 1938, in *Facts About Current English Usage*, Albert H. Marckwardt and Fred G. Walcott reported on the actual practice of writers in using the locutions evaluated in Leonard's poll.

As methods for systematic study of usage became established, some scholars spoke out against the classroom approach to "good English." Robert C. Pooley criticized it in *Grammar and Usage in Textbooks in English* (1933) and *Teaching English Usage* (1946). C. C. Fries' *American English Grammar* (1940) provided evidence that educated writers of standard English showed more variation in usage than had been assumed. Information on actual usage from a wide variety of scholarly sources was brought together and summarized in Margaret M. Bryant's *Current American Usage* in 1962. More evidence was provided in *Computational Analysis of Present-Day American English* (1967) by Henry Kučera and W. Nelson Francis.

These works and others built up a picture of what educated users of American English say and, more especially, write. But for many people who are interested in usage, what *is* is not nearly so important as what *should be.* Most of the popular guides to usage are conservative—that is, they prescribe usages and constructions that this *Index* associates with formal English. Roy H. Copperud's *American Usage: The Consensus* (New York: Van Nostrand, 1970) brings together recommendations (often conflicting) from six guides—Theodore M. Bernstein, *The Careful Writer* (New York: Atheneum, 1965); Roy H. Copperud, *A Dic¹ tionary of Usage and Style* (New York: Hawthorne, 1964); Bergen Evans and Cornelia Evans, *A Dictionary of Contemporary*

American Usage (New York: Random, 1957); Rudolf Flesch, *The ABC of Style* (New York: Harper, 1964); Wilson Follett, *Modern American Usage: A Guide,* ed. and completed by Jacques Barzun (New York: Hill, 1966); and H. W. Fowler, *A Dictionary of Modern English Usage,* 2nd ed., rev. by Sir Ernest Gowers (New York: Oxford Univ. Press, 1965) – as well as from Bryant's *Current American Usage* (New York: Funk, 1962), *Webster's Third New International Dictionary of the English Language* (Springfield, Mass.: Merriam, 1961), the unabridged edition of the *Random House Dictionary of the English Language* (New York: Random, 1966), and *The American Heritage Dictionary of the English Language* (Boston: American Heritage and Houghton, 1969).

The appearance of *Webster's Third,* as the edition is popularly known, offered clear proof that, for an articulate minority, concern about usage is intense. The publishers of the dictionary had decided to apply usage labels much more sparingly than in the past, on the grounds that the primary role of a dictionary was to record usage, not evaluate it, and that it was often impossible to label with any precision words taken out of context. Praised by many scholars, the decision was attacked in newspaper editorials and magazine articles as an abandonment of standards. More recently the polling technique introduced into usage study in the 1930s has been borrowed by publishers. Panels made up of journalists, novelists, columnists, commentators, and others concerned with verbal communication have registered mixed opinions on individual items for *The American Heritage Dictionary* and *Harper's Dictionary of Contemporary Usage* by William and Mary Morris (New York: Harper, 1975).

What this concern with the etiquette of usage indicates is that the writer should be aware of the attitudes of his audience – which are not always consistent with the audience's own usage. Most disputes involve matters of divided usage within standard English. Judgments vary, and as letters to the editors of newspapers and periodicals frequently reveal, conservative attitudes are often passionately held. Such letters also reveal that while word watching can make anyone's reading more interesting and his writing both richer and more precise, it can also be an unfortunate obsession. It is bad when the watcher (and listener) insists on "correcting" the usage of others. It is much worse when he makes usage the criterion for judging not only their educational and social level but their character and intelligence.

Like every writer, you must make your own choices. But they should be intelligent choices, based on sound information. The best safeguard against avoidable bias is awareness of some principles of selection; the principle proposed in this *Index* is appropriateness. And there is the intangible called taste. If, like most of us, you find some locutions too stuffy or too crude, you can simply not use them. Although no one can control the usage of others, everyone can control his own.

See *Writer's Guide,* pp. 289–96.

utilize

Utilize means "put to use." The verb *use* is almost always preferable.

V

Verb-adverb combinations

In "I looked up at the top of the tree," the verb *look* is used in its ordinary sense and is modified by the adverb *up*. In "I looked up the word in the dictionary," *looked up* is a verb meaning "investigated," a meaning not explained by a literal use of the two words. A person may *break out* (literally) of jail or *break out* with measles; he can *look after* a departing car or *look after* the children. In each of these pairs of expressions, the first has a verb modified by an adverb in its ordinary meaning, and the second is really a different verb, with a meaning of its own, composed of two elements. The second word in these two-word verbs, commonly referred to as a particle, can sometimes have more than one position in a sentence: I *looked up* the word in a dictionary; I *looked* the word *up* in a dictionary.

Hundreds of such verb-adverb combinations are in use, most of them one-syllable verbs with adverbs like *about, around, at, by, down, for, in, out, through, to, up, with.* They are widely used in general English and often give an emphatic rhythm differing from the more formal *investigate (look into), sacrifice (give up), surrender (give up).* This pattern is now the most active way of forming new verbs. When the combinations develop meanings beyond what their elements imply, they are separately entered in dictionaries.

Reference: Dwight Bolinger, *The Phrasal Verb in English* (Cambridge, Mass.: Harvard Univ. Press, 1971).

verbal, oral

Although *verbal* is widely used to mean "spoken," many word watchers insist on *oral* for that meaning. See *oral, verbal.*

Verbals

The parts of a verb that function as nouns or adjectives are called verbals. For their various uses see Gerunds, Infinitives, Participles.

Verbs

1. Forms. If we exclude *be* and the modal auxiliaries, all verbs can be identified by their capacity to add to the base form (*ask, sing, tear*) the suffix *-ing* (*asking*), the suffix *-s* (*asks*), and the suffix *-ed* (*asked*) or use some other change in form as the equivalent of the *-ed—sing, sings, singing, sang, sung; tear, tears,* *tearing, tore, torn. Be* has eight forms *(be, am, is, are, was, were, being, been); can, may, must,* and other modal auxiliaries have only one or two forms. We recognize verbs by their form and sentence position even when we don't know their meaning. In "I am sure that his words will coruscate," we know that *am, will,* and *coruscate* are verbs — *am* and *will* because we have already learned their forms, functions, and meanings, and *coruscate* because it depends on *will,* even if we have no notion of its meaning.

Verbs fall into two classes, a closed one (no new ones are added) whose function is primarily grammatical, and an open one (new ones are constantly added) whose lexical meaning is important. In "He got hurt," *got* performs the grammatical function of showing past tense and passive voice, and *hurt* carries the lexical meaning. See Auxiliaries, Gerunds, Infinitives, Participles, Parts of Speech, Principal parts of verbs, Tenses of verbs, Voice.

2. Function. The syntactic function of verbs is typically to form the predicate of a clause or sentence — that is, to join with a subject, and perhaps an object, to form a single construction. For convenience we are using *verb* instead of some more specific word like *predicator* to indicate this function as well as to indicate the part of speech. See Agreement, Linking verbs, Objects, Subjects, Transitive and intransitive verbs.

3. Verbs and style. The rhetorical function of a verb is usually to comment on the topic of a sentence. Generally speaking, the important action in a sentence should be in the main verb after the topic-subject has been stated. In the sentence "The possibility of a decision in regard to an investigation of reasons for student transfers exists," the one verb is *exists;* it states only that the very long and complicated topic-subject is there for the reader to consider. But the important action is not that a possibility exists; it is that someone may decide to investigate why students transfer: [The president?] may decide to investigate why students transfer. This sentence has three verbs: *decide, investigate,* and *transfer.* Those are the crucial actions in the sentence and should be represented in verbs, not in the abstract nouns related to the verbs.

Too often the main verb of a sentence is a lexically empty verb like *make, have, give,* and *get,* and abstract nouns related to lexically full verbs are subjects or objects. Unless there is good reason to keep a sentence abstract and impersonal, it usually should be rewritten with the abstract nouns changed into lexically vivid verbs:

The *intention* of the teacher is to make a selection of the best papers. *Better:* The teacher *intends* to select the best papers.

See Absolute phrases, Conditional clauses, Nominalization, Passive voice, Subjunctive mood, Tense, Verb-adverb combinations. References: Robert L. Allen, *The Verb System of Present-*

Day English (New York: Humanities Press, 1966); Joos; Long and Long, Chs. 23–30; F. R. Palmer, *A Linguistic Study of the English Verb* (Coral Gables: Univ. of Miami Press, 1968); Quirk et al., Chs. 3, 12.

Vernacular

Vernacular once meant "the local language as opposed to Latin." In England the word was used to refer to natural spoken English as opposed to formal literary English, and this usage gained social and political overtones in the United States. Vernacular humor – that is, comic writing in the English of the farm and the frontier – often celebrated Jacksonian democracy, rural interests, and naturalness and ridiculed the East, city ways, and "fancy" language. Since Twain and Whitman, it has been impossible to flatly oppose the literary language to the vernacular language, for the vernacular has been more important to American literature than the formal or academic. Thus while *vernacular* is still encountered as a term for nonstandard English, it is also the term for a literary style derived from the speech of particular classes or regions. See Colloquial English.

very

1. As a qualifier. *Very* is so much used as a qualifier that it may weaken the expression it is meant to intensify. The *Emporia Gazette* once described its war upon *very* this way:

"If you feel you must write 'very,' write 'damn.'" So when the urge for emphasis is on him, the reporter writes "It was a damn fine victory. I am damn tired but damn well – and damn excited." Then, because it is the Emporia (Kan.) Gazette, the copy desk deletes the profanity and the quotation reads: "It was a fine victory. I am tired but well – and excited." That's how the Gazette attains its restrained, simple, and forceful style. Very simple.

2. With past participles. The argument against using *very* before a participle is that a participle is not an adjective but a verbal, conveying not a quality but an action, and therefore cannot be modified by *very* ("extremely"), which is indicative of a degree of quality. By this argument, an adverb of degree, such as *much* or *greatly*, must stand between *very* and the participle (not "very distressed" but "very much distressed"). But in general usage many participles, both present and past, have for a long time been compared like adjectives and freely modified by *very* and *too: disturbing, more disturbing, very disturbing, too disturbing*. With past participles a scale can be set up: some take *very* (very tired), some *much* (much improved), some either (very pleased, much pleased), some neither (brightly [*not* very *or* much] lighted). References: Bryant, pp. 222–23; Copperud, p. 276; Long, pp. 58–59.

viable

Viable was originally used for newborn infants in the sense "capable of living" and then extended to ideas, institutions, and plans with the metaphysical senses "capable of growth," "capable of sustaining itself in existence," and "capable of being put into practice." As a vogue word, *viable* developed more new senses than the dictionaries could keep up with; but in many contexts it means no more than "workable": a viable program, a viable organization.

Vogue words

Particular words and expressions are constantly enjoying great popularity in one social or professional group or another, but a true vogue word is one that has moved into general usage and there become a fad. Some begin in the slang of the black ghetto or the campus and find their way into the copy of advertising writers; others start in the academy or the bureaucracy and become clichés through the efforts of journalists and commentators. As P. A. Duhamel has said, "The jargon of the day can so fascinate some speakers that they will repeat it mindlessly, substituting incantation for communication" *(Boston Herald-Advertiser)*. Writers are not immune to this weakness.

Some vogue words and expressions have little specific meaning to begin with in the contexts in which they appear. At various times "like," "you know?" "see?" and "right?" have been used in place of grunts as conversation fillers. Worse, in that the speaker or writer often believes he is saying something, are expressions like "That's the name of the game," "That's the bottom line," "It's a whole new ballgame," and "That's what it's all about." Other vogue words lose what force and meaning they had *(actually, basically, meaningful, relevant)* and become counter words. Still others take on so many meanings in so many different contexts as to become almost meaningless *(scenario, concept, massive, one-on-one)*. The thing that all vogue words and expressions have in common is that they have become a bore. Writers should make every effort to avoid using them.

See Cliché, Counter words, Triteness.

Voice

1. Forms. *Voice* is a term borrowed from the grammars of the classical languages, where it usually differentiates distinctive endings on verbs. In English, *passive voice* refers to constructions made with the past participle and some form of the verb *be* (was killed); all other verb forms are *active*.

	Active	Passive
Present:	he asks (is asking)	he is asked (is being asked)
Future:	he will ask	he will be asked
Perfect:	he has asked	he has been asked
Infinitives:	to ask, to have asked	to be asked, to have been asked
Participles:	asking, having asked	being asked, asked, having been asked.

Get is also used for the passive, especially in informal English:

If he should get elected, we'd be lost.
Our house is getting painted.

2. Definition. The traditional semantic definition is often a useful guide in identifying active and passive verbs, but there are many exceptions. When the subject of a verb is the doer of the action or is in the condition named by its verb (and predicate), the verb is traditionally said to be in the active voice: The congregation sang "Abide with Me"; They will go swimming; His father gave him a car. When the subject of a verb receives the action, the verb is said to be in the passive voice: "Abide with Me" was sung by the congregation; He was given a car by his father; They had been caught.

There are, however, patterns in English that are formally active but semantically passive to the degree that the subject actually "receives" the action: Your car drives easily; This wood doesn't burn as well as that wood; I received one rebuff after another. According to generative-transformational theory, these patterns and the formal passive with a form of *be* and the past participle of the verb result from transformations of a deep structure in which the noun phrase that moves into the subject position is in some sense originally an object. This is clearest in the passive, where the change involves just three simple steps. The direct object becomes the subject, a form of *be* and the past participle are added to the verb, and the original subject becomes the object of the preposition *by:*

The truck   pulls   the car.
The car   is pulled   by the truck.

Other transformations are responsible for the other illustrative sentences. In each case, somewhere in the deep structure the apparent subject has been an object, a "receiver" of an action. See Deep structure.

3. Active vs. passive. Some verbs have no passive version (She resembles her mother), and some are seldom used in the active (She bore four children); but most verbs can be put in either voice. In much written English, as in spoken English, the active voice is more common and more natural because we are accustomed to the actor-action-goal pattern of expression. Active verbs that are not just fillers in a sentence are usually more direct and lively than the corresponding passive:

Passive: The idea that we should leave was suggested by Kevin.
Active: Kevin suggested that we should leave.

Though the passive occurs less frequently than the active, it is legitimately used when the action is more important than the agent of the action, when the agent is unknown or unimportant, or when continuity of idea or emphasis requires shifting the agent to the end of the sentence. See Passive voice 3.

References: Copperud, pp. 207–208; Jespersen, Ch. 12; Joos; Long and Long, pp. 273–77, 285–90.

W

wake

English is oversupplied with verbs for waking from sleep (intransitive) and waking someone else from sleep (transitive). Most common is *wake* (*woke* or *waked; woke, waked,* or *woken*), to which *up* is frequently added in general writing. *Awaken* (*awakened, awakened*) is almost as common but somewhat more formal. *Awake* (*awoke* or *awaked; awoke, awaked,* or *awoken*) is rather formal. *Waken* (*wakened, wakened*) is least used.

want

Except in the rather rare sense "have need" (They want for the bare necessities of life), *want* should not be followed by *for:* I want [for] you to go. Nor should it be followed by a *that* clause: I want that you should go.

Want for "ought, had better" — You want to review all the notes if you're going to pass the exam — is informal.

Want in, want out, without a complementary verb, is seen in general and informal writing but not in formal. References: Bryant, pp. 224–25; Copperud, p. 279.

way, ways

Way in the sense "far" is established in general writing, though not in formal:

A stock can be selling at two cents and be way overpriced. – Thomas W. May, *Atlantic*

It goes way back to his red-baiting days. – T.R.B., *New Republic*

There is some prejudice against the use of *ways* to mean "distance" (a little way[s] down the road).

we

We is frequently used as an indefinite pronoun in expressions like "we find" and "we feel," to avoid passive and impersonal constructions. It is also used to mean "I and others," as in writing for a group or institution. And there is the *we* of the newspaper editorial page, the royal *we* of kings and popes, the corporate *we* of business letters, and, particularly since the spread of radio-television interview and "talk" shows, the *we* that can only mean "I," as in a singer's "We always draw well in Las Vegas."

We for *I* has been taken up by ordinary individuals, with no hint of publicity agents, teammates, or bureaucratic associates, on the peculiar grounds that it is more modest than *I*. But the ambiguity of *we* for *I* is even worse than the condescension of *we* for *you* as in the kindergarten *we* (We won't lose our mittens, will we?) and the hospital *we* (How are we feeling this morning?).

well, good

Well is either an adjective (He looks well) or an adverb (She swam well); *good* is an adjective (a good feeling). See *good, well.*

what

When a predicate nominative connected to a *what* clause by a linking verb is singular, the verb is singular: What I wish to discuss is the responsibility of students. When the predicate nominative is plural, usage is divided:

What we are getting is old answers to old questions. – Daniel Boorstin, *Look*

What he wanted were people who could stimulate. . . . – Anthony Starr, *Esquire*

When *what* is the subject of its clause and the *what* clause is the subject of the sentence, usage is consistent if the *what* clause, linking verb, and predicate nominative agree in number: What is needed is a change; What are needed are changes. But when the *what* clause is singular and the predicate nominative is plural, the linking verb may be either singular or plural:

What is required is neither military bases, pacts, nor conspiracies. – Anatole Shub, *Foreign Affairs*

Still, what holds all his work together are stylistic qualities. – Richard Kostelanetz, *New York Times Magazine*

See *but that, but what.*

when, where

Although the *when* or *where* clause is probably the standard form for defining in informal usage and occurs often in general contexts, there is strong prejudice against it: Welding is when [*or* where] two pieces of metal are heated and made into one. The grammatical argument is that an adverbial clause may not serve as the predicate complement of a noun, which requires as its complement another noun or a noun phrase or clause.

whether

Or is required after *whether* when *whether* introduces a complete or elliptical adverbial clause: Whether [he is] right or not, we owe him respect. In noun clauses, *or not* may be used for emphasis, but it is not strictly necessary:

Whether readers find him successful will depend on their patience. – Charles F. Mullet, *American Historical Review*

If the child at home wonders whether he is loved, the pupil in school wonders whether he is a worthwhile person. – Robert Dreeben, *Harvard Educational Review*

When the alternatives are fully expressed, *or not* is redundant: Whether or not the move is good or bad is debatable.

Repeating *whether* after *or* can be usefully explicit when the alternatives are long and complex, as in some formal contexts.

See Conditional clauses; *if, whether.* References: Copperud, pp. 284 – 85; Fries, p. 217.

which

1. For broad reference. The use of *which* to refer to the whole idea of a preceding clause (They plan to tear it down, which is a pity) is well established; but objections are properly raised when the reference is so loose that the *which,* at first reading, seems to refer only to the preceding word: She liked the book, *which* was puzzling. Similarly, a reader should not have to grapple with two *which*'s, one of specific and one of broad reference, in a single short sentence: I worked Saturdays to earn money *which* was owed on the car, *which* pleased my parents.

2. In the genitive. *Whose* as the genitive of *which* is older and less cumbersome than *of which* and is preferred by most writers: "a pattern whose outlines are clearly visible" rather than "a pattern the outlines of which are. . . ." Reference: Pooley, pp. 167–69.

3. In parallel clauses. The coordinating conjunctions *and* and *but* connect equivalent *which* clauses having the same antecedent. Sometimes a writer omits the relative pronoun before the first clause only to find that he needs it before the second: "It seems to hold as much promise for American politics as the second-hand legislative reforms [   ] Sinclair propounded in his novels, and which successive Democratic administrations enacted" (Andrew Kopkind, *New York Times Book Review*). In such cases, insertion of *which* will provide balance.

Sometimes an adjective *which* clause, which is subordinate, is mistakenly attached to a main clause by *and* or *but:* "I took to my heart the memorable statement in Joseph Pulitzer's will, now reprinted every day on the editorial pages of the *St. Louis Post-Dispatch*, and which I subsequently tacked to the wall of my office" (Willie Morris, *North Toward Home*). This sentence could be construed as another case of equivalent clauses, to be revised by inserting *which is* before *now;* but it seems more likely that the writer intended to have the single *which* clause ("the memorable statement in Joseph Pulitzer's will . . . which I . . . tacked to the wall") and inserted the *and* to provide some separation from "the editorial pages of the *St. Louis Post-Dispatch*." In careful writing, a conjunction before a single adjective clause should be avoided, even at the cost of considerable revision. See Subordination 2.

4. *Which* or *that*. For the choice between *which* and *that* as relative pronouns, see *that.*

Reference: Copperud, pp. 15–16.

while

As a temporal conjunction, *while* means "during the time that": While the rest were playing cards, he was studying. In general English it is also used to mean "although" or "whereas" (While the cast is talented, the play is a bore) and to introduce the second of two clauses where *though* or *but* might stand (The beagle was a thoroughbred, while the rest of the pack were mongrels). There is some prejudice against *while* when no sense of time is involved. References: Bryant, pp. 231–32; Copperud, p. 284; Fries, pp. 236–37.

who, whom

Ideally, function determines form: *who* is used for subjects and *whom* for objects. In all varieties of English, subjects are consistently rendered as *who* except when they are immediately followed by the subjects of interspersed clauses. Then what *The New Yorker* used to refer to as The Omnipotent Whom is common, as if the pronoun rather than its clause were the object of the interspersed clause: "a solemn old man whom American officials thought might just possibly make a decent guide" (Theodore H. White, *Saturday Review*). As subject, *who* is the right form in such constructions.

Where *whom* is called for, formal usage observes the proprieties, but informal and general often break the traditional rule. General usage permits *who* in questions like these:

And who was the hard sell aimed at? – Mary McCarthy, *New York Review of Books*

Who are they trying to impress? – Bruce Price, *Washington Post*

And though general usage much prefers *whom* in the object function at the beginning of dependent clauses, it sometimes accepts informal *who*: "How [elections] come out depends on who the voters have to choose between" (James Q. Wilson, *Commentary*).

The reason educated writers accept *who* as object when they would recoil from objective *I, we, he, she*, and *they* is that *who* is so often in subject territory, preceding the verb. When the pronoun functions as subject, function and position are in harmony, and *who* is the natural choice. When the pronoun functions as object, function and position are at odds. In formal contexts most writers take the trouble to ignore position and let function determine form. In casual conversation, position is allowed to determine form. General usage usually favors the demands of function except when the pronoun introduces the whole sentence (Who can we turn to?). In college writing, subject *who* and object *whom* are normally the appropriate choices, even though *whom* may sound pedantic in some contexts.

See *one of those who*. References: Bryant, pp. 232–34; Copperud, pp. 285–86; Long and Long, pp. 343–46; Pooley, pp. 68–72; Edward Sapir in Hungerford, Robinson, and Sledd, pp. 327–36.

whose

Whose is interchangeable with *of which* and often the better choice. See *which* 2.

will, shall

Whether pointing to the future and expressing determination, prohibition, or obligation or simply indicating the future, *will* is more common than *shall* with all three persons. See *shall, will.*

-wise

This suffix has long had a limited currency in forming adverbs from nouns *(edgewise, lengthwise, slantwise)*. Some years ago it increased in faddish use, especially in an abstract rather than a special sense *(average-wise, budget-wise, legislation-wise, tax-wise)* until new *-wise* words became a joke. Now both the overuse and the ridicule have died down. When a noun has no established adjectival form, a *-wise* coinage may serve a need and have the virtue of concision. But often the *-wise* word lacks precision *(production-wise)*; sometimes it represents no saving *(economy-wise* versus *in economy)*; and it may simply duplicate an existing word *(drama-wise* for *dramatically)*. The connotation of jargon is a further liability. Reference: Copperud, p. 287.

with

According to formal rules, a singular subject followed by a *with* phrase (or *along with, together with)* takes a singular verb: The sheriff along with his three deputies was [*not* were] the first to reach the scene. In general and informal English *with* is often treated as if it created a compound subject. Reference: Copperud, pp. 287–88.

woman, lady

An adult human female is a woman. She may or may not be a lady—"Miss Hepburn is always a lady, a person of integrity" (Edwin Wilson, *Wall Street Journal*)—just as a man may or may not be a gentleman.

Wordiness

Replace the wordy expressions with more compact and exact ones.

There are two cures for wordiness—surgery and treatment. Surgery means excision, simply cutting out words. Treatment means repair, rewriting.

1. Cut out deadwood. Deadwood is the type of wordiness that contributes nothing but clutter:

At [the age of] forty he was a handsome [looking] man.

He was aware [of the fact] that he had failed.

The architecture [of the buildings] and the landscaping [of the grounds] speak of town pride.

[It also happened that] we were the same age.

He kept things moving in [the field of] basset breeding throughout [the entirety of] his career.

The most common deadwood consists of unnecessary phrases like "green *in color*," "seven *in number*," "rectangular *in shape*" and clichés like "in the business world" and "in the field of economics," which we often use without thinking. But good writing requires thought, and when a first draft is revised, every phrase should be looked at closely. Does "green in color" mean anything more than "green"? Doesn't "in business" say everything that "in the world of business" says?

Sometimes a phrase that contributes nothing to the meaning of a sentence nevertheless fits its rhythm or has some other stylistic justification. Perhaps adding "in my life" to "for the first time" provides a desired emphasis even though it's tautologous. But, in general, simply eliminating deadwood is a step toward a compact, direct, honest prose style.

2. Compress inflated passages. When deadwood is involved, no replacement is necessary, but loose, unfocused expression often demands rewriting:

The reason that I'm telling all this is because I want to demonstrate in the clearest way possible that the cultural background of my family was of such a nature as to encourage my interest in the reading of books, magazines, etc.
Rewritten: All this shows that my family background encouraged me to read.

Using unnecessary words produces flabby writing. You can often improve a first draft greatly by reducing long-winded phrases and other circumlocutions to single words that are more direct, more emphatic, and just as clear:

Instead of		
in this day and age	today
at this point in time	now
during the time that	while
in the event that	if
at the conclusion of	after

See Nominalization, Passive voice.

wo Word order

Change the order of words or other elements so that the meaning is clearer or the phrasing is more natural or more effective.

The placing of words and word groups in a sentence is the most important means of showing their grammatical relationships. Word order plays a major role in style, particularly in achieving emphasis.

1. Interrupted constructions. Keep your subjects close to your verbs. When a word or words interrupt a construction, the effect is usually clumsy unless the interrupter deserves special emphasis:

Between subject and verb: Newspaper headlines *in these trying and confused times* are continually intensifying our fears.
More natural: In these trying and confused times, newspaper headlines are. . . .

2. Wandering modifiers. Keep your modifiers close to the words they modify. When modifiers are separated from their head-words, the result is frequently awkward, sometimes misleading:

Bob recovered from exhaustion plus what apparently was a bug making the rounds following two days' bedrest.—Grace Lichtenstein, *New York Times*
Better: Following two days' bedrest, Bob. . . .

Her uncle, King Leopold, was even unable to influence her.
Better: Even her uncle. . . .

I decided that if I moved in the direction of the apple tree growing beside the fence calmly, I might make it before the bull charged.
Better: . . . moved calmly in the direction. . . .

3. Word order and emphasis. Don't change normal word order unless you have a reason for doing so. As a rule an element shifted from its usual position receives increased emphasis, as when the object is put before subject and verb:

Object first: I was surprised to find Salinger's novel on the list. *That book* I read when I was fourteen.
Predicate adjective first: Lucky are the ones who need no longer worry.

See Ambiguity, Dangling modifiers. Reference: Fries, Ch. 10.

Words
Index articles containing general discussions of words and their uses include Abstract language, Diction, Figurative language, Origin of words, Slang, Synonyms, and Vogue words.

world
Inflated phrases with *world*—"the business world," "the fashion world," "the publishing world," "the world of science (economics, finance, politics . . .)"—can usually be collapsed: After graduation he went into [the world of] advertising. "Today's modern world" means "today." In other cases, more specific language is preferable: This is especially true in the world of jazz [*better:* among jazz musicians]. *Area, field,* and *realm* are misused in the same way.

would, should
In indirect discourse, *shall* as well as *will* is likely to be reported as *would:* She said, "We shall see"; She said that we would see. See *should, would.*

would have, would of
Writing *would of* for *would have* is nonstandard. See *have* 3.

ww Wrong word

Replace the word marked with one that says what you mean.

No word is right or wrong in itself. As a correction symbol, *ww* means that the word does not convey a meaning that makes sense in context. In the sentence "What he said showed real comprehensibility of the problems of Asia," *comprehensibility* does not make sense; it's the wrong word. *Comprehension* would be the right word. In "Some people remain stagnant to the lessons of life," *stagnant* needs replacing; *oblivious* is one possibility. In "I remember explicitly my first puff of a cigarette," *clearly* would be a good choice to replace *explicitly.* Errors like this occur when the writer is attempting to use words whose meaning he is not sure of, when he confuses words of similar sound, or when he simply writes too hurriedly and fails to proofread his work. See Careless mistakes.

X

 Correct the obvious error.

See Careless mistakes.

Xmas

X is the first letter of the Greek word for Christ. It has been used for centuries as an abbreviation in the word *Xmas,* pronounced exactly like *Christmas.* Today, however, *Xmas* is most likely to be pronounced *eks'mus,* and for many its popularity with advertisers has given it unpleasant commercial connotations. Except for purposes of irony, *Xmas* is inappropriate in serious writing.

Y

yet

Yet is both an adverb (The books haven't come yet) and a coordinating conjunction roughly equivalent to *but:* His speech was almost unintelligible, yet I found that I enjoyed it.

you

In giving instructions, as in a how-to essay, *you* is often a good stylistic choice (Then you glue the bottom strip . . .), certainly preferable to repeated use of the passive. As an impersonal pronoun, *you* is more common than *one* in general usage and not at all rare in formal:

In a sense, Richard III, as Shakespeare sees him, is the little boy who has found out that God does not strike you dead when you tell a lie. — Arnold Edinborough, *Shakespeare Quarterly*

There are at least three ways to treat any philosophical work: (1) You may inquire into its background, its history. . . . — Frederick Sontag, *Journal of Religion*

Writers should avoid switching back and forth between *you* and *one* and take care that their *you, your* is clearly indefinite, not personal. "Your parents depend on alcohol and pills to get them through the day" might better be "Our parents. . . ."

See *one, they* Reference: Bryant, pp. 238–39.

youth

As a collective noun, *youth* meaning "young people in general" can be followed by either singular or plural verbs and pronouns. In American usage the singular construction is much the more common: "Russian youth wants to avoid military confrontation as sincerely as American youth does" (George Feifer, *New York Times Magazine*). But when *the* precedes *youth*, a plural verb is often desirable to show clearly that more than a single person is meant: The increase in tuition made education too expensive for the youth who were most in need of it.

Though the collective use includes both sexes, *youth* meaning "a young person" ordinarily refers to a young man, and the ordinary plural is *youths*.

Youth has been so overused by journalists and commentators that sometimes almost any alternative—*young man* (or *men*), *boy(s), adolescent(s), young people, girls and boys*—would be welcome. See *kid*.

✓ A correction symbol indicating approval: "good idea," "well expressed," and so on.

Acknowledgments

From "Songs of Outlaw Country" by Pete Axthelm, *Newsweek,* April 12, 1976. Copyright © 1976 by Pete Axthelm. Reprinted by permission of The Sterling Lord Agency, Inc.

From "Two on the Isle" by Caskie Stinnett, *Atlantic,* October 1976. Copyright © 1976 by The Atlantic Monthly Company. Reprinted by permission of Harold Matson Co., Inc.

From "Rugby Is a Better Game" by Allen Jackson, *Atlantic,* November 1952. Copyright 1952 by The Atlantic Monthly Company, Boston, Mass. Reprinted with permission.

From "The Poisoning of the West" by Jack Olsen, *Sports Illustrated,* March 8, 1971. Reprinted by permission of the author.

From "A Beginner's Guide to the Martial Arts" by Victoria Pellegrino, *Ms.,* December 1974. Reprinted by permission of the author.

From "Eyewitness Testimony" by Robert Buckhout, *Scientific American,* December 1974. Reprinted by permission.

From "A New Solution for the CIA" by I. F. Stone. Reprinted with permission from *The New York Review of Books,* February 20, 1975. Copyright © 1975 NYRev. Inc.

"Plan a Fund-Raiser That Really Makes Money." Reprinted with permission from *Changing Times Magazine,* © 1976 Kiplinger Washington Editors, Inc., February 1976.

From "Of Thee I Sing" by Martha Weinman Lear, *The New York Times Magazine,* July 4, 1976. © 1976 by The New York Times Company. Reprinted by permission.

From "Women's Lib Plays in Peoria" by Susan Jacoby, *Saturday Review,* February 8, 1975. © 1975 by Saturday Review/World, Inc. Reprinted by permission.

692 Acknowledgments

From "The Sting of Polish Jokes" by Michael Novak, *Newsweek,* April 12, 1976. Copyright 1976 by Newsweek, Inc. All rights reserved. Reprinted by permission.

From "On Being a Scientist" by Mitchell Wilson, *Atlantic,* September 1970. Copyright © 1970 by Mitchell Wilson. Reprinted by permission of International Creative Management.

From "The Men in the Middle" by John Kifner, *The New York Times Magazine,* September 12, 1976. © 1976 by The New York Times Company. Reprinted by permission.

From *Pieces of the Frame* by John McPhee. Reprinted with the permission of Farrar, Straus & Giroux, Inc. Copyright © 1974, 1975 by John McPhee. "Firewood" appeared originally in *The New Yorker.*

From "Cruel Lib" by D. Keith Mano, *Newsweek,* September 8, 1975. Copyright 1975 by Newsweek, Inc. All rights reserved. Reprinted by permission.

From "In Defense of Flirting" by Anne Taylor Fleming, *Newsweek,* April 26, 1976. Copyright 1976 by Newsweek, Inc. All rights reserved. Reprinted by permission.

From "I. B. Singer: False Messiahs and Modern Sensibility" by Irving Howe. Copyright © 1966 by Random House, Inc. Reprinted from the *Introduction to Selected Short Stories of Isaac Bashevis Singer* by permission of the publisher.

From "The Nightmare of Going Mad" by Joy Gould Boyum, *The Wall Street Journal,* July 6, 1976. Reprinted with permission of The Wall Street Journal, © Dow Jones & Company, Inc., 1976. All rights reserved.

"On Our Birthday—America as Idea" by Barbara Tuchman, *Newsweek,* July 12, 1976. Copyright 1976 by Newsweek, Inc. Reprinted by permission of Russell & Volkening, Inc., as agents for the author.

From "Small Bombs and Big Bombs" by Norman Cousins, *Saturday Review*, June 27, 1970. © 1970 by Saturday Review Corp. Reprinted by permission.

From "On Political Maturity" by Robert M. Hutchins, *Change*, November 1974. Reprinted by permission of Change Magazine.

From "The Peripatetic Reviewer" by Edward Weeks, *Atlantic*, March 1971. Copyright © 1971 by The Atlantic Monthly Company, Boston, Mass. Reprinted with permission.

From "Carbide Pollution Assailed by Nader" by Ben A. Franklin, *The New York Times,* October 15, 1970. © 1970 by The New York Times Company. Reprinted by permission.

From "Closeup: Record Has Subtle Moments" by Charles C. DuBois, *Centre Daily Times*, September 24, 1976. Reprinted by permission.

From "Are Colleges Worthy of the Young?" by Alan Pifer. Reprinted with permission of the author and *The Chronicle of Higher Education,* July 7, 1975. Copyright © 1975 by Editorial Projects for Education, Inc.

From "Drums Under the Window" by Denis Donoghue. Reprinted with permission from *The New York Review of Books,* October 14, 1976. Copyright © 1976 NYRev. Inc.

From "The Nocturnal Game" in SCORECARD, ed. Robert W. Creamer, *Sports Illustrated,* October 11, 1976, p. 23. © Time, Inc.

From "Stopping by Woods on a Snowy Evening" from *The Poetry of Robert Frost*, edited by Edward Connery Lathem. Copyright 1923, © 1969 by Holt, Rinehart and Winston. Copyright 1951 by Robert Frost. Reprinted by permission of Holt, Rinehart and Winston, Publishers, the Estate of Robert Frost, and Jonathan Cape Ltd.

"The Blushing Bride" from *I Know What I Like* by Georgina Coleridge. Copyright © 1959 by Chatto and Windus; 1963 by Georgina Coleridge. Reprinted by permission of Curtis Brown Ltd.

General Index

Italic type is used in this index for entries on particular words and constructions; it also designates the assignments appearing throughout the Guide *under the headings "For Analysis," "For Writing," "For Punctuating."*

Program paragraph, 106
Progressive verb forms, 606
Pronouns, 587, 588–89, 607–09
  agreement of, 401–02
  ambiguous, 406
  case of, 435–36
  demonstrative, 475
  intensive, 537
  interrogative, 537, 588, 608
  personal, 587, 592, 607
  possessive, 599
  reciprocal, 608, 616
  reference of, 617–18
  reflexive, 607–08, 618
  relative, 589, 608, 619–20
  repetition of, 152
Pronunciation, 281
Proof in argument, 164
  discovering, 171–92
  fallacies in, 192–95
  See also Deduction, Induction.
Proofreading, 21, 22, 348, 353, 434,
  609
Proper adjectives, 609
Proper names, 433
Proportion, 123–24
proved, proven, 609
provided, providing, 609
Psychologese, 610
Psychological point of view, 43–44,
  598
public, 610
Punctuation, 266–78, 610–11
  for clarity, 276, 450
  close or open, 267
  between coordinate clauses, 271,
    445–47, 629
  at end of sentence, 268–69, 489
  of interrupters, 274–75, 449, 470,
    582
  between main elements of sen-
    tence, 270–71, 450–51
  with quotation marks, 276, 615
  in series, 275–76, 449–50, 630
  and style, 266–67
  of subordinate elements, 273–74,
    448
  For Punctuating, 269, 272–73, 277
Punctuation marks
  apostrophe, 268, 412–13
  brackets, 268, 425
  colon, 268, 272, 443–45
  comma, 240, 268, 270, 271, 273–74,
    275, 445–51
  dash, 240, 268, 272, 274, 275,
    469–70

ellipsis, 268, 345, 371, 487
exclamation mark, 268, 269, 500
hyphen, 268, 280–81, 457, 482–83,
  529–30, 589
parentheses, 268, 274, 275, 582
period, 268, 591
question mark, 268, 269, 350, 612
quotation marks, 268, 276, 613–15,
  660
semicolon, 229, 268, 271, 629–30
Puns, 307, 611
Purpose in writing, 3, 10–12, 42, 129,
  315, 348–49
  For Writing, 325

Q

Qualifiers, 588, 611–12
Question mark, 268, 269, 350, 612
Questions, 268, 612–13
  rhetorical, 116, 626
  as topic sentences, 135
  for transition, 111
Quotation marks, 268, 276, 613–15,
  660
Quotations, 115, 463
  in argument, 189
  and colons, 444
  use of ellipses in, 487
  methods of indicating, 613
  in research paper, 330, 345–46,
    350–51, 354
  For Analysis and Writing, 351–52

R

raise, rear, 615
reaction, 615
Reader. See Rhetorical situation,
  audience in.
Reading, 314–16
  close, for critical writing, 314
  as resource for writing, 7
  taking notes on, 314, 315, 343–47,
    622
Reading aloud, 21, 314–15
real, really, 615–16
rear, raise, 616
reason is because, 616
Reciprocal pronouns, 608, 616
reckon, 616
Red herring, 194, 502
Reduced clauses, 440–41, 616
Reductio ad absurdum, 197

Correction Chart

To the student: When one of these correction symbols calls attention to a weakness in your essay, look up the *Index* article that discusses the problem, and make the revision. The symbols in the chart are arranged alphabetically; page numbers for the articles follow the instructions.

ab Write out this word. Or use the standard abbreviation. 387

abst Make this word or passage more concrete or more specific. 390

adj Reconsider your choice of adjective. 395

adv Correct the form or change the position of the adverb. Or reconsider your choice of adverb. 398

agr Make the verb agree with its subject or the pronoun with its antecedent. 400

amb Make your meaning unmistakable. 406

apos ⌄ Insert or remove an apostrophe as required. 412

awk, k Rewrite this passage to make the phrasing smoother and more effective. 418

beg Revise the beginning of your essay to make it lead more directly and smoothly into your subject or to arouse your reader's interest. 420

cap Capitalize the word marked. 432

case Correct the mistake in case. 435

cf Revise this sentence to correct the comma fault. 451

coh Make clear the relation between the parts of this sentence or between these sentences or paragraphs. 441

colon ⁏ Use a colon here. Or reconsider the use of this colon. 443

comma ⌄ Insert or remove comma here: between independent clauses, 445; with preceding or following elements, 448; with non-restrictive modifiers, 448; with interrupting and parenthetical words and phrases, 449; in lists and series, 449; for clarity, 450; for emphasis, 450; with main sentence elements, 450; in conventional uses, 451; with other marks of punctuation, 451.

comp Correct the fault in comparing the adjective or adverb marked. 454

concl Revise the ending of your paper to round out the discussion. 458

conj Make this conjunction more accurate or more appropriate to the style of the passage. 460

coord Correct the faulty coordination. 465

d Replace this word with one that is more exact, more appropriate, or more effective. 478

det Develop this passage more fully by giving pertinent details. 477

div Break the word at the end of this line between syllables. 482

dm Revise the sentence so that the expression marked is clearly related to the word it is intended to modify. 468

emp Strengthen the emphasis of this passage. 488

fig Replace this trite, inconsistent, or inappropriate figure of speech. 504

form Make this word or passage less formal, more appropriate to your style, subject, and audience. 512

frag Make this construction a grammatically complete sentence, or join it to a neighboring sentence. 513

glos See this *Index* for an article on the word marked.

id Replace this expression with standard idiom. 531

inf Make this word or passage less informal, more appropriate to your style, subject, and audience. 536

ital Underline to indicate italics. 539